Encyclopedia of
CONFLICT
Resolution

Encyclopedia of
CONFLICT
Resolution

Heidi Burgess
Guy M. Burgess

ABC-CLIO

Santa Barbara, California
Denver, Colorado
Oxford, England

Library of Congress Cataloging-in-Publication Data

Burgess, Heidi.
    Encyclopedia of conflict resolution / Heidi Burgess and Guy M. Burgess.
        p.   cm.
    Includes bibliographical references and index.
    1. Conflict management—Encyclopedias.   2. Dispute resolution
(Law)—Encyclopedias.   I. Burgess, Guy M., 1949–   .   II. Title.
HM136.B783   1997
303.6'9'03—dc21   97-8637
                                                                                    CIP

ISBN 0-87436-839-1

02 01 00 99 98   10 9 8 7 6 5 4 3 2

ABC-CLIO, Inc.
130 Cremona Drive, P.O. Box 1911
Santa Barbara, California 93116-1911

Typeset by Letra Libre

This book is printed on acid-free paper.
Manufactured in the United States of America

Contents

Introduction

The Field of Conflict Resolution

Although people have been resolving conflicts as long as they have existed, conflict resolution as a unique field is relatively new. In one sense, it can be traced back to a group of scholars and practitioners who responded to World War I with efforts to try to prevent a recurrence of worldwide, violent conflict. Leading scholars from international relations and other fields began to apply scientific methods to investigate the causes and processes of conflict and to try to develop ways to avoid conflict escalation and its destructive results. This research was stalled during World War II, but it began again even more intensely after the war.

In the early 1950s, scholars such as Herbert Kelman, Kenneth Boulding, and Anatol Rapoport founded the Research Exchange on the Prevention of War. They organized workshops, ran symposia, and published a journal, which in 1957 became the *Journal of Conflict Resolution,* still one of the leading journals in the field.

Another strand of what has come to be called the field of dispute resolution arose in the 1920s and 1930s, when collective bargaining was widely implemented in the labor-management context to try to control the violent labor conflicts that were commonplace in the early part of the twentieth century. In addition, arbitration came to be widely used as a means of resolving disputes over contract interpretation and implementation.

A third conflict resolution strand came from the civil rights and other popular empowerment movements of the 1960s. More and more people in the 1950s and 1960s tried to remedy injustice and take control of public decision-making processes rather than leaving decisions to be made by bureaucrats alone. These movements—the civil rights movement, the women's movement, and the environmental movement, among others—increased the level of public conflict in this country; however, they spurred the development of new approaches to conflict resolution as well.

Finally, the increased level of conflict generated a large increase in the number of civil lawsuits filed. This led to an overburdened court system and a search for faster, less costly ways to resolve disputes. A multitude of alternative dispute resolution (ADR) procedures were developed in the 1960s, 1970s, and 1980s as part of what became known as the ADR movement. Some of these procedures, such as arbitration and mediation, were not new but were being applied much more widely than before. Others—such as summary jury trials and regulatory negotiation—were new concepts that were developed specifically in response to the dispute resolution "crisis" of the 1970s and 1980s.

The Conflict/Dispute Resolution Knowledge Base

Because its roots are so diverse and its applications so widespread, it is difficult for people who are interested in this new field to find information about the conflict resolution "knowledge base." Textbooks are available, but each tends to examine only one aspect of the field and to be written from one theoretical perspective. For example, one leading textbook is *Dispute Resolution: Negotiation, Mediation, and Other Processes.* Its authors are Stephen Goldberg, Frank Sander, and Nancy Rogers, three professors of law who focus almost exclusively on alternative dispute resolution and its legal aspects. Another leading source is known as the Conflict Series, four books written by John Burton and Frank Dukes, who focus primarily on deep-rooted conflicts and advocate the use of the human needs approach for conflict analysis and resolution. Few books cover the breadth of the field—in part because it is so large but also because it is growing so rapidly.

We had been working to make the broad conflict resolution knowledge base more accessible, both for our own use and for others'. When Henry Rasof, an editor at ABC-CLIO, approached us about writing an encyclopedia of conflict resolution, we were intrigued. We had not considered the idea before, but it was consistent with our interest in providing easy access to the broader conflict resolution knowledge base. It would be a daunting task, no doubt, but one that seemed well worth the effort. Thus, this project was born.

Scope of the Book

In this volume we define *conflict resolution* broadly. Although many scholars make a distinction between the terms *conflict* and *dispute,* this book covers both. It includes long-running, deep-rooted conflicts and short-term, negotiable disputes. It covers all the contexts in which disputes and conflicts occur—from the most basic two-party personal relationships between spouses or parents and children to superpower nuclear confrontations. We address labor-management issues; environmental and public policy conflicts; business negotiations; victim-offender reconciliation; and tensions between social groups divided along racial, ethnic, gender, cultural, or lifestyle lines. This comprehensiveness recognizes that in spite of their obvious differences, the many types of human conflict have much in common.

Deciding what knowledge was central to the field and should be included in the book was a difficult task. We cover what we consider to be the central concepts, such as conflict and dispute, escalation, interests, and positions. Likewise, we include the primary and subsidiary conflict resolution techniques. Primary techniques are the most common ones: negotiation, mediation, and arbitration. Subsidiary techniques are those such as active listening or I-messages that are used as part of the major processes. We also include techniques such as med-arb (a combination of mediation and arbitration) and mini-trials, both of which are stand-alone processes but are not used as widely as the primary techniques.

Other entries discuss current ethical issues such as the certification of mediators and the meaning of mediator neutrality, major dispute and conflict resolution organizations and journals, and important people—both scholars and practitioners of dispute resolution processes—who have had a significant impact on the field's development. Space limitations prevented us from including everyone we might have wished to mention.

Last, the encyclopedia includes a number of events and cases. These include important historical events such as the negotiation of the Camp David Accords between Israel and Egypt and the Persian

Gulf War fought after Iraq invaded Kuwait. As these two examples illustrate, we chose both conflict resolution successes and failures to illustrate what can go right and what can go wrong in dispute resolution efforts. Other cases are not of great historical importance from the general public's point of view but are important to the dispute resolution field. Examples include the passage of the Administrative Dispute Resolution Act of 1990 and the Dartmouth Conferences, which brought U.S. and Soviet citizens together throughout the Cold War to try to break down stereotypes, develop a degree of mutual understanding and trust, and eventually develop alternative approaches to resolving the superpower standoff. Other cases are not historically important, but they provide good examples of theoretical ideas and concepts that are included elsewhere in the book. For example, there is a case on a school system that used dispute system design to deal with its recurring racial and ethnic conflicts, another case on labor-management negotiations in the airline industry, and a third case examining divorce mediation.

Intended Audience and Uses

The text is intended for a wide variety of uses and users. It contains information to help people sort through the many dispute resolution options available and to get a better idea of what each is, how each works, and what the advantages and disadvantages of alternative approaches are. The volume also explains common words and concepts that dispute resolution consumers might hear, such as *caucuses, principled negotiation,* and *zero-sum conflicts.* Although we use language that nonprofessionals can understand, the presentation is sufficiently detailed that beginning professionals, who may be knowledgeable about one aspect of the field but know very little about another, will also find this volume

useful. We also provide information for consumers, such as how to obtain professional assistance, what to ask for, what to watch out for, and how to get training in this area. Although some of this information is included in the main entries (in the entry on mediator qualifications, certification, and training, for example), more information is available in the appendixes, which include lists of dispute resolution organizations with contact information, sources for mediator referrals, training providers, and university-based programs, among others.

Our goal is to provide a broadly accessible reference that gives readers quick answers to key questions without forcing them to wade through large quantities of information. Recognizing that readers may need more detailed follow-up information, we included references directing them to the field's important works and cross-referenced the entries extensively, allowing readers to follow a string of entries to get a more complete picture of an area of knowledge. One of the most difficult aspects of writing this volume was limited space—we always wanted to write more on a topic. Cross-references were one way to deal with this problem; rather than duplicating information that related to two entries, we put it in just one place, with cross-references between the two.

For readers who would like to use this volume as a primer on the conflict resolution field, we suggest beginning with the entries on alternative dispute resolution, mediation, arbitration, and negotiation and then following the links to other entries, repeating the process until a point of natural closure is reached. Ambitious readers might want to browse through the entire volume. We learned a great deal in writing it; we hope our readers will learn a great deal as well.

Finally, the volume can be used by people who want to look up one or two entries and then move on. Although the cross-references provide more depth, each entry stands alone and can be understood without going further.

Alternative Perspectives

As the conflict resolution field is continually evolving, many unanswered questions and debates remain. The diversity of its participants leads to a wide variety of views on almost every topic. People disagree about what is good or bad to do; they even disagree about the meanings of fundamental terms. In cases in which important differences of opinion exist, we tried to present competing views. However, we kept within the conflict resolution/dispute management arena. Other fields, such as psychology, diplomacy, political science, and law, have different perspectives on the nature of conflict that we could not address due to space and time constraints. Readers should also be cautioned that this is not a legal text; those who need legal advice should consult a lawyer or a legal reference and not rely solely on this book.

Acknowledgments

We want to thank all the people and organizations that helped with this book. We thank Henry Rasof and ABC-CLIO for convincing us to write and produce it, and we thank the William and Flora Hewlett Foundation for providing the funds to allow us to do so. (The Hewlett Foundation has also funded most of our other work, which gave us the background knowledge to undertake this project.)

We also want to thank the graduate students who provided draft entries and research assistance: Emma Zitter-Smith, Tanya R. Glaser, T. A. O'Lonergan, and Mariya Yevsyukova. (The list of entries they drafted is in Appendix 5.) Thanks also to Erica Tarpy, a law student who did a review of the legal ADR literature; and to law professor Emily Calhoun, who advised us on a number of the legal entries.

Lastly, we want to thank Quinn Doody, Katy Orton, Danielle Munsell, and Kathy Ottman, who tirelessly edited, proofread, corrected, and printed a seemingly endless stream of entries. They did a tremendous job—this volume would not have been possible without them.

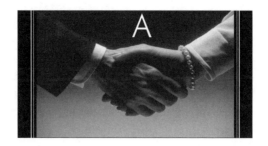

Academy of Family Mediators

The Academy of Family Mediators (AFM) is a nonprofit educational organization founded in 1981 by a group of leading mediators to support professional and public mediation education. The academy has developed, and continues to refine, criteria for mediator education, training, and ethical practice in cooperation with other state, regional, and national conflict resolution organizations. The academy seeks to elevate mediation practice and expand mediation opportunities. It also sponsors a national mediator referral system to help people identify mediators in their area and provides information about mediation training programs. AFM holds annual conferences and has a wide selection of educational materials, books, videotapes, audiotapes, and professional publications for sale. It also publishes the journal *Mediation Quarterly* as well as a quarterly newsletter, *Mediation News,* for its members.

See also: Appendix 1 for contact information.

Active Listening

Active listening is a way of listening to and interacting with another person that improves interpersonal understanding. Rather than listening with one ear, while watching and thinking about something else, active listening requires the listener to give the speaker his or her complete attention. The listener then repeats in his or her own words what the speaker just said. This as-sures the speaker that the person listening has really paid attention and has understood. The listener does not have to agree with the speaker—he or she only needs to understand what the other person believes or feels. Only after this is done should the listener explain what he or she thinks or feels.

Active listening improves communication in several ways. First, it allows the immediate correction of misunderstandings. Second, it tends to open people up, encouraging them to tell more. If two people are in conflict, the tendency is for each one to contradict or deny what the other person says. This tends to make people defensive, and they either become aggressive or withdraw. They do not continue to talk openly if they are attacked for doing so. If, however, they feel like someone is really listening with open ears and an open mind, they are likely to explain more about how they feel and why. This often reveals information about underlying interests and needs that allows the conflict to be resolved.

Consider the following scenario:

Child: I don't want to do my homework. It's dumb!
Parent: No, it's not. It's important that you learn math so that you can do well in school and get into a good college.
Child: I don't care how I do in school. I hate school! Leave me alone!

1

This kind of exchange is common, but it doesn't go anywhere. The homework probably won't get done, and the interpersonal understanding between parent and child will be nil. If the parent uses active listening, however, the exchange could be different:

Child: I don't want to do my homework. It's dumb!

Parent: You don't want to do your homework because you think it won't teach you anything important.

Child: No, it's not that. I know it's important, but I have so much of it and I really don't understand the math. I've been trying and trying and I don't seem to get it.

Parent: Hmm. You sound frustrated and tired.

Child: Yeah, I am. Maybe I'll take a break for half an hour and then try again. Can I have a snack to give me some energy?

Parent: Sure. Then maybe we can work on the math together.

Although each of these conversations begins in the same way, they end very differently. In the first situation, the parent turns the child off, stops communication, and fails to get what he or she wants (a completed homework assignment). In the second situation, the parent uses active listening to draw the child out. This improves the parent's understanding of the situation and enables him or her to offer appropriate assistance. In the end, the homework will probably get done, and the communication and the strength of the relationship between the parent and child will be maintained (or even improved).

See also: Communication; Interpersonal Conflict; Misunderstandings; Parent-Child Conflict.

References and Further Reading: Moore, Christopher W., 1986, *The Mediation Process;* Tillet, Gregory, 1991, *Resolving Conflict: A Practical Approach;* Ury, William, 1991, *Getting Past No: Negotiating with Difficult People,* 37–39.

Adjudication

Adjudication of civil disputes involves the resolution of a conflict by a court or other formal body that makes a judgment based on evidence presented (Gifis 1991, 7). The distinguishing characteristic of adjudication is that it requires disputants to present reasoned arguments and proof of their claims (Fuller 1978).

Adjudication can take place outside the formal court system. Arbitration, for instance, is considered an adjudicatory process, as are private judging and mini-trials. Court-based adjudication is usually considerably more formal than arbitration and other alternative dispute resolution (ADR) processes that occur outside the courts. As the field of alternative dispute resolution has developed, many people have come to use the term *adjudication* to refer only to litigation carried out in court.

Court-based adjudication of civil cases occurs when one person—believing that he or she has suffered a wrong—files legal charges against another (i.e., sues). If the case goes to trial, a judge—or, frequently, a jury—will listen to testimony and evidence presented by both sides and make a decision. The losing party is permitted to ask a higher court to reverse the decision (i.e., appeal) and frequently does so. However, if no appeal is filed, this decision is binding on both parties.

Court-based adjudication differs from ADR processes in a number of ways. First, it is not voluntary. If one person decides to sue another, the defendant cannot refuse to participate. In contrast, individuals can usually refuse to participate in ADR processes (unless they have contractually agreed to do otherwise, as in binding arbitration). Second, court-based adjudication is subject to appeal, whereas arbitration generally is not. Third, the decision maker in court-based adjudication generally lacks specialized expertise in the subject matter of the dispute. In some ADR processes (e.g., arbitration), the decision maker typically does have such specialized knowledge. Finally, court-based adjudication is a public process, whereas ADR adjudicatory processes are private.

The parties' needs determine whether court-based adjudication or some other process is superior. In addition to the foregoing considerations, parties should consider the following factors.

First, court-based adjudication usually results in a decision that one party is right and the other party is wrong; in other words, it lays blame. This characteristic also tends to mean that the outcome is a win-lose proposition, with the winner taking all and the loser losing everything.

Second, court-based adjudication is generally seen as a power-balancing mechanism. Individuals can sue corporations; abused wives can sue abusive husbands. The person filing a lawsuit does not need the agreement of the defendant to get a fair hearing in court. However, to the extent that legal rules are biased in favor of the more powerful sectors of society to begin with, the power-balancing capacity of court-based adjudication is undercut.

Third, court-based adjudication provides strict rules of procedure and evidence. It dictates what can and cannot be said and how the process unfolds. It ensures that one side does not dominate the discussion. However, by excluding hearsay and other evidence considered inadmissible, court-based adjudication may preclude parties from discussing some matters that they would like to discuss.

Fourth, in court-based adjudication, professionals (lawyers) speak for the conflicting parties. This may be beneficial to those who need help preparing or presenting their cases. It is a disadvantage, however, to others. For example, some parties may wish to avoid the adversarial, blaming, all-or-nothing argumentation of lawyers, especially when future cooperation with the other party to the conflict is important (e.g., in child custody matters). These parties may prefer to argue their cases themselves in more informal processes and to give lawyers only the role of consultants.

Fifth, in court-based adjudication, control of the outcome is not in the hands of the parties. Between the time charges are filed and the date of the trial—or even after a decision is made and a case is appealed—lawyers usually attempt to negotiate a solution to the conflict. But if a settlement cannot be negotiated, the decision of the judge or jury stands and is binding. In either event, decision making tends to be one step removed from the people who must live with the decision, and creative solutions tend to be more difficult to achieve. Sometimes the real, underlying problem between the parties is overlooked.

Sixth, court-based adjudication can be used to set a legal precedent that affects a broad range of persons and interests. If a plaintiff believes that a law is invalid and wants to prevent the application of that law not only to him- or herself but also to all other persons, court-based adjudication may be a good option.

Seventh, court-based adjudication tends to be very slow. The time between filing charges and the hearing can be months or even years. For some people, delay can be beneficial. For those who need a prompt resolution that enables them to resume their normal lives or businesses, however, it can be a disadvantage.

See also: Adversarial Approach; Alternative Dispute Resolution; Arbitration; Mediation; Mini-trial; Private Judging.

References and Further Reading: Black, Henry Campbell, 1990, *Black's Law Dictionary;* Fuller, Lon, 1978, "The Forms and Limits of Adjudication"; Gifis, Steven H., 1991, *Law Dictionary;* Goldberg, Stephen B., Eric D. Green, and Frank E. A. Sander, 1985, *Dispute Resolution;* Tillet, Gregory, 1991, *Resolving Conflict: A Practical Approach.*

Administrative Conference of the United States

The Administrative Conference of the United States (ACUS) was an independent federal advisory agency established by Congress in 1968 to help improve federal administrative processes. It became one of the strongest advocates for the increased use of alternative dispute resolution (ADR) at the federal level; however, it was eliminated by Congress in 1995, when the 1990 Administrative Dispute Resolution Act expired. In 1996, however, Congress passed a new Administrative Dispute Resolution Act, which permanently established and extended the provisions of the earlier act. It also called on the president to designate an agency or create an interagency committee to carry out the work that had formerly been done by the ACUS. Thus the ACUS's functions, if not its structure, will continue.

In 1990, the ACUS called for every federal department and agency that had significant interaction with the public to establish an ombudsman's office. According to Commissioner Marshall Berger, "Experience shows that it [an ombudsman] can increase cooperation with government and reduce occasions for litigation. Equally important, the ombudsman can provide high-ranking decision makers with the information needed to identify and treat systemic problems before they get out of hand" (Brown 1993, 171).

The ACUS was also a key player in obtaining passage of the Administrative Dispute Resolution Act of 1990. This act required every federal agency to consider the use of ADR processes whenever possible to resolve disputes that might otherwise be litigated. The act also required agencies to train their personnel in negotiation techniques and to appoint several senior officials in each agency to act as dispute resolution specialists. The ACUS was given a specific role in training federal officials to implement the act and was to report to Congress periodically on the agencies' success in implementing ADR procedures. The ACUS was also instrumental in the passage of the 1990 Negoti-

ated Rulemaking Act, which encouraged federal agencies to use negotiated rulemaking or regulatory negotiation (regneg) whenever possible in their rulemaking procedures.

See also: Administrative Dispute Resolution Acts of 1990 and 1996; Alternative Dispute Resolution, Institutionalization; Federal Use of Alternative Dispute Resolution; Negotiated Rulemaking Act of 1990; Ombudsman.
References and Further Reading: Administrative Conference of the United States, 1986, *Agencies' Use of Alternative Means of Dispute Resolution;* Administrative Conference of the United States, 1992, *Recommendations and Reports,* vol. 1; Brown, Brack, 1993, "Public Organizations and Policies in Conflict: Notes on Theory and Practice"; Dauer, Edward A., 1994, *Manual of Dispute Resolution.*

Administrative Dispute Resolution Acts of 1990 and 1996

The Administrative Dispute Resolution Act of 1990 authorized and encouraged federal agencies to use alternative dispute resolution (ADR) processes as much as possible to informally resolve agency disputes. The act defined alternative dispute resolution as "any procedure that is used, in lieu of an adjudication . . . to resolve issues in controversy, including, but not limited to settlement negotiations, conciliation, facilitation, mediation, factfinding, mini-trials, and arbitration, or any combination thereof" (5 *U.S. Code* §571 et seq.). Such procedures may be used whenever the parties involved agree to their use. In addition, the act requires training in negotiation for government personnel and requires the appointment of senior agency officials as dispute resolution specialists.

However, the act cautioned that agencies should *not* use ADR when its use is likely to preclude important outcomes. For example, since ADR does not set precedents, the act suggests that it should not be used in cases in which the setting of precedent is important. Likewise, it should probably not be used if the matter significantly affects persons or organizations that are not parties to the proceeding or if a full public record of the proceeding is important and cannot be obtained with ADR. The act also discouraged the use of ADR if such use would inhibit the agency's continuing jurisdiction over an important matter.

The 1990 act contained a five-year "sunset" provision, which meant that the act had to be reauthorized in 1995 to stay in effect. This did not occur, but Congress did pass a new and expanded act in 1996, also called the Administrative Dispute Resolution Act. The 1996 act permanently reauthorized the provisions of the earlier act, along with the provisions of the 1990 Negotiated Rulemaking Act, which had also been passed for a five-year trial period.

See also: Alternative Dispute Resolution; Alternative Dispute Resolution, Institutionalization; Negotiated Rulemaking Act of 1990.
References and Further Reading: Brown, Brack, 1993, "Public Organizations and Policies in Conflict: Notes on Theory and Practice"; Dauer, Edward A., 1994, *Manual of Dispute Resolution;* Goldberg, Stephen B., Eric D. Green, and Frank E. A. Sander, 1985, *Dispute Resolution.*

Administrative Procedure Act (APA)

The Administrative Procedure Act is a federal act, first passed in 1946, that defines and regulates the decision-making procedures to be used by all federal agencies. Before the passage of this act, procedures varied greatly from agency to agency, and many people charged that particular agencies were not protecting individual rights or the public interest. According to Gifis (1991, 12), the APA "brought coherence and judicial character to formerly haphazard procedures." The act provides guidelines for the rulemaking process (whereby an agency issues rules that define how it operates and carries out its statutory obligations). The APA also designates procedures for administrative hearings, judicial review, and public participation in federal agency decision-making processes.

Although the APA was a considerable improvement over previous administrative policies, in the 1960s and beyond these policies came under attack for being too rigid and especially for discouraging adequate public involvement in administrative processes. One result, among others, was the passage of the 1990 Negotiated Rulemaking Act and the 1990 Administrative Dispute Resolution Act, both of which relaxed APA procedures sufficiently to allow for—and even encourage—the use of negotiated rulemaking and other forms of alternative dispute resolution by administrative agencies in all their activities that affect the public.

See also: Administrative Dispute Resolution Acts of 1990 and 1996; Negotiated Rulemaking Act of 1990.
References and Further Reading: Davis, Kenneth Culp, 1972, *Administrative Law Text;* Gellhorn, Ernest, 1972, *Administrative Law and Process in a Nutshell;* Gifis, Steven H., 1991, *Law Dictionary.*

ADR
See Alternative Dispute Resolution.

Adversarial Approach

The adversarial approach to conflict is the approach typically taken when one views an opposing person or group as an adversary to be defeated. It is a competitive and confrontational way of engaging in conflict.

People using an adversarial approach tend to define the situation in judgmental terms. Thus, an attempt is made to blame the opponent for a wrong and to force the opponent to make amends. When lawyers use an adversarial approach in court (as the court-based adjudication process essentially requires them to do), they tend to frame the conflict as an all-or-nothing situation in which their clients are right and the opposing parties are wrong. Further, lawyers and others using the adversarial approach often use a confrontational and accusatory tone, which may escalate the conflict and worsen relations between the parties, even as the conflict is being resolved.

If a conflict involves the distribution of scarce resources, the adversarial approach usually assumes a win-lose situation: whatever one side gets, the other doesn't get. (This is also referred to as a zero-sum situation, because any plus for one side is a minus for the other.)

Although an adversarial approach may result in an adequate and fair outcome in many cases, it has significant drawbacks. One is the escalation of conflict and damage to relationships referred to above. Another is the loss of potential integrative or win-win solutions in which the parties work together as partners to solve a joint problem. This allows them to explore the differences between their positions (what they say they want or need) and their interests (what they really want or need). Often their interests are complementary, even though the positions are contradictory. When this occurs, an integrative approach to conflict resolution usually results in a better outcome than does an adversarial approach.

An example of this situation is a story commonly told in introductory classes on conflict management: Two children are squabbling over an orange. They engage in an adversarial battle, both explaining to the mother why one deserves the orange and the other doesn't. Exasperated, the mother cuts the orange in half and gives half to each child. This is a fair—and probably acceptable—outcome if the children both wanted to eat the orange. But in this story, one child wanted to eat the orange and the other wanted to use the rind for an art project. Had the children inquired about each other's reasons for wanting the orange (i.e., their interests), they would have determined that both could have gotten 100 percent of their interests met, not half, as they got from pursuing the adversarial approach.

When interests are consistent or compatible, integrative processes can often yield better outcomes than adversarial processes. In situations in which interests are contradictory, however, adversarial processes may be necessary. They can also be helpful in obtaining the leverage necessary to force an unwilling party to negotiate.

See also: Adjudication; Bargaining, Integrative and Distributive; Win-Win, Win-Lose, and All-Lose Outcomes; Zero-Sum, Positive-Sum, and Negative-Sum Games.
References and Further Reading: Rothman, Jay, 1992, *Confrontation to Cooperation: Resolving Ethnic and Regional Conflict;* Susskind, Lawrence, and Jeffrey Cruikshank, 1987, *Breaking the Impasse.*

Advocacy

Advocacy has two different meanings in the conflict resolution context. Lawyers use the term to describe what they do for their clients—they advocate, or represent their clients' interests, in negotiation, arbitration, and other adversarial proceedings. The term can also refer to what parties themselves do—they advocate a position in a negotiation, mediation, or political or legal process. In this sense, advocacy is closely related to community organizing and empowerment and is linked to efforts to bring about social change and remedy injustice. This kind of advocacy involves the identification of problems, interests, and goals (i.e., advocated solutions) as well as the implementation of the strategy and tactics necessary for achieving those goals (Kramer and Specht 1969, 8–9).

In some ways, advocacy and conflict resolution are similar. Both advocates and conflict resolvers (mediators, especially) share the goals of social justice and empowerment. They also share the goal of resolving conflicts by creating change, although the kind of change they seek may be different. Their methods differ as well.

First, mediators always work for both parties at the same time, trying to craft solutions that meet the needs of both parties simultaneously. Advocates usually work with one party only; they see the interests of that party as primary and will use any strategy or process—mediation or other-wise—to achieve their goals. Many advocates are suspicious of mediation and other conflict resolution processes based on consensus; some see it as a tool of oppression and co-optation, not empowerment and justice.

The goals of advocates and mediators are also different. Mediators are usually seeking win-win outcomes, whereas advocates are usually seeking a win for their side and don't particularly care about the outcome for the other side. Although this sounds crass, it is practical when facing situations that are not amenable to win-win solutions.

Similarly, mediators often try to equalize power differences between the parties, whereas advocates support this approach only if they begin with less power than the opponent. Since most advocates seek victory, not consensus, they reject power equalization efforts if they believe that they have the upper hand (Cunningham 1990, 35). Mediators also tend to focus more on the primacy of process, and advocates are more concerned about outcomes. Advocates see the process as a strategy for achieving their goals; it is not the goal itself.

Although community organizing and advocacy have been extremely successful in some areas in bringing about social change and improved justice, some observers of recent political processes see advocacy as the antithesis of collaborative problem solving and successful decision making. For instance, Larson and Chrislip observe that advocacy and grassroots organizing, as perfected in the 1960s and 1970s, empowered many veto groups and enabled them to stop the "old boys' network" from achieving its goals. These veto groups made leadership much more difficult, they say, because there was no longer a prevailing hierarchy. "No one has the authority to override others, yet many people are empowered to say no" (Larson and Chrislip 1994, 20–21). The result has been public policy gridlock.

"Numerous constituencies from all sectors have formed associations around common grievances, staking out every imaginable position on major issues. Each is convinced of the righteousness of its cause. Paranoid and hostile, they battle each other from mutually exclusive positions, their conflicting aims fragmenting power and political will. Most represent legitimate concerns, but few, unfortunately, speak for the broader interest of society" (Larson and Chrislip 1994, 21). This approach, they argue, invites polarization and detracts from our ability to solve complex public policy problems. "With no consensus, advocacy groups focus more on stopping others from implementing their solutions than on finding ways to solve problems. As advocacy oversimplifies and divides, it focuses attention on parochial interests rather than on the broader good" (Larson and Chrislip 1994, 22).

Although many advocates continue to use a divide-and-conquer strategy, others are becoming increasingly interested in consensus building and related approaches to problem solving. The Nature Conservancy, for instance, has long relied on negotiation and consensus-building efforts to achieve its environmental goals. Other environmental groups are beginning to use these strategies as well, realizing that consensus processes and advocacy do not need to be antithetical. If both advocates and third-party interveners learned more about the other's approaches, they would be more successful in their own.

See also: Collaborative Leadership; Collaborative Problem Solving; Community Organizing; Empowerment; Mediation; Persuasion.

References and Further Reading: Alinsky, Saul, 1971, *Rules for Radicals: A Practical Primer for Realistic Radicals;* Cunningham, Helen V., Mark A. Chesler, and Barbara Israel, 1990, "Strategies for Social Justice: A Retrieval Conference: Report on Grassroots Community Organizing and Conflict Intervention"; Kahn, Si, 1982, *Organizing: A Guide for Grassroots Leaders;* Kramer, Ralph M., and Harry Specht, 1969, *Readings in Community Organization*

Practice; Larson, Carl E., and David D. Chrislip, 1994, *Collaborative Leadership.*

Alinsky, Saul

Saul Alinsky was a community organizer who worked with poor and minority groups, training them in the techniques of community organization and nonviolent direct action. He helped them organize what he called "power blocs of the poor" to put pressure on governmental agencies and corporations to change their policies. One of his better-known efforts was in Rochester, New York, where he successfully pressured the Eastman Kodak Corporation and other local employers to hire more blacks. Another well-known campaign, which was undertaken by his Chicago Woodlawn organization, pressured the city and landlords to improve slum housing.

Although trained in the fields of criminology and conflict resolution, Alinsky was more of a conflict stimulator than a conflict resolver and was incarcerated several times for his civil disobedience. Working as a facilitator rather than a leader, Alinsky recruited local people whom he trained to lead his citizens organizations. In all his organizing, he emphasized group interests but personalized social problems—showing recruits how the social problems affected them and how they could organize to effect change. Using provocative language and strong speaking skills, he heightened people's anger with a target ("the villain") and trained them to initiate conflicts in order to force social change.

In the 1960s, Alinsky began working with the middle class, because he believed that significant social change could be brought about only by a well-organized majority. In 1968, he founded the Mid-America Institute, which trained middle-class activists to organize their own communities.

In addition to organizing and teaching, Alinsky wrote several books about his approach that became classics. These included *Reveille for Radicals* (1969, first published in 1946), which described his advocacy strategies for the poor, and *Rules for Radicals* (1971), which focused on middle-class organizing tactics.

See also: Community Organizing; Empowerment; Nonviolence.

References and Further Reading: Alinsky, Saul, 1969, *Reveille for Radicals;* Alinsky, Saul, 1971, *Rules for Radicals: A Practical Primer for Realistic Radicals;* Bailey, R., 1974, *Radicals in Urban Politics: The Alinsky Approach;* Finks, P. David, 1984, *The Radical Vision of Saul Alinsky;* Fisher, Robert, 1994, *Let the People Decide: Neighborhood Organizing in America;* Horwitt, Sanford D., 1989, *Let Them Call Me Rebel: Saul Alinsky, His Life and Legacy.*

Alternative Dispute Resolution

Alternative dispute resolution (ADR) is a broad term that encompasses all forms of dispute resolution other than court-based adjudication. Negotiation, mediation, and arbitration are all considered to be forms of ADR, as are many other related processes such as mini-trials, med-arb, private judging, ombudsmanship, neutral expert fact-finding, and summary jury trials.

Although both mediation and arbitration can be traced back hundreds of years, what has become known as the ADR movement began in the United States in the late 1960s. This was a time of considerable civil turmoil; it was also a time when the laws protecting individual rights were expanded, making it possible for many more people to use the courts for redress of grievances (especially in civil rights and environmental cases). The result was an apparent increase in civil suits that clogged court dockets, caused lengthy delays, and, in some cases, led to procedural errors. ADR was developed, at least in part, in an attempt to overcome these problems. By using negotiation, mediation, or arbitration, disputants could resolve many conflicts more quickly and less expensively than they could through court-based adjudication. This took part of the potential caseload away from the courts, thereby helping to mitigate the problem of case overload.

Other benefits of ADR have been touted as well. For instance, ADR is considered more user-friendly. It usually involves the disputants more directly in the dispute resolution process than adjudication (which relies on lawyers to represent clients and judges to make decisions). ADR often allows the conflicting parties to define both the process and the substance of any settlement to be reached. This increase in disputant involvement leads to greater satisfaction with the outcome. It also increases compliance with the decision in many cases. ADR is also seen as superior because it is more cooperative and less competitive or adversarial than court adjudication. This minimizes conflict escalation and hard feelings and tends to improve the relationship between the conflicting parties, rather than worsening it. This is especially important in situations in which the adversaries must continue to interact after the conflict is settled. Hostile and adversarial court proceedings often push disputants farther apart, making future cooperation (over child custody issues, for instance) more difficult.

Early in the movement, ADR was seen as a way to get communities as a whole involved in local dispute resolution processes. Neighborhood justice centers were intended to get local citizens involved in providing justice for themselves, instead of relying on outside professionals (lawyers and judges) to impose justice on them. Many people believe that this goal has not been achieved, but the potential to reap such benefits remains.

Although many ADR practitioners (mediators and arbitrators) believe that the advantages of ADR far outweigh the disadvantages, other scholars and lawyers have serious concerns about ADR processes. One concern is that ADR is a tool of the dominant class: it simply sugarcoats and perpetuates the domination of the weak by the powerful. Related to this is the charge that ADR provides second-class justice, with first-class justice being that provided by the courts (i.e., legal representation, carefully crafted rules of procedure and evidence, and due process). Those who cannot afford this class of justice can use ADR, which provides no such protections.

Likewise, ADR is believed to encourage compromise. This is fine in some cases but is inappropriate in cases of serious injustice, value-based conflicts, or conflicts that involve violence, confrontation with authorities, or defiance of legal norms. A final problem is one of precedent and community impact. Usually, ADR settlements are private. There is no public record of decisions, no public scrutiny or even awareness of repeated problems. Thus, if a large corporation is allowed to use ADR to privately settle multiple disputes over one defective product, there is no incentive or requirement that the product be improved or that the corporation's behavior change. A court ruling on a defective product, however, can force the company to remedy all the problems with the faulty product and can impose a high enough cost that the company is likely to be more careful in designing and testing its products in the future.

In balance, ADR is useful and even superior to court-based adjudication in many cases; however, it has enough problems that its use should be considered carefully. In general, ADR is best applied when the power of the two parties is roughly equal, when the continuing long-term relationship between the parties is important, when the precedents are clear, and when a cooperative or compromise outcome makes sense. Adjudication may be superior when a party seeks to test a law or set a precedent, when one party is significantly less powerful than the opponent, when a public outcome is desired, and when the case is so complicated that full discovery, rules of procedure, and rules of evidence are needed to yield a just outcome. Other criteria are important as well; further information can be found in the subsequent additional entries on ADR, the entries on each type of ADR and adjudication, and in the references.

See also: Adjudication; Arbitration; Med-Arb; Mediation; Mini-trial; Negotiation; Neutral Expert Fact-Finding; Ombudsman; Private Judging; Summary Jury Trial.
References and Further Reading: Dauer, Edward A., 1994, *Manual of Dispute Resolution;* Fiss, Owen M., 1984, "Against Settlement"; Goldberg, Stephen B., Eric D. Green, and Frank E. A. Sander, 1985, *Dispute Resolution;* Riskin, Leonard L., and James E. Westbrook, 1987, *Dispute Resolution and Lawyers;* Scimecca, Joseph A., 1993, "Theory and Alternative Dispute Resolution: A Contradiction in Terms?"; Singer, Linda R., 1990, *Settling Disputes: Conflict Resolution in Business, Families, and the Legal System.*

Alternative Dispute Resolution, Barriers to Use

Although alternative dispute resolution (ADR) is highly effective in many situations, barriers often prevent it from being used as much as it could be. These barriers include a lack of knowledge about ADR options. Few ADR providers have sufficient funds for advertising; thus information about the processes themselves and about providers tends to be primarily word-of-mouth.

Further, at least in the United States, the courts tend to be the socially acceptable way to prosecute disputes. People know about courts; they know how they work. Mediation and arbitration are less familiar and hence less trusted than traditional court-based adjudication. Although some lawyers are familiar with and supportive of the use of ADR in many situations, others are not comfortable with its use. Like the parties they are being asked to represent, many lawyers choose to avoid ADR processes, believing that the court is the best venue for obtaining justice. Lawyers in particular, but other parties as well, tend to be better trained in the techniques of adversarial argument than they are in consensus building or problem-solving negotiation. Therefore, they may

prefer dispute resolution processes that use the adversarial approach.

Since the use of ADR is usually voluntary, all the disputants must agree to use it. If one side wants mediation but the other wants to go to court, court wins. Courts or statutes may require that parties try mediation, but none requires that a settlement be reached. Thus, even in mandatory mediation, a party who prefers a court-based process can just refuse to settle and force the issue to go to court.

Other factors inhibit the use of ADR as well. For example, if the parties think that they have strong cases that can easily be won in court, they may be hesitant to enter the less predictable realm of mediation. Why settle when you can win outright? Likewise, if parties think that they can prevail using another power option (e.g., a strike, an election, or a lobbying campaign), they are likely to choose that approach over an ADR process that may require compromise. The same is true if the dispute involves inherently nonnegotiable issues. Deep-rooted moral conflicts over abortion or gay rights or high-stakes, unavoidable win-lose conflicts over the allocation of scarce resources are examples of issues that are not amenable to compromise. Parties confronting these issues usually choose adjudicatory processes over ADR for the resolution of their disputes.

Finally, if one party would benefit from delay or would benefit by imposing higher process costs on the opponent, it will choose adjudication over ADR. The same is true for parties wanting to set a precedent for future cases, which ADR generally does not do. Thus, ADR is possible only when it has potential benefits for all the parties and when the parties are cognizant of its existence and the likely benefits it can provide.

See also: Alternative Dispute Resolution; Alternative Dispute Resolution, Ethical Issues; Alternative Dispute Resolution, Institutionalization; Intractable Conflicts.
References and Further Reading: Dauer, Edward A., 1994, *Manual of Dispute Resolution;* Goldberg, Stephen B.,

Eric D. Green, and Frank E. A. Sander, 1985, *Dispute Resolution*, 12–13; Goldberg, Stephen B., Frank E. A. Sander, and Nancy H. Rogers, 1992, *Dispute Resolution: Negotiation, Mediation, and Other Processes.*

Alternative Dispute Resolution, Ethical Issues

Alternative dispute resolution (ADR) gives rise to a number of ethical questions. Some relate to particular forms of ADR, others to ADR in general. One of the key questions regarding ADR in general is whether it provides second-class justice. Some observers believe that ADR is not as fair as the process provided by the traditional legal system because it is much less formal, is not always bound by substantive law, and is private (hence not open to public scrutiny). Although many people view these characteristics as benefits, other observers see them as costs and argue that ADR is used only by those who lack the money, the time, or the knowledge to use the better system—the courts. This view is at least partially supported by data that reveal that the bulk of community mediation center clients are the poor who have no other access to the justice system (Abel 1982).

Ironically, others see the court system as the second-class process and private alternatives, such as private judging, as the first-class alternative. This view argues that private judging has all the procedural safeguards of the courts yet is almost always much faster; it has the further benefit of allowing the disputants to choose the judge, which they cannot do in the public system. These observers question whether the rich should be allowed to buy a gold-plated process while others are left with bogged-down courts that take too many procedural shortcuts to try to cut caseloads—yet still remain terribly slow. It has also been argued that private judging is harming the public judicial process by siphoning off the best judges and taking the steam out of needed reform measures. The

suggestion has also been made that ADR is replacing a good but overburdened system with an inferior system, rather than putting the effort into fixing the problems of the court system to make it work more effectively.

Other ethical questions revolve around particular processes. With both mediation and arbitration, there are questions about the qualifications and certification of providers. Since the field is still quite new, there are no standard procedures for training or certification. Anyone can hang a sign on the door, proclaiming themselves to be a mediator or an arbitrator. Although most have some training, few have a great deal of training and experience when they start practicing. Hence the quality of service is highly variable.

Questions of neutrality and impartiality are also problematic in mediation and arbitration. Although it is assumed that a mediator or arbitrator should be both neutral and impartial, in practice this can be hard to accomplish. Mediators often take a liking or disliking to one or more of their clients. Should they then withdraw from the case because they can no longer act impartially? Answers to this question differ from person to person. Suppose the mediator realizes that one party is overpowering another, or that one party is lying or otherwise subverting the process. Should he or she expose the problem or not? To preserve the fairness of the process, the mediator would have to, yet to do so is a violation of the standard of confidentiality, another cornerstone of most mediation codes of ethics. What if the parties agree to a settlement that appears to the mediator to be grossly unfair to one of the parties, or perhaps to a third party who is not at the table (to the children in a divorce situation, for example)? Should the mediator try to convince the parties to alter their agreement? Or should the mediator withdraw from the process (thereby absolving him- or herself of responsibility) and allow the parties to finalize the agreement with another mediator or on their own?

These questions relate to another ethical question regarding the mediator's role in directing the process. Some mediators argue that they are process consultants only, that they should never get involved in the substantive debate. Others take an active role, highlighting areas of common ground, proposing solutions to problems, drafting settlement agreements (before the parties agree to the terms), and then trying to "sell" these agreements to the parties. No consensus has been reached on which approach is more appropriate, although activist mediators (those who take an active role in the substance of the discussions) are probably more common than transformational mediators (those who focus on the process and leave the substance to the parties themselves).

These are but a few of the many unresolved ethical questions surrounding ADR. Although they often pose problems for third-party interveners and their clients, most mediators and arbitrators are aware of the ethical challenges they face and diligently try to make the best decision in each case. Clients should explore the ethical approaches and assumptions of a mediator before hiring that person, and they should feel comfortable with the approach the mediator intends to take.

See also: Alternative Dispute Resolution, Institutionalization; Arbitration, Ethical Issues; Mediation, Ethical Issues; Mediation Models; Mediator Selection.

References and Further Reading: Abel, Richard, 1982, *The Politics of Informal Justice: The American Experience;* Burton, John, and Frank Dukes, 1990b, *Conflict: Practices in Management, Settlement and Resolution,* 186–88; Bush, Robert A. Baruch, 1992, *The Dilemmas of Mediation Practice: A Study of Ethical Dilemmas and Policy Implications;* Folberg, Jay, and Alison Taylor, 1984, *Mediation: A Comprehensive Guide to Resolving Conflicts without Litigation,* 244–90; Gibson, Kevin, 1989, "The Ethical Basis of Mediation: Why Mediators Need Philosophers"; Kolb, Deborah M., and Associates, 1994, *When Talk Works: Profiles of Mediators;* Tillett, Gregory, 1991, *Resolving Conflict: A Practical Approach,* 145–59.

Alternative Dispute Resolution, Institutionalization

The use of alternative dispute resolution (ADR) has become more common over the last 25 years. Used in only a few settings (labor-management negotiations, for instance) in the 1950s, it has now spread to almost every U.S. institution, from the family and church to the schools, the workplace, government agencies, and the courts. Family and divorce mediation are now common throughout the United States, and a number of state and local jurisdictions require that mediation be attempted in divorce or child custody cases before they are brought before the court. Many schools nationwide are using peer mediation to help teach students conflict resolution skills, enabling them to handle their own conflicts without the intervention of teachers or principals. Although such school-based programs were relatively rare ten years ago, they are now commonplace at all levels, from kindergarten through high school. The most successful programs involve the teachers and school administrators as well as the students. Everyone is trained in dispute resolution practices, and they use these practices to resolve the many kinds of conflicts that arise within school settings.

Dispute resolution programs are also much more common in workplace settings than they were 20 or 30 years ago. Ombudsman offices are common, as are streamlined grievance procedures that are based on the ADR concepts of mediation, arbitration, and dispute systems design. In addition to being used to resolve employee-employer and coworker conflicts, ADR is frequently used to resolve consumer and commercial dispute between businesses. Many contracts contain mediation or arbitration clauses, requiring the use of one of these processes to resolve disputes before turning to the courts. This has caused ethical problems, because some industries require consumers to submit to a board of arbitrators created by the industry itself. Whether such mediators or arbitrators can still act fairly is a matter that is under scrutiny. Businesses tend to favor these processes, however, because they are much faster than court-based alternatives, and they are usually private. That prevents the publication of sensitive information, be it trade secrets or the faulty nature of a company's product. (The avoidance of class-action claims in cases in which they are justified is one drawback of ADR processes.)

Finally, ADR has become increasingly commonplace in government agencies, from the local to the federal level, especially in the executive and judicial branches. By July 1995, 18 states had established state offices of dispute resolution to implement and oversee a wide variety of state-based ADR programs. These offices were established largely because of government administrators' concerns about the rising cost of litigation. ADR is also seen as a way of showing "an increasingly skeptical public that [government] can be innovative and consumer-responsive" (Khor 1995b, 1).

Also common at the state or local level are court-based ADR programs designed to lighten burgeoning caseloads. One common approach is called court-annexed arbitration. This is a mandatory but nonbinding form of arbitration that is required by statute or court rule in about 20 states and several federal district courts for particular kinds of cases—money claims under certain amounts (typically $50,000 to $150,000) or automobile damage claims. Disputants are required to try arbitration before proceeding to trial. However, if they are not satisfied with the arbitrators' findings, they can request a new trial (trial de novo). Other alternatives to court-based adjudication that can be suggested by lawyers or judges include early neutral evaluations, summary jury trials, and special master mediators.

Although some federal agencies began experimenting with regulatory negotiation and other forms of ADR in the late 1970s, ADR became widely used at the federal level in the 1990s following the passage of several key acts, including the Civil Justice Reform Act of 1990, the Negotiated Rulemaking Act of 1990, and the Administrative Dispute Resolution Act of 1990. The Civil Justice Reform Act required, among other things, that federal judges establish advisory committees to help the courts deal with the problems of court congestion and delay and to consider the possible use of ADR to mitigate these problems. Similarly, the other two acts encouraged, and in some instances required, federal agencies to use ADR processes in rulemaking, enforcement, and other activities affecting or involving the public. Although some federal agencies use ADR much more than others, the trend toward its increasing use continues across all governmental levels.

See also: Administrative Dispute Resolution Acts of 1990 and 1996; Civil Justice Reform Act of 1990; Court-Annexed Alternative Dispute Resolution Procedures; Federal Use of Alternative Dispute Resolution; Negotiated Rulemaking Act of 1990; Ombudsman.

References and Further Reading: Fowler, Mary Candace, 1995, "Uncle Sam's In-House 'Efficacy Experts' Report Savings from ADR"; Khor, Karen, 1995b, "Cost-Savings Propel Proliferation of States' Conflict-Resolution Programs"; Laue, James, 1987, "The Emergence and Institutionalization of Third Party Roles in Conflict."

The Alternative Newsletter

The Alternative Newsletter is a highly useful and detailed resource on dispute resolution. Originally sponsored by the Association of American Law Schools, the newsletter is now independent. Edited and distributed by James Boskey of the Seton Hall Law School in Newark, New Jersey, the newsletter is intended to be used primarily by lawyers. However, it is written in easy-to-understand English and contains a wealth of information likely to be valuable to anyone interested in the field of dispute resolution—lawyer or not. It comes out three times a year and is available on disk or on paper.

Topics covered include a listing and review of new books in the field of alternative dispute resolution (ADR) and a fairly complete listing of ADR articles published since the last issue of the newsletter. Also included are lists of new ADR organizations, upcoming training programs, meetings and conferences, job opportunities, and short news items related to ADR topics. This newsletter can help a person stay abreast of ADR developments better than any other single publication.

American Arbitration Association

Founded in 1926 as a public service, non-profit organization, the American Arbitration Association (AAA) provides alternative dispute resolution (ADR) services as well as educational and training services. Although the AAA does not decide cases, it provides a forum in which disputes can be heard by a roster of over 20,000 neutral parties. It operates 36 offices nationwide and maintains an international arbitration network.

The AAA offers a variety of ADR services, including arbitration, mediation, mini-trials, fact-finding, election services, insurance ADR, ADR for business, and court-referred mediation. The AAA also serves as a resource for other conflict resolution institutions by operating the largest ADR library and offering continuing education and training for staff, neutrals, and conflict resolution professionals.

As stated in its bylaws, "the objectives of AAA are to study, research, promote, establish and administer procedures for the resolution of disputes of all kinds." The AAA has tested and established many of the current rules and procedures for ADR processes.

Membership in the AAA is open to all who are interested in voluntary dispute settlement. Currently, AAA members include companies, unions, associations, law firms, arbitrators, and individuals. The AAA draws financial support from member contributions, which supplement income derived from administrative charges for services.

The AAA has published several videotapes and books on ADR. It also issues pamphlets updating ADR procedures and produces several quarterly journals.

See also: Alternative Dispute Resolution; Arbitration Appendix 1 for contact information.
References and Further Reading: American Arbitration Association, World Wide Web Home Page, http://www.adr.org.

American Bar Association, Dispute Resolution Section

The American Bar Association (ABA) is the primary professional association for lawyers in the United States. Its members include practicing and nonpracticing lawyers, judges, court administrators, law teachers, and public attorneys (e.g., public defenders and government attorneys). It not only represents the interests of its members, it also addresses many issues of public concern: child abuse, governmental corruption, juvenile crime, pollution, and costly and ineffective justice, among others.

In 1993, the ABA created a Dispute Resolution Section. The purposes of this section are to study and implement improved methods of dispute resolution, including court-annexed and court-directed dispute resolution processes and other private and community-based alternative dispute resolution (ADR) processes. It also provides an ADR clearinghouse, technical assistance, and public and professional education programs. The section publishes the *Dispute Resolution Magazine* three times a year for its members and collaborates on the *Ohio State Journal on Dispute Resolution*, which also comes out three times a year—twice with articles on dispute resolution topics, and once with a bibliography of recent publications in the field.

References and Further Reading: American Bar Association, World Wide Web Home Page, http://www.abanet.org/dispute/home.html.

American Bar Association Practice Standards for Lawyer Mediators in Family Disputes

In 1984, the American Bar Association (ABA) adopted a set of standards that define acceptable practice for lawyers who act as mediators in family disputes. The standards listed in this document include the following: (1) The mediator has a duty to describe the mediation process and its cost before parties agree to mediate. (2) The mediation is confidential, meaning that the mediator will not disclose information obtained from the participants during the mediation without the prior consent of both parties. (3) The mediator must be impartial. (4) The mediator must make sure that the participants' decisions are based on sufficient knowledge and information. (5) The mediator has a duty to suspend or terminate the mediation if continuing it would harm one or more of the participants. (6) The mediator has a duty to advise each participant to obtain legal review prior to reaching an agreement. Each of these items is elaborated on, giving mediators direction about how they should go about fulfilling these obligations and what related obligations they have in these areas.

See also: Divorce Mediation; Mediation, Ethical Issues; Model Standards of Conduct for Mediators.

References and Further Reading: American Bar Association, 1984, "ABA Standards of Practice for Lawyer Mediators in Family Disputes."

Amnesty and Forgiveness

Like apology, amnesty and forgiveness are important tools for bringing about reconciliation in a variety of conflict situations. "Forgiveness is not 'giving up,' or 'letting the other off the hook.' It is a self-realiza-tion that allows one to develop a sense of compassion" (McFarland 1995, 1).

In deep-rooted international or internal ethnic conflicts (such as those in the Middle East or the Balkans), reconciliation cannot occur until all sides are willing to forgive the others for their wrongdoing. According to Montville (1993, 112), "Transactional contrition and forgiveness between aggressors and victims is indispensable to the establishment of a new relationship based on mutual acceptance and reasonable trust." Such forgiveness is hard—especially if one is forgiving unspeakable violence, as occurred in the Balkans. However, over the long run, it can help heal wounds and allow people to get on with their personal, social, and political lives. "The more common misperception is that by performing acts of revenge, one's hurt will go away. This notion blocks people from coming out of their pain and moving on" (McFarland 1995, 10). Forgiveness does not come quickly or naturally, however. People need time to mourn their loss and to heal to some extent before they are ready to forgive.

One of the dilemmas of conflict resolution is whether to institutionalize forgiveness in the form of granting amnesty for war crimes, or whether such crimes should be prosecuted. In some cases, one side insists on prosecuting war criminals (for instance, when many Nazis were tried for war crimes after World War II). In other cases, wars can be ended (and many deaths and atrocities avoided) if all sides are granted amnesty from prosecution. This was the case in the Nicaraguan conflict between the Sandinistas and the Contras, which was ended with the Esquipulas Agreement of 1987. Among other provisions, this agreement granted amnesty to all insurgents. Paul Wehr tells a moving story about this process: "Time and again, the spirit of reconciliation was evident in the way Sandinistas dealt with their opposition. By way of illustration, Interior Minister Tomas Borge came upon a National Guard officer who had only months before the Sandinista victory tortured, raped, and killed Borge's wife. He took the officer out of the line, who undoubtedly feared he would be executed immediately. Instead, according to the account, Borge told him, 'My revenge will be to pardon you'" (Wehr and Nepstad 1994, 89). The South African offer of amnesty to perpetrators of political violence during the apartheid era is another example. Without amnesty, the successful transition to the new democratic structure would have been much less likely.

See also: Apology; Communal Conflicts; Ethnic and Racial Conflicts; International Conflict; Reconciliation; Truth and Reconciliation Commission, South Africa.
References and Further Reading: Curle, Adam, 1995, "Forgiveness?"; McFarland, Daniel, 1995, "Consultation on Reconciliation: New Directions in Peacebuilding"; Montville, Joseph, 1993, "The Healing Function in Political Conflict Resolution"; Schmidt, Janet P., 1995, "Mediation and the Healing Journey toward Forgiveness"; Wehr, Paul, and Sharon Erickson Nepstad, 1994, "Violence, Nonviolence, and Justice in Sandinista Nicaragua."

Anger and Anger Management

Anger is a natural human reaction that is an autonomic (hence unavoidable) response in some situations, and a chosen response in others. If it is constructively expressed and effectively managed, anger can be beneficial. It can open lines of communication; it can alert the angry person and others that there is a problem that needs to be solved. This creates an opportunity for reconciliation and the development of mutually beneficial (win-win) solutions.

Often, however, anger is not effectively managed and is expressed in destructive ways. The common result is escalated anger and conflict, harmed or destroyed relationships, and mounting social, psychological, and even economic costs. Rather than opening channels of communication, destructive anger can block communication completely. It discourages the target

from responding with empathy, encouraging retaliation instead. Thus learning how to express anger constructively and to manage its effects are essential for effective conflict management and resolution.

Response to Anger

Perhaps the most important rule of effective anger management is understanding that people always have a choice about how they will respond to an anger-provoking situation. Even when anger is completely justified, as when a child is killed or a person is treated in an abhorrent way, the angry respondent has a choice of retaliating (which usually makes matters worse) or expressing anger in a way that is more likely to lead to a constructive response. Retaliation usually feeds the conflict spiral, increasing the intensity of the anger on both sides and leading to a continued and worsening conflict. In international situations, this can eventually lead to war; in interpersonal conflicts, it can lead to severed relationships and, at times, interpersonal violence. Constructive anger management, in contrast, de-escalates conflicts; it allows the offending party to understand that he or she has made a mistake and to take steps to remedy the situation. This can lead to improved outcomes and successful long-term relationships.

Self-Awareness

The first step toward constructive anger management, according to Gary Hankins, author of *Prescription for Anger,* is developing improved self-awareness. The more you are able to identify and predict what situations make you angry and how you typically respond, the more you will be able to modify your response to make it constructive. "Anger management is NOT the process of avoiding or eliminating anger, rather it is the process of using your self-awareness to make your anger work for you, rather than against you" (Hankins

1988, 139). If you understand what typically makes you angry, people will not be able to "push your buttons" or knock you off balance. You will be prepared for any tricks they might try and will have a pre-planned effective response to most anger-provoking situations. Even when anger hits you by surprise, such self-awareness can help you respond in a more effective way, as you become aware of what you are doing and how that will affect your opponent and your relationship overall.

The Fishbowl Technique

Another trick for successfully managing anger is what Hankin calls the "fishbowl technique." Here you step back and away from an anger-provoking situation as it is going on and observe it as if you were watching fish from outside the fishbowl. Rather than reacting immediately and impulsively, step back and watch your own and your opponents' moves to see who is doing what and what the response to each statement is. This allows you to plan a response that is likely to be most effective for you, while doing as little damage to the relationship as possible.

Conflict theorist William Ury (1991) makes a similar suggestion: "Go to the balcony," he says, whenever you get angry. Step away and assess what is happening, why it is happening, and what you can do to turn the process your way. This is opposite to our normal tendency, Ury points out, which is to strike back, give in, or leave. Yet none of these responses is as likely to get us what we need as a calm and rational approach, which is possible to implement if we "go to the balcony" or use the fishbowl technique to calm down and plan a constructive response.

Relaxation Techniques

Other techniques for calming down include deep breathing, counting, or using rapid relaxation. Rapid relaxation, as de-scribed by Hankin, involves four steps. First is refocusing attention away from the provocation toward a desired resolution. Second is relaxing with calming self-talk. Third is reevaluating—putting the situation into perspective and analyzing how important it really is. Is it important enough to risk your life, a treasured relationship, a job, your health, or your reputation? Probably not. The fourth step is re-freshing—becoming aware of the physical, emotional, and mental power you can attain by calming down and maintaining your self-balance and control.

Rational Emotive Therapy

Similar to rapid relaxation is Albert Ellis's technique of rational emotive therapy, or RET. This theory suggests that anger is a result of your response to a situation, not the situation itself. So you can control your anger by controlling your thoughts. RET focuses especially on dispelling destructive, "irrational" ideas and replacing them with constructive, "rational" thoughts. These thoughts can then be used to develop a constructive response to anger-creating situations.

I-Messages

In addition to controlling their own anger, parties to conflict can often behave in ways that limit their opponents' anger as well. One widely taught technique is the use of "I-messages" rather than "you-messages" to express dissatisfaction with another. I-messages explain one's own feelings: "I feel insecure when I don't know what is going to happen next." In contrast, you-messages are accusatory: "You never tell me what's going on!" By putting blame on the other, you-messages encourage anger and self-defensive responses. I-messages encourage empathy and joint problem solving.

See also: De-escalation; Empathy; Escalation; I-Messages; Negotiation, Breakthrough.

References and Further Reading: Ellis, Albert, 1996, *Better, Deeper, and More Enduring Brief Therapy: The Rational Emotive Behavior Therapy Approach;* Hankins, Gary, 1988, *Prescription for Anger;* Ury, William, 1991, *Getting Past No: Negotiating with Difficult People.*

Apology

Apologizing can be a powerful tool in conflict resolution, one that is sometimes essential to reconciliation. According to a number of international conflict scholars, including Joseph Montville, apologies are absolutely essential in the resolution of violent ethnic or religious conflicts, such as those occurring in the Middle East or in the Balkans. In those situations, it is essential that both sides listen to and acknowledge their responsibility for the grievances of their opponents. Only by accepting their appropriate moral responsibility for the opponents' suffering can healing and reconciliation take place. This then allows for the "establishment of a new relationship based on mutual acceptance and reasonable trust" (Montville 1993, 112). Such recognition of responsibility and apology are rare in deep-rooted, protracted conflicts but can sometimes be fostered by parties engaging in cooperative problem-solving efforts, particularly problem-solving workshops designed by Herbert Kelman (Kelman and Cohen 1976), John Burton (1987), and others.

Apologies are also useful—and often easier to obtain—in interpersonal conflicts. Typical steps in problem-solving negotiation involve first listening to the grievances of the other side and then acknowledging those grievances. Acknowledgment does not necessarily imply agreement with that view, but simply acceptance of the fact that it exists. If, however, one party agrees that he or she was in error, at least in part, and is willing to apologize for that error, that can go a long way toward mending relationships and encouraging the other side to then accept responsibility for his or her part of the problem. As in international cases, apology paves the way for the development of cooperative solutions and the reestablishment of trust and strong working relationships.

See also: Amnesty and Forgiveness; Collaborative Problem Solving; Ethnic and Racial Conflicts; Problem Solving, Analytical; Reconciliation; Trust and Trust Building; Truth and Reconciliation Commission, South Africa; Value Conflicts.

References and Further Reading: Burton, John, 1987, *Resolving Deep-Rooted Conflict: A Handbook;* Kelman, Herbert, and Stephen Cohen, 1976, "The Problem-Solving Workshop: A Social Psychological Contribution to the Resolution of Conflict"; Montville, Joseph, 1993, "The Healing Function in Political Conflict Resolution"; Rothman, Jay, 1992, *Confrontation to Cooperation: Resolving Ethnic and Regional Conflict;* Ury, William, 1991, *Getting Past No: Negotiating with Difficult People.*

Appropriate Dispute Resolution

The term *appropriate dispute resolution,* as distinct from alternative dispute resolution, emphasizes the belief that there is no one-size-fits-all dispute resolution process. Appropriate dispute resolution begins by assessing the conflict to determine which strategy is best suited to the situation. In some cases, the most appropriate approach may be one of the many processes that seek voluntary agreement between the parties—for instance, negotiation, mediation, or med-arb. In other cases, voluntary approaches may be inappropriate. For example, many believe that family mediation should not be used once family disputes become violent. Instead, the conflict should be handled as a criminal matter. In still other cases, the most appropriate approach is one that combines mandatory elements with voluntary ones. For example, victim offender mediation processes may be used once a court determines guilt. Similarly, sensitivity training might be required for people found guilty of sexual harassment. In cases involving serious violations of fundamental human rights in which the perpetrator is unwilling to admit guilt or remedy the situation, the most appropriate approach may involve some type of nonviolent direct action rather than compromise.

Although many people still use the term *ADR* to refer to alternatives to the court system, it is also commonly used in the sense of appropriate dispute resolution, suggesting that no one alternative is better than another in all circumstances.

See also: Alternative Dispute Resolution; Conflict Assessment; Multidoor Courthouse.

Arbitration

Arbitration is a dispute resolution process in which the disputing parties present their case to an impartial third party, who then issues a judgment. Like court-based adjudication, (i.e., litigation), arbitration is an adversarial rather than a cooperative process. However, it is usually not as formal as court-based adjudication. Technically, litigation is an arbitration process, but the term *arbitration* is usually reserved for private processes in which an independent arbitrator issues the decision.

Although it is applied in a variety of settings, arbitration is most commonly used in labor-management, commercial, and consumer conflicts. In 1985, more than 95 percent of all collective bargaining contracts contained a provision for final and binding arbitration to resolve labor-management disputes over such things as discipline, discharge, promotions or demotions, productivity, pensions, and seniority (American Arbitration Association 1996; Goldberg, Green, and Sander 1985, 189).

An example of a consumer case that might be arbitrated is a situation in which a consumer believes that a car repair shop damaged his or her car instead of fixing it and refuses to pay, demanding instead that the shop pay for the additional repairs needed from another shop. An arbitrator would listen to the arguments of both sides and then come to a decision—for instance, that the shop was not at fault and that the car owner should pay his or her debt in full, or that the shop was indeed at fault and should make the necessary repairs for free or reimburse the owner for the costs of obtaining the repairs elsewhere. Although these hypothetical outcomes are all-or-nothing, arbitration awards can be compromises as well. For example, the arbitrator might conclude that the shop did not do its job as well as it should have, but that it is not liable for further damage. Therefore, the arbitrator might say that the car owner owes the shop nothing, but the shop does not owe the consumer anything either.

Arbitration differs from mediation in that mediators do not make decisions; they only help the parties come to a decision themselves. Although an arbitrator's decision is usually final and binding, the disputing parties still control the range of issues to be resolved and often many of the procedural aspects of the process (although these are sometimes predetermined in a contract).

Most arbitration is voluntary; the disputants agree to enter into the process either after the dispute has occurred or beforehand through a contract or similar agreement. Many commercial and consumer contracts—for instance, health insurance contracts and brokerage agreements—contain a clause requiring that arbitration be used to resolve any disputes that arise in the implementation of the agreement.

Unlike adjudication, in which one party sues and the other party is forced to respond, both parties to a conflict must agree to arbitration in order for it to occur. Once a contract stipulating the use of arbitration to resolve disputes is signed, however, arbitration becomes mandatory. In either situation, once such an agreement is made, the arbitrator's ruling is final. (This contrasts with mediation, in which the final agreement can be rejected.) In addition, according to the U.S. Arbitration Act and the

Uniform Arbitration Act (which has been adopted in almost every state), arbitration rules are enforceable.

Types of Arbitration

Several variations of the basic arbitration model exist. Among them are high-low arbitration, in which the limits of the award are set before the hearing; final-offer arbitration, in which the arbitrator must pick one of the parties' final offers; and advisory arbitration, which is similar to regular arbitration, but the decision is not binding. Another nonbinding form of arbitration is court-annexed arbitration. This kind of arbitration, initiated by the judicial system to remedy court overloads, is mandatory but not binding. This means that some kinds of cases in particular jurisdictions—for instance, cases involving monetary damages under $50,000—are required to go to arbitration before they can be litigated. If the parties accept the arbitrator's finding, the case is settled. If one or both parties reject the ruling, they have a right to a new trial (called a trial de novo) in which the case is heard in a regular court. Many jurisdictions discourage such appeals by requiring that a party that fails to win more in court than it was offered in arbitration pay court costs or even an additional penalty.

The Arbitration Process

The arbitration process varies considerably from case to case but typically follows several general steps. First, the parties agree to use arbitration and choose an arbitrator (or sometimes a panel of three arbitrators). A large number of for-profit firms provide arbitrators, as do several nonprofit and government organizations, for instance, the American Arbitration Association (AAA) and the Federal Mediation and Conciliation Service (FMCS; limited to labor disputes). The AAA, for example, gives parties a list of possible arbitrators, along with short bi-

ographies of each. Both parties indicate their choices in order and cross out any on the list whom they find unacceptable. The AAA then compares the two lists and chooses the arbitrator who best matches the parties' selections. In other cases, each party chooses one arbitrator, and those two arbitrators jointly select a third.

Most often, arbitrators are chosen for their particular experience and expertise. Commercial arbitrators are often lawyers, businesspeople, or professors who have expertise in the area of the dispute (computer software, construction, telecommunications, and so forth). Labor arbitrators are usually experienced in labor law or labor relations.

After the arbitrator is selected, he or she talks with the parties to learn what the conflict is about. Sometimes a preliminary hearing is held to clarify the issues in dispute, the uncontested facts, and the procedures to be used for the rest of the process. The arbitrator also gathers information about the case through written documents and summaries of each side's position. Usually the written information is supplemented by oral information presented in a full hearing. This hearing can be formal— almost like a court hearing—or it can be informal; it depends on the arbitrator's style, the parties' wishes, and any requirements detailed in the agreement to arbitrate. Usually, both parties present their arguments and respond to their opponent's arguments and any arbitrator questions. They often present witnesses, who may be cross-examined.

After the hearing, the arbitrator (or arbitration panel) considers the evidence and makes a decision, which may be an all-or-nothing outcome or a compromise, depending on the facts of the case. If necessary, the decision may be explained in a written document. In traditional arbitration, this decision is binding—it cannot be appealed except in rare circumstances. In court-annexed arbitration or advisory arbitration, however, the decision is not binding unless both parties agree to it. If they do not, the parties are free to pursue litigation or any other dispute resolution procedure.

Advantages of Arbitration

Arbitration has a number of advantages over both adjudication and mediation in many instances. First, it is more flexible than adjudication. The parties can choose the arbitrator themselves, who may be an expert in the field, whereas a judge is unlikely to have the appropriate technical expertise. Thus, arbitration is especially suited to complex and highly technical commercial disputes.

Second, the timing of the hearing can be adjusted to meet the parties' needs. In most cases, the process can be completed much more quickly than is possible through the courts. Since time is usually money, a faster process has double benefits in many cases.

Third, arbitration is private. Although the parties may disclose what happened afterward (unless they mutually agree not to), the documents and the hearing itself are closed to outsiders. This can help preserve positive working relationships. It also permits the protection of trade secrets and other information that parties (especially businesses) would prefer be kept private.

Fourth, most arbitration decisions are final and binding. This means that the case will be brought to a close quickly. It will not be drawn out for years and years through an endless (and costly) appeals process.

Many of these benefits are provided by mediation as well, but arbitration works in cases in which mediation does not. Mediation does not work well, for instance, in cases that revolve around questions of fact or legal interpretation. In these instances, an adversarial process is often more effective. Arbitration is also superior to media-

tion when the relationship between the parties has completely disintegrated. Mediation requires at least some degree of communication, cooperation, and trust. If these factors are absent and cannot be rebuilt by a mediator, either arbitration or litigation is likely to be the process of choice.

Disadvantages of Arbitration

Arbitration does have disadvantages, however. Like adjudication, it is adversarial in nature. It does not rebuild relationships, and it does nothing to foster trust between the disputing parties. Rather, arbitration can encourage the continued escalation of the conflict as the parties attempt to present their own versions of the story in the strongest possible terms while belittling or disputing the facts presented by the other side. In addition, the decision-making authority is taken away from the parties themselves. Some see this as disempowering and ultimately less satisfying than a process, such as mediation, that allows the conflicting parties to tailor the outcome to best meet their interests and needs.

Others decry arbitration for being too informal and potentially unjust. Since arbitration decisions are not appealable, the arbitrator has broad powers, which can potentially be abused. Some charge that arbitrators tend to look for compromise solutions, even when doing so doesn't make sense, in an effort to please both parties so that they will be chosen as arbitrators again. Others charge that arbitrators tend to make win-lose decisions based on obvious criteria, without carefully looking into the parties' interests to ferret out possible win-win outcomes. Since arbitration usually simplifies and shortens many aspects of court adjudication (limiting discovery and the presentation of testimony), some charge that arbitration fails to provide due process. Like mediation, arbitration also fails to produce a public record of the proceedings, which is important in some cases.

Whether these costs and shortcomings of arbitration are worth the benefits depends on the particular situation and the interests and concerns of the parties involved.

See also: American Arbitration Association; Arbitration, Final-Offer; Arbitration, High-Low Contract; Commercial Disputes; Consumer Disputes; Court-Annexed Alternative Dispute Resolution Procedures; Federal Mediation and Conciliation Service; Labor-Management Relations and Conflict; Mediation.

References and Further Reading: American Arbitration Association, World Wide Web Home Page, http://www.adr.org; Folberg, Jay, and Ann L. Milne, 1988, *Divorce Mediation: Theory and Practice;* Goldberg, Stephen B., Eric D. Green, and Frank E. A. Sander, 1985, *Dispute Resolution;* Tillet, Gregory, 1991, *Resolving Conflict: A Practical Approach.*

Arbitration, Advisory

Advisory arbitration is similar to regular arbitration, except that it is used for advisory purposes only—the outcome is not binding. Its purpose is to give parties information about the likely result of a case without risking the finality of an unfavorable outcome. Advisory arbitration can help clarify the legal ramifications of the case and the likely judicial or arbitrated outcome for all parties. Once such a clarification is obtained, parties and their lawyers are in a much better position to negotiate an outcome that parallels the likely adjudicated outcome yet saves time and money. In addition, the parties can fine-tune the agreement to better meet their needs while staying close enough to the predicted adjudicated outcome so that all the parties will agree to the negotiated settlement.

See also: Arbitration; Early Neutral Evaluation; Mini-trial; Neutral Expert Fact-Finding; Summary Jury Trial.
References and Further Reading: Dauer, Edward A., 1994, *Manual of Dispute Resolution.*

Arbitration, Commercial

Arbitration is particularly common in commercial disputes, that is, in disputes between private businesses. Commercial arbitration can be traced back to eighteenth-century England, where merchants preferred it to adjudication, because they could resolve disputes according to their own customs rather than public law. In the United States, arbitration has been commonly used to resolve commercial disputes since the late nineteenth century (Goldberg, Green, and Sander 1985, 280–82).

Typical issues that are arbitrated involve problems with delayed shipments, incomplete shipments, quality of goods delivered, or claims of contract violations. Rather than taking the other party to court, businesses often prefer to use arbitration because it is quicker, less costly, and more private. Frequently, an agreement to arbitrate disputes is made in the initial contract, before any disputes arise. In other cases, no such arrangement is made, but the parties agree to use arbitration when the dispute occurs.

Although arbitrators can be found in a number of ways, they are often provided by the American Arbitration Association (AAA), the leading commercial arbitration organization in the United States. The AAA trains and certifies arbitrators and provides lists of qualified arbitrators to anyone requesting arbitration assistance. The parties generally have ten days to examine the list (which contains names and biographical information), cross off any people they consider unacceptable, and indicate their preferences regarding the others. The AAA then uses these preferences to choose an arbitrator who is acceptable to both sides.

The next step is often a preliminary hearing, which may be requested by either party or the arbitrator to clarify the issues, determine contested and uncontested facts, and discuss the exact process that will be used. Often a contract specifies that AAA procedures will be followed, in which case the procedural rules are set. When such a stipulation is not made, arbitrators have considerable flexibility regarding the level of formality of the process; therefore, they often discuss the options with the parties involved.

The next step is the regular arbitration hearing, in which each side presents its case in an effort to prove that its argument is correct and the other is wrong. Parties may represent themselves or may have lawyers represent them. Generally, the procedures are the same as those used in adjudication (though often greatly streamlined and simplified). Each party makes an opening statement, discusses remedies sought, provides witnesses, and makes a closing statement, summing up its position. After both sides do this, the arbitrator considers the evidence and makes a decision, which is binding. Unless requested otherwise by the parties, the decision requires no oral or written justification.

Because it is a simplified version of adjudication, arbitration is often a quicker and less costly way to get the same result. It is also useful when the dispute is highly complicated or technical. Unlike judges, who are usually experts in the law but not in the substantive issue in dispute, arbitrators can be both. Alternatively, a panel of three arbitrators can be chosen, one or two having expertise in the substantive matter of the case, the other having procedural or legal expertise. In such a case, a majority decision must be made by the panel members, and that decision is binding.

See also: American Arbitration Association; Arbitration; Commercial Disputes.

References and Further Reading: American Arbitration Association, 1991, *A Commercial Arbitration Guide for Business People;* Coulson, R., 1985, "Code of Ethics for Arbitrators in Commercial Disputes"; Goldberg, Stephen B., Eric D. Green, and Frank E. A. Sander, 1985, *Dispute Resolution.*

Arbitration, Court-Annexed

Court-annexed arbitration is mandatory arbitration that parties in some jurisdictions are required by law to try for particular kinds of civil cases before they may bring those cases to trial. Unlike traditional arbitration, which is voluntary but binding, court-annexed arbitration is mandatory but not binding. If either of the parties does not like the arbitration award, that party is free to appeal the award through a trial in court (called a trial de novo, in legal terminology). Many jurisdictions, however, try to limit such appeals by charging a hefty fee to parties that do not improve their arbitration award at the trial. (The assumption is that if they come out the same or worse, the appeal was frivolous.)

Developed initially in Pennsylvania in 1952, court-annexed arbitration has become increasingly popular as a way to mitigate judicial backlogs. Typical cases that are required to use court-annexed arbitration are civil cases seeking monetary remedies below a certain threshold, which ranges from about $15,000 to $150,000. Some jurisdictions specify the type of cases as well: automobile injury cases, for example. Often exemptions are possible for inappropriate cases, and litigants who do not fall under the mandatory categories can choose to use the procedure on a voluntary basis as well.

The decision-making processes used in court-annexed arbitration are similar to those in traditional arbitration. The parties choose their own arbitrator from lists supplied by the court or by private organizations, such as the American Arbitration Association. The arbitrator reviews written documents, holds a hearing, and renders a decision, which he or she delivers to the parties and files with the court. If neither party requests a trial de novo within a predetermined period (30 days, for example), the decision is deemed final and is enforceable just as if it were obtained in a regular trial.

According to Nolan-Haley (1992), participants generally perceive court-annexed arbitration to be fair, but it is not clear whether it significantly reduces judicial time and costs. Nevertheless, increasing numbers of local, state, and federal courts are adopting such procedures. By 1985, 24 states and 19 federal districts used court-annexed arbitration or were actively considering it. This number has continued to grow, and in 1990, 33 states had court-annexed arbitration or mediation programs; by 1994, the number of such programs was in the hundreds (Dauer 1994, 13-2).

See also: Adjudication; Arbitration; Court-Annexed Alternative Dispute Resolution Procedures.

References and Further Reading: Burton, Lloyd, and John McIver, 1991, "A Summary of the Court-Annexed Arbitration Evaluation Project"; Dauer, Edward A., 1994, *Manual of Dispute Resolution;* Nolan-Haley, Jacqueline M., 1992, *Alternative Dispute Resolution in a Nutshell;* Sherman, E., 1995, "Court-Mandated Alternative Dispute Resolution: What Form of Participation Should Be Required?"

Arbitration, Ethical Issues

Arbitrators are guided by one or more codes of ethics developed by leading arbitration associations. The Code of Ethics for Arbitrators in Commercial Disputes was developed jointly by the American Arbitration Association (AAA) and the American Bar Association. There is a separate but similar code of ethics for labor arbitrators that was developed by the AAA, the Federal Mediation and Conciliation Service, and the National Academy of Arbitrators, which is a private group of about 600 of the nation's top labor arbitrators.

The commercial code of ethics requires that arbitrators first "uphold the integrity and fairness of the arbitration process" (Coulson 1985, 196). This means that they must be neutral and impartial and should avoid any actions that suggest that they are not. They must not be swayed by outside pressure, by fear of criticism, or by self-interest. Further, the code states that they should prevent delaying tactics, harassment of parties, or other "abuses or disruption" of the arbitration process. They are required to make their decisions "in a just, independent, and deliberate

manner" (Coulson 1985, 199). The code also states that arbitrators should maintain the confidentiality of information given to them.

The code of ethics for labor arbitrators is similar. It sets out the qualifications necessary for labor arbitrators and their responsibilities, which include neutrality and impartiality, confidentiality, and avoidance of delay, just as the commercial code requires. Other items in the labor arbitration code include determination of fees, responsibilities to administrative agencies, and methods for conducting hearings and issuing decisions (Leap 1995).

See also: Alternative Dispute Resolution, Ethical Issues; Arbitration; Arbitration, Commercial; Arbitration, Labor; Mediation, Ethical Issues.

References and Further Reading: Coulson, R., 1985, "Code of Ethics for Arbitrators in Commercial Disputes"; Goldberg, Stephen B., Frank E. A. Sander, and Nancy H. Rogers, 1992, *Dispute Resolution: Negotiation, Mediation, and Other Processes;* Leap, Terry L., 1995, *Collective Bargaining and Labor Relations.*

Arbitration, Final-Offer

Final-offer arbitration is a special form of arbitration in which the arbitrator may not compromise but is required to choose the final offer of one of the parties to the dispute. This encourages parties to be reasonable, since they know that the most reasonable of the two (or more) offers will be selected.

This technique is often used in baseball salary disputes—in fact, some texts refer to the process as baseball arbitration. It is superior, in this context, to traditional arbitration because it prevents both parties from making outlandish demands in an effort to get the arbitrator to split the difference. Rather, the parties are encouraged to make reasonable demands. Often, in the process of determining what is reasonable, the disputing parties are actually able to work out an agreement without arbitration. Even when they cannot, however, the arbitrator is usually presented with two fairly reasonable offers rather

than two extreme positions that are hard
to reconcile.

See also: Arbitration; Collective Bargaining; Labor-
Management Relations and Conflict.
References and Further Reading: Adams, Charles W.,
1987, "Final Offer Arbitration: Time for Serious Consider-
ation by the Courts"; Goldberg, Stephen B., Eric D.
Green, and Frank E. A. Sander, 1985, *Dispute Resolution;*
Ury, William L., Jeanne M. Brett, and Stephen B. Gold-
berg, 1991, "Designing an Effective Dispute Resolution
System."

Arbitration, High-Low Contract

High-low contract arbitration is a variation on traditional arbitration in which
the parties agree to limit the range of
possible outcomes before they enter into
the arbitration process. This protects the
plaintiff (the person complaining) from
the fear that he or she will get nothing at
all; it also protects the defendant (the
person being complained about) from
having to pay an exorbitant award. These
limits reduce the risks of arbitration and
may encourage reluctant parties to enter
the process. Another advantage of high-
low contract arbitration is that the
process of setting the limits for awards
initiates a cooperative discussion between the parties before the arbitration
takes place. This may pave the way for
settlement through negotiation, making
arbitration unnecessary.

See also: Arbitration; Arbitration, Final-Offer.
References and Further Reading: Goldberg, Stephen B.,
Frank E. A. Sander, and Nancy H. Rogers, 1992, *Dispute
Resolution: Negotiation, Mediation, and Other Processes.*

Arbitration, Labor

In union-management grievance disputes,
binding arbitration is almost always used
as the ultimate dispute resolution mechanism after a variety of less formal approaches are tried. "If collective bargaining
agreements were written in clear, unambiguous language and grievance procedures allowed the resolution of contractual

disputes at the earliest possible stage, then
there would be little need for labor arbitrators," writes Terry Leap, an expert on
labor-management relations (Leap 1995,
435). However, he observes, this is seldom
the case. Contracts are ambiguous, so frequent disputes arise regarding proper interpretation. Although many such disputes
are resolved at earlier stages of the grievance process, some are sufficiently difficult
to sort out that binding arbitration is necessary for resolution. Feuille and Kolb
(1994) estimate this number to be somewhere between 2 and 20 percent.

Typical disputes involve charges of inappropriate promotion, demotion, or discharge or disputes over working conditions, disciplinary measures, or employee
compensation. In addition to being used to
settle questions of right and wrong, arbitration is commonly used in the labor-management context to resolve impasses in
bargaining over new contracts.

Although labor arbitration has a long
history, it has risen in prominence since
World War II, because arbitrators have
been able to address the issues and meet
the challenges of an ever-changing labor-
management climate. Labor arbitration
has been seen as a constant: a trusted
means that both labor and management
can rely on to render timely, fair, and effective decisions. Although other dispute resolution mechanisms (such as mediation)
have also been tried to resolve labor-management disputes, arbitration remains the
method most highly utilized and trusted.

The process of labor arbitration is similar to that of other types of arbitration (e.g.,
commercial arbitration). An arbitrator is
chosen, and a hearing is held. The hearing is
fairly formal—much like a court hearing—
although procedures can be simplified
somewhat if both parties and the arbitrator
agree. Evidence is presented and witnesses
are called and cross-examined; exhibits are
presented, all in an effort to persuade the
arbitrator that a particular side is right and

the other is wrong. The arbitrator listens to the evidence, reads the collective bargaining agreement, then makes a determination. He or she issues an opinion within a specified time (usually 30 days) after the hearing, and this opinion is binding.

Although this finding can conceivably be a compromise, more often it is a determination that one side is right and the other is wrong. Thus the result is usually a win-lose outcome, not an integrative win-win outcome. For this reason, some industries have been trying to use labor mediation as opposed to arbitration, believing that the result is more likely to meet the needs of both sides and to improve the relationship between the sides—which arbitration generally does not do. Despite the fact that labor mediation has worked well in the few places it has been used, it is still a much less popular approach than arbitration in the grievance resolution arena.

See also: Arbitration; Collective Bargaining; Labor-Management Relations and Conflict; Mediation.
References and Further Reading: Feuille, P., and D. M. Kolb, 1994, "Waiting in the Wings: Mediation's Role in Grievance Resolution"; Leap, Terry L., 1995, *Collective Bargaining and Labor Relations.*

Arbitrator

An arbitrator is a person who performs arbitration, a form of alternative dispute resolution in which a neutral third party listens to the arguments of both sides of a dispute and then renders a decision, which is generally final and binding. Unlike judges, who usually have no expertise in the particular topic in dispute, arbitrators are often chosen for their expertise in a particular area. For example, people with a dispute relating to construction would likely choose an arbitrator who is also a general contractor, an architect, or a lawyer specializing in construction issues. People with a health insurance dispute might prefer to use someone familiar with medicine, the insurance industry, or both. By having a neutral who is already an expert on the topic, the parties do not have

to spend nearly as much time educating the arbitrator about the technical aspects of the dispute. They also can have more confidence that the decision will be based on a sound technical understanding of the issues, which may not be true if the decision were made by a judge or a jury of laypeople.

Although parties are free to find an arbitrator on their own, they often turn to one of several major organizations that provide arbitration services and lists of arbitrators. One is the American Arbitration Association, which has a list of over 20,000 arbitrators who are experts in a wide variety of fields. Other organizations providing references to arbitrators include the Better Business Bureau and the Federal Mediation and Conciliation Service (limited to labor disputes).

One ethical problem that has arisen in recent years is that some sales contracts specify that disputes will be arbitrated by a person drawn from a board of arbitrators assembled by the industry selling the product. For example, insurance companies maintain their own arbitrators to arbitrate insurance disputes; financial service organizations do the same. Consumers and consumer advocates have charged that such arbitrators are not neutral—they are trained and sometimes paid by the industry and thus tend to take the industry's side in a dispute. Although this problem still arises in some cases, more and more contracts specify that the arbitrator will be provided by a neutral organization.

See also: American Arbitration Association; Arbitration; Arbitration, Ethical Issues; Better Business Bureau; Federal Mediation and Conciliation Service.
References and Further Reading: American Arbitration Association, World Wide Web Home Page, http://www.adr.org; Goldberg, Stephen B., Eric D. Green, and Frank E. A. Sander, 1985, *Dispute Resolution;* Tillet, Gregory, 1991, *Resolving Conflict: A Practical Approach.*

Arias Sánchez, Oscar

Oscar Arias Sánchez was the president of Costa Rica from 1986 to 1990, during which time he acted as the primary mediator of the Esquipulas Agreement, which negotiated an end to the wars in Nicaragua, El Salvador, and Guatemala. For this effort, he was awarded the Nobel Peace Prize in 1987.

Arias Sánchez was an exceptional leader for many reasons. First, he held a Ph.D. and was a noted scholar in both political science and economics. He taught at the University of Costa Rica and published many books and articles in his fields of expertise. Arias Sánchez won the presidential election in 1986 by insisting that Costa Rica not be drawn into any war in Central America. Soon after being elected, Arias became an active peace broker, trying to bring all the warring Central American factions together.

Building on an earlier peace plan that had not been successful (the Contadora Pact), Arias developed a new peace plan that was broader in scope. The ten-point plan called for immediate cease-fires in all the guerrilla wars in the region (Nicaragua, Guatemala, and El Salvador), the end of insurgents' use of outside countries for their guerrilla efforts, national reconciliation commissions that worked for negotiated settlements of all the regional disputes, amnesty for insurgents, repatriation of refugees, the end of states of emergency, the protection of human rights, democratization of the political systems in the region, and continuing regional consultations in summit meetings. Although they were initially reluctant, Arias was able to sell this plan to regional leaders as well as to international leaders, including those in the U.S. Senate and eventually to President Reagan (though Reagan opposed the plan initially). After much prodding and fine-tuning, the five Central American heads of state met in Guatemala City in August 1987, where they signed the peace plan. The plan went into effect three months later, on 7 November 1987.

In awarding the Peace Prize, Nobel Chairman Aarvik highlighted two points about the Arias peace plan that had most impressed the committee. First was that it was the product of Central American presidents themselves, who wanted outside intervention to cease. Second was the fact that the plan coupled democracy with peace. Arias had long advocated the indivisibility of those two concepts. Speaking at the Nobel ceremony, he declared, "Peace is a never-ending process. It is an attitude, a way of life, a way of solving problems and resolving conflicts. We seek in Central America not peace alone, not peace to be followed some day by political progress, but peace and democracy, together, indivisible, an end to the shedding of human blood, which is inseparable from an end to the suppression of human rights" (Abrams 1988, 252).

See also: Amnesty and Forgiveness; Human Rights; International Conflict; Mediation, International; Reconciliation.
References and Further Reading: Abrams, Irwin, 1988, *The Nobel Peace Prize and the Laureates: An Illustrated Bibliographical History, 1901–1987;* Anglade, Christian, 1988, "President Arias of Costa Rica"; Kidder, Rushworth M., 1994, *Shared Values for a Troubled World: Conversations with Men and Women of Conscience;* Wehr, Paul, and Sharon Erickson Nepstad, 1994, "Violence, Nonviolence, and Justice in Sandinista Nicaragua."

Arms Control and Disarmament

Efforts to implement arms control or disarmament have occurred sporadically throughout recorded history, often following the development of new, more destructive weapons or after an especially destructive war. According to Luttwak (1994), one of the earliest efforts to limit the scope of war was organized by Greek tribes in the eighth century B.C. and sought to limit the type of actions one army could take against another. More extensive limitations were implemented in the 1600s after the Thirty Years' War in Europe, limiting warfare to combat by armed forces, requiring the humane treatment of prisoners, and outlawing pillage. These rules were followed throughout the 1700s, making war "a relatively limited and civilized 'game of kings.'"

The next significant move toward controlling weapons was the Hague Conferences. The First Hague Conference was convened by Nicholas II of Russia in 1889. Twenty-six nations drafted a series of regulations regarding the conduct of war and also established the Permanent Court of Arbitration for the arbitration of international disputes. The Second Hague Disarmament Conference was held in 1907. Fewer agreements were made this time, although additional arbitration courts were established. These courts did not have enforcement power, however, and were unable to prevent the deteriorating international conditions from erupting into World War I.

Following World War I, U.S. President Woodrow Wilson spearheaded the establishment of the League of Nations. The league was to "establish reasonable limits on the military forces of each country and submit them for consideration to the member governments" (Luttwak 1994). Again, however, compliance was voluntary, and the short-lived league was largely ineffective. Several other disarmament efforts were made between World War I and World War II, including the Washington Naval Conference, which limited the naval power of signatory countries; the Kellogg-Briand Pact, which renounced war as an instrument of foreign policy; and a world disarmament conference convened by the League of Nations in 1932, which sought the progressive elimination of offensive weapons. Lack of agreement about how this might be done prevented this conference from having a significant impact as the nations of Europe and Asia began the slide toward World War II.

The horrors of World War II and the threat of a more extensive nuclear war stimulated many more efforts at arms control and disarmament—especially regarding nuclear weapons—in the 1960s through 1990s. At the same time, however, the United States and the Soviet Union were locked in an intractable arms race,

only sporadically slowed by arms limitation agreements. In the late 1960s, after the Cuban Missile Crisis, for instance, the United States and the Soviet Union ratified SALT I—the Strategic Arms Limitation Agreements—which limited the size and the composition of the nations' nuclear weapons arsenals. A continuation of these agreements—SALT II—was not ratified by the U.S. Congress, however, due to the Soviet invasion of Afghanistan and the consequential demise of détente. In 1987, however, President Reagan and Soviet leader Mikhail Gorbachev signed an agreement limiting intermediate-range nuclear forces (INF). The treaty, which was ratified in 1988, required the phased destruction of all U.S. and Soviet intermediate-range missiles. In July 1991, Gorbachev and President Bush signed the START I agreement, which called for the reduction of strategic nuclear weapons by about 25 percent. Although Soviet weapons were dispersed when the Soviet Union dissolved in late 1991, Bush and Russian President Boris Yeltsin signed the START II agreement in 1993, which called for the elimination of many more of the nations' nuclear warheads. Both START I and START II called for the control of conventional weapons as well.

See also: Détente; International Conflict; League of Nations; Strategic Arms Limitation Talks.
References and Further Reading: Luttwak, Edward, 1994, "Arms Control, International"; McLauchlan, Gregory, 1996, "Stepping Back: Nuclear Arms Control and the End of the Cold War."

Association of American Law Schools, Section on Alternative Dispute Resolution

The Section on Alternative Dispute Resolution of the Association of American Law Schools (AALS) was founded in 1983 following a conference on the subject convened by Professor Frank E. A. Sander at Harvard Law School. Since that time, the section has conducted at least one educational session (and usually two or more) at the annual AALS meeting. The program for a particular year is selected by the chair of the section, with the assistance of other section members. In addition, the section has twice conducted midyear educational meetings at which the teaching of alternative dispute resolution (ADR) and ADR skills have been considered.

From 1983 to 1995, the section sponsored *The Alternative Newsletter*. The newsletter was created by James Boskey of Seton Hall Law School and continues to be published by him as an independent publication. It is designed to provide a wide range of information on developments in ADR in the United States and around the world.

See also: The Alternative Newsletter; Appendix 1 for contact information.

Association of Family and Conciliation Courts

The Association of Family and Conciliation Courts (AFCC) is an international association of family courts, established in 1963, to improve court services to couples and their children. In addition to evaluating and improving court-based services, the association seeks to "provide an interdisciplinary forum for the exchange of ideas and the development of solutions to problems of family discord" (Association of Family and Conciliation Courts 1996, 1). This goal reflects the association's recognition that family disputes have an emotional impact that cannot be completely resolved through any court process. Thus, the association encourages judges and lawyers to get together with counselors, mediators, and other professionals who work with families to establish programs to help them resolve their disputes in a variety of ways, including mediation and conflict prevention.

The association's membership includes over 1,600 courts, judges, lawyers, mediators, custody evaluators, and mental health professionals from the United States, Canada, Australia, New Zealand, Great Britain, and other countries.

In addition to producing a journal, the *Family and Conciliation Courts Review,* it has produced a wide variety of informational material for couples and families. One brochure called "Parents Are Forever" is a widely used source of information about divorce for parents, discussing issues such as custody and visitation. Other publications and videos address a wide variety of family problems, including abuse, conflict management, and parenting.

See also: Appendix 1 for contact information.
References and Further Reading: Association of Family and Conciliation Courts, 1996, "An Invitation [to Join]."

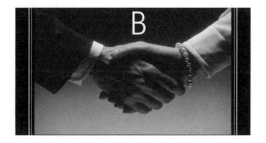

Balance of Power

The term *balance of power* was originally developed to describe power relationships between sovereign nation-states in the international system. However, the term can be extended to any set of individuals or groups who have a conflict of interest and who maintain a relationship based on a power balance between them. For example, if one child is consistently the underdog in family squabbles, parents often try to empower that child so that he or she can defend him- or herself better in the future, perhaps deterring further attacks. Essentially, this is maintaining family peace through the balance of power.

At the international level, a balance of power is said to exist when all nations in a system are deterred from attacking the others because they fear that they will lose or at least be greatly harmed by the effort. The problem with the balance-of-power approach to international stability is that it can break down for a variety of reasons. First, a potential aggressor must be convinced that a nation would defend itself fully if attacked. However, according to Pruitt and Rubin (1986, 84), "history reveals many failures in this regard." Iraq's invasion of Kuwait and the Japanese attack on Pearl Harbor are two examples of such failures. Second, basing stability on mutual threat is like "fighting fire with fire" (Pruitt and Rubin 1986, 85). It runs the risk of escalating the conflict, with only a small wind necessary to blow the situation out of control. Third, threats that are intended to be deterrents can actually be interpreted as aggressive signals. This can provoke a counterattack (actually a first strike) when the perceived "aggressor" was only trying to deter aggression from the other side. Thus, deterrence can actually cause aggression rather than deter it.

Jay Rothman and many other political scientists have observed that the notion of balance of power no longer makes much sense. This is true, in part, because of the end of the Cold War and the superpower standoff; it is also true because of the widespread rise of nationalistic and ethnic movements within nation-states, which brings the very concepts of sovereignty and statehood into question. Rothman suggests that the notion of balance of power should be replaced with the notion of "power of balance." Rather than viewing the world as organized with a coercive balance of power between sovereign nation-states, it should be viewed as a set of ethnic and other "identity groups" that gain individual power through balance and cooperation. Power "becomes a vehicle whereby people gain the ability to fulfill their own needs, not, as is usually meant by power, to coerce others to do that which they would otherwise not do" (Rothman 1992, 45).

See also: Cold War; Communal Conflicts; Deterrence; Empowerment; International Conflict; Morgenthau, Hans; Power Balancing.

References and Further Reading: Pruitt, Dean G., and Jeffrey Z. Rubin, 1986, *Social Conflict;* Rothman, Jay, 1992,

Confrontation to Cooperation: Resolving Ethnic and Regional Conflict; Wright, Quincy, 1965, *A Study of War.*

Ballot Initiatives

Ballot initiatives are proposed laws or constitutional amendments that are developed by citizen groups or businesses and then submitted to the voters for acceptance or rejection. Although they are found across the country, initiative processes are much more common in the western and Midwestern states, with California being the leader in numbers of initiatives put forward each year.

Initiatives are a unique form of democracy and conflict resolution, as they allow all the citizens of a state or locality to vote on an issue of contention and thereby "resolve" it. However, initiatives often fail to bring the hoped-for resolution, because they tend to spawn counterinitiatives (either simultaneously or later) and constitutional challenges.

Initiatives have several other problems as well. First, they tend to favor special interests, especially those that are well funded. So many signatures are needed to get an issue on the ballot that most successful initiatives pay people to collect signatures—up to $5 a signature in some cases. After the issue is on the ballot, a substantial advertising campaign is necessary to win its approval. Thus, grassroots organizations without much money cannot succeed at this process.

Another problem with ballot initiatives is that they are often confusing, and voters do not really understand what they are voting on. This is not necessarily the fault of the voters. Ballot initiatives are often worded in such confusing ways that even lawyers and courts debate the intended and actual meanings. This results in people voting for laws that they did not intend to approve, which leads to further disillusionment with the legislative process and more conflict rather than less. Nevertheless, most citizens favor the continued use of ballot initiatives. According to Eugene C. Lee, a political scientist from the University of California, "They view it as sort of a whip, something to hold over the head of the Legislature. . . . There's something fundamentally important about it" (quoted in Reinhold 1990, A16).

See also: Citizen Participation; Referendum.
References and Further Reading: Cronin, Thomas, 1989, *Direct Democracy: The Politics of Initiative, Referendum, and Recall;* Magleby, David B., 1984, *Direct Legislation: Voting on Ballot Propositions in the United States;* Reinhold, Robert, 1990, "Ballot Becomes a Burden in California."

Bargaining, Integrative and Distributive

Bargaining or negotiation can be carried out in one of two ways: cooperatively or competitively. Cooperative approaches are usually called integrative bargaining, because they seek to integrate the interests of each side with the interests of the opposition. Competitive approaches are usually called distributive bargaining, because they seek to distribute the outcome between two competitive parties.

Integrative bargaining works only in situations in which the interests of the parties are not diametrically opposed—in other words, when win-win outcomes are actually attainable. (An example of integrative bargaining might be a negotiation over the sale of a house. The seller wants a high price; the buyer a low one. But the seller may also want a quick sale, whereas the buyer is in less of a hurry. An integrative outcome would be one in which the price is lowered a bit, so the buyer wins, and the sale is done quickly, so the seller wins as well.)

In zero-sum situations—when the only way one person can win is if the other person loses—distributive bargaining tactics are required. (An example of this situation would be the same seller-buyer story if the buyer has nothing to offer the seller other than money. In this case, the two parties' interests are diametrically opposed—the more money one person gets, the more the other loses.)

These two situations call for different negotiating tactics. The most common form of integrative bargaining is principled negotiation—the approach popularized by Roger Fisher and William Ury in their best-selling book *Getting to Yes*. Here, parties focus on identifying common interests and developing options for mutual gain. If it is done creatively, Fisher and Ury argue, almost all conflicts can be resolved in an integrative way.

Many other conflict theorists disagree, arguing that at least half of bargaining situations are distributive, not integrative. In distributive bargaining, relative power and good tactics are key to success. Identifying interests is helpful, since the parties want to be sure that the settlement achieves their underlying interests, but seeking options for mutual gain is simply a waste of time. Instead, efforts should be focused on building up one's power, thereby strengthening one's negotiating position, and using a good strategy that will likely outsmart or outargue the opponent. There are countless theories on how this is best done, but the key to all of them is maximizing one's own interests regardless of the outcome for the other.

See also: Negotiation; Principled Negotiation and *Getting to Yes;* Win-Win, Win-Lose, and All-Lose Outcomes.
References and Further Reading: Fisher, Roger, and William Ury, 1981, *Getting to Yes* (2nd ed. with Bruce Patton, 1991); Raiffa, Howard, 1982, *The Art and Science of Negotiation;* Schellenberg, James A., 1996, *Conflict Resolution—Theory, Research, and Practice.*

Bargaining, Interest-Based and Positional

Interest-based bargaining is an approach to bargaining or negotiation in which the parties focus on their underlying reasons for wanting something (called interests) rather than simply negotiating opposing positions (as is done in positional bargain-ing). A child and a parent might negotiate over homework, for example, by discussing starting times. If they use positional bargaining, the child might say, "I'll start at 7:00"; the parent demands 4:00, and they settle (perhaps) on 5:30, which may not really meet the interests of either party, because that allows the child very little time to work before dinner.

If they use interest-based bargaining, however, the child might say, "I need some time to relax after basketball practice," and the parent might say, "If you wait until 7:00, you are so tired that you work more slowly and don't get it done." They might agree that the child will do an hour right after school (before basketball practice) and then finish up what is left after dinner. That meets the parent's interests (that the homework is finished and dinner is not disturbed) and meets the child's need to relax after practice.

Often conflicts that appear to be win-lose can be changed to win-win if the disputants use interest-based bargaining rather than positional bargaining. An extension of interest-based bargaining is what Roger Fisher and William Ury (1981) call "principled negotiation." This adds a few extra principles to the fundamental idea of negotiating interests, not positions, to make win-win outcomes even more likely. The concepts of integrative bargaining and distributive bargaining are also related (and sometimes used interchangeably). However, it is possible to use interest-based bargaining in distributive situations, so the terms are not exactly synonymous.

See also: Bargaining, Integrative and Distributive; Principled Negotiation and *Getting to Yes.*
References and Further Reading: Fisher, Roger, and William Ury, 1981, *Getting to Yes* (2nd ed. with Bruce Patton, 1991).

BATNA

BATNA is an acronym invented by Roger Fisher and William Ury that stands for "best alternative to a negotiated agreement." Before you can make a wise decision about whether or not to accept a negotiated agreement, you must know what your alternatives are. If your best alternative, your BATNA, is worse than the negotiated agreement, you should accept the agreement. But if your BATNA is better than the offer you have negotiated, you should withdraw from the negotiations and pursue your alternative.

For example, it makes sense to buy a car when the negotiated price is less than your BATNA (in this case, what you would expect to pay for a comparable car elsewhere). If the negotiated price is higher than your BATNA, you should reject the offer and either go elsewhere or ask the dealer to make a lower offer. To be an effective negotiator, it is essential to know your BATNA. Without such knowledge, as Fisher and Ury point out in *Getting to Yes,* you are negotiating with your eyes closed.

It is also helpful to know your opponent's BATNA. This gives you a guide to the range of offers that might be acceptable. Again, using the car example, if you know that someone else has offered $4,500 for a used car, you might offer $5,000 if you really want it, but you would be wasting money if you went as high as $6,000. Before you offer $5,000, however, you should be sure that you cannot get a comparable car for less money from another source.

This example is simple, but assessing BATNAs is often complicated. It is important to consider all factors involved in the transaction, not just money. In addition to the price of a car, for example, you need to consider the time involved in buying another car, the possibility of fixing up your existing car, the relative safety of competing cars, the possibility of using public transportation, and service and reliability issues. Relationship issues may also play a role. Is this dealer one you trust, whereas the alternative seller is unknown or even disreputable? If so, paying more money may be worth it.

In important negotiations, it is often possible and helpful to try to improve your BATNA before you enter into negotiations. This is especially important when you are negotiating with others (such as representatives of a large corporation) who appear to have more power. Even if your opponent has more money, more knowledge, or more prestige, the most important source of power is having a good alternative to an agreement. If you can walk away from an agreement easily because you have a good alternative but your opponent (for example, an automobile dealer who needs customers) does not, that gives you the power to negotiate a deal in your favor.

These principles apply to all negotiation processes, not just simple purchases. International negotiations often break down because one or both parties decide that the alternatives to agreement (for example, war) are superior to accepting the demands of the opposing side. Complex, multiparty negotiations are especially difficult to conclude, as an agreement must be found that is superior to all the parties' BATNAs. Consider, for example, a case in which 20 parties sit down at a negotiation table with a mediator and hammer out an agreement for disposing of hazardous waste in a community. If only one of those parties believes that a better outcome can be achieved through litigation, that party can undermine the whole process by withdrawing from the negotiation and suing one or more of the other parties in an effort to fully prevail. Knowing and manipulating your BATNA is critical to success in all types of negotiation.

See also: Negotiation, Limits to; Principled Negotiation and *Getting to Yes;* Reality Testing.

References and Further Reading: Fisher, Roger, and William Ury, 1981, *Getting to Yes* (2nd ed. with Bruce Patton, 1991).

Better Business Bureau

Better Business Bureaus (BBBs) are local nonprofit organizations supported by dues paid by local businesses. They work to promote consumer satisfaction with their members and with business in general by encouraging the use of ethical business practices and efficient dispute resolution.

BBBs provide a variety of services to their members and to the public. These include reliability reports on businesses, information about charities, other consumer information, and dispute resolution services—including mediation, arbitration, and conciliation (a process in which BBB staffers clarify each side's view of a dispute to the other and transmit offers for resolution back and forth by mail or phone.) Typical types of disputes handled include complaints about contract violations, unethical sales practices, unsatisfactory service, failure to perform warranty work, misleading advertising, and billing problems. The BBB does not handle complaints about employment practices or discrimination.

The BBB Care Program for dispute resolution involves over 5,000 mediators, arbitrators, and support staff. The service is offered in over 100 local BBBs, and over 58,000 businesses have committed themselves to this process for dispute resolution. Whenever a consumer submits a complaint to the BBB, the BBB asks the consumer to contact the company personally first, to see if the company will rectify the problem on its own. If it does not, the consumer is asked to submit the complaint to the BBB in writing; the BBB then follows up by forwarding the complaint to the company and requesting a response. It continues to facilitate communication between the company and the consumer, either in writing or by phone, until a resolution is reached. BBB staff also assist in the process of writing up agreements and verifying compliance. If simple conciliation is not successful, the BBB offers both mediation and arbitration as well. Many companies have agreed in advance to submit unsettled disputes to BBB arbitration and to be bound by the results of that process. All the BBB's dispute resolution services are provided at low cost to members and are free to consumers.

See also: Arbitration; Conciliation; Consumer Disputes; Mediation; Appendix 1 for contact information.
References and Further Reading: Council of Better Business Bureaus, World Wide Web Home Page, http://cbbb.org/bbb/bbb.html.

Boulding, Elise

Elise Boulding, a world-renowned sociologist, peace activist, and peace researcher, has been working in these fields for over 50 years. One of the most active leaders in the conflict resolution and peace research fields, Dr. Boulding helped found the International Peace Research Association (IPRA), the Consortium on Peace Research, Education, and Development (COPRED), and the United States Institute of Peace (USIP). She also helped develop several global peace-building programs within the United Nations Educational, Scientific, and Cultural Organization (UNESCO) and the United Nations University.

Born in Oslo, Norway, in 1920, she immigrated to the United States as a small child. She married Kenneth Boulding in 1941, and they raised five children. As a result of that experience, she not only honed her peacemaking skills but also developed a lifelong interest in children and parenting, family issues, and the role of women in society. Women, she believes, have a special role in peacemaking—in the home, in the community, and in the world. She has written extensively about this role and has authored hundreds of books and articles on peace, consensus building, conflict resolution, development, and international cooperation.

Dr. Boulding has studied, taught, and traveled worldwide. Her close friend and colleague Kevin Clements, former director of the Asian-Pacific Peace Research Association and now director of the Institute for Conflict Analysis and Resolution at George Mason University, described Dr. Boulding's achievements at a ceremony at which she received the Global Citizen Award from the Boston Research Center for the 21st Century: "Elise Boulding regards the whole world as her home and has devoted herself unstintingly to its care and nurture. Elise has a philanthropic spirit that transcends the narrow bounds of nation, race, and region; she knows that one of the fundamental roles of the peacemaker is to see and realize wholeness where there is fragmentation and division. To this end, she derives great joy and delight from building networks and weaving relationships between peoples of all races and religions" (Clements 1995, 10–11).

See also: Boulding, Kenneth; Consortium on Peace Research, Education, and Development; International Peace Research Association; United States Institute of Peace.
References and Further Reading: Boulding, Elise, 1990, *Building a Global Civic Culture: Education for an Interdependent World;* Boulding, Elise, Clovis Brigagao, and Kevin Clements, 1991, *Peace Culture and Society: Transnational Research and Dialogue;* Clements, Kevin, 1995, "Elise Boulding, Global Citizen"; Roberts, Nancy L., 1991, "Elise Björn-Hansen Boulding"; *Who's Who of American Women, 1995–1996.*

Boulding, Kenneth

Although an economist by training, Kenneth Boulding was a true Renaissance scholar who devoted his life to what he called "human betterment." A significant portion of human betterment, in Boulding's view, involved the pursuit of stable peace between nations and the amicable resolution of conflict between individuals. One of the founders of the scholarly field of conflict resolution, Boulding left a legacy of books and articles that has had a profound influence.

One of his most important insights was his distinction among the three sources of power: threats, exchange, and love. Boulding clearly demonstrated that threats and force are often not the best way for people to advance their interests. He was particularly worried about the belief that the best way to keep the peace was through the system of continuing threat and counterthreat called deterrence. He believed that such a strategy would produce an intense and unstable arms race that would eventually escalate into war.

Boulding believed that the cycle of threat, counterthreat, and war could be broken by the establishment of stable peace, which he defined as a relationship between nations (or other social groups) in which the possibility of violent confrontation or war was so remote that it did not enter into anyone's calculations. He saw a region of stable peace extending from Western Europe through North America to Japan and Australia. With the end of the Cold War, he had hoped that the region could be expanded to include the countries of the former Soviet bloc.

Boulding also felt that the history of peace has never really been written. Instead, peace has been viewed almost universally as a nonevent and therefore not worthy of study or teaching. He tried to improve our understanding of peace as a positive process, not merely as the absence of war. As an occasion for this kind of reflection, he proposed a national holiday to celebrate the Rush-Bagot agreement that demilitarized the Great Lakes and initiated stable peace between the United States and Canada.

A prolific writer, Boulding's most important conflict-related books include *The Economy of Love and Fear, Human Betterment, Three Faces of Power, Stable Peace,* and *Conflict and Defense.*

See also: Boulding, Elise; Deterrence; Power; Stable Peace.
References and Further Reading: Boulding, Kenneth, 1962, *Conflict and Defense: A General Theory;* Boulding, Kenneth, 1973, *The Economy of Love and Fear: A Preface to Grants Economics;* Boulding, Kenneth, 1978b, *Stable Peace;* Boulding, Kenneth, 1985, *Human Betterment;* Boulding, Kenneth, 1989, *Three Faces of Power.*

Boutros-Ghali, Boutros

Boutros Boutros-Ghali, the sixth secretary-general of the United Nations (UN), was elected to a five-year term on January 1, 1992. Before that, he served as deputy prime minister for foreign affairs in Egypt (May–December 1991) and minister of state for foreign affairs (October 1977–May 1991). As secretary-general, Boutros-Ghali's primary goals were to strengthen the UN and to further its efforts in preventive diplomacy, peacemaking, peace building, and peacekeeping in the post–Cold War era. He set out his plan for doing this in a report entitled *An Agenda for Peace*, published by the UN in June 1992 (revised edition 1995). This report defines Boutros-Ghali's vision for the role and functions of the UN in a new era—one that has seen a massive increase in UN peacekeeping and observer operations.

In 1995, Boutros-Ghali issued *An Agenda for Development* as a companion volume to *An Agenda for Peace*. This report set out five foundations of development: peace, the economy, the environment, society, and democracy. All these factors are interlinked, he stressed, and all must be addressed simultaneously if sustainable development is to occur. The protection of human rights was his third priority as secretary-general.

Boutros-Ghali advocated a strong UN role in furthering the cause of democracy in the world's newly democratic states. He provided UN observers for democratic elections in over 40 nations, including 2,100 observers in the April 1994 South African elections—the largest electoral assistance operation ever undertaken by the UN.

Although the secretary-general attempted to restructure and reform the UN bureaucracy, he was faulted by the United States and others for failing to make effective changes. The United States opposed his bid for a second term as secretary-general and hence he was replaced after only one term by Kofi Annan, who took over as secretary-general on January 1, 1997.

See also: Diplomacy, Preventive; Peace Building; Peacekeeping; Peacemaking; United Nations.

References and Further Reading: Boutros-Ghali, Boutros, 1995, *An Agenda for Development;* Boutros-Ghali, Boutros, 1995, *An Agenda for Peace;* United Nations, 1996, "Boutros Boutros-Ghali United Nations Secretary-General."

Brainstorming

Brainstorming is a procedure used in negotiation, mediation, or consensus-building efforts to generate options for settlement. Rather than examining the positions of the parties, which are often far apart, the mediator or facilitator reframes the problem into a question and then asks the parties to come up with as many answers as possible, while withholding judgment about the merits of the ideas expressed.

For example, parties to a conflict over the design and size of a proposed shopping center might be asked to consider what type and size of stores would be best for the neighborhood and for the developers. Rather than limiting themselves to their initial positions (e.g., big new mall versus no change), disputants are asked to think of all the possible options for mutual satisfaction. Suggestions are recorded on newsprint or a blackboard—somewhere where everyone can see—and participants are urged to build on and modify initial ideas as long as the result yields more options, without dismissing any (evaluation of options is done later).

Brainstorming often starts slowly but picks up momentum as people become more comfortable with one another and with the process. In addition to generating creative new ideas for settlement, brainstorming tends to improve interpersonal and intergroup relations and communication. It also helps change adversaries into collaborators, who switch from a competitive to a cooperative mode of problem solving.

See also: Adversarial Approach; Collaborative Problem Solving; Framing; Interests and Positions.

References and Further Reading: Moore, Christopher W., 1986, *The Mediation Process;* Susskind, Lawrence, and Jeffrey Cruikshank, 1987, *Breaking the Impasse;* Tillet, Gregory, 1991, *Resolving Conflict: A Practical Approach.*

Burton, John

John Burton is one of the most important scholars in the conflict resolution field today. A former Australian diplomat, Burton has written extensively on international relations and conflict resolution topics for almost 50 years. Samuel Lewis, former president of the United States Institute of Peace, described Burton as the field's "first leading explorer and one of its most ardent spokesmen before students, scholars, and governments since its beginnings in the late 1950s" (Lewis 1990, viii). Many of Burton's books and articles have greatly influenced the development of conflict resolution and related fields. For example, his book *Peace Theory* (1962) helped establish the field of peace studies; *Conflict and Community* (1969) was one of the seminal books that started the field of conflict resolution; *World Society* (1972) created a new paradigm in international relations theory; and *Deviance, Terrorism and War* (1979) was the first of many books setting out his theory of human needs, which he and others have developed into a generic theory of conflict and its resolution. A more recent four-volume series (1990), coauthored and edited with Frank Dukes, attempts to map the entire field of conflict settlement, management, and resolution from both a theoretical and a practical point of view. Covering interpersonal, intergroup, and international conflicts, this series is one of the best overviews of the field.

Burton is one of the leading proponents of human needs theory—a theory of conflict that argues that most deep-rooted conflicts are caused by the denial of one or more fundamental human needs (e.g., security, identity, recognition). Although interests are negotiable, human needs, Burton says, are not. Individuals or groups that are denied access to these needs will fight ceaselessly until they are attained and will not trade them for anything. Therefore, the only way to resolve such conflicts is to identify and provide the desired needs, usually through major socioeconomic and political changes in or between societies.

In addition to his work in diplomacy, writing, and teaching, Burton has been active as a third-party intermediary trying to help diverse groups throughout the world resolve their conflicts. Working with groups from Lebanon, Cyprus, Northern Ireland, and Sri Lanka, for example, he has developed and held what he calls "problem-solving workshops," where participants from all sides of a conflict sit down with conflict scholars to analyze the fundamental needs underlying their conflict and identify ways in which those needs could be met that would satisfy all (Burton 1987).

See also: Needs; Problem Solving, Analytical.
References and Further Reading: Burton, John, 1962, *Peace Theory: Preconditions of Disarmament;* Burton, John, 1969, *Conflict and Community: The Use of Controlled Community in Ireland;* Burton, John, 1972, *World Society;* Burton, John, 1979, *Deviance, Terrorism and War: The Process of Solving Unsolved Social and Political Problems;* Burton, John, 1987, *Resolving Deep-Rooted Conflict: A Handbook;* Burton, John, 1990a, *Conflict: Human Needs Theory;* Burton, John, 1990b, *Conflict: Resolution and Provention;* Burton, John, and Frank Dukes, 1990a, *Conflict: Practices in Management, Settlement and Resolution;* Burton, John, and Frank Dukes, 1990b, *Conflict: Readings in Management and Resolution;* Lewis, Samuel W., 1990, "Foreword to the Series."

C

Camp David Accords (Israeli and Egyptian)

The Camp David Accords (signed 17 September 1978) were the product of a historic 13-day negotiating session (5–17 September 1978) among Israel, Egypt, and the United States. The leaders and a few of their closest advisers assembled at Camp David, the presidential retreat in Maryland, to undertake the negotiations and emerged from their isolation nearly two weeks later with the framework for peace between Israel and Egypt. This achievement had barely seemed possible five years earlier, when Israel and Egypt were fighting the last of their four wars, or even five days before the conference began, when the entrenched positions of both sides made it difficult to imagine that the leaders could sit at the same table, let alone agree on any issues of substance.

Leading Up to Camp David: A Grim History of War

The grievances that necessitated the negotiation of peace between Israel and Egypt had been accumulating for years. Since the formation of the State of Israel, the entire Arab world had refused to recognize Israel's existence as a country. Rather, the new state was viewed as a continuation of the colonialism from which the Arab states had been trying to free themselves for most of the twentieth century. The injection of Israel into territory already claimed by the Arabs who lived there, and the indignation of Muslims worldwide who saw the proclamation of the State of Israel as an annexation of one of their holiest regions, created bitter conflict. The Israelis were forced to fight a difficult War of Independence (1948) to wrest their state from the British and the Arabs. This war, compounded by the murder of more than six million European Jews in the Holocaust, did not leave the Israelis disposed to much flexibility on the question of their right to exist as a nation. To the Israelis, the conflict revolved around the denial of two fundamental human needs: security and identity.

Over the next 25 years, the region suffered three major wars between Israel and its neighbors: Egypt, Jordan, and Syria. The 1967 War left Israel in control of the West Bank of the Jordan River, the Sinai Peninsula, the Golan Heights, and perhaps a million Palestinians. The War of Attrition waged by Egypt against Israeli forces during 1969 and 1970 left all sides debilitated. Then in the October 1973 War, the Syrian and Egyptian armies moved on Israel in an attempt to reclaim their territory lost in 1967, only to take heavy losses and regain nothing. Egypt was perhaps the most affected by these wars. In addition to causing heavy losses of life and territory, the three defeats jeopardized Egypt's standing as a leader in the Arab world and exacerbated the often shaky position of its leaders. The wars exacted a terrible toll on the economies of all the combatants, fueled an un-precedented arms race, and generally dominated the politics of the countries involved to the exclusion of all else.

During this time, attempts at peace had little success. The United Nations made several strong statements condemning the violence on all sides, notably in Resolutions 242 and 338, but did not have much influence on the combatants. All sides endorsed the idea of an end to aggression but then accused the other of being the aggressor. U.S. and Soviet influence in the area was occasionally able to moderate the degree of belligerence, but both countries pumped vast supplies of arms into the region in the name of their strategic interests. A major U.S.-Soviet peace initiative, the Rogers Plan of 1969, died an ignominious death after all parties except the United States and Jordan refused to sign it. The bright spots of diplomacy in the area before 1978 had been limited to temporary cease-fires and keeping the Suez Canal open, at least intermittently.

The Thaw

In 1977, secret negotiations between Egyptians and Israelis came to a climax with Anwar al-Sadat's acceptance of the Israeli offer to meet with any Arab leader any place, any time. Although this was little more than a ceremonial visit, Sadat's trip to Jerusalem was a dramatic step in principle, signaling a change from the harsh rhetoric that had previously characterized the Israeli-Arab relationship and indicating both parties' new willingness to try to deal with each other in a more dignified way. Leaders of the two countries continued to have highly publicized meetings that resolved nothing but moved the parties closer to a breakthrough than they had ever been.

Jimmy Carter

Soon after his inauguration in 1977, President Jimmy Carter decided that the Mid-

dle East would have a high priority in his foreign-policy agenda. He arranged to have separate personal meetings with the leaders of Israel, Egypt, Jordan, Syria, and Saudi Arabia, during which he laid the groundwork for U.S. involvement in the peace process, based on the United States' mutual friendship with all sides. Especially important was Carter's reaffirmation of the United States' long-standing "special" relationship with Israel, which helped allay Israeli fears, and Carter's personal chemistry with President Sadat. Although the positions of the two sides were diametrically opposed, Carter had found a working relationship with both of them.

However, before the United States was able to convince the two sides to meet, Menachem Begin was elected prime minister of Israel. Begin was a member of the Likud Party, traditionally a more conservative and hawkish party than the Labor Party, which had ruled Israel since its formation. Some thought that this election marked the end of any hope for peace. Surprisingly, however, President Carter found an even greater personal affinity with Begin than he had had with his Labor predecessor Yitzhak Rabin, and a meeting among the three leaders and their top aides was arranged. There was a disappointing lack of interest from other Arab leaders, but it was hoped that the example of good-faith bargaining set by Egyptian-Israeli negotiations would induce other Arab leaders to follow suit.

The Camp David Meetings

The Egyptian delegation arrived at Camp David first, optimistic and ready to work. Like Carter, Sadat wanted to use the opportunity of the Camp David meetings to address the most important parts of the conflict in the Middle East directly and to resolve as much as possible.

The Israeli delegation was not of a similar mind when it arrived. Prime Minister

Begin and his advisers and aides were much less optimistic. They had the upper hand in the military situation at the moment, so they were not inclined to make many concessions. Nor did they expect the Egyptians to be willing to give in much. Further, they believed that a firm stance accurately represented the views of Begin's Likud Party and the Israeli people as a whole. Consequently, they (like most of Carter's State Department and U.S. National Security staff) expected the Camp David meeting to be only a beginning, or at best a framework for future negotiations between the parties. They were not yet ready to settle any of the major issues in dispute.

Carter rejected this position out of hand. He told Begin "that we three principals could not expect others to settle major issues later if we could not do so now, and that all the controversial questions should be addressed among us directly" (Carter 1982, 330). Begin agreed to try to negotiate on a wider scale but made no promises.

The three principal leaders met alone for the first and last time of the entire negotiation on the morning of 6 September. The tone of the meeting was exceedingly negative, with Sadat presenting a draft document that he had previously approved with other Arab leaders for Begin's perusal. Begin kept calm for the rest of the meeting but was in fact enraged by what he saw as the unreasonable demands being made by the Egyptians. He felt that there was nothing new in the document, which he saw as a rehashing of the positions the Israelis had rejected for years. Carter agreed that the document was harsh but reminded Begin of the pressures that Egypt was already under for breaking ranks with the other Arab nations, and he emphasized Sadat's stated willingness to negotiate on nearly all the points of the document. Begin, however, remained upset. From then on, Carter met with the leaders separately or with their aides, since it was clear that Begin and Sadat could not or would not be able to put aside their antagonisms long enough to engage in successful face-to-face negotiating.

Shuttle diplomacy was still possible, however. Sadat's personal relationship with Carter was such that he nearly always endorsed Carter's suggestions, even over the objections of his advisers. Carter thus believed that he could readily bargain with or for Sadat personally. To deal with Begin, Carter relied on Begin's aides to use their influence. Generally, if he could sway them, they would use their influence to persuade Begin. Carter considered this approach to be superior to putting Sadat and Begin together again, as that would only exacerbate already astronomical tensions.

Carter's Negotiating Approach

Carter's approach to the Camp David meetings flew in the face of all conventions as to how international negotiations were to be conducted. In rejecting the Geneva Conference–legalistic approach, Carter set the stage for a highly personal set of negotiations that would be interspersed with sightseeing, biking, hiking, and movie watching. Each delegation had its own cabin, and the cabins were separated by a considerable distance, allowing the delegations to remain apart when they so desired but to see each other regularly as part of camp life. The context of these meetings was important to Carter, who wanted the Israelis and Egyptians to see each other as people, not as teams of adversaries. Carter further stipulated that there would be no time limits on the negotiations and no media contact. The press was given one briefing a day by Carter's press secretary, Jody Powell. Carter wanted to create an atmosphere of fluidity inside Camp David so that concessions that might provoke strong public reaction could be suggested with impunity, thus encouraging creativity in both the content of negotiations and the delegations' dealings with each other on a personal level.

In preparation for the Camp David meetings, Carter had ordered briefing books that contained psychological and personal assessments of Sadat and Begin. The actual points of conflict had been established and postured upon for months and even years before the conference, and Carter trusted his advisers (principally Secretary of State Cyrus Vance and National Security Adviser Zbigniew Brzezinski) to handle the legal and historical points at issue. Carter concentrated on enhancing his trust and empathy with each man.

Carter pushed hard for each side to be as flexible as possible and to think creatively about long-lasting problems. He encouraged each to understand the pressures the other faced and how far each had come to get where they were now. He frequently stressed the consequences of failing to reach an agreement—for their nations and for themselves. Once, for example, when Sadat threatened to leave, Carter explained to him "the extremely serious consequences of his unilaterally breaking off the negotiations: that his action would harm the relationship between Egypt and the United States, he would be violating his personal promise to me, and the onus for failure would be on him. . . . I told him it would damage one of my most precious possessions—his friendship and our mutual trust" (Carter 1982, 392). It was a series of such personal appeals that kept the negotiations going.

Substantive and Procedural Points of Dispute

The leaders needed to decide the scope of their negotiations before any real bargaining could take place. It was unclear from the start whether the Egyptians were negotiating on their own behalf or on behalf of the entire Arab world. They hoped to do the latter, but that proved to

be impossible, so they limited their aspirations as the meetings went on. The Israelis indulged in some deliberate obfuscation of their interests, aiming for the best possible bargaining position. There continued to be confusion about the scope and intent of the negotiations until the final draft was typed. Within this muddled context, the U.S. delegation sought to clarify and simplify separate issues, perceiving that it was the sweeping generalizations of previous rhetoric that had separated the two sides, rather than absolutely intractable demands.

The Parties' Interests: The Egyptians were absolutely committed to reclaiming the Sinai Peninsula, the withdrawal of all Israeli settlers from the peninsula, and the establishment of peace under the terms of UN Resolution 242. The Israelis wanted a guarantee of their security, an acknowledgment of their right to exist, the end of the trade embargo by Arab nations, access to the Suez Canal and the Straits of Tiran, and the establishment of peace. In Sadat's role as unofficial spokesman for the Arab world, he also felt obligated to address the other Arabs' interests: the rights of Palestinians, the status of the West Bank and Jerusalem, and the return of the Golan Heights to Syria.

Evolving Agreements: As the parties negotiated through Carter, the positions of both sides slowly softened, revealing many compatible interests. Sadat agreed early on to the establishment of regular diplomatic relations between Israel and Egypt and the end of the embargo, with the acknowledgment of Israel's right to exist implicit in these agreements. Sadat tried to negotiate on behalf of the other Arabs regarding the West Bank and the Golan Heights, but Israel insisted that negotiations over those issues take place with Jordan and Syria directly. Israel consented to address the rights of the Palestinians in the Camp David agreement, though only by calling for negotiations among Jordan, Israel,

Egypt, and elected representatives of the Palestinian people within five years. (Israel refused to accept the leadership of the Palestine Liberation Organization as legitimate as long as the PLO charter called for the elimination of Israel.) Sadat agreed, thereby dispatching his duty as spokesman for the Arab world while reaching another agreement with Israel. The major remaining conflicts were the language of the peace accord and the withdrawal of Israeli settlers from the Sinai.

The withdrawal from the Sinai was particularly contentious for two reasons. There had been some misinterpretation as to how many troops Sadat would move back into the Sinai and where they would be placed, should he reclaim it. Israel was not actually committed to keeping the Sinai, but it was concerned that the return of the Sinai would bring an Egyptian military presence that could be dangerous. Once that issue was clarified by the drawing of a line beyond which Egyptian equipment could not be moved and the creation of a monitoring mechanism to ensure this, there remained the problem of the thousands of Israelis who had moved to the area while it was in Israel's possession. Sadat wanted immediate dismantling of the settlements, whereas the Israeli time frame ranged from 20 years to never. Begin was finally convinced to bring the matter before the Knesset (Israeli parliament) for a vote. In the end, this was enough for Sadat on the issue of settlements, but there was still the problem of Resolution 242.

Resolution 242, adopted by the UN Security Council on 22 November 1967, speaks to "the inadmissibility of the acquisition of territory by war," a phrase that the Egyptians thought thoroughly condemned the Israelis. The Israelis, however, asserted that they had taken the Golan, West Bank, and Sinai in their own defense after the Arabs had attacked Israel. This became a problem at Camp David when Egypt (and

Carter) wanted the final accords to refer to Resolution 242 and its sister Resolution 338 as the basis of their negotiations. The Israelis believed that this would set a precedent that would require them to relinquish the Golan Heights and the West Bank, which they continued to deem essential to their security until a comprehensive peace could be established. In the end, all references to Resolution 242 remained in the accords, as the basis of peace and future negotiations in the region. The Israelis were placated by the caveat that all their security issues would be addressed in the context of future negotiations. This also facilitated better relations between Israel and the outside world, which had condemned it for effectively rejecting the authority of the United Nations and the world community.

Carter tirelessly traveled back and forth between the delegations, searching for the true interests underlying the stated positions. He cajoled, he pressured, he reassured, he used all his personal skills and his official position to generate concessions from both sides. When significant progress was made, he began to draft a final agreement. After 23 revisions, the negotiations were concluded. The agreements were not as comprehensive as Sadat and Carter had originally wished, but most observers believed that they were definitely the best possible at the time. The resulting Camp David Accords were signed by Sadat and Begin on 17 September 1978.

The Aftermath
The Knesset vote on the Camp David Accords took place on 28 September 1978, with the final tally being 84 in favor of the agreement, 19 opposed, and 17 abstentions. Peace was negotiated between the two countries under the Framework for Peace contained in the accords, and a formal peace treaty was signed by Egypt and Israel on 26 March 1979. The spirit of co-

operation that produced this peace never extended beyond Egypt and Israel, however, and the issues of the Golan Heights, the West Bank, Jerusalem, and the rights of the Palestinians were not substantively addressed again until the Madrid Conference of 1992.

Jimmy Carter was defeated by Ronald Reagan in the 1980 presidential elections. Anwar al-Sadat was assassinated on 6 October 1981 by Egyptian members of the Muslim Brotherhood, a fundamentalist group opposed to the peace with Israel. Egypt itself was deemed a pariah among its neighbors, was kicked out of the Arab League, and lost aid money it had depended on from other Arab states. The peace between Israel and Egypt, however, has endured. There is an Israeli embassy in Cairo and an Egyptian embassy in Tel Aviv. The Sinai is the sovereign possession of Egypt, still patrolled by a multinational force under the auspices of the UN. Israeli and Egyptian ships alike ply the waters of the Suez Canal and the Straits of Tiran. But most importantly, neither side has lost a single citizen's life in war against the other since the adoption of the Camp David Accords.

See also: Bargaining, Interest-Based and Positional; International Conflict; Mediation; Oslo Accords, Middle East Peace Process; Single-Text Negotiating; United Nations Mediation of the Egyptian-Israeli Negotiations at Kilometer 101.
References and Further Reading: Babbitt, Eileen F., 1994, "The Power of Moral Suasion in International Mediation"; Carter, Jimmy, 1982, *Keeping Faith: Memoirs of a President;* Goldschmidt, Arthur, 1988, *Modern Egypt: Formation of a Nation-State;* Quandt, William B., 1993, *Peace Process: American Diplomacy and the Arab-Israeli Conflict since 1967.*

Carnegie Endowment for International Peace

The Carnegie Endowment for International Peace is an operating (not grantmaking) foundation established in 1910 in Washington, D.C., with a gift from Andrew Carnegie. It conducts research; holds discussions, study groups, and conferences;

and produces publications on international affairs and U.S. foreign policy. Through these activities, it seeks to "invigorate and extend both expert and public discussion on a wide range of international issues" (Carnegie Endowment for International Peace 1996, 1), including migration of peoples, nuclear nonproliferation, regional conflicts, multilateralism, democratization, and the use of force.

In 1993 the endowment established a public policy research center in Moscow to promote collaboration among scholars in the United States, Russia, and other former Soviet states. The Moscow center also holds seminars, workshops, and study groups that attract international participants from academia, government, journalism, nongovernmental organizations, and the private sector.

In addition to its research reports and public educational materials, the endowment publishes the quarterly journal *Foreign Policy*.

References and Further Reading: Carnegie Endowment for International Peace, 1996, "Carnegie Endowment for International Peace: Staff and Projects 1996–97."

Carter, Jimmy

Jimmy Carter (James Earl Carter Jr., born 1 October 1924) rose to the presidency of the United States (1977–81) after an early career as a state senator and later as governor of Georgia. His presidency was noteworthy both for its general activism in foreign policy and for Carter's personal involvement in the negotiation of the Panama Canal Treaty (signed September 1977), the Camp David Accords (negotiated September 1978), the formal peace treaty between Egypt and Israel (confirmed March 1979), and the SALT II treaty with the Soviet Union (negotiated 1977 to 1979, signed July 1979 but rejected by Congress September 1979).

Although he was defeated in the 1980 presidential election, Carter did not retire from the international stage. In 1982, he accepted a professorship at Emory University in Atlanta, Georgia, and there founded the Carter Center. Carter now lends his time and resources, along with the substantial resources of the Carter Center, to the promulgation of democracy and human rights and the improvement of people's lives both in the United States and abroad.

The former president has personally traveled to and monitored elections in Panama (May 1989 and May 1994), Nicaragua (February 1990), the Dominican Republic (May 1990), Haiti (December 1990), Zambia (October 1991), Guyana (October 1992), Paraguay (May 1993), and Mexico (August 1994). He also continues to participate directly in the resolution of international conflicts, such as talks between the government of Ethiopia and the Eritrean People's Liberation Front (convened in 1989), talks with North and South Korean leaders about nuclear disarmament (held in June 1994), negotiation of the terms of departure for Haiti's military regime (September 1994), negotiation of a four-month cease-fire and the resumption of peace talks between Bosnian Muslims and Serbs in the former Yugoslavia (December 1994), and the negotiation of a four-month cease-fire in the ongoing civil war in the Sudan (March 1995).

See also: Camp David Accords (Israeli and Egyptian); Carter Center; International Conflict.
References and Further Reading: Carter Center World Wide Web Home Page, http://www.emory.edu/CARTER_CENTER.

Carter Center

The Carter Center was founded by Jimmy Carter and Rosalynn Carter in 1982. It is a nonpolitical, nonpartisan organization associated with Emory University and the Carter Presidential Library in Atlanta, Georgia. In the words of former president Carter, the center is "dedicated to helping create a world governed by the peaceful resolution of conflict and respect for every individual's human rights" and "to help[ing] individuals acquire the tools they need to improve their own lives" (Carter Center home page). To this end, the center engages in research on international and domestic conflict and other societal issues and seeks solutions to these conflicts and issues through conferences, programs, and direct negotiation.

Examples of the center's work abroad include the monitoring of democratic elections around the world, efforts to curb diseases such as guinea worm and river blindness, the establishment of the International Human Rights Council, and ongoing work in development in several African, Latin American, and Caribbean nations.

Domestically, the Carter Center has developed antiviolence programs, set up a loan fund for small businesses, and done work in the area of mental illness awareness. The many Carter Center programs are run by a full-time staff of over 300 people as well as numerous volunteers and interns.

References and Further Reading: Carter Center World Wide Web Home Page, http://www.emory.edu/CARTER_CENTER.

Caucuses

Caucuses are meetings that mediators hold with one party at a time to discuss some aspect of the process or the substance of the mediation session. Most often, caucuses are held when something is not going well—when the parties are stuck and unable to move forward, when one or both of the parties are engaging in behaviors that are unnecessarily upsetting to their opponents, or when emotions are getting too strong and a cooling-off time is likely to be of benefit.

Caucuses allow disputants to vent their feelings without angering the other side. If an angry party expresses those feelings in the presence of the mediator, the mediator can help that person deal with the anger effectively and reframe the presentation to the opponent to avoid making the other side angry as well.

Caucuses are also useful if parties seem to be pursuing questionable negotiating strategies or positions. Mediators can explain why a certain strategy might lead to trouble; they can also ask probing questions to try to get the parties to examine their positions carefully to see why they want what they are asking for and whether their aspirations (or expectations) are realistic (this is commonly referred to as "reality testing"). Mediators can also use caucuses as mini training sessions. For example, they can give a quick lesson on communication skills, focusing on such key concepts as I-messages or active listening. Or they can review the four principles of principled negotiation, helping disputants to reframe their arguments in terms of interests rather than positions and getting them to focus on the problem, not the people involved.

In general, the discussions between parties and the mediator in caucuses are confidential. However, when appropriate, the mediator may ask a party to reveal what was discussed in the caucus, or the mediator may ask the party for permission to do so.

Although most mediators use caucuses, some believe that mediation needs to be an open process and that meeting with just one side risks creating feelings of distrust. To be sure, if caucuses are held, the mediator should take care to meet with both sides, not just one, and to pay equal attention to the issues and concerns of each party, both in the caucus sessions and in the joint sessions.

See also: Active Listening; Cooling-off Period; I-Messages; Mediation; Mediation, Ethical Issues; Principled Negotiation and *Getting to Yes;* Reality Testing.

References and Further Reading: Bush, Robert A. Baruch, and Joseph P. Folger, 1994, *Promise of Mediation;* Folberg, Jay, and Alison Taylor, 1984, *Mediation: A Comprehensive Guide to Resolving Conflicts without Litigation;* Moore, Christopher W., 1986, *The Mediation Process.*

Children's Creative Response to Conflict

Children's Creative Response to Conflict (CCRC) is a nationwide program that provides materials and training to teach conflict resolution and related topics to children in school. Begun in New York City in 1972, CCRC now runs programs throughout the United States and abroad, offering workshops for parents, families, children, and teachers. The main themes include cooperation, communication, affirmation, conflict resolution, mediation, problem solving, and bias awareness. Although CCRC is broader in scope than some competing programs, CCRC trainers believe that children must feel secure in themselves and their relationships before they can work constructively on conflict resolution. Thus, the CCRC approach first works on open communication, cooperation, and sensitivity to others' feelings and needs in an effort to create a warm and caring classroom atmosphere. Once this is done, CCRC trainers suggest moving on to more traditional conflict resolution skills, such as problem solving and mediation. To help teachers and administrators create such a program, CCRC provides workshops and educational materials on all these topics as well as ideas about how the CCRC themes, materials, and techniques can be integrated into daily classroom activities and the overall curriculum.

See also: Community Board of San Francisco; School Conflict; School Conflict Resolution Programs.

Citizen Participation

The term *citizen participation* refers to a wide variety of processes designed to allow citizens to become involved in the governing process at the local, state, and federal levels. These processes include public hearings and meetings, advisory committees, neighborhood councils, citizen courts, and ballot initiatives, among others.

Beginning with the antiwar movement in the 1960s and the environmental movement in the 1970s, citizen participation has become a much more prevalent—and troublesome—aspect of U.S. politics. Increasing numbers of citizens are demanding involvement in many decisions that used to be made by bureaucrats and "experts" alone.

The advantage of such involvement is that decisions—when they are made—usually better reflect the interests and concerns of the public that will be affected by the decisions. The disadvantage, however, is that citizen participation can seriously slow down the decision-making process, often to the point where no decisions are made or implemented at all. This commonly occurs as people with widely differing values come to loggerheads over controversial issues and challenge any decision that is made, either through administrative appeal or in court. Such challenges can tie up decisions for years, preventing any progress on the problem that the decision was intended to address.

Nevertheless, given the extent to which governmental decisions affect our lives, public involvement in the governing process is essential. Therefore, it must be undertaken carefully, with processes designed to help citizens understand the issues and participate in decision making in meaningful ways.

Although it has far more costs than benefits, the most common form of citizen participation is the public hearing. This is an open meeting, usually held by a governmental agency, to inform the public about a proposed plan of action and get public responses to it. The problem with public hearings is that they are most commonly held after a plan of action has already been formulated, and the only citizens who tend to come are those who are opposed to the plan. The government representatives typically sit at tables in the front of a room (often a large auditorium), and the citizens stand up, one after another, for hours, making impassioned one- or two-minute speeches about how the government plan is bad or, occasionally, good. Although such an exercise may give the government agency some idea of the sentiment of the opposition, it rarely provides a representative view of the public-at-large. It also gives a superficial image of public concerns.

Other forms of public participation are more useful but much more time-consuming as well. Having citizens serve on decision-making or advisory bodies is one way that they can become more meaningfully involved in the governance process. But such participation requires a great deal of time and knowledge, or a willingness to learn all the technical information that is required to understand the complex society in which we live. Some research suggests that this form of citizen involvement can lead to serious conflicts when citizens clash with expert committee members, whose knowledge and reasons for making decisions are very different.

Ballot initiatives are another form of citizen participation that has greatly increased in popularity over the last decade. Here, citizens groups collect signatures to put laws or constitutional amendments on the ballot. Thus, citizens take over the role of legislatures. Although this allows citizens to have a much greater say on issues that affect them than they have with representative government, most people end up voting on a large number of issues that they do not fully understand. Further, initiatives tend to oversimplify problems and solutions. Therefore, they rarely lead to effective remedies to problems.

See also: Ballot Initiatives; Collaborative Leadership; Collaborative Problem Solving; Public Meetings and Hearings; Public Policy Conflicts; Referendum; Scientific and Technical Disputes.

References and Further Reading: Chrislip, David D., 1995, "Transforming Politics"; DeSario, Jack, and Stuart Langton, 1987, *Citizen Participation in Public Decision Making;* Fischer, Frank, 1993, "Citizen Participation and the Democratization of Policy Expertise: From Theoretical Inquiry to Practical Cases."

Citizens' Radiation Monitoring Program

In March 1989, the Three Mile Island (TMI) nuclear generating plant near Harrisburg, Pennsylvania, suffered a loss-of-coolant accident. Because of a combination of a defective valve and human error, the reactor's core was severely damaged and a small amount of radioactive material was released into the atmosphere. The maximum exposure to people living near the plant was estimated to be about twice that of average yearly background radiation levels (Gray 1989, 16).

Although the amount of radiation released was not expected to have any significant health impacts, residents were frightened by the incident. Their fear was heightened when Metropolitan Edison (Met Ed), the plant's operator, proposed to release small amounts of radioactive krypton gas into the atmosphere as a first step toward cleanup. The Nuclear Regulatory Commission (NRC) agreed with Met Ed that such a release would not further endanger the health and safety of the public. However, public distrust of both Met Ed and the NRC was extremely high, and most of the public strongly opposed such a release. The NRC held public hearings in an effort to explain to people what would happen and why they should not be concerned. Facts and figures coming from the NRC were neither understandable nor credible, however, and public distrust and fear escalated.

In response to these concerns, the U.S. Department of Energy (DOE) brought together representatives from several federal, state, and local agencies to establish the Citizens' Radiation Monitoring Program. The purpose of the program was to "ensure that citizens in the vicinity of TMI received accurate and credible information about radiation levels during the purge" (Gray 1989, 17). The assumption was that citizens were more likely to believe information that they generated themselves than information provided by the NRC or Met Ed.

Twelve communities that lay within five miles of TMI nominated four citizens each to serve as monitors. Rather than selecting scientists, these people were teachers, secretaries, engineers, housewives, police officers, and retirees. They were all given an intensive "crash course" on radiation, its effects, and detection methods, and they were trained to operate the monitoring equipment and interpret the findings for their communities. Results of this monitoring were posted daily and were released to the media and to the participating local, state, and federal agencies. As a result, public trust in the process was increased considerably, and Met Ed was able to conduct the purge of krypton gas. The people who served as monitors learned a lot about nuclear power and its risks and benefits and were able to transfer this knowledge to others in their communities. According to Gray (1989, 21), "Had the NRC proceeded with the purge without community guarantees about credible information, the conflict would only have escalated, probably to the level of violence."

This case is one of many that illustrate the importance of citizen involvement in public decision-making processes. Without such involvement, there tends to be a much higher level of distrust of public decisions, and escalated conflicts are likely to occur. The case also illustrates the importance of translating complex technical data into information and language that ordinary citizens can easily understand. Once this was done and the information was generated by trusted people, the conflict was essentially resolved, and the reactor was successfully cleaned up to the benefit of both the plant operators and the community at large (Gircar and Baratta 1983).

See also: Citizen Participation; Environmental Conflicts; Public Policy Conflicts; Scientific and Technical Disputes.
References and Further Reading: Gircar, B. G., and A. J. Baratta, 1983, "Bridging the Information Gap: Radiation Monitoring by Citizens"; Gray, Barbara, 1989, *Col-*

laboring: Finding Common Ground for Multiparty Problems.

Civil Justice Reform

The civil justice system provides a forum for the resolution of disputes between private parties (e.g., those that pertain to contracts or personal injuries). If one person sues another for failing to uphold a contract or for compensation for injuries sustained in an automobile accident, for example, they become involved in the civil justice system.

The civil justice system has been criticized in the last two decades for its alleged failures to provide either efficient or fair results. Many critics talk of a "litigation explosion," which has overburdened the courts so badly that cases are delayed for years. Others complain that cases are rushed through the system in ways that lead to unfair outcomes, or that the delays themselves constitute denial of justice.

Other concerns with the civil justice system involve the equity of awards in personal-injury cases. The news is filled with stories of people who have won exorbitant awards—millions of dollars for damages that resulted from spilled coffee, for example—whereas others who were seriously harmed from gross negligence were paid little or nothing. The result, critics charge, is an increase in insurance rates (to cover the costs of the occasional huge award) as well as an increase in the costs of products that everyone buys. Another result is the curtailment of research and new product development. Work on new vaccines and contraceptives, for example, has been greatly slowed due to manufacturers' fears of being sued if anything goes wrong with their new products. Other types of drugs are believed to be safer and thus better business risks.

Other observers, such as law professor Marc Galanter (1983), argue that the litigation explosion is largely a myth, that most of the increase in caseload is traceable to a few major problems—asbestos litigation or breast-implant litigation, for example. Many consumer advocates also defend the tort system, saying that it is simply doing its job, compensating people for real harm done and punishing offenders so that they are deterred from wrongdoing in the future.

Nevertheless, concern about the inadequacies of the civil justice system have spurred many reforms, primarily of two types: procedures for expediting the movement of cases through the regular court system, and procedures for diverting cases out of the court system to alternatives.

Expediting Procedures

Procedures that have been developed to move cases through the system more quickly include special "fast tracks" for particular kinds of cases; the use of judicial "adjuncts" such as magistrates to hear cases; procedures to limit and simplify pretrial activities such as motions, pleadings, and discovery; limits on requests for delays of trials or hearings; "docket cleaning" (the dismissal of inactive cases); and penalizing disputants who settle at the last minute, after courtrooms and juries have been assigned. Although such procedures have apparently helped somewhat, the evidence of improved efficiency is not as strong as some had hoped.

Diversion Procedures

Other civil justice reforms divert cases out of the courts into alternative systems. This has been done by offering voluntary, or in some cases mandatory, alternatives: mediation, arbitration, judicial settlement, or early neutral evaluation, for example. Some states hold "settlement weeks" in which large numbers of parties are encouraged to engage in settlement conferences before trial. Many states also require arbitration or mediation of certain types of cases before trial. For example, mandatory mediation of child custody cases is fairly common, as is mandatory arbitration of civil suits seeking monetary damages below a specified amount.

The two types of procedural reforms may overlap. For example, some states provide private judges or "parajudicials" to adjudicate certain classes of cases. Other states require medical malpractice cases to be screened by a panel of experts to determine whether the case is serious or frivolous and, if serious, to promote settlement before a full trial.

Benefits of Reform

Advocates of reform cite many benefits beyond faster case processing and diminished court caseloads. The reforms extend a forum for seeking justice to populations whose access to the traditional judicial system has previously been limited. In addition, the reforms substitute integrative (win-win) procedures for adversarial (win-lose) procedures and often replace procedures that are controlled by external "experts" (lawyers and judges) with procedures that are controlled by the disputing parties themselves. When parties are encouraged to resolve their own disputes through mediation and related processes rather than through litigation, disputants tend to be more invested in the decision that is made and are thus more likely to carry it out. They are also likely to learn conflict resolution skills that will benefit them over the long term.

Costs of Reform

Although the popularity of alternative dispute resolution (ADR) has grown steadily over the last two decades, a number of people have voiced serious concerns about its societal implications. Some are concerned that such procedures constitute the denial of constitutional due process, equal protection, or jury trial rights, since ADR processes replace jury trials. Others question the institution of a two-track system—a "first-class" system for those who can afford it, and a "second-class" system for those who cannot. A third criticism revolves around the issue of social control. Although some see ADR as a means of extending justice to populations that are usually left out of the regular justice system, others see it as extending the arm of state control into more private aspects of people's lives. A similar charge is that ADR—mediation especially—is a means of sugarcoating injustice and perpetuating the status quo, especially in disputes between one lower-power and one higher-power party.

Despite all these concerns, however, client satisfaction with alternative procedures has generally been fairly high, and more and more reform measures are being instituted at all levels of the justice system.

See also: Alternative Dispute Resolution, Institutionalization; Criminal Justice; Due Process; Tort Reform.
References and Further Reading: Abel, Richard L., 1982, *The Politics of Informal Justice: The American Experience;* Drivon, Laurence E., and Bob Schimdt, 1990, *The Civil War on Consumer Rights;* Galanter, Marc, 1983, "Reading the Landscape of Disputes: What We Know and Don't Know (and Think We Know) about Our Allegedly Contentious and Litigious Society"; Matthews, Roger, 1988, *Informal Justice?;* Menkel-Meadow, Carrie, 1991, "Pursuing Settlement in an Adversary Culture: A Tale of Innovation Co-Coped or 'The Law of ADR'"; Resnick, Judith, 1995, "Many Doors? Closing Doors? Alternative Dispute Resolution and Adjudication."

Civil Justice Reform Act of 1990

The Civil Justice Reform Act (CJRA) of 1990 was passed to relieve some of the congestion in the courts and remedy some of the alleged abuses and malfunctions of the traditional civil justice system. The CJRA required every federal district court to conduct a self-study of costs and delays related to its court processes and to develop a plan for civil case management that would reduce those costs and delays as much as possible. This self-study was to be undertaken with the assistance of an advisory group, which was to assess the condition of the civil and criminal dockets in the district; identify the principal causes of delay and excess costs; and make recommendations, which the courts were free to accept or reject, for dealing with these problems (Dunworth and Kakalik 1994).

The act also required ten pilot districts to adopt six predefined principles of case management, which were to be independently evaluated to determine their effectiveness. The six principles were (1) the differential management of cases (meaning that simple cases would be handled differently from complex cases); (2) early and ongoing judicial control of pretrial processes, such as discovery and pretrial motions; (3) special monitoring and judicial control of complex cases; (4) cost-effective discovery through cooperation and voluntary exchange of information; (5) good-faith efforts to resolve discovery disputes before filing motions; and (6) diversion of cases, when appropriate, to alternative dispute resolution (ADR) programs. These changes were to be implemented by January 1992 by the ten pilot districts; the other 84 federal districts were to implement such changes before December 1993.

According to the RAND Institute for Civil Justice, which carried out the independent evaluation, "Not everyone agrees that the mandated case-management principles in the pilot program have merit. Some see them as overly rigid and controlling—a type of assembly-line justice that prevents the system from adapting to the needs of individual cases. Others think the principles so vague and permissive that pilot districts will be able to comply with the legislative requirements by retaining most of their existing policies" (RAND 1996).

Despite these concerns, the initial RAND report was quite positive. In general, it said that the advisory groups "approached their mission with dedication and conscientiousness." Although some district judges met with, or were actually members of, the advisory groups, they all operated quite independent of the court's control. Nevertheless, RAND reported that "most courts accepted their advisory group's recommendations for change" (RAND 1996). The nature and the volume of changes actually made varied greatly from district to district. Some districts were highly aggressive, implementing a large number of changes designed to significantly streamline procedures; others made only minor adjustments to programs that they considered to be effective already. Overall, the RAND study suggested that "implicit policy changes may be as important as explicit ones." Many judges and lawyers believe that the process of implementing changes has "raised the consciousness of judicial officers, clerks, and lawyers," resulting in many subtle changes in procedures that ultimately will help limit costs and delays (RAND 1996).

See also: Alternative Dispute Resolution; Civil Justice Reform; Tort Reform.

References and Further Reading: Dunworth, Terence, and James Kakalik, 1994, "Preliminary Observations on Implementation of the Pilot Program of the Civil Justice Reform Act of 1990"; RAND Institute for Civil Justice, 1996, "Research Brief: Evaluating the Civil Justice Reform Act of 1990."

Civil Law and Litigation

Civil law (as opposed to criminal law) involves disputes between private parties. A civil dispute may be adjudicated in a court, but the court only listens to the arguments of both sides and makes a judgment. It does not determine guilt or innocence and apply a punishment, as occurs in criminal cases.

A civil lawsuit begins when one party (the plaintiff) files a petition against another party (the defendant). If the judge believes that the plaintiff's petition lacks any merit, he or she may simply dismiss the case without holding a hearing or a trial. If a hearing is necessary, however, each party has a chance to obtain information from the opposing side (through a process called discovery) before the hearing. More formal presentation of evidence occurs during the trial itself. The evidence may be presented to a judge or to a jury, depending on the nature of the case. Parties are almost always represented by attorneys in both pretrial hearings and the trial itself. The losing party generally has a right to appeal the decision to a higher court. Most cases are settled before a trial actually occurs, although a small percentage do go through the whole process. The term *civil law* may also refer to the law created by legislative action (Congress or state legislatures), as opposed to common law, which is based on commonly held principles of justice and rationality and is enforced by judges' interpretation of the law on a case-to-case basis.

See also: Adjudication; Common Law; Criminal Justice; Settlement Conference.
References and Further Reading: Gifis, Steven H., 1991, *Law Dictionary;* Schellenberg, James A., 1996, *Conflict Resolution—Theory, Research, and Practice.*

Civil Rights Act of 1964

The Civil Rights Act of 1964 was the result of a decade of intense activity on the part of both blacks and whites, working to increase Americans' awareness of the civil rights problem and then assembling large coalitions of individuals and organizations to lobby Congress for effective legislation.

Nonviolent Action

Following the Supreme Court's 1954 decision on school desegregation (*Brown v. Board of Education,* 347 U.S. 483 [1954]), blacks began a series of nonviolent efforts designed to bring the discrimination problem into the public view. Best known (and most effective) of these activities were the Montgomery bus boycott in 1955 and

1956, which was the beginning of Martin Luther King's prominence in the civil rights movement; the sit-ins at southern lunch counters throughout the South; and the freedom rides, in which blacks and whites rode interstate buses together to test the federal government's and the southern states' resolve to enforce the Supreme Court's desegregation rule for interstate transport.

All these efforts involved thousands—even tens of thousands—of people and brought the hypocrisy of discrimination to Americans' television screens day after day. Added to that were scenes of black children being verbally and physically attacked as they tried to enter previously all-white schools; clashes between state officials and federal troops that Attorney General Robert Kennedy called upon to enforce the school and bus desegregation rules; and ultimately the August 1963 March on Washington, in which nearly 200,000 people, black and white, gathered in the nation's capital to protest the injustice of racial discrimination. This was the site of Martin Luther King's "I Have a Dream" speech, where, indeed, "the sons of former slaves and the sons of former slave owners" sat down together, as King prophesied, not yet to "share the table of brotherhood" but to demand that such a table be created.

Congressional Action

As these events were occurring, organizations throughout the North and the South were preparing a massive effort to shepherd a comprehensive civil rights bill through Congress. Although Congress had been largely apathetic or even hostile to the cause of civil rights since the Reconstruction era, it could no longer take such a position. A coalition of Republicans and Democrats in the House of Representatives worked with several outside groups (the Leadership Conference on Civil Rights, the

National Council of Churches, and the Justice Department, especially) to put together a strong bill in the House. All attempts to weaken it were defeated, and it passed by a vote of 290 to 130.

A similar bipartisan coalition was established in the Senate, where civil rights proponents had to overcome the traditionally hostile Judiciary Committee and a southern state filibuster to get the bill passed. The key party in the Senate effort to pass the bill was Republican Everett Dirksen, GOP minority leader. Dirksen controlled the votes needed to stop the filibuster. Although he was a proponent of civil rights in general, Dirksen had a number of reservations about the House bill, which had been forwarded directly to the Senate floor. Civil rights proponents inside and outside the Senate worked with Dirksen for weeks, as the southern filibuster continued. Robert Kennedy negotiated with Dirksen, GOP members of the House pushed for the bill's passage, and finally Dirksen agreed, offering only a few minor amendments to save face. When Dirksen agreed, the needed votes were obtained, and the Senate voted 71 to 29 to stop the filibuster. A week later, the bill was passed by a vote of 73 to 27. It was later signed into law by President Lyndon B. Johnson.

Significance of the Act

This bill was noteworthy for a number of reasons. It was the first significant piece of civil rights legislation to be passed by Congress since 1875. (In 1957 and 1960, Congress enacted limited civil rights bills, but these addressed only voting rights, and the first was not even effective, necessitating the second.) The 1964 Civil Rights Act was also the first act to attack all forms of discrimination. It prohibited discrimination in places of public accommodation and in programs receiving federal funds. It also prohibited discrimination in employment and established the Equal Employment Opportunity Commission (EEOC). It barred unequal voting rights and lowered literacy requirements so that more blacks could vote. It also established the Community Relations Service (CRS) as part of the Department of Justice, to help communities prevent and effectively resolve racial, ethnic, and other civil rights conflicts.

See also: Community Relations Service; King, Martin Luther, Jr.; Montgomery Bus Boycott; Nonviolence. *References and Further Reading:* Carson, Clayborne, 1991, *The Eyes on the Prize: Civil Rights Reader—Documents, Speeches, and Firsthand Accounts from the Black Freedom Struggle, 1954–1990;* Dittmer, John, George C. Wright, and W. Marvin Dulaney, 1993, *Essays on the American Civil Rights Movement;* Lytle, Clifford M., 1966, "The History of the Civil Rights Bill of 1964"; Matusow, Allen J., 1984, *The Unraveling of America: A History of Liberalism in the 1960s;* Weisbrot, Robert, 1990, *Freedom Bound: A History of America's Civil Rights Movement;* Whalen, Charles, and Barbara Whalen, 1985, *The Longest Debate: A Legislative History of the 1964 Civil Rights Act.*

Civilian-Based Defense

Civilian-based defense (also called civilian defense, social defense, or nonmilitary defense or resistance) refers to the defense of a territory or a way of life using civilian resistance (as opposed to military resistance) and civilian means of struggle (as opposed to military means of struggle) (Sharp and Jenkins 1990). Thus civilian-based defense relies on social, economic, political, and psychological weapons, rather than on traditional military weapons, to discourage or defeat a foreign military invasion, occupation, or coup.

According to Gene Sharp and Bruce Jenkins (1990, 6), "These nonviolent weapons are used to wage widespread noncooperation and to offer massive public defiance. The aim is both to deny the attackers their objectives and to make impossible the consolidation of their rule, whether in the form of foreign administration, a puppet regime, or a government of usurpers."

Although civilian-based defense is far less common than military defense, it has been used in a number of cases, including the German resistance to the Kapp Putsch in 1920, the French opposition to a coup attempt against Charles de Gaulle in 1961, the German attempt to defend the Ruhr from French and Belgian invasion and occupation in 1923, and the Czech struggle against the Soviet invasion in 1968. Civilian-based defense was also used by Norwegians to resist the Nazis and, most recently, by Lithuanian and Russian citizens in 1991, when the Lithuanians were fighting for their independence from the Soviet Union and the Russians prevented the coup against Gorbachev.

Like other forms of nonviolence, civilian-based defense works because the real power of a society rests not in its rulers but in its people. Rulers, even the most tyrannical, can exercise their power only if they have popular support. If that support is withdrawn or withheld, would-be rulers lose their legitimacy to rule. Although the government may not crumble immediately, the loss of legitimacy "sets in motion the weakening or disintegration of the rulers' power" (Sharp and Jenkins 1990, 25).

Sharp and Jenkins list two key factors that are necessary for successful civilian-based defense. First is noncooperation. Citizens must overtly and actively express their rejection of the tyrannical government or the invading army by refusing to cooperate with its demands, even if that means violent reprisals. Noncooperation can be social; for instance, citizens can socially boycott the invaders by refusing to look at them or talk to them, or they can withdraw from normal social activities (school attendance or sporting events, for example). More common is economic noncooperation: citizens can implement boycotts of goods or businesses, or they can go on strike. Political noncooperation can also contribute to effective defense. Examples include civil disobedience, the boycott of governmental activities, and the maintenance or establishment of "alternative" governmental structures. Although none

of these activities alone will prevent an invading force from occupying and ruling a country, extensive and coordinated noncooperation can be effective in preventing successful invasion.

Second, Sharp and Jenkins contend that citizens must act together as a group, not as individuals. Individuals can easily be divided and conquered, but massive protests by groups and institutions are more difficult to control. A few people refusing to work is ineffective, but whole unions or cities refusing to work is much more damaging. Likewise, individual resisters can be thrown in jail, but whole cities of resisters are much harder to repress.

Although nonviolent direct action has been successful in hundreds of cases worldwide, few nations have seriously considered relying on civilian defense as an alternative to military defense. One problem, pointed out by Vogele (1993), is that civilian defense is hard to quantify and demonstrate in advance, making it difficult to use for deterrence. However, as more people become aware of how it works and its potential to successfully defend against attack (perhaps even better than military defense), its use as a deterrence strategy will increase. Given the potential effectiveness of civilian defense and the increasing ineffectiveness of military action, more and more scholars and politicians are considering the application of civilian defense as a supplement to or a replacement for military defense.

See also: Deterrence; Nonviolence; Sharp, Gene.
References and Further Reading: Boserup, Anders, and Andrew Mack, 1975, *War without Weapons: Non-Violence in National Defense;* Koch, Koen, 1984, "Civilian Defense: An Alternative to Military Defense?"; Naess, Arne, 1974, "Nonmilitary Defense"; Sharp, Gene, and Bruce Jenkins, 1990, *Civilian-Based Defense: A Post-Military Weapons System;* Vogele, William B., 1993, "Deterrence by Civilian Defense."

Clausewitz, Karl von

Karl von Clausewitz (1780–1831) was a Prussian soldier and military theorist. According to Correlli Barnett (1972, 301), "[he] was the first man to make conceptual sense of war as a social and political activity and to deduce its governing principles. Clausewitz is the starting point of all later theorizing about war, and often the finishing point as well. He significantly influenced the German and French general staffs before 1914; he is the fountainhead of present-day Communist thinking about war [as well]." According to Edward de Bono (1976, 136), his influence continued into World Wars I and II and beyond; Hitler's strategy of blitzkrieg, for instance, was based on Clausewitzian principles. After World War II and the advent of nuclear weapons, military strategy changed significantly. Nevertheless, a number of political and military strategists of the 1950s have been labeled "neo-Clausewitzian." These include Human Kahn and Henry Kissinger, who advocated a rational nuclear strategy parallel to Clausewitz's rational (prenuclear) military strategy. The emphasis in both cases was the use of war as an extension of political process and that, despite the risk of nuclear annihilation, nuclear war "should still be contemplated as an act of policy by world leaders" (Bono 1976, 136).

Clausewitz is best remembered for his three-volume treatise *On War,* in which he elaborated on the now famous statement that "war is only a continuation of state policy by other means" (Bono 1976, 134; Clausewitz 1943). In the contemporary era, this is generally interpreted to mean that Clausewitz was a proponent of war as a method of conflict resolution. Actually, he was not. He stressed that war should not be taken lightly and should be used only under certain limited circumstances when politics had failed and when the conditions were right for military victory. Thus, he stressed the importance of being able to predict the outcome of a military conflict before it begins—an approach that was not as common in his day as one might expect. He also stressed that war must be directed by politicians, not generals, although the two must work in close concert if the war is to be successful.

See also: Kissinger, Henry A.
References and Further Reading: Barnett, Correlli, 1972, "Karl Maria von Clausewitz"; Bono, Edward de, 1976, *The Greatest Thinkers;* Clausewitz, Karl von, 1943, *On War.*

Coalition Building

Coalition building is an important way for parties in conflict to increase their power. Highly evident in political processes, building coalitions of people or interest groups can be beneficial in many other circumstances as well. For example, environmental groups can argue much more forcefully for environmental protection if they band together in a unified coalition with one another and with other interest groups (neighborhood organizations, for instance) than they can acting independently or, worse, in opposition to one another. Likewise, citizens who want action from their city government are in a much stronger position if they form a coalition of people from different areas who share similar concerns.

The benefits of coalition building are not only the increased number of people who become involved in a cause but also the fine-tuning of the goals and strategies that it encourages. If people or groups must agree on their goals and strategies, they usually have to give them more careful thought and debate than they would if they were acting alone. This encourages people and groups to consider the legitimacy of their goals and tactics and to question the efficacy of approaches that might otherwise go unquestioned. Although maintenance of the coalition takes time and effort and can require groups to compromise on some of their interests or goals, the effort is often more than repaid in terms of increased power in relation to the opposition or the outside world as a whole.

See also: Advocacy; Collaborative Problem Solving.
References and Further Reading: Folger, Joseph P., and Marshall Scott Poole, 1984, *Working through Conflict: A Communication Perspective;* Ury, William, 1991, *Getting Past No: Negotiating with Difficult People.*

Cold War

The Cold War was the monumental struggle between the United States and its allies and the Soviet Union and its partners that began shortly after the end of World War II and continued until the dissolution of the Soviet Union in 1989. Based on fundamental ideological differences, a deep-seated distrust of each other, and an escalating arms race, the Cold War shaped the international world order for over 40 years and profoundly influenced the politics and economies of many nations.

Just as Karl von Clausewitz defined war as the continuation of policy by other means, Zbigniew Brzezinski, President Jimmy Carter's national security adviser, described the Cold War as "warfare by other (non-lethal) means.... Nonetheless," he said, "warfare it was. And the stakes were monumental.

"Geopolitically the struggle, in the first instance, was for control over the Eurasian landmass, and eventually, even for global preponderance. Each side understood that either the successful ejection of the one from the western and eastern fringes of Eurasia or the effective containment of the other would ultimately determine the geostrategic outcome of the contest.

"Also fueling the conflict were sharply conflicting, ideologically motivated conceptions of social organization and even of the human being itself. Not only geopolitics, but philosophy—in the deepest sense of the self-definition of mankind—were very much at issue" (Brzezinski 1993, 10).

Although the Cold War is usually said to have started after World War II, problems between the United States and the Soviet Union can be traced back to 1918–20, when the United States sent over 10,000 troops to Russia to oppose the communist takeover. The communist revolution was successful, but the United States refused to recognize the new government until 1933. The two nations set aside their rivalry to join forces to combat Adolf Hitler in World War II, but tensions developed quickly after the end of the war when Joseph Stalin sought Soviet security by using the Red Army to control most of Eastern Europe. The United States countered this move with the Marshall Plan, designed to strengthen the economies of Western and Central Europe, and with the establishment of the North Atlantic Treaty Organization (NATO) to defend the West against the apparently growing "Soviet threat."

Western fears of the USSR and communism increased even further in 1949 and 1950, when the Soviets exploded an atomic bomb and communists took over in China. Shortly thereafter, the United States became embroiled in the Korean War—the first of many attempts to keep communist control from spreading further. (Later wars were fought in Vietnam, Cambodia, Nicaragua, and the Middle East.)

The arms race fueled by the Cold War was expensive and dangerous—costing both the United States and the Soviet Union billions of dollars, and bringing questionable security at best. Many peace advocates thought that the arms buildup was a greater threat to the United States than the Soviets were and advocated bilateral or even unilateral arms reductions in an effort to diminish the ever-growing threat of nuclear war.

This threat became frighteningly real in 1962, when the Soviets attempted to put missiles in Cuba. Following a short standoff, during which President John F. Kennedy threatened nuclear retaliation, the Soviets agreed to withdraw their missiles in return for Kennedy's promise not to invade Cuba. Both nations were sufficiently frightened by this episode that they began a period of de-escalation, commonly called détente. This period lasted from 1963 to 1980, when the Soviets invaded Afghanistan and the United States elected Ronald Reagan president. These events reignited the arms race and the Cold War until 1985, when Mikhail Gorbachev came to power in the Soviet Union. Gorbachev sought to ease tensions with the West while relaxing internal controls within the Soviet system as well. Within four years, Gorbachev's policies of glasnost and perestroika led to the downfall of communism, first in the Soviet satellite nations, and then in the Soviet Union itself, which was dissolved into many independent states. Although most observers consider the dissolution of the USSR to mark the end of the Cold War, both the United States and Russia (as well as several other former Soviet states) maintain significant nuclear arsenals. Thus, although the tensions of the Cold War are significantly reduced, the threat of nuclear war is not absent.

See also: Arms Control and Disarmament; Cuban Missile Crisis; Détente.
References and Further Reading: Brzezinski, Zbigniew, 1993, "The Cold War and Its Aftermath"; Feber, Walter La, 1994, "Cold War"; Hill, Kenneth L., 1993, *Cold War Chronology: Soviet-American Relations, 1945–1991;* Kennan, George F., 1983, *The Nuclear Delusion: Soviet-American Relations in the Atomic Age.*

Collaborative Leadership

Collaborative leadership is a new form of leadership that differs from authoritative or charismatic leadership in that collaborative leaders have no formal power or authority. Rather, they have people skills that enable them to effectively convene and facilitate collaborative problem-solving groups. Collaborative leaders come from many roles and many backgrounds; they are not necessarily in traditional leadership positions—local government officials, managers, or department chairs—but are people who understand and are committed to the collaborative process for solving problems.

According to Barbara Gray, an expert on collaboration, "[collaborative] leaders need a vision of what collaboration can accomplish, sensitivity and the ability to develop relationships with diverse stakeholders, and a sense of optimism and process literacy, that is knowledge of the process tools, both human and organizational, for designing effective collaborations. Cultivating leaders with these special competencies is essential [for effective collaborative problem solving]" (Gray 1989, 279).

According to Carl Larson and David Chrislip, who wrote a book on the topic, collaborative leaders are particularly effective in four ways. First, they can inspire the commitment and action of others. "What makes collaborative leaders unique is that they catalyze, convene, energize, and facilitate others to create visions and solve problems" (Larson and Chrislip 1994, 138). Second, rather than ruling, collaborative leaders act as peer problem solvers. Thus, they don't tell people how to solve problems, but they direct a process that helps people work out solutions themselves. Third, they are good at building broad-based involvement. Collaborative leaders make every effort to identify all the stakeholders and get them to the table. They also work hard to keep those people involved. Finally, collaborative leaders sustain hope and participation. When people get frustrated or angry and consider dropping out, a good collaborative leader convinces the participants of the value of their participation, both to themselves and to the process, in an effort to keep everyone talking. They set incremental and obtainable goals, and they celebrate each small success to encourage continued participation and enthusiasm.

This kind of leadership is becoming increasingly essential in the 1990s. Leaders can no longer lead by authority alone; too many people distrust their leaders, the decisions are too complex to be made unilaterally, and many advocacy groups hold veto power that can stymie any top-down decision. The only way to get things done in the political climate of the 1990s is to collaborate with all the potentially affected interest groups and get them to buy into the decision that is made. This process requires the development and training of an entirely different set of leaders and leadership skills.

See also: Collaborative Problem Solving; Consensus Building.
References and Further Reading: Bryson, John M., and Barbara C. Crosby, 1992, *Leadership for the Common Good: Tackling Public Problems in a Shared-Power World;* Gray, Barbara, 1989, *Collaborating: Finding Common Ground for Multiparty Problems;* Larson, Carl E., and David D. Chrislip, 1994, *Collaborative Leadership;* Strauss, David, 1993, "Facilitated Collaborative Problem Solving."

Collaborative Problem Solving

Collaborative problem solving (also called consensus building or collaboration) is a conflict resolution process used primarily in complex, multiparty disputes to enable those with a stake in a problem to work together to develop a mutually acceptable solution. Examples of collaborative problem-solving efforts include the international negotiations over limiting chlorofluorocarbons (CFCs) to protect the ozone layer and the National Coal Policy Project, which brought together coal extractors, coal users, and environmentalists to develop new approaches to coal policy and environmental protection that met the needs of both sides.

Although still viewed skeptically by some leaders and many advocacy groups, collaborative problem solving is rapidly gaining interest as traditional decision making no longer seems capable of resolving public conflicts or solving social problems. According to consensus-builder David Strauss, people are finally figuring out that traditional win-lose decision making is actually lose-lose decision making. "Once we recognize we are only pulling each other down, there will be an interest

in moving to a more collaborative win/win approach" (Strauss 1993, 31).

Typically, collaborative problem solving moves through a number of phases. These include (1) participant identification and recruitment; (2) start-up, process design, and participant education; (3) problem definition and analysis; (4) identification and evaluation of alternative solutions; (5) decision making; and (6) implementation.

Participant Identification

It is critical that all current and potential stakeholders be involved in the process. Participants must include all the individuals and groups that have power to make or implement decisions, those who have an interest in the problem or the outcome, and those who have the power to block decisions or their implementation.

Start-up and Process Design

Although the convener may suggest an initial process, participants must be involved in most, if not all, of the process decisions and buy into the process if it is to be successful. Although a facilitator can make suggestions, moderate discussions, and enforce ground rules, ultimately it is the participants themselves who must make the ground rules, set the agendas, and make the procedural (as well as substantive) decisions.

Problem Definition and Analysis

Often, when faced with complex problems, different groups define the problem differently. One of the first steps of consensus building is to reach agreement on what the problem is and what is causing it. Only then can work begin on designing solutions.

Identification and Evaluation of Alternative Solutions

Brainstorming is frequently used to identify alternative solutions, which are then evaluated in terms of their ability to solve the identified problems and meet the needs of each of the parties.

Decision Making

In collaborative problem solving, decisions are made by consensus, not by vote. This means that everyone must agree. To attain such consensus, alternatives must meet the parties' needs sufficiently so that each one believes that the outcome is a win for him or her as well as for all the other parties involved. The outcome must also be better than that which could be attained by any party through another process. If one party thinks that he or she can get a better result by force (for instance, by suing someone), most likely that is what will happen. This usually causes the collaborative process to break down.

Implementation

The last phase of collaborative problem solving is implementation. Frequently, the implementation phase involves continued monitoring by the collaborative problem-solving group and a reconvening of that group to iron out problems as they occur.

Determinants of Success

Barbara Gray, author of a definitive book on the subject, cites five factors that are critical to the success of consensus building. First, the stakeholders must be interdependent. If one stakeholder can go off alone and obtain what is needed without participating in the process, that stakeholder will do so, which usually causes the process to break down (if it starts at all). Second, differences between participants must be dealt with in constructive ways. That means that differences in values as well as in interests and needs, must be recognized, worked with, and appreciated for what they are. Destructive at-

tempts to subvert some groups' differing interests or needs in favor of one's own undermine the potential for success. Third, all the parties must jointly own the process. This means that all the parties must be involved in making both process and substantive decisions. Fourth, the participants assume a collective responsibility for implementing any agreements that are reached. This means that, through collaboration, the stakeholders restructure the socially acceptable rules for dealing with one another and the problem in the future. Rather than fighting over issues in an adversarial forum, successful collaborative processes set up a means to continue collaborative problem solving for the initial problem and related issues in the future. Last, Gray says, collaboration must be an emergent process. This means that it changes its structure and form over time, often going from an amorphous, poorly organized group of participants to a much more cohesive organization and problem-solving entity (Gray 1989).

See also: Bargaining, Integrative and Distributive; Brainstorming; Environmental Conflicts; Framing; Mediation; Montreal Protocol on Substances that Deplete the Ozone Layer; Public Policy Conflicts; Rationality.

References and Further Reading: Gray, Barbara, 1989, *Collaborating: Finding Common Ground for Multiparty Problems;* Larson, Carl E., and David D. Chrislip, 1994, *Collaborative Leadership;* Strauss, David, 1993, "Facilitated Collaborative Problem Solving."

Collective Bargaining

Collective bargaining is a negotiation process used by organized labor unions and employers to determine the terms and conditions of employment of all union members. Established in 1935 by the National Labor Relations Act (NLRA; also called the Wagner Act), collective bargaining provides an organized and generally effective way for labor and management to resolve their natural conflict and to reach agreement on issues such as wages, hours, benefits, and employment conditions. The NLRA requires that each side bargain in good faith, stating that parties should deal with each other with "open and fair minds and sincerely endeavor to overcome obstacles existing between them" for the purpose of avoiding labor unrest and disruption of the "free flow of commerce" (29 *U.S. Code* §§151 et seq.).

Although usually thought of as contract negotiations alone, collective bargaining also involves negotiations over the interpretation and application of the contract once it is established (called contract administration) and informal discussions of issues of mutual concern between union representatives and employers (called informal joint consultation).

Contract Negotiations

In union-management contract negotiations, there are usually a number of inconsistent—or even incompatible—interests that must be negotiated. Unions usually want higher pay, better benefits, more job flexibility, and more job security, whereas employers usually want to give in as little as possible on all these issues in the interests of reducing labor costs. Other interests at stake are mutual: both workers and employers want the firm to stay financially viable (so the workers maintain their jobs); to do this, they both probably want to produce a good-quality product. Negotiations typically involve trade-offs and compromises, with each side giving up something it wants in an effort to get something else it deems even more important, although occasionally win-win solutions can be found to apparently win-lose situations. Often in collective bargaining negotiations, the less important issues are decided first, which creates a climate of compromise and mutual trust. That paves the way for the discussion of more difficult issues.

Although each side has a negotiating team, usually one team member is the spokesperson. This provides clarity and consistency within the negotiations. Each side also has a recorder who records what is said and any agreements that are reached. The negotiations can be extremely complex, involving highly technical data and myriad issues. Usually the union makes a proposal to the employer first; then the employer responds with its own proposal. The give-and-take can last weeks, or even months, punctuated by periods of stalemate and apparent inactivity, followed by intense negotiation, especially if a strike deadline looms. Usually negotiations begin several weeks or months before the previous contract runs out, allowing parties sufficient time to negotiate a new one. Despite media images to the contrary, negotiations are usually successful within the given time period, and strikes are averted. However, strikes and lockouts (in which employers prevent unionized workers from working) are the ultimate power strategies if negotiations fail.

Contract Administration

Contract administration is the process used by unions and management to resolve disputes relating to the collective bargaining agreement. Examples of such disputes include whether an employee was unfairly terminated or demoted, whether an employee was asked to work more overtime than allowed, or whether the working conditions were appropriate. Rather than employees facing supervisors on their own, union representatives handle the negotiations with employers over such disputes. This is usually done in a multistep grievance procedure that starts informally with the immediate supervisor and goes up a ladder of formality until the last step, which is almost always binding arbitration conducted by an independent labor arbitrator (such as one provided by the American Arbitration Association).

Informal Joint Consultation

Informal joint consultation is the process whereby union representatives and employers meet informally to discuss mutual concerns and sometimes to engage in collaborative or joint problem solving rather than adversarial bargaining. Although still limited in its use, many observers believe that the cooperative approach is much more effective, even in contract negotiations, than the traditional adversarial approach to bargaining, especially given the pressures of increased governmental regulation, foreign competition, and declining union membership. Often, many of the contractual issues can be resolved before formal contract negotiations through such informal consultation, leaving only a few of the most difficult issues to be dealt with through the adversarial process.

See also: Arbitration; Dispute Systems Design; Labor-Management Relations and Conflict; Workplace Conflict and Grievance Procedures.
References and Further Reading: Colosi, Thomas R., and Arthur E. Berkeley, 1986, *Collective Bargaining: How It Works and Why;* Leap, Terry L., 1995, *Collective Bargaining and Labor Relations;* Weiss, David S., 1996, *Beyond the Walls of Conflict: Mutual Gains Negotiating for Unions and Management.*

Collective Security

Collective security refers to a system of international cooperation among nations in which the governments of all states join together to prevent any one of them from attacking or conquering another. Thus, according to Thomas Weiss (1993, 3), "no government could with impunity undertake forceful policies that would fundamentally disturb" the peace and security of the others. Although the term has been used in many different ways, in general, the concept assumes that there are some internationally established norms of international behavior—most importantly, a norm against armed aggression—that the community of nations (or a subset of this community) is willing to defend. Thus "collective security obliges states to put their troops where their rhetoric is" (Butfoy 1993, 2).

Although there is some confusion in the way the terms are used, most scholars differentiate between *collective security* and *collective defense.* Collective defense usually refers to alliances in which one group of nations pledges to defend its own group against outsiders. Thus, both the North Atlantic Treaty Organization (NATO) and the Warsaw Pact are examples of collective defense, not collective security. According to Butfoy (1993, 2), "The catchphrase in collective security is 'all for one, and one for all,' [while] for alliances it is usually 'us against them.'"

Both the League of Nations and the United Nations (UN) tried to establish regimes of collective security. Although the UN has been more successful than the League of Nations was, it too was quickly shackled in its efforts by the political pressures of the Cold War. Now that the Cold War is over and the concept of collective security was tested successfully in the Persian Gulf War, interest in this form of international cooperation has been renewed.

Proponents of collective security argue that it is an effective deterrent to aggression as well as a more effective response to actual aggression than is possible when states must act on their own. For example, Kuwait acting alone was virtually helpless defending itself against Iraq. The UN coalition, however, forced Iraq to withdraw from Kuwait in only a few days of military action.

Collective security also is said to promote trust and cooperation among nations rather than the distrust and competition promoted by balance-of-power or anarchistic arrangements. Proponents also argue that collective security provides an alternative to what has been called the "security dilemma." This refers to the situation that occurs when states attempt to increase their own security by building up arms and hence threatening other states, which respond by doing the same. This arms race ultimately reduces the security of both states instead of increasing it (Kupchan and Kupchan 1995).

For these reasons as well as others, proponents of collective security argue that its time has come. They would like to see the United Nations take a new, stronger role in enforcing norms of peaceful cooperation among nations and implement enforcement actions, such as the Persian Gulf War, much more frequently in an effort to maintain international peace and security.

Many other diplomats and international relations scholars believe that the concept of collective security is misguided, however. It is seen as conceptually muddled (due to the confusion between this and related terms) and naively unrealistic. It suggests what nations ought to do, but as the UN example illustrates, it is not necessarily what they actually do. States are unlikely to honor their commitments to defend other nations if these commitments are contrary to their own self-interest or are too expensive.

Another concern is that collective security arrangements, if implemented as designed, would be inflexible. They would require intervention when other means of defense might be more effective. They assume that a military response is most appropriate in an age when many more effective solutions to conflict are possible. In addition, some suggest that the requirement that all nations come to the aid of one will turn minor wars into major wars. Others oppose such arrangements because they work to maintain the status quo, assuming that any change is bad. In the current context, some consider the notion to be simply a cover for Western, especially U.S., hegemony.

See also: League of Nations; United Nations.
References and Further Reading: Butfoy, Andrew, 1993, "Collective Security: Theory, Problems and Reformulations"; Downs, George W., 1994a, *Beyond the Debate on Collective Security;* Downs, George W., 1994b, *Collective Security beyond the Cold War;* Gordenker, Leon, and

Thomas G. Weiss, 1993, "The Collective Security Idea and Changing World Politics"; Kupchan, Charles A., and Clifford A. Kupchan, 1995, "The Promise of Collective Security"; Weiss, Thomas G., 1993, *Collective Security in a Changing World: A World Peace Foundation;* Zartman, I. William, and Victor A. Kremenyuk, 1995, *Cooperative Security: Reducing Third World Wars.*

Co-mediation

Co-mediation is done by a team of mediators rather than one mediator. This can be useful in a variety of circumstances, because two people can bring different types of expertise to the table. Further, their different personal characteristics may increase interpersonal understanding and trust. For example, a family mediation program in Boulder, Colorado, uses co-mediation in all its parent-teen mediation sessions. One mediator is an adult, the other a teen. Teen clients relate better to the peer mediator than they would to an adult and therefore tend to open up more and work in a more positive way to achieve results.

The same is true in other types of conflicts as well: divorce mediators sometimes work in teams of one man and one woman, or one lawyer-mediator and one therapist-mediator. This gives them a broader perspective on many issues than either would have alone. Mediators of multiethnic or multiracial conflicts often try to form teams, with one mediator representing the race or ethnicity of each of the parties.

Co-mediation is also used to train new mediators. Typically, most mediators start with a 40-hour training program. They then need considerable experience in real-life settings before they are comfortable with—and good at—mediation. Serving as a co-mediator with a more skilled mediator is a common and effective way to build skills without sacrificing the services provided to the client.

See also: Divorce Mediation; Mediation.
References and Further Reading: Kovach, Kimberlee K., 1994, *Mediation: Principles and Practice;* Singer, Linda R., 1990, *Settling Disputes: Conflict Resolution in Business,*

Families, and the Legal System; Slaikeu, Karl A., 1996, *When Push Comes to Shove: A Practical Guide to Mediating Disputes.*

Commercial Disputes

Commercial disputes are disputes between businesses over nonperformance of contracts, failure to provide specified goods or services, delays, cost overruns, and other business matters. These issues seldom involve important, precedent-setting legal issues, but rather verification of contract terms and compliance and establishment of methods of remedy, if such is necessary.

Many commercial disputes are resolved through arbitration or mediation rather than litigation. There are several advantages to these approaches. First, both mediation and arbitration are private. Therefore, business problems and trade secrets do not need to be made public. Second, both processes tend to be faster and less expensive than litigation. This is important to businesses that need to get matters resolved as quickly as possible. Third, in both processes, disputants can choose their own neutral party. This allows them to choose someone who has expertise in the area of the dispute, freeing the disputants from the task of "educating" the judge or jury, and enhancing the likelihood that a sensible decision, based on the actual facts of the case, will be made. Fourth, mediation especially, but arbitration as well, helps disputants resolve disputes in a businesslike way. This allows them to continue a good business relationship with their opponent in the future.

Many commercial contracts contain clauses that provide for mandatory arbitration or mediation of disputes. Such clauses are especially common in purchase and sales agreements, leases, licensing agreements, partnership agreements, franchises, joint-venture and loan agreements, and shipping contracts. Often, the arbitra-

tion or mediation is done by a neutral intermediary from the American Arbitration Association, although other organizations, such as the CPR Institute for Dispute Resolution and the Better Business Bureau, have mediation and arbitration programs as well (American Arbitration Association 1989, 1991; Coulson 1993).

See also: American Arbitration Association; Arbitration, Commercial; Better Business Bureau; Consumer Disputes; CPR Institute for Dispute Resolution.
References and Further Reading: American Arbitration Association, 1989, *A Guide to Mediation for Business People;* American Arbitration Association, 1991, *A Commercial Arbitration Guide for Business People;* Coulson, Robert, 1993, *ADR in America: Alternatives to Litigation.*

Common Ground

Common ground is anything that the parties to a dispute share. It may be common values or beliefs, common associations, or common interests or needs. Finding common ground is essential if a collaborative, win-win outcome is to be developed.

At times, the areas of common ground are easily ascertained. For instance, if a person wants to buy a car and a car dealership wants to sell one, they have a common interest in finding a price that suits them both. If parents are arguing over the appropriate curriculum to be used in a neighborhood school, they also have a common interest—the best possible education for their children—although there may be considerable disagreement about what that means.

At other times, areas of common ground are elusive. In the abortion debate, most pro-choice advocates perceive no common ground between themselves and pro-life (antiabortion) advocates. Indeed, the values held by both are contradictory, yet many abortion activists (pro and con) can agree on several things: that children should be loved and well cared for, and that the need for abortions should be minimized by preventing unwanted pregnancies (how to do that, however, remains an area of dispute).

Areas of common ground provide the foundation for successful collaboration and the development of mutually acceptable agreements. The more areas of common ground, the easier it is, generally, to develop a solution to a conflict that is acceptable to all. When common ground is perceived to be absent, successful negotiation of a conflict is all but impossible. Even in the most difficult cases, some common ground can usually be found. For example, although the areas of common ground in the abortion controversy are not wide enough to allow a win-win solution to the debate, they do provide some areas in which opposing groups might work together to achieve a common goal.

See also: Collaborative Problem Solving; Interests and Positions; Intractable Conflicts.
References and Further Reading: Common Ground Network for Life and Choice, 1995, *News from the Common Ground Network for Life and Choice* (spring); Gray, Barbara, 1989, *Collaborating: Finding Common Ground for Multiparty Problems;* Pruitt, Dean G., 1991, "Strategic Choice in Negotiation."

Common Law

Common law is a system of jurisprudence that originated in England and was adopted by the United States. Common law itself consists of principles and rules that derive their authority from common usage or custom or from judicial decrees that enforce that usage or custom. Largely determined by judges' interpretation of the law, the principles are determined by judicial precedent combined with the social needs of the community. For this reason, common law changes as community needs change (Schellenberg 1996, 163).

See also: Civil Law and Litigation.
References and Further Reading: Gifis, Steven H., 1991. *Law Dictionary;* Schellenberg, James A., 1996, *Conflict Resolution—Theory, Research, and Practice.*

Commons

The commons refers to resources that are owned by the community as a whole and are not the property of any individual or group. Such common property resources include public lands, air and water, and many publicly owned facilities—highways, parks, and public buildings, for example. A strong temptation exists for individuals to exploit these resources for maximum personal gain while giving little, if any, thought to the long-term sustainability or equity of such exploitation. This pursuit of short-term, individual self-interest threatens to produce what Garrett Hardin called the "tragedy of the commons." In his classic illustration, livestock owners seeking to build their herds (and their personal wealth) grazed ever-larger numbers of animals on the commons—the common grazing area owned by the community as a whole. For a time, this strategy advanced everyone's interests, but it eventually led to tragedy when overgrazing resulted in the complete destruction of the grasslands on which the livestock and the community depended. The herds died, along with the wealth of all members of the community (Hardin 1968).

This parable illustrates a tragedy that constantly threatens modern society. We overuse our resources, pollute our water and air, and overrun our parks. To avoid destroying these common resources, people need to limit their demands on the commons to levels that are sustainable over the long-term. Since people do not generally limit themselves voluntarily, the community that owns the commons must develop a set of generally accepted procedures for sharing scarce community resources. Institutions responsible for managing the commons on behalf of U.S. society, for example, include the Environmental Protection Agency, the National Park Service, the U.S. Forest Service, and the Bureau of Land Management, among others. Conflicts involving the management of these resources are the principal focus of environmental and public policy disputes.

See also: Environmental Conflicts; Public Policy Conflicts.

References and Further Reading: Brann, Peter, and Margaret Foddy, 1987, "Trust and Consumption of a Deteriorating Common Resource"; Hardin, Garrett, 1968, "The Tragedy of the Commons"; Ostrom, Elinor, 1990, *Governing the Commons: The Evolution of Institutions for Collective Action.*

Communal Conflicts

Communal conflicts are conflicts between ethnic, religious, linguistic, or regional groups, either within or across nation-state boundaries. Typically, the conflicts focus on one or all groups' desire for cultural, religious, ethnic, or national self-determination and security. Examples include the Bosnian conflict, the Rwandan conflict, the Northern Ireland conflict, and the Quebec-Canadian conflict.

Although communal conflicts have existed as long as people have, they have become especially prominent since the end of the Cold War. During the Cold War, the superpowers largely divided up the world into two territories ("ours" and "theirs"), and most communal conflicts were suppressed or hidden under the overarching superpower standoff. In the communist countries especially, government control was so strong that ethnic groups dared not fight with one another; they were repressed by the communist state. Once communism fell, long-standing conflicts between groups could again surface, and they became particularly important in many regions where different groups jockeyed to fill the political vacuum left by the communists or to attain their independence.

Communal conflicts seem to be among the most difficult to resolve or even manage. Institutions (particularly the United Nations) have been developed to moderate international conflict, but they have no jurisdiction over conflicts within one nation-state. These conflicts are also difficult to manage because they tend to be deep rooted and involve fundamental human needs for identity and security. Although many international conflicts are resolved by compromise, fundamental needs cannot be compromised. Therefore, coercion or violence is common in these situations.

Conflict resolution specialists do not agree on how best to manage such conflicts. Many believe that the conflicts need to be approached analytically with what is called analytical problem solving. Here, groups of influential people from all sides (often not formal leaders, however), sit down together and analyze the fundamental nature of the conflict. They then work together to develop plans to mitigate or resolve the conflict that address the fundamental identity and/or security problems. Although this approach holds much promise, it is slow and hard to scale up so that the leaders as well as the citizens of the affected groups accept and implement the solutions that have been developed.

Other people advocate peace-building measures that bring individual members of opposing groups together in cooperative projects. This way, they get to know and trust one another, and slowly over time, as enough people become involved in such efforts, normal relationships between the groups are established. Other people advocate the pursuit of more traditional negotiation, mediation, and peacekeeping. No approach seems to work easily or well, however, as most communal conflicts tend to be intractable.

See also: Ethnic and Racial Conflicts; Intractable Conflicts; Peace Building; Problem Solving, Analytical.
References and Further Reading: Gurr, Ted Robert, and Barbara Harff, 1994, *Ethnic Conflict in World Politics;* Kriesberg, Louis, 1993, "Preventive Conflict Resolution of Inter-Communal Conflicts"; Lederach, John Paul, 1994, *Building Peace: Sustainable Reconciliation in Divided Societies;* Rothman, Jay, 1992, *Confrontation to Cooperation: Resolving Ethnic and Regional Conflict.*

Communication

Communication is a central element in all conflicts. Poor communication often creates or exacerbates conflict, and conflict inhibits and distorts communication. Thus, improving communication, both before and during conflicts, is essential to conflict prevention and effective management or resolution.

Communication Problems

In the simplest sense, communication involves a sender, a receiver, a message, a means of communication, and an environment in which the message is being sent. Problems can arise in any of these areas. The person sending the message may not have good communication skills and may not be able to express him- or herself effectively. He or she may be confused about what to say or how to say it and may end up sending an ambiguous or misleading message to the receiver. This can create a conflict if the receiver thinks that a message is hostile or accusatory or threatening when it really isn't (or wasn't intended to be). At other times, people intentionally mislead the listener, believing that a lie (or failure to disclose a fact) will better protect their interests than telling the truth.

At the same time, the receiver may not have (or may not be using) good listening skills. People tend to have stereotypes about other people—preconceptions about what others think and what they are likely to say. For this reason, people tend to hear what they expect to hear, no matter what was actually said. If the message is ambiguous, they are especially likely to interpret it according to their own stereotypes, and if they are engaged in a conflict, these stereotypes will likely be negative. When engaged in a heated exchange, people also tend to plan their responses while their opponents are talking rather than focusing on what is being said. Although they may get the broad outline of the ideas being expressed, they are likely to miss the nuances or hidden messages in any communication that they are not really focused on.

A brochure put out by the Workskills Program lists the "seven fatal filters" that prevent effective listening: (1) perceptions—beliefs about the situation that override what you hear; (2) judgments—opinions about the speaker that color what he or she says; (3) conditioning—the way you learned to listen (most of us never did); (4) assumptions—jumping to conclusions about what is being said; (5) environmental distractions—noisy environment, other people around, other things to attend to; (6) physical—if one person has a hearing problem; and (7) internal filters—a preoccupation with yourself, what you will say next, or what you think about what the other is saying. In order to listen effectively, these filters need to be removed (Workskills Program 1991).

The process of communication is also extremely important. Is it done face-to-face in a calm and cooperative atmosphere? Or is it done in an emotional exchange in which tone of voice and nonverbal cues override the substance of what was said? Equally problematic is communication through third parties—unless those third parties are acting in a mediation role. Communication through the media or through rumors, for example, can lead to serious misunderstanding and unnecessary escalation of tensions.

Communication Skills

One way to remove many of the filters that inhibit good communication is to engage in active listening—a technique in which a person listens attentively to another person's story and then repeats the essentials, emphasizing feelings as well as facts, back to the speaker. This gives the speaker a chance to correct any misunderstandings and a chance to elaborate if ideas were missed. Only after this exchange occurs does the other person explain his or her own point of view.

In heated or emotional conflicts, the parties are often so angry with each other that effective communication is no longer possible. In this case, a mediator can be helpful in several ways. The mediator can act as a messenger, sending messages back and forth between the two parties who cannot meet face-to-face. The mediator can also work individually with the parties to help them understand what the other person thinks and why. In addition, the mediator can help parties frame their messages in the most constructive ways.

For example, one skill frequently taught by mediators is the use of "I-messages" instead of "you-messages." "You-messages" are accusatory—they say "you did this, you did that," and they tend to generate a defensive reaction. "I-messages," however, say "I feel this when . . .," which tends to elicit empathy and understanding rather than defensiveness and opposition. People engaged in conflicts do not need a mediator to learn such skills. However, if they don't have them, mediation is a good way not only to solve the immediate problem but also to gain some lifelong communication and conflict management skills.

See also: Active Listening; I-Messages; Mediation; Misunderstandings.

References and Further Reading: Borisoff, Deborah, and David A. Victor, 1989, *Conflict Management: A Communication Skills Approach;* Folberg, Jay, and Alison Taylor, 1984, *Mediation: A Comprehensive Guide to Resolving Conflicts without Litigation,* 100–29; Hocker, Joyce L., and William W. Wilmot, 1985, *Interpersonal Conflict;* Tillett, Gregory, 1991, *Resolving Conflict: A Practical Approach,* 21–31.

Communication, Cross-Cultural

Communication in conflict is always difficult, but it is especially difficult and problem prone in cross-cultural situations. Anyone who has tried to translate from or to a foreign language knows that translation is a tricky and difficult process. Different cultures often have subtle differences in meaning for apparently identical words. Although words denoting concrete objects (e.g., *foot* or *bus*) are easily translated accurately, more abstract and complex terms, such as *justice, equality,* or *leadership,* are especially prone to misinterpretation, as are critical conflict-related terms such as *compromise, agreement,* or *mediation,* which can mean different things in different languages and cultures.

Not only are people's languages different, but their entire way of perceiving and responding to the world can be different. The way we see and interpret things is not biological but cultural. We have a culturally derived framework of meaning; we relate things we see and hear to our own set of experiences, expectations, and understandings. When those experiences and expectations are different, the meaning we give to a particular event is also different. As a result, it is easy for us to misinterpret things that are said or seen if they are coming from, or are set in, a culture that differs from our own.

Stella Ting-Toomey describes three types of cultural constraints that cause communication problems in cross-cultural situations. First are cognitive constraints—frames of reference or belief systems that discourage people from thinking or addressing a problem in a particular way. Second are behavior constraints—norms that govern appropriate verbal and nonverbal behavior in a particular situation. Third are emotional constraints, which dictate the appropriate emotional response to a given problem. All these can lead to statements or behaviors that seem threatening, hostile, or disinterested when they are nothing of the kind. Alternatively, people can be thought to agree to something when they really do not (Ting-Toomey 1985).

Correcting misunderstanding can also be difficult, even when one is aware that the potential for misunderstanding is high. It is possible to carry out a lengthy conversation, engage in active listening in which one confirms one's interpretation of what the other has said, and still be unaware that critical words are being used in very different ways. Great care and patience are necessary in such situations to make sure that the messages being sent are the same as the messages being received.

Skilled mediators can sometimes help resolve such communication problems by acting as interpreters, buffers, or coordinators. As interpreters, they can translate the subtleties of meaning to people who might not otherwise understand the cultural biases of the opposing side. As buffers, mediators can prevent inappropriate outbursts and can shield parties from situations that threaten their identity, self-image, or "face." As coordinators, mediators adjust the timing and tempo of the negotiations to synchronize opposing negotiation styles. They can identify when the time is ripe for negotiation or concession and when it is not (Cohen, 1996).

Cross-cultural mediators should be aware of their own impact on the communication process. If a mediator is of the same culture as one of the parties but not the other, there is a tendency for the party of a different culture to view the mediator with suspicion and for the mediator to misinterpret that party more often than the other. If the mediator is of a different culture from both parties, three translations are involved in every communication, not two. This makes the potential for misunderstanding even higher, and the skills of the mediator need to be correspondingly higher as well.

See also: Active Listening; Communication; Ethnic and Racial Conflicts; International Conflict.

References and Further Reading: Avruch, K., P. Black, and J. Scimecca, 1991, *Conflict Resolution: Cross-Cultural Perspectives;* Cohen, Raymond, 1996, "Cultural Aspects of International Mediation"; Duryea, Michelle Lebaron, 1992, *Conflict and Culture: A Literature Review and Bibliography;* Samovar, L. A., and R. E. Porter, 1985, *Intercultural Communication: A Reader;* Ting-Toomey, Stella, 1985, "Toward a Theory of Conflict and Culture."

Community Board of San Francisco

The Community Board Program is a nonprofit organization founded in 1976. It was one of the first community mediation pro-

grams and still serves in that capacity, providing community mediation services in the San Francisco area. The Community Board also offers conflict resolution–related program development and training assistance to schools, juvenile correctional facilities, and other agencies nationwide. The goal of these processes is not only to resolve the immediate conflict but also to teach the people involved how to deal more effectively with other conflicts in the future. One of the main assumptions of the Community Board that makes it unique is its focus on community building and empowerment as well as conflict resolution. Thus, the purposes of the organization are to "promote the theory and practice of conciliation and mediation as effective forms of dispute resolution, and to develop the capacity of neighborhoods, institutions and other types of 'communities' to express and resolve their own conflicts" (Community Board flier).

The Community Board is especially interested in teaching conflict resolution skills to youth and families. It has developed a peer mediation program for children in elementary through high school that is used across the country. Classroom conflict resolution curricula have also been developed, field-tested, and published for a national school audience. The Community Board Program has developed a peer mediation model for juvenile correctional facilities as well.

See also: Community Justice Centers; Mediation, Community; School Conflict Resolution Programs; Appendix 1 for contact information.

Community Justice Centers

Community justice centers (also called neighborhood justice centers) provide mediation services for people in the neighborhood. Many are directly or indirectly associated with the court system and receive referrals of minor criminal cases. (Typical cases include assault, minor theft, and harassment—mostly between people who know each other.) Other centers are community based; they are run by a city or a freestanding nonprofit organization. Although these centers take minor criminal cases, many of their cases are civil: disputes between landlords and tenants, between businesses and customers, between employers and employees. Many are so minor that they would never get into the formal justice system. Typical problems handled include disputes between neighbors over loud stereos and barking dogs, between teens and parents over curfews or other rules, and between roommates over lifestyle differences or expense and chore sharing.

Initially developed in a few urban locations in the 1970s with federal money, neighborhood justice centers continue to expand all over the country, providing mediation in more than 100,000 cases a year (Drake and Lewis 1988). Although the federal government no longer funds these centers (because they are no longer seen as innovative), most are still able to squeak by, getting funding from local and state governments, private donations, and, in some cases, fees from clients, although most centers strive to provide their services for free. Most maintain a small paid staff and use a large number of volunteer mediators who get 20 to 40 hours of training and then apprentice with experienced mediators to better learn the skill.

Although funding continues to be a problem for many centers, they continue to exist because they provide a useful service not offered anywhere else. For poor people, who make up a large portion of community justice centers' caseloads, the centers' free mediation service is often the only conflict resolution forum available. This has caused some observers to accuse such centers of providing "second-class justice" for the poor, with "first-class justice"—that provided by the regular justice system—reserved for the rich.

However, many people believe that the type of dispute resolution offered by these centers—mediation—is superior to court adjudication for both the rich and the poor because it is less adversarial and allows people to work out solutions to their problems themselves. The result tends to be that the solutions make more sense to the parties, are better complied with, and empower the parties to resolve future disputes in a more constructive way. In addition, parties who engage in mediation usually maintain or improve their relationship, whereas those in litigation often worsen it (Davis 1982; McGillis 1986; Singer 1990).

For example, according to Daniel McGillis, community justice centers are seen by many to be superior to the courts for processing minor criminal cases, because "complainants very often withdrew their complaints as [the] trial neared because their opponent was a neighbor, relative, or acquaintance. The complainants were not seeking incarceration for the adversary or a fine (paid to the state); they wanted changed behavior, an apology, or money paid to them as restitution for the harm done" (McGillis 1986, 5). Mediation in community justice centers routinely provides such outcomes; courts generally do not. As a result, according to McGillis and many other observers, mediation clients tend to be quite satisfied with both the process and the result—which is not at all true for the traditional adversarial justice system.

Despite the avowed benefits and client satisfaction, however, most community justice centers still have difficulty recruiting clients. Those tied to the courts and receiving large numbers of court referrals do better, but those that rely on word of mouth have trouble. Many people have tried to determine why this is so, but no one knows for sure. The leading hypothesis is that the courts and court-based processes are simply better known and better trusted. In addition, according to Susan Silbey and Sally

Merry (and others), citizens do not voluntarily use alternatives as much as mediators would like because disputants want vindication and "truth." They want an advocate to help them argue their side of the case and a third party to declare the other side wrong. "They go to court for an advocate and to get justice; they do not respond eagerly to the opportunity to take the problem back into their own hands" (Silbey and Merry 1984, 153). Considerable research shows, however, that those who are willing to take the problem back end up with better solutions and are more satisfied than those who do not.

See also: Adjudication; Community Board of San Francisco; Mediation, Community.
References and Further Reading: Davis, Robert, 1982, "Mediation: The Brooklyn Experiment"; Drake, William, and Michael Lewis, 1988, "Community Justice Centers—A Lasting Innovation"; McGillis, Daniel, 1986, *Community Dispute Resolution—Programs and Public Policy;* Silbey, Susan S., and Sally Engle Merry, 1984, "What Do Plaintiffs Want? Re-examining the Concept of Dispute"; Singer, Linda R., 1990, *Settling Disputes: Conflict Resolution in Business, Families, and the Legal System.*

Community Organizing

Community organizing is a process in which a professional "change agent" or "community organizer" helps a group of individuals or entire groups, organizations, or a community as a whole engage in collective action to address social problems. It involves identifying problems, diagnosing causes, formulating solutions and interim goals, planning and organizing people and processes to address the problems, and developing strategies and tactics designed to accomplish change (Kramer and Specht 1969, 8). These strategies can involve writing letters and telephoning government officials, circulating petitions, forming work groups, doing research, making public presentations about the problem, working on committees to formulate solutions, recruiting new organization members, fund-raising, and direct action. The goal is to form a larger organization that can wield increas-

ing amounts of power within the community to accomplish the changes that will address the social problems of concern.

According to Saul Alinsky—one of the best-known community organizers and author of *Rules for Radicals,* the "Bible" of 1960s and 1970s grassroots community organizing—community organizing "is for those who want to change the world from what it is to what they believe it should be. *The Prince* was written by Machiavelli for the Haves on how to hold power. *Rules for Radicals* is written for the Have-Nots on how to take it away" (Alinsky 1971, 3).

Ralph Kramer and Harry Specht distinguish two forms of community organizing—community development and social planning. Community development involves efforts to mobilize people who are affected by a social problem to solve that problem themselves. The focus here is on building new organizations and new coalitions among people who have not worked together previously and to empower those people with new skills and new ways of approaching problems that they haven't recognized or used before.

Social planning, in contrast, involves integrating different existing organizations into a coalition that then works together to more effectively address a social problem. The major characteristic of this approach is that it is undertaken by people who are already linked with community agencies and organizations—thus, they are bound by the goals and policies of those agencies as well as by their own, and they have professional knowledge and skills that the people in the first case do not have but can learn (Kramer and Specht 1969, 10–11).

Depending on the problem to be addressed, the people involved, and the relationship to other issues, the strategies and tactics of community organizing can be very different. When the needed changes are not controversial and when the actors and those being acted upon are largely in agreement, collaborative or consensus-based strategies can be used quite effectively. When the values and interests of the parties are considerably different, consensus building is often supplemented by or replaced with campaigns of persuasion and recruitment linked with mild coercion. When there is a wide gap between the values, interests, and goals of the parties, and when it is clearly a win-lose situation, outright confrontation is usually the strategy of choice (Kramer and Specht 1969, 202). Such confrontations often involve nonviolent action of some sort (marches, protests, strikes, or boycotts, for example). No matter what set of tactics is chosen, the goals are usually to recruit more members for the coalition, to gain power, and to implement the social or political changes desired. The strategy may involve conflict resolution, or it may actually involve conflict creation and escalation, which is intended to ultimately result in a victory for the community activists over those advocating the status quo.

See also: Advocacy; Alinsky, Saul; Coalition Building; Communal Conflicts; Escalation.
References and Further Reading: Alinsky, Saul, 1971, *Rules for Radicals: A Practical Primer for Realistic Radicals;* Cunningham, Helen V., Mark A. Chesler, and Barbara Israel, 1990, "Strategies for Social Justice: A Retrieval Conference: Report on Grassroots Community Organizing and Conflict Intervention"; Kahn, Si, 1982, *Organizing: A Guide for Grassroots Leaders;* Kramer, Ralph M., and Harry Specht, 1969, *Readings in Community Organization Practice.*

Community Policing

Community policing is a new approach that tries to establish a positive, cooperative relationship among the police department, police officers, and citizens of the community. The key to this approach is collaboration between the police and citizens. Police and citizens work together to determine what citizens want and expect from the police department and to assess how the department might best meet those goals. The police then work jointly with the community to accomplish the goals.

According to the Sanford, Maine, Police Department (1996), one of thousands of departments nationwide that practice community policing, community policing is a "customer-oriented approach to building partnerships to make communities safe and liveable. It's problem solving at the level closest to the problem. It's channeling all the police resources to the neighborhood level to help solve problems and build self-reliant neighborhoods."

Community policing is especially useful and important in the effort to curb youth violence. Without such an approach, the relationship between police and troubled teens tends to be negative. Common problems include racial and cultural differences, value differences, lack of trust, little or no contact between police officers and youths except in negative (enforcement) situations, and high levels of anger. Youth-focused community policing increases positive contact between the police and youth and gives youth an opportunity to work with the police and community leaders in an effort to set local priorities and improve their own quality of life. This empowers the youth, increases their self-esteem, and improves their sense of personal efficacy. These personal changes are often sufficient to allow (and encourage) teens to renounce gang activities and become more involved in socially positive endeavors.

See also: Collaborative Problem Solving; Mediation, Community; Police-Citizen Conflicts.
References and Further Reading: Johnson, Tim, 1996, "Community Policing: America's Best Chance to End Youth Violence"; Sanford, Maine, Police Department, 1996, "Community Policing," World Wide Web Home Page, http://www.biddeford.com/~pdcommun.html.

Community Relations Service

The Community Relations Service (CRS), part of the U.S. Department of Justice, was created in 1964 as part of the Civil Rights Act. Its goals are to help communities reduce racial and ethnic tensions, prevent the development of ethnic and racial conflicts, and help resolve such conflicts peacefully if they do start. This is done through conciliation, mediation, technical assistance, and training. In addition to providing these services to local governments, the CRS provides such assistance to law enforcement agencies, schools, nonprofit agencies and community groups, prison administrators, local businesses facing ethnic and racial problems, and judges (who may refer suits concerning racial or ethnic discrimination to the CRS as an alternative to litigation).

Although many of the conflicts that the CRS becomes involved in are relatively low-profile, some are extremely visible and volatile. For example, the CRS went to Los Angeles to try to stop the violence that followed the first Rodney King trial; it went back before the second (federal) verdict was released to try to prevent a recurrence. The CRS is active in all the major U.S. cities, helping schools avoid harmful racial incidents, helping police maintain positive relationships with the diverse populations they serve, and helping communities work together to solve joint problems without breaking down along racial or ethnic lines.

Although the CRS can intervene in a conflict on its own initiative, it prefers to be invited in by one of the disputing parties or an interested third party. Either way, before they formally intervene, CRS personnel talk to as many people as possible to assess all sides' points of view. Once they understand who the players are and what the issues and problems are, they develop an intervention plan to help the parties resolve the conflict peacefully.

Often this is done through conciliation, an informal process in which the CRS works with the parties individually to open channels of communication, help people understand the grievances and fears of the other side, and do whatever else it can to ease tension, increase mutual trust, and develop solutions to problems that are considered fair by all. If this doesn't work, the next step is mediation, which is a more for-

mal process carried out by representatives of each party who sit down with a CRS mediator to review the issues and then craft and implement a solution that is considered fair to all. All these services are provided free and are available on short notice if an emergency arises.

The Community Relations Service has ten regional offices scattered around the country. Its headquarters is in Washington, D.C.

See also: Conciliation; Ethnic and Racial Conflicts; Mediation; Appendix 1 for contact information.

References and Further Reading: Department of Justice, Community Relations Service, 1989, *The Community Relations Service: Assistance in the Resolution of Community Disputes Based on Race, Ethnic or National Origin;* Department of Justice, Community Relations Service, 1991, *Avoid Racial Conflict: A Guide for Municipalities.*

Compromise

Many conflicts are resolved by compromise—both parties give up something that they want in order to get something else that they want. This is necessary if the conflict is structured in a win-lose way—if there is a fixed amount of an item (money, land, or time, for instance) to be divided up, and whatever one party gets, the other loses. (An example of this would be negotiations over the price of a house. The seller may ask for $200,000; the buyer may offer $180,000; they can compromise on $190,000. Neither got exactly the price they wanted, but they did exchange the house.)

Alternatively, parties in conflict may have several interests or concerns. They may then negotiate a compromise whereby they attain some of their interests but not others. Thus, a union may negotiate a new contract that includes provisions for a higher wage, more vacation, and better health insurance coverage. In exchange, it may agree to longer hours per week and less flexibility regarding benefits packages. Most negotiation and mediation processes are based on compromises. It is expected that each party will give up some of what it wants to achieve an agreement that is acceptable to all.

Some conflict resolution scholars are critical of this approach, arguing that people should not have to make concessions if they are honest about their real wants and needs. Rather, they should use integrative bargaining (a win-win approach) or analytic problem solving to design a solution that comes close to giving the parties all of what they need.

See also: Bargaining, Integrative and Distributive; Mediation; Negotiation; Problem Solving, Analytical; Win-Win, Win-Lose, and All-Lose Outcomes.

References and Further Reading: Burton, John, 1987, *Resolving Deep-Rooted Conflict: A Handbook;* Susskind, Lawrence, and Jeffrey Cruikshank, 1987, *Breaking the Impasse.*

Conciliation

The term *conciliation* is used in several ways. Some people use it as a synonym for mediation—meaning a process in which a neutral facilitator meets with the parties to help them clarify the issues, seek common ground, and negotiate a settlement of their dispute. Others see conciliation as a different, less formal process in which a third party works with the disputants to correct misunderstandings, reduce fear and mistrust, and improve communication between the disputing groups. Used in this way, conciliation stops short of mediation, in that it does not involve formal negotiation between the parties.

For example, the Better Business Bureau (BBB) offers three different dispute resolution options: conciliation, mediation, and arbitration. It uses the term *mediation* in the traditional sense, but it uses *conciliation* to refer to a less intrusive process. In BBB conciliation, the neutral party simply talks to each side to understand his or her view of the problem (which generally involves a consumer dispute with a business) and then communicates the consumer's view of the problem to the business and the business's view of the situation to the consumer. The neutral party also passes along offers made by either side to resolve the problem. This process usually occurs by telephone or mail, rather than in a face-to-face meeting, as is done in mediation. Although it is simple, such a process, according to the BBB, "frequently settles the matter simply and quickly."

The Community Relations Service (CRS), an arm of the U.S. Department of Justice formed to help communities avoid or limit racial and ethnic conflicts, makes a similar distinction between conciliation and mediation. Conciliation is the less formal process, in which the CRS talks to people on all sides of a conflict to gather and exchange information, corrects rumors, improves communication, works with each side to increase trust, and explores opportunities for resolution. If this does not solve the conflict, the CRS offers a more formal mediation process in which representatives of all sides sit down together to develop a solution with the help of a CRS mediator.

Still other people see conciliation as a part of mediation. According to mediation expert Christopher Moore (1986, 124), "*Conciliation* is the psychological component of mediation in which the third party attempts to create an atmosphere of trust and cooperation that is conducive to negotiation. . . . Conciliation is an ongoing process that occurs throughout negotiation." This is done by correcting misperceptions, reducing fear, improving communication, and increasing trust so that the parties can then negotiate effectively during the later stages of the mediation process.

See also: Better Business Bureau; Community Relations Service; Facilitation; Mediation.

References and Further Reading: Council of Better Business Bureaus, World Wide Web Home Page, http://cbbb.org/bbb/bbb.html; Department of Justice, Community Relations Service, 1989, *The Community Relations Service: Assistance in the Resolution of Community Disputes Based on Race, Ethnic or National Origin;* Moore, Christopher W., 1986, *The Mediation Process.*

Confidentiality

Most mediator codes of conduct specify that all aspects of the mediation process are confidential. This means that neither the parties nor the mediator may reveal information that is disclosed in the mediation session to outside parties (including courts). Often mediators ask clients to sign a waiver or consent form before beginning mediation in which they agree that they will not reveal the proceedings to outsiders and will not subpoena the mediator or his or her records in any adversarial process that might arise during or after the mediation sessions.

In addition, mediators are bound to maintain the confidentiality of information obtained in caucuses, unless the person giving the information agrees to its disclosure. This can cause procedural or ethical problems for the mediator. For example, a disputant may reveal that he or she lied in a joint session. Should the mediator reveal this problem, or cut off the mediation because it occurred? Most ethical codes are ambiguous on such points. Even without such dilemmas, mediators may find it hard to maintain the image of impartiality when they are known to be privy to private information. Even if that information is not actually used to manipulate the process, the suspicion that this might occur can diminish trust and inhibit progress. This is one reason that some mediators try to avoid caucusing as much as possible, believing that all aspects of the process should be visible to all participants.

See also: Mediation, Ethical Issues; Mediator Impartiality and Neutrality.
References and Further Reading: Gibson, Kevin, 1992, "Confidentiality in Mediation: A Moral Reassessment"; Kovach, Kimberlee K., 1994, *Mediation: Principles and Practice;* Moore, Christopher W., 1986, *The Mediation Process.*

Conflict and Dispute

In common usage, the terms *conflict* and *dispute* are often considered synonymous.

Many conflict resolution experts, however, find it useful to use the terms in more precise ways. In this sense, *conflict* refers to a long-term, underlying disagreement that divides two or more parties; *dispute* refers to individual episodes within this long-running conflict. For example, consider the never-ending conflict between the poorer inner cities and the richer suburbs. This conflict may be manifested as a dispute over the propriety of a citywide tax to support inner-city scientific and cultural facilities such as museums, zoos, and performing arts centers. Or the dispute may focus on efforts to lobby state legislators to spend more money on inner-city social programs and less on suburban freeways. Still another dispute might revolve around whether a new baseball franchise should be named for the inner city or the larger region (e.g., should it be the Denver Rockies or the Colorado Rockies?). Each of these individual disputes is resolved, but the underlying conflict continues.

Other examples of long-term underlying conflicts include those between abortion supporters and opponents; between advocates and opponents of homosexual lifestyles; between different racial, ethnic, and religious groups; and between those who believe that the natural habitats should be preserved for their own sake and those who believe that natural resources should be used to advance human interests.

It is generally unreasonable to expect to resolve deep-rooted, underlying conflicts over the short term. True conflict resolution requires changing people's underlying values, which takes a long time. For example, Martin Luther King and the civil rights movement were able to persuade most Americans to abandon the policy of segregation. Most people now truly believe that discrimination against minorities is wrong. Nevertheless, racial conflict still exists in this country as we debate how to remedy past wrongs and how to move forward.

Individual dispute episodes within an overall conflict are routinely resolved in ways that set policies at least temporarily (until the next dispute episode reopens the issue and raises the possibility of policy change). In some cases, dispute episodes are resolved through negotiation and compromise. In other cases, they are resolved through some type of "power contest" such as litigation, election, political lobbying, strike, or military action. A principal goal of the alternative dispute resolution movement has been to increase the proportion of disputes that are resolved through some form of negotiation and decrease the percentage that rely on power contests. In many cases, alternative dispute resolution processes are more likely to be successful after the balance of power is clarified and everyone has a clear image of their alternatives to a negotiated agreement.

See also: Conflict Resolution, Conflict Management, and Dispute Settlement.

References and Further Reading: Burton, John, 1990b, *Conflict: Resolution and Provention;* Burton, John, and Frank Dukes, 1990a, *Conflict: Practices in Management, Settlement and Resolution.*

Conflict Assessment

To resolve or manage a conflict successfully, one needs to understand what that conflict is about and who is involved. This is done by conducting a conflict assessment (also referred to as conflict analysis or conflict mapping). Typical questions that should be answered in such an assessment include the following:

1. Who are the parties? Who is directly involved, and who is not involved but potentially affected?
2. What are their positions, that is, what do they say they want?
3. What are their underlying interests? In other words, what do they really want (which may or may not be the same as what they are asking for directly)? Are the issues primarily over substance, process, or both?
4. What is the conflict history and setting? How did it start? What are the major events or outside factors that have an influence on the conflict or its outcome? Is it part of a long-running conflict, or is this a new issue that has not arisen before?
5. What are the dynamics of the conflict? Is it rapidly escalating, involving more and more people or issues, or more extreme tactics? Is it simmering under the surface without really coming to a head? Is it fueled by misunderstanding, rumor, or fears?
6. How are the parties approaching the conflict? Are they trying to use persuasion or negotiation to influence the other side? Are they relying on power strategies to force a solution in their own favor? If so, what power strategies are different sides using? What do they expect (or hope) to win?
7. What are each side's sources of power? What is the power balance (i.e., who is more powerful than the other)?
8. What is the potential for settlement or resolution of this conflict? Are there possible win-win outcomes, or are the differences deep rooted and nonnegotiable? Are the parties willing to talk or consider a compromise? Is there a neutral third party who might be able to act as an arbitrator or mediator? Would such a process be accepted by the parties in dispute?

Mediators and other third-party neutrals typically make such an assessment before they begin any intervention process. Parties to a conflict can also benefit immensely by conducting such an analysis on their own. This helps them to see more clearly what is going on and why, and it helps them make more informed decisions about which strategies are likely to serve them well and which are likely to fail or even harm them over the long run.

See also: Interests and Positions; Parties; Power.
References and Further Reading: Deutsch, Morton, 1973, *The Resolution of Conflict: Constructive and Destructive Processes;* Hocker, Joyce L., and William W. Wilmot, 1985, *Interpersonal Conflict;* Tillett, Gregory, 1991, *Resolving Conflict: A Practical Approach.*

Conflict Prevention

Conflict prevention involves activities designed to keep conflict from developing between individuals or groups as well as activities that seek to prevent a dispute from becoming violent. Such activities can be proactive, meaning that they seek to predict conflict long before it occurs and eliminate the causes of such conflict before it develops. Leading conflict resolver John Burton advocates what he calls "conflict provention," which goes beyond isolating and removing sources of conflict to actively promoting conditions that foster cooperation (Burton 1989). Alternatively, conflict prevention can simply involve a heightened awareness of brewing conflict and efforts to contain or resolve such conflicts quickly before they escalate to violence.

The latter approach is easier and hence more common. In the international arena, many governments as well as the United Nations, have instituted a variety of early warning systems—basically, data collection efforts—that are intended to assess the stability of different ethnic groups and political regimes around the world. The purpose is to develop a sense of where violence is likely to develop so that measures can be instituted to prevent or limit this eruption, when possible.

Depending on the phase of the potential or actual conflict, a large variety of preventive measures are possible. For example, when conditions appear ripe for conflict but none has yet broken out, dialogues between individuals or groups can improve interpersonal and intergroup understanding. Communication and conflict resolution training and the development of dispute settlement procedures and institutions are also important. At the intergroup level, efforts to reduce inequality between groups and to increase the interdependence of groups are useful as well.

Once a threat has been made or low-level violence has erupted, other measures are called for. These include deterrence (demonstrating that the threat will be answered with a counterthreat), reassurance (that the threatening party has nothing to fear from the other and hence should not attack), crisis management, and external mediation or other conflict intervention.

See also: Crisis Management; Deterrence; Diplomacy, Preventive; Peace Building; Peacekeeping.
References and Further Reading: Burton, John W., 1989, "On the Need for Conflict Prevention"; Kriesberg, Louis, 1993, "Preventive Conflict Resolution of Inter-Communal Conflicts"; Siccama, Jan G., 1996, "Conflict Prevention and Early Warning in the Political Practice of International Organizations."

Conflict Resolution, Conflict Management, and Dispute Settlement

The term *conflict resolution* is used broadly to refer to any process that is used to end a conflict or dispute in a peaceful way. (War is seldom considered to be a means of conflict resolution, although it does indeed resolve conflicts once it is over.) Used in this way, *conflict resolution* refers to all judicial processes and alternative dispute resolution techniques—negotiation, mediation, arbitration—as well as consensus building, diplomacy, analytical problem solving, and peacemaking. In short, it involves all nonviolent means of solving interpersonal, intergroup, interorganizational, or international problems. But just as many conflict resolution theorists make a distinction between the terms *conflict* and *dispute,* many also make a distinction among *conflict resolution, conflict management,* and *dispute settlement.*

Conflict resolution refers to a relatively stable resolution of a deep-rooted conflict that is obtained by identifying the underlying sources of that conflict (usually fundamental human needs or value differences) and then instituting socioeconomic and/or political changes that allow the values or needs of all sides to be met simultaneously. An example is the resolution of the long-standing Israeli-Egyptian conflict with the Camp David Accords. There, both sides' fundamental need for security (and Israel's need for identity) was met by the acceptance of the other's right to exist and the return of Egyptian land in exchange for a promise of future peaceful relations between the countries (which has now held for almost 20 years).

Dispute settlement refers to the elimination of differences of interests either by negotiation or compromise (hence through negotiation or mediation) or by an authoritative decision made by an outside party (an arbitrator, judge, or jury) that determines who is right. Wage and benefit packages can be negotiated between labor and management; juries can determine that a doctor did or did not engage in malpractice—these are dispute settlements. Dispute settlement provides a solution to a particular immediate problem, generally involving differences in interests or a dispute over rights involving two or more parties. According to conflict theorist John Burton, "'disputes' involve negotiable interests, while 'conflicts' are concerned with issues that are not negotiable, issues that relate to ontological human needs that cannot be compromised. Accordingly, 'settlement' refers to negotiated or arbitrated outcomes of disputes, while 'resolution' refers to outcomes of a conflict" (Burton 1993, 55).

Conflict management refers to the management of conflict processes. It may not result in ultimate resolution because resolution of deep-rooted conflicts is often hard to attain. However, conflicts can be managed to make them less destructive and more productive. Goals can

be clarified, communication can be improved, facts can be sought and verified, procedures can be improved to be more equitable and accessible. In situations in which people share fundamental values, conflict management is often all that is needed to settle a dispute or even resolve a conflict. However, when deep-rooted values or needs are in opposition, conflict management falls short of obtaining ultimate resolution.

See also: Alternative Dispute Resolution; Camp David Accords (Israeli and Egyptian); Conflict and Dispute.
References and Further Reading: Burton, John, 1987, *Resolving Deep-Rooted Conflict: A Handbook;* Burton, John, 1993, "Conflict Resolution as a Political Philosophy"; Diamond, Louise, 1994, "On Developing a Common Vocabulary."

Conflict Resolution Center International, Inc.

The Conflict Resolution Center International (CRCI) is a resource center that assists people who are working to resolve conflicts in their own communities. It is especially concerned with community and neighborhood disputes and racial, ethnic, and religious conflicts. It publishes a journal, *Conflict Resolution Notes,* that is available both in hard copy and over the Internet (through ConflictNet). CRCI also has developed a large listing of conflict resolution resource people, both service providers (e.g., mediators and facilitators) and trainers. If contacted by mail, phone, or E-mail, for a small fee, CRCI will identify all the service providers (and/or trainers) who match particular needs and are in the appropriate geographic area. It also maintains an extensive library of conflict resolution materials that are indexed and annotated.

See also: Appendix 1 for contact information.

Conflict Styles

Conflict styles are how a person responds to conflict. Typical styles are competitive, collaborative, compromising, and accommodating. Often a person uses one style in certain situations routinely but relies on a different approach under other circumstances or with different people. For instance, a person might be highly competitive at work or in school, trying to win as much and as often as possible, with little regard for the impact on his or her opponent. The same person may be much more collaborative or accommodating in family situations, when love or respect between family members calls for a different conflict approach.

Each of these conflict styles has advantages and disadvantages. Competition, for example, helps push people to work hard and to be creative and productive. However, competition can harm the relationship between parties because it focuses on maximum gain for one person, usually at the expense (loss) of the other.

Collaboration is the best approach to use when one wants to find a solution to a problem that meets the interests or needs of both parties. It is much better than competition at protecting or even building relationships; it also is likely to result in decisions that are followed, because all the parties will benefit from the decision and will support it as their own. However, collaboration can take considerable time and energy and often fails to yield a settlement at all if the problem is not amenable to win-win problem solving.

Compromise is sometimes quicker than collaboration, and it gets each side at least some of what it wants. It is easy and has a certain obvious logic to it—a simple "we'll just cut the apple in half" psychology that is defensible and often acceptable to all. However, compromising usually results in half solutions for everybody: no one gets what they really want or need; rather, they get only half. Thus, it can be viewed as a lose-lose approach rather than a win-win approach, especially if the issue is important.

Accommodating is giving in to the other side. At times, when the issue is unimportant or one realizes that the other side is right, this is the best approach. It maintains or even improves the relationship with the other side and doesn't utilize resources in a losing fight. However, if a person habitually accommodates others, that person will never get his or her own needs met and is likely to be taken advantage of or overpowered in almost all situations. By becoming aware of one's habitual style and assessing the costs and benefits of that approach, one can become more flexible and better match one's response to the particular situation.

See also: Collaborative Problem Solving; Compromise; Win-Win, Win-Lose, and All-Lose Outcomes.
References and Further Reading: Hocker, Joyce L., and William W. Wilmot, 1985, *Interpersonal Conflict*, 37–66; Kilmann, Ralph H., and Kenneth W. Thomas, 1976, "Interpersonal Conflict-Handling Behavior as Reflections of Jungian Personality Dimensions."

ConflictNet, PeaceNet, and the Internet

Conflict resolution information is becoming abundant on the Internet. Particularly useful information sources are ConflictNet and PeaceNet. ConflictNet offers current information on critical issues in the conflict resolution field, current legislation, conflict resolution conferences, training opportunities, service providers, and membership and professional organizations of interest to conflict resolution professionals. The ConflictNet web site on the Internet also has many links to other conflict resolution organizations and has numerous on-line discussion groups.

PeaceNet connects a network of people interested in peace, social and economic justice, human rights, and the struggle against racism. It provides a clearinghouse for information on these topics and includes access to on-line publications, discussion groups, academic programs, and conferences.

Many other organizations also provide conflict resolution information and even mediation services on-line. Useful web sites are being added constantly, so users should use one of the excellent web-search services to find out what is currently available. On-line discussions on conflict resolution topics are available through a number of conflict listserves, Internet newsgroups, and ConflictNet and PeaceNet conferences. Also available on many sites are announcements and descriptions of professional training opportunities and college and university degree programs in conflict-related fields, including on-line distance-learning courses. Other accessible information sources include bibliographic search systems; free on-line publications; links to libraries, on-line bookstores, and journal article distribution services through which conflict materials can be obtained; conflict resolution service providers; and conflict- and peace-related research institutes.

See also: Diplomacy, Virtual; Appendix 1 for contact information.

Consensus

Consensus is a quarterly newsletter published by the MIT-Harvard Public Disputes Program, part of Harvard Law School's Program on Negotiation. The newsletter describes successful cases of negotiation and consensus building in environmental, social, and other public policy disputes in the United States and Canada. The newsletter is sent to over 35,000 federal, state, and municipal officials in those two countries in an effort to "promote a better understanding of dispute resolution techniques, to encourage the use of these techniques in the public sector, and to serve the public good." The newsletter is also available on-line through ConflictNet.

In addition to its lead articles, which are usually case histories of successes, each issue of *Consensus* includes a section entitled "Practitioner's Notebook," which dis-

cusses issues of interest to conflict resolution practitioners and is published in conjunction with the Public Policy Sector of the Society for Professionals in Dispute Resolution. Each *Consensus* also contains an extensive listing of public policy conflict resolution providers in the United States and Canada.

See also: Program on Negotiation at Harvard Law School; Society of Professionals in Dispute Resolution; Appendix 1 for contact information.

Consensus Building
See **Collaborative Problem Solving.**

Consortium on Peace Research, Education, and Development

The Consortium on Peace Research, Education, and Development (COPRED) is a nonprofit organization, founded in 1970, to bring together conflict resolution and peace researchers, educators, and activists. Its members include 600 individuals (students, educators, mediators, peace activists, and religious leaders, among others) and 150 organizations (university peace studies programs, professional associations, institutes, foundations, and peace activist organizations). COPRED holds an annual conference and several regional meetings and undertakes a variety of projects. It also publishes a bimonthly newsletter called *Peace Chronicle* and a scholarly journal called *Peace and Change: A Journal of Peace Research.*

See also: Appendix 1 for contact information.

Consumer Disputes

Consumer disputes are disputes between businesses and their customers over poor products or services, failure to uphold contracts, or the business's failure to meet the customer's expectations. Typical problems involve automobile repairs or purchases, landlord-tenant disputes, and problems with mail-order products.

These disputes tend to have three characteristics that influence the way they are resolved. First, there is a large power disparity between the individual consumer and the business. Often the business is a huge corporation with an entire legal department that specializes in dealing with customer disputes (among other things). The consumer does not have a lawyer on retainer and is inexperienced in handling disputes of this kind. Second, the stakes for the company are usually small (at least in dollar amounts), whereas they can be quite large for the consumer. Third, the consumer may be relatively ignorant about the technical aspects of the product or the service in dispute (Goldberg, Green, and Sander 1985). These three factors make it relatively easy for the business to overpower the consumer and prevail in any dispute between the two. However, consumers are getting somewhat wiser and more forceful, due in part to public education programs and consumer advocates. Given the importance of maintaining a good public image, many companies are cooperating with a variety of consumer dispute resolution programs or are establishing their own.

Public Consumer
Dispute Resolution Programs

Originally, most consumer disputes that were not easily resolved were taken to small-claims court (some still are). However, businesses tend to have an advantage in that forum, because they are more familiar with the procedures and have easy access to technical advice. It is ironic, but true, that the worst offenders often do best in small-claims court, because they are the most experienced at "playing the game."

Other public dispute resolution procedures are not so slanted. For example, many states have consumer protection departments within the attorney general's office. These departments often mediate complaints over the phone or in person and act as an advocate for the consumer if the business is clearly at fault. Media consumer action lines also act as mediators and consumer advocates. When they see a company acting in a negligent way, they can use the threat of negative publicity to force the business to do what is necessary to remedy the problem. Neighborhood justice centers also handle consumer disputes through mediation. Although power disparities still exist in these forums, research shows that they are not as significant in influencing the outcome as they are in typical adjudicatory processes.

Private Consumer Dispute
Resolution Mechanisms

In addition to the public processes, many companies have set up their own internal or private processes to handle consumer disputes. The Magnuson-Moss Warranty Act of 1975 says that industries can create their own arbitration procedures. If these procedures meet certain standards of fairness as set out by the Federal Trade Commission, the consumer must try arbitration before going to court. The arbitration decision, however, is not binding.

The Better Business Bureau (BBB) also runs a variety of industry-sponsored dispute resolution programs. It provides conciliation, mediation, and binding arbitration for all types of consumer disputes and operates the BBB-Line, which has contracts with many automobile manufacturers (including General Motors) to provide dispute resolution services for automobile users.

One of the main controversies relating to consumer disputes is that some companies and industries have set up arbitration panels made up of their own experts and force clients (often unwittingly) to sign contracts that specify that these panels will be used to provide binding arbitration in the event of disputes. Even worse than in small-claims court, this creates a biased dispute resolution system in which the arbitrators are likely to decide cases in favor of the company. Although this problem has become sufficiently visible and controversial that some companies have switched to more neutral procedures, many still use industry experts, claiming that they are the only ones who have the necessary expertise to make wise and fair decisions.

Questions that consumers should consider when examining industry-run dispute resolution processes include the following (Goldberg, Green, and Sander 1985): (1) Who appoints the arbitrator—the industry or a neutral third party (such as the American Arbitration Association)? (2) Is the arbitrator independent of the business or industry? (3) Does the consumer have the right to present his or her case in person? (4) Are consequential damages possible? (For example, if the consumer misses work time because his or her car is improperly repaired, can the consumer be reimbursed for lost pay?) (5) Is the decision binding on either or both parties? (In some cases, the decision is binding only on the business, not on the consumer.) Even if the answer to some of these questions is negative, the process may still be a fair one. However, consumers should be wary of these issues and understand that the system can be stacked in favor of the industry.

See also: Better Business Bureau; Community Justice Centers; Landlord-Tenant Disputes.
References and Further Reading: Goldberg, Stephen B., Eric D. Green, and Frank E. A. Sander, 1985, *Dispute Resolution,* chap. 9; McGillis, Daniel, 1987, *Consumer Dispute Resolution: A Survey of Programs;* Singer, Linda R., 1990, *Settling Disputes: Conflict Resolution in Business, Families, and the Legal System,* 87–110.

Contingency Fees

Contingency fees are fees paid to lawyers that are conditional on them winning the case. In some kinds of cases, such as personal-injury cases, lawyers do not charge their clients for services up front but take a percentage—sometimes a large percent-

age—of the award if they win. This has the advantage of allowing people who are unable to pay for a lawyer to pursue their cases. However, it has the disadvantage, some charge, of encouraging excessive awards, as juries award enough for the plaintiff to be compensated for his or her injuries, even after the lawyer takes a large cut "off the top." Some observers also believe that contingency fees encourage lawyers to take questionable cases, because every once in a while, one will pay off with a huge reward. Others argue that the contingent fee system gives an incentive to attorneys not to file frivolous or weak cases, since there will be a fee only when the attorney wins a case. Some even argue that the system causes attorneys to be overly cautious and to refuse to represent plaintiffs who have meritorious cases but ones that are especially expensive to litigate.

See also: Civil Justice Reform; Tort Reform.
References and Further Reading: Brickman, Lester, 1989, "Contingent Fees without the Contingencies: Hamlet without the Prince of Denmark?"

Contract

A contract is an agreement between two or more parties that, if correctly framed, is enforceable through the courts. Contracts generally involve an exchange of some kind—one party agrees to give another party some kind of goods or services in exchange for something else. For example, a contract may specify that a builder will build an addition to a house within a certain time frame and conforming to written specifications in exchange for payment of a certain amount. Or a contract may be drawn up between coauthors of a book, stipulating that each will write certain parts of the book and, in exchange, each will receive a certain percentage of the advance and royalties.

Contracts are the safest way to finalize agreements, as most contracts are enforceable by the judicial system. If one party violates a contract, the other party can sue the offender in court and thus force the violator to either live up to the contract or otherwise reimburse the plaintiff (the person initiating the suit) for his or her losses. If an agreement is not formalized in writing as a contract, a legal remedy is much more difficult to obtain.

See also: Civil Law and Litigation; Tort.
References and Further Reading: Gifis, Steven H., 1991, *Law Dictionary;* Moore, Christopher W., 1986, *The Mediation Process.*

Conversion

Conversion is the process through which parties to a conflict change their opinions on an issue and adopt their opponent's point of view. Conversion requires either fundamental changes in an individual's moral beliefs or a willingness to accept more generous principles regarding the distribution of wealth and power. When the conflict involves only a small number of individuals, conversion can truly resolve the underlying long-term conflict. For example, parents who are initially completely opposed to a child's choice of friends may change their minds once they get to know the friends better. This resolves the conflict completely.

In the case of large-scale, social policy conflicts, however, conversion is unlikely to result in complete resolution, because conversion is an individual process. The conversion of an individual merely changes the number of people who are supporting each side of the conflict. Although such a shift of allegiances can lead to significant changes in the balance of power and the outcome of particular social policy disputes, the underlying tension will remain until virtually everyone on one side has been converted. For example, in the last 40 years, large numbers of people have converted toward more environmentally sensitive positions. More and more disputes—over the construction of new facilities, air-

and water-quality programs, and habitat preservation—are settled with environmental values in mind. Nevertheless, environmental conflicts remain a major source of tension in our society.

Partial conversion also plays an important role in moderating conflict. If people believe that an opponent's position is truly abhorrent, they are likely to devote considerable resources to opposing it, thereby prolonging and intensifying the conflict. With partial conversion, however, people are likely to see the issue as more ambiguous. They might even believe that the other side has some valid points. This can reduce the intensity of the conflict significantly. For example, many white males limit their opposition to affirmative-action policies because they are partially (though certainly not completely) persuaded that such policies are a legitimate remedy for years of discrimination. This has limited the intensity of the backlash against affirmative action, allowing it to be implemented in many settings.

See also: Conflict Resolution, Conflict Management, and Dispute Settlement; Environmental Conflicts; Interpersonal Conflict; Persuasion; Power; Public Policy Conflicts.
References and Further Reading: Bond, Doug, 1993, "Nonviolent Direct Action and the Diffusion of Power"; Sharp, Gene, 1973, *The Politics of Nonviolent Action;* Wehr, Paul, Heidi Burgess, and Guy Burgess, 1994, *Justice without Violence.*

Cooling-off Period

When a conflict becomes emotional or escalates, it is often useful to call for a cooling-off period, or a time of disengagement, that is long enough to let all the parties calm down, review what has happened, and consider their next steps carefully before they reenter the fray. This is equally useful and important in interpersonal disputes, labor-management disputes, and most other types of disputes.

In interpersonal disputes, for example, it is almost impossible to negotiate effectively when one person is so angry that he or she cannot think—or talk—calmly or rationally. If a party is violent, if he or she is screaming and lashing out, it is impossible to initiate constructive problem solving or conflict resolution until all the disputants have calmed down enough to think and to listen. Thus, a cooling-off period is essential if the problem is to be resolved.

The same is true in labor-management negotiations. If contract negotiations have become difficult and heated, the parties (or an external third party, such as the Federal Mediation and Conciliation Service) may call for a cooling-off period (which might be 30 or 60 days), after which time negotiations or mediations begin anew. This not only gives negotiators time to reevaluate their positions, it may also move them closer to the contract deadline, which is often an additional impetus to conclude the negotiations successfully to avoid a strike.

See also: Anger and Anger Management; Deadlines; Emotions in Conflict; Escalation; Interpersonal Conflict; Labor-Management Relations and Conflict.
References and Further Reading: Hankins, Gary, 1988, *Prescription for Anger;* Ury, William, 1991, *Getting Past No: Negotiating with Difficult People.*

Cooperative Problem Solving
See **Collaborative Problem Solving.**

Coser, Lewis

Lewis Coser is a sociologist who wrote one of the key books on conflict theory, entitled *The Functions of Social Conflict.* Based largely on the earlier work of sociologist Georg Simmel, Coser postulates that conflict is not dysfunctional (as most sociologists in the 1950s maintained) but is a normal and necessary part of all social systems, enabling groups to form and persist, adapt and change.

Conflict with an external enemy helps groups become more cohesive, Coser argues. It helps define the group structure and preserve group identity. It also encourages the establishment of associations and

coalitions between individuals and groups and helps establish and maintain a balance of power that keeps social systems stable.

Coser suggests that all societies need what he calls "safety valve institutions"— institutions and norms that allow for the controlled release of anger and hostility. If no such safety valve is present, anger and hostility will build until they explode, destroying relationships and, at times, groups, organizations, or entire societies in the process. For this reason, Coser maintains that conflict is not dysfunctional; rather, rigid social structures that do not permit or encourage conflict are dysfunctional, because these structures tend to rip apart when tensions build, allowing conflicts to emerge from beneath the political or social repression.

See also: Balance of Power; Simmel, Georg.
References and Further Reading: Coser, Lewis A., 1956, *The Functions of Social Conflict.*

Costing

Parties to conflicts make decisions concerning the positions they want to pursue and the strategies they want to use, based on an assessment of the likelihood of success and the probable cost of pursuing the issue. Parties often underestimate the costs of conflicts and overestimate the prospects for success. This, in turn, leads them to pursue strategies that do not advance their interests. Often, it is politically difficult for those involved in strategy-making decisions to challenge the optimistic "can-do" attitudes of others.

To combat this problem, conflict professionals use "costing" processes to help the parties systematically and realistically assess the costs and benefits of alternative approaches. Costing may be done with a lawyer or mediator who asks difficult questions about the parties' expectations. It is important that intangible factors such as personal anxiety, damaged relationships, and the long-term reinforcement of animosities be considered, in addition to more tangible costs such as legal fees and potential casualties (in military confrontations).

Costing may also involve independent, objective assessments of available options. For example, a group that is unhappy with school board policies might decide to abandon its recall efforts after a poll demonstrates that the group will most likely not acquire the signatures needed to place the issue on the ballot. Similarly, a group might elect to abandon legal appeals after receiving an estimate of costs and the likelihood of success.

See also: BATNA; Conflict Assessment; Negotiation Loopbacks; Reality Testing.
References and Further Reading: Hocker, Joyce L., and William W. Wilmot, 1985, *Interpersonal Conflict,* 107–29; Moore, Christopher W., 1986, *The Mediation Process.*

Court-Annexed Alternative Dispute Resolution Procedures

Court-annexed alternative dispute resolution (ADR) procedures are formally connected to the courts. In some instances, litigants are required to try ADR before they can initiate litigation. This is common in medical malpractice cases, which are often sent to a screening panel before they can be filed in court. Similarly, divorce cases with custody disputes are frequently sent to mediation before a court will agree to hear them. In other situations, the court may select cases to refer to mediation or arbitration, or it may require the participation of a reluctant party if the opposing party requests the use of ADR.

Types of Court-Annexed ADR

Most commonly, cases are referred to one of five processes: court-annexed arbitration, early neutral evaluation, summary jury trial, mediation, or special master mediation. Court-annexed arbitration is usually mandatory, but unlike regular arbitration, it is not binding. About 20 states and a few district courts require court-annexed arbitration to be used in particular kinds of cases—for instance, automobile injury cases or money claim cases under a certain dollar amount. Although procedures vary, standard arbitration procedures are usually followed, which are adversarial in nature but are less formal and much faster than a typical trial.

In early neutral evaluation, a neutral expert assesses the facts of a case in an effort to help the parties settle before a trial. If they cannot reach a settlement, the neutral expert can help the parties tailor the case for the most effective trial and may help facilitate the discovery process.

Summary jury trials are another form of early neutral assessment. Here a judge and a jury hear a simplified version of the case and issue an advisory verdict, which the parties can then agree to accept or reject. If they reject the verdict, they revert to a standard trial process.

Mediation is a very different procedure. In mediation, a neutral third party facilitates settlement discussions but does not recommend a particular decision. Rather, the mediator helps the parties better communicate, clarify the issues, look for areas of common ground, and devise a solution that meets both sides' interests. Thus, in mediation, the disputants have much more control over the process and the substance of the decision than they do in the other procedures.

Special master mediation is a hybrid type of mediation used in particularly complex, multiparty cases. The special master may act as a typical mediator or may simply help organize large and complex cases so that they can be more effectively handled by the court.

Advantages of Court-Annexed ADR

Court-annexed ADR has a number of advantages. First is the reduction in court caseloads. Before the advent of ADR, the courts were getting increasingly bogged down in what seemed to be ever-increasing caseloads. With the use of alternative processes and incentives to settle out of court, the courts can be reserved for the cases that really need them.

Second, in many instances, alternative procedures yield better results. This is often true in situations in which the parties need to maintain a workable future relationship (such as divorce when there are children involved). Mediation, in particular, helps improve relationships, whereas the adversarial process in court often damages relationships even further and makes compliance with the final settlement terms less likely. Mediation also has the advantage of keeping the decision in the parties' hands. This enables disputants to emphasize those aspects of the case that are important to them and to reach agreements that contain what they need. Courts do not always do this. Although disputants tend not to choose alternative processes voluntarily, those who are forced into them often agree in the end that they are satisfied with the outcome.

Third, ADR requires money. It is hard to keep small ADR programs financially viable, but if programs can be enlarged by making their use mandatory, they become much more cost effective for everyone. In addition, as they become better used and better known, it is hoped that voluntary ADR use will increase.

Disadvantages of Court-Annexed ADR

The biggest concern with court-annexed ADR is that it denies parties their due process—it denies them their day in court. Although almost all mandatory ADR processes are nonbinding, they often have significant incentives built in to encourage the parties to accept the outcome. In addition, it can be argued that some cases are not appropriate for ADR, yet the procedures require that ADR be tried anyway.

This is a waste of time and money, since the case will inevitably end up in court anyway.

See also: Alternative Dispute Resolution, Institutionalization; Arbitration, Court-Annexed; Early Neutral Evaluation; Mediation; Special Masters and Magistrates; Summary Jury Trial.

References and Further Reading: Goldberg, Stephen B., Frank E. A. Sander, and Nancy H. Rogers, 1992, *Dispute Resolution: Negotiation, Mediation, and Other Processes;* Plapinger, Elizabeth, Margaret L. Shaw, and Donna Stienstra, 1993, *Judge's Deskbook on Court ADR;* Sander, Frank E. A., 1993, "The Courthouse and Alternative Dispute Resolution"; Sherman, E., 1995, "Court-Mandated Alternative Dispute Resolution: What Form of Participation Should Be Required?"

CPR Institute for Dispute Resolution

CPR Institute for Dispute Resolution (formerly the Center for Public Resources) is a nonprofit alliance of 550 global corporations and major law firms, established in 1979, to develop alternatives to the high cost of litigation facing business and government. Its purpose is to assist law departments and law firms to incorporate alternative dispute resolution (ADR) into their regular business.

Eight hundred fifty U.S. corporations with 2,800 subsidiaries have signed the CPR Corporate Policy Statement of Alternatives to Litigation, in which they pledge to explore ADR when involved in disputes with other signatories. In addition, 1,500 law firms have signed the CPR Law Firm Policy Statement on Alternatives to Litigation, in which they pledge to be knowledgeable about ADR options and to discuss these options with their clients.

CPR also maintains panels of distinguished neutrals, which include 600 of the nation's leading lawyers, former judges, and law professors, who provide ADR services to CPR members and the public. Since CPR panels are considered to be a public resource, CPR offers to secure third-party assistance on a pro bono or reduced-fee basis for parties to "disputes of public significance" if the parties lack adequate funds to pay in full.

CPR has also developed a number of industry-specific programs to help resolve conflicts in the areas of banking, construction, food, franchise, health, insurance, oil and gas, securities, and utilities. It publishes a news journal entitled *Alternatives* as well as books, practice tools, model procedures, forms, clauses, and videotapes. In addition to providing services in the United States, CPR collaborates with law firms and corporate lawyers in Europe and trains lawyers from the new democracies and developing countries in ADR skills.

See also: Appendix 1 for contact information.

Criminal Justice

Criminal justice is the part of the justice system that involves crimes, as opposed to civil justice, which involves violations of contracts or personal injuries. Although conflict resolution and alternative dispute resolution (ADR) procedures are more widely applied in the civil justice system, they have been used in the criminal justice system as well.

One application of ADR in the criminal justice system is victim-offender reconciliation. In this process, an offender—most often one who has already admitted to or has been found guilty of a crime—meets with his or her victim face-to-face to work out a plan for restitution and to reach some kind of interpersonal reconciliation. This is thought to benefit the individuals involved as well as the justice system, in a number of ways. First, the traditional criminal justice system focuses most of its attention on the job of prosecuting and punishing the criminal. The victim is, at best, ignored; often the victim is further traumatized and exploited in the trial process itself. Victim-offender reconciliation is seen by many proponents to support and empower the victim much more than the traditional criminal justice system does.

Second, when the victim and offender can meet face-to-face, the nature of the restitution is often more appropriate than when the restitution is established by a judge or a probation officer, who may not know enough about the people involved or about the case to be helpful. In addition, as in other forms of mediation, when the parties to the event work out a solution together, it is more likely to be implemented than if the solution is imposed by an outside third party.

Third, victim-offender reconciliation is considered by some to be a better way of limiting crime. Traditional criminal justice is based on the notion of punishment, which is intended to deter others, take the criminal off the streets, and rehabilitate him or her. Studies have shown that none of these goals are really met by the current system. Victim-offender reconciliation, it is argued, may actually meet those goals better than the traditional system.

Although not commonly considered dispute resolution, plea bargaining can also be seen as a form of negotiation. In plea bargaining, offenders plead guilty to a lesser crime than the one they are charged with to avoid a trial and the chance of being found guilty of the greater crime (and hence receiving a harsher punishment). Although some people object to this process and feel that it lets criminals "get off," it has become increasingly necessary to mitigate serious overcrowding problems—both in the court system and in prisons.

See also: Victim-Offender Reconciliation Programs.
References and Further Reading: Kennedy, Leslie W., 1990, *On the Borders of Crime: Conflict Management and Criminology;* Simpson, Mary, 1996, "A Story of Victim-Offender Reconciliation"; Umbreit, Mark S., 1995, *Mediating Interpersonal Conflicts: A Pathway to Peace,* 135–63.

Crisis Management

Crisis management techniques are designed to reduce the risk that rapidly changing conflict situations will escalate into highly destructive confrontations that undermine the interests of all parties. In crisis situations, events can proceed so rapidly that the parties are forced to respond before they clearly understand what they are responding to.

The most serious crisis situations arise when opposing military forces are arrayed against each other. If one side believes that the other is mobilizing its forces for an attack, it is likely to feel compelled to respond with an equal mobilization or attack of its own, believing that the best defense is a strong offense.

When events proceed so quickly that there is little time for fact-finding, responses tend to be based on worst-case assumptions. Such situations can quickly escalate into all-out confrontations that no one really wants. Barbara Tuchman's book *The Guns of August* offers a frightening case study of how the crisis following the assassination of Archduke Ferdinand escalated into World War I.

William Ury's book *Beyond the Hotline* addresses crisis management strategies designed to deal with an even more serious problem—the nuclear confrontation between the United States and the former Soviet Union. To reduce the risk that relatively simple misunderstandings could escalate into nuclear war, Ury's plan called for the United States and the Soviet Union to create closely linked crisis-control centers with the ability to give each other up-to-the-second information on the status of their respective military forces. This strategy would allow unintentionally provocative actions to be explained and even reversed before they led to tragedy (Ury 1985).

A similar approach can be used in less serious situations. For example, the Community Relations Service of the U.S. Department of Justice organizes crisis-response teams in racially divided communities. Composed of community leaders from various constituency groups,

these teams promptly investigate racial incidents and provide their constituents with accurate information. Although such teams cannot resolve all problems, they can reduce the risk that inaccurate and incomplete information acted on in the urgency of the moment will unnecessarily complicate the situation.

See also: Community Relations Service; Cooling-off Period; Escalation; Misunderstandings.
References and Further Reading: Brecher, Michael, and Patrick James, 1988, "Patterns of Crisis Management"; Tuchman, Barbara Wertheim, 1962, *The Guns of August;* Ury, William L., 1985, *Beyond the Hotline: How Crisis Control Can Prevent Nuclear War.*

Cuban Missile Crisis

The Cuban Missile Crisis was a standoff between the United States and the Soviet Union that took place in 1962, when the Soviets began to place medium-range nuclear weapons and warheads in Cuba, threatening the U.S. mainland. The crisis began when photographic proof of the missiles was brought to the attention of President John F. Kennedy. He responded by threatening a naval blockade of all Soviet shipments to Cuba unless the Russians removed the missiles. They did not.

Kennedy ordered the U.S. Navy to establish a blockade, effective on 24 October. At 10:00 that morning, two Soviet ships were detected nearing the barrier. The U.S. Navy also determined that a Russian submarine had moved into position between the two surface ships. The U.S. aircraft carrier *Essex* ordered the Soviet submarine to surface; if it refused, it was to be attacked.

Robert Kennedy, the president's brother and the U.S. attorney general, wrote of the incident later: "I think these few minutes were the time of gravest concern for the President. Was the world on the brink of holocaust? Was it our error? A mistake? Was there something further that should have been done? Or not done? His hand went up to his face and covered his mouth. He opened and closed his fist. His face seemed drawn, his eyes pained, almost gray. . . . We had come to the time of final decision" (Kennedy 1969, 69–70).

At 10:25 the Russian ships stopped. The president immediately ordered that they were not to be stopped or intercepted but allowed to turn back. Robert Kennedy wrote: "Then we were back to the details. The meeting droned on. But everyone looked like a different person. For a moment the world had stood still, and now it was going around again" (Kennedy 1969, 129)

As Dean Pruitt and Jeffrey Rubin (from whom this description is taken) point out, this is a classic example of a conflict that escalated higher and higher, until it reached the point of stalemate. The stalemate was caused not by lack of resources or lack of will, but rather by both sides' unwillingness to move any closer to the brink of nuclear holocaust. Both sides had the capacity to continue the struggle, but neither dared do so.

Shortly after the military standoff, U.S. and Soviet leaders negotiated an agreement in which the United States promised not to invade Cuba, and the Soviets committed to withdraw or destroy their Cuban missiles (Pruitt and Rubin 1986, 128–29).

See also: Cold War; Escalation; Stalemate; Threats.
References and Further Reading: Kennedy, Robert F., 1969, *Thirteen Days: A Memoir of the Cuban Missile Crisis;* Pruitt, Dean G., and Jeffrey Z. Rubin, 1986, *Social Conflict.*

Dahrendorf, Ralf

Ralf Dahrendorf is one of the leading sociologists in the study of conflict in the second half of the twentieth century. He is often called a neo-Marxist because he agrees with Marx that conflict is the primary method of organizing society and fostering social change. However, unlike Marx, Dahrendorf believes that any groups in society can conflict with each other, not just economic classes.

The key determining factor of conflict potential, according to Dahrendorf, is power differentials. Inevitably, he argues, one individual or group or society has more power and acts as a leader; the others have less power and are subordinate. In any such situation, the interests of the leader and subordinate are different and are likely to be in conflict.

Some conflicts can be resolved, but Dahrendorf claims that domination conflicts never are. They "can only be regulated, he argued, not resolved, because the structural basis of conflict is never eliminated. . . . To think [as did Marx] that class conflicts can be resolved through some form of violent struggle is, for Dahrendorf, an illusion. Such struggles may change those who have temporary positions of power, but their general effect is to exacerbate the conflict and make it more difficult to manage—not to resolve it" (Schellenberg 1996, 86).

See also: Domination Conflicts; Escalation; Intractable Conflicts; Marx, Karl.

References and Further Reading: Dahrendorf, Ralf, 1957, *Class and Conflict in Industrial Society;* Schellenberg, James A., 1996, *Conflict Resolution—Theory, Research, and Practice.*

Dartmouth Conferences

The Dartmouth Conferences were unofficial annual conferences of high-level officials, scholars, and policy analysts from the United States and the Soviet Union who met in an effort to improve superpower relations. Begun in 1960, just after the Soviets shot down the United States' U-2 spy plane over Soviet territory, the conferences were intended to diminish the rising tensions between the two nations. The first meeting, which was held at Dartmouth College in New Hampshire, was sponsored by the Kettering Foundation, the Institute for USA and Canada Studies, and the Soviet Peace Committee. Later conferences were supported by many other major foundations as well.

For a long time, the conferences were held behind closed doors; they were off the record, with no official standing. However, conclusions reached were transmitted to decision makers in both governments. In 1988, the meetings were opened up to more public participation, but they remained unofficial citizen or "track two" diplomacy, as opposed to the official "track one" diplomacy, which was being carried out by government officials simultaneously.

In 1995, Harold Saunders, the Kettering Foundation's director of international affairs, wrote, "During the 1980s, the participants in the Dartmouth Conference Regional Conflicts Task Force gradually found a systematic way of working together. As one Russian participant said, 'we began together as ideological enemies. But somehow we learned to penetrate each others' consciousness'" (Saunders 1995, 5).

According to Paul Olczak and Dean Pruitt (1995), these conferences were successful in laying the foundation for effective de-escalation when the motivation for ending the Cold War was finally realized, and they were essential in enabling Gorbachev to successfully execute that de-escalation in the late 1980s.

Even after the end of the Cold War, the Dartmouth conferees have continued to meet to try to ameliorate the many communal conflicts that are developing around the world. They developed a five-stage process of sustained dialogue that is now being implemented in Tajikistan and in Baton Rouge, Louisiana (with regard to race relations there). Together with the Kettering Foundation, they are working to establish this process in other locations as well.

See also: Cold War; Diplomacy, Citizen, Track Two, and Multitrack; Pugwash Conferences on Science and World Affairs.

References and Further Reading: Burton, John, and Frank Dukes, 1990a, *Conflict: Practices in Management, Settlement, and Resolution;* Olczak, Paul V., and Dean G. Pruitt, 1995, "Beyond Hope: Approaches to Resolving Seemingly Intractable Conflict"; Saunders, Harold, 1995, "Sustained Dialogue Comes Home."

De-escalation

De-escalation is a reduction in the intensity of a dispute or conflict that typically occurs either after a rapid intensification of hostilities or after what Saadia Touval and William Zartman (1985) call a "hurting stalemate" (a situation in which neither party can win, but both are being harmed by continuing the fight). In the first case, a conflict may move quickly from a minor incident to violence or, in the international context, to the threat of war. At this point, the parties are faced with a decision: Should they continue with the conflict, which is likely to be costly, or should they back down from the brink and try to solve it? Many factors influence such a decision: the perceived costs and benefits of continuing the escalation, the resources available to each side, the salience of the issues in dispute, the level of anger and distrust between the parties, and the response of others to the situation. If the costs of continuing the conflict exceed the expected benefits, if sufficient resources are unavailable, or if the issues are relatively unimportant, the parties will likely try to de-escalate the conflict. However, if anger and distrust run high, if the issues are important, or if victory is seen as critical, the conflict is likely to continue and even grow.

Usually, de-escalation is much harder to initiate than escalation. Escalation often occurs automatically: if people do what comes naturally in a conflict, they tend to strike back at any provocation. This often results in escalation, even when none is intended. De-escalation, in contrast, takes careful thought and a great deal of work. It requires careful choreography and a receptive audience. It also requires careful timing. If de-escalation is attempted at the wrong time, it is likely to fail.

Steps toward De-escalation

De-escalation usually occurs in a series of steps. First is the signaling by one or both parties that they are ready to explore the possibility of settlement. This may be accompanied or preceded by an attempt to determine the likely reception of such a suggestion by the other side. Such probing or signaling must be done carefully, as it can be construed as a sign of weakness and encourage the opponent to press even harder. In highly heated conflicts, it often helps to have such an inquiry made by a neutral third party, who does not suggest that the inquiry is actually coming from the opposition.

The second stage is exploratory discussions about the format and agenda of negotiations (often referred to as prenegotiation). Here, the parties sit down together, with or without a third-party intermediary, and investigate the possibility of negotiation. Questions to be answered include: Can the parties talk to each other effectively? Are there interests that might be negotiated? Will the parties suspend the hostilities while the negotiations are taking place? In escalated conflicts, such exploratory discussions may be difficult to initiate or hold without third-party assistance. With skillful assistance, however, the parties can often better assess their own options, the options of their opponents, and likely avenues for mutual accommodation.

The third phase of de-escalation is negotiation, where the parties actually sit down together, explore their interests and needs in depth, and try to work out a solution that meets all the parties' interests and needs as much as possible. This can be done by focusing on each party's interests and using principled negotiation as a model. Alternatively, the focus can be put on the parties' needs, using analytical problem solving as the method of choice.

The fourth phase is concluding and sustaining agreements. In order to conclude an agreement, the proposed settlement must give each party at least as many benefits as it expected to obtain by continuing the confrontation. If the negotiated settlement falls short of that goal for any party, that party is likely to withdraw from the negotiations and continue the fight. For this reason, settlement negotiations cannot take place until the conflict is "ripe." Such ripeness typically occurs after a hurting stalemate or a rapid escalation of a conflict that threatens to cost the parties more than they think they stand to win. In either case, they have a strong incentive to negotiate a solution.

In highly escalated conflicts, these phases are usually best attempted with the assistance of a third-party mediator, who will help the parties communicate more effectively, explore their interests and options, assess those options, and develop one solution that is best for all.

GRIT

Another approach to de-escalation is called GRIT, which stands for gradual reciprocal initiatives in tension reduction. This strategy, proposed by Charles Osgood, starts when one disputant makes a minor concession that does not substantially weaken his or her position. The intention is to encourage the other side to make a matching concession. If the opponent does so, the first disputant then makes a second concession, encouraging a matching response. If the opponent does not respond initially, Osgood suggests that the first disputant continue making overtures for de-escalation by making one or two more minor concessions in the hope of encouraging a positive response from the other side. This is a relatively low-risk way to turn an escalation process around and to signal to the opponent that the party wants to negotiate without appearing to be weak. It also is a way to deescalate a conflict without relying on a mediator's assistance.

See also: Costing; Crisis Management; Escalation; GRIT; Principled Negotiation and *Getting to Yes;* Problem Solving, Analytical.

References and Further Reading: Kriesberg, Louis, Terrell A. Northrup, and Stuart J. Thorson, 1989, *Intractable Conflicts and Their Transformation;* Kriesberg, Louis, and Stuart J. Thorson, 1991, "Timing the De-escalation of International Conflicts"; Osgood, Charles E., 1962, *An Alternative to War or Surrender;* Pruitt, Dean G., and Peter J. Carnevale, 1993, *Negotiation in Social Conflict: Escalation, Stalemate, and Settlement;* Touval, Saadia, and I. William Zartman, 1985, *International Mediation in Theory and Practice.*

Deadlines

Deadlines are action-forcing provisions incorporated into agreements between contending parties and between those parties and intermediaries. They specify the date and time by which various actions must be taken. Without such deadlines, it is easy for agreements to be subverted by parties who simply never get around to doing what they promised to do.

Deadlines can apply to procedural or substantive issues. For example, the terms of an agreement to mediate a dispute might require that each party formally respond to proposals made by the other party within two weeks. Substantive deadlines might require that a settlement be paid on or before a specific date or that the developer of a new residential community complete construction of a community park by a particular time.

To be effective, deadlines must be enforceable. For example, if a party to the mediation referred to above fails to respond in two weeks, the other party or the mediator must have some recourse, such as terminating the mediation and seeking legal relief. Similarly, if the developer doesn't complete the construction of the community park on time, he or she might be threatened with the loss of future building permits. Without such action-forcing mechanisms, negotiations can go on indefinitely, and agreements can be violated without consequences.

References and Further Reading: Carpenter, Susan L., and W. J. D. Kennedy, 1988, *Managing Public Disputes.*

Defense Base Closure and Realignment Commission

The purpose of the Defense Base Closure and Realignment Commission was to provide a fair process for the closure and realignment of U.S. military installations. Earlier attempts at base closures and realignment had been stymied by partisan politics. The commission was an attempt to avoid political conflict and achieve a nonpartisan and fair solution to the problem of excess and obsolete military bases.

Up until the end of the Vietnam War, base closings were under the authority of the Department of Defense; at the end of that war, the military shut down a large number of bases. At that time, Congress, "eager to protect the interests of their constituents," enacted legislation requiring the Department of Defense to notify Congress of intended base closings or realignments and to complete onerous environmental evaluations. Consequently, base closures nearly ceased, and the military's facilities exceeded the needs of its shrinking personnel roster. In 1990, Secretary of Defense Richard Cheney proposed a series of base closures, but Congress rejected his recommendations as having been politically influenced. The Defense Base Closure and Realignment Act was passed in 1990 to break the impasse.

Structure

The Defense Base Closure and Realignment Act authorized the president, in consultation with Congress, to appoint an independent eight-person commission. The act instructed the president to consult with the majority leaders of the House and Senate regarding four of the nominees and with the minority leaders regarding two. The president nominated the remaining two independently and appointed the chair. A commission was appointed for a single term of Congress, and the act provided for the appointment of a commission in 1991, 1993, and 1995. Of the 1993 commissioners, four had served in the military, two were retired military officers, three held high-level management positions in private industry, two had been elected to the House of Representatives, two had served on the 1991 commission, and each had extensive experience in government administration.

The task of the commission was to review and analyze the list of bases recommended for closure or realignment by the Department of Defense. To this end, the act instructed the secretary of defense to first submit a force-structure plan to Congress and to the commission. The force-structure plan outlines the military's anticipated activities and personnel needs. Second, the Department of Defense had to develop and submit to Congress a set of criteria to be used in selecting bases for closure. Finally, the secretary of defense had to submit a list of bases recommended for closure to the commission.

The commission then reviewed proposed base closings and recommended a series of closures in its final report. The final report was submitted to the president, who could either approve it or return it to the commission to be revised and resubmitted. If the president approved the final report, it was forwarded to Congress. Congress could not amend the report. Unless Congress rejected the report by a joint resolution of disapproval, the commission's final report became law. If the report was rejected by either the president or Congress, the base closure process would be terminated for that year.

Deliberative Process and Central Issues

The act specified that in order to change any of the secretary's recommendations, the commission must find that they "deviated substantially from the force-structure plan and final selection criteria." In 1991, 1993, and 1995, there were eight selection criteria. The first four criteria related to military value and were given priority. The other mitigating criteria assessed the estimated return on investment for each proposed base closure, the effect on the local economy and infrastructure, and the environmental impact. The commission, with the assistance of staff from the General Accounting Office and a number of other government agencies, reviewed the Department of Defense recommendations and the justifications for those recommendations. The 1993 commission added bases to the list of installations under consideration for closure.

The act further instructed the commission to hold public hearings on the Department of Defense recommendations. The 1993 commission held 11 hearings in Washington, D.C., and 17 regional hearings across the country. The 1995 commission held 29 hearings. All hearings were open to the public, and a number were televised. The commission received and responded to hundreds of thousands of letters from citizens. Commissioners and staff made over 100 fact-finding visits to bases under consideration. Regarding this process, the 1993 commission observed, "Most important, the communities were given a seat at the table." In their final reports the commissions presented their reviews of both the military's concerns and the communities' concerns.

Outcome

All three commissions succeeded in producing final reports that were acceptable to the president and Congress. The 1991 commission recommended 34 base closures and 48 realignments. In 1993, the commission recommended 130 base closures and 45 realignments. The 1995 commission closed or realigned 132 bases.

Although it adds a layer of bureaucracy to an already overburdened government structure, the use of an independent commission to make decisions that are too politically "hot" for Congress to handle is a useful conflict resolution mechanism. It is especially useful in distributive conflicts such as these, in which the gains or losses have to be distributed fairly, avoiding the "not in my backyard" (NIMBY) problem.

Similar independent commissions have been formed to deal with other controversial topics, such as Social Security reform. Not all have been successful, but they do provide a way of using consensus building and related alternative dispute resolution techniques as a supplement to the traditional legislative decision-making process.

See also: Distributional Conflicts; Federal Use of Alternative Dispute Resolution; Legislative Process; NIMBY, LULU, and NOPE.

References and Further Reading: Defense Base Closure and Realignment Commission, 1993, *Report to the President;* Defense Base Closure and Realignment Commission, 1995, *Report to the President.*

Democracy

Democratic processes are seldom thought of as conflict resolution structures, but they are exactly that. Democracy is essentially a grand dispute resolution system that establishes a set of institutions and procedures to be followed to resolve both private and public disputes. Democratic procedures include the democratic election of legislative bodies (for example, Congress, state legislatures, and city councils). These institutions, in turn, make public policy based on their own majority-rule voting processes (at times requiring a two-thirds or three-fourths majority). The policies set by the legislatures are then implemented by the government's executive branch.

In order to protect individuals from the "tyranny of the majority," democratic societies also guarantee a broad range of individual rights and liberties, including rights of due process. In the United States, these rights are embodied in the Bill of Rights and several other key amendments to the U.S. Constitution.

In democratic societies, the principle of majority rule with the protection of individual rights is enforced through the judicial system. In the United States, this involves a complex local, state, and federal court system with multiple levels of appeal, culminating with the U.S. Supreme Court. The Supreme Court is responsible for protecting democratic institutions as well as resolving disputes between citizens and between citizens and the government.

Democratic processes are also used to govern many nongovernmental organizations—corporations and citizen groups, for example. Such organizations commonly have bylaws and follow the democratic rules of procedure, such as those outlined in *Robert's Rules of Order.* Although these principles do not resolve all disputes, they provide a process through which most disputes can be addressed.

Ironically, however, democracy also creates conflict, because it tolerates and even encourages diverse views. Thus, people in democracies can think and say what they please—a privilege not found in authoritarian regimes. This makes conflicts more visible than they are in nations where people are told what to think and where speech and the press are controlled. Democracy can also be frustrating; people are allowed to speak their minds, but decisions are made by a majority vote (i.e., win-lose). This means that losers' interests are not represented in the final decision. The result is often dissatisfaction and continuing controversy, even after decisions are made.

Frustration with the win-lose nature of traditional democratic decision making has led to a number of experiments with alternative structures. Increasing numbers of local decisions are being made collaboratively, using a variety of consensus-building processes instead of traditional win-lose decision making. Likewise, both state governments and federal agencies have used regulatory negotiation for a number of years, in an effort to use win-win negotiating processes instead of win-lose administrative and judicial decision making as a way of setting and enforcing environmental standards.

Other aspects of most Western democracies that contribute to effective conflict resolution are the principles of individual liberty, private property, and market mechanisms for controlling the economy. Many conflicts are avoided, or at least limited, by social institutions that grant individual freedom to a large number of human activities. In most aspects of social, economic, and cultural life in the United States and other democracies, people are free to do what they please, as long as they do not infringe on the rights of others. If others do not approve, they are told to mind their own business.

The institution of private property is another crucial dispute resolution mechanism, because it gives individuals the freedom to use their own possessions as they wish. Similar to personal liberty, property rights are not absolute—rules have been established that govern how property can be used so that its use does not infringe on the rights of others. Zoning regulations and pollution control laws are examples of limits on private property rights.

Although some democracies limit the operation of market mechanisms, many rely on economic markets as another institutional dispute resolution mechanism. Rather than making political decisions about who is to work at what jobs, produce what products, at what cost, market mechanisms are used to make these decisions "automatically." Again, although market mechanisms have problems, they also avoid a great deal of potential conflict.

Without respect for individual freedom, private property, and the free market, the frequency and intensity of conflicts could increase dramatically. Thus, these principles are as central to effective democratic institutions as the fundamental political structures discussed above.

See also: Collaborative Leadership; Collaborative Problem Solving; Referendum; Regulatory Negotiation; Rights.
References and Further Reading: Baker, Pauline H., 1996, "Conflict Resolution versus Democratic Governance: Divergent Paths to Peace?"; Strauss, David, 1993, "Facilitated Collaborative Problem Solving."

Demonstrations

Demonstrations are one form of direct action used in an attempt to persuade people that they should change their behavior. The purpose of demonstrations is usually to draw attention to a problem. The intended audience may be the adversary, one's allies, or neutral third parties who can influence the course of events by endorsing one side or another. The more that demonstrations remain nonviolent and focused on legitimate problems, the more effective they are likely to be. If they degenerate into violence or if they focus on a problem that is not considered legitimate, they are less likely to bring about desired results.

The summer 1963 March on Washington, for example, was a nonviolent demonstration in which over 200,000 people—white and black—assembled in the nation's capital to express their opposition to racial discrimination. This was where Martin Luther King gave his "I Have a Dream" speech, which drew widespread national and even international attention and applause. The result of that speech and that march—together with many other demonstrations and acts of civil disobedience—was the 1964 Civil Rights Act, which greatly improved the status of minority groups in the United States.

See also: Civil Rights Act of 1964; Gandhi, Mahatma; King, Martin Luther, Jr.; Nonviolence; Persuasion; Violence.
References and Further Reading: Holmes, Robert L., 1990, *Nonviolence in Theory and Practice;* Sharp, Gene, 1973, *The Politics of Nonviolent Action.*

Détente

The term *détente* refers to the reduction of tension between nations. Most often, the term has been used to describe a period of improved relations between the United States and the Soviet Union that started to some extent in the 1950s after the death of Stalin and continued in the 1960s, as a reaction to the Cuban Missile Crisis. Détente ended between 1979 and 1980 with the Soviet invasion of Afghanistan and the election of Ronald Reagan, a hard-line anticommunist, to the U.S. presidency.

In the 1950s, both nations developed hydrogen bombs, intercontinental ballistic missiles, and satellites. With this kind of technology, it was clear that either side could completely annihilate the other and that nuclear war would be suicidal. In addition, the arms race was crippling the economies of both nations and alienating third-world nations that wanted an end to the Cold War. This led to the beginning of a policy of peaceful coexistence, which was supported in principle by Soviet Premier Khrushchev and U.S. Presidents Eisenhower and Kennedy. A number of agreements provided evidence of such a policy: the Korean armistice (1953), the Antarctic Treaty (1959), and the International Geophysical Year Agreement (1958).

Relations between the two countries deteriorated again in the early 1960s, climaxed by the Cuban Missile Crisis in 1962. This was an extremely frightening event for both the Soviets and the Americans. Never before (nor since) had the superpowers been so close to the brink of nuclear war. After the crisis was resolved, the importance of avoiding similar crises and backing down from the hair-trigger nuclear standoff seemed critical to the leaders (as well as to the general populations) of both nations. Thus détente was reestablished in an effort to avoid a nuclear war.

A related purpose of the 1960s détente was to limit the nuclear arms race. Neither side was willing to discuss nuclear disarmament, but they were willing to negotiate ways to limit the arms race and prevent the spread of nuclear weapons to other nations. In addition, they hoped that détente would stimulate both nations' economies. The United States began to sell much-needed grain and technology to the Soviets and thereby expanded its worldwide market.

The relationship between the two nations was not, however, one of peace. The fundamental social, economic, and political differences between the two nations remained. Efforts to address these fundamental conflicts were not even considered. Rather, the two nations simply agreed to pursue that conflict in nonmilitary ways. "Détente, as the parties themselves saw it, was a policy to regulate a fundamentally irreconcilable relationship" (Wallensteen 1985, 3).

Détente was more successful in the 1960s than it had been in the 1950s. In 1963, U.S. and Soviet decision makers agreed to a limited nuclear test ban treaty, agreed that the United States would sell the Soviets grain, and agreed to establish the "hot line" for crisis communication between the two nations' leaders. These agreements were followed by lengthy negotiations on the issue of nuclear proliferation, which resulted in the 1968 nonproliferation treaty. More agreements were made in the early 1970s: the first Strategic Arms Limitation Treaty (SALT I, 1972) and the Helsinki Accords (1975). Progress slowed, however, in the late 1970s, and détente essentially ended when the Soviets invaded Afghanistan in December 1979 and Reagan was elected president in 1980.

See also: Arms Control and Disarmament; Cold War; Strategic Arms Limitation Talks.
References and Further Reading: Froman, Michael, 1991, *The Development of the Idea of Détente: Coming to Terms;* Kriesberg, Louis, 1992, "The U.S.-USSR and Middle East Cases"; Wallensteen, Peter, 1985, "Focus on American-Soviet Détente: What Went Wrong?"

Deterrence

Deterrence refers to actions taken by one party to prevent an attack by another. The term is usually used in the context of international conflicts. The United States and the Soviet Union, for instance, relied on a strategy of deterrence to prevent nuclear war. By building up their nuclear arsenals to the point where they could sustain a first strike and still counterattack with devastating force, both countries were relatively secure in the notion that the other would not intentionally start a nuclear war (although both were concerned that one could start by accident).

Although deterrence is based on threats (one side threatens to harm another if it is harmed), not all threats deter. Deterrence works best, observes Roger Fisher, when it is used to maintain the status quo. It does not work nearly as well to encourage change. Fisher attributes this to what he calls "governmental inertia," or "the tendency of a bureaucracy to keep doing what it has been doing" (Fisher 1994, 19). In the case of U.S.-Soviet relations, deterrence was intended to prevent the Soviets from attacking Western Europe—an action that they had not yet taken. This, Fisher observes, was an "easy choice." Inertia already favors the status quo; there is no need to formulate or defend a new decision, no need to persuade others, make a commitment, or gather more data. All the parties need to do is to continue what they were doing.

Although deterrence did prevent a nuclear strike by the Soviets, it did not stop Serbian aggression in Bosnia, pacify Somalian warlords, or end North Korea's quest for nuclear weapons. "Each of these cases," observes Fisher, "has demonstrated an apparent inability of the United States and the United Nations—despite obvious military and economic superiority—to deal effectively with such conflicts. Sanctions have been threatened and applied, without success" (Fisher 1994, 17). The difference, Fisher observes, is that these are not cases of deterrence failure but of "compellence" failure. "We seek to influence a group of leaders to make a new decision—a decision to change an ongoing course of action. Yet in most cases, we have essentially been trying to use the same methods of influence as we did for deterrence, namely making threats and demands from a distance. When we seek to bring about a change in behavior, the methods used in deterrence rarely work" (Fisher 1994, 17–18).

Other problems with deterrence are that it is costly and risky. Threats need to be credible, so the United States not only had to build up a huge arsenal of nuclear weapons but also had to convince the Soviets that it might use them. The gamesmanship involved in maintaining the nuclear deterrent brought the two superpowers to the brink of nuclear war on several occasions—the best known being the Cuban Missile Crisis. Even though they backed away from the brink every time, as long as the two nations had nuclear weapons aimed at each other, there was a small possibility that they would be fired. According to mathematical laws, if something is possible and one waits long enough, it eventually will happen. For that reason, maintaining peace through nuclear deterrence suggests that sometime in the future deterrence will fail, and we will be faced with nuclear war.

See also: Balance of Power; Boulding, Kenneth; Cold War; Cuban Missile Crisis; International Conflict.
References and Further Reading: Fisher, Roger, 1994, "In Theory Deter, Compel, or Negotiate?"; Sur, Serge, 1993, *Nuclear Deterrence: Problems and Perspectives in the 1990s;* White, Ralph K., 1987, "Deterrence and Tension Reduction."

Dialogue

In the conflict management field, the term *dialogue* refers to a method of getting people who are involved in an emotional, deep-rooted conflict to sit down together with a facilitator and to talk and listen, with the goal of increasing mutual understanding and, in some cases, coming up with joint solutions to mutual problems.

Jay Rothman (1992) describes four different types of dialogue processes. The first is positional dialogue, in which disputants sit down together and talk, but they define the problem in adversarial, "us versus them" terms. They blame each other for the conflict and voice mutually exclusive positions.

Second is human relations dialogue, in which parties meet to break down fears and dispel stereotypes and to develop trust and friendships with people from the opposing side. A large part of the process involves learning why people feel the way they do about the disputed issue and coming to understand that intelligent and worthy human beings can feel that way without being stupid or evil.

The third kind of dialogue is activist dialogue, in which parties who normally oppose each other, but who share some common interests, make an effort to work collaboratively with their customary opponents to further a common goal. Blacks and Koreans working together to rebuild riot-damaged Los Angeles and Palestinians and Israelis working together on a jointly managed farm are two examples of activist dialogue.

The fourth kind of dialogue is problem-solving dialogue. Here, adversaries are brought together by a panel of facilitators who help them develop a common definition of their problem and then go on to generate solutions that will meet the needs of all sides. Problem-solving dialogue thus focuses on fundamental human needs (security and identity, for instance), whereas other forms of dialogue focus more on interests and values.

One example of the human relations approach to dialogue is that used by the Cambridge, Massachusetts, Public Conversations Project (PCP), one of the leading proponents and practitioners of dialogue processes in the United States. This project, begun by a group of family therapists, applies traditional therapy techniques to highly escalated and emotional public policy conflicts. Focused initially on abortion, they have expanded their work into many other areas of concern: international population and development, environ-

mental protection, race relations, and homosexual rights, for example.

The PCP defines dialogue as "an exchange of perspectives, experiences, and beliefs in which people speak and listen openly and respectfully. In political debates, people speak from a position of certainty, defending their own beliefs, challenging and attacking the other side, and attempting to persuade others to their point of view. They generally speak not as individuals, but as representatives of a position defined by the dominant discourse. In dialogue, participants speak as unique individuals about their own beliefs and experiences, reveal their uncertainties as well as certainties, and try to understand one another" (Becker et al. 1994, 3). Unlike some dialogue facilitators, the PCP does not urge participants to seek common ground, because it has found that this concept frightens people away before they begin. Rather, it asks participants to engage in a new kind of conversation, one that is open to listening, understanding, and learning in a new way.

To facilitate this conversation, the PCP creates a structured situation and asks a carefully designed set of questions that encourages participants to get to know and understand one another and their beliefs in a deeper way than is possible in a normal setting. Although people do not change their minds about the issue in this process—people do not change from being pro-choice to pro-life—they do change their minds about the people involved in the dialogue and frequently about the opposition as a group. The goal (which is usually achieved) is to get participants to understand that these deep-rooted, emotional public policy questions (such as abortion) are not black and white issues but are highly complex issues with multiple "right" answers. Participants come to respect people on both sides of the debate and understand that those who hold opposing views are not, by definition, evil. This is a long way from resolving the abortion controversy, but it is also a big step toward personal reconciliation of this and other hotly debated issues.

Another form of dialogue is policy dialogue that is held to investigate possible changes in public policies regarding various political issues. The National Coal Policy Project, carried out during the energy crisis in the 1970s, was an example of a policy dialogue designed not to resolve a specific dispute but to get environmentalists and coal interests together to discuss future changes in environmental policies regarding coal extraction and use in the United States. As described by Barbara Gray, the National Coal Policy Project as well as other policy dialogues, convened parties "to explore differences, clarify areas of disagreements, and search for common ground without the expectations that binding agreements will emerge" (Gray 1989, 180).

Richard Schwartz uses the term *dialogue* similarly when discussing its use in international conflicts. Dialogue is a common approach to what has come to be known as "track two diplomacy," which involves citizens (rather than leaders or decision makers) of opposing countries who meet to break down stereotypes and develop ways to solve mutual problems. Although their recommendations are not binding, grassroots dialogue groups can affect official decision making if the people involved have credibility and adequate links to decision makers.

Schwartz cites four ways that dialogue can contribute to conflict resolution. First, it demonstrates that people from opposing sides can learn from one another. Second, it encourages the formation of and linkage with other dialogue groups, which spreads the goodwill further and enhances the sense of efficacy of participants. Third, dialogue groups can collect, reinvent, or generate creative ideas that might contribute to a solution, and they can then publicize these ideas to decision makers and their own populations. Fourth, they can obtain access to influential or powerful people who might be able to implement their ideas.

See also: Collaborative Problem Solving; Diplomacy, Citizen, Track Two, and Multitrack; Intractable Conflicts; National Coal Policy Project; Problem Solving, Analytical; Public Conversations Project.

References and Further Reading: Becker, Carol, Laura Chasin, Richard Chasin, Margaret Herzig, and Sallyann Roth, 1994, "From Stuck Debate to New Conversation on Controversial Issues: A Report from the Public Conversations Project"; Gray, Barbara, 1989, *Collaborating: Finding Common Ground for Multiparty Problems;* Rothman, Jay, 1992, *Confrontation to Cooperation: Resolving Ethnic and Regional Conflict;* Schwartz, Richard, 1989, "Arab-Jewish Dialogue in the United States: Toward Track II Tractability."

Diplomacy

Diplomacy refers to the political institutions and processes through which nations interact with one another. Basically, it involves all the business that one nation might need to undertake with another, including formal and informal negotiations, establishment of trade policies, and exchange of citizens (student exchanges, visitors, and so forth). Typically, diplomacy is conducted by professional foreign service officers, although ambassadors may be appointed who are not career diplomats but distinguished professionals from business, politics, or academia. Most diplomats operate out of embassies in foreign countries, although some work in the home country in the State Department (or similar agency) or in the United Nations. In addition to engaging in day-to-day bilateral diplomacy (negotiations between two nations), diplomats are called on to negotiate multinational agreements, such as the treaty to limit the production of chlorofluorocarbons to protect the atmosphere's ozone layer.

According to Stanley Michalak, ancient Greece was the first civilization to develop an orderly system of diplomacy between its city-states. Diplomatic activity declined during the Middle Ages but was reestablished during the Italian Renaissance, when many of the current diplomatic practices were developed. These included a system of permanent ambassadors to foreign countries; foreign offices that supported these ambassadors and set foreign policy; standard protocols, privileges, and immunities for diplomats; and the concept of extraterritoriality, which means that an embassy is considered to be governed by the laws of the home country, not the laws of the state in which the embassy is located (Michalak 1994).

When nation-states began to take shape in seventeenth-century Europe, diplomacy between them became especially important. Based on what is now known as the realist theory of political relations, diplomats negotiated with others to gain power and further their nations' interests. Diplomacy at that time was primarily an adversarial process (as it is now). Diplomats tried to maintain power over weaker nations and maintain a balance of power with other nations of equal status. This balance of power was considered essential to maintaining peace.

Although several efforts have been made to alter the adversarial, power-based approach to diplomacy, none has yet been successful. The first such effort was that championed by Woodrow Wilson, who called for a 14-point plan of open diplomacy and collective security to be established by the League of Nations. Congress rejected the concept of the League of Nations, however, and it quickly failed.

A second somewhat similar attempt to revise diplomatic functions was made with the creation of the United Nations (UN) after World War II. The UN, too, was to be based on the notions of collective security and international governance. Although the UN still exists, it has never been able to fulfill its intended mission, first due to the Cold War, and second due to an unwillingness of nations to cede some of their sovereignty to the world body.

Given the problems with the UN system and the problems encountered in the effort to enforce world peace at the end of the Cold War, many political scholars and diplomats are calling for a revision of diplomatic procedures. More and more attention is being given to "track two" or "citizen diplomacy," which involves private citizens (not formal diplomats) of disputing nations meeting to engage in joint problem solving. Unlike traditional diplomacy, which still tends to be adversarial, track two diplomacy can be much more collaborative, as the citizen diplomats are not bound by official state policies, expectations, or political pressures. Citizen diplomats can be much more flexible, bold, and aggressive in pursuing new ideas than can formal diplomats. If the ideas make sense, they can take them to the formal diplomats and decision makers, who can move forward on the ideas even though they would have seemed too extreme had they been proposed by the diplomats themselves.

See also: Adversarial Approach; Collaborative Problem Solving; Collective Security; Diplomacy, Citizen, Track Two, and Multitrack; International Conflict; League of Nations; Montreal Protocol on Substances that Deplete the Ozone Layer; United Nations.

References and Further Reading: Diamond, Louise, and John McDonald, 1991, *Multi-Track Diplomacy: A Systems Guide and Analysis;* Evans, Gareth, 1993, *Cooperating for Peace: The Global Agenda for the 1990s and Beyond,* chap. 5; Michalak, Stanley J., 1994, "Diplomacy"; Rothman, Jay, 1992, *Confrontation to Cooperation: Resolving Ethnic and Regional Conflict.*

Diplomacy, Citizen, Track Two, and Multitrack

Citizen diplomacy refers to unofficial contacts between people of different nations, as opposed to official contacts between governments. It can involve simple exchanges of people (student exchanges, for instance), international religious activities (through the World Council of Churches, for example), or scientific and cultural exchanges (international scientific meetings, traveling art exhibits, musical performances, and so forth). The purpose, most often, is to foster interpersonal understanding and cooperation.

The term *track two diplomacy* is also commonly used to refer to such unofficial international contacts; however, this term is more narrowly defined. Track two diplomacy, as described by Joseph Montville (who invented the term), refers to unofficial negotiations or discussions on topics normally negotiated officially, for instance, arms control or resolution of an ongoing conflict. Track two is "in no way a substitute for official, formal, 'track one' government-to-government or leader-to-leader relationships," Montville states. "Rather, track two activity is designed to assist official leaders by compensating for the constraints imposed on them by the psychologically understandable need for leaders to be, or at least be seen to be, strong, wary, and indomitable in the face of the enemy" (Montville 1987, 7). The Dartmouth Conferences and the Pugwash Conferences, both held to improve U.S.-Soviet relations, are two examples of track two diplomacy, as are the analytic problem-solving workshops held by Herbert Kelman, John Burton, and others.

Louise Diamond and John McDonald (1991) developed the term *multitrack diplomacy* because citizen diplomacy can actually take any of eight forms: (1) professional conflict resolution efforts; (2) international business contacts; (3) citizen exchanges; (4) international research, education, and training; (5) activism; (6) religious contacts between people of different nations; (7) international contacts within the funding community; and (8) public opinion and communication programs.

All these efforts can further interpersonal understanding and cooperation and can enhance official efforts at international reconciliation. Sometimes, however, citizen efforts are designed to oppose official government policy. The city of Boulder, Colorado, for instance, adopted a "sister" city in Nicaragua during the Sandinista-Contra war as a way of expressing support for the Nicaraguan people and countering the official U.S. government efforts to support the Contras against the Sandinista government.

See also: Dartmouth Conferences; Diplomacy; Needs; Oslo Accords, Middle East Peace Process; Problem-Solving, Analytical; Pugwash Conferences on Science and World Affairs; Track Two Preventive Diplomacy in the South China Sea.

References and Further Reading: Burton, John, and Frank Dukes, 1990a, *Conflict: Practices in Management, Settlement and Resolution;* Diamond, Louise, and John McDonald, 1991, *Multi-Track Diplomacy: A Systems Guide and Analysis;* Montville, Joseph, 1987, "The Arrow and the Olive Branch: A Case for Track Two Diplomacy."

Diplomacy, Preventive

Preventive diplomacy is undertaken in an effort to avoid, or at least contain, international conflicts and to keep them from escalating into full-blown war. The goal is similar to that of peacekeeping or "preventive deployment," which involves the use of military personnel to establish or maintain a cease-fire. However, preventive diplomacy involves diplomatic rather than military efforts to control conflicts.

Specific approaches to preventive diplomacy include "the full range of 'peaceful means' described in Article 33 of the UN Charter, i.e., 'negotiation, enquiry, mediation, conciliation, arbitration, judicial settlement, resort to regional agencies or arrangements,' . . . all of which are described in detail in the Handbook on the Peaceful Settlement of Disputes between States, prepared by the UN Secretariat" (Evans 1993, 61).

Gareth Evans argues that the United Nations can and should devote a much greater proportion of its efforts to preventive diplomacy, as this is more cost effective and humane than waiting for conflicts to escalate and then trying to cool them down. Although sovereign nations are unlikely to be willing to submit their disputes to arbitration or judicial settlement, Evans suggests that negotiation, conciliation, and mediation—all processes in which the disputants themselves maintain control—can be used more often and more successfully than has been the case in the past. This is especially true if intervention happens early in the conflict, before it has escalated to armed warfare. Although the United Nations is likely to be one of the most effective purveyors of preventive diplomacy, regional organizations, private mediators (such as Jimmy Carter), and various nongovernmental organizations (for example, the Mennonite Conciliation Service) are also important sources of assistance in preventive diplomacy efforts.

See also: Carter, Jimmy; Conflict Prevention; Crisis Management; De-escalation; Diplomacy; Mediation, International; Mennonite Conciliation Service; Peacekeeping; Track Two Preventive Diplomacy in the South China Sea; United Nations.
References and Further Reading: Evans, Gareth, 1993, *Cooperating for Peace: The Global Agenda for the 1990s and Beyond.*

Diplomacy, Virtual

Virtual diplomacy is undertaken with the help of electronic communication. A relatively new field, electronic diplomacy is flourishing in the late 1990s, spurred by rapid advances in telecommunications technologies and the Internet. Still, its origins go back at least as far as the "hot line" that connected the United States and the Soviet Union by telephone during the height of the Cold War.

The recent development of the Internet and the World Wide Web is dramatically speeding the flow of information and drastically diminishing the cost of information transfer. By reducing the need for expensive foreign travel, electronic technologies are permitting the rapid expansion of a broad range of international communities, including many nongovernmental organizations formed around collaborative business ventures and among people with similar social and political interests. Many of these individuals and or-

ganizations are engaging in a broad array of informal diplomatic activities. Although some of these activities involve formal government officials, others fall under the rubric of citizen diplomacy. Many of these virtual communities see the promotion of peaceful international relationships as key to advancing their interests. This is leading groups to intervene in all stages of the peacemaking process—from conflict limitation and avoidance, through efforts to bring about the cessation of hostile confrontations, to the rebuilding of communities torn apart by conflict. Electronic communication has facilitated all these efforts, as it unites people around the globe quickly and inexpensively and gives them access to an enormous base of information to use in their problem-solving efforts.

See also: Communication, Cross-Cultural; Diplomacy; Diplomacy, Citizen, Track Two, and Multitrack.
References and Further Reading: United States Institute of Peace, Forthcoming, *Virtual Diplomacy: Conference Proceedings.*

Discovery

Discovery is a legal term for the procedure used by attorneys to obtain information relating to a lawsuit. Through discovery, lawyers can obtain copies of important documents, deeds, and other information held by the opposing side that are important to the case. Since opposing parties can be extremely slow in providing such information, the discovery process can take a long time. Recent amendments to the federal rules of civil procedure attempt to eliminate some of these difficulties by, for example, requiring early disclosure of certain types of information. In addition, many forms of alternative dispute resolution use streamlined processes designed to make discovery easier and faster for all parties.

See also: Civil Justice Reform; Court-Annexed Alternative Dispute Resolution Procedures; Tort Reform.
References and Further Reading: Gifis, Steven H., 1991, *Law Dictionary.*

Dispute

See **Conflict and Dispute.**

Dispute Resolution Access: A Guide to Current Research and Information

Dispute Resolution Access is a newsletter published by the Community Board Program in San Francisco, one of the first and still one of the most prominent neighborhood dispute resolution organizations in the country. In addition to providing dispute resolution services to local citizens, the San Francisco Community Board has been a leader in providing conflict resolution training and training materials to people around the country and elsewhere in the world. Consistent with this broader educational interest, the Community Board publishes this newsletter in an effort to "bring current dispute resolution research, policy papers, evaluations, articles, and other useful information" to dispute resolution professionals throughout North America.

Published twice a year, the newsletter contains abstracts of papers and other research findings organized by topic. Frequent topics include community dispute resolution, court-related dispute resolution, culture and ethnicity, the environment, family/divorce, gender, international conflict, labor and organizational conflict, mediation, negotiation, peace, public policy, and schools. In addition, the newsletter often contains a substantial article written by one of the leaders of the field on a topic of current interest.

See also: Appendix 1 for contact information.

Dispute Review Boards

First set up in 1979, dispute review boards (DRBs) are used in the construction industry to resolve disputes between owners and contractors and, at times, between contractors and subcontractors. They can be used in conjunction with or indepen-

dent of a partnering agreement, which is another dispute resolution process commonly used in the construction industry.

Typically, DRBs consist of a standing panel of three neutral parties who are knowledgeable about the particular project and construction procedures. Typically, each party selects one neutral, and these two neutrals jointly select a third. All neutrals must be approved by the owner and the contractor. Although the primary function of the DRB is to help the parties resolve disputes without litigation, the DRB is involved in the project continuously, even if no disputes occur. It meets regularly to monitor project progress and thus is already familiar with the situation should a dispute develop. If and when it does, both parties prepare position papers that they present to the board. The board reads them, holds an informal hearing, and issues a recommendation for the resolution of the dispute. Although this recommendation is not binding, it typically carries considerable weight, in part because the neutrals are trusted, and in part because their recommendations are generally considered admissible evidence in any subsequent litigation or arbitration.

The American Society of Civil Engineers tracked the performance of DRBs on 166 projects. It found a high success rate—the boards heard 225 disputes and resolved 208 of them. Only one dispute submitted to a DRB ultimately went to litigation (Augustine 1994). Thus, DRBs provide a quick and cost-effective way of resolving construction disputes before they escalate and hamper project completion.

See also: Commercial Disputes; Partnering.
References and Further Reading: Augustine, Mary Jane, 1994, "Dispute Prevention and Resolution in the Construction Industry"; Fisher, Timothy S., 1994, "Dispute Review Boards: A Blueprint for Success."

Dispute Settlement

See **Conflict Resolution, Conflict Management, and Dispute Settlement.**

Dispute Systems Design

Dispute systems design is a strategy for handling the continuing stream of disputes that confront all large organizations and society as a whole. First advanced by William Ury, Jeanne Brett, and Stephen Goldberg in *Getting Disputes Resolved* (1988), the process helps organizations develop an overall dispute handling system with different mechanisms for each type of dispute. The system assesses the special circumstances involved in each dispute and directs the contending parties to the most appropriate dispute handling mechanism. The approach envisions three types of disputes and dispute resolution procedures: interest based, rights based, and power based.

Ury, Brett, and Goldberg maintain that well-functioning dispute handling systems resolve most disputes through interest-based negotiation (or mediation). For example, employees concerned about better working conditions and managers concerned about increased productivity might well be able to negotiate a package of workplace changes that both sides agree would lead to a more pleasing and productive working environment. In other words, there are win-win solutions to these disputes that advance the interests of all parties.

Dispute systems design recognizes, however, that some disputes cannot and should not be resolved in this way. These disputes revolve around questions of who is morally or legally right. For example, employees might argue that they cannot be dismissed from their jobs because they are pregnant or because they test positive for HIV. To deal with such disputes, a dispute handling system would include separate rights-based mechanisms. Ideally, these processes would quickly and inexpensively determine who is right and who is not and then help the parties "loop back" to an interest-based approach to conclude a settlement. Examples of such loop-back processes include mini-trials, advisory arbitration, summary jury trials, and procedures for sharing information. Should these efforts fail, Ury, Brett, and Goldberg advocate some type of arbitration as a way of making a final rights determination, which is less costly than conventional litigation.

Dispute systems designers also recognize that there are yet other disputes that cannot be resolved with rights-based or interest-based techniques. In these situations, the dispute is so deeply rooted that the parties are unwilling to compromise unless forced to do so; they are committed to using all their power in an attempt to prevail. Such power contests may involve strikes, lockouts, elections, public demonstrations, or even violence or military action. For example, labor and management may conclude that the only way to break a stalemate on long-term job security issues is to strike. Again, a well-designed dispute system would try to encourage a loop back to interest-based approaches with techniques such as cooling-off periods or third-party intervention. When this fails, designers would try to encourage lower-cost power contests. For example, symbolic strikes are preferable to all-out confrontations. They also encourage the parties to be prudent in their use of force in order to reduce the risk of backlash or of things spinning out of control.

According to Ury, Brett, and Goldberg, a good dispute handling system resolves most disputes through interest-based mechanisms, with a much smaller number of disputes being resolved by rights-based processes and even fewer by power-based approaches. They contrast this situation with "distressed systems," in which organizations use interest-based processes relatively infrequently and rely excessively on rights-based and power-based approaches to dispute resolution.

See also: Bargaining, Interest-Based and Positional; Dispute Systems Design for Families; Dispute Systems Design

for Schools; Negotiation, Loopbacks; Power; Principled Negotiation and *Getting to Yes;* Rights.
References and Further Reading: Ury, William L., Jeanne M. Brett, and Stephen B. Goldberg, 1988a, *Getting Disputes Resolved: Designing Systems to Cut the Costs of Conflict.*

Dispute Systems Design for Families

Dispute systems design is the formulation, in advance, of a method for the resolution of disputes that occur frequently and predictably in interpersonal, intergovernmental, and international relationships. Disputes following divorce, such as alimony and child support payments and child custody issues, are examples of such predictable and frequent disputes for which one might profitably design a dispute resolution system in advance. Without such a system, such recurring disputes are usually handled on a case-by-case basis. Each incident can become painful, protracted, and costly, escalating rather than diminishing the conflict between the couple.

A case study of dispute systems design in one divorce case is described by Joan Kelly (1989): The Browns, a divorcing couple, were mired in a continuing battle over the financial responsibility and care for their minor child. The conflict showed no signs of resolution within the traditional adversarial divorce process, so the Browns turned to mediation in an effort to structure a new form of coparental relationship to replace the failed marriage. Through mediation, the Browns hoped not only to resolve the immediate disputes regarding the divorce but also to design a system within which future disputes could be resolved.

The Browns worked with a mediator, who suggested that they use the five tenets of dispute systems design: (1) focus on the interests of all parties, including the child; (2) build in "loop-backs" (i.e., returns) to mediation and negotiation; (3) arrange procedures in a low-cost to high-cost se-

quence; (4) provide the necessary motivation, skills, and resources; and (5) anticipate future disputes and resolve them now.

The mediator asked the Browns to consider the methods by which they wanted to resolve future disputes. They both agreed, in principle, to use the least costly methods available. They were then asked to consider the tools they would need to resolve future conflicts. They agreed that a detailed custody and parenting agreement would be useful to address important issues. If properly done, it would also offer a framework for minimizing future disputes.

In their discussions, the mediator helped the Browns predict disputes that were likely to arise and devise ways to handle such problems in advance. For example, they agreed that future disputes over when the child would be with each parent were likely. In response, the Browns developed a detailed agreement in lieu of the usual provision of "reasonable visitation by the father." The Browns then identified other areas of probable future conflict and structured similar agreements. Further, they agreed to use a sequence of dispute resolution procedures in future custody disputes arising out of their child's changing needs during adolescence. Rather than immediately turning to the courts, they agreed to try to resolve future conflicts themselves and, if that failed, to try mediation before resorting to an adversarial process.

Through the mediation process, the Browns acquired the communication and negotiation skills to resolve postdivorce conflicts without the help of a mediator. After three years, they reported that although their anger toward each other had not diminished, they were in conflict less often because their dispute resolution system was working. Although they may have to return to mediation in the future, their case illustrates a typical outcome. Divorcing couples who use mediation to settle immediate issues and plan for the resolution of future disputes are more likely to abide by their agreements (since they made them themselves) and tend to develop the communication and conflict resolution skills that enable them to work out unforeseen difficulties in the future more effectively than couples who rely on an expert (a lawyer or the court) to make the decisions for them. Because of these advantages, the Association of Family Mediators asserts that mediation and family-oriented dispute systems design should be formally incorporated into all state-run institutionalized divorce processes.

See also: Academy of Family Mediators; Dispute Systems Design; Divorce Mediation; Family Conflict.
References and Further Reading: Kelly, Joan B., 1989, "Dispute Systems Design: A Family Case Study."

Dispute Systems Design for Schools

In almost all relationships and organizations, similar disputes tend to happen again and again. Rather than dealing with each one as if it were the first and last, conflict professionals have developed the notion of dispute systems design—the process of designing a system or procedure, in advance, that can be used to resolve the continuing series of disputes as they arise.

John Murray (1989) describes one such system developed in the 1980s for a school system in a moderately sized southern city, referred to by the pseudonym "Central City." In response to court-imposed desegregation, the Central City school district experienced the phenomenon of "white flight" from the district. This resulted in a predominantly (60 to 70 percent) black student body in the district schools. The school district pursued an aggressive desegregation plan by initiating litigation against neighboring, predominantly white school districts. The resultant rulings required the continual monitoring of the school board by lawyers and a federal judge. More significantly, there was an escalation in the number and severity of confrontations between blacks and whites, citizens and school board members, and teachers and administrators.

Realizing that something had to be done, the school board held a retreat at which the members became familiar with collaborative problem-solving theory and skills. Following this retreat, a follow-up session was held, jointly facilitated by the staff of a local foundation (which had funded the retreat) and the Conflict Clinic at George Mason University. The goal was to begin designing a dispute resolution system for the school district.

Due to court intervention, the district had an uncoordinated tripartite decision-making structure. The governing body of the district was the federal district court judge and his appointed referee. The second level of decision making was the increasingly contentious and factious school board. Finally, decision making was also done in the community by business leaders, families, and students. Due to the adversarial nature of the court governance of the district, there was little communication among the three parties.

The Conflict Clinic advised that five guiding principles be followed in the design of a dispute resolution system. First, the problem should be defined by the parties, not their attorneys. Second, the depth of the problem should be determined, to enhance the probability that the parties had identified the root of the problem. Third, there had to be a commitment to a process controlled by the participants. Fourth, the process being established had to be linked to the tripartite decision-making structure. Finally, it was imperative that all major interests be represented.

A broad-based, representative community group was formed. In the first meeting, the group developed a common definition of the problem and formed three committees that would meet monthly to address the three problems identified. One committee worked to design a process that allowed people holding extreme positions (typical of this community) to work together. The second committee focused on incorporating communication skills enhancement into the process and increasing the understanding of minority cultures. The third committee examined ways of developing community leadership and support for the school district, in the hope of increasing community residents' input and giving them some control in the decision-making process.

The community group served as a means of resolving disputes at the lowest, and possibly most efficient, level. It informed both the school board and the court, because it was able to accurately represent the extreme positions of the community. Further, the school board and the court recognized the significance of this community group in the implementation of the district's and the court's decisions. Most significantly, the group earned the legitimacy and credibility necessary to design a dispute resolution system that may ultimately change the existing balance of power in the community and thus change the nature of the political structure.

See also: Dispute Systems Design; School Conflict Resolution Programs.
References and Further Reading: Murray, John S., 1989, "Designing a Disputing System for Central City and Its Schools."

Distributional Conflicts

Distributional conflicts involve disputes over who gets what or who gets how much. These conflicts tend to be structured in a win-lose (also called zero-sum) way. This means that the more one party gets, the less the opponent gets. Examples of such win-lose distributional conflicts are labor-management disputes over issues such as wages and benefits, conflicts between nations over land, and conflicts between coworkers over prime vacation times. In each of these cases, a win for one means a loss for the other. If employee wages go up,

management profits go down. If the Israelis control Jerusalem, the Palestinians do not. If one worker gets to go on vacation over the Fourth of July, the other workers cannot.

Negotiation theorists disagree on the best way to handle such distributional conflicts. One school of thought, led by Roger Fisher and William Ury, inventors of the concept of "principled negotiation," argues that any conflict, including distributional conflicts, can be solved cooperatively. By separating the people from the problem, focusing on interests rather than positions, inventing options for mutual gain (which they claim are almost always feasible), and relying on objective criteria, negotiators can come up with win-win outcomes to most apparently win-lose distributional conflicts (Fisher and Ury 1981).

Other negotiation theorists disagree. Many conflicts are not amenable to principled negotiation, they contend, no matter how much the parties would like to try. These conflicts are inherently zero-sum conflicts, in which there is no way to "expand the pie" or otherwise meet everyone's interests or needs simultaneously. Distributive negotiation strategies are very different from integrative negotiation strategies, and they should be based on a careful dance between one's "reservation price"—the minimum or maximum one can accept—and the opponents' reservation price. Various negotiating gambits can be used to try to get a better idea of an opponent's real reservation price and then to negotiate a result that is closer to one's own end than to the opponent's. Important strategies include knowing one's options and reservation price, estimating as accurately as possible the opponent's options and reservation price, knowing how high (or low) to make the initial offer, and knowing how quickly to move up or down in relation to concessions made by the other side. The strategies recommended for distributional bargaining are more complex than those that Fisher and Ury suggest for principled negotiation, yet the situations can be sufficiently difficult that simple answers are hard to come by. Although other factors contribute to making conflicts difficult to handle, high-stakes distributional conflicts are often resistant to resolution (Raiffa 1982; Schelling 1960).

See also: Bargaining, Integrative and Distributive; Principled Negotiation and *Getting to Yes;* Territorial Conflicts.
References and Further Reading: Goldberg, Stephen B., Eric D. Green, and Frank E. A. Sander, 1985, *Dispute Resolution;* Raiffa, Howard, 1982, *The Art and Science of Negotiation;* Schelling, Thomas C., 1960, *Strategy of Conflict;* Fisher, Roger, and William Ury, 1981, *Getting to Yes* (2nd ed. with Bruce Patton, 1991).

Divorce Mediation

Divorce mediation is perhaps the best known and most used form of mediation in the United States. It began in the late 1950s, as increasing numbers of judges, lawyers, and families came to realize that the traditional adversarial process of divorce did not yield effective solutions to problems of child custody and visitation and tended to exacerbate tensions between couples rather than reduce them. In response to these concerns, many counties established what were called "domestic relations departments" to work with couples in what has now become known as the therapeutic mediation model. "This model emphasized a discussion of the marriage, the reasons for the divorce, exploration of the potential for reconciliation, and a focus on the future relationship between the couple" (Milne 1983, 22). In the 1970s, other mediators began focusing on the legal issues of divorce, and the first divorce mediation training programs were established. The field grew quickly; divorce mediation is now widely available and used nationwide.

Most observers believe that mediation of divorce is usually superior to adjudication, for a variety of reasons. First, it is a much more cooperative process that empowers the parties to solve their own problems rather than disempowering them, as the judicial process does. In mediation, the couple can work together cooperatively to define their interests and needs; they can develop solutions to issues of property division, child custody, and visitation that more nearly meet their needs than any solutions a court is likely to develop. Since the solution is better—and was developed by the parties themselves—they are more likely to abide by it than they are a court-imposed settlement. In addition, mediation is usually much quicker and less costly and tends to improve the relationship between the parties, enabling them to work together in the future (on continuing parenting or business issues, for example).

Divorce mediation typically takes several sessions, held over a period of weeks. At the beginning, the mediator explains the process and how it differs from court adjudication. He or she explains the ground rules and usually stresses the need for each side to retain legal counsel to advise them during the process and before a final settlement is signed. (This is necessary because mediators, even if they are lawyers, cannot dispense legal advice to mediation clients.)

The mediator then undertakes fact-finding: he or she gathers information about assets, liabilities, income, monthly budgets, property, and the like. This is documented by both sides and agreed on. The parties then go into the "softer" issues, such as child custody, visitation, and related issues. All the facts as well as the underlying emotional issues, are put on the table, discussed, and usually resolved. This differs greatly from legal adjudication, which tends to deal with only the essential legal aspects of the case and to ignore or even repress the emotional aspects of the situation. Thus, mediation allows for a more complete airing and resolution of the issues, which generally results in more compromise and more flexibility than does a court decision. Given the greater satisfaction of the parties, mediation tends to resolve more issues for a longer period than does legal adjudication.

Divorce mediation is not appropriate in all cases, however. It is not suitable in situations of abuse or when one party is at a great disadvantage in negotiating skills or power. It is also not suitable when one party simply seeks vengeance or refuses to listen or compromise. Problems also arise when one party wishes to prolong the relationship and thereby drags the mediation on forever in an effort to forestall the divorce. Despite these drawbacks, however, mediation is usually worth a try. Usually little is lost; if mediation fails, the parties are free to pursue court adjudication. Given the low cost and potential benefits, a number of states require divorcing parties to try mediation before adjudication, especially if issues of child custody are involved.

See also: Dispute Systems Design for Families; Family Conflict; Gender Conflict; Interpersonal Conflict; Mediation; Mediation and Therapy; Mediation Models; Power Balancing.

References and Further Reading: Burton, John, and Frank Dukes, 1990a, *Conflict: Practices in Management, Settlement and Resolution,* 38–44; Folberg, Jay, and Alison Taylor, 1984, *Mediation: A Comprehensive Guide to Resolving Conflicts without Litigation,* 147–89; Milne, A. L., 1983, "Divorce Mediation: The State of the Art"; Singer, Linda R., 1990, *Settling Disputes: Conflict Resolution in Business, Families, and the Legal System,* 31–56; Umbreit, Mark S., 1995, *Mediating Interpersonal Conflicts: A Pathway to Peace,* 87–113.

Domination Conflicts

Domination conflicts develop when one person, group, or nation tries to dominate another. Conflicts between siblings, schoolchildren, coworkers, racial groups, and nations often center on domination issues. Although it is not necessary for any one person or group to dominate the other, most social structures are based on domination-submission relationships.

According to a theory of domination-submission conflicts developed by Pat Patfoort (1995), these relationships tend to develop from individual differences that become linked with value judgments. Differences in race, culture, language, religion, job, income, housing, athletic ability, intellectual ability, gender, beauty, height, and weight become factors that are associated with goodness or badness. This gets translated into patterns of discrimination against the "inferior" person or group. Subordinate groups usually do not accept the validity of this discrimination, however. They fight to have their values predominate—to become the dominant group instead of the subordinate group. Thus, there is continuous conflict between dominant and subordinate individuals and groups—a continuous testing of status and a continuous attempt by the underdogs to turn the relationship upside down (Patfoort 1995).

As long as the energy in a conflict is directed toward developing or maintaining power over another, domination conflicts cannot be resolved. They will go on indefinitely, because one group (it doesn't matter which one) will always be on the bottom. The individual or group holding the bottom position may change over time, but as long as someone is on the bottom, the conflict will continue.

The only way to resolve domination conflicts is to change the structure of the relationship so that it becomes one of equals rather than unequals. Feminist theorists (and others) developed the idea of "power with" and "power to" as opposed to "power over." "Power with" is the power one develops by working collaboratively with one's opponent, and it gives one the "power to" solve the mutual problem. This is usually more successful, advocates claim, than continuing to strive for "power over," which just continues the domination-submission conflict indefinitely.

Although this makes good sense theoretically, it is often difficult to implement. Few individuals or groups in the dominant position are willing to relinquish that power, and few subordinate groups are willing to suggest an equal relationship rather than a reversal of roles. For that reason, domination conflicts tend to be highly intractable.

See also: Ethnic and Racial Conflicts; Intractable Conflicts; Power.
References and Further Reading: Patfoort, Pat, 1995, *Uprooting Violence: Building Nonviolence: From Nonviolent Upbringing to a Nonviolent Society.*

Due Process

Due process is the legal process guaranteed by the Fifth and Fourteenth Amendments to the U.S. Constitution. These amendments state that no person "shall be deprived of life, liberty, or property without due process of law." This guarantee applies to both civil and criminal rights. It ensures that public employees cannot be terminated without following a carefully defined process; nor can prisoners be disciplined or students expelled arbitrarily. Similarly, although the government can use the right of eminent domain to take private property that is needed for public use (for example, to build a road), the owner must be fairly compensated for the loss.

One of the unresolved issues in the dispute resolution field is whether alternatives to the traditional adversarial judicial system actually provide due process. Some critics claim that all the efforts to streamline the judicial process deny defendants their constitutional rights. Others believe that alternative dispute resolution actually protects those rights better than the courts, as they are more accessible, more participatory, and more efficient than the court system.

See also: Alternative Dispute Resolution; Alternative Dispute Resolution, Ethical Issues; Justice.
References and Further Reading: Matthews, Roger, 1988, *Informal Justice?;* Pennock, J. Roland, and John W. Chapman, 1977, *Due Process.*

Early Neutral Evaluation

Early neutral evaluation (ENE) is a court-annexed alternative dispute resolution (ADR) procedure. It was first used in the federal courts of the Northern District of California but is now used in many other federal and state courts as well. Private parties also use it.

ENE was originally intended to be a process that fell somewhere between mediation (in which discussion between parties is facilitated by a neutral third party) and nonbinding arbitration (in which a third party reviews the positions of the parties and recommends a particular outcome). It was intended to give each party an incentive to evaluate the strengths and weaknesses of his or her own case, focus on real areas of dispute, and develop efficacious approaches to discovery. It was also intended to give parties an early opportunity to negotiate a settlement. It has been found to be most useful in complex cases with multiple parties, a high level of animosity between parties, complex legal issues, many pretrial disputes, or liability that might exceed $50,000 (Dauer 1994, 13–21).

Cases can be selected for ENE in a variety of ways. ENE can be one of the ADR procedures available through a multidoor courthouse (a one-step intake center where disputants are referred to the most appropriate dispute resolution forum). It can be recommended by a judge or by one or both of the trial attorneys. Sometimes courts require that some form of ADR be used, and ENE is one of the choices offered. At other times the judge may specifically require that the parties use ENE before a case is tried in court.

After a case is chosen for ENE, a neutral party is appointed. Sometimes this appointment is made by a judge, but often the parties agree on the selection. The job of the neutral is to read about and listen to the facts of the case, recommend how the case can be streamlined through the justice system, and suggest how it might be settled.

Typically, each party writes a short position paper that outlines the fundamental facts of the case, emphasizing how the matter can be expedited. After the neutral considers these positions, he or she holds a hearing to discuss settlement possibilities and possible expediting procedures, should the case continue to trial. In one evaluation of ENE, it was found that in over 70 percent of the cases, "something good" happened (Dauer 1994, 13–21). This means that the case was settled or that the parties agreed to a more efficient approach to discovery or developed better-focused issues to be considered in the trial. In all, Dauer contends that ENE is low cost and low risk and often provides significant benefits.

See also: Court-Annexed Alternative Dispute Resolution Procedures; Tort Reform.
References and Further Reading: Dauer, Edward A., 1994, *Manual of Dispute Resolution;* Rosenberg, Joshua, and Jay H. Folberg, 1994, "Alternative Dispute Resolution: An Empirical Analysis."

Economic Conversion

One of the keys to successful peacemaking is a strategy for converting war-related industries to civilian production. Military conflicts are complicated activities that can be pursued only with the support of large-scale social institutions. They require large numbers of soldiers, sailors, and airmen, along with many civilians to provide military equipment and support services. Inevitably, these people become economically dependent on continuing confrontation and military tension. Even in peacetime, arms races have the same effect: jobs are generated by efforts to deter potential aggressors, and the arms race must be continued to maintain those jobs. The result is what President Dwight Eisenhower called the military-industrial complex—a group of people with a direct financial interest in continuing confrontation.

An important component of efforts to reduce military tensions is a workable mechanism for converting military institutions to peaceful applications. It is important that military forces see peace as an opportunity rather than as a threat to their economic well-being. This is what economic retraining programs try to do. Besides retraining, they involve job placement and efforts to help communities that are dependent on military installations. In addition to providing well-deserved help for those who protected the society during times of military confrontation, these programs reduce the risk that unemployed military forces, feeling abandoned by society, may turn against those they once protected (this latter risk is of special concern in the countries of the former Soviet Union).

See also: Arms Control and Disarmament.
References and Further Reading: Klein, Lawrence R., Fuchen Lo, and Warwick J. McKibbin, 1995, *Arms Reduction: Economic Implications in the Post–Cold War Era;* Melman, Seymour, 1970, *The Defense Economy: Conversion of Industries and Occupation Civilian Needs.*

Emotions in Conflict

Emotion is usually a major source—and outgrowth—of conflict. When people are in conflict, in addition to being angry, they may feel shame, confusion, fear, distrust, powerlessness, apprehension, or many other negative emotions. If these emotions are effectively managed by the parties themselves or by a mediator, they can contribute to conflict resolution. If they are not effectively managed, they can feed back into the conflict, heightening tensions and causing further escalation and possibly stalemate.

In their classic book *Getting to Yes,* Roger Fisher and William Ury (1981, 17) urge disputants to "separate the people from the problem." The intent of this suggestion is to get people to focus on the substantive aspects of the problem they share, rather than on their anger with one another. This encourages a rational approach to joint problem solving rather than an emotional approach, which may heighten tensions and make problem solving more difficult.

However, complete suppression of emotions can be frustrating to disputants who, rightly or wrongly, see emotions as being a central part of the problem. If emotions are truly a central part of the conflict, any dispute settlement process that suppresses or ignores the emotional component will likely be ineffective. A process such as transformative mediation, which deals directly with relationships and emotions, or analytic problem solving, which deals directly with deep-rooted feelings and needs, is a more appropriate approach. But even these approaches cannot be started until emotions are brought under control to some extent. For example, if a conflict has erupted into violence, the violence must be stopped and emotions cooled down somewhat before any effective conflict resolution process can be started.

If emotions are not a central part of the conflict but an outcome, they can often be addressed (or suppressed) within the context of problem-solving mediation. Often mediators allow parties to "vent" their emotions early in a mediation session—either privately with the mediator or openly to the opposition. Such venting can have several beneficial effects: it can clarify to the mediator and to the opposition how strongly something has affected the other party or how strongly he or she feels about a situation; it also help the disputants release pent-up frustrations and have the satisfaction of at least being "heard." But venting is also dangerous. It can easily increase tensions, make the opponent excessively defensive or hostile, and detract from a constructive, problem-solving atmosphere. Gary Hankins, an expert on anger and anger management, cites several research studies that found that letting anger out just makes people more angry. "Letting it out isn't purging, it is practicing" (Hankins 1988, 265). This suggests that venting has the potential of increasing the anger of the person venting as well as that of the opponent.

Certainly, if it is going to be tried, venting must be done carefully, to prevent it from escalating a conflict further. Often it helps to establish ground rules for communication—prohibiting direct personal attacks or name-calling, for example—to try to limit the escalation of emotions. Mediators can also reframe statements to make them less volatile and to facilitate interpersonal understanding after emotional outbursts. Humor can also help defuse an emotional situation, getting parties to relax after a difficult interchange.

Sometimes, mediators choose to suppress emotions by asking the parties to focus on the substantive problem, not on their negative feelings about the opponent. They may even keep the parties separate and use shuttle diplomacy, in which the mediator carries messages back and forth between the parties, not bringing them together until their emotions have been brought under control.

See also: Anger and Anger Management; Cooling-off Period; Escalation; Mediation; Mediation Models; Problem Solving, Analytical; Venting Anger.

References and Further Reading: Burton, John, 1987, *Resolving Deep-Rooted Conflict: A Handbook;* Carpenter,

Susan L., and W. J. D. Kennedy, 1988, *Managing Public Disputes;* Fisher, Roger, and William Ury, 1981, *Getting to Yes* (2nd ed. with Bruce Patton, 1991); Hankins, Gary, 1988, *Prescription for Anger;* Montville, Joseph, 1993, "The Healing Function in Political Conflict Resolution"; Moore, Christopher W., 1986, *The Mediation Process;* Olczak, Paul V., and Dean G. Pruitt, 1995, "Beyond Hope: Approaches to Resolving Seemingly Intractable Conflict."

Empathy

Empathy is the ability to understand and reflect the emotions and feelings of others. The ability to feel and express empathy toward an opponent can go a long way toward managing one's own and one's opponent's anger as well as resolving the conflict that promoted the anger. Gary Hankins urges people to manage their anger by trying to show respect and empathy for their opponents. The more willing they are to meet the needs and desires of others, and the less concerned they are about constantly gratifying themselves, the better people can control their own anger and resolve conflicts that tend to be anger provoking (Hankins 1988).

Empathy is particularly important in deep-rooted, needs-based conflicts, in which feelings of identity, security, and recognition are often central. Jay Rothman advocates problem-solving workshops as a means of encouraging disputants to develop both "emotional empathy" and "analytic empathy." Emotional empathy is what happens when "parties come to identify with each other and with each other's hurts, hopes, and fears." Analytic empathy goes further, to the point that parties "come to understand the power and the depth of their adversaries' motivation, hurts, hopes and fears" (Rothman 1992, 20–21). They may not believe that these feelings are rational or correct, but with analytic empathy, they will realize that these beliefs are real and that they will have to meet the needs of the other side in order to get their own needs met. Thus, analytic empathy leads to an understanding of the interdependence of adversaries. This helps guide disputants away from positional or interest-based bargaining and toward collaborative problem solving and integrative solutions to mutual problems.

Showing empathy is also an important skill for mediators. Mediators must become sensitized to their own feelings as well as to the feelings of others and become proficient at active listening, an approach that reframes statements in terms of feelings. This legitimates the feelings expressed in a mediation session and helps parties better deal with those feelings as well as with the substantive aspects of the dispute.

See also: Active Listening; Framing; Needs; Problem Solving, Analytical; Transformation.
References and Further Reading: Folberg, Jay, and Alison Taylor, 1984, *Mediation: A Comprehensive Guide to Resolving Conflicts without Litigation,* 74–99; Hankins, Gary, 1988, *Prescription for Anger;* Rothman, Jay, 1992, *Confrontation to Cooperation: Resolving Ethnic and Regional Conflict.*

Empowerment

The term *empowerment* is used in several related but different ways. In all cases, it means giving a party more power in a conflict. How this is done, however, varies. One approach to empowerment is community organizing and advocacy assistance. In this situation, a person (often a lawyer or community organizer) works with one side in a conflict to help that party define its goals, interests, and conflict strategy. The advocacy adviser helps disputants obtain the technical information they need, raise money or obtain other necessary resources, form coalitions, negotiate, lobby, litigate, or campaign more effectively for their position. By doing these things, the disputants are empowered to act more effectively on their own behalf.

A second approach is similar but is done by a mediator in the context of a mediation session. Knowing that mediation works better and results in better outcomes when the parties have roughly equal amounts of power, mediators often help empower the lower-power party to achieve a balance of power at the negotiating table. This can be done overtly, by giving the lower-power party more assistance than the other party is given, or it can be done covertly by manipulating who talks when, what is discussed when, or which options are emphasized and which are ignored, thereby giving more attention to the interests of the lower-power side.

This type of empowerment can cause ethical problems for both the mediator and the parties to the mediation process, as it is difficult for a mediator to empower one side yet remain neutral and impartial. Despite this difficulty, however, many mediators feel comfortable taking this empowerment role when one party is clearly at a disadvantage in the negotiations.

A third approach to empowerment is that advocated by R. Baruch Bush and Joseph Folger (1994), who call for the empowerment of both parties through transformative mediation. Unlike problem-solving mediation, which focuses on dispute resolution as the ultimate goal, transformative mediation focuses on empowerment and recognition. Empowerment, in this sense, means restoring disputants' "sense of their own value and strength and their own capacity to handle life's problems" (Bush and Folger 1994, 2). Transformative mediation is a technique designed to do this as well as to encourage the parties to recognize or empathize with the situation or problem that the opponent faces. Often such empowerment and recognition lead to resolution, but not always. In either case, however, it encourages the transformation of the relationship and the personal growth of the parties involved.

See also: Advocacy; Mediation, Ethical Issues; Mediation Models; Power; Power Balancing; Transformation.
References and Further Reading: Bush, Robert A. Baruch, and Joseph P. Folger, 1994, *Promise of Mediation.*

Enemy Image

The term *enemy image* refers to the negative stereotypes that individuals and groups commonly have of their opponents. The opposing group is seen as unremittingly evil—capable of no good intentions or acts. At the same time, one usually views oneself as entirely good; any negative acts are caused by pressures brought about by the enemy.

Psychologists attribute such assumptions to what they call "projection." Projection is a way of increasing one's self-esteem by taking one's own undesirable characteristics (e.g., aggression or selfishness) and projecting them onto the opponent (Rothman 1992, 16). This raises one's own self-image and, in the case of groups, increases group cohesion and identity. The cost, however, is the continuation or even escalation of the conflict, which can have destructive results.

When Anwar al-Sadat (then president of Egypt) traveled to Jerusalem in 1977, he gave a speech to the Israeli Knesset, saying that although some walls between Egypt and Israel had begun to fall, "there remains another wall . . . a psychological barrier between us, a barrier of suspicion, a barrier of rejection; a barrier of fear, of deception, a barrier of hallucination without any action, deed or decision" (quoted in Rothman 1992, 16). This psychological wall, Sadat said, constituted 70 percent of the problem. Although Sadat was referring to the conflict between Israel and Egypt, he could have been describing the conflict between Israel and the Palestinians; between the Tutsis and the Hutus in Rwanda, Burundi, and Zaire; or between the Turks and the Greeks on Cyprus. Enemy images—which cause fear and insecurity—are the driving force among ethnic groups locked in destructive conflicts around the world.

See also: Camp David Accords (Israeli and Egyptian); Communal Conflicts; Ethnic and Racial Conflicts; Stereotyping.

References and Further Reading: Rothman, Jay, 1992, *Confrontation to Cooperation: Resolving Ethnic and Regional Conflict;* Volkan, Vamik, 1985, "The Need to Have Enemies and Allies."

Environmental Conflicts

Environmental disputes and conflicts involve public policy questions about human interaction with the natural environment. Examples include disputes over air and water quality, biodiversity, outdoor recreation, natural hazards, toxic chemicals, public lands management, and land use. Often these conflicts focus on management of the commons—resources that belong to the society as a whole and not just to a few private individuals (such as air, water, and public lands). As such, these conflicts tend to focus on the activities of a number of governmental institutions—such as the National Park Service, the Forest Service, the Bureau of Land Management, and the Environmental Protection Agency at the federal level, and similar agencies and organizations at the state and local levels—that are responsible for environmental protection.

Because the commons belong to everyone, environmental conflicts often involve large numbers of well-organized interest groups as well as ad hoc citizens groups that are organized to deal with specific situations. As a result, these disputes tend to involve large numbers of parties, each pursuing different interests and strategies. When one or more groups pursue a rights- or power-based approach (by litigating or seeking political action), the dispute can become protracted and expensive.

Environmental conflicts have additional characteristics that make their resolution especially challenging. For example, disputes frequently concern dangers that cannot be directly perceived by the general public. For example, most toxic materials can be detected only by experts using sophisticated equipment. Further, the health and environmental impacts of these materials can be determined only by complex scientific studies that often contain a lot of uncertainty. Adding to the confusion, competing experts make contradictory statements regarding the nature and severity of the problem. Members of the general public, and often decision makers as well, have no way of knowing whom to believe.

The nature of environmental problems often requires that corrective actions be taken before the full extent of the problem is readily apparent. Otherwise, the remedy will be ineffective or vastly more expensive. (An example is the avoidance of the greenhouse effect. If we wait to respond until we know for sure that it is happening, it will be too late. If we make substantial changes in our fossil fuel use now, we may be severely hampering our lifestyle and economy for a problem that does not really exist.)

In addition, environmental disputes frequently involve deep moral disagreements concerning the appropriate relationship between humans and nature. Although some people believe that humans have a right, or even an obligation, to exploit the natural world for their own benefit, others think that we have an obligation to protect the environment from human intrusion. Like other moral disagreements, these fundamental value differences make compromise difficult.

Over the last several decades, more and more agencies have been trying to avoid environmental standoffs by implementing a variety of consensus decision-making processes: negotiated rulemaking, permitting, and enforcement, for example. The Environmental Protection Agency has been one of the leaders in implementing negotiated rulemaking, a process whereby all the potentially affected parties develop new agency rules regarding environmental protection through a consensus-based process that tries to meet everyone's interests and

needs. This approach has been highly successful in preventing lawsuits over new regulations and has improved compliance with regulatory decisions as well. The U.S. Forest Service has also had considerable success in utilizing consensus building to draft and implement forest management plans that simultaneously meet the needs of a diverse set of forest users.

See also: Citizens' Radiation Monitoring Program; Collaborative Problem Solving; Montreal Protocol on Substances that Deplete the Ozone Layer; National Coal Policy Project; Negotiated Rulemaking at the Maine Department of Transportation; NIMBY, LULU, and NOPE; Public Policy Conflicts; Scientific and Technical Disputes.
References and Further Reading: Carpenter, Susan L., and W. J. D. Kennedy, 1988, *Managing Public Disputes;* Susskind, Lawrence, and Jeffrey Cruikshank, 1987, *Breaking the Impasse.*

Escalation

Escalation is an increase in the intensity of a conflict. Although escalation is often unintentional, conflicts can escalate very quickly, changing from relatively minor disputes to bitter confrontations. Unfortunately, de-escalation is usually much harder to achieve.

According to Dean Pruitt and Jeffrey Rubin, five changes are typical as a conflict escalates. First, the parties' tactics change from ones that are relatively light and inoffensive to ones that are heavier and more confrontational. Second, the number of issues in conflict tends to increase. A conflict may start out focused on one issue, but as it escalates, the parties bring more and more grievances into debate. Third, the focus of the conflict changes from specific to more global concerns. Fourth, more and more parties get involved. People take sides, form coalitions, and seek allies. Fifth, parties change from wanting to win for their own sake to wanting to beat the other. In very escalated conflicts, the disputants can get to the point where their primary goal is to bring harm to the opponent rather than to gain victory for themselves (Pruitt and Rubin 1986, 7–8).

The Cold War between the United States and the Soviet Union was a prime example of an escalated conflict. During World War II, the two countries were allies. This cooperation broke down shortly after the end of the war when Joseph Stalin, distrustful of the West and seeking Soviet security, sought to impose communist governments on the surrounding Eastern European countries. The United States saw this communist expansion as a threat and countered with the Marshall Plan (a light tactic designed to strengthen the economies of Western European democracies) and an effort to rebuild and unify West Germany. These moves further threatened the Soviets, who had been at war with Germany twice in the previous 30 years and who therefore wanted Germany to remain permanently weak. The USSR responded first with protest (a light tactic), then with minor provocative acts, and then with a full blockade of Berlin (a heavy tactic). The United States staged the Berlin airlift to free Berlin from Soviet control (certainly an assertive tactic) and formed the North Atlantic Treaty Organization (NATO), which eventually led to the rearmament of West Germany (a very heavy tactic). Throughout this time, and almost continuously until 1989, "issues proliferated, the parties became increasingly absorbed in the struggle; more and more elements of the relationship between the superpowers were affected; and goals changed from self-advancement to subverting the adversary" (Pruitt and Rubin 1986, 88–89).

Escalation can happen just as easily in interpersonal disputes—between siblings or married couples, for example. In all cases, a minor event gets blown out of proportion and ends up becoming a major, protracted conflict.

Several factors contribute to escalation. Among these is the tendency to respond to a conflict of interest in a competitive way. Typically, if both parties to a conflict are competitive, they will start by applying light tactics but will likely increase the intensity of the tactics to heavier and heavier ones—in part in an effort to defend themselves, and in part in an effort to win—until one of them is able to prevail.

Several conflict theorists refer to this process as a "conflict spiral." Susan Carpenter and W. J. D. Kennedy (1988) describe the process of conflict spiral as it commonly occurs in a public policy dispute. Typically, after a problem develops, people take sides, their positions harden, dialogue stops, and perceptions get distorted. The conflict moves beyond the initial parties and issues to involve more and more people and interest groups and to require increased resource and time commitments on all sides. At early stages of conflict, before the intensity increases, citizens group activities include telephone calls, letter writing, and informal meetings. Once the conflict escalates, however, citizens groups form coalitions, more radical or militant leaders take over, and tactics become more confrontational, including litigation, nonviolent direct action, or even violence.

Although conflicts escalate very quickly, de-escalation is much more difficult. Parties do not want to back down for fear of looking weak, so they tend to maintain their provocative positions or escalate the conflict further, even when they realize that they cannot win. Often, de-escalation is possible only after a damaging stalemate—a situation in which both sides have been locked in a costly struggle for a long time. Eventually, one or both parties are likely to conclude that continuing the dispute costs more than it is worth, and one or both will take steps (with or without the help of a third party) to de-escalate the dispute and eventually settle it.

See also: Anger and Anger Management; Cold War; Cooling-off Period; Crisis Management; De-escalation.

References and Further Reading: Carpenter, Susan L., and W. J. D. Kennedy, 1988, *Managing Public Disputes;* Pruitt, Dean G., and Jeffrey Z. Rubin, 1986, *Social Conflict.*

Ethnic and Racial Conflicts

Ethnic and racial conflicts are conflicts between individuals and/or groups that are stimulated primarily by group membership and differential treatment based on that group membership. Thus, in addition to sharing certain physical and cultural traits, racial and ethnic groups are seen as politically, socially, and psychologically different and thus worthy of different treatment. Examples include conflicts between whites and people of color within the United States; conflicts between the Serbs, Croats, and Muslims in the Balkans; the conflict between the Tutsis and the Hutus in Burundi and Rwanda; and the conflict between the Turks and the Greeks on Cyprus.

Current Upsurge in Ethnic Conflicts

Although such conflicts have been going on throughout human history, racial and ethnic conflicts have become particularly prominent in the 1990s, following the end of the Cold War. According to John McDonald, in the three years following the fall of the Berlin Wall (November 1989), the world suffered 82 violent conflicts that killed over 1,000 people each. Three of these were international wars; the other 79 were intrastate racial or ethnic conflicts (McDonald 1995, 2).

McDonald attributes this rise to a number of factors: "people's loss of identity, loss of language, religion and customs, poverty, starvation, overpopulation, lack of water, other environmental issues, etc." But he emphasizes the loss of other forms of political organization that tended to suppress many of these conflicts. In the early 1900s, he points out, most of the world was dominated by great empires: the Ottoman and Austro-Hungarian Empires (which collapsed after World War I), the Japanese Empire (gone after World War II), and the British, French, Dutch, Bel-

gian, and Portuguese Empires, all of which disappeared between 1945 and 1975. Finally in 1992 the Soviet Empire collapsed. "Most current ethnic conflicts were generated by policies established during the days of Empire. Today there is no power available to keep the lid on the pot, so it boils over, and people get burned" (McDonald 1995, 2).

Intractability of Ethnic Conflicts

Ethnic and racial conflicts tend to be difficult to manage or resolve for a variety of reasons. First, these conflicts affect both personal and group identities as well as interests and worldviews. Thus, they are extremely complex and deep rooted. Threats to a group are direct threats to each member of the group. Further, threats to an individual's identity are as fundamental—and serious—as any threat that can be made. Such threats cannot be ignored but will be resisted and countered in all ways possible, because identity is a fundamental human need.

Second, ethnic and racial conflicts are characterized by ethnocentrism—the process of group identification through which groups define themselves as "good" and outsiders as "bad." Although such processes lead to group cohesion and increased internal effectiveness, they escalate conflicts with outside groups, who are almost always considered to be inferior, if not less than human. This bias leads people to perceive any actions of outsiders as malevolent. Even conciliatory actions are likely to be interpreted as "tricks," not real efforts at peace building. Further, groups tend to assume that outsiders' hostile actions are caused by the outsiders' bad character, not the situation they are faced with or a deviant individual who does not represent the group as a whole.

Third, racial and ethnic conflicts tend to perpetuate themselves. Individual and group identities become so intertwined with the conflict that maintaining the conflict is often considered safer than pursuing peace. People who pursue peace are seen as traitors to the cause. Further, conciliatory gestures are often thought to be too risky, as they might signal weakness or the intention to give in.

Also problematic is the fact that racial and ethnic conflicts tend to create what Joseph Montville calls a "psychology of victimhood." One side believes that it has been the victim of violent and traumatic aggression that was completely unjustified. Even if this aggression has stopped, the fear remains that the aggressor might strike again. Often this sense of victimhood exists on both sides. This is true with the Palestinians and the Israelis; the Serbs, Muslims, and Croats in the former Yugoslavia; and the Catholics and Protestants in Northern Ireland. In these situations, neither side is willing to make peace until restitution is given for past atrocities, but after a while, this becomes impossible (Montville 1993, 113).

Management and Resolution of Ethnic Conflicts

In addition to the problems listed above, ethnic conflicts are hard to manage or resolve because there are no institutions empowered to do so. The United Nations (UN) is empowered to intervene in international conflicts—conflicts between two sovereign nation-states—but it is not empowered to intervene within one state, unless specifically requested to do so by the government. Usually the government does not make such a request; governments want to handle internal affairs themselves. Even when the UN does intervene with peacekeepers, these forces are at best able stop the killing; they cannot force the parties to resolve the conflict or implement a lasting peace.

Recognizing the limitations of the UN in these matters, Secretary-General Boutros Boutros-Ghali issued a report in 1995 called *An Agenda for Peace,* which urged the UN and its member states to reconsider the nature and the role of sovereignty in the "new world order." In order to effectively deal with burgeoning racial and ethnic conflicts, Boutros-Ghali called for three activities to supplement the UN's traditional peacekeeping role: preventive diplomacy—efforts to prevent disputes from arising or from escalating; peacemaking—conflict resolution efforts to bring hostile parties to agreement; and postconflict peace building—efforts to rebuild war-torn societies both economically and socially.

A number of experts suggest that ethnic conflicts can be resolved only if the parties and intermediaries change their focus from reconciling interests to identifying and meeting fundamental human needs—most notably security and identity—which are at the root of almost all racial and ethnic conflicts. The most common way to do this is through problem-solving workshops—a setting in which unofficial representatives of all parties sit down together with a panel of scholars to analyze the root causes of their conflict and then identify ways that these root causes can be addressed. This usually involves a process of reconciliation (acknowledgment of one's own past errors and the forgiveness of the errors made by the other side) as well as structural and procedural changes designed to recognize and meet the identity and security needs of all sides.

Although most international conflict experts agree on the need for all these activities, few see any of them as a panacea. Many ethnic conflicts remain intractable, despite all efforts. The best that can be hoped for, in many cases, is the management of the conflict so that it remains below violent levels and a continuing effort to address individual dispute episodes in ways that resolve the problem fairly for the parties involved.

See also: Conflict and Dispute; Dispute Systems Design for Schools; Identity Conflicts; Israeli-Palestinian Women's Workshop; Montgomery Bus Boycott; Peace Building; Peacekeeping; Peacemaking; Problem Solving, Analytical. *References and Further Reading:* Boutros-Ghali, Boutros, 1995, *An Agenda for Peace;* McDonald, John W., 1995, "Why Ethnic Conflict?"; Montville, Joseph, 1993, "The Healing Function in Political Conflict Resolution"; Ross, Marc Howard, 1992, "Ethnic Conflict and Dispute Management: Addressing Interests and Identities, Getting to an Accord."

Face Saving

Face saving involves maintaining a positive self-image. Often conflict or conflict resolution processes can threaten this self-image, especially if one side is forced to admit that it was at fault or is weaker than the other side. The threat of loss of face alone can prevent a conflict from being resolved.

To avoid this problem, it is important to allow one's opponents to make concessions without appearing to have backed down. Just by changing the wording in an agreement (but not the substance), one can often make it seem fair and avoid the image that anyone has "lost." Negotiation expert William Ury (1991, 105) suggests, "go slow to go fast." By this he means don't try to get everything at once; rather, follow a slow, step-by-step process. If the opponent resists such a process, don't push too hard. Don't ask for a final commitment until all the benefits and safeguards are laid out on the table. Then the opponent can focus on what he or she has gained, not on what he or she has lost. This allows opponents to respect themselves (for their own negotiating skills) and present a strong face to their constituents. Power is useless "if it drives your opponent into a corner and makes him resist you with all his might. Leaving him a way out is a time-honored precept" (Ury 1991, 128).

Ury also stresses that opponents should be allowed to feel as satisfied as possible at the end of any negotiation. "Although you may feel elated at your success," he says, "don't crow. In the wake of the Cuban Missile Crisis, President Kennedy issued strict instructions to his Cabinet officers not to claim victory. He did not want to make it harder for Premier Khrushchev to justify to his comrades his decision to withdraw the missiles." In other words, he wanted to leave Khrushchev a way out, a way to save face before his comrades. Had he not done this, Khrushchev likely would have refused to remove the missiles at all, and as recent documents have shown, we could easily have been facing nuclear war (Ury 1991, 134).

See also: Cuban Missile Crisis; I-Messages; Negotiation, Breakthrough; Negotiation Strategy.
References and Further Reading: Ury, William, 1991, *Getting Past No: Negotiating with Difficult People.*

Facilitation

Facilitation is a form of assisted negotiation, similar to mediation. Mediation, however, usually involves only a few (often two) parties, whereas facilitation typically is used for multiparty meetings or consensus-building processes. Like a mediator, the facilitator focuses on the meeting or negotiation process, not on the substance. The facilitator works with the parties to make sure that all the appropriate parties are at the table, and he or she helps the group establish and enforce ground rules and an agenda. The facilitator uses active listening to ensure that each speaker is understood and sees that every participant is given a chance to speak. Often, facilitators record what is said on large pieces of newsprint, which is displayed prominently in the meeting room. This keeps a public record of the discussion, which helps people better focus on the agenda and see areas of common ground. (Some facilitators have an assistant, called a recorder, who keeps the written record of the proceedings, allowing the facilitator to attend more completely to the discussion.) Unlike many mediators who make substantive suggestions, facilitators usually limit themselves to regulating the process. Facilitators also usually work with all the parties face-to-face, whereas mediators frequently rely on caucuses with individual parties and even shuttle diplomacy to bring about an agreement.

Facilitators commonly run meetings within one organization as well as consensus-building processes among many parties. A panel of facilitators is used to conduct analytic problem-solving workshops, held to help those involved in deep-rooted, intractable conflicts focus on the core issues of their conflict and identify ways to change the social, economic, and/or political structure to better meet the needs of all the parties involved.

See also: Collaborative Problem Solving; Mediation; Problem Solving, Analytical.

References and Further Reading: Burton, John, 1987, *Resolving Deep-Rooted Conflict: A Handbook;* Doyle, Michael, and David Straus, 1976, *How to Make Meetings Work: The New Interaction Method;* Schwarz, Roger M., 1994, *The Skilled Facilitator: Practical Wisdom for Developing Effective Groups;* Strauss, David, 1993, "Facilitated Collaborative Problem Solving."

Fact-Based Disputes

Disputes often involve factual disagreements that can potentially be resolved by independent objective analysis. In such fact-based disputes, the disagreement centers around perceptions and judgments about something that happened in the past, a current condition, or a potential fu-

ture event. For example, two roommates may disagree about who paid last month's rent and who didn't (a past event). Teachers might disagree about the amount of homework to give students because they don't agree on how many other assignments and commitments their students have (a current condition). Neighbors might disagree about supporting a new housing development because they have different perceptions of the likely effects that such a development would have on their own property values (a future event).

In many cases, these kinds of disputes can be completely resolved through joint fact-finding. The landlord can be contacted to confirm who paid the rent, or a canceled check can be produced. The teachers can survey their students to find out how much time they are spending on homework and how many other afternoon and evening commitments they have. Neighbors can hire an expert consultant to help them assess the likely effect of a new subdivision on their own property values.

Other factual disputes are not so easily handled. Many scientific or technical disputes involve issues with a high degree of uncertainty. For example, scientists seldom agree about the level of risk related to hazardous materials or the best way to accomplish environmental protection. Some scientists are conservative, saying that any risk is too much and that any decisions made should keep the risk as close to zero as possible. Others are much less concerned; they believe that the benefits of commercial and industrial activities are much greater than the small potential risks that might occur as side effects. Thus, they tend to downplay any hazards from toxic emissions or waste disposal.

Although there are no firm scientific answers to such questions, a variety of techniques has been developed to resolve such disputes sufficiently to make a decision. Science courts, data mediation, joint fact-finding, and neutral expert fact-finding are all techniques designed to address such scientific or technical questions and to develop answers that are sufficiently credible to both sides that they can be used as a basis of decision.

See also: Citizens' Radiation Monitoring Program; Joint Fact-Finding; National Coal Policy Project; Neutral Expert Fact-Finding; Risk and Uncertainty; Scientific and Technical Disputes.

References and Further Reading: Cormick, Gerald W., and Alana Knaster, 1986, "Mediation and Scientific Issues: Oil and Fishing Industries Negotiate"; O'Brien, David M., 1987, *What Is Due Process? Courts and Science-Policy Disputes;* Susskind, Lawrence, and Jeffrey Cruikshank, 1987, *Breaking the Impasse;* Tillett, Gregory, 1991, *Resolving Conflict: A Practical Approach,* 136–44.

Falkland Islands (Malvinas) Conflict

The conflict between Great Britain and Argentina over the Falkland Islands dates back to the 1700s, when both Britain and Spain claimed sovereignty over the region. In the early 1800s, Argentina became independent from Spain and claimed the Falklands (which the Argentinean government called the Malvinas). The British did not recognize this claim and, in 1833, sent two warships to take the islands by force. The British were successful, and the islands have been inhabited by about 2,000 British colonists ever since.

Although Argentina continued its formal claim over the islands, it did nothing to confront the issue again until the mid-1960s, when anticolonial movements were growing worldwide. Given this impetus, Argentina renewed its claim to the Malvinas and was able to get the United Nations (UN) to pass a resolution in 1965 that called for negotiations toward a "peaceful solution to the problem" (Schellenberg 1996, 119). Negotiations began in 1966.

According to James Schellenberg, early discussions "appeared to assume an eventual transfer of the Falklands to Argentine sovereignty" (1996, 120). However, negotiations dragged on for years without significant progress. In 1973, Juan Perón came to

power in Argentina and asserted Argentinean claims over the Malvinas once again. When Margaret Thatcher was elected prime minister of Britain in 1979, she too took a harder stand on the sovereignty issue than had her predecessor and was spurred on by the Falkland population, which made it clear that they wanted to remain under British rule.

In 1981, a new military triumvirate came to power in Argentina and made Malvinas sovereignty a high priority. On 2 April 1982, the Argentine military launched a full-scale invasion of the Malvinas, quickly forcing the small British army unit to surrender. The UN quickly called for Argentina to withdraw, but it refused. The British again sent warships to the area and began their own invasion on 21 May. Fierce fighting continued for over three weeks involving 39,000 men. Britain finally prevailed but suffered over 1,000 casualties (255 dead and 777 wounded). The Argentineans reported 652 men dead or missing.

Although armed conflict has not occurred again, the sovereignty issue is not considered resolved by either side, and normal relations between the two countries is still elusive. Immediately after the war, both Britain and Argentina made conciliatory gestures designed to reduce tensions. Representatives of the two governments met off and on with mediators, but the sovereignty issue has never been successfully confronted. Part of the problem, according to C. R. Mitchell, is that neither side took the concessions of the other seriously. "Unfortunately, in each case, the target of the conciliatory gesture seemed clearly not to perceive the initiative in question as genuine and worthy of direct reciprocation" (Mitchell 1991, 411). For example, in 1985, the British unilaterally announced the end of their ban on Argentine imports. Although this benefited Argentina, it also benefited the British economy. Thus, it was not seen as a significant concession and was not reciprocated. Likewise, in November 1986, Argentina offered to "establish the formal ending of hostilities" with Great Britain (Mitchell 1991, 415). The offer was rejected by Britain, however, which believed it to be "a cunning attempt to lure Britain into discussions about sovereignty by indirect means" (Mitchell 1991, 415). The standoff still continues over a decade later, clearly illustrating that force rarely solves a problem once and for all but only temporarily settles a dispute (sometimes at great cost), leaving the underlying conflict to continue to smolder until "fire" breaks out again sometime in the future.

See also: Conflict and Dispute; International Conflict.
References and Further Reading: Mitchell, C. R., 1991, "A Willingness to Talk: Conciliatory Gestures and De-Escalation"; Schellenberg, James A., 1996, *Conflict Resolution—Theory, Research, and Practice.*

Family Conflict

Although some families try to repress conflict, family conflict is ubiquitous. No matter how much love and caring exists between family members, whenever two or more people live together and depend on each other as much as most family members do, conflicts are inevitable. However, these conflicts need not be destructive. If conducted in a respectful and caring way, conflict can help family members understand one another better; it can help create more effective means of interaction; and it can allow spouses, parents, or siblings to negotiate solutions to problems that meet everyone's needs. Alternatively, family conflict can be very destructive, both to the individuals and to the relationships.

Families that deal with conflict in constructive ways usually communicate openly about their disagreements in a respectful and accommodating way. Although they may not have read Fisher, Ury, and Patton's book *Getting to Yes,* they tend to follow their rules for negotiating: separating the people from the problem

and trying to meet everyone's interests and needs, not just demanding their own way with no concern for others. Conflict in these families tends to be limited to specific situations and is generally resolved in a way that allows the disputants to feel that their needs were met (at least as much as possible) and that their relationship with the other is maintained or even strengthened.

Families locked into destructive conflict tend to do the opposite. They focus on personalities as much as or even more than on issues, acting as if the people, not the issues, are the problem. They use positional bargaining—insisting that one side win at the expense of the other. They tend to try to overpower the opponent by using manipulation, threats, deception, or even violence. Conflicts in these families tend to continue over time, often stuck in repeating, destructive patterns that push people further and further apart rather than bringing them closer together.

Although these dynamics can be present in other kinds of conflicts, several factors make family conflict different from other kinds of conflict. First, the parties are already highly emotionally engaged; therefore, family conflicts can become intense very quickly. Second, the parties are involved in a long-term relationship, whether they want to be or not. Parents are always parents, children are always children, siblings are always siblings, regardless of whether they live together. The relationship between family members is permanent, although the nature of the relationship will change. Third, families generally operate by their own rules and resent and resist outside interference. Whether they operate by consensus building and negotiation or by the power of one or both parents over the rest of the family, these patterns tend to be strongly ingrained. When they are dissatisfied, observes Linda Singer (1990, 31), "family members often take the law into their own hands. Unhappy teenagers defy parental authority or run away. Separated parents deny visiting rights to ex-spouses or fail to pay court-ordered child support." Thus, even the legal system, when it tries to intervene in family disputes, is often unsuccessful in bringing about a lasting resolution. For this reason, more families have been turning to alternative dispute resolution—especially mediation—to help them deal with family issues that they cannot resolve themselves.

Conflicts between Husbands and Wives

When mediators speak of family conflict, most often they are referring to conflict between husbands and wives. Although the vast majority of such conflicts are resolved amicably between the parties themselves, a significant number of couples turn to outsiders for assistance either in managing or resolving their conflict or in dissolving the marriage. Family therapists work with partners individually and with couples together to try to improve their interpersonal communication, understanding, and trust. Mediators also work on such issues, but much of their work involves helping couples negotiate the terms of divorce. Relatively rare in the 1960s, divorce mediation has become increasingly common as lawyers, judges, and clients have come to realize that the highly formal and adversarial process typical of the courts fails to adequately resolve many of the relationship issues tied up with divorce. Mediation provides a friendlier, more flexible process that allows the parties to develop solutions for themselves that usually meet their needs better than do solutions imposed by a court. In addition, mediation is more empowering to the parties, enabling them to take control of their own lives rather than putting such monumental decisions as child custody in the hands of a stranger who does not know any of the people involved.

Divorce mediation is not appropriate for all couples, however. When there has been abuse or when one party is much stronger than the other, mediation may yield an unfair result. Mediation is also inappropriate when one side wants to prove the other side wrong and is seeking vengeance as much as a resolution.

Parent-Child Conflicts

Also ubiquitous are parent-child conflicts, which are characterized by a discrepancy of power between the parties—at least when the children are relatively small. However, children quickly learn that they have more power than they think, and they can get locked into power struggles with their parents in which no one wins. Different parenting experts have different solutions to such problems, but most advocate firm rules when necessary and negotiation whenever possible. Just as in adult conflicts, if parents and children can listen respectfully to the other, attend to the interests and needs of the other, and work out a solution that meets everyone's needs, the conflict will probably be resolved constructively. But if the child and the parent try to outwit or overpower the other or, at the extreme, resort to violence to control the other, damage will be done to the individuals involved (especially the child) and to the relationship, over both the short and the long term.

Sibling Conflicts

One of parents' greatest frustrations is the constant conflicts born of sibling rivalry. These conflicts parallel couples' conflicts in that the power between siblings is closer to equal than it is in parent-child conflicts, but the rivalry between children is often greater than it is between adults, provoking conflicts more often. Again, parenting experts disagree on the best methods of controlling sibling conflicts, but most suggest that children be allowed to work out as many of their conflicts as possible themselves, rather than having the parents jump in all the time. This gives children experience in negotiating and problem solving that they would not get if the parents solved the children's problems. However, children must be taught the skills of negotiation and cooperative problem solving; they should not be left to battle it out with their siblings in whatever way seems to work.

See also: Divorce Mediation; Parent-Child Conflict; Principled Negotiation and *Getting to Yes.*
References and Further Reading: Fisher, Roger, and William Ury, 1981, *Getting to Yes* (2nd ed. with Bruce Patton, 1991); Rubin, Jeffrey Z., and Carol Rubin, 1988, *When Families Fight;* Singer, Linda R., 1990, *Settling Disputes: Conflict Resolution in Business, Families, and the Legal System,* 31–56.

Federal Arbitration Act

The Federal Arbitration Act (FAA) of 1947 authorizes federal and state courts to enforce contractual agreements to arbitrate. This federal law preempts the various state arbitration laws and so provides for more uniform enforceability of agreements to arbitrate. The FAA applies to all contracts "involving commerce." It states that written provisions in such commercial contracts to settle disputes by arbitration "shall be valid, irrevocable, and enforceable." The awards resulting from such arbitration are enforceable by court order. The FAA also provides arbiters in such cases with the power to subpoena witnesses and documents.

Enforcement of contractual agreements to arbitrate has become more vigorous since the mid-1980s. Legal alternative dispute resolution scholar Edward Dauer (1994, chap. 20, p. 1) observes, "While courts in the early part of the twentieth century were reluctant to enforce arbitration clauses for fear that they would be validating the ouster of their own jurisdiction, courts today have expressed what seems to be almost a preference for extrajudicial dispute resolution procedures."

See also: Arbitration; Arbitration, Commercial; Uniform Arbitration Act.
References and Further Reading: Dauer, Edward A., 1994, *Manual of Dispute Resolution.*

Federal Mediation and Conciliation Service

The Federal Mediation and Conciliation Service (FMCS) was established as an independent agency of the U.S. government by the Labor Management Relations Act in 1947 to preserve and promote "labor-management peace" (Federal Mediation and Conciliation Service 1995, 5). To do this, the FMCS provides mediation, arbitration, preventive mediation, education, and training in conflict resolution and collaborative processes to companies and unions in an effort to prevent or minimize conflicts between the two groups. In addition, the FMCS offers its expertise to local, state, and federal government agencies, with the goal of helping to resolve administrative disputes and regulatory controversies without litigation. The FMCS has also begun to offer its assistance to foreign governments, which are increasingly requesting training and technical assistance in effective industrial relations and cooperative labor management. In 1995, the FMCS trained almost 400 leaders from 85 countries in cooperation with other U.S. governmental agencies (the Departments of State and Labor, the Agency for International Development, and the U.S. Information Agency, for example).

See also: Collective Bargaining; Labor-Management Relations and Conflict.
References and Further Reading: Federal Mediation and Conciliation Service, 1995, *Transformation: Forty Eighth Annual Report.*

Federal Use of Alternative Dispute Resolution

The use of alternative dispute resolution (ADR) in the federal government has grown rapidly over the last 15 years, part of a growing acceptance and use of ADR in many sectors of U.S. society. ADR is used by the federal government in a variety of ways, both internally and externally. Internally, many agencies use ADR to resolve employee disputes through mediation, arbitration, and/or ombudsman offices. Many agencies also have in-house training of middle- and upper-level personnel in mediation and other dispute resolution processes. The intent is to provide employees with skills they can use to resolve disputes both within and outside their organizations. External uses of ADR include negotiated rulemaking, enforcement actions, the issuance and revocation of licenses or permits, and the settlement of litigation brought by or against federal agencies.

The Federal Aviation Administration was the first federal agency to use negotiated rulemaking (also called regulatory negotiation, or "reg-neg"), through which outside parties—those to be regulated, concerned interest groups, and the general public—can negotiate with the agency on the details of regulations to be issued. Although reg-neg is not always appropriate, most agencies that have implemented it have been pleased with the outcome. The rules issued are sound and are usually not challenged, which is uncommon with traditional rulemaking procedures. (Without negotiated rulemaking, the agency issues the rules itself and is usually challenged in court by those who oppose the proposed regulations. This costs the agency and the opponents a lot of money and time and delays the implementation of needed regulations, sometimes for several years.)

The Environmental Protection Agency (EPA) was the first federal agency to apply ADR to enforcement actions, using mediation to enforce environmental regulations. Although some environmental advocates and agency staff members fear that this is a softening of the EPA position toward violators, proponents argue that re-

quired corrective actions are taken, and usually more quickly than if the cases had been handled in court (which can take several years).

These types of efforts have been stimulated in the 1990s by the passage of several key pieces of legislation: the 1990 and 1996 Administrative Dispute Resolution Acts (ADRAs), the 1990 Negotiated Rulemaking Act, and the 1991 Administrative Procedure Technical Amendments Act (APTA). All these acts encouraged federal agencies to implement ADR procedures as widely as possible in their policy-making and enforcement activities, with the intent of streamlining these activities and cutting costs. Although many federal agencies and employees were unfamiliar with ADR when these acts were passed, ADRA called for widespread training of federal employees in ADR techniques. As a result, knowledge of and comfort with these processes has been increasing in many federal agencies over the last several years.

The federal government also has several agencies whose specific mission is the provision of ADR services. The Federal Mediation and Conciliation Service (FMCS) supplies mediation and other dispute resolution services to businesses and unions involved in labor-management disputes; the Community Relations Service does the same for communities and public and private organizations that need help dealing with racial and ethnic disputes. The FMCS also provides training in ADR to other federal, state, and local agencies that want to learn more about how to implement ADR in their own organizations. The Administrative Conference of the United States (ACUS) was another organization that played a critical role in establishing and promoting the use of ADR in the federal government. Established in 1964, the ACUS was an independent federal advisory agency that promoted ADR and was instrumental in getting critical ADR legislation passed.

See also: Administrative Conference of the United States; Administrative Dispute Resolution Acts of 1990 and 1996; Alternative Dispute Resolution, Institutionalization; Community Relations Service; Federal Mediation and Conciliation Service; Negotiated Rulemaking Act of 1990; Regulatory Negotiation.
References and Further Reading: Dauer, Edward A., 1994, *Manual of Dispute Resolution;* Segal, Phyllis N., 1993, "'Reinventing Government' Includes ADR"; Susskind, Lawrence E., 1993b, "When ADR Becomes the Law: A Review of Federal Practice."

Fisher, Roger

Roger Fisher is the Samuel Williston professor of law emeritus at Harvard Law School. Fisher was a founder and former director of the Harvard Negotiation Project, one of the first and most distinguished research institutions in the fields of negotiation and dispute resolution. Fisher is widely acknowledged as one of the world's leading authorities on negotiation. His best-known work is the best-selling book *Getting to Yes: Negotiating Agreement without Giving In,* which he first published in 1981 with William Ury. A second edition was released in 1991 with Ury and Bruce Patton as coauthors. This book sets out the principles of what the authors call "principled negotiation"—a way to negotiate win-win agreements through integrative bargaining. The book was an instant success, as it was full of useful information and was presented in language that anyone could understand.

Fisher has authored countless other books and articles over the years, including *Beyond Machiavelli: Tools for Coping with Conflict* (coauthored with Elizabeth Kopelman and Andrea Kupfer Schneider) and *Getting Together: Building a Relationship That Gets to Yes* (coauthored with Scott Brown). In addition to teaching and writing, Fisher has done extensive consulting and training with governments, corporations, and individuals worldwide and has helped mediate many international disputes.

See also: Principled Negotiation and *Getting to Yes;* Ury, William.

References and Further Reading: Fisher, Roger, and Scott Brown, 1988, *Getting Together: Building a Relationship that Gets to Yes;* Fisher, Roger, Elizabeth Kopelman, and Andrea Kupfer Schneider, 1994, *Beyond Machiavelli: Tools for Coping with Conflict;* Fisher, Roger, and William Ury, 1981, *Getting to Yes* (2nd ed. with Bruce Patton, 1991).

Follett, Mary Parker

All but forgotten until recently, Mary Parker Follett is now being "revived" and dubbed by some the mother of the dispute resolution field. Writing in the 1920s, Follett was the first to develop the concept of integrative bargaining, which she suggested was one of three primary ways to deal with conflict. The other two were domination and compromise. In domination, one side imposes its will on the other; with compromise, both sides give up something to get something else. In integrative bargaining, win-win solutions are developed in which each side gains without the other side losing. This mutual-gains approach has been widely adapted by most contemporary conflict resolution theorists and practitioners—it forms the basis of Roger Fisher and William Ury's *Getting to Yes*—and it underlies the human needs approach to deep-rooted conflicts. (Human needs theorists do not advocate the negotiation of interests, but they do advocate developing integrative ways to meet all the parties' needs.)

According to contemporary theorist Deborah Kolb, Follett was also an early advocate of what is now being called "transformative" conflict resolution. Although she was interested in outcomes, she was even more concerned about process and relationships. Rather than focusing on the parties' "enlightened self-interests," as many contemporary mediators and theorists do, Follett emphasized the importance of focusing on the relationship between the disputants and the process that they use to deal with the dispute.

See also: Bargaining, Integrative and Distributive; Compromise; Conflict Styles; Domination Conflicts; Needs;

Transformation; Win-Win, Win-Lose, and All-Lose Outcomes.
References and Further Reading: Davis, Albie M., 1991, "An Interview with Mary Parker Follett"; Kolb, Deborah M., 1995, "The Love for Three Oranges or: What Did We Miss about Ms. Follett in the Library?"; Rothman, Jay, 1992, *Confrontation to Cooperation: Resolving Ethnic and Regional Conflict.*

Framing

Framing is a complex and often muddled process in which disputants define what a conflict is about and how it should be approached. It is through this process that parties transform vague feelings of frustration into actual positions to be attained. People frame conflicts in differing ways, based on their interests, values, needs, and underlying worldviews. Just as culture, education, job, lifestyle, and life experiences alter people's views of the world, these factors also influence the way they define conflict situations. This, in turn, can lead them to visualize different and often incompatible solutions. For example, ranchers in a small community may view a proposal to build a new ski area as a threat to their way of life, whereas the would-be developers see it as a way of bringing prosperity and security to an economically declining area. One party defines the issue in terms of economics and the need for recreational opportunities for city dwellers, and the other defines it in terms of lifestyle and quality-of-life factors for people living in the rural community.

Another kind of framing problem occurs when people frame disputes that have a potential win-win outcome as win-lose situations. When people decide that resources are fixed, they try to claim as much for themselves as possible. Often, collaborative problem solving allows the development of options that expand the available resources, thus allowing all the parties to get what they want or need. For example, water is a scarce resource in the western United States, and water conflicts are common as different users compete for what appears to be a limited supply. In recent years, however, several efforts have been made to cooperatively develop and fund water conservation programs that have yielded surplus water for agricultural or metropolitan use. By instituting cooperative conservation programs and "water trades," parties that were previously locked in battles over water rights were able to meet their needs.

Another problem is that people tend to frame disputes according to the resources and skills that they have. Although there are many exceptions, lawyers often see disputes as win-lose situations that need to be pursued through the adversarial process, whereas mediators see the same situations as potentially win-win situations that would profit from mediation or collaborative problem solving.

To overcome framing problems, people need to make an effort to look at problems as others see them and to consider alternative solutions that might not correspond to their usual approach. (This is often called "reframing.") In collaborative problem solving and mediation, the facilitator or mediator helps the parties do this as a prelude to negotiation; parties can try to do the same themselves, with or without the participation of people from the other side. Often, if parties work together to jointly frame a conflict, a solution that meets the needs of all sides but was not obvious before will become apparent.

See also: Bargaining, Integrative and Distributive; Collaborative Problem Solving; Conflict Assessment; Win-Win, Win-Lose, and All-Lose Outcomes.
References and Further Reading: Gray, Barbara, 1989, *Collaborating: Finding Common Ground for Multiparty Problems;* Ury, William, 1991, *Getting Past No: Negotiating with Difficult People.*

Future Disputes Clause

A future disputes clause is a section of a contract that specifies how disputes that arise out of that contract will be resolved.

Typically, a future disputes clause specifies that either mediation or arbitration will be used to settle any disagreements relating to the contract. To be effective, however, a future disputes clause must also specify when, where, how, and by whom the mediation or arbitration will take place. The American Arbitration Association recommends that the following standard clause be inserted into contracts calling for arbitration of disputes:

"Any controversy or claim arising out of or relating to this contract, or the breach thereof, shall be settled by arbitration administered by the American Arbitration Association in accordance with its [applicable] Rules, and judgment upon the award rendered by the Arbitrator may be entered in any court having jurisdiction thereof" (American Arbitration Association 1991). This clause has consistently been supported by courts. The advantage of having a clause like this in a contract is that it avoids the threat of lengthy and costly lawsuits for both parties. It also assures both parties that any arbitration done will be fair and impartial, which is sometimes not the case if the arbitration is provided by an arbitrator who is chosen by the industry or business that is involved in a dispute with a consumer.

See also: American Arbitration Association; Arbitration; Arbitration, Ethical Issues; Conflict Prevention; Mediation.
References and Further Reading: American Arbitration Association, 1991, *A Commercial Arbitration Guide for Business People;* American Arbitration Association, World Wide Web Home Page, http://www.adr.org.

Galtung, Johan

Johan Galtung helped create the field of peace research and is still one of its leading figures. He founded and directed the first peace research center, the International Peace Research Institute, in Oslo, Norway, for ten years. He also founded the *Journal of Peace Research.* He has consulted extensively with many United Nations agencies and has served as a visiting professor worldwide. He has written 50 books and over 1,000 articles on peace, justice, and violence.

One of Galtung's primary theoretical contributions to the field is his concept of structural violence, which is violence perpetrated by the social structure or institutions of a society, not by traditional weapons. Systematic discrimination against a particular ethnic or racial group, for instance, is what Galtung calls structural violence. In his view, this prevents peace just as much as traditional violence does.

Galtung also advocates a positive notion of peace. Thus, rather than seeing peace as an absence of violence or war, he suggests that it be conceptualized in a positive way—as a presence of the right to self-determination, identity, security, and justice.

See also: International Peace Research Association; Peace; Structural Violence.
References and Further Reading: Galtung, Johan, 1975–80, *Essays in Peace Research;* Galtung, Johan, 1995, *Choose Peace;* Galtung, Johan, 1996, *Peace by Peaceful Means;* Lawler, Peter, 1995, *A Question of Values: Johan Galtung's Peace Research.*

Game Theory

Game theory is a way of studying decision making by using simplified situations, called games, to model complex human predicaments and responses. Most games involve two or more players, each of whom has to make one or more decisions involving at least two choices. For instance, in the simplest games, two players are faced with two choices. The amount they win or lose is dependent not only on their own choice but also on the choice the other player makes. The best-known game of this type is the prisoner's dilemma game, which is commonly used to investigate the interplay between cooperation and competition. The game's name and structure come from a hypothetical situation involving two prisoners who are accomplices and are imprisoned for the same crime. Held in separate locations, each is asked to confess. The game payoffs are rigged so that each player wins the most if he or she confesses and his or her opponent does not. (Confessing is the competitive approach, and staying silent is the cooperative approach.) Thus, if one player is competitive and one is cooperative, the competitive player wins. But if they both confess (they are both competitive), they both lose. The best outcome for the two of them is obtained if neither confesses (i.e., they cooperate with each other). In this case, they do better than they would if both confessed, but not as well as one would do if one confessed and the other stayed silent. Sometimes the game is played only once; more often it is played over and over with the same people to see if their strategies change over time, becoming either more competitive or more cooperative.

Although this is a simple story, it is replayed in many different forms in real life. Arms races are essentially prisoner dilemma games, for example. If one side arms itself heavily (the competitive response) and the other does not, the side that is stronger wins (at least in terms of security, if not in terms of costs). If both sides build up their arms, however, it diminishes rather than increases their security, costs them a lot, and gains nothing. The cooperative response is for both sides to disarm, which will lead to mutual security. But this option cannot be taken unless one trusts the other side—which seldom happens in the game or in real life.

One of the leading game theorists, Robert Axelrod, organized two "tournaments" in which other game theorists submitted mathematical solutions for obtaining the optimal result in a repetitive prisoner's dilemma game. In both cases, the winning approach was that developed by game theorist Anatol Rapoport, who developed the "tit for tat" approach. This approach calls for the "prisoner" to be cooperative on the first move and then to match his or her opponent on each subsequent move. This strategy did better than any other approach proposed, as it tended to encourage the growth of trust and cooperation, whereas other approaches stimulated a competitive response more frequently in one or both players.

Although the games used in game theory experiments are very simple, they provide a way of understanding, modeling, and predicting typical human responses to conflict situations. Proponents like game theory because it is a way of stripping the complexity away from human decisions and making the decision-making process more easily seen and understood. Critics, however, see this as a fatal flaw: the games are so oversimplified, they charge, that the lessons learned reveal very little about human decision making and actual conflict situations.

See also: Conflict Styles.

References and Further Reading: Axelrod, Robert, 1984, *The Evolution of Cooperation;* Pruitt, Dean G., and Peter J. Carnevale, 1993, *Negotiation in Social Conflict: Escalation, Stalemate, and Settlement,* 14–27; Schellenberg, James A., 1996, *Conflict Resolution—Theory, Research, and Practice.*

Gandhi, Mahatma

Mahatma Gandhi was the leader of India's nonviolent struggle for independence from the British. Although he was preceded by several important advocates of nonviolence (for instance, Christ, Leo Tolstoy, and Henry David Thoreau), from whom he drew many of his ideas, many modern observers consider Gandhi to be the father of modern nonviolent resistance.

Born in Porbandar, India, in 1869, Gandhi studied law in London and was admitted to the British bar. He returned to India for a short time but then took a job in an Indian law office in Durban, South Africa, where he stayed for 20 years, working and protesting to improve the life of Indian immigrants to South Africa. This is where he first developed the policy of passive resistance to and noncooperation with unjust laws and discriminatory practices, which he then applied in India's struggle for independence.

Central to Gandhi's nonviolence strategy was a belief in *satyagraha,* which is generally translated as "soul force" or "truth force." Gandhi also referred to it as "the law of suffering," because it was based on the use of voluntary suffering to confront an opponent—in a very human way—with the terrible consequences of his or her violence or oppression (Seifert 1965). Linked to satyagraha was *ahimsa*— the refusal to do harm, even when harmed by another. Gandhi insisted that his followers refrain from violence in their thoughts as well as in their actions. "A satyagrahi," he maintained "must never forget the distinction between evil and the evil-doer. He must not harbor ill-will or bitterness against the latter. He may not even employ needlessly offensive language against the evil person, however unrelieved his evil might be. For it is an article of faith with every satyagrahi that there is no one so fallen in this world but can be converted by love. A satyagrahi will always try to overcome evil by good, anger by love, untruth by truth, himsa by ahimsa. There is no other way of purging the world of evil" (Gandhi 1971, 95).

Gandhi was imprisoned and beaten many times for his efforts in South Africa and later in India, but he steadfastly maintained his nonviolent stance. This approach generated respect for his views and increased his political power. His efforts in South Africa resulted in significant sociopolitical changes that benefited the Indian minority in that country, such as recognition of Indian marriages and abolition of the poll tax for Indian citizens.

After succeeding in his nonviolent struggle in South Africa, Gandhi returned to his homeland in 1915, where he again utilized satyagraha in the Indian struggle against British rule. In 1919, Britain passed the Rowlatt Acts, which gave Indian colonial leaders emergency powers to put down "revolutionary" activities. This so angered the Indian population that millions of Indians became Gandhian satyagrahis—members of Gandhi's nonviolent struggle for justice.

Gandhi and the satyagrahis engaged in numerous campaigns against unjust British laws and practices. Boycotting British goods, the satyagrahis initiated a wide variety of cottage industries in an effort to reverse the poverty created by British industrial hegemony. They marched to the sea to make salt as a protest against the British salt tax. Gandhi often fasted for political purposes: to stop Muslim-Hindu violence,

to stop anti-British violence, to improve the lot of the untouchables, and to quell the riots that ensued after India was partitioned into India and Pakistan. His fasts were effective because he was so popular, and the British feared that a revolution would start if Gandhi were allowed to die from his hunger strikes. In January 1948, at the age of 79, Gandhi was killed by an assassin.

Although he was unaware of the theory behind many of his practices, Gandhi's nonviolent tactics were extremely powerful in obtaining his demands without escalating the conflict more than necessary. For example, when conflicts escalate, issues tend to proliferate. Gandhi prevented this by taking on only one campaign at a time. He therefore prevented the conflict from spreading from one issue to another to another until it was so entangled as to be out of control. Similarly, he prevented the intensification of hostility by insisting that all opponents be treated with respect. He also engaged in slow, step-by-step escalation, always providing an opportunity for negotiations or de-escalation between each step. These approaches prevented rapid and uncontrollable escalation, which quickly makes conflicts unmanageable and often unwinnable as well (Wehr 1979).

See also: Escalation; King, Martin Luther, Jr.; Nonviolence; Tolstoy, Lev (Leo) Nikolayevich.
References and Further Reading: Bondurant, Joan V., 1965, *Conquest of Violence: The Gandhian Philosophy of Conflict;* Gandhi, Mohandas K., 1971, "Non-Violence"; Seifert, Harvey, 1965, *Conquest by Suffering: The Process and Prospects of Nonviolent Resistance;* Weber, Thomas, 1992, "Conflict Resolution and Gandhian Ethics"; Wehr, Paul, 1979, *Conflict Regulation.*

GATT Negotiations

The General Agreement on Tariffs and Trade (GATT) is a series of multilateral agreements signed by over 100 countries on the reduction of barriers to trade. GATT was the product of a 1947 conference in Geneva that explored the idea of an international trade organization. Although the original concept lacked support, the idea of mutual negotiation of trade agreements led to seven subsequent rounds of negotiation, up to the most recent Uruguay Round convened in 1986. The original focus of GATT was purely on tariffs, but it was expanded during the Tokyo Round of negotiations (1973–79) to include other nontariff barriers to trade.

The institutional structure of GATT is minimal. It includes the Council of Representatives, made up of GATT signatory countries and acting as GATT's executive body; various committees and working groups dealing with specific or ongoing issues of concern requiring study and consultation; panels, which are used for dispute arbitration when other consultative measures have failed; the Consultative Group of Eighteen, which is constituted of both developed and developing countries; and the director general, who acts as the chairperson of the actual negotiations, mediates discussion and negotiation of policy disputes, and oversees the GATT Secretariat—the research and administrative arm of the organization.

The goal of these multilateral negotiations on trade is to increase the gains of each country by ensuring mutualism. Tariffs and other regulations, such as packaging and marketing restrictions, quotas, or unreasonable customs procedures, are thought by most economists to detract from the overall gains inherent in trade. The reduction of these barriers allows countries to specialize in goods in which they have a comparative advantage. A further disadvantage of trade barriers is the lose-lose process of retaliation: if one country erects a trade barrier, raising the price and reducing the competitiveness of a foreign good, the foreign country is likely to erect a barrier of its own to compensate for the losses suffered from the original tariff.

Because unilateral trade barrier reduction can have damaging effects on any econ-omy, it is unlikely that any country will take unilateral action. Hence GATT focuses on increasing the benefits of trade by negotiating agreements that are likely to be accepted by all countries and that hold each country to the same standards, thereby resolving issues leading to retaliatory measures. GATT enforces this principle of nondiscrimination by requiring the GATT signatories to accord any trade concession given to one country to all countries "immediately and unconditionally"—a condition also known as most-favored-nation status. GATT further stipulates that all goods, once they have entered a country, must be treated equally with the goods of the country itself, a condition known as national treatment.

There are a number of exceptions to these rules that have been included in the formal agreements. Certain unilateral actions are protected, such as the use of tariffs or other regulation by developing countries with relatively weak economies. Developed countries may also take measures to protect industries in the areas of national security and infant industries and take temporary measures to protect industries that are threatened by extreme market fluctuations. Countries also have recourse to bilaterally negotiated voluntary export agreements and restraints that bypass the conventions of GATT. A number of products are not included under GATT protocols due to a lack of agreement by negotiating countries, especially in the area of agriculture, an industry that has historically been subsidized by many nations.

GATT relies on the voluntary compliance and self-enforcement of agreed-upon measures. It has no formal institutional mechanism for penalizing violating countries other than exclusion from negotiations or withdrawal of most-favored-nation status and the privileges accompanying it. The agreements reached are subject to ratification by the national governmental body of each nation, and no sovereignty is conceded to GATT as an organization. Proponents of

GATT point out that tariffs on a world level have dropped considerably on average, reaping benefits for consumers worldwide. Critics are divided into two camps. One argues that GATT does not make trade free enough and is too complicated. The other camp maintains that workers (especially in developing countries) are disproportionately and negatively impacted by GATT concessions and that GATT undermines the role of the state in providing for the health of its own economy through legislation and regulation. Whatever the truth of these arguments, the GATT negotiations are expected to continue and are seen as beneficial by its signatories.

See also: International Conflict.

References and Further Reading: Caves, Richard E., Jeffrey A. Frankel, and Ronald W. Jones, 1990, *World Trade and Payments: An Introduction*; Colas, Bernard, 1994, *Global Economic Co-operation: A Guide to Agreements and Organizations;* Van Bergeijk, Peter A. G., 1994, *Economic Diplomacy, Trade and Commercial Policy.*

Gender Conflict

Gender conflict is multifaceted. In part, it derives from different styles that men and women tend to have toward work, toward play, toward problem solving, and toward relationships. In part, it derives from stereotypes that are deeply ingrained in U.S. (and many other societies') culture. Women are still seen as generally subservient to men and are expected to maintain their "proper place." Indeed, many gender issues relate directly to stereotypes about power: men are seen as powerful, women as submissive. The acceptance of male domination of females brings about many of the problems we now call gender conflicts: discrimination against women (especially in the workplace), differential pay for women and men, and sexual harassment and abuse.

Power Issues and Gender Stereotypes

In U.S. society as well as most others, men still tend to hold the powerful positions, women the less powerful roles. This is due, at least in part, to gender stereotypes that still pervade both men's and women's thinking. Men are generally seen as stronger (both physically and emotionally), more rational, more capable of making wise decisions. Thus, they are seen as more capable leaders and are allowed to move up organizational hierarchies into leadership roles more often than women are. Women are generally seen as weaker, more emotional, and hence incapable of making wise decisions. Thus, they are kept in less powerful positions where they can support the men. These stereotypes are reinforced by biology—women must take time off from work to have babies, whereas men can work right through the event—and by social structures that still have women taking on the major responsibility for child care. This tends to take women away from their work more than it does men, again making them "less capable" of holding powerful jobs that require 100 percent commitment.

Over the last several decades, increasing numbers of women and some men have come to challenge these stereotypes and the discriminatory structures they have created. Although expressing stereotypical images of women is less acceptable in U.S. culture than it used to be, people still largely act as though the stereotypes are true. For this reason, women still tend to hold less powerful positions, tend to get paid less for equal jobs, and tend to be listened to in a different way.

Power and stereotypes also affect one's interpretation of outside events. Although more and more organizations are formulating increasingly strict sexual harassment policies, behavior that many men consider to be completely normal and acceptable is viewed by women as harassment. Many feminists even charge that rape is viewed differently by women and men. What men consider to be acceptable sexual behavior, women do not. And although these norms are changing, they have not changed sufficiently to allow women to defend themselves without getting further injured in the process. Most women dare not publicly charge someone with sexual harassment or rape, for fear of what will happen to them if they do. A leading mediator, Albie Davis, echoed the observation of many when she said, "I have not encountered one instance where it's been safe for a woman to raise the issue of sexual harassment either formally or informally. They always suffer extreme emotional and professional damage. To enter the sexual harassment realm is to sign up for a major life trauma" (Davis and Rifkin 1994, 3).

Conflict Styles

Conflicts between the sexes are further complicated by the fact that women seem to handle conflict differently than men do. Although it is a stereotype, just as those discussed above, many feminist scholars observe that women and men have different negotiating styles. Deborah Kolb points out three such differences. First, women tend to focus more on relationships, while men focus more on substantive issues. Thus women's goals in a negotiation tend to be on mending relationships, whereas men want to focus on solving the substantive problem. Second, women tend to take a broader and longer-term view of situations than do men, who tend to focus on the specifics of the immediate situation. Third, men and women communicate differently. Men try to reason, to argue, to debate. Women, Kolb says, tend to ask questions, tell stories, listen, and empathize. Although each of these styles has its benefits and costs, the result, when they are combined, is that men dominate and women remain submissive. This is one of the reasons that some observers believe that divorce mediation is not fair to women; they tend to be exploited in the

process, it is argued, because they cannot negotiate at an even table with men.

See also: Divorce Mediation; Power; Power Balancing.
References and Further Reading: Davis, Albie M., and Janet Rifkin, 1994, "A Conversation between Friends"; Kolb, Deborah M., 1994, "Is It Her Voice or Her Place that Makes a Difference? Gender Issues in Negotiation"; Taylor, Anita, and Judi Beinstein Miller, 1994, *Conflict and Gender.*

Generational Conflict

Conflicts between generations are common. At the personal level, they take the form of parent-child conflicts, which exist from childhood through adulthood. Interestingly, conflicts between adult children and parents are often similar to conflicts between young children and parents; they center on questions of appropriate behavior and control—in other words, who makes decisions for whom. When children are young, parents are expected to dictate behavioral expectations and make choices for their children, although children will resist. At some point, however, children are expected to grow up and take control of their own behavior and lives. If parents continue to intervene after a child has grown up and left home, conflict usually results. The same is true if a child refuses to grow up and depends on parental support or guidance long into adulthood.

Other generational conflicts involve changes in norms and lifestyles. Things that are appropriate—even required—of one generation are frightening or appalling to another. In order for children to be accepted by their peers, they often have to do things that upset their parents. This is part of the adolescent process of breaking away from the parents and becoming independent adults. Nevertheless, the generational conflicts it creates can be severe.

Family therapists and conflict resolution specialists advise that generational conflicts be handled in the same way that other interpersonal conflicts are handled—with interest-based bargaining.

Rather than taking a strong stand and refusing to budge, most conflicts can be handled better if both parent and child are willing to listen attentively to each other and try to develop a win-win approach that meets the needs of both people. By negotiating the solutions to problems, children are also more likely to obey the final decision rather than defy it, as they are likely to do if it is imposed unilaterally.

Generational conflicts also occur at the community and societal level. This is the problem of generational equity, of using the resources or money of one generation to support another. An example of this is the government debt: to pay for services for current citizens, the United States has borrowed vast sums of money that must be paid back by people who are not yet born. The exploitation of nonrenewable resources and wilderness ecosystems so that they will no longer be available for future citizens' use is another source of generational inequity and conflict.

See also: Environmental Conflicts; Family Conflict; Generational Equity; Parent-Child Conflict; Public Policy Conflicts.

References and Further Reading: Halpern, Howard Marvin, 1992, *You and Your Grown up Child: Nurturing a Better Relationship;* Kirshenbaum, Mira, and Charles Foster, 1991, *Parent-Teen Breakthrough: The Relationship Approach;* Kotlikoff, Laurence J., 1992, *Generational Accounting: Knowing Who Pays, and When, for What We Spend.*

Generational Equity

Generational equity problems arise when the legitimate interests of future generations are not adequately protected by current decision-making and conflict resolution processes. Such problems commonly arise because future generations are simply not around to participate in these processes and protect their interests. As a result, there is a strong tendency to enlarge the current pie (thereby avoiding immediate win-lose conflicts) by borrowing from the future.

For example, short-term budget conflicts are frequently limited by reducing the amount spent on long-term infrastructure maintenance. This leaves additional money for distribution in the current budget cycle but increases the amount that future generations will have to spend to repair or replace neglected bridges, highways, water systems, and factories. Other generational equity questions arise from reductions in spending for education or the exploitation of natural resources at levels that cannot be sustained over the long term. The same process is responsible for the enormous federal budget deficit—the deficit is produced by decisions to distribute more money to current generations, to be repaid by future ones.

The only way to prevent generational inequity problems is to be sure that someone is effectively representing future interests in current conflict resolution and decision-making efforts. Although some individuals are willing to do this, institutions that are mandated to protect future interests are often in a stronger position to act effectively. For example, environmental protection and resource management agencies, educational institutions, research and development organizations, and departments responsible for corporate investment decisions are charged with the responsibility of protecting future interests. Yet they are confronted with other institutions that have shorter-term goals and often successfully press for current spending over future investment.

Any society that neglects the generational equity problem is likely to deteriorate over time, as future citizens will have to devote more and more of their resources to paying for their parents' activities. For this reason, some people suggest that it makes sense to think of society as something that we are borrowing from our children, rather than something that we have inherited from our parents.

See also: Distributional Conflicts; Environmental Conflicts; Public Policy Conflicts; Win-Win, Win-Lose, and All-Lose Outcomes.

References and Further Reading: Kotlikoff, Laurence J., 1992, *Generational Accounting: Knowing Who Pays, and When, for What We Spend.*

Gorbachev, Mikhail Sergeyevich

Mikhail Gorbachev was general secretary of the USSR in the late 1980s. He gained international prominence for his domestic policies of perestroika (Russian for "restructuring") and glasnost ("openness") as well as for his foreign policies, which advocated peaceful coexistence with the West by pursuing negotiations, not confrontation. Decried by many in the Soviet Union, Gorbachev was applauded in the West because he brought an end to the Cold War and, inadvertently, contributed to the dissolution of the Soviet Union itself.

Through perestroika, Gorbachev began moving the Soviets toward a more free-market economy. Glasnost eased media censorship, released political dissidents, and reexamined the standard version of Soviet history. Gorbachev was committed to political pluralism and cited the right to self-determination in his decision to take no military action when the Warsaw Pact countries overthrew their communist governments. This soon led to the end of communist rule in most of the Warsaw Pact countries and then in the Soviet Union itself.

In addition to participating in the summit meetings with President Ronald Reagan that resulted in the signing of the Intermediate Nuclear Forces (INF) Treaty, Gorbachev promoted the reunification of Germany and ended the ten-year Soviet-Afghanistan standoff. He received the Nobel Prize for Peace in 1990 for his contributions to changes in East-West relations. However, he was threatened by a right-wing coup in August 1991 and then was forced to resign from the presidency in December of that year, on the eve of the dissolution of the USSR and the ascendancy of Boris Yeltsin as president of Russia.

See also: Cold War
References and Further Reading: Kaiser, Robert G., 1991, *Why Gorbachev Happened: His Triumph, His Failure, and His Fall;* Sheehy, Gail, 1991, *Gorbachev: The Making of the Man Who Shook the World.*

GRIT

GRIT, a concept first developed by C. E. Osgood (1962), stands for graduated and reciprocated initiatives in tension-reduction, which he and others later simplified to gradual reduction in tension. GRIT starts when one side to a conflict makes a unilateral concession to the other side or otherwise makes a move designed to increase trust between the two disputing parties. Ideally, this concession is unambiguous and open to complete verification so that the opponent can be sure that it is not a trick. The concession should also be accompanied by a clear message that a similar concession from the other side is desired or even expected.

If the opponent responds positively, the first party makes a further concession, requesting a matching response, and the process continues, so that the conflict slowly de-escalates through a series of unilaterally initiated moves. Even if the opponent does not respond positively, Osgood suggests that the first party try again, each time making a concession that does not hurt itself deeply or make it appear weak but does indicate a willingness to cooperate if the opportunity is given.

An example of GRIT in international conflict resolution is Egyptian President Anwar al-Sadat's surprise trip to Jerusalem to meet with Israeli officials in 1977. Before his trip, Israel and Egypt had been at war repeatedly since Israel's founding in 1948. Egypt, like all other Arab states, was seen by Israel as hostile and evil—out to destroy Israel at the first opportunity.

Sadat announced before his historic trip that his reasons for going to Jerusalem (then the capital of Israel) were to increase trust and to diminish tensions between the two nations. Indeed, the trip succeeded in doing so and paved the way for the Camp David negotiations the next year.

See also: Camp David Accords (Israeli and Egyptian); De-escalation; Peace Building; Sadat, Anwar.
References and Further Reading: Lindskold, S., 1978, "Trust Development, the GRIT Proposal, and the Effects of Conciliatory Acts on Conflict and Cooperation"; Osgood, Charles E., 1962, *An Alternative to War or Surrender;* Osgood, Charles E., 1966, *Perspective in Foreign Policy;* Pruitt, Dean G., and Jeffrey Z. Rubin, 1986, *Social Conflict;* Ryan, Stephen, 1995, *Ethnic Conflict and International Relations.*

Ground Rules

Ground rules are the rules of conduct or behavioral guidelines that govern negotiating. Often, ground rules are unspoken, but when several parties are engaged in a negotiating process or when the dispute is particularly contentious, having formal, agreed-on ground rules is important. According to environmental conflict managers Susan Carpenter and W. J. D. Kennedy (1988, 118), "Nearly every managed program dealing with public disputes uses some form of ground rules. . . . Ground rules explicitly spell out behavior and procedures that people normally consider to be fair but sometimes abandon in carrying on a fight." For example, ground rules may state that everyone is allowed to speak, but no one may speak for more than five minutes at a time. Another ground rule might prohibit personal attacks or questioning a disputant's motives.

Carpenter and Kennedy describe three types of ground rules. Some rules regulate disputant behavior. Examples are requirements that disputants treat each other with respect, honor other people's values and beliefs, keep their agreements, and approach conflicts as "problems to be solved" rather than "battles to be won" (Carpenter and Kennedy 1988, 118).

Other ground rules regulate process. Examples include rules that state that everyone is expected to be on time for meetings and that the facilitator will propose an agenda for each meeting that will be approved by the group and then must

be followed. Other procedural ground rules might require that the same negotiator represent each party at every meeting (so that people do not have to keep bringing the newcomer up to speed), that observers are or are not welcome, or that the meetings are or are not open to the public or the press.

Still other ground rules may define the scope of the discussions. In a dispute over the development of a new ski area, participants may agree to discuss the environmental, economic, and social impact of the proposed development but not other aspects of the nearby communities' growth management plans. Some ground rules may set out the kinds of technical information that will be used in the discussions and how these data will be obtained. Will the group have access to proprietary data? If so, the ground rules need to specify how those data will be kept confidential. If not, ground rules should specify how needed data will be obtained from other sources.

Ground rules are usually drafted beforehand by the person or people planning the meeting. The meeting facilitator must then get approval from all the parties before going on to other substantive business. Without complete approval, ground rules are meaningless, because a meeting cannot be run successfully with rules that do not apply to all participants.

Generally, if a meeting involves many parties and is ongoing (e.g., takes place over several sessions), ground rules need to be put in writing. If only a few parties are involved and the meeting is a one- or perhaps two-time event, the ground rules can be agreed on orally. In either case, the meeting facilitator should remind the parties of the ground rules before each meeting and should remind parties again should a rule be violated. Occasionally, more forceful measures, such as ejecting a participant from a meeting, are necessary to enforce ground rules, but such extreme measures are seldom needed. Most people follow approved ground rules without needing reminders, and those who need reminders usually respond quickly when one is given. Ground rules therefore allow for orderly and constructive discussion of agenda items. Without such ground rules, meetings can quickly degenerate into unfocused diatribe and conflict escalation rather than constructive problem solving or conflict resolution.

See also: Collaborative Problem Solving; Environmental Conflicts; Procedural Conflicts; Public Policy Conflicts.

References and Further Reading: Carpenter, Susan L., and W. J. D. Kennedy, 1988, *Managing Public Disputes;* Gray, Barbara, 1989, *Collaborating: Finding Common Ground for Multiparty Problems.*

Health Care Conflicts

The health care system in the United States is beset with conflicts. Conflicts arise between patients and caregivers over treatment choices and implementation (i.e., accusations of malpractice); among patients, caregivers, and the insurance industry over costs and coverage; between caregivers and treatment facilities regarding working conditions and expectations; and between caregivers in different roles—doctors and nurses, for instance. Other conflicts involve questions of access to care: Who should pay for indigent care? How much and what kind of care should the poor receive? How much and what kind of care should be provided to the middle class and the affluent, perhaps at the expense of giving care to others?

Although some of these conflicts are relatively simple to resolve, many are not. Often the stakes are extremely high—involving life or death. Financial costs can be exorbitant as well. Added to this are fundamental value and religious differences that make compromise all but impossible. If a patient's family wishes a loved one to die with dignity, without artificially prolonging the process with medical intervention, and the patient's doctor and hospital believe that all possible treatments should be implemented to save lives, there will be a serious conflict. Further complicating the situation is the number of parties involved—a patient, the patient's family, the health care providers (doctors, nurses,

technicians, hospitals, nursing homes, and so forth), the insurance industry, and in some cases the government (which pays for indigent and elder care). In addition, health care conflicts often involve highly technical issues as well as questions of risk and uncertainty. Doctors often explain that medicine is not a science, but rather an art. They can do their best to treat patients properly, but the result is never assured. Patients who expect "perfect" results are often disappointed, even angered, when the outcome is not as they expected.

The way in which medical conflicts are resolved has been changing over the last two decades. In the 1970s and earlier, most of these conflicts were resolved by "experts." Doctors made treatment decisions for patients, who rarely questioned those decisions. Insurance companies decided what was and was not covered and paid accordingly. When disputes occurred, they were generally resolved by the courts. A jury would listen to expert testimony and then make a decision regarding a medical malpractice claim or a claim that an insurance company had violated its contract. Negotiation, mediation, and other alternative dispute resolution processes were rare.

In the last 20 years, however, this trend has changed markedly. As health care costs have risen, consumers and insurance companies have become increasingly concerned about treatment options, costs, and access to care. They have demanded a greater role in the decision-making process and have insisted on dispute resolution mechanisms that reflect such involvement. As a result, many more health care conflicts are being resolved with mediation or consensus building, in which all the parties work together to come up with a resolution that will satisfy everyone.

One example of this trend is reflected in the way many hospitals are dealing with ethical conflicts regarding treatment choices. Whereas such choices used to be made by doctors alone, now ethical disputes are usually referred to ethics committees made up of people from different stakeholder groups (doctors, administrators, and patient advocates, for instance). Although these committees may still engage in "expert decision making," increasing numbers use mediation to help the parties agree on treatment decisions. This approach is also being used in medical malpractice cases and insurance disputes. Large-scale consensus-building processes have also been used successfully in some states to implement statewide health care reform, addressing issues such as access to care and cost containment.

See also: Collaborative Problem Solving; Public Policy Conflicts; Risk and Uncertainty; Tort Reform.
References and Further Reading: Khor, Karen, 1995a, "Conflicting Trends Are Causing Ethical Dilemmas in Health-Care Industry: Hospitals and Nursing Homes Test Mediation for Impartial, Informed Solutions"; Slaikeu, Karl A., 1989, "Designing Dispute Resolution Systems in the Health Care Industry."

Hewlett Foundation, William and Flora

The William and Flora Hewlett Foundation has been one of the leading organizations in conflict resolution funding since the mid-1980s. It makes grants for conflict resolution work in five categories: theory development; practitioner organizations; promotion of the field; consensus building, public participation, and policy making; and international conflict resolution.

To encourage the development of theory and the establishment of conflict resolution as a legitimate scholarly discipline, the foundation has given general support grants to about 20 interdisciplinary university-based centers that focus on theory development and the improvement of practice. The foundation's grants to practitioner organizations are intended to support the development of new methods, the evaluation of ongoing programs, and the dissemination of conflict resolution services to traditionally underserved populations.

To promote the field, the foundation has supported organizations that train potential users of dispute resolution or otherwise promote the field as a whole. To encourage better public decision making, Hewlett has supported efforts at policymaking reform and public policy conflict prevention. The foundation also supports a few organizations that are working on the international application of conflict resolution techniques and the development of practice-relevant theory related to intergroup conflicts around the world.

See also: Appendix 1 for contact information.

Human Needs and Human Needs Theory
See **Needs.**

Human Rights

The United Nations' Universal Declaration of Human Rights was unanimously adopted in December 1948 as a "nonbinding statement of aspirations" (Forsythe 1995, 298). This declaration states that all nations owe their citizens fundamental human rights and freedoms. According to the declaration, personal, civil, political, economic, social, and cultural rights should be limited only by a recognition of the rights and freedoms of others and by the requirements of morality, public order, and the general welfare. The declaration also specifies that citizens have the right to life, liberty, and security of person; to freedom from arbitrary arrest and to a fair trial; to be assumed innocent until proved guilty; to privacy within their own homes and correspondence; to freedom of movement and place of residence; to nationality and asylum; to ownership of property; to freedom of thought, conscience, religion, opinion, and expression; to freedom of association, peaceful assembly, and participation in government; to social security, work, rest, and an adequate standard of living; to education; and to participation in the social life of the community.

Following passage of this declaration, the UN began to negotiate more specific rules that would be used to accomplish these aspirations. Negotiations were difficult, as governments and cultures in different parts of the world had different interpretations of what constituted inalienable human rights. Whereas the West emphasized the primacy of civil and political rights, the communist countries and the less developed world emphasized the importance of social, economic, and cultural rights. This debate continued for over 20 years until two covenants—the International Covenant on Civil and Political Rights and the International Covenant on Economic, Social, and Cultural Rights—were drafted, opened for signature, and finally took effect (for consenting states) in 1976.

These covenants gave the principles in the Universal Declaration the strength of international law and thus gave the UN the authority to enforce that law. Due to political pressure and widespread resistance, however, the UN's enforcement measures have been inconsistent and only partially effective. Nevertheless, the importance of protecting human rights has become a more high-profile issue worldwide, and most states are making an effort to comply with the provisions of the UN declaration and covenants. Further, it is almost uniformly accepted that diplomatic pressure (from either the UN or other nation-states) intended to protect human rights is not a violation of sovereignty or inappropriate interference in a state's internal affairs. Rather, the UN declaration, together with the covenants and other agreements developed later, confirm that the international community has not only the right but also the obligation to protect human rights worldwide.

See also: International Alert; United Nations.
References and Further Reading: Donnelly, Jack, 1989, *Universal Human Rights in Theory and Practice;* Forsythe, David P., 1995, "The UN and Human Rights at Fifty: An Incremental but Incomplete Revolution."

I-Messages

I-statements or I-messages are ways of communicating a problem to another person that are less accusatory than "you-messages." The focus in I-messages is on one's own feelings or how a problem affects oneself. The focus in you-messages is what is wrong with the other person or what the other person did. For example, if a parent is angry because her child stayed out later than she was supposed to, the parent could express this anger with a you-message: "You were supposed to be home by 11:00 and it is after 1:00! You are so irresponsible!" The response from the child is likely to be defensive: "I am not! Your 11:00 deadline was unreasonable!" This is likely to degenerate into a heated argument, leave both the parent and the child angry, and fail to solve the problem or improve the relationship between the two. The alternative I-message might be: "I got really worried about you. I was afraid that you'd been in an accident or that something else terrible had happened. I wish you had called to let me know what was going on." This kind of message is likely to yield a more sympathetic and helpful response, such as "I'm sorry, Mom. I'll be more careful to watch the clock next time." Although this may not completely solve the problem, it makes the child more aware of her parent's feelings and needs. She is also more likely to try to meet those needs in the future, since she was treated respectfully in this exchange and her rela-

tionship with her mother was reinforced, not diminished.

Learning I-messages is difficult, because you-messages often come much more naturally. We tend to see our problems as being caused by other people and tend to hide our fears and feelings. Thus, defining a problem in terms of "you" is often much easier than phrasing it in terms of "I." However, if a person makes the effort to explain his or her needs and feelings without accusing the other person of being the cause of the problem, the chances of resolving the conflict are much greater.

See also: Active Listening; Communication; Interpersonal Conflict.

References and Further Reading: Gordon, Thomas, 1970, *Parent Effectiveness Training;* Ury, William, 1991, *Getting Past No: Negotiating with Difficult People.*

Identity Conflicts

Identity conflicts involve an assault on a person's or a group's fundamental sense of self. Such assaults are so profoundly threatening that these conflicts tend to escalate quickly, becoming intractable. Terrell Northrup, one of the leading scholars on identity conflicts, explains that identity is fundamental because it involves not only one's sense of who one is but also how one relates to the rest of the world. "It is a system of beliefs or a way of construing the world that makes life predictable rather than random. . . . The alternative, a random world with no rules, would be deeply frightening and impossible to operate in" (Northrup 1989, 55).

Identity, Northrup says, also includes a sense of security—the feeling that one is safe physically, psychologically, socially, and spiritually. When this sense of safety is violated, the defensive response is rapid and strong. This is true for all levels of conflict between individuals, groups, organizations, even nations. Identity is the primary issue in almost all racial and ethnic conflicts; it is also an issue in the abortion and gay rights conflicts, as people identify with others who hold similar beliefs (Christians, gays, feminists, and so forth). Identity can also be an issue in interpersonal conflicts, for instance, in spousal abuse cases in which men see women as their "property," to do with as they see fit, or in conflicts between parents and children, when each sees the other as threatening to his or her own sense of self.

In all these cases, when identity is threatened, the threatened party tends to become both aggressive and defensive. Victims tend to reinforce and rigidify their own sense of righteousness, while simultaneously defining the threatening party as evil or as less than human. (Such dehumanization is common in most domination-submission conflicts, in which the dominant group sees the submissive group as subhuman and thus deserving of differential treatment.) Even short of dehumanization, in identity conflicts, everything one's own group does tends to be seen as good, and everything the other group does is considered bad—even when the two groups are doing the same thing.

When such views become ingrained (and they do so quickly), they are hard to reverse. Whereas parties to tractable conflicts are generally willing to sit down together to work things out, parties to identity conflicts are generally unwilling to take that step, because even sitting down with the opponent is a threat to one's own identity. Eventually, the conflict itself becomes central to the identity of the individual or group. Many sociologists believe that all groups are defined in terms of who they are not, rather than who they are. Thus, maintenance of the conflict becomes essential for identity maintenance, making conflict resolution all the more unlikely.

Although these (and other) factors make identity conflicts difficult to de-escalate, de-escalation can be brought about, Northrup suggests, with proper techniques used at the proper time. Traditional negotiation or mediation usually does not work in identity conflicts, because the parties will not even agree to come to the table. Psychological strategies that aim at altering the sense of identity—of one's self or of the other—Northrup argues, are also likely to be unsuccessful, because identity is too fundamental to be altered in this way. Yet "second-level" techniques, which target the relationship between the disputants, can help get parties together in a way that slowly builds up mutual understanding and trust. Eventually, negative stereotypes break down, and the sense of threat to one's identity diminishes to the point where groups agree to sit down and negotiate the substantive issues in dispute. This, however, is a long, slow process that may take years—or even generations—to come about.

See also: Communal Conflicts; Domination Conflicts; Enemy Image; Ethnic and Racial Conflicts; Intractable Conflicts; Israeli-Palestinian Women's Workshop; Needs; Problem Solving, Analytical.

References and Further Reading: Northrup, Terrell A., 1989, "Dynamic of Identity"; Smith, Anthony, 1986, "Conflict and Collective Identity: Class, *Ethnie,* and Nation"; Smyth, Leo F., 1994, "Intractable Conflicts and the Role of Identity."

Interest Groups

Interest groups consist of people who have a particular cause in common. In order to advance their interests, they form formal or informal associations with other individuals with similar interests and jointly attempt to advance their goals. The Environmental Defense Fund, as its name implies, is an association of people interested in defending the environment. Similarly, the Chamber of Commerce is a group seeking to expand commerce and business opportunities, and the National Association for the Advancement of Colored People seeks to advance the interests of black Americans. By pooling their resources, these interest groups are able to vigorously advocate their positions in a broad array of conflict situations. Such interest groups and their professional representatives often constitute the principal parties to many large-scale public policy conflicts.

Although the primary goal of all interest groups is to protect and enhance the interests of their membership, their approaches vary greatly. Some rely heavily on power-based strategies—litigation, elections, even nonviolent direct action—to attain their goals. Others try to use consensus processes or even market mechanisms to buy what they want. The Nature Conservancy, for instance, protects land by buying it.

Although interest groups are vigorous advocates for their own causes, they can make decision making more difficult. Often they act as veto groups: they have enough power to block a proposed action but not enough power to implement another one. Disputes between powerful interest groups can create a stalemate that prevents decisions from being made and hence problems from being solved.

Another problem with interest groups is that many tend to be very loosely organized with a surprisingly diverse membership. This creates questions about who can legitimately speak for or represent a particular interest and whether a promise made by a "representative" of any particular interest group can be considered binding on the group as a whole.

See also: Advocacy; Interests and Positions; Parties.
References and Further Reading: Carpenter, Susan L., and W. J. D. Kennedy, 1988, *Managing Public Disputes;* Larson, Carl E., and David D. Chrislip, 1994, *Collaborative Leadership;* Susskind, Lawrence, and Jeffrey Cruikshank, 1987, *Breaking the Impasse.*

Interests and Positions

Interests are the things people really want in a conflict, and positions are what they say they want. Although it might appear that these should be the same, they often are not. To illustrate the difference between the two concepts, many negotiation trainers tell a story about two children fighting over an orange. Their mother gets tired of the fight, cuts the orange in half, and gives one half to each. But this satisfies neither child, because one needed the whole orange peel for an art project, and the other wanted the whole orange to eat. Although each child's position was "I want the orange!" one's interest was food and the other's interest was art. Thus, their interests were completely compatible, even though their positions were diametrically opposed. By failing to investigate the underlying reasons for their positions, neither child got what he or she wanted.

Although this is a simple story, the same dynamic is repeated constantly. Most people involved in conflict engage in what is called positional bargaining—arguing over positions, not the underlying interests. A key to successful problem-solving negotiation or mediation is moving away from a focus on the positions to examine the underlying interests. Often, it is found, these are compatible, even when stated positions are not. Although entire courses can be focused on how to identify and negotiate interests, a simple guideline is to ask an opponent why he or she has a particular position. Several layers of "whys" often reveal fundamental interests (as well as values and needs) that can be met through a negotiated solution (Fisher, Ury, and Patton 1991).

See also: Bargaining, Interest-Based and Positional; Needs; Negotiation; Principled Negotiation and *Getting to Yes;* Value Conflicts.
References and Further Reading: Fisher, Roger, and William Ury, 1981, *Getting to Yes* (2nd ed. with Bruce Patton, 1991).

Intermediary or Third Party

The terms *intermediary* and *third party* both refer to a person or group of people who come into a conflict to help the disputing parties analyze, manage, or resolve their dispute.

Types of intermediaries include consultants and facilitators, mediators, and arbitrators. Consultants and facilitators are usually the least powerful. They help parties identify the source of the conflict, analyze the conflict, and decide how to handle it. Facilitators help establish productive communication between the parties, often relaying messages and offers back and forth or facilitating problem-solving meetings.

Mediators are typically more powerful than facilitators. They bring the parties together, design an agenda for problem solving, structure communication, and meet with the parties both separately and together in an effort to improve the parties' relationship or resolve the dispute. (Transformative mediators focus more on the relationship, and problem-solving mediators focus more on resolving the problem.)

Arbitrators are the most powerful type of intermediary, as they are empowered to actually make a decision. In most cases, the decision of the arbitrator is binding—that is, it cannot be appealed. In this sense, arbitrators are even more powerful than judges and juries, whose decisions can usually be appealed to a higher court.

See also: Alternative Dispute Resolution; Arbitration; Facilitation; Mediation.
References and Further Reading: Dugan, Marie A., 1987, "Intervener Roles and Conflict Pathologies"; Laue, James, 1987, "The Emergence and Institutionalization of Third Party Roles in Conflict."

International Alert

Founded in 1985, International Alert (IA) is an independent international nongovernmental organization (NGO) dedicated to resolving violent conflicts and promoting peace and social justice. IA focuses on conflicts within countries, particularly ethnic conflicts. IA also emphasizes the early detection and prevention of violent conflict. The organization's commitment to peace is coupled with a commitment to support human rights and promote social justice.

IA works extensively with other NGOs and with governmental bodies to convene meetings, seminars, and conferences. Examples of such work include offering funding and holding training seminars for women's peace organizations in Burundi and arranging problem-solving seminars for local government officials in Dagestan (in the former Soviet Union). IA has also worked directly with conflicting parties to facilitate negotiations and bring parties to the table. In Sierra Leone, an IA special envoy participated directly in the negotiated release of rebel-held hostages, thus paving the way for further negotiations between the political factions.

See also: Ethnic and Racial Conflicts; International Conflict; Peace Building; Appendix 1 for contact information.
References and Further Reading: International Alert, 1996, *On the Alert*, no. 6 (May).

International Association of Conflict Management

The International Association of Conflict Management (IACM) was founded in 1984 to encourage research and training in conflict management and dispute resolution. IACM is an interdisciplinary and international association; its members come from over 28 countries and more than 15 disciplines, including sociology, psychology, communication, business, political science, international relations, public administration, and economics. The association holds an annual conference and publishes a newsletter called *Signal*.

See also: Appendix 1 for contact information.

International Conflict

The term *international conflict* is applied in several related but very different ways.

One distinction is between private- and public-sector international conflicts.

Private-Sector Conflicts

Private-sector international conflicts are conflicts between individuals or organizations from different nations. These conflicts have all the characteristics of domestic interpersonal or interorganizational conflicts, with the added complication of differing cultures, traditions, sometimes languages, and legal systems. One of the problems in these circumstances is an ambiguity regarding which country's laws and courts should be used to resolve the dispute. Often, simultaneous cases occur in both countries, which makes collecting any judgment especially difficult.

One common approach to avoiding jurisdictional problems is the inclusion of an arbitration clause in international contracts. This clause can specify the procedures to be used by the parties acting independently, or it may specify that an international organization be called on to provide arbitration services. (Organizations that provide international arbitration include the International Chamber of Commerce in Paris, the Arbitration Institute of the Stockholm Chamber of Commerce, and the International Court of Arbitration administered by the World Business Organization.)

This approach still leaves problems unaddressed: for instance, many people and organizations from less-developed countries refuse to abide by Western legal systems. In an attempt to overcome this problem, the United Nations Commission on International Trade Laws (UNCITRAL) developed a uniform set of culturally neutral arbitration rules for use on a worldwide basis. Although these approaches make international civil and commercial conflicts less difficult, there are still significant conflict resolution problems.

Public-Sector Conflicts

Other international conflicts are those between governments or other public entities. Traditionally, both political scientists and conflict resolution scholars considered these kinds of international conflicts to involve sovereign nation-states. These conflicts can range in severity from minor disagreements on joint policies (for instance, trade policies) to extremely broad-based differences affecting all segments of two (or more) nations' interactions. The extreme is war, defined by Quincy Wright (1965, 698) as the "simultaneous conflict of armed forces, popular feelings, jural dogmas, and national cultures so nearly equal as to lead to the extreme intensification of each."

In recent years, however, especially after the end of the Cold War, an increasing number of "international" conflicts have actually involved different ethnic groups within individual states. Examples are Bosnia, Rwanda, Sri Lanka, and Chechnya. In most of these cases, the issue has been one of sovereignty for particular ethnic groups or full and equal participation in the social, economic, and political life of a country. A growing number of international relations scholars have pointed out that this is not really a new occurrence, but rather a new way of looking at what has been happening in many parts of the world all along. Rather than viewing the nation-state as the most important actor in these conflicts, many scholars are now looking at "identity groups"—racial, ethnic, or other subnational groups that are seeking to assert their own identity and rights within the boundaries of one or more nation-states.

Both kinds of international conflict are qualitatively different from other types of conflict, because there is no effective legal remedy that the parties can turn to for support or assistance. Although the UN intervenes in a few international conflicts, it cannot intervene in conflicts internal to one state, and the efficacy of its intervention, when it occurs, is mixed at best.

The most commonly used resolution methods include diplomacy, international mediation, nonviolent pressure (for instance, sanctions), and military force. Diplomacy generally refers to negotiations carried out by formal representatives (diplomats). This process can be bilateral or multilateral (i.e., involving only two nations or several nations). It can be done very informally, with off-the-record conversations ending with a handshake, or very formally, ending in a treaty that is ratified by the signatory governments.

When direct negotiations fail, an impartial third party may be asked to mediate the conflict. Typically, these mediators are high-profile people such as the secretary-general of the United Nations, high-ranking officials in other neutral countries (for instance, a Norwegian statesman played a major role in facilitating the Israeli-Palestinian negotiations in 1993–95), or independent statesmen, such as Jimmy Carter. Other people who provide international conflict resolution assistance are not high-ranking officials but "citizen diplomats." Often these are members of the peace churches—Mennonites or Quakers, for instance—who act as facilitators of international negotiations at both the grassroots and the official levels.

Also increasing in use is what is called "track two" diplomacy, or unofficial discussions among private citizens who are outside the official diplomatic structure but interested in exploring new possibilities for peacemaking. A particularly interesting approach in use for about 20 years is the analytical problem-solving workshop. These workshops involve private citizens working with a panel of conflict scholars who help them analyze the underlying needs and interests involved in the conflict and then go from there to explore options for meeting all sides' needs simultaneously. Although these workshops are usually held with private citizens rather than diplomats (which allows people to explore options that formal representatives would be precluded from considering), an effort is made to involve people who are connected to the power establishment so that the group's findings will be considered by those in decision-making roles.

The outcome of all these methods is highly unpredictable, although nonviolent options are often more successful than they are expected to be, and violent options less successful. Many international conflicts resist all resolution efforts for years and then suddenly transform into conflicts that are amenable to negotiation. The Cold War between the United States and the Soviet Union, for example, seemed to resist all efforts at resolution. Leaders on both sides understood the danger and futility of the continuing arms race but were unable to stop it. Then, in 1989, the Soviet Union dissolved, and the Cold War did as well.

Other breakthroughs occurred in 1996. For instance, significant headway was made in both the Middle East and the Balkans, although much tension and conflict remain in both regions. Even the most intractable of international conflicts may become "ripe" for resolution. In other cases, avoidance of escalation into war is the best that can be achieved.

See also: Camp David Accords (Israeli and Egyptian); Carter, Jimmy; Cuban Missile Crisis; Falkland Islands (Malvinas) Conflict; Mediation, International; Montreal Protocol on Substances that Deplete the Ozone Layer; Peace Building; Peacekeeping; Peacemaking; Persian Gulf War; Track Two Preventive Diplomacy in the South China Sea; United Nations; United Nations Mediation of the Egyptian-Israeli Negotiations at Kilometer 101.

References and Further Reading: Azar, Edward E., and John W. Burton, 1986, *International Conflict Resolution: Theory and Practice;* Goldberg, Stephen B., Frank E. A. Sander, and Nancy H. Rogers, 1992, *Dispute Resolution: Negotiation, Mediation, and Other Processes;* Kriesberg, Louis, 1992, "The U.S.-USSR and Middle East Cases"; Kriesberg, Louis, Terrell A. Northrup, and Stuart J. Thorson, 1989, *Intractable Conflicts and Their Transformation;* Kriesberg, Louis, and Stuart J. Thorson, 1991, "Timing the De-escalation of International Conflicts"; Perlman,

Lawrence, and Steven C. Nelson, 1983, "New Approaches to the Resolution of International Commercial Disputes"; Rivkin, David, 1991, "International Arbitration"; Rothman, Jay, 1992, *Confrontation to Cooperation: Resolving Ethnic and Regional Conflict;* Wright, Quincy, 1965, *A Study of War.*

International Court of Arbitration

The International Court of Arbitration, administered by the World Business Organization, provides arbitration of international commercial disputes. Hundreds of parties, arbitrators, and lawyers from countries representing every economic, political, and social system have used the services of the court. During 1994, 384 new requests for arbitration were submitted to the court; by the end of that year, 801 cases were pending.

The organization publishes a bulletin twice a year with a special supplement and also publishes a set of rules for international conciliation and arbitration. In order to respond to the specific needs of maritime disputes, the court and the Comité Maritime International jointly prepared a set of rules appropriate for maritime arbitration.

Also affiliated with the court is the Centre for Expertise, which was founded in 1976 for the purpose of appointing or proposing experts in connection with business transactions. Its scope of activity covers the technical, financial, and services sectors.

See also: Arbitration; Arbitration, Commercial; International Conflict; Appendix 1 for contact information.

International Court of Justice

The International Court of Justice (ICJ), also called the World Court, is the principal judicial entity of the United Nations (UN). Established in 1946, it is seated at the Peace Palace at the Hague. It is the successor to the Permanent Court of International Justice, part of the League of Nations.

The ICJ's main objective is "to achieve international peace and security in the world community of sovereign states." It does this by deciding legal cases between nations; private parties may not bring cases before the court. (International commercial cases are usually handled by the International Court of Arbitration or other similar bodies.) The court interprets treaties, settles questions of international law, and resolves disputes over reparation for violations of international obligations. Further, the UN may ask the court for an advisory opinion on any legal matter.

Jurisdiction of the court is neither compulsory nor universal; it depends on the consent of the states that are parties to a particular dispute. Disputes can come before the court in one of two ways. The disputing parties may have an agreement specifying that disputes be submitted to the court. Alternatively, one party may request the court's intervention on the basis that a second party is required by the terms of a treaty to accept the authority of the ICJ in a particular situation.

The decision of the ICJ is final and binding; no appeal can be made. However, the court has little enforcement power. Although the UN Security Council is empowered to take measures to enforce court decisions, it does not have the money, personnel, or will to do so in every case. For that reason, compliance with court decisions is largely voluntary.

In 1985, President Ronald Reagan withdrew the United States from its former policy of automatic compliance with ICJ decisions. Many other major powers—including the former Soviet Union, China, France, and West Germany (now the united Federal Republic of Germany)—had already done the same and thus considerably weakened the authority of the court.

See also: International Court of Arbitration; International Law; League of Nations; United Nations.

References and Further Reading: Singh, Nagendra, 1989, *The Role and Record of the International Court of Justice;* United Nations, 1992, *Handbook on the Peaceful Settlement of Disputes between States.*

International Law

International law governs relations between nation-states. It is composed of international treaties and conventions, general customs, and generally accepted principles of law and equity. Although few organizations are empowered to enforce international law, nations are expected to comply with international laws, and they generally do. If they do not, they are likely to damage their international relationships. In addition, the violated state may complain to the United Nations (UN), which may issue a declaration condemning the violation or may act to remedy the situation (as occurred when Iraq invaded Kuwait in 1990). However, the UN has insufficient money, personnel, and will to intervene in all violations of international law. Thus, it is the responsibility of the states to follow prescribed rules and principles.

Since the beginning of the nineteenth century, much international law has been written in international conferences. The Congress of Vienna in 1815 reorganized Europe after the defeat of Napoleon. It also established rules for the behavior and treatment of international diplomats, which are followed to this day. The Conference of Paris in 1856 adopted the Declaration of Maritime Law and allowed for the addition of new signatories to previously signed treaties. The 1899 Hague Conference adopted the Convention for the Pacific Settlement of International Disputes and created the Permanent Court of Arbitration. This court served as an important instrument for international arbitration for many years.

At the end of World War I, the Treaty of Versailles established the Permanent Court of Justice and the League of Nations, both intended to be instruments of international conflict resolution and designed to prevent the escalation of hostilities to the level that caused World War I. The United States objected to the collective security provisions in the Treaty of Versailles and thus never signed it or joined the League of Nations, which severely weakened its effectiveness.

The Treaty of Versailles was followed by the Kellogg-Briand Pact (also called the Pact of Paris for the Renunciation of War), signed in 1928. This agreement was ratified by over 60 nations, including Germany and Japan, but it was powerless to prevent World War II. At the end of that war, the League of Nations was replaced with the United Nations, which has actively sought to codify and enforce international law. The UN Charter established the International Court of Justice to adjudicate international disputes and charged the General Assembly with the responsibility of furthering the development of new international laws. The General Assembly created the International Law Commission and the Commission on International Trade Law to help in those activities. Perhaps the most notable of the new international laws created as a result of such UN work are the Law of the Sea, governing the peaceful use of the world's oceans, and the chlorofluorocarbon treaty, limiting the use of ozone-destroying chemicals.

See also: Collective Security; International Conflict; League of Nations; Mediation, International; Montreal Protocol on Substances that Deplete the Ozone Layer; Peace of Westphalia; United Nations.
References and Further Reading: Falk, Richard, 1991, "International Law in a Fragmented World: The Challenge of New Issues and New Actors"; Wright, Quincy, 1965, *A Study of War.*

International Negotiation Network

The International Negotiation Network (INN) is a network of eminent persons, conflict resolution practitioners, and diplomats established by the Carter Center to provide third-party assistance (mediation), expert analysis and advice, training workshops, and media attention, when needed, to help facilitate the constructive resolution of international conflicts. The INN has been active in the Balkans, Ethiopia, Liberia, and Sudan, among other places. Members include Jimmy Carter, Oscar Arias Sánchez (Nobel Peace Prize winner and former president of Costa Rica), Javier Perez de Cuellar (former UN secretary-general), Hans Dietrich Genscher (former vice chancellor and minister of foreign affairs, Federal Republic of Germany), and Desmond Tutu (Nobel Peace Prize winner and president of the All Africa Conference of Churches). The INN is part of the Carter Center's Conflict Resolution Program.

See also: Carter Center; Appendix 1 for contact information.

International Peace Research Association

The International Peace Research Association (IPRA) is an independent international nongovernmental organization, founded in 1965 out of a widely felt need to apply the tools of social science to develop a better understanding of peace processes. The purpose of IPRA is to "advance interdisciplinary research into the conditions of peace and the causes of war and other forms of violence" (IPRA brochure). Toward this end, IPRA promotes national studies and teaching related to world peace, facilitates contacts and cooperation between scholars and educators throughout the world, and facilitates and encourages the worldwide dissemination of peace research results.

IPRA members come from over 70 countries, representing all the regions of the world. Members participate in working groups examining topics such as communication, conversion of industrial facilities from military to civilian uses, defense and

disarmament, ecological security, food policy, human rights and development, internal conflict resolution, international conflict resolution, nonviolence, peace building in crisis areas, peace education, peace movements, refugees, religious conflict, and women and peace.

See also: Peace Research; Appendix 1 for contact information.

Interpersonal Conflict

Interpersonal conflict occurs between individual people—parents and children, siblings, friends, coworkers, even strangers. Most such conflicts are routine and hardly noticed. Children argue about what game to play, but they usually work it out themselves. Husbands and wives disagree about minor choices all the time—where to go out to dinner, what to do over the weekend, how to handle a rebellious child.

Most interpersonal conflicts are resolved without really thinking about it. In some situations, one side acquiesces to the other, feeling that the problem is not worth arguing about. In other situations, the parties talk it out—negotiate, essentially—in an effort to meet both sides' needs. Conflict becomes a problem only in the small number of situations in which it escalates—when both people are highly invested in the dispute and are unwilling to work out an amicable solution. This is typically the type of conflict that gets noticed, because it is destructive. Thus, this is the kind of interpersonal conflict that needs an active conflict resolution effort.

Conflict Elements

According to Joyce Hocker and William Wilmot (1985), interpersonal conflicts have a number of typical elements. First, they involve an overt struggle. Both people realize that they are in a conflict, and they express that conflict in their communications with the other party. Second, the people in conflict usually believe that they have incompatible goals. One person believes that he cannot have what he wants or needs if the opponent gets what she wants or needs. This is not necessarily the case; it is quite possible that by redefining the problem, or "enlarging the pie" to be divided, both disputants can get their needs met. If this is recognized initially, there will be no conflict. The third element of interpersonal conflicts is perceived scarce rewards. The assumption is made that there is not enough of something to go around. Again, this may not be true, but perceptions drive conflicts, not reality.

In addition, parties in conflict must be interdependent and must interfere with each other in some way. If a party is in no way dependent on another, no conflict will exist—they will simply ignore each other. The same is true for interference. If parties have opposing goals, but each pursues his or her own goal without interfering with the other, no overt conflict will exist. Conflict develops only when one side tries to achieve his or her goal at the expense of the other person.

Like relationships themselves, interpersonal conflicts vary in intensity, importance, and investment. When they involve minor issues with acquaintances, conflicts are usually low in intensity and investment. When they involve major issues with family members, the intensity, importance, and investment can be extremely high, because the potential loss—of the substance of the dispute, of the relationship between the people, or both—is critical.

Conflict Timing
Gregory Tillet (1991) observes that interpersonal conflicts are more likely to occur at critical stages in a relationship: during initiation, when internal or external events force a change in the nature of the relationship, and at the end. Each of these situations causes stress and requires responses

that differ from normal patterns, thereby increasing the chance of misunderstanding and deviation from what is expected.

Conflict Effects
Interpersonal conflicts can be either constructive or destructive, depending on how they are handled. If they are handled in a cooperative, problem-solving way, the outcome is most likely to be positive. People can generate new solutions to problems, learn, grow emotionally, and strengthen their relationships. Conflicts are destructive only if the disputants are hurt by the conflict, which happens more often if the conflict is handled competitively and is allowed to escalate or spiral out of control. In this case, people become increasingly invested in the conflict and often change their goals from trying to win to trying to hurt the other person. Although escalated conflicts can still be resolved, resolution is usually harder to obtain and is likely to leave one or even both parties worse off than they were when they started. For this reason, escalated conflicts are usually more destructive than constructive.

Conflict Styles
Most people tend to rely on preset responses or conflict styles when they are faced with a dispute. These styles can be ranked according to one's aggressiveness and one's propensity to cooperate.

People who are neither aggressive nor cooperative tend to avoid conflicts. They change the subject or avoid a person in an effort to make the conflict go away. Sometimes this works, but often it does not. Ignoring a problem will not solve it unless one side eventually accommodates the other or finds another way to meet his or her goal.

People who are less aggressive and highly cooperative tend to accommodate the other; they tend to go along with whatever the other person wants. This is fine if the issue is not important or when the relationship is more important than the issue in dispute. However, accommodation can create problems if the issue is one that really matters to people on both sides. It can also be a problem if this is the only way that a person can deal with a conflict, because that person will always be taken advantage of.

People who are highly aggressive deal with conflict in a competitive way. Using positional bargaining, they seek to win as much as they can for themselves, with little or no regard for the outcome of the other. This works fine when this sort of behavior is expected and when substantive outcomes are more important than relationship issues. However, the competitive approach can lead to an escalated conflict and potentially a hurting stalemate, in which each side continues to hurt the other without either side being able to prevail.

The fourth possibility is high aggressiveness and high cooperation. Such a person has a strong concern for his or her own outcomes but a strong concern for the outcomes of the other as well. This approach stimulates collaboration or principled negotiation—a problem-solving approach that typically yields productive outcomes for both sides (especially if the other party uses this style as well).

The final possibility is moderate levels of aggressiveness and cooperation, which tends to lead to compromise. Unlike collaboration, which yields win-win outcomes, compromise typically yields half-win outcomes. This means that disputants give up half of what they want to get the other half. (Collaboration works to develop solutions that meet most or all of both parties' needs.) Compromise is useful when collaborative solutions are simply not possible. However, when values in conflict are strong, compromise is often seen as impossible as well (for example, few people will compromise on their positions about abortion or gay rights).

Conflict Management and Resolution

One's approach to conflict typically determines which mode of conflict management or resolution one is most comfortable with. People who tend to avoid conflict may prefer a conflict resolution forum where the problem is solved for them. They are more likely to rely on lawyers to argue their case in court than they are to try to work out their problems themselves through negotiation or mediation. Ironically, very competitive people may react the same way, although competitive people may first try negotiation to overpower their opponent. If this does not work easily, however, highly competitive people are likely to use adversarial dispute resolution mechanisms—typically litigation or arbitration—to force the other side to capitulate.

However, many people have come to realize that adversarial processes have as many costs as they do benefits; in addition, they tend to be very expensive and slow. As a result, more and more people—especially compromisers and collaborators, but others as well—are turning to alternative dispute resolution mechanisms such as mediation to manage or resolve disputes that they cannot negotiate themselves. Mediation is becoming an increasingly common way to resolve marital conflicts (to prevent or facilitate divorce), parent-child conflicts, workplace conflicts, and peer conflicts in schools. In addition, increasing numbers of schools are teaching children how to mediate their own disputes, which may yield a higher percentage of adults who tend to deal with interpersonal conflicts in collaborative ways.

See also: Adversarial Approach; Collaborative Problem Solving; Compromise; Conflict Styles; Dispute Systems Design for Families; Divorce Mediation; Family Conflict; Mediation; Workplace Conflicts and Grievance Procedures.
References and Further Reading: Hocker, Joyce L., and William W. Wilmot, 1985, *Interpersonal Conflict;* Tillett, Gregory, 1991, *Resolving Conflict: A Practical Approach,* 104–14.

Intractable Conflicts

Intractable conflicts are ones that are highly resistant to resolution; they do not respond to traditional or alternative dispute resolution processes. Examples include conflicts based on deep-rooted value differences (for instance, abortion or gay rights), conflicts revolving around high-stakes distributional issues (for example, the federal budget deficit or changes in spending on social programs), and conflicts over a person's or group's position in the socioeconomic hierarchy (many racial and ethnic conflicts are of this type). Although these examples are all public policy conflicts, other kinds of conflicts can be intractable as well. Many international conflicts—the Middle East, Bosnia, Rwanda, the Cold War, Northern Ireland—were highly intractable for many years (and most continue to be). Interpersonal conflicts can also be intractable—witness destructive marital conflicts or the never-ending rivalry between siblings. The common factor that distinguishes many intractable conflicts from more tractable ones is that intractable conflicts are often inherently win-lose. Abortions are either easier to get or harder to get. We spend more on social programs, or we spend less. Although tractable conflicts can often be resolved with solutions that give both sides what they want, most intractable conflicts are structured so that a win-win outcome is not possible.

At times, intractable conflicts are transformed into disputes that can be resolved. This generally happens after a prolonged and damaging stalemate. Eventually the parties may decide that continuing the conflict is doing more harm than good, and they agree to negotiate a settlement. The end of apartheid in South Africa is one example of a highly intractable conflict that was transformed in the 1990s with the implementation of the National Peace Accord. Other intractable conflicts are not "ripe" for resolution. In these conflicts, both sides still think that they can win outright. Therefore, they pursue the conflict for months, years, even centuries, without giving in. Even when such intractable conflicts cannot be transformed, they can be conducted in more or less constructive ways.

It is important to consider how tractable a conflict is likely to be, because tractable conflicts are managed differently than intractable conflicts. Tractable conflicts can be resolved through litigation, negotiation, or mediation. Intractable conflicts cannot be resolved with those methods. If conflicts are likely to be intractable, disputants and potential third-party intermediaries should determine how they can confront the conflict most constructively and least destructively, rather than focusing on how to resolve it. Thus, conflict resolution is not always the appropriate goal. Conflict management is more appropriate and potentially more successful in the case of intractable conflicts.

Rather than being completely tractable or intractable, disputes can be ranked on a continuum from simple to impossible to resolve. For example, simple contract disputes in which one party says that a contract was violated and the other disagrees are usually relatively easy to handle. Parties or their lawyers present the case to a judge, a jury, or an arbitrator, who listens to both sides and then makes a decision in favor of one party or the other. At the other extreme, the conflict over abortion in the United States is probably impossible to resolve. Laws will be passed that make abortions either easier or harder to get. But the value differences and the strongly held beliefs of the pro-life and pro-choice factions are unlikely to change sufficiently so that abortion is no longer an issue of political contention.

Most conflicts fall somewhere between these two extremes. For example, many environmental conflicts are fought for years, but they are eventually resolved. Family conflicts can also smolder for a long time but may eventually be resolved by negotiation, mediation, or, not uncommonly, dissolution of the family.

Many factors contribute to a conflict's placement along the tractability continuum. Among those factors that make a conflict more intractable are the presence of deep-rooted value differences, an unavoidable win-lose outcome, high stakes, the presence of alternatives that are perceived to be better than any obtainable negotiated settlement (see BATNA), large numbers of parties, large numbers of issues, and complex issues. If a conflict has many of these complicating factors, it is likely to be intractable. If it has none, it should be resolvable. If it has only one or two, it may be resolvable with effort. However, some of these factors (especially deep-rooted value differences and high stakes) can make a conflict intractable, even if none of the other factors are present.

See also: Conflict and Dispute; *Roe v. Wade.*
References and Further Reading: Burgess, Heidi, and Guy Burgess, 1993, "Confronting Intractable Conflicts in Constructive Ways"; Kriesberg, Louis, Terrell A. Northrup, and Stuart J. Thorson, 1989, *Intractable Conflicts and Their Transformation;* Kriesberg, Louis, and Stuart J. Thorson, 1991, "Timing the De-escalation of International Conflicts."

Israeli-Palestinian Women's Workshop

In 1987 and 1992, the Center for International Affairs at Harvard University sponsored a set of workshops designed to bring together politically active Israeli and Palestinian women. The workshops were informal, and the women involved held no official positions. These workshops were intended to foster working trust among the participants and to allow them to analyze the conflict as a shared problem and generate new approaches to its resolution. These workshops also offered researchers an opportunity to analyze and evaluate the interactive problem-solving approach to

conflict resolution. Researchers investigated both the effect that the workshops had on the participants and the impact that such workshops might have on the larger negotiation process.

Researchers started from the premise that stable peace requires a transformation of the relationship between the communities in conflict. This process of transformation can be described in three stages. First, each side must acknowledge and question its stereotypes of the other. The workshop participants showed evidence of reaching this first stage. For example, one of the workshop participants was a prominent member of a right-wing religious party. She effectively challenged stereotypes held by both Palestinian women and more left-wing Israeli women. Workshop participants "commented on the value of hearing a 'reasonable' voice from that end of the political spectrum" (Babbitt and d'Estree 1996, 523).

In the second stage, the parties actually revise their stereotypes in a direction that is more conducive to negotiating and problem solving. The parties begin to develop a working trust. Researchers also saw evidence of second-stage development. The workshops showed that both sides labored under external constraints and internal division. Palestinian participants felt that it was helpful to understand the factors constraining Israeli women. Seemingly inconsistent behavior on the part of the Israelis could now be seen as consistent, given this improved understanding. In turn, the Palestinian women were willing to discuss differences within their own group. One Israeli participant took this openness to show "a level of trust, both in the process and [in] the Israeli participants" (Babbitt and d'Estree 1996, 525), that she had not observed in Palestinians previously. In the third stage, the parties cement their changes in assumptions and attitude. This results from their continuing interaction and the repeated confirmation that the new information and interpretations are a valid reflection of the other side's character and intent.

In assessing the potential impact of such workshops on the larger negotiation process, the researchers were particularly interested in two questions. First, how did the participants apply the understanding gained from the workshop to the political arena? Follow-up interviews with the participants revealed two changes in their political activities. Participants tended to maintain contact with one another, exchanging information and facilitating networking and coalition building across conflict lines. Participants also showed an increased sensitivity to the concerns of the other community.

Second, researchers considered the potential of unofficial problem-solving workshops to contribute to official negotiations. Researchers observed that improved understanding, trust, and coalition building are valuable contributions in any stage of the negotiating process. In particular, though, these workshops "presaged the disagreements that were to occur later, and with more vehemence, in the real negotiations" (Babbitt and d'Estree 1996, 527). For example, the workshops revealed internal differences within the Palestinian community, differences that might have been more fruitfully explored and clarified in the presence of the participants' developing trust.

Researchers also asked whether women had a unique role to play in the peace process. Although lacking comparative data, researchers speculated that the presence of shared experiences among the participants, such as child rearing, bound them together as women. These shared experiences may have served as a foundation on which to build further shared understandings and from which to develop a working trust.

See also: Diplomacy, Citizen, Track Two, and Multitrack; Problem Solving, Analytical; Stereotyping; Transformation; Trust and Trust Building.

References and Further Reading: Babbitt, Eileen, and Tamra d'Estree, 1996, "An Israeli-Palestinian Women's Workshop"; Rothman, Jay, 1992, *Confrontation to Cooperation: Resolving Ethnic and Regional Conflict.*

Jamestown Area Labor Management Committee

The Jamestown Area Labor Management Committee (JALMC) is one of many collaborative efforts between labor and management undertaken in an effort to improve labor-management relations, revitalize businesses and their host communities, and attract new businesses to areas that are suffering from declining economies or populations. Collaboration is also intended to help businesses and their host communities to compete more successfully in the global marketplace.

Although this type of collaborative effort is becoming increasingly popular in the 1990s, the JALMC was started much earlier and, according to Barbara Gray (1989, 195), is the "most long-standing and successful labor management collaboration." The JALMC is composed of the general managers and top union representatives of all the manufacturing firms in the Jamestown, New York, area. It came together in 1972 at the urging of Jamestown's mayor, who was also active on the committee.

The JALMC has taken initiatives to offset economic decline, improve working conditions in the factories, and encourage industrial development in the community (Trist 1983). The results have been a marked improvement of what had been a "very bitter industrial relations climate," the rescue of numerous businesses and the attraction of thousands of new jobs to the area, the introduction of shop-floor democracy in several factories, and "a network to support shared innovation and training among the participating firms" (Gray 1989, 195).

Gray attributes the JALMC's success to several factors, including a focus on the revitalization of existing plants, a separation of collective bargaining from the JALMC agenda, and the skillful leadership of the mayor and a representative of the local machinists union. This kind of collaboration between labor and management is becoming much more common and important, as global competition makes sustaining U.S. industries and jobs increasingly difficult.

See also: Collaborative Problem Solving; Labor-Management Relations and Conflict.
References and Further Reading: Gray, Barbara, 1989, *Collaborating: Finding Common Ground for Multiparty Problems;* Trist, E. L., 1983, "Referent Organizations and the Development of Interorganizational Domains."

Joint Fact-Finding

Joint fact-finding is a useful technique for resolving fact-based disputes. It is usually used in collaborative problem solving or consensus-building processes, but it can be used in other settings as well. In collaborative processes, the parties sit down together and ask themselves what they know and don't know about the issues to determine what they need to clarify in order to make informed decisions. Then they work together to find the answers by forming working groups, consulting with neutral outside experts, or otherwise jointly engaging in the fact-finding process in such a way that everyone agrees on the facts once they are obtained.

For example, parties might disagree about the best way to meet a city's future transportation needs. Some might advocate the construction of new roads; others might wish to widen roads that currently exist; still others might advocate the development of light rail or expanded bus routes and schedules. To effectively deal with these issues, the parties might first sit down together and look at what they know. Do they know the current capacity and use rates of area roads and alternative transportation systems? Do they know (and agree on) future population projections? Do they agree on the effect of these projections on transportation use? Most likely, uncertainty will exist in all these areas. Teams can then form to investigate these different issues. When necessary, neutral experts—considered trustworthy by all sides—can be consulted to provide or interpret information for the team or for the group as a whole. Although not all factual disputes can be completely resolved in this way, the level of disagreement is likely to be significantly diminished and the decision-making process correspondingly enhanced.

See also: Citizens' Radiation Monitoring Program; Environmental Conflicts; Fact-Based Disputes; Neutral Expert Fact-Finding; Public Policy Conflicts; Scientific and Technical Disputes.

References and Further Reading: Singer, Linda R., 1990, *Settling Disputes: Conflict Resolution in Business, Families, and the Legal System,* 15–30; Susskind, Lawrence, and Jeffrey Cruikshank, 1987, *Breaking the Impasse.*

Journal of Conflict Resolution

The *Journal of Conflict Resolution* (*JCR*) is published six times a year by Sage Publications. One of the leading journals in the field, *JCR* was also the first journal that focused on the topics of conflict resolution,

war, and peace. It was started shortly after World War II by a small group of scholars including Herbert Kelman, Kenneth Boulding, and Anatol Rapoport, who formed the Research Exchange on the Prevention of War.

Coming from diverse disciplines, this group was interested in applying scientific techniques to the problem of avoiding war. They formed working groups, held meetings, and published a journal, which became the *Journal of Conflict Resolution* in 1957. According to Kelman, publication of the journal helped move the field of peace research in a professional direction. The journal united international relations scholars with the earlier "nonspecialist" scholars who had been involved in the initial research exchange. It also led to the creation of the Center for Research on Conflict Resolution at the University of Michigan, a focal point for early U.S. peace research.

JCR is still an interdisciplinary journal of social scientific theory and research on human conflict. It focuses on both international and intergroup conflict within and between nations. In addition to theoretical articles and reports on basic research, it includes reports about innovative practical applications of conflict resolution processes.

See also: Boulding, Kenneth; Kelman, Herbert; Peace Research; Rapoport, Anatol; Appendix 1 for contact information.

Justice

Justice can be defined in many ways. Sometimes justice refers to getting a fair outcome. If a person engages in a criminal activity and is caught and convicted, justice is said to be served if the criminal is punished consistently with societal norms and with the punishment of similar offenders. If the offender receives too harsh a sentence or no punishment at all, people are likely to charge that an injustice has occurred.

In other cases, justice refers to the fair distribution of scarce resources (commonly referred to as distributive justice). Within this category, scholars distinguish among three approaches: equity, equality, and need. When justice is defined in terms of equity, people are rewarded in proportion to what they put into a particular situation. This suggests that people who work harder should earn more money or get better grades, and that sports stars should get greater rewards than other players who do not contribute as much to the team's success.

Justice may also be defined in terms of equality: everyone gets the same thing, regardless of input. An example is equalized school funding. When tax dollars are collected from everyone in a state and distributed evenly, so that poor school districts get just as much money as rich districts, the principle of equality, rather than equity, is being followed. Similarly, if spots on a sports team are distributed by lottery rather than skill, or if everyone gets to play and positions are rotated, the principle of equality is being followed.

If justice were defined in terms of need, poor school districts would be given more money for education than rich districts, because the children in those districts need lower student-teacher ratios, more time in school, and more special programs.

Since there is no one definition of justice or fairness that is "right," deciding how to make important distribution decisions can be controversial. A strong argument for each approach can be made, and little basis is available for determining which argument is more "just" than the others.

In addition to defining justice in terms of outcome, some definitions emphasize the importance of how a decision is made. This is referred to as procedural justice. Just as distributive justice can be defined in terms of equity, equality, and need, procedural justice can be defined in terms of neutrality, standing, and trust (Folger, Sheppard, and Buttran 1995). Neutrality requires that decisions be made by an honest, unbiased decision maker who considers accurate and appropriate facts. Standing refers to social position or status within a group or within a process. If people are denied standing, they are denied participation in a decision. If they are concerned about or likely to be affected by the decision, the denial of participation is likely to lead to charges of injustice. Trust involves the belief that the intentions of third-party decision makers are benevolent, that they want to treat people in a fair and reasonable way (Tyler and Lind 1992, 142). If disputants lack trust in the third-party decision maker, they too are likely to assert that the decision is unfair.

Different approaches to justice meet different goals. People who are most concerned with financial success and economic productivity tend to emphasize equity and neutrality, whereas those who are most concerned with social relationships and the cohesiveness of groups tend to see equality and standing as most important. Trust and need are the factors stressed by people who are most concerned with nurturing and care of the individual. However, these assessments change as the situation changes. Thus, justice tends to be a slippery concept that is highly important but difficult to grasp (Folger, Sheppard, and Buttran 1995).

See also: Peace; Structural Violence.

References and Further Reading: Bunker, Barbara Benedict, Jeffrey Z. Rubin, and Associates, 1995, *Conflict, Cooperation, and Justice: Essays Inspired by the Work of Morton Deutsch,* 441; Folger, Robert, Blair H. Sheppard, and Robert T. Buttran, 1995, "Equity, Equality, and Need: Three Faces of Social Justice"; Tyler, T. R., and E. A. Lind, 1992, "A Relational Model of Authority in Groups."

Kelman, Herbert

Herbert Kelman was one of the founders of the field of dispute resolution and is still one of its leading figures. Kelman received his doctorate from Yale University in 1951. In the early 1960s, he became a professor of psychology at the University of Michigan, where he was also a research psychologist with the Center for Research on Conflict Resolution. He later became a professor of social ethics at Harvard. His work in social psychology explores social influence and attitude change. His interest in conflict resolution focuses on international problems, particularly the Arab-Israeli conflict.

Kelman is best known to the field of conflict resolution for his development and implementation of analytical problem solving and problem-solving workshops. Analytical problem solving takes an analytical or scholarly approach to examining the fundamental nature of conflict, including underlying sources, history, and dynamics. It teams disputants with scholar-facilitators to do this analysis as a precursor to the formal negotiations. Problem-solving workshops provide an unofficial setting in which parties to a conflict can explore their perceptions of the conflict and of each other. The goal is to develop a better mutual understanding of the situation and to establish a working trust between the participants.

See also: Israeli-Palestinian Women's Workshop; Problem Solving, Analytical; Trust and Trust Building.

References and Further Reading: Kelman, Herbert, 1965, *International Behavior: A Social Psychological Analysis;* Kelman, Herbert, and Stephen Cohen, 1976, "The Problem-Solving Workshop: A Social Psychological Contribution to the Resolution of Conflict."

Kettering Foundation and National Issues Forums

The Kettering Foundation is an operating (not grant-making) foundation that works to improve the public policy-making process from the local through the international level. It is especially interested in getting the public involved in the policy-making process. To do this, the foundation has formulated what it calls "new rules of engagement," through which people can interact to "turn unproductive relationships into more constructive ways of working together" (Kettering Foundation Web Site). These rules of engagement are for use by the conflicting parties themselves, not third parties, and are designed to be used for situations in which traditional negotiation and mediation are unlikely to be successful.

For example, one of Kettering's most successful programs is its National Issues Forums—nonpartisan discussions about controversial public policy issues, based on the tradition of early American town meetings. Since 1982, Kettering has run forums on topics such as affirmative action, freedom of speech, family values, youth violence, abortion, health care, and racial inequality. In 1995 and 1996, locally sponsored forums were held in almost 200 communities in 37 states.

Unlike ordinary public meetings or hearings in which people talk at one another without listening, National Issues Forums are moderated to encourage thoughtful consideration of all the views expressed. By reading and discussing background materials supplied by Kettering, participants inform themselves and one another, identify and evaluate a broad range of policy alternatives, and work to develop a common perspective on the issue that is geared toward effective action.

"National Issues Forums put the public back into politics, not by helping to elect candidates or advancing special interests, but by enhancing the public's ability to make choices well" (Kettering Foundation Web Site). After participating in National Issues Forums, people are usually better able to identify and evaluate alternative policies, and they try much harder to understand the ideas of others who have different values or assessments of the problem. Thus, participants tend to become more open-minded and form new personal bonds across racial, class, and other group lines.

Kettering has published the results of its work in a variety of forms. It develops study guides and exercises for use in schools, colleges, and universities; it publishes a journal, the *Kettering Review;* and it publishes a variety of reports.

See also: Dialogue; Public Conversations Project; Value Conflicts; Appendix 1 for contact information.

King, Martin Luther, Jr.

Martin Luther King Jr. is considered by many to be the greatest black leader of the twentieth century. Born in Atlanta, Georgia, in 1929, King grew up under segregation in the South. Although his own family was relatively well-off, he saw the oppressive poverty, violence, and injustice suffered by many southern blacks. Like many other blacks, he devoted his life to a quest for justice, and he did so through a steadfast commitment to nonviolence, an approach he began to espouse during his college years.

After college, King decided to follow his father into the ministry. He received his bachelor of divinity degree from Crozer Theological Seminary in 1951 and went on to earn his doctorate in systematic theology at Boston University in 1955.

While pursuing his graduate studies, King was appointed pastor of the Dexter Avenue Baptist Church in Montgomery, Alabama. A gifted orator, he quickly became famous as the leader of the 1954 Montgomery bus boycott and, after that, as one of the most respected leaders of the early civil rights movement in the South. He later formed the Southern Christian Leadership Conference in order to pursue black civil rights at the national level. King received the Nobel Peace Prize in 1964 and continued to be a central figure in the civil rights movement until his assassination in 1968.

It was in the Montgomery boycott that King first put into action the theory of nonviolent resistance, which he had encountered in Henry David Thoreau's "Essay on Civil Disobedience" as an undergraduate. Although he was moved by Thoreau's work, it was not until he entered the seminary that King launched a concerted effort to find a solution to the problem of social injustice. There, King studied Mahatma Gandhi's writing in depth. He was profoundly influenced by Gandhi's philosophy of nonviolent resistance, called satyagraha. He was also influenced by U.S. theologian Reinhold Niebuhr. Niebuhr's critique of pacifism led King to understand nonviolent resistance as an active, rather than passive, response to evil.

In his essay "Pilgrimage to Nonviolence," King described his philosophy of nonviolent resistance. Central to King's philosophy was an emphasis on love, understanding, and redemptive goodwill. Nonviolent resistance is not passive acceptance of evil; it is an active but loving confrontation of evil and injustice. The nonviolent resister does not seek to defeat and humiliate the opponent but to awaken the opponent's sense of moral shame, win the opponent's understanding, and ultimately build a shared community. To achieve this goal, the resister must refrain from not only physical violence but also mental violence, or hate. He or she must always seek to see the opponent's humanity. Resistance, King said, is to be directed "against the forces of evil rather than against persons who happen to be doing evil" (King 1966, 391). Underlying King's approach was the belief that "the universe is on the side of justice" (King 1966, 395). Although nonviolent resistance can be used simply as a tactic, King, like Gandhi, saw even greater potential for nonviolence as a way of life. An ethic based on love, understanding, and nonviolent resistance to evil, he believed, could make a profound contribution to world peace.

See also: Ethnic and Racial Conflicts; Gandhi, Mahatma; Identity Conflicts; Montgomery Bus Boycott; Nonviolence.
References and Further Reading: Colaiaco, James A., 1988, *Martin Luther King, Jr.: Apostle of Militant Nonviolence;* King, Martin Luther, Jr., 1958, *Stride toward Freedom;* King, Martin Luther, Jr., 1964, *Why We Can't Wait;* King, Martin Luther, Jr., 1966, "Pilgrimage to Nonviolence"; King, Martin Luther, Jr., 1967, *Where Do We Go from Here: Chaos or Community?*

Kissinger, Henry A.

Henry Kissinger served as national security adviser and secretary of state under President Richard Nixon and was the leader of U.S. foreign policy during that time. Kissinger followed the policy of realpolitik, instituting a foreign policy that was pragmatic, not ideological, and focused on maintaining international stability by maintaining the balance of power. He negotiated with anyone—enemies or allies—and did whatever it took to protect U.S. interests.

Yet Kissinger also acted as a mediator when he believed that it was in the United States' interests to do so. He was the first to make widespread use of shuttle diplomacy—moving back and forth between adversaries, facilitating the exchange of messages when parties in conflict were unwilling or unable to meet in person. He used this approach extensively in the Middle East, for example. Through shuttle diplomacy, Kissinger mediated a cease-fire in the 1973 Middle East war, persuaded Israel to withdraw its troops from Egypt, and convinced the Organization of Petroleum Exporting Countries (OPEC) to end its oil embargo. These efforts likely contributed to President Jimmy Carter's ability, in 1978, to mediate the Camp David Accords.

In addition, Kissinger participated in secret meetings that resulted in the January 1973 cease-fire agreement between North Vietnam and the United States, for which he shared the Nobel Peace Prize (with Le Duc Tho) in 1973. Kissinger is also credited with helping to normalize relations with the Soviet Union, opening the People's Republic of China to the West, and laying the groundwork for Nixon's 1972 signing of the Strategic Arms Limitation Treaty (SALT I). Nevertheless, Kissinger's (and Nixon's) foreign policies and strategies were opposed by many Americans. Along with Nixon, Kissinger was blamed for broadening the U.S. war in Vietnam and authorizing both the secret bombing of Cambodia and the terror bombing of Hanoi in 1972. He was also criticized for allowing covert CIA operations in South America and Africa—even while he was engaged in negotiations in those regions.

See also: Cold War; Détente; Diplomacy; Morgenthau, Hans; United Nations Mediation of the Egyptian-Israeli Negotiations at Kilometer 101.
References and Further Reading: Isaacson, Walter, 1992, *Kissinger: A Biography;* Kissinger, Henry, 1994, *Diplomacy;* Shawcross, William, 1979, *Sideshow: Kissinger, Nixon, and the Destruction of Cambodia.*

Labor-Management Negotiations: The Air Canada/IAM Case

Labor-management negotiations tend to be highly routinized, but at the same time, they can be difficult. Several factors present obstacles to successful negotiations. The 1987 negotiations between Air Canada and the International Association of Machinists (IAM) present a case in point.

First, most labor-management negotiations take the form of a zero-sum game. This means that whatever the union gains, management loses. This trade-off is not always necessary—sometimes unions make demands that cost the company little or no money (or vice versa)—but usually the negotiations revolve around money-related issues such as wages, benefits, or working conditions. Thus, the more one party wins, the more the other loses. This win-lose structure makes the application of principled negotiation considerably more difficult.

Factors external to the company and the union—and hence completely outside the negotiators' control—can also complicate negotiations. As an example (drawn from a case study originally written by Bryan Downie in 1991), negotiations between Air Canada and its machinists (represented by IAM) broke down in October 1987. The issues were wages and pensions. Although a tentative agreement had been reached in September, the rank-and-file union members were not scheduled to

vote on the agreement until October. By the time they did so, the Canadian autoworkers had negotiated a completely separate labor agreement with Chrysler Canada for indexed pensions—the first such agreement in the history of Canadian labor. (With indexed pensions, pension benefits increase when the consumer price index increases.) Although the original agreement reached by the Air Canada and IAM negotiators gave IAM members the same benefits received by other Air Canada unions, it did not include indexed pensions. Since Chrysler workers had just received indexing, the IAM members thought that they could hold out for indexed pensions too. They therefore rejected the settlement and threatened to strike if an agreement on indexing could not be reached.

Air Canada could not afford to give in, because it had already negotiated a considerable increase in pension benefits, and any more concessions would make its labor costs much higher that its main competitor's. Further, if IAM pensions were indexed, all the other unions that worked with Air Canada would want their pensions indexed too, which could cost the company enormous sums of money. The company, therefore, refused the indexing demand.

According to Canadian law, before a union can strike, it must attempt mediation. One of the best labor mediators in Canada was brought in but could not reach an agreement. IAM threatened and then carried out a rotating strike (striking a different site each day), and when that didn't work, the union struck the whole company, shutting it down completely for 19 days shortly before the Christmas travel season.

Although neither side had been willing to negotiate further before the strike, the threatened loss of the Christmas season brought both sides back to the bargaining table in mid-December. By that time, concessions that had been unacceptable earlier became tolerable. The mediator designed a solution that offered the union an indexed pension, but in such a way that it did not cost the company significantly more money. Thus, both sides were able to claim to their constituencies that they had won, and the second settlement was ratified without trouble.

This case illustrates a number of characteristics that are common not only in labor-management negotiations but also in many other kinds of negotiations. One is the concept of "ripeness." Negotiations can break down at one time and then succeed later, when the parties finally realize that they will be hurt more by continuing the stalemate than by reaching an agreement. This was not true for either side in early December, when the potential benefits of a strike surpassed the expected costs. However, once the strike threatened to cut into Christmas profits, both the company and the union members—who earned overtime pay during the holidays—wanted to reach an agreement and go back to work.

Face saving is another important concept illustrated in this case. The agreement finally reached was one that both labor and management could call a victory. It was not as good as either side had wanted, but it met their most important needs. Thus, neither side had to admit that it had lost.

Another "trick" used by the mediator at the end was to change the people involved in the negotiations. Often it helps just to bring in new faces—people who are not battle-weary and who do not have personal grudges against the others. In this case, the mediator went further by bringing in the top company management into the negotiations. This signaled to the union that the company meant business, and the dispute was settled relatively quickly with this change of personnel.

Downie concluded his case study as follows: "The Air Canada/IAM case documents that timing, process, symbols, information and face-saving are as important, if not more so, than substance. Where there is an impasse, they seem to be at the crux of the settlement process" (Downie 1991, 185). Negotiators and mediators must be cognizant of all these issues and be able to play one against the other in order to successfully conclude what might appear to be a simple negotiated agreement.

See also: Collective Bargaining; Face Saving; Labor-Management Relations and Conflict; Mediation; Negotiation and Mediation; Timing and "Ripeness"; Principled Negotiation and *Getting to Yes;* Win-Win, Win-Lose, and All-Lose Outcomes.
References and Further Reading: Downie, Bryan M., 1991, "When Negotiations Fail: Causes of Breakdown and Tactics for Breaking the Stalemate."

Labor-Management Relations and Conflict

Labor and management have a fundamental conflict of interest that is currently highly managed and structured by laws and collective bargaining agreements. This structure has many benefits. It has routinized labor-management conflict sufficiently that lengthy strikes are relatively uncommon, and violence, which used to be commonplace, is now rare. However, the structure also has disadvantages. Especially problematic is the inherent adversarial nature of most collective bargaining and grievance procedures. These procedures discourage and, at times, even preclude more collaborative problem-solving approaches to labor-management relations that theoretically could benefit both sides.

The current structure of labor-management relations began to take shape after World War I. Before that time, there were few unions; most employees negotiated terms of employment directly with the employer. Robber barons and even smaller employers held all the economic and political power; workers had none. Consequently, workers, especially newly freed slaves and recent immigrants—people with little training and power in the society—were highly vulnerable and badly exploited.

Disgust with the situation eventually led to a number of protective laws enacted by the states and the federal government. These included laws regulating the maximum number of hours worked and minimum wages for women and children (later extended to men) and laws providing workers' compensation, social security, unemployment insurance, disability insurance, and other similar protections.

Other laws protected employees' right to form and participate in labor unions. The first such act was the Railway Labor Act of 1926, which regulated the collective bargaining process in the railroad industry. A 1934 amendment established the National Mediation Board, which was empowered to conduct certification elections to certify union representation of employee groups. This was followed in 1935 by the National Labor Relations Act (the Wagner Act), which was passed to reduce work stoppages caused by union-recognition disputes and to legitimate the collective bargaining process to better equalize the power between employers and employees. This act established the right of employees in all industries engaged in interstate commerce to form or join unions and established those unions' right to engage in collective bargaining and to strike. The National Labor Relations Board (NLRB) was established to enforce the

provisions of the act, but it did not have any mediation or conciliation functions.

Misconceptions about and problems with the Wagner Act led to the passage of the Labor Management Relations Act (Taft-Hartley Act) in 1947. This act went beyond the Wagner Act to protect both labor and management from abuses perpetrated by the other. It also created the Federal Mediation and Conciliation Service to help resolve labor-management conflicts.

These acts (and others) established the current highly structured relationship between employers and unions based on the collective bargaining agreements (or contracts) that are negotiated by union and management leaders once every few years. In addition to setting wages, working conditions, benefits, and the like, most collective bargaining agreements contain detailed regulations regarding appropriate behavior of workers and management in a variety of situations. These details give rise to what is called "contract administration," the process of resolving disputes over whether the collective bargaining contract has been followed correctly. Such disputes are usually handled by a multilevel grievance procedure that starts with an employee speaking to his or her supervisor and ends with binding arbitration between management and union representatives who act on behalf of the employer and the employee. (Several steps are available in between these end points.)

Typically, both contract negotiations and grievance resolution are done in an adversarial way. Contract negotiations are usually conducted using positional bargaining, with unions and management trading concessions while trying to increase their power. Sometimes negotiators take a more integrative or problem-solving approach, negotiating on the basis of interests rather than positions, but this is still relatively rare in the labor-management arena.

Similarly, although grievances are sometimes resolved by mediation, arbitration is much more common. In arbitration, the assumption is made that one party is right and the other is wrong, and an adversarial process is used to distinguish between the two. Mediation, in contrast, looks at the interests behind both stories and tries to solve the problem without necessarily assigning blame.

Since the outcome of adversarial conflict resolution processes is highly dependent on relative power, the balance of power between unions and management is always in contention. The Taft-Hartley Act was passed, in part, because many thought that the Wagner Act gave unions too much power. Even after the Taft-Hartley Act was passed, however, the power of unions continued to grow until the 1980s, when various economic conditions began to erode that power base. Foreign competition altered the U.S. economy and employers' viability, as did the shift from manufacturing to service-sector jobs. Both of these economic changes diminished the power of unions and forced them to relinquish more than they gained (in some industries, at least). Union membership in the 1990s is down considerably as a result of these trends.

Another result of these economic pressures has been a change in labor-management relations from a highly adversarial structure to a more collaborative relationship. Although the inherent conflict of interest between labor and management still exists, both sides realize that one cannot exist without the other, and neither can thrive without the cooperation of the other. For this reason, increasing numbers of employers are altering the adversarial nature of their collective bargaining, grievance review, and even decision-making processes. Integrative approaches are being tried more frequently in all these areas, with variable success. Examples of such cooperation include the establishment of labor-management problem-solving committees developed to work out problems that cannot be adequately addressed in the 30-day contract negotiation period. More and more contracts are including only vague references to certain items—safety and health issues or pension program administration, for instance—and are referring such items for resolution through these labor-management committees. Another example is what is called "relationship by objective." This is a cooperative approach on the part of management to work out problems with unions using collaborative or integrative techniques, rather than the traditional adversarial processes. A third trend is what is called codetermination. This is the involvement of workers in what used to be management decision making. Widespread in Europe, codetermination is growing in popularity in the United States as well.

However, some observers believe that the success of such integrative ventures is limited by the fundamental structure of labor-management relations. Contract negotiators may use integrative bargaining to work out a contract, but the rank and file must still approve the contract that results. If the contract does not "win" enough concessions from the other side, it may not be approved. Although sophisticated union and management leaders may recognize the superiority of cooperation over competition, negotiation trainer Charles Heckscher observes that most workers believe that competition has worked for them in the past; thus they tend to reward it in the present. Negotiators who hold out for all they can get are likely to be rewarded and retained; ones who are seen as weak (because they compromise) are likely to be released. This kind of attitude among the rank and file makes innovation in the labor-management relations area difficult. Others are not nearly as negative, citing many successful collaborative agreements and processes in contract negotiation, administration, and business decision making.

See also: Arbitration, Labor; Bargaining, Integrative and Distributive; Collective Bargaining; Federal Mediation and Conciliation Service;
References and Further Reading: Heckscher, Charles C., 1993, "Searching for Mutual Gains in Labor Relations"; Kovach, Kenneth, 1987, "New Directions in Labor Relations"; Leap, Terry L., 1995, Collective Bargaining and Labor Relations; Weiss, David S., 1996, Beyond the Walls of Conflict: Mutual Gains Negotiating for Unions and Management.

Landlord-Tenant Disputes

Disputes between landlords and tenants are common over such issues as rent payment, maintenance of the rental property, damage to the rental property, and return of security deposits at the end of a rental relationship. When the parties cannot resolve these disputes by themselves, they have several options available. One is to take the case to court—often small-claims court, but sometimes the regular courts. Another option is mediation. Many community mediation programs routinely mediate landlord-tenant conflicts for free. Some jurisdictions even require that mediation be attempted before a case will be heard in court.

See also: Community Justice Centers; Consumer Disputes; Mediation, Community.
References and Further Reading: Singer, Linda R., 1990, Settling Disputes: Conflict Resolution in Business, Families, and the Legal System.

Laue, James Howard

Until his death in 1993, James Laue was one of the leaders in academic and applied conflict resolution. Laue, who was white, began his career with the primarily non-white Community Relations Service. He was friends with and was trusted by Martin Luther King and Roger Wilkins, along with many other black leaders. He mediated civil rights disputes in Selma, Alabama, and helped resolve the Memphis, Tennessee, garbage collectors strike. From the Community Relations Service, he went on to help found one of the first university-based conflict resolution practice centers in the United States: the Conflict Clinic, which is still one of the leading public policy and environmental dispute resolution organizations in the United States. A leader in international conflict resolution as well, in 1979, Laue was asked by President Jimmy Carter to be vice chairman of a commission to establish a national peace academy (which ultimately was established as the United States Institute of Peace). In 1987, he went to George Mason University to become the first educator in the United States to hold an endowed chair in the newly developed field of conflict resolution.

In a memoir of Laue, Roger Wilkins wrote, "when I grew up, I entered the world and began to work, as so many black people do, to make America keep her promises, I found that there were far fewer white Americans who had that passionate Jeffersonian dream etched deeply in their souls as I had once thought. But Jim Laue had it. . . . And I also thought, and do now think, that a life is not defined by its most glorious moments, by the times when you are on the stage, and the lights are on you, and you do something fine. I believe, rather, that a great life is the life where the person goes the distance for her or his beliefs and ideas and where the fidelity to those beliefs and those ideas is worked out in the private places where we really live our lives. . . . Jim Laue was a man possessed with a dream of a decent society and a decent world. Jim Laue was a man of passion who wrested every bit of result from the great store of innate ability that he had. Jim Laue was my friend. Jim Laue went the distance" (Wilkins 1993, 5).

See also: Community Relations Service; Environmental Conflicts; Ethnic and Racial Conflicts; King, Martin Luther, Jr.; Public Policy Conflicts; United States Institute of Peace.
References and Further Reading: Laue, James H., 1993, "Resolution: Transforming Conflict and Violence"; Wilkins, Roger, 1993, "My Friend Jim Laue."

Law and Society Association

The Law and Society Association (LSA) was founded in 1964 by a multidisciplinary group of scholars interested in the place of law in social, political, economic, and cultural life. Members include lawyers and scholars from the fields of sociology, political science, psychology, anthropology, economics, and history. Members share a common commitment to developing theoretical and empirical understanding of law as it relates to other social institutions and to developing the interdisciplinary field of sociolegal studies.

The LSA publishes the quarterly *Law and Society Review* and a regular newsletter. The newsletter contains information about the association and developments in the field. It also publishes information about opportunities for research funding, educational programs, and conferences.

The LSA's annual meeting usually draws over 700 people. A graduate student workshop is held in conjunction with the annual meeting, and a week-long summer institute is held to introduce new scholars to the field.

See also: Appendix 1 for contact information.

League of Nations

The League of Nations was an international organization devoted to maintaining international peace through collective security. It began in 1920 and was effectively replaced in 1945 by the United Nations (the league ceased operations in 1946). The League of Nations came about as part of the negotiated peace that ended World War I. President Woodrow Wilson formulated a peace plan based on fourteen points, one of which was the formation of a general association of nations. This peace plan was accepted by the Allies and by the Axis powers and formed the basis for the Treaty of Versailles, which formally ended World War I. Despite Wilson's prominent role in founding the League of Nations, the United States objected to its call for collective security and never officially joined. Although the United States attended the league's meetings on an unofficial basis, its refusal to join considerably lessened the league's effectiveness. Despite the U.S. position, Wilson received the Nobel Peace Prize in 1920 for his efforts to establish the League of Nations.

The league did have some successes. It contributed to improving health and labor conditions around the world, aiding World War I refugees, and preventing the escalation of a few international disputes, such as a territorial dispute between Finland and Sweden and a border dispute between Greece and Bulgaria. However, the major powers were unwilling to submit their disputes to the league for resolution; it was therefore unable to prevent a number of major disputes from escalating and was completely powerless to prevent the occurrences that led to World War II. The league became smaller and weaker through the 1930s and 1940s and was finally officially dissolved in 1946, ceding authority to the United Nations.

See also: Collective Security; International Conflict; United Nations; Wilson, Woodrow.
References and Further Reading: Northedge, F. S., 1986, *The League of Nations: Its Life and Times 1920–1946;* Scott, George, 1973, *The Rise and Fall of the League of Nations.*

Legislative Process

Although not commonly considered a conflict resolution mechanism, democratic legislative processes are an effective way to resolve public policy conflicts at the local, state, and federal levels. Since they operate by majority vote and the will of the majority becomes binding, legislative decisions can be made with much less than consensual support. However, the passage of bills does not always mean that losers will give up the fight. Often, they continue their political efforts in the hope of reversing or altering a decision in a future legislative session. Nevertheless, decisions are made, programs are implemented, and disputes are temporarily settled, if not permanently resolved.

Often, a great deal of negotiation occurs before a bill is passed. A bill usually goes through many revisions—in a sense, a single-text negotiation process—though at times, several different versions of a bill are under consideration simultaneously. One common tactic is for legislators to trade votes on different issues. Thus, a senator may agree to vote for another senator's important bill if that senator will do the same for the first one's pet bill. This is a broader way of negotiating interests than would be possible if only one issue at a time were considered. Public input into the deliberations is usually limited to speaking at public hearings and writing or calling legislators in an effort to influence their vote. Most public-interest organizations have lobbyists whose sole job is to keep track of bills under consideration and to try to persuade legislators to vote "correctly" on the bills that the lobbyists care about.

On controversial issues, legislative negotiation can become adversarial. Positional bargaining is far more common than interest-based bargaining, though both are used. Some experiments have been undertaken with procedures similar to the regulatory negotiation process used by administrative agencies to make rules and regulations. However, the statutory authority of elected officials and the requirement of a majority vote on all bills make public involvement in legislative negotiation more difficult than it is in the case of administrative agencies.

See also: Bargaining, Interest-Based and Positional; Conflict and Dispute; Environmental Conflicts; Public Policy Conflicts; Regulatory Negotiation.
References and Further Reading: Field, Patrick, 1994, "State Legislators Use Consensus-Building to Resolve Issues, Involve Citizens, Develop Legislation"; Olson, David, 1980, *The Legislative Process: A Comparative Approach.*

Legitimacy

Legitimacy is a measure of the degree to which a dispute resolution process is regarded as fair. It is a term that may be applied to decision-making or dispute resolution processes as well as to the outcomes of such processes. For example, the following are usually regarded as legitimate: honest elections utilizing a duly constituted democratic process, litigation based on generally accepted laws, use of minimum force by police officers working to control criminal behavior, defensive application of military force, and mutually acceptable negotiated agreements. Illegitimate approaches to disputes include loophole-based litigation, rigged elections, use of the police to terrorize and intimidate political opponents, military conquest, and negotiation processes that pressure parties into accepting unwanted agreements. Legitimacy is important from a conflict resolution perspective, because the pursuit of legitimated positions is less likely to provoke intense conflict.

Standards of legitimacy are not absolute, however. Differing legal, political, and moral traditions produce significant differences of opinion concerning what is and is not legitimate. The more diverse a society, the greater the difficulty in finding legitimating principles that everyone can support. For example, differing moral beliefs account for wide variations in the legitimacy of policies that favor abortion and homosexuality. There are also intense differences concerning the principles upon which wealth is distributed. Some Americans believe in the principle of equal opportunity, and others advocate the pursuit of equality of outcomes. Legitimating principles are also subject to self-serving interpretations, with people much more likely to find fault with processes that yield unfavorable results for themselves.

See also: Common Ground; Procedural Conflicts; Value Conflicts.

References and Further Reading: Burton, John, and Frank Dukes, 1990b, *Conflict: Readings in Management and Resolution,* 117–44; Deutsch, Morton, 1973, *The Resolution of Conflict: Constructive and Destructive Processes;* Merwe, Hugo van der, and Dennis J. D. Sandole, 1993, *Conflict Resolution Theory and Practice: Integration and Application;* Thomas, George M., Henry A. Walker, and Morris Zelditch Jr., 1986, "Legitimacy and Collective Action."

Litigation
See **Adjudication.**

Machiavelli, Niccolo

Born in 1469, Niccolo Machiavelli served as a diplomat for the Republic of Florence. His writings range over history and military and political theory, but he is best known for his book *The Prince*, which is essentially a handbook of strategy for the successful ruler. Machiavelli is notorious for having favored political expediency over moral integrity. While discussing "In What Manner Princes Should Keep Their Word," he advises his readers, "A prince should stick to the path of good but, if the necessity arises, he should also know how to follow evil." This willingness to use strategic deceit is expressed by the term *Machiavellian.*

See also: Alinsky, Saul; Diplomacy; Power.
References and Further Reading: Machiavelli, Niccolo, 1985, *The Prince;* Ridolfi, Roberto, 1963, *The Life of Niccolo Machiavelli.*

Mandela, Nelson

Nelson Mandela was born in South Africa in 1918, the son of a tribal chief. Mandela joined the African National Congress (ANC) in 1944 and was instrumental in leading the ANC toward more active, though still nonviolent, opposition to apartheid. In 1961, in response to police violence, Mandela helped organize an underground paramilitary organization to wage a campaign of sabotage. When his relationship to this group was discovered, Mandela was charged with treason. He was convicted and in 1964 was sentenced to life in prison. As a political prisoner, Mandela served as a symbolic rallying point for antiapartheid groups throughout the world.

In the face of increasingly violent clashes between the government and antiapartheid protesters, President Frederik Willem de Klerk freed Mandela in 1990. Mandela had been in negotiation with the South African government from prison as early as 1986. After his release, he was elected president of the ANC and led the congress in formal negotiations with the South African government to end apartheid. Mandela's leadership proved decisive in turning the increasingly militant ANC away from insurrection and back toward negotiation. South Africa achieved a negotiated end to apartheid in 1993. Nelson Mandela was elected president of South Africa in the nation's first free elections, held in 1994.

Despite nearly three decades in prison, Nelson Mandela shows no bitterness and refuses to demonize the opposition. From his early days in the ANC to the present, Mandela's goal has been to end domination and achieve true democratic reform. His negotiations have been marked by an avoidance of racial politics, a pragmatic flexibility regarding means coupled with a steadfast commitment to his goals, and a patient tenacity and personal conviction.

See also: Ethnic and Racial Conflicts; Nonviolence; Truth and Reconciliation Commission, South Africa; Tutu, Desmond.

References and Further Reading: Benson, Mary, 1986, *Nelson Mandela;* Mandela, Nelson, 1965, *No Easy Walk to Freedom;* Mandela, Nelson, 1986, *The Struggle Is My Life;* Mandela, Nelson, 1994, *Long Walk to Freedom.*

Marshall, George

George Marshall first rose to prominence as army chief of staff during World War II, from 1939 to 1945. After the war, he served as secretary of state (1947–49) and secretary of defense (1950–51) under President Harry Truman. Marshall, however, is best known as the author of the Marshall Plan, the blueprint for the reconstruction of post–World War II Europe. Unlike the punishing Treaty of Versailles, which ended World War I but was so costly to the Axis powers that it led to World War II, the Marshall Plan extended economic aid to Germany as well as to the formerly allied European nations. Through substantial grants and loans from the United States, Great Britain, France, and West Germany made dramatic gains in prosperity. Europe's recovered prosperity contributed to its political stability. By rebuilding Europe's markets, the Marshall Plan also contributed to postwar prosperity in the United States.

Marshall won the Nobel Peace Prize in 1953 for his plan. He was the first soldier to be so honored. As secretary of defense, Marshall also helped to create the North Atlantic Treaty Organization (NATO).

See also: Cold War; Peace Building.
References and Further Reading: Ferrell, Robert, 1966, *George C. Marshall;* Moseley, Leonard, 1982, *Marshall, Hero for Our Times;* Pogue, Forrest, 1963–73, *George C. Marshall.*

Marx, Karl

Karl Marx was a German political philosopher and revolutionary who, together with Friedrich Engels, developed the theory of "scientific socialism," otherwise known as communism. They collaborated on the *Communist Manifesto* (published in 1948), which was the first formal statement of communist principles. Marx further developed these principles in his later works, among them *Das Kapital.*

Central to Marx's philosophy was the notion of class struggle. He saw class conflict as the source of all social and political organization as well as all social and historical change. Throughout history, he observed, humans have been divided into classes on the basis of their relationship to the "means of production." By this he meant that there was a dominant class that owned the land in agricultural societies or the businesses in industrial societies. Then there were the laborers, who worked for the owners. The relationship between these two groups, Marx observed, was perpetual exploitation, as the owners accumulated all the fruits of their workers' labor (what Marx referred to as "surplus value") and the workers were given only subsistence wages.

Marx preached that the traditional exploitative relationship between owner and worker would eventually collapse. The greed and competition of capitalism would eventually destroy the system itself, paving the way for a socialist system and what he called the "dictatorship of the proletariat." (The proletariat is the working class, and the bourgeoisie is the businessperson-owner class in Marx's terms.)

Although Marx was never very influential during his lifetime, Marxist social, economic, and political thought has had a vast influence around the world, in both practical and theoretical terms. Many social scientists and conflict scholars still focus on class and related divisions (such as race, ethnicity, and gender) as key elements in social organization and conflict processes. In practical terms, Marx's analysis of capitalist economy, class struggle, and surplus value has become the foundation for modern socialist thought. His notion of revolution has been the impetus for many socialist and communist revolutions, including the Russian revolution led by Lenin.

See also: Domination Conflicts.
References and Further Reading: Coser, Lewis A., 1971, *Masters of Sociological Thought: Ideas in Historical and Social Context;* Giddens, Anthony, 1971, *Capitalism and Modern Social Theory: Analysis of the Writings of Marx, Durkheim and Max Weber;* Marx, Karl, 1936, *Capital, A Critique of Political Economy;* Marx, Karl, and Friedrich Engels, 1955, *The Communist Manifesto;* Schellenberg, James A., 1996, *Conflict Resolution—Theory, Research, and Practice.*

Med-Arb

Med-arb is a conflict resolution technique, most commonly used in labor-management contract negotiations, that combines elements of mediation and arbitration. Most often, union and management representatives sit down with a "med-arbiter" who first acts as a mediator, trying to help the parties negotiate an acceptable contract. If the parties fail to reach agreement, or if they can agree on some terms of the contract but not on others, the intermediary is empowered to act as an arbitrator and issue a binding decision on elements of the contract that could not be mutually agreed to.

Many observers find this process helpful. It gives the parties the benefit of trying to work things out themselves but provides a solution if they are unable to do so. In this sense, med-arb provides the best of both approaches. According to one highly experienced labor negotiator, "The med-arb process is really mediation with 'muscle.' In the hands of an experienced and capable med-arbiter, it usually results in the parties reaching agreement on most, and in many cases all, of the issues. It forces the parties to move toward each other in the bargaining process by advancing their honest positions" (quoted in Goldberg, Green, and Sander 1985, 265).

Others believe that med-arb compromises both approaches. Parties to a mediation disclose things that they would not disclose to an arbitrator. Thus, parties to med-arb may not bargain in good faith (because they do not want to reveal real interests or bottom lines). If they do, the arbitrator may well learn facts that he or she should not use in making an arbitration decision. Yet once such facts are revealed, they are hard (perhaps impossible) to ignore. Recognizing this possible conflict of interest, some med-arb processes call for a different person to act as an arbitrator if the need develops.

See also: Arbitration; Collective Bargaining; Labor-Management Relations and Conflict; Mediation.
References and Further Reading: Burton, John, and Frank Dukes, 1990a, *Conflict: Practices in Management, Settlement and Resolution;* Goldberg, Stephen B., Eric D. Green, and Frank E. A. Sander, 1985, *Dispute Resolution.*

Media Role in Conflict

In large-scale, societal-level conflicts involving many people and interest groups, the print and broadcast media provide one of the most important means through which the parties learn about the issues and communicate with one another (in addition to the internal communication mechanisms of organized interest groups). However, in the United States the media exercise their important communication role in a highly competitive environment in which print and broadcast media are in a constant struggle for advertising dollars. This means that their first objective is to provide people with the news that they want. In spite of the work of many conscientious reporters and news organizations, it can be difficult to separate objectively reported facts from entertaining stories. Often sensational and negative events are highlighted more than positive ones because they are more "interesting." This tendency to highlight rare, sensational events, people, and statements and to emphasize controversy rather than consensus tends to escalate conflicts.

The telecommunications revolution and the dramatic increase in the number of channels offering news have created another problem, often referred to as "narrowcasting," in that news is increasingly directed toward small niche markets and tends to tell people what they want to hear. Unlike the "broadcasting" of the 1950s and 1960s, when Walter Cronkite was the "most trusted man in America," each market now may hear a different version of the truth, and no single source is trusted by the majority of people. This increases the degree to which contending groups misunderstand one another and thus heightens the potential for conflict.

A third problem with media involvement in conflict is that some negotiations are best carried out in private. Many difficult public policy and international negotiations would be impossible if every issue and idea raised were reported to the public. Often negotiators must slowly feel their way through a set of controversial and potentially explosive public issues before they come up with an agreement that they can "sell" to the public. If the public is allowed to watch such a process unfold, the outcry can derail the discussions in their beginning stages.

Still, in spite of these problems, the traditions of free speech and freedom of the press provide an abundant flow of information, which ensures that public disputes are resolved on a much more informed basis than they would be in a society without these traditions.

See also: Communication; Diplomacy, Citizen, Track Two, and Multitrack; Escalation; Ground Rules; Misunderstandings.
References and Further Reading: Baumann, Melissa, and Hannes Siebert, 1993, "The Media as Mediator"; Koppel, Ted, 1996, "The Perils of Info-Democracy"; Young, Christopher, 1991, *The Role of the Media in International Conflict.*

Mediation

Mediation is one of the primary methods of alternative dispute resolution (ADR). It involves the intervention of a neutral third-party mediator in the negotiation process. The mediator's role is to *assist* the disputing parties to communicate effectively, analyze the dispute, and develop a mutually acceptable solution. Unlike arbitrators, who listen to both sides in a conflict and then make a decision, a mediator has no decision-making authority. Rather, mediators help the disputants arrive at their *own* decisions about possible terms of settlement.

Several aspects of this definition are important. First is the notion that mediation is basically negotiation. It is not therapy, and it is not advocacy; it is just assisted negotiation. Second, the mediator is usually an impartial neutral party. This means that he or she is not connected in any way to any of the disputing parties, nor does he or she have an interest or a stake in the outcome. Third, the mediator does not have the authority to make a decision. The mediator only guides the disputants through the negotiation process: he or she helps the parties define the problem and the parties' interests, understand the views of the other, and craft a settlement that is agreeable to all.

In practice, mediation does not always correspond to this ideal definition. Deborah Kolb (1994), a leading scholar in the Harvard Program on Negotiation, argues that this definition is largely a myth. Mediation is not always done by neutral third parties; sometimes the mediator is connected to one or both sides but is accepted by both because he or she is trusted. Jimmy Carter, for instance, had strong ties to both Israel and Egypt but was trusted by Menachem Begin and Anwar Sadat to mediate the Camp David Accords.

At other times, a mediator may be covertly partial to one side and may try to influence the outcome accordingly. This is sometimes done if a mediator perceives one party to be a much less skillful negotiator than the other, but with an equally righteous or even more righteous claim. The mediator may then try to equalize the power of the parties by "fine-tuning" the process to favor the lower-power party's position.

Even when mediators do not take sides, they often form opinions about the nature of a fair settlement. Some mediators feel strongly that they should keep such feelings to themselves and let the parties make their own decisions. Others are much more directive, trying to convince the parties of the value of the mediator's solution. Thus, although they may not have the authority to impose a solution, they are in an extremely powerful position to steer the parties in one direction or another.

Styles of Mediation

In their 1994 book *The Promise of Mediation,* R. Baruch Bush and Joseph Folger distinguish between problem-solving mediation and transformative mediation. Problem-solving mediation emphasizes finding a solution and generating mutually acceptable settlements. (Others refer to this as settlement-oriented, agreement-centered, or bargaining mediation.) Derived from the labor-management collective bargaining model, this approach is by far the most common one in use in the 1990s.

This was not always the case, however. When mediation first became popular in the United States in the 1960s, it was developed, at least in part, as a means of empowering traditionally low-power groups to take control of their own lives. Thus developed what Bush and Folger call transformative mediation, or mediation that transforms the people involved by empowering them to understand their own needs as well as the needs of their opponent, and to "exploit the opportunities for moral growth inherently presented by conflict" (Bush and Folger 1994, 84). (Others refer to this as relationship-centered or therapeutic mediation.) Although transformative mediation was advocated by several of the early leaders of the mediation movement in the 1960s, it fell out of favor in the 1970s and 1980s. In the 1990s it is enjoying

something of a resurgence, as more and more people examine the "myths" of mediation and realize that mediation is not exactly what it is generally thought to be.

Application Settings

Although mediation is used in various forms throughout the world, the model described here is most prevalent in the United States, Western Europe, Australia, and New Zealand. Its most common applications include family conflicts (especially divorce and child custody cases); labor-management conflicts (including contract disputes and employee grievances); landlord-tenant, neighborhood, and community conflicts; and minor criminal cases (such as vandalism, petty theft, or assault) that are referred to mediation by the courts. Mediation is also used in institutional settings such as prisons and schools. Peer mediation programs, in which elementary and secondary school students are trained to mediate conflicts between peers on the playground and in the classroom, have been implemented in hundreds of schools nationwide. Although few scientific evaluations have been completed on these programs, anecdotal evidence suggests that peer mediation reduces the time teachers need to spend on discipline (giving them more time to teach the curriculum). Many teachers and principals also report a reduction in overall student violence following the implementation of peer mediation programs.

In addition to interpersonal conflict applications, mediation is used successfully in large-scale public disputes. For example, many environmental conflicts over issues such as facility siting and hazardous waste management have been successfully mediated. Mediation is also used to resolve international conflicts. The Camp David Accords are one well-known example of successful international mediation. Other examples include the 1993 Oslo declaration of principles on the Israeli-Palestinian conflict mediated by Norwegian diplomats, Pope John Paul II's mediation of Argentina and Chile's dispute over the Austral area, and Algeria's mediation between the United States and Iran to obtain the release of the American hostages.

Mediation Steps

Mediation techniques vary from one mediator to another, but most follow some variation of the following steps. First, contact is made with the disputing parties. Often one or both of the disputants contact the mediator and ask for assistance; sometimes, the mediator offers assistance on his or her own initiative. If one party asks for help and the mediator thinks that the case is appropriate for mediation, he or she then contacts the other party or parties to see if they are willing to participate. Before undertaking the mediation, the mediator talks with each of the parties individually to explain how mediation works, to learn the basic parameters of the case, to develop rapport with the parties and establish a degree of trust, and to plan an approach. A date, time, and place for the mediation are set, and the parties get together for the beginning of the process.

Usually, mediation sessions begin with a discussion of the agenda and ground rules. Some mediators suggest the ground rules and an agenda and ask for the parties' concurrence; others let the parties develop the ground rules and the agenda themselves, with help as needed from the mediator. The next step involves definition of the issues. Often, different issues are important to different parties. Getting everyone's issues on the agenda is critical for success.

After defining the issues, most mediators help the parties separate their underlying interests and needs from their stated positions. Often in negotiations, people demand things that exceed what they really want, assuming that this will give them ne-

gotiating room. Mediators try to switch people from this typical positional bargaining mindset to a more integrative approach, where they explore true interests and options for meeting everyone's interests simultaneously. Eventually, the mediator helps the parties generate a variety of options for settlement, assess those options, and fine-tune one so that it best meets the interests of all disputants. This agreement is then put in written form for all the parties to sign.

Differences in approach center around a few controversial questions. One is the degree to which the mediator should become involved in the substance of the discussions. Some mediators stress that they are process consultants only. They help keep the meeting on track; they orchestrate who talks when and what topics are discussed, but they do not suggest settlement options themselves or otherwise enter the substantive discussions. Other mediators take an active role in clarifying interests, highlighting areas of common ground that are being overlooked, molding those commonalities into options for settlement, and then "selling" their preferred approach to the parties. Neither approach is right or wrong, although one approach may be more appropriate in one situation than in another, and some parties may feel more comfortable with one style than with another.

A second divergence is how mediators deal with power differentials. Parties in conflict are seldom equal in power. Most often, some are better negotiators than others, some are more experienced or knowledgeable than the others, some have better alternatives than others. Very uneven power can yield an extremely unfair result. For instance, a financially wise husband can outnegotiate his naive and traditionally subservient wife into accepting a divorce settlement that is strongly in his favor. Some mediators feel that it is appropriate to intervene in such situations, either by empowering the wife to better support her own interests or by urging her to seek outside assistance. (Most divorce mediators urge parties to have a lawyer review their agreement before they sign it.) Others feel that such intervention is inappropriate, as it calls into question the mediator's neutrality. This question has no easy answers. Disputants should discuss power differentials with the mediator before the process begins, if it is an area of concern. If the mediator's answer is not satisfactory, clients should seek another mediator who advocates a more acceptable approach.

Bush and Folger's steps for transformative mediation are somewhat different. As in problem-solving mediation, transformative mediation starts with an opening statement from the mediator, who explains what mediation is and how it works and gets the parties' agreement to participate. The parties are then asked to participate in the formation of the ground rules. From there, the process is very loose. The mediator tries to get each of the parties to explain the conflict and his or her concerns for the other, the primary goal being improved mutual understanding and acceptance of the legitimacy of both sides' "stories." Unlike problem-solving mediators, who tend to make generalizations about what the conflict is about, transformative mediators "microfocus on the parties' contributions," staying in a "responsive posture" (Bush and Folger 1994, 192–93). When the discussions stall, the mediator tries to get the process going again by broadening the agenda. He or she asks questions to try to get the parties to see the other side's issues more clearly or understand what might be behind an earlier statement. Unlike problem-solving mediation, which often tries to narrow discussions down to the point where they focus on a particular solution, transformative mediation is a widening process that tries to maximize opportunities for the parties' empowerment and mutual recognition (which, according to Bush and Folger, are the primary goals of transformative mediation).

Advantages of Mediation

Mediation, when practiced by a skilled mediator, has many advantages over alternative forms of dispute settlement. The advantages over litigation are cost (it is usually much less expensive) and speed (it usually, but not always, proceeds more quickly than litigation does). Unlike the all-or-nothing, win-lose character of most adversarial processes, mediation allows parties to seek and find more creative solutions to their problems that are more likely to address their underlying needs and satisfy all the parties simultaneously. Thus, rather than parties having to compromise, or give up some of what they wanted, mediators can help them find integrative solutions that "expand the pie" and provide most or all of what each party really desires.

Given that the parties themselves are involved in formulating the solution to their problems, these solutions are often more appropriate and workable. This means that compliance with the results may be higher and the solutions longer-lived than those imposed by an outside third party, such as a court.

Other advocates of mediation stress the personal empowerment that results from the process. People who have poor conflict management skills can learn more effective approaches for handling disputes, which they can apply not only in the current case but again and again throughout their lives. In addition, mediation tends to maintain or even strengthen the relationship between the parties. Rather than increasing the hostility between disputants, as adversarial processes often do, mediation helps the parties see the other's point of view and come to respect the validity of that view. This can be beneficial when a continuing relationship is necessary, be it with a landlord, a boss, or an ex-spouse.

Disadvantages of Mediation

Mediation has its disadvantages, however. One, referred to earlier, is that it is not always what it seems. Mediators sometimes claim to be neutral and impartial but are actually highly invested in the outcome of the case. They may manipulate the process, the substance of the discussions, or both in an effort to get a result they deem to be fair or wise. Thus, although not as coercive as some processes, mediation is not always as voluntary and participant-directed as it may appear.

In addition to having the potential for mediator exploitation, there is the potential for parties with more power to obtain a resolution that is greatly in their benefit. Thus, mediation is seen by some representatives of advocacy groups as simple co-optation. Although some mediators claim that participants "leave their power at the door," this is seldom true. In situations with significant power differentials, other processes may safeguard the rights and interests of low-power parties better than mediation would.

Another disadvantage of mediation is that it provides only an individual solution to what may be a collective problem. Thus, people with defective cars can mediate individual cases and get their cars fixed, but the company will not be forced to fix all the defective cars. Similarly, individual African Americans could have used mediation to resolve early civil rights conflicts— for example, school integration or shared public transportation. This might have gotten one person into a school or one group of people better seats on the bus, but without the precedent-setting legal cases such as *Brown v. the Board of Education* or massive direct action such as the Montgomery bus boycott, civil rights for all U.S. citizens would have been further delayed.

A final charge leveled against mediation is that it denies citizens their due process. Since many mediators are not lawyers, they cannot render legal opinions. Nor are they bound by the law the way judges and juries are. This gives parties to mediation the flexibility to consider solutions to problems that would not be considered within the generally narrow confines of the law. But it does not give parties the protection of those laws either. As a result, some lawyers and advocates charge that mediation (and other forms of ADR) provide only "second-class justice." The protections of the courts are used by the rich, and the poor are relegated to inferior ADR processes.

One of the strongest advocates of mediation, Larry Susskind, agrees that mediation does not always achieve the ideal outcome. But the key question, he says, is "compared to what?" Mediation is not better in every case. Sometimes the courts yield a better result. Sometimes direct action is more effective. But very often, mediation yields the best result for all— lower-power parties included. Only by comparing mediation with the realistically available alternatives can one decide whether mediation is likely to be the best approach to any particular conflict.

See also: Co-mediation; Divorce Mediation; Mediation, Community; Mediation, Court-Based; Mediation, Ethical Issues; Mediation, History of; Mediation Models.

References and Further Reading: Abel, Richard, 1982, *The Politics of Informal Justice: The American Experience;* Bush, Robert A. Baruch, and Joseph P. Folger, 1994, *Promise of Mediation;* Folberg, Jay, and Alison Taylor, 1984, *Mediation: A Comprehensive Guide to Resolving Conflicts without Litigation;* Kolb, Deborah M., and Associates, 1994, *When Talk Works: Profiles of Mediators;* Kressel, K., and D. Pruitt, 1989, *Mediation Research: The Press and Effectiveness of Third-Party Intervention;* Moore, Christopher W., 1986, *The Mediation Process;* Nader, Laura, 1979, "Disputing without the Force of Law"; Susskind, Lawrence, 1994, "Activist Mediation and Public Disputes."

Mediation, Community

Over 700 communities currently provide some kind of community mediation program. Although the structure and purposes of these programs vary widely, most are based on the assumption that many minor civil and criminal complaints that otherwise tend to flood the courts can be more effectively and less expensively resolved through mediation. Given this assumption, community mediation centers (also called neighborhood justice centers) have been developed to provide free or low-cost mediation services for local citizens involved in interpersonal disputes. Typical kinds of disputes handled include those between landlords and tenants, neighbors, roommates, parents and teens, and merchants and consumers. Some centers branch out into areas such as land-use disputes, traffic disputes, or other community-level concerns.

The nature of the disputes handled by community mediation centers depends in part on their sponsorship. Many are run as an adjunct to the justice system, which is their major source of referrals. Disputants in minor civil and criminal cases are encouraged or, in some cases, required to try mediation before they come before the court for adjudication. Other community mediation programs are run by nonprofit agencies that are independent of the justice system. Although these programs may get some referrals from the courts, most of their referrals come from other sources—social service agencies, schools, word of mouth, and so forth.

Both kinds of community mediation centers usually rely on volunteer mediators, although most have a few paid staff members who do training and/or administer the program. Funding for these centers comes from a variety of sources: local or state governments, foundation grants or other gifts, and a few by federal contracts and grants. Some charge a fee to offset the cost of some or all of their services. (Federal funding was more common in earlier years than it is now.)

The goals, and hence the mediation styles, used by these centers vary widely.

Many centers are modeled after the San Francisco Community Board Program—one of the first community mediation programs established in the United States. The purpose of the Community Board Program was to give dispute resolution authority back to the citizens of the community. It was seen as an empowerment process, giving community members control over their own affairs rather than ceding that control to an external authority—the courts. Related goals were enhancing the sense of community, empowering local decision making, reducing violence, and increasing intergroup and interpersonal cohesiveness and mutual understanding. These goals relate closely to the transformative approach to mediation advocated by R. Baruch Bush, Joseph Folger, and others (Bush and Folger 1994).

Other community mediation programs are designed to relieve court congestion and provide an alternative to adversarial, court-based dispute resolution processes. Such centers tend to focus more on problem-solving mediation using interest-based bargaining and the development of win-win solutions (as opposed to the win-lose approach of the courts). They tend to deemphasize the primacy of relationship and process issues or the personal and community empowerment issues that the Community Board model stresses.

Although community mediation has become increasingly popular nationwide, and client satisfaction appears to be high, some critics question its validity or effectiveness. The criticism is similar to that of other forms of mediation: it provides "second-class justice," while "first-class justice" is provided by the courts; or it microfocuses on personal problems without examining the broader social issues that those personal problems are part of (this charge is less valid for the Community Board model than for the problem-solving model, perhaps). Proponents of community mediation, however, argue that it gives control of dispute resolution back to the people involved in the disputes. It teaches people how to handle their own problems, both over the short term and over the long term, and it enables people to develop win-win solutions to their problems that would not have been accomplished had the dispute been resolved in an adversarial setting such as the courts.

See also: Mediation; Mediation, Court-Based; Mediation, History of; Mediation Models.

References and Further Reading: Burton, John, and Frank Duke, 1990a, *Conflict: Practices in Management, Settlement and Resolution;* Bush, Robert A. Baruch, and Joseph P. Folger, 1994, *Promise of Mediation;* Duffy, K., P. V. Olczak, and J. G. Grosch, 1991, *Community Mediation;* Goldstein, Susan, 1987, *Cultural Issues in Community Mediation, 1983;* Pruitt, Dean G., 1995, "Process Outcome in Community Mediation."

Mediation, Court-Based

Many community mediation programs are to some degree court based or court connected. The strength and significance of this connection vary widely, depending on the type and quality of services provided.

In many instances, courts have established mediation programs in an effort to reduce their trial caseloads. They may encourage litigants who seem likely to be able to settle out of court to try mediation; in other cases, mediation is mandated. (Mandatory mediation is not final, however. The parties always have the option of going back to court if an agreement cannot be reached.)

At times, mediation is required for other reasons. For example, many judges realize that mediation is better suited than the courts for resolving child custody disputes, because mediation allows parents to consider issues that the court might not look at and to work things out in a way that makes sense to the parties, which does not always happen in court. Therefore, a number of judicial districts require divorcing parties to try mediation before going to court for the resolution of child custody disputes.

Although there is a great deal of diversity from district to district, most court-based mediation programs have some commonalities. First, they tend to deal with cases that would be litigated if they were not mediated. This includes divorce and child custody disputes and consumer and commercial disputes, among others. Many are also involved with victim-offender mediation—a process for dealing with minor criminal cases outside the court system.

Often, court-based mediation programs have larger caseloads than other community mediation programs. This may mean that they are more financially viable, but it also may mean that they are more bureaucratic and regimented. For instance, there tends to be more pressure in the large court-based mediation programs to process cases quickly. Mediators may be encouraged to complete cases within an hour or two, and certainly to press for resolution in the first meeting, instead of conducting a series of meetings, as is usually done in private divorce mediation and in many other kinds of community mediation cases.

Also, given the pressure by the courts to come to a resolution quickly, court-based mediators are more likely than private or community mediators to be strongly directive, even going so far as to arbitrate cases that cannot be resolved by the parties themselves. (Arbitrators make the decision for the parties, whereas mediators help the parties come to a decision themselves.)

Another difference in some court-based programs is that attorneys may negotiate for their clients during mediation. This almost never occurs in private or community mediation; those processes pride themselves on offering an alternative to courts that allows parties to speak for themselves rather than through their lawyers. Yet some court-based programs allow or even encourage attorneys to be at the mediation table with their clients, which makes the process more courtlike than independent mediation programs. In this sense, court-based mediation is a middle point between adjudicatory process and private mediation, which is much less formal, less constrained by time, and perhaps less directive.

See also: Arbitration; Mediation, Community; Mediation Models; Victim-Offender Reconciliation Programs.
References and Further Reading: Folberg, Jay, and Alison Taylor, 1984, *Mediation: A Comprehensive Guide to Resolving Conflicts without Litigation;* Mastrofski, Jennifer Adams, 1990, "Mediation in Court-Based Systems: More Variations than Similarities."

Mediation, Ethical Issues

Mediators face many ethical dilemmas in their practice. In a report prepared for the National Institute of Dispute Resolution, mediator Robert A. Baruch Bush lists nine categories of ethical dilemmas. The first involves staying within the limits of one's competency. Mediators not only must be skilled in the mediation process but also should be somewhat familiar with the kind of dispute they are mediating. How much skill and knowledge they need is controversial. Mediators who focus exclusively on process argue that having substantive knowledge of an issue is not necessary and can even lead to excessive mediator intervention in the substance of the arguments. Activist mediators, in contrast, who intend to become involved in the substantive debate, believe that strong substantive expertise is essential for good mediation.

A second issue is neutrality and impartiality. Should mediators who have a relationship with one side but are accepted by both sides agree to take a case? Should mediators who don't know the clients but share group affiliation take the case? (For example, can a white mediator mediate for a black and a white disputant?) After a mediator accepts a case, what happens when the mediator develops a particular like or dislike for a party? Should he or she withdraw from the mediation?

A third dilemma involves the maintenance of confidentiality. Generally, all discussions in mediation are considered confidential, but what happens when the mediator learns about a past or impending act of violence or other crime? What should the mediator do if he or she learns something in caucus that would significantly affect the negotiations if the other party knew (for instance, if the mediator learns that one party is misconstruing the facts or otherwise misleading the other party in order to obtain a favorable settlement)? Some mediators ask for permission to disclose the information; others may simply disclose it without permission; others may do neither, believing that confidentiality is primary.

A fourth issue is ensuring informed consent. This is especially problematic when one party may be overtly or covertly coerced into participating or agreeing to a particular settlement or is incompetent to negotiate effectively on his or her own behalf. Should the mediator try to remedy this situation, or should he or she withdraw from the process?

A fifth issue is the degree to which a mediator should direct the process and intervene in the substance of the dispute. Some mediators become heavily involved in both, directing the parties to what they believe to be fertile areas for discussion, and drafting agreements that they then sell to the parties. Others take a nondirective approach. Which is ethically superior?

A sixth issue is separating mediation from therapy and legal advice. Many mediators are lawyers; others are therapists. Both legal advice and counseling can be important in particular conflict situations, but should they be provided by the mediator? Most codes of ethics suggest that they should not. Thus, the mediator, when acting as a mediator, should not provide either counseling or legal advice (even to both parties), but rather should refer the parties to outsiders for such services. Others feel that as long as the service is provided to both, it is acceptable.

The seventh issue involves avoiding doing harm to the parties during mediation. How does a mediator know when mediation will make a bad situation worse? Or when it will cause the disclosure of confidential information? What should a mediator do in such cases?

The eighth issue involves abuse of the mediation process. What can (and should) the mediator do when a party lies, conceals information, or engages in intimidation of the other party?

Last, how can mediators avoid conflicts of interest—with the courts or other referring agencies, or with themselves? (The more cases they settle, the better they look, and the more cases they will get in the future, so there is an incentive to close their eyes to ethical problems and just get the settlement.)

Bush reports (and most mediators agree) that none of these issues has been resolved. Several agencies have promulgated codes of conduct for mediators in various areas, but none specifically deals with each of these issues. They are a constant topic of debate in training and professional meetings, and most mediators are at least aware of the issues and are trying to come to terms with them in a way that they find fair (Bush 1992).

See also: Alternative Dispute Resolution; American Bar Association Practice Standards for Lawyer Mediators in Family Disputes; Mediation; Mediation Models; Mediator Impartiality and Neutrality; Model Standards of Conduct for Mediators.

References and Further Reading: Bush, Robert A. Baruch, 1992, *The Dilemmas of Mediation Practice: A Study of Ethical Dilemmas and Policy Implications;* Folberg, Jay, and Alison Taylor, 1984, *Mediation: A Comprehensive Guide to Resolving Conflicts without Litigation,* 244–90; Kolb, Deborah M., and Associates, 1994, *When Talk Works: Profiles of Mediators;* Stephens, William O., John B. Stephens, and Frank Dukes, 1995, "The Ethics of Environmental Mediation"; Touval, Saadia, 1995, "Ethical Dilemmas in International Mediation."

Mediation, History of

Mediation has a long history. Its use was documented in China over 2,000 years ago,

and the Bible refers to Jesus as a mediator between God and man. Before the Renaissance, the Catholic Church acted as the primary dispute resolution mechanism in Western Europe; Jewish rabbis did the same for their communities. In many parts of Africa, disputes have long been resolved by a *moot,* or neighborhood meeting, in which an elder or respected community member acts as mediator.

Similar traditions were established early in American history. Native Americans used a form of mediation to solve interpersonal and tribal conflicts. Early immigrants (especially the Puritans, Quakers, Chinese, and Jews) also used mediation to resolve interpersonal disputes. By the early 1700s, however, the use of mediation declined, as communities became more mobile and institutions and commerce became more complex. This led to an increasing reliance on common law and litigation, as opposed to negotiation and consensual forms of conflict resolution.

Rapid industrialization and labor unrest of the late nineteenth and early twentieth centuries brought a renewed interest in quick dispute resolution mechanisms. The U.S. Department of Labor was established in 1913, with "commissioners of conciliation" to help resolve labor-management disputes. (In 1947, they became the Federal Mediation and Conciliation Service.) In the 1960s, the Community Relations Service was established by the Department of Justice to help provide conciliation and mediation of civil rights disputes.

The use of formal mediation has expanded exponentially since that time. Spurred by the increased congestion of and dissatisfaction with the courts, more people and organizations are turning to alternatives, especially mediation (and in some contexts, arbitration) to resolve their disputes. Hundreds of neighborhood justice centers have been established nationwide since the 1960s to provide faster, more accessible, and less adversarial resolution of interpersonal and community disputes using mediation. The Association of Family and Conciliation Courts was founded in 1963 to promote court-connected family mediation as a supplement or an alternative to family litigation. The first court-based dispute resolution forum was established in Ohio in 1971. Funded by the Law Enforcement Assistance Administration, it provided law students to act as mediators in minor criminal cases. By the 1980s and 1990s, the use of mediation had expanded into almost all conflict resolution settings and was used quite routinely in some (family and labor-management disputes are still the most prevalent application settings).

See also: Alternative Dispute Resolution; Alternative Dispute Resolution, Institutionalization; Mediation.
References and Further Reading: Folberg, Jay, and Alison Taylor, 1984, *Mediation: A Comprehensive Guide to Resolving Conflicts without Litigation;* Kovach, Kimberlee K., 1994, *Mediation: Principles and Practice;* Moore, Christopher W., 1986, *The Mediation Process.*

Mediation, International

Mediation is used often in international conflicts, especially when the disputes are protracted and complex and when the parties' own conflict resolution efforts have reached an impasse. In a study of the 78 international conflicts that occurred between 1945 and 1986, Jacob Bercovitch found that 56 percent were mediated—some successfully, many not.

Although it is common, international mediation is difficult for many reasons. International conflicts tend to involve many issues and complexities. They are often highly escalated, with emotions, costs, and risks high on all sides. Although there is a rudimentary set of international laws, there is little universally accepted law, nor a universally accepted international body that can limit or control international disputes. For this reason, mediation is one of the few dispute resolution mechanisms that parties to international conflict can use, other than surrender or continued hostility, both of which are often unacceptable.

The very factors that make mediation attractive also tend to limit its success, however. For example, Bercovitch found that mediation is more likely to be successful in low-intensity disputes. "Protracted and intense international disputes," he states, "are not particularly conducive to mediation or any other form of third party intervention" (Bercovitch 1991, 23). This suggests that conflicts should be mediated before they escalate, but mediation also does not work if it is tried too early. Parties must "test their strength," according to Bercovitch, before they are ready to sit down to serious negotiations. (This corresponds to other scholars' focus on the issues of timing and "ripeness." Ripe moments appear and disappear quickly, so mediation that works at one stage of a conflict is not likely to work either earlier or later.)

Other factors likely to influence the success of international mediation are the nature of the parties, the issues involved, and the mediator. The mediator must be highly skilled and highly respected. Having a mediator with power over the disputing parties is an additional help. Typical international mediators are representatives of the United Nations (often the secretary-general), representatives of regional organizations, or a third country. Sometimes mediation is carried out by informal, non-state third parties (such as Mennonites and Quakers), whose long-standing reputation as skilled peacemakers gives them credibility. However, Bercovitch found that such informal mediators are often not as effective as mediators who have the power to reward cooperation and "punish" obstinacy. (Jimmy Carter's mediation at Camp David is one example of mediation "with clout.") Sometimes, however, mediators without clout do better. Norway, for example, was able to mediate an agreement between the Palestinians and the Israelis when the United States could not, because it was able to provide trusted and truly impartial mediators and a private setting.

Like other forms of mediation, international mediation involves difficult ethical dilemmas. One is whether to settle for an end to the fighting or to hold out for a truly just settlement. Sometimes holding out for justice means far more casualties than accepting a cessation of hostilities. However, when an unjust settlement is obtained, it is more likely to break down quickly, spawning renewed violence and even war. Although similar dilemmas occur in other types of disputes, the human costs of protracted conflict in the international sphere make such decisions especially difficult.

See also: Camp David Accords (Israeli-Egyptian); Diplomacy; International Conflict; Mediation; Oslo Accords, Middle East Peace Process; United Nations Mediation of the Egyptian-Israeli Negotiations at Kilometer 101.

References and Further Reading: Bercovitch, Jacob, 1991, "International Mediation and Dispute Settlement: Evaluating the Conditions for Successful Mediation"; Touval, Saadia, 1995, "Ethical Dilemmas in International Mediation"; Touval, Saadia, and I. William Zartman, 1985, *International Mediation in Theory and Practice.*

Mediation, Problem-Solving
See **Mediation Models.**

Mediation, Transformative
See **Mediation Models; Transformation.**

Mediation and the Law

Mediation is one form of alternative dispute resolution. In this case, *alternative* usually means alternative to litigation. Indeed, mediation differs from litigation and other adversarial forms of dispute resolution in critical ways. First, mediation is much less formal than adjudication. It does not follow legal rules of procedure, nor is it bound by legal precedent or substantive law. The parties themselves, rather than a judge or arbitrator, decide what constitutes an agreeable resolution of the dispute. This gives the parties more flexibility to craft a solution to their problem that really meets their needs. However, mediation lacks the legal guarantees of due process and fairness that are characteristic of the judicial system.

Second, mediated agreements are not always legally enforceable, as are adjudicated settlements. Although some mediated agreements, such as divorce settlements, require court approval, most do not. They rely largely on the goodwill and trust between the parties to ensure that the agreement is followed. Often mediators encourage the parties to formalize their agreement in the form of a contract to make it legally enforceable. When a contract is drawn up and signed, any disputant who thinks that the contract has been violated can sue the violator for breach of contract, just as in any other contractual agreement.

Other mediated agreements come about after the parties become involved in a judicial process but before the court hearing takes place. In this instance, the parties' lawyers may stipulate the terms of the agreement to the court, and the court has the option of approving these terms in its final decree. (This is what occurs in divorce mediation, for example.)

Other mediated settlements, however, are not formalized as contracts or court decrees. They may consist of an oral exchange of promises, a partial or full payment of the amount of money or goods promised, or an informal written agreement, such as a memorandum of understanding between the parties. Although these approaches to implementation are more consistent with the informality of the rest of the mediation process (and hence may be more consistent with the effort to build trust and enhance the relationship), parties must be aware that the implementation and enforcement of the provisions of the agreement are generally their responsibility alone.

See also: Adjudication; Contract; Divorce Mediation.
References and Further Reading: Folberg, Jay, and Alison Taylor, 1984, *Mediation: A Comprehensive Guide to Re-*

solving Conflicts without Litigation; Moore, Christopher W., 1986, *The Mediation Process.*

Mediation and Therapy

Many mediators (especially family mediators) are trained therapists as well as mediators, and their style of mediation likely reflects this training. Many engage in therapeutic or transformative mediation, which is relatively nondirective and empowering (hence similar to therapy). Even problem-solving mediation, which is more directive and controlling, is similar to therapy in its reliance on improved communication and human relations skills.

Nevertheless, mediation differs from therapy in a number of important ways. First, the purposes of the two processes are different. The purpose of mediation is to resolve conflict. A neutral third party helps the disputants communicate more effectively, define the problem, brainstorm solutions, and develop an agreement that is acceptable to both. Mediation is highly task focused and issue oriented. The purpose of therapy, in contrast, is personality and behavioral change. It is focused on the individual (or in family therapy, on the family unit). The goal is to improve relationships, improve social and psychological functioning, and enhance personal well-being. "The work is client focused, generally emotion oriented and emphasizes behavioral change" (Bradshaw 1995, 238).

Another difference is that therapy requires the development of a detailed history of the client and the problem, whereas mediation does not. Although mediation may examine the past somewhat, it emphasizes looking forward toward solutions and new relationships. Also, mediation is usually short term, focusing on one problem that needs to be solved. Therapy is often longer term and focuses on individual behaviors that need to be changed.

Despite these differences, however, some styles of mediation are similar to some approaches to therapy, and it is easy for mediators, especially those who were originally trained as therapists, to blur the line between the two processes, using both simultaneously or sequentially if doing so is likely to be helpful. One ethical dilemma facing mediators and therapists is how much these roles should be separated, and to what extent they can be allowed to overlap. Should a therapist offer his or her clients divorce mediation if family therapy is unsuccessful in saving their marriage? Likewise, should a therapist-mediator use therapy to help parties who are at an impasse in mediation alter their approach and perhaps move forward in a different way?

Several ethical codes suggest that the division between therapy and mediation should be complete and clear. Mediators should not engage in therapy, nor should they agree to mediate a case if they have served as a therapist for one or both of the parties before the mediation started. The purpose of this division is to ensure the mediator's actual and perceived impartiality. Other observers believe that such rigid rules are unnecessary and, at times, even detrimental to the clients' welfare. If a therapist-mediator can offer both services simultaneously and effectively, some observers feel that this is both legitimate and effective.

These questions arise most often in the context of family mediation, although they occasionally develop in other situations as well. People considering using mediation and/or therapy should be clear about their goals and the services they want the third party to provide. They should also be aware of the problem of impartiality if a therapist offers mediation and give careful consideration to whether this is in the best interests of both parties. Often, switching from therapy to mediation makes sense, but it may be appropriate to find a different mediator and not use the therapist.

See also: Divorce Mediation; Family Conflict; Interpersonal Conflict; Mediation, Ethical Issues; Mediation Models; Mediator Selection; Mediator Qualifications, Certification, and Training.

References and Further Reading: Bradshaw, William, 1995, "Mediation and Therapy"; Dworkin, Joan, Lynn Jacob, and Elizabeth Scott, 1991, "The Boundaries between Mediation and Therapy: Ethical Dilemmas."

Mediation Models

The term *mediation* can apply to a wide variety of approaches to conflict resolution. The only commonalities among various models is that one or more third parties act as a mediator who somehow works with the parties (or their representatives) to help them deal with their dispute. The goals and methods of this process can differ widely, depending on the nature of the problem, the type of mediator, and the setting.

Perhaps the most common form of mediation is variously referred to as problem-solving mediation, settlement-oriented mediation, or agreement-centered mediation. Here, the mediator's main goal is to obtain a settlement of the immediate dispute. This is done by working with the parties together (although individual caucusing is common) to get them to agree on the nature and the specific details of their conflict. (This is usually done by defining the parties' interests.) The mediator then helps the parties brainstorm alternative solutions, evaluate the alternatives to determine how well they meet each of the party's interests and needs, and finally choose one solution that best meets the interests of all sides. The role of the mediator in this process is to help the parties communicate effectively, define the problem in terms of interests rather than positions, invent options for mutual gain, and draft a mutually acceptable agreement.

Problem-solving mediators vary in their degree of involvement in the substantive issues when compared with other kinds of mediators (especially therapeutic or transformative mediators). Problem-solving mediators tend to be more manipulative and directive regarding both the process and the substance of the discussions. Most problem-solving mediators highlight points of consensus, and some actually propose settlement options or even draft full settlement agreements (before the parties direct them to do so, following the parties' ideas). This is good for parties who need a lot of help, but it is not good for parties who are competent negotiators themselves and who want to maintain control of the process and the substance of the discussions.

A variant of problem-solving mediation is labor-management mediation (which came first and provided the basis on which problem-solving mediation was built). The difference between problem-solving mediation and labor-management mediation is that labor-management mediation is often more highly structured, with procedural precedents, traditions, and regulations. Both the mediators and the negotiators are professionals who negotiate on behalf of their constituencies (labor or management), not on behalf of themselves. Thus, the negotiators are not empowered to ratify an agreement; usually, the agreement must be approved by the owners and workers after the mediation session concludes.

Another mediation model is what R. Baruch Bush and Joseph Folger call transformative mediation. This type of mediation focuses primarily on improving the relationship between the parties. If an agreement to the conflict is reached, that is a side effect of the improved relationship, not the primary purpose of the mediation. Transformative mediators take a nondirective role in both the process and the substance of the discussions. As Bush and Folger (1994) explain, they verbally "follow the parties around," emphasizing opportunities during the discussion for empowerment and recognition of the parties. Unlike problem-solving mediators, who often work to empower the low-power disputant only, transformative mediators work to empower all the parties to better analyze and understand the conflict, the choices available to them, and how they might best deal with the situation they face. They also encourage the parties to recognize the concerns, fears, and interests of the other— not necessarily agreeing with these feelings, but recognizing that they exist, are legitimate, and must be addressed if a solution is to be obtained. By stressing empowerment and recognition rather than immediate problem solving, transformative mediators try to transform the relationship between the parties over the long term rather than trying to solve the immediate dispute.

Therapeutic mediation is similar to transformative mediation in that it attempts to transform relationships between the parties. Therapeutic mediation does not, however, focus on empowerment and recognition. Rather, it focuses on all the psychological and emotional causes of the conflict and attempts to deal with these underlying causes in order to obtain settlement of the overlying issue.

A fifth mediation model is what Jay Folberg and Alison Taylor refer to as supervisory mediation. This is an informal, authority-based mediation that occurs when a superior (a parent, a boss, a teacher, or a coach) mediates a dispute between two or more subordinates. The key difference in this situation is that the mediator is usually not a professional mediator but is someone who is empowered to enforce a decision. Thus, the supervisory mediator engages in a process similar to med-arb, in which the mediator tries to help the parties reach a mediated agreement, but if they cannot, he or she acts as an arbitrator to impose the solution that he or she thinks is best.

All of these models of mediation (with the exception of supervisory mediation) assume that the mediator is both neutral and impartial. This means that the mediator is not connected to any of the parties and is not biased in favor of one or another. Although this is the predominant mode of mediation in North America, it is not necessarily the case in other countries and other cultures. Central American cultures, for instance, frequently use mediators who are "insider-partials." These mediators are known to be more sympathetic to one side than the other, but they are trusted by both sides because of their personal distinction and institutional prominence. An example of an insider-partial mediator is Oscar Arias Sánchez, who mediated the end of the Nicaraguan Sandinista war with the Contras as part of his Esquipulas Agreement (Wehr and Nepstad 1994).

See also: Arias Sánchez, Oscar; International Conflict; Labor-Management Relations and Conflict; Med-Arb; Mediation.

References and Further Reading: Bush, Robert A. Baruch, and Joseph P. Folger, 1994, *Promise of Mediation;* Folberg, Jay, and Alison Taylor, 1984, *Mediation: A Comprehensive Guide to Resolving Conflicts without Litigation;* Wehr, Paul, and Sharon Erickson Nepstad, 1994, "Violence, Nonviolence, and Justice in Sandinista Nicaragua."

Mediation Quarterly

Mediation Quarterly is one of the leading mediation journals published in the United States. It is sponsored by the Academy of Family Mediators, but its topics go beyond family disputes to all types of interpersonal disputes. The goal of the journal is to "advance professional understanding of mediation from an interpersonal perspective." To do this, it publishes articles on mediation theory, research, and practice. It also has occasional special issues that focus on particularly controversial and important topics in the mediation arena.

See also: Academy of Family Mediators; Appendix 1 for contact information.

Mediator Impartiality and Neutrality

In the standard North American approach to mediation, the mediator is usually expected to be both impartial and neutral. Impartiality, according to Christopher Moore, refers to the mediator's attitude toward the parties; he or she must not favor one side over the other, but must value and treat each equally. Neutrality refers to the relationship between the mediator and the disputants. Ideally, the mediator has not had a previous relationship with any of the parties, nor should he or she expect a future relationship to result from the mediation process.

"The need for impartiality and neutrality does not mean that a mediator may not have personal opinions about a dispute's outcome," according to Moore. "No one can be entirely impartial. What impartiality and neutrality do signify is that the mediator can separate his or her opinions about the outcome of the dispute from the desires of the disputants and focus on ways to help the parties make their own decisions without unduly favoring one of them" (Moore 1986, 15).

Although this rule is advocated in most mediation training programs and codes of ethics, it is often not practiced in reality. Impartiality becomes a problem, especially in problem-solving mediation, when one party is significantly less powerful than the other. Many mediators try to correct this situation by working to empower the low-power party, which strongly calls into question their neutral stance.

Impartiality is also compromised when mediators take a highly directive role in the mediation process, suggesting not only procedures to be used but also substantive decisions to be made. This is an inevitable outcome of problem-solving mediation, according to R. Baruch Bush and Joseph Folger (1994, 76): "mediators are told to solve problems but to refrain from the very kinds of moves that are necessary to do so. Or, they are told to control process but not influence content, though the distinction easily blurs in actual practice. In short, problem-solving mediation from a neutral stance is increasingly recognized as practically impossible to do, under any meaningful definition of neutrality." For this reason, among others, Bush and Folger favor transformative mediation, in which mediators take special care to avoid any directive actions and thus can stay neutral more easily.

Other cultures do not place nearly as strong an emphasis on mediator impartiality or neutrality. Central American cultures, for example, frequently use "insider-partial" mediators—mediators who are involved in the conflict and are known to favor one side over the other. They are trusted by both sides, nevertheless, because of their status in the community and their reputation for fairness. Because they are part of the community, insider-partial mediators have a stronger interest in forging an agreement that will last, and if problems arise, they will still be around to help work them out. Neutral-impartial mediators who are external to the conflict and/or to the community cease their involvement with the parties once the final agreement is signed. For this reason, insider-partials are trusted more in some cultures, whereas outsider-impartial mediators are generally more highly trusted in the United States (Wehr and Nepstad 1994).

See also: Empowerment; Mediation; Mediation, Ethical Issues; Mediation Models.

References and Further Reading: Bush, Robert A. Baruch, and Joseph P. Folger, 1994, *Promise of Mediation;* Moore, Christopher W., 1986, *The Mediation Process;* Wehr, Paul, and Sharon Erickson Nepstad, 1994, "Violence, Nonviolence, and Justice in Sandinista Nicaragua."

Mediator Qualifications, Certification, and Training

In the United States, there is no standard certification process for mediators, although the issue has been under consideration for a number of years. The Society of Professionals in Dispute Resolution (SPIDR) has been at the center of the debate. Although it strongly supports the notion that mediators must be qualified, it has found after lengthy deliberation that there is no one definition of "qualified" that is adequate for all situations. For this reason, the SPIDR has refrained from developing a national certification procedure.

A number of states, however, have established certification requirements for mediators who are associated with state or local courts or are listed on state-run mediator referral lists. A number of conflict resolution organizations (such as the American Arbitration Association and the Academy of Family Mediators) do their own certification of mediators.

Most mediators' qualifications include a mix of academic training, practical skill, experience, knowledge of the particular subject in dispute (e.g., divorce, water law, medical malpractice), and personality. Some are trained specifically as mediators; others supplement training as lawyers, therapists, social workers, businesspeople, or scholars, for instance, with training as mediators. Although other fields stress academic training over other qualification criteria, SPIDR has found "impressive evidence that some individuals who do not possess these credentials [academic degrees] make excellent dispute resolvers" (Society of Professionals in Dispute Resolution 1989, 12–13).

Most mediators have at least some practical training in mediation. Typical training programs run from 20 to 80 hours or more. A few universities offer undergraduate and graduate degrees in conflict management, although most mediators have not gone through such programs. Many mediation training programs require additional internships or co-mediation experience in which the mediator-in-training co-mediates with an experienced mediator for months or even years to gain experience.

Some mediator qualifications cannot be taught but are more innate. Some people are better listeners, better problem solvers, better synthesizers of diverse or even divergent ideas than others. Therefore, reputation is often the best guide to a mediator's qualifications. Potential mediation clients should consider what they want from a mediator, get a list of possible people from one or more providers, talk to the mediator, check references, and then make a decision as to whether that person is likely to meet their needs.

People seeking mediation training should check out the available training programs just as carefully, as there are no requirements for trainers either. Since training is often as lucrative as mediation, some mediators with relatively little experience offer training as a way to supplement their income. Potential clients should therefore be careful to investigate the experience and reputation of the training provider. State offices of mediation and major dispute resolution organizations (such as the American Arbitration Association, the Academy of Family Mediators, and SPIDR) have lists of reputable training providers in cities nationwide. A short list of trainers is also given in Appendix 4 of this book.

See also: Academy of Family Mediators; American Arbitration Association; Mediation; Society of Professionals in Dispute Resolution; Appendix 4 for a list of training providers.

References and Further Reading: Folberg, Jay, and Alison Taylor, 1984, *Mediation: A Comprehensive Guide to Resolving Conflicts without Litigation,* 233–43; Honeyman, Christopher, 1993, "A Consensus on Mediators' Qualifications"; Society of Professionals in Dispute Resolution, 1989, *Report of the SPIDR Commission on Qualifications;* Society of Professionals in Dispute Resolution, 1996, *Ensuring Competence and Quality in Dispute Resolution Practice.*

Mediator Selection

Selecting a good mediator can be tricky. Mediators differ greatly from one another in their backgrounds, training, skills, and styles. Parties looking for a mediator should consider several people and learn quite a bit about them before making a selection. This can be done by getting information about the organizations the mediators belong to, by interviewing the mediators themselves, and by talking to people who have used their services in the past (mediators should be willing to give references). Lists of recommended mediators can also be obtained from a variety of organizations at the local and state levels. The local bar association, for instance, may have lists of attorney-mediators; family counselors and family courts usually have lists of family mediators; the American Arbitration Association has lists of mediators as well as arbitrators; and state-level dispute resolution organizations may maintain lists of mediators.

When choosing a mediator, one should be sure that the mediator has considerable experience and training in the kind of dispute involved. Since there is no uniform process of certifying mediators, anyone can advertise as a mediator, even those who have had little or no training or experience. The best mediators will have gone through a variety of training programs and will have been practicing in the appropriate areas for several years.

One should also investigate the mediator's style. How much control does the mediator give to the parties? Does the mediator set the ground rules and force the parties to follow them, or do the parties help design the ground rules and the process? Does the mediator tend to direct the process but let the parties control the substance of the discussions? Or does the mediator tend to become active in the substance of the dispute, suggesting—or even pushing—his or her own solutions? Neither of these approaches is right or wrong. They are just different styles, each of which will suit particular people and particular cases more than others. Some people want or need the mediator to take a strong substantive and procedural role; they want

someone with substantive expertise to help craft new options and sell those options—if they seem good—to the opposition. Others want minimal control. They simply want a forum and perhaps a third-party observer and facilitator to help move the discussions along at a reasonable pace and to keep people on their good behavior. Disputants should examine their own needs and then match those needs to the style of the mediator they are considering.

Other concerns are mediator cost, availability, potential conflict of interest, and reputation. Are they known to be neutral and fair? Reasonably priced? Available when they are needed? Do they have any connections or past activities that would constitute a conflict of interest?

The last item to consider is that the mediator must be approved by both parties. If one side finds a mediator, that mediator may then be willing to help convince the other party to come to the table. But if the other party prefers a different mediator, the parties will have to resolve that decision before the mediation can proceed.

See also: Mediator Qualifications, Certification, and Training. *References and Further Reading:* American Arbitration Association, World Wide Web Home Page, http://www.adr.org; Carpenter, Susan L., and W. J. D. Kennedy, 1988, *Managing Public Disputes;* Kovach, Kimberlee K., 1994, *Mediation: Principles and Practice;* Kubey, Craig, 1991, *You Don't Always Need a Lawyer.*

Mennonite Conciliation Service

The Mennonite Conciliation Service (MCS) is a network of Mennonites committed to peacemaking and reconciliation of conflicting parties. Run by the Mennonite Central Committee, the MCS provides resources, training, networking, and intervention in the United States and around the world in an effort to transform destructive conflict into constructive conflict, growth, and change.

The MCS publishes a journal called *Conciliation Quarterly,* which focuses on issues of conflict transformation from the interpersonal to the international level. It conducts workshops and training seminars on diverse topics: conflict theory, conflict theology, mediation, facilitation, team building, and problem solving. MCS staff and network members (who include Christians from the Brethren in Christ faith) also provide third-party intervention services (mediation, facilitation, and consulting) to individuals, groups, and congregations both in the United States and elsewhere.

MCS's guiding principles are both spiritual and practical: members believe that "positive conflict transformation requires both the use of our best skills as well as the guiding presence of God's spirit" (Mennonite Central Committee brochure). They work simultaneously for harmony and justice, negotiated agreements, and forgiveness. Along with the Brethren and the Quakers, the Mennonites have been a leading force for nonviolent conflict resolution worldwide.

See also: Appendix 1 for contact information.

Mini-trial

A mini-trial is an alternative dispute resolution process that combines aspects of negotiation, mediation, and adjudication. It is most commonly applied in business disputes when direct negotiations have reached an impasse. Although the process was first developed by Eric Green, a business mediator, the term *mini-trial* was first used by a *New York Times* reporter to describe settlement negotiations in a patent infringement case between TRW and Telecredit (Nolan-Haley 1992). The mini-trial has also been used successfully in product liability, employee grievance, and antitrust disputes.

Although the steps in a mini-trial vary from one situation to the next, most mini-trials involve three stages. The first stage involves the exchange of key documents and relevant written information before the hearing. The second stage is the hearing process, which is conducted by a neutral third party—often a retired judge or a technical expert in the appropriate field—who serves on a hearing panel along with executives—not lawyers—from each side of the dispute. These executives must have decision-making authority for the organizations involved.

During the hearing, attorneys for each side present a summary of the case for the executives and the neutral third party. Usually this summary is much shorter than it would be in a regular trial, and it is usually presented in narrative form, rather than through the examination and cross-examination of witnesses. The goal is to review the key aspects of the case quickly and then move on to the third—decision-making—phase of the process. In the third phase, the administrators on the hearing panel try to negotiate a settlement, based on the information presented during the hearing. If the administrators cannot come to an agreement, they often solicit the assistance of the neutral party. The neutral may assist in the process of the negotiations, may suggest the framework or even the details of an agreement, or both. The administrators make the final decision whether to settle or not. If a settlement is reached, the process is binding. If no settlement is reached, the parties are free to pursue other dispute resolution options, such as traditional arbitration or adjudication.

The advantages of this process are that it is much faster (typically one to four days) and usually less expensive than a traditional trial, and it gives the principals in the conflict control over the outcome. Mini-trials often work better than negotiations or mediation involving representatives of organizations who are not decision makers, because the people involved in the mini-trial are empowered to make a decision. There is no need to educate constituents or convince decision makers of the benefits of settlement terms that someone else developed. Further, since the executives participating in the mini-trial have usually not been involved in earlier negotiations, they may not be entrenched in their positions and may be more open to new options than previous negotiators.

One disadvantage of mini-trials is that the presentation of evidence is truncated. Therefore, it can be argued that due process is not protected. Also, the speed of the process is a disadvantage to parties who would benefit from delay. However, the risks of the process are low. Either party may withdraw from the process at any time, and even if the case is not settled, the effort is not wasted, because it helps all the parties prepare for the ensuing trial.

See also: Arbitration; Early Neutral Evaluation; Mediation; Negotiation; Private Judging; Summary Jury Trial;
References and Further Reading: Dauer, Edward A., 1994, *Manual of Dispute Resolution;* Goldberg, Stephen B., Frank E. A. Sander, and Nancy H. Rogers, 1992, *Dispute Resolution: Negotiation, Mediation, and Other Processes;* Kolb, Deborah M., and Associates, 1994, *When Talk Works: Profiles of Mediators;* Nolan-Haley, Jacqueline M., 1992, *Alternative Dispute Resolution in a Nutshell;* Susskind, Lawrence, and Jeffrey Cruikshank, 1987, *Breaking the Impasse.*

Misunderstandings

Misunderstandings and misperceptions are common sources of conflict and conflict escalation. They develop from unrealistic stereotypes that disputants have about each other, media reports that focus on sensational and unrepresentative aspects of a conflict, lack of time for the parties to find out what is really happening, cultural and educational differences that influence how parties interpret specific situations, people's tendency to assume the worst when confronted with incomplete or unreliable information, and deliberate misinformation and deception.

Misperceptions cause problems because they make parties behave differently than they would if they better understood the situation. For example, an accident may be interpreted as a malicious act and provoke an inappropriately aggressive response; a well-intended question or comment might be interpreted as an attack and provoke a counterattack instead of an honest answer.

In heated conflicts, misunderstanding and misperception tend to be common, as people often jump to conclusions based on partial facts (which correspond to their expectations), and they often fail to attend to information that runs counter to their stereotypes and assumptions. The result is that they misinterpret the interests or goals of their adversaries, overlook or disregard key stakeholders, misinterpret (or fail to examine) relevant technical facts and outstanding uncertainties, and miscalculate the costs and potential benefits of pursuing the conflict in different ways. For example, people who are very angry may pursue expensive litigation, even though they have little probability of victory; or they may try to push a proposal through an administrative decision-making process without assessing the strength of the opposition and preparing to deal with it.

Baby boomers remember with both fear and amusement a scene in which Soviet Premier Nikita Khrushchev took off his shoe and pounded it on the table during a United Nations address. The United States interpreted this as an act of a fanatic trying to intimidate the West. According to William Ury, it was actually Khrushchev's attempt "to be one of the guys." Having heard that Americans love passionate political debate, he was just trying to be passionate and look like an American (Ury 1991, 25–26).

Strategies for limiting misunderstandings include active listening, facilitated dialogues and meetings, the development of enhanced public writing and speaking skills, commitments by the media to provide the community with accurate information (and avoid inflammatory reporting), recognition by the parties of the dangers of stereotyping, and a commitment to take the time needed to obtain reliable information. Also of use are rumor-control teams composed of opinion leaders representing important constituency groups who agree to investigate rumors and publicly report the facts (along with outstanding uncertainties).

See also: Active Listening; Communication; Communication, Cross-Cultural; Crisis Management; Dialogue; Media Role in Conflict; Stereotyping.
References and Further Reading: Deutsch, Morton, 1973, *The Resolution of Conflict: Constructive and Destructive Processes;* Ury, William, 1991, *Getting Past No: Negotiating with Difficult People.*

Model Standards of Conduct for Mediators

The current "Model Standards of Conduct for Mediators" was developed from 1992 to 1994 by a committee representing three organizations: the American Arbitration Association (AAA), the American Bar Association (ABA), and the Society of Professionals in Dispute Resolution (SPIDR). According to the AAA, the purpose of the committee was to "develop a set of standards to serve as a general framework for the practice of mediation." The standards were seen as an effort to further develop the field—as the beginning, not the end, of a consideration of the ethical questions surrounding mediation practice. They were intended to perform three functions: guide the conduct of mediators, inform parties to mediations, and promote public confidence in mediation. The standards are intended to apply to all forms and types of mediation; however, at times, their implementation may be affected by laws or contractual agreements. The standards, as written, were approved by the AAA and SPIDR as well as by the Litigation and Dispute Resolution Sections of the ABA (the ABA as a whole has not taken a position on the standards).

Topics covered include the following:

1. Self-determination. This means that mediation is voluntary and the parties can withdraw at any time.

2. Impartiality. Mediators must remain impartial and evenhanded throughout the process.

3. Conflicts of Interest. Mediators must disclose all potential conflicts of interest with the parties or the issue and must avoid the appearance of such conflicts of interest even after the mediation process is over.

4. Competence. A mediator must have the necessary qualifications to do a good job.

5. Confidentiality. The mediator is expected to "maintain the reasonable expectations of the parties with regard to confidentiality." This means that confidentiality can be determined on a case-by-case basis with the parties, but the mediator is bound to follow the agreed-upon guidelines.

6. Quality of the Process. The mediator is expected to conduct the mediation "fairly, diligently, and in a manner consistent with the principle of self-determination of the parties."

7. Advertising. Mediators are directed to be truthful in advertising their services.

8. Fees. Mediators must fully disclose and explain their fees before the mediation begins.

9. Obligations to the Process. Mediators have a duty to improve the practice of mediation, which includes educating the public about mediation, making it more accessible, and improving their own professional skills and abilities.

See also: Mediation; Mediation, Ethical Issues.
References and Further Reading: American Arbitration Association, 1996, "Model Standards of Conduct for Mediators," World Wide Web Home Page, http://www.adr.org.

Montgomery Bus Boycott

The Montgomery bus boycott was one of the most well-known and successful acts of nonviolent direct action undertaken by blacks in the struggle for civil rights in the 1950s and 1960s. The boycott began on 5 December 1955, four days after a black seamstress named Rosa Parks was arrested for refusing to relinquish her seat on a Montgomery, Alabama, city bus to a white passenger. Although hers was a spontaneous decision without political intention at the time, many blacks had been frustrated by the city bus company's segregation rules and had been planning a boycott or other protest action at the first appropriate opportunity. Shortly after Parks's arrest, black leaders assembled and planned their response—a citywide boycott of the buses until black demands for fair treatment were met. The boycott was organized by the newly formed Montgomery Improvement Association (MIA), which chose a young preacher named Martin Luther King Jr. to be its leader.

MIA demands at the time were surprisingly limited. The organizers were not ready to press for full desegregation of the buses when the boycott commenced but limited their aspirations to three: greater courtesy on the part of bus drivers toward black passengers, employment of black bus drivers for predominantly black routes, and a more flexible seating arrangement that would allow blacks to sit in the front of the bus if the "black" seats in the back were full and seats in the "white" section were empty.

Despite the limited nature of these demands, they were quickly rejected by the white city leaders at the initial negotiating session on 8 December 1955. The bus company offered to make every other bus on black routes a "black only" bus, but this solution was not accepted by black leaders, and negotiations broke down. Further negotiating sessions were held on 17 and 19 December and on 9 January 1956. None were successful; discussions broke down each time in interpersonal hostilities and technical disagreements.

After the last negotiating session in January 1956, the white leaders attempted to break the boycott through coercion. They forbade the black taxi companies to give rides for bus fares, they arrested drivers in the massive car pool that was organized after the taxi companies were effectively closed down, and they faked an "agreement" and published an announcement in the local newspaper that the boycott was over. Someone even bombed King's house in an attempt to frighten him into submission. None of these coercive tactics succeeded. They just further strengthened the blacks' will to prevail and pushed them to the point where they demanded—and eventually won—full desegregation of the buses through the U.S. Supreme Court.

The decision came on 13 November 1956 but was not actually implemented in Montgomery until 20 December, which was when the boycott was officially over. Despite the Supreme Court ruling, considerable violence followed as blacks were beaten and shot and black leaders' houses and churches were bombed. Slowly, however, the violence subsided, and the civil rights movement—and Martin Luther King Jr.—focused efforts on other cities and events.

See also: Ethnic and Racial Conflicts; King, Martin Luther, Jr.; Nonviolence; Power.
References and Further Readings: Branch, Taylor, 1988, *Parting the Waters.*

Montreal Protocol on Substances that Deplete the Ozone Layer

The chlorofluorocarbons (CFCs) treaty (formally called the Montreal Protocol on Substances that Deplete the Ozone Layer) was created in Montreal in 1987. It is the first international agreement whose purpose is to avert global environmental disaster, and it is one of the most successful international consensus-building efforts ever undertaken. The treaty limits, and seeks to eventually eliminate, the production of CFCs, which are chemicals that destroy stratospheric ozone. The ozone layer protects the earth from the sun's ultraviolet (UV) radiation. Without such protection, increased UV radiation is expected to cause many harmful effects, including increased skin cancers, suppression of the immune system, and eye disorders. Increased UV radiation is expected to harm plants and animals as well.

The negotiations over this treaty, like many other international environmental negotiations, were complex and difficult. Discussions were initiated by the United Nations Environment Programme (UNEP) in 1985 in Vienna, the same year the "ozone hole" over Antarctica was discovered. At the Vienna Convention, "governments committed themselves to protect the ozone layer and to co-operate with each other in scientific research to improve understanding of the atmospheric processes" (Ozone Secretariat).

Difficult negotiations continued for two years, at which time the Montreal Protocol was signed by 48 countries. It has been amended twice so far—once in London in 1990, and again in Copenhagen in 1992. Currently, 155 countries are parties to the Vienna Convention and Montreal Protocol, including over 100 developing countries as well as the United States (which is the largest CFC producer).

Given the global nature of the problem, many stakeholders were involved, including producers of CFCs in the United States and abroad, environmental organizations, the UNEP, scientists, and many governments from both the North and the South. The CFC producers were willing to acknowledge the veracity of the evidence about the harmfulness of CFCs, but they wanted to be sure that the time frame for their elimination was financially feasible. Developing countries, too, accepted the scientific data, especially since the problem seems to be worse in the Southern Hemisphere. However, they did not want the treaty to limit their ability to develop. Careful negotiations enabled the interests of all the parties to be respected and the goal of ozone protection to be met. According to the Ozone Secretariat, the organization formed to oversee the implementation of the treaty, "the Protocol is constructively flexible; it can be tightened as the scientific evidence strengthens, without having to be completely renegotiated. Indeed, it sets the 'elimination' of ozone-depleting substances as its 'final objective.'" Although the protocol was considered to be only a first step, it has been immensely successful. Again according to the Ozone Secretariat "once it was agreed, events developed with astonishing speed. New scientific evidence showed that very much tighter and greater controls would be needed, and governments and industry moved further, and faster, than anyone would have believed possible."

Barbara Gray quotes Richard Benedict, one of the U.S. negotiators who helped write the treaty, as saying that several factors made the treaty possible. These included: "(1) close cooperation between policy makers and scientists; (2) an evolutionary step-by-step process of consensus building; (3) the enlightened self-interest of U.S. chlorofluorocarbon manufacturers, who agreed to a ban; (4) skillful leadership within several constituencies; (5) the absence of blame among industry and environmental organizations in the United States; and (6) a model role by the United Nations Environmental Program, which served as convener for the negotiations" (Gray 1989, 275).

See also: Collaborative Problem Solving; Environmental Conflicts; International Conflict; Public Policy Conflicts.
References and Further Reading: Gray, Barbara, 1989, *Collaborating: Finding Common Ground for Multiparty Problems;* Ozone Secretariat, World Wide Web Home Page, http://www.unep.org/unep/secretar/ozone/abtozsec.htm.

Morgenthau, Hans

Hans Morgenthau was a political scientist who wrote a classic book entitled *Politics among Nations*, published in 1948. This book is considered the bible of political realism, a theory of power politics that dominated the field of international relations from the 1940s through the 1980s. Although many current political scientists now question the assumptions of political realism, many others still hold this view. No doubt this book is the source of many contemporary beliefs about international relations.

Key to Morgenthau's theory is the notion that the world is made up of sovereign nation-states that control their citizens and try to pursue their national interests by using their power to impose their will on other states. Relations between states are thus determined by the relative power (or balance of power) among nations. When nations are more powerful than their neighbors and opponents, they work to keep it that way. If they are less powerful, they do what they can to increase their own power and diminish their opponents' through alliances, weapons development, or trade. Thus, politics is dominated by power struggles between states. The dominators try to maintain their position; the dominated try to reverse it.

As contemporary political scientist A. J. Groom explains, "Realism responded to a felt need. It explained the coming catastrophe of the 1930s, the global military confrontation of the first part of the 1940s, and the virulence of the Cold War thereafter. Its very simplicity and its starkness were attractive. It was an explanation of a world in conflict, and it assumed there could be no other world. Therein lay its difficulty, because it could not explain everything" (Groom 1997).

In the 1960s and later, critics of realism began to emerge. Criticism centered around the focus on nation-states as the sole actors in the international system. Subnational groups, international organizations, corporations, churches, and other institutions all played a significant role in determining the world order. In addition, modern politics seemed to demonstrate the importance of cooperation as well as coercion, as exemplified by the formation of the European Community. Nevertheless, many of Morgenthau's ideas still seem to make sense in many instances. As long as national leaders and diplomats act according to Morgenthau's assumptions, their actions will continue to make those assumptions true.

See also: International Conflict.
References and Further Reading: Groom, A. J., 1997, "Approaches to Conflict and Cooperation in International Relations: Lessons from Theory for Practice"; Morgenthau, Hans, 1960, *Politics among Nations;* Rothman, Jay, 1992, *Confrontation to Cooperation: Resolving Ethnic and Regional Conflict.*

Mother Teresa

Mother Teresa (Agnes Gonxha Bojaxhiu) was a Catholic nun who received the Nobel Peace Prize in 1975 for her exceptional service to the poor. Born in Macedonia but later living in Calcutta, India, Mother Teresa saw herself and her order, the Missionaries of Charity, as tools in God's hands. As such, members of the order act toward the poor as Mother Teresa believed all would act toward Jesus Christ if he were alive today.

In 1928, she joined a religious order and took the name Teresa. She was sent to India, where she began teaching in Calcutta. Mother Teresa began working with the city's poor in 1948 and formed the Missionaries of Charity in 1952. The order provides food for the poor and operates hospitals, schools, orphanages, youth centers, and shelters for lepers and the dying destitute. The 4,000 women in the order take vows of poverty, chastity, and obedience in addition to service to the poor. The Missionaries of Charity now has branches in 50 Indian cities and 30 other countries. In addition to the Nobel Prize, Mother Teresa received the 1971 Pope John XXIII Peace Prize and the Jawaharlal Nehru Award for International Understanding in 1972. She died in September 1997.

References and Further Reading: Chawla, Navin, 1992, *Mother Teresa;* Hitchens, Christopher, 1995, *The Missionary Position: Mother Teresa in Theory and Practice.*

Multidoor Courthouse

The term *multidoor courthouse* refers to a place, which may or may not be an actual courthouse, where people can go to get a dispute handled in a variety of ways. In a multidoor courthouse, people with problems first talk to an intake person. By listening and asking questions about the problem, the intake person suggests the most appropriate forum for addressing the problem: regular litigation, small-claims court, mediation, or arbitration, for example. If the intake person is sufficiently knowledgeable and skilled, this initial screening can save disputants much time and money by matching the problem to the process that is likely to be most effective. However, people must be able to choose a different process from the one recommended if they so desire or to change processes midstream if the initial course of action is not working effectively (Goldberg, Sander, and Rogers 1992).

See also: Alternative Dispute Resolution; Arbitration; Mediation.

References and Further Reading: Goldberg, Stephen B., Frank E. A. Sander, and Nancy H. Rogers, 1992, *Dispute Resolution: Negotiation, Mediation, and Other Processes.*

Myrdal, Alva

Alva Myrdal was the first recipient of the Einstein Peace Prize in 1980. Two years later, she received the Nobel Peace Prize for her efforts to promote world disarmament. Elected to the Swedish Parliament in 1962, she served for the next 11 years as a member of the Swedish cabinet and as member of the Swedish delegation to the United Nations General Assembly. During this period, she also served as the head of the Swedish delegation to the UN Disarmament Committee in Geneva.

Myrdal's early work focused on education and the family, emphasizing population control. Although these issues remained important to her, in 1961 she shifted her attention to the promotion of international peace and disarmament. Myrdal's approach to peace emphasizes the role of the social sciences in understanding the sources and dynamics of violence and the importance of grassroots resistance to militarism and violence.

See also: Arms Control and Disarmament; Peace; United Nations.

References and Further Reading: Myrdal, Alva, 1980, "Statement by Alva Myrdal upon Receiving the International Award from the Albert Einstein Peace Prize Foundation, 29 May 1980"; Myrdal, Alva, 1982, *The Game of Disarmament.*

National Association for Community Mediation

The mission of the National Association for Community Mediation (NAFCM) is "to support the maintenance and growth of community-based mediation programs and processes, to present a compelling voice in appropriate policy making, legislative, professional, and other arenas, and to encourage the development and sharing of resources for these efforts" (National Association for Community Mediation 1996). Activities undertaken by NAFCM include the publication of the quarterly *NAFCM News* and the monthly *Update* (for members only) and a membership directory that includes not only names and numbers but also detailed descriptions of program services. NAFCM also maintains an information clearinghouse, engages in extensive networking with local and regional community mediation organizations, and engages in projects intended to improve and promote community mediation programs nationwide. NAFCM has developed training modules in conflict resolution that are used by NAFCM mediation centers to train over 8,000 AmeriCorps members in the management and resolution of personal, interpersonal, and intergroup conflict. The focus in these modules is on effective communication and problem solving—key aspects of all mediation efforts.

See also: Mediation, Community; Mediation, Court-Based; Appendix 1 for contact information.

References and Further Reading: National Association for Community Mediation, 1996, *NAFCM News.*

National Association for Mediation in Education

The National Association for Mediation in Education (NAME) has grown since its founding in 1984 to become the primary national and international clearinghouse for information, resources, technical assistance, and training in school- and university-based conflict resolution. Services provided by NAME include classroom curricula, videos and other teaching aids, program evaluation tools, and other publications designed to help teachers and school administrators implement effective school-based conflict resolution programs. It publishes a newsletter, *The Fourth R,* which includes columns for teachers, students, and researchers. It also holds an annual conference, provides technical assistance to school-based programs, and undertakes research and evaluation relating to school conflict resolution efforts. Freestanding until December 1995, NAME then became part of the National Institute for Dispute Resolution (NIDR). Although it is now combined with NIDR, its goals remain largely the same: to advance the field of conflict resolution and to implement effective conflict resolution programs in schools nationwide.

See also: National Institute for Dispute Resolution; School Conflict Resolution Programs.

National Association of Labor-Management Committees

The National Association of Labor-Management Committees (NALMC) provides assistance to industry-specific groups with the goal of furthering labor-management cooperation. The NALMC was formed in 1977 as an association of local and regional committees. Soon after it was founded, the NALMC helped ensure the passage of the 1978 Labor-Management Cooperation Act, whose purpose was to "provide workers and employers the opportunity to study and explore new and innovative joint approaches to achieving organizational effectiveness . . . and explore ways of eliminating potential problems which reduce the competitiveness and inhibit the economic development of the plant, area, or industry" (NALMC brochure).

The association offers ongoing education programs, access to an extensive library of videos, the quarterly newsletter *Forward Thinking,* and workshops in the area of health care as it relates to labor and management roles. It also cosponsors, with the U.S. Department of Labor and the Federal Mediation and Conciliation Service, the biannual National Labor-Management Conference.

See also: Arbitration, Labor; Federal Mediation and Conciliation Service; Jamestown Area Labor Management Committee; Labor-Management Relations and Conflict; Workplace Conflict and Grievance Procedures; Appendix 1 for contact information.

National Coal Policy Project

The National Coal Policy Project (NCPP) was one of the first efforts made to bring together a large group of stakeholders to engage in consensus building and collaborative problem solving in the public policy-making arena. Although the NCPP was not as successful as many later collaborative problem-solving efforts, it forged new ground and illustrated—through both its successes and its failures—the potential benefits of multiparty consensus-building processes.

The NCPP began in 1976 in response to the environmental and economic tensions spawned by the 1973 Arab oil embargo. Following the oil embargo, there was a resurgence of interest in the United States in coal as an energy source. Environmentalists, however, expressed concern over the potential impacts of increased extraction and use of coal and the lack of clear regulations on those issues. At the same time, industry faced uncertainties about the future of coal use. Both environmentalists and industry were, at this point, dissatisfied and frustrated with the prospects of resolution within the traditional system. Neither side was winning long-term victories, and both were faced with the prospect of a long, expensive conflict yielding an uncertain outcome at best. These concerns prompted the proposal, in 1976, of the NCPP. The NCPP was to serve as an alternative to the traditional legislative and judicial forums for airing disputes over the extraction and use of coal as an energy source.

Gerry Decker, of Dow Chemical Company, and Larry Moss, former chair of the Federal Energy Administration's Environmental Advisory Committee (and former Sierra Club member), persuaded several environmental and industry groups to participate in a test meeting to investigate the possibility of a productive dialogue between the two groups. Although the first several meetings were heated and difficult, they made sufficient progress to convince most of the participants that continuing the meetings was worth their time. Thus, they sought and obtained funding for a formal process, which lasted four years. The initial meeting established two caucuses, one representing the interests of environmentalists, and the other representing industry interests. Five task forces were also formed, focusing on mining, transportation, air pollution, energy pricing, and fuel utilization and conservation. A plenary group, comprising the caucus chairs and the task forces' chairs and cochairs, was given responsibility for the plenary discussions and final approval of task force recommendations. The project as a whole was assisted by staff provided by Georgetown University.

One of the biggest problems the NCPP faced (which continued to haunt it throughout the process) was the selection of participants. Although the topics to be discussed were broad, the organizers decided to limit participation to only two groups: environmentalists and representatives of coal-producing and coal-consuming industries. Other interest groups—for instance, union representatives and government officials—were not invited to participate, although government representatives were invited to be observers, without voting power. These decisions were made for a variety of reasons, but most importantly, the NCPP conveners wanted to keep the group small enough to be manageable. They saw this as an initial experiment; therefore, they were interested in being able to facilitate productive discussions and develop consensus recommendations. They were less interested in ensuring that those recommendations were implemented—the step that was jeopardized by limiting the number of participants. In addition, not all those who were invited chose to participate. Many of those in powerful positions thought that they had nothing to gain by participating.

The first official meeting of the NCPP was in January 1977. Many topics were identified for discussion, including the development of new emissions control technology, coal transportation options, the siting of new coal-fired power plants, mine reclamation, environmental impacts of coal slurry pipelines, federal regulations on surface mining of coal, citizen participation and reduction of delays in energy facility siting, and energy pricing. Each task force set its own agenda and obtained its own data. In many cases, this required joint fact-finding to develop a data set that was credible to all participants. In several cases, task forces took field trips together to collect data and observe conditions. Although the task force meetings were open to the public, few observers came. This allowed the discussions to be more frank and wide ranging than they might have been in a more public forum, and it made negotiating easier. In February 1978, the NCPP released its first set of recommendations. Some of these recommendations were effective in influencing governmental policy, but many were not, as the NCPP had not established the necessary links to people in power, nor had it involved all the stakeholders, which is necessary if one is to have actual policy impact.

In December 1978, the NCPP initiated a second phase to deal with unresolved issues. Three task forces worked in a manner similar to those in phase one and issued recommendations in March 1980. Some of these later recommendations were implemented, but others were not, for the reasons cited earlier.

Despite its failure to have significant immediate impact, the NCPP did have the long-term impact of showing that complex, protracted, multiparty public policy disputes could be effectively addressed using consensus-building processes. Techniques for doing so were refined over the next 10 to 15 years, and now, collaborative problem solving is relatively common in federal, state, and local governments. In addition, the NCPP is seen as the forerunner to the concept of regulatory negotiation, which has also become widespread over the last decade.

See also: Collaborative Problem Solving; Environmental Conflicts; Public Policy Conflicts; Regulatory Negotiation.
References and Further Reading: Carter, L. J., 1977, "Coal: Invoking the 'Rule of Reason' in Energy-Environment Crisis"; Gray, Barbara, 1989, *Collaborating: Finding Common Ground for Multiparty Problems.*

National Conference on Peacemaking and Conflict Resolution

The National Conference on Peacemaking and Conflict Resolution (NCPCR) is one of the largest and most important conferences on the topic of peace and conflict resolution in North America. Held every two years at different locations, this conference brings together hundreds of conflict resolution professionals, practitioners, researchers, students, and teachers for six days of workshops, seminars, panel discussions, and networking. Founded in 1982 to provide a forum for researchers and practitioners from different settings to exchange ideas, the conference has grown in size every year, reaching 2,200 participants in 1995. Topics covered range from international peacemaking to interpersonal conflict resolution. Advocates as well as intermediaries are encouraged to attend; this has fostered an interesting dialogue between these two groups, which tend to have different approaches to peace and justice questions. Over the years, the conference has sought increased ethnic, racial, and international diversity as well. Although primarily North American in scope, increasing numbers of participants come from overseas. Conference offices are located at George Mason University in Fairfax, Virginia.

See also: Appendix 1 for contact information.

National Institute for Dispute Resolution

The National Institute for Dispute Resolution (NIDR) is a nonprofit corporation founded in 1983 that aims to advance the conflict resolution field by offering technical assistance, educational programs, consulting, demonstration projects, publications, and limited grants. It serves as a clearinghouse for dispute resolution information of many kinds.

NIDR's primary areas of interest include public policy dispute resolution, quality-of-justice issues, and youth conflict resolution. The public policy program emphasizes mediation, facilitation, negotiated rulemaking, and policy dialogues on public decision-making processes at the local to the international level. NIDR's work on quality-of-justice issues promotes the continued integration of alternative dispute resolution mechanisms into the traditional legal system. The youth program promotes multicultural understanding, prejudice reduction, and violence prevention.

NIDR's services include DR Search, a customized research service designed to find the latest dispute resolution information. DR Search can also identify dispute resolution providers in a particular community. NIDR also runs workshops on particular dispute resolution skills, offers technical assistance for both public and private organizations on the institutionalization of dispute resolution within organizations, and provides assistance in evaluating dispute resolution services nationwide.

NIDR publishes *NIDR News,* a bimonthly newsletter that reports on dispute resolution developments and has a calendar of upcoming events, and *FORUM,* a magazine devoted to the stimulation of debate about the use of conflict resolution techniques. The institute also publishes books, research reports, teaching and training materials, and videotapes.

See also: Appendix 1 for contact information.

National Labor Relations Board

The National Labor Relations Board (NLRB) is a federal body that handles complaints and charges of unfair labor practices. The NLRB consists of a five-member board, an independent general counsel, and a group of regional and residential offices located throughout the United States. Board members are appointed by the president (with Senate confirmation) for five-year terms.

Labor complaints are investigated by regional office staff members. Hearings are conducted by administrative law judges employing the rules of evidence and procedure of the U.S. district courts. Their recommendations may be appealed to the NLRB itself, which then renders a binding decision. This decision may be appealed through the U.S. courts of appeal and, rarely, to the U.S. Supreme Court.

A compliance officer at the regional level ensures that the board's orders are followed. If necessary, the officer can seek court-ordered enforcement and contempt charges. The board also oversees certification elections through which employees select a union to represent them. Once a union is so certified, the NLRB ensures that the employer bargains with the chosen union.

One of the problems with the NLRB is that its efforts can be circumvented by legal maneuvering and by companies that are willing to pay fines and continue practices in contempt of the board's orders. Further, the presidentially appointed board is not immune to the political, social, and economic ideology of the president. Board members appointed by Republican presidents tend to be more conservative and pro-management, whereas Democratic appointees more often favor unions. The result is policy inconsistency, reversal, and considerable controversy. Nevertheless, the NLRB is one of the many institutions established by the federal government to bring peace and order to the workplace. Taken together, these institutions have been successful, and labor-management relations are much improved over the situation in the early 1900s, when severe labor strife and even violence were common.

See also: Collective Bargaining; Labor-Management Relations and Conflict.

References and Further Reading: Leap, Terry L., 1995, *Collective Bargaining and Labor Relations.*

National Peace Foundation

The National Peace Foundation (NPF) is a private, nonpartisan, nonprofit organization founded in 1982. The foundation lobbied for the establishment, in 1984, of the United States Institute of Peace and worked thereafter on its strengthening and expansion. The foundation's overall mission is to "promulgate peace building and conflict resolution on every level from the community, to the regional, to the national and international" (NPF brochure).

Since 1988, the foundation has taken a more activist approach to peace and democracy building. It carries out dialogues, seminars, conflict resolution training, and mediation programs in the United States and abroad. All these activities are based on the fundamental belief that "individuals as well as organizations and governments, can be instrumental in reconciling conflicting interests and building amicable relationships" (NPF brochure). The foundation periodically bestows its Peacemaker Award on outstanding individuals who exemplify this tenet. *Peace Reporter* is the regular publication of the foundation.

See also: United States Institute of Peace; Appendix 1 for contact information.

Needs

Psychologist Abraham Maslow postulated that all people are driven to fill certain fundamental human needs. In addition to the purely biological need for food and shelter, Maslow (1943) argued that humans also seek safety and security, love, a sense of belonging to a group, self-esteem, and self-actualization (the ability to achieve one's goals). This idea has been adapted to conflict resolution theory by John Burton, Herbert Kelman, and others who suggest that most protracted or intractable conflicts are not over interests but rather over fundamental human needs. If individuals or a group of people (a particular ethnic group, for example) are denied security, identity, recognition, or equal participation within a society, they will be driven by a fundamental psychological imperative to fight for these needs. The only way to resolve conflicts over fundamental human needs is to change the structure of the society so that these needs are fulfilled for all groups. If they are not, the conflict will continue.

Although conflicts over material interests (such as money or territory) tend to lead to win-lose outcomes in which one party wins what its opponent loses, conflicts over human needs are not inversely related. Rather, human needs are inexhaustible and tend to reinforce one another. Thus, the greater the sense of security and legitimate identity one party has, the more it is willing to allow the same sense of security and identity to the opponent. This is clearly illustrated in the Israeli-Palestinian conflict. When the conflict was described as focusing on territory alone, no progress toward peace was made. However, once the Palestine Liberation Organization (PLO) and the Israelis acknowledged each other's right to exist (identity), the sense of security increased for both sides, and progress started to be made on territorial disputes.

See also: Interests and Positions; Problem Solving, Analytical.
References and Further Reading: Burton, John, 1990b, *Conflict: Resolution and Provention;* Kelman, Herbert C., 1982, "Creating the Conditions for Israeli-Palestinian Negotiations"; Maslow, Abraham, 1943, "A Theory of Human Motivation."

Negotiated Rulemaking
See **Regulatory Negotiation.**

Negotiated Rulemaking Act of 1990

The Negotiated Rulemaking Act was one of two key acts passed in 1990 to institute alternative dispute resolution in the federal government (the second was the Administrative Dispute Resolution Act). The Negotiated Rulemaking Act legitimizes and encourages the use of negotiated rulemaking (also called regulatory negotiation, or "reg-neg") by federal agencies. This process allows agencies to negotiate with the parties to be regulated and other interested people and organizations before establishing new regulations. By doing so, the agency can develop rules and regulations that are acceptable to outside interest groups and are thus less likely to be challenged in court (as regulations almost always are otherwise).

The use of regulatory negotiation is considered by many to be highly beneficial, as it avoids the costly and adversarial nature of traditional rulemaking and yields regulations that are perceived as more legitimate and thus more likely to be followed. Some observers are uncomfortable with the approach, because it allows the "wolves" to help make the regulations to protect the "chickens." However, since all interest groups are involved in the process, most people believe that the outcomes are generally fair to all sides, not a sellout to the regulated parties.

See also: Federal Use of Alternative Dispute Resolution; Regulatory Negotiation.
References and Further Reading: Brown, Brack, 1993, "Public Organizations and Policies in Conflict: Notes on Theory and Practice"; Weissman, Steven, 1996, "'Reg-Neg' Can Work, but Pitfalls Remain."

Negotiated Rulemaking at the Maine Department of Transportation

Environmental policy making can be a difficult and contentious process. It involves many interest groups, each of which seeks policies that are in direct opposition to the interests of other parties. Often the result is a standoff and a continuation of the status quo. Alternatively, the regulatory agency listens to all the competing demands and then does its best to develop a policy that meets most of the groups' interests in some way. However, since no one's interests are fully met, one or more groups invariably sue the agency, adding tremendous time and public expense to the policy-making process.

An alternative approach that has become increasingly popular over the last 20 years is regulatory negotiation, or negotiated rulemaking. Here, the policy-making agency sits down with interest groups to negotiate rules in advance. The goal of the process is not to force people to accept the agency's wishes but to allow interested parties to work with the agency to develop a consensus on how the rules should be written. This is a much less contentious process, and it results in rules that are more readily accepted by the regulated parties, usually without any follow-up lawsuits.

In 1991, the Natural Resources Council of Maine (NRCM) was joined by other environmental groups in opposing a proposal to widen the turnpike in the southern part of the state. When they were unable to become significantly involved in the planning process or to stop the proposal, they sought and passed a public referendum that required the Maine Department of Transportation (MDOT) to write new rules regarding state transportation policy. The policy was to cover a variety of modes of transportation, be environmentally sound, and improve public participation in the decision-making process.

Although they had won the referendum, the NRCM and its environmental allies realized that they would have to work with the MDOT to implement their plans. The MDOT also realized that the referendum had changed the rules of the policy-making game and that it would have to work with the NRCM and other citizens groups much more effectively in the future. For that reason, when the NRCM and its allies suggested that a consensus-based regulatory negotiation process be used to develop the new rules, the MDOT agreed. It assembled a group of 58 representatives

from environmental and business interests and state agencies, and they worked together for a year to develop a new transportation policy for the state. According to Sandra Bogdonoff, the Transportation Policy Advisory Committee (T-PAC), which wrote the rules, "provides a model for consensus building and public participation for state government policy" that not only resulted in new rules but also opened lines of communication, formed new alliances, and created a "perception of shared stewardship of Maine's transportation policy" (Bogdonoff 1995, 151).

MDOT told the negotiators that they needed to meet three requirements. First, the rules had to be completed by the preset deadline. Second, the rules had to be agreed to unanimously. Third, the rules had to be workable, in the judgment of MDOT. The facilitators suggested a two-tier structuring of T-PAC. The entire committee would give input to a steering committee, which would be responsible for writing the rules based on the group's input.

The second meeting of T-PAC began the development of a shared knowledge base; the third meeting formulated a list of goals. The facilitators then asked the group to break into task forces, one for each part of the act. Committee members resisted such assignments, however, deciding instead to form task groups according to interests. Thus, there was an environmental group, a business group, and the MDOT group. Each of these groups chose negotiators to work with the other groups for the actual rule drafting. The negotiators had trouble proceeding, but once the facilitators circulated an outline of the rules, based solely on the referendum, the environmental negotiators took the outline and wrote a first draft. The MDOT developed a second version, and comparisons were made. The full group then worked together, sometimes word by word, to develop a consensus version, which was approved by the MDOT and the public.

In addition to achieving its short-term goals, the regulatory negotiation also resulted in a long-term change in the way transportation decision making occurs in Maine. Regional committees were formed to model the T-PAC process at the regional level. At both the state and the regional levels, transportation planning is now more inclusive, more consensual, and less contentious.

See also: Collaborative Problem Solving; Environmental Conflicts; Facilitation; NIMBY, LULU, and NOPE; Public Policy Conflicts; Regulatory Negotiation.
References and Further Reading: Bogdonoff, Sandra, 1995, "Consensus Building to Write Environmentally Responsive Rules for Maine's New Transportation Policy."

Negotiation

In many ways, negotiation is the fundamental form of dispute resolution. Generally voluntary, negotiation simply involves a discussion between disputing parties for the purpose of reaching a settlement of their dispute. Although people are usually unaware of what they are doing, most social interaction involves negotiation: unless one lives alone, one negotiates the distribution of household chores, what will be cooked (and eaten) for dinner, who will do what in the evening and over the weekend. If one is to live successfully with others—in a house, at work, in a community—one must be able to negotiate effectively.

Negotiation can take many forms. In 1981, Roger Fisher and William Ury published a seminal book entitled *Getting to Yes* (updated in 1991) that distinguished between two prominent forms of negotiation: positional bargaining and interest-based bargaining. Positional bargaining is competitive. Typically, one party takes an opening position, the other counters with an opposing offer, and the two parties haggle until something between the two opening positions is agreed on. The goal is to get the most for oneself, with little or no concern for the outcome of the other. (Frequently the parties assume that the more one side gets, the less the other side gets, so they try to get as much as they can for themselves.)

For example, a union may open contract negotiations demanding a 10 percent wage increase and an increase in job security and medical benefits. Management may counter with a 5 percent increase, less job security, and stable medical benefits. The two sides will debate the merits of their positions and illustrate their power (by threatening a lockout or a strike, for example) until an agreement, which is usually somewhere between the two extremes, is reached.

Although this approach to negotiation is common, Fisher and Ury believe that it fails to yield optimal results because the parties work against each other instead of together and end up compromising in ways that violate their underlying interests (the things they really want or need), which may not be represented or protected by their stated positions. For instance, union negotiators may know that a 10 percent raise would make the company financially unstable, but they ask for it anyway because they know that they will have to back down in the negotiations. But their demand for such an extreme wage increase may focus the discussion on wages instead of on job security, which might be a bigger concern.

A better approach, Fisher and Ury maintain, is interest-based bargaining (in *Getting to Yes* they call it "principled negotiation"), which focuses on the underlying interests of the parties, not their opening positions. Interests are what the parties really want, not what they say they want. For example, in the above case, the workers might want job security much more than the 10 percent raise, and they might want a raise not just for the money but because the money can buy them a better quality of life. If the company can provide a better quality of life by providing a better working environment and more job security, it might be able to meet the employees' interests better with a smaller raise, while keeping the company financially strong. Unlike positional bargaining, which assumes that interests are diametrically opposed, interest-based bargaining assumes that at least one of the interests of the parties is the same—to reach an agreement. Thus, Fisher and Ury urge negotiators to view each other as allies attacking a common problem rather than as enemies attacking each other.

The skills and strategy required for the two kinds of negotiation are different. People engaged in positional bargaining need to judge who should make the first offer, how high or low that offer should be, if and when they should make concessions, and what those concessions should be. They also must focus on power—theirs and their opponent's. They need to increase their power to influence the opponent as much as possible, while trying to diminish their opponent's power over them. The key to power is alternatives: If negotiators have good alternatives to an agreement, they can ask for whatever they want and walk away if they don't get it. If negotiators really need an agreement because they don't have any good alternatives, their power to get the agreement they want is greatly reduced.

In interest-based bargaining, the process is rather different. Usually the parties start by defining their interests. They examine the extent to which the interests are compatible and the extent to which they are opposed. They then work in the areas of compatibility to develop options for mutual gain. By brainstorming settlement options together and refining them in a cooperative manner, parties to interest-based bargaining often come up with win-win solutions that positional bargaining would overlook. However, this is possible only in situations in which interests are compatible. If they are not, a more competitive strategy is considered by many to be the tactic of choice.

Many observers believe that negotiation is the best dispute resolution option available, because it allows the parties to maintain control over both the process and the substance of their dispute and any settlement agreement. This enables the parties to define the issues, their interests and needs, and solutions that work for them. Also, when people are involved in forging an agreement themselves, they are more likely to stick to it than if it is imposed on them by someone or something else.

However, not all people can successfully negotiate a solution to all problems. Sometimes the problems are too complex or controversial; sometimes too many people or too many issues are involved; sometimes relationships have gotten so bad that the parties cannot communicate effectively or will not even sit down together to talk. In these circumstances, mediation (which is assisted negotiation) or adjudication may be the dispute resolution mechanism of choice.

Even when one of these approaches is chosen, however, the ultimate outcome is usually obtained through negotiation. Mediation is simply negotiation that is facilitated by a third party who helps direct the process. Although adjudication is very different from negotiation, about 95 percent of cases filed are settled out of court (through negotiation) before the trial takes place. However, this negotiation is done by lawyers, negotiating on their clients' behalf. If people really want to maintain control of the process and substance of their own dispute, negotiations between the parties themselves is generally the superior dispute resolution method.

See also: Adjudication; Bargaining, Integrative and Distributive; Mediation; Principled Negotiation and *Getting to Yes.*
References and Further Reading: Breslin, J. William, and Jeffrey Z. Rubin, 1991, *Negotiation Theory and Practice;* Fisher, Roger, and William Ury, 1981, *Getting to Yes* (2nd ed. with Bruce Patton, 1991); Raiffa, Howard, 1982, *The Art and Science of Negotiation.*

Negotiation, Breakthrough

Breakthrough negotiation is an extension of principled negotiation that was developed by William Ury, coauthor of *Getting to Yes,* in his sequel *Getting Past No.* Designed to overcome some of the obstacles to principled negotiation described in *Getting to Yes,* breakthrough negotiation involves five rules that supplement the fundamental rules of principled negotiation so that the system will work, as Ury puts it, "with difficult people."

The first rule of breakthrough negotiation is to avoid reacting to provocations, or, as Ury puts it, "go to the balcony." He urges people to retreat to "the balcony" (or any place close to, but away from, the negotiating table) whenever things get heated or negotiations become stalled. This allows the negotiator to step back, calm down, think, and carefully strategize without allowing the situation to escalate further (as it can do when a disputant simply reacts without thinking in either a defensive or an aggressive way).

The second step is to disarm one's opponents by "stepping to their side." When they put up obstacles, don't run right into them, Ury says, but go around them. Use active listening to acknowledge opponents' feelings, I-messages to express your own; agree whenever you can, and stand up for yourself—respectfully—when you cannot. In this way you can deflect attacks and provocations, rather than countering them with more of the same, which simply escalates a conflict and makes resolution more difficult to attain.

The third step is to change the negotiating game. Don't simply respond to ultimatums or positional bargaining with the same game; rather, change the game to a problem-solving one by asking questions such as Why? Why not? What if . . . ? or What makes that fair? Negotiate about the process of negotiation, identify your opponent's tricks when you see them, but don't fall for them. Urge that the problem be framed in terms of "we" rather than "you" and "I."

The fourth step is to make it easy for the opponent to say yes, and the fifth step is to make it hard to say no. "Bring them to their senses," says Ury, "not to their knees." Usually, when people refuse to agree, it is because they think that they have a better alternative available than the one they can get from negotiation. If this is true, you will have to beat this alternative, but if it is not, Ury advises, you have to educate them about the reality—about the consequences of saying no. All these techniques are designed to make principled negotiation work in situations in which most people assume that it will not work, to forge win-win agreements when none are apparent, and to turn enemies into partners who can work together to solve mutual problems.

See also: Active Listening; I-Messages; Principled Negotiation and *Getting to Yes;* Ury, William.
References and Further Reading: Fisher, Roger, and William Ury, 1981, *Getting to Yes* (2nd ed. with Bruce Patton, 1991); Ury, William, 1991, *Getting Past No: Negotiating with Difficult People.*

Negotiation, Limits to

Not all disputes can be solved with negotiation—for example, those that involve deep-rooted values or nonnegotiable, fundamental human needs. Americans do not negotiate their beliefs about the morality of abortion, nor do Palestinians or Israelis negotiate their fundamental right to exist. The only way that deep-rooted value- or needs-based conflicts can be resolved is if ways are found to meet all the parties' needs simultaneously or to honor each party's values equally. When values are diametrically opposed, however, as they are in the abortion controversy, the best that can be done is to find a middle ground and expect the struggle to continue. Conflicts involving deep-rooted value differences and struggles over fundamental needs (such as identity or security) are usually highly intractable. Related disputes can be temporarily settled, but the underlying conflict usually cannot be permanently resolved.

In addition, negotiation works only when all the disputants consider a mutual agreement to be their most desirable alternative. If any party believes that it has a better alternative, it is likely to pursue that option instead. For example, if a developer asks an environmental group to sit down and negotiate the design of a new shopping center so that it is environmentally sound, the environmental group may do so if it thinks that making design changes is the greatest impact it is likely to have on the outcome. However, if the group thinks that it can go to court and block the construction of the center altogether, it is likely to do so. This is what Fisher and Ury call the "BATNA," or "best alternative to a negotiated agreement." If any disputant's BATNA is better than the negotiated settlement, it will not agree to a negotiated solution; rather, it will pursue its BATNA.

Overcoming the BATNA limit requires that all parties have similar expectations regarding the likely result of alternative dispute resolution mechanisms. In other words, they must agree on the likely outcome of a lawsuit, an election, civil disobedience, or whatever strategies are available for prosecuting a conflict. Based on such expectations, they can then negotiate an agreement that is similar to the expected outcome of the alternative processes and save themselves the transaction costs.

Negotiation also reduces the risk that the expected outcome will not be realized. For example, if the parties can agree on the likely outcome of court-based litigation, they can negotiate an agreement that closely parallels the expected verdict. This is done all the time when parties settle out of court before a trial. They usually take the case far enough in the process that they can predict its outcome. At that point, there is no reason to push the process further; rather, the situation is "ripe" for negotiation.

However, when there is disagreement or uncertainty regarding the probable outcome of alternative dispute resolution mechanisms, the situation is not ripe for negotiation. Before negotiation can succeed, these uncertainties must be clarified. Parties will be inclined to try an alternative approach to negotiation if they do not achieve their goals through alternative dispute resolution.

See also: Alternative Dispute Resolution, Barriers to Use; BATNA; Intractable Conflicts; Negotiation; Negotiation and Mediation, Timing and "Ripeness"; Principled Negotiation and *Getting to Yes.*

References and Further Reading: Arrow, Kenneth, Robert H. Mnookin, Lee Ross, Amos Tversky, and Robert Wilson, 1995, *Barriers to Conflict Resolution;* Fisher, Roger, and William Ury, 1981, *Getting to Yes* (2nd ed. with Bruce Patton, 1991).

Negotiation, Principled
See **Principled Negotiation and** *Getting to Yes.*

Negotiation and Mediation, Cross-Cultural

Negotiating or mediating with people from other cultures is often more difficult than negotiating with someone of one's own culture and often requires different negotiating (and mediating) strategies. In addition to possible language barriers and other communication problems, people from different cultures have different expectations regarding appropriate negotiation and conflict resolution practices.

For example, a distinction is often made between low-context and high-context cultures. People from low-context cultures (which include the United States, Canada, and Western European countries) tend to see conflict as a struggle between competing interests, which they approach in a rational, businesslike way. They tend to use direct, explicit language, tackle the problem head-on, and use either competitive (positional) bargaining or integrative (problem-solving) negotiation to deal with the issue directly.

The North American model of mediation reflects this approach. Americans manage their conflicts as they manage their businesses. Parties are urged to "buy into" a mediation process that is ready-made. The process helps them define their problem, identify alternative solutions, and choose the one that fits best. "They go through the procedure in assembly-line fashion," with the "production manager" being the mediator (LeResche 1990, 78).

People from high-context cultures (which include Japan, China, Latin America, and other traditional, collectivist, and honor-based cultures) see conflict as a problem of relationships as much as interests. They need a much slower, more relationship-oriented process, one that caters to their preference for indirect and non-verbal communication that protects relationships and face.

Because of the importance of relationships and community values, traditional cultures often prefer third-party interveners who are part of the community and even part of the conflict itself, rather than the external neutral so commonly used in North American mediation. Thus they use "insider-partial" mediators who are involved in the conflict and may even be partial to one side or another. Because these people are respected in the community and are known to be fair, they are trusted as mediators by both sides. In addition, since they are members of the community who will be present over the long term, they have more invested in the solution than does an outsider who comes in to help the parties solve a problem and then leaves.

Unlike other conflict resolution professionals from the United States, who try to import the North American model to other parts of the world, John Paul Lederach is respected by many mediators for de-

veloping and teaching what he calls the "elicitive model" of conflict resolution. Lederach consults and trains people around the world by helping them utilize their own culture and skills to better resolve their conflicts in their own way, rather than trying to get them to be more like Americans.

See also: Communication, Cross-Cultural; Conflict Styles; Mediation, Ethical Issues; Mediation Models; Neutrality and Impartiality; Rationality.
References and Further Reading: Lederach, John Paul, 1990, "Training on Culture: Four Approaches"; LeResche, Diane Neumann, 1990, "Procedural Justice of, by, and for American Ethnic Groups: A Comparison of Interpersonal Conflict Resolution Procedures Used by Korean-Americans and American Community Mediation Centers with Procedural Justice Theories."

Negotiation and Mediation, Timing and "Ripeness"

In the course of most disputes, there will be times when prospects are good for agreement-based resolution and times when the chances for agreement are bleak. Frequently, mediators talk about the concept of "ripeness": some conflicts are "ripe" for negotiation or resolution, and others are not.

Although it is possible to create ripeness, one must usually wait until it occurs. At that point, a person has to be able to recognize the ripeness of the conflict situation and be prepared to move quickly to pursue opportunities for agreement.

In general, chances of agreement are best when one or more of the parties have become frustrated by their inability to succeed through alternative measures. This may happen after the parties have battled to a stalemate or have received reliable estimates of the costs of continued confrontation. It may also come with personnel changes on one or more sides, since new negotiators may not harbor the distrust or hostility developed in earlier confrontations. There may also be external deadlines that will penalize the parties if they fail to reach an agreement by a certain time—the expiration of a labor contract, for example.

The key is to take advantage of these opportunities when they present themselves. If a ripe moment is overlooked, the conflict does not necessarily stay ripe. It may take a considerable amount of time before the opportunity for resolution returns.

See also: BATNA; Negotiation, Limits to.
References and Further Reading: Kriesberg, Louis, and Stuart J. Thorson, 1991, "Timing the De-escalation of International Conflicts"; Zartman, I. William, 1985, *Ripe for Resolution.*

Negotiation Journal

The *Negotiation Journal: On the Process of Dispute Settlement* is published quarterly by Plenum Publishing in cooperation with the Program on Negotiation at the Harvard Law School. One of the leading dispute resolution journals, the *Negotiation Journal* targets a wide audience: lawyers, diplomats, politicians, policy makers, businesspeople, labor negotiators, and scholars. Articles are solicited from a wide range of people as well; practitioners, theorists, researchers, advisers, and teachers are all encouraged to submit articles for publication. Regular features include columns about current topics, book reviews, research reports, case studies, reports of educational innovations, and articles about the theory and practice of dispute settlement.

Although it often focuses on success stories, the journal also reports failures, since the editors believe that as much—or even more—can be learned from failure as from success. The overall goal of the journal is the development of better techniques for dealing with conflict and differences through the negotiation process. However, the editors recognize that negotiation is not always feasible or advisable. Thus, the journal examines broader issues as well: when negotiation is or is not appropriate or possible, when third-party intervention is appropriate, and when negotia-

tion might be used to resolve disputes that have previously been settled through other (for instance, adversarial) means. "Most generally, our approach to negotiation is guided by the view that it is ultimately more important to pose wise questions than to obtain wise answers. To this end, we are interested in and responsive to new, varied, and unusual approaches to the negotiation process."

See also: Program on Negotiation at Harvard Law School.

Negotiation Loopbacks

Conflicts can generally be resolved in one of two ways: through negotiation of interests or through the imposition of force. Often conflicting parties try negotiation, and when that fails, they use a force-based strategy to get their needs met. Negotiation loopbacks occur when the parties to a conflict abandon legal, political, or other power strategies and return to the negotiating table. Roger Fisher and William Ury's classic theory of principled negotiation argues that the parties should not accept a negotiated agreement if they believe that an alternative is available that will yield a better result. Thus, negotiation efforts commonly fail because one or more parties believe (often incorrectly) that they have a better alternative—litigation, a strike, an election, a military campaign—which they then pursue (Fisher, Ury, and Patton 1991; Ury, Brett, and Goldberg 1988a).

Although it may be sensible for the parties to pursue these alternatives for a while, they do not necessarily have to take them to the "bitter end." They need follow them only long enough to find out who the winners and losers will be. Once this is clear, it is usually to the parties' advantage to "loop back" to a negotiation process and conclude an agreement that closely parallels everyone's expected outcome. Although this negotiation loopback does not change the fundamental outcome of the dispute, it allows for fine-tuning to fit the settlement more closely to the parties' needs. It also substantially reduces many of the transaction costs (time, money, damaged relationships, and, in some cases, loss of life).

The most common example of negotiation loopbacks is when people settle lawsuits out of court. After pretrial discovery and hearings, the lawyers for both sides can often predict the likely outcome of a trial. Rather than taking the time, expense, and risk of a trial, however, they negotiate a settlement with the other side, based on their expectations of the outcome of the trial. Such out-of-court settlements occur in almost 95 percent of cases that are filed.

See also: Interests and Positions; Power; Principled Negotiation and *Getting to Yes;* Rights.
References and Further Reading: Fisher, Roger, and William Ury, 1981, *Getting to Yes* (2nd ed. with Bruce Patton, 1991); Ury, William L., Jeanne M. Brett, and Stephen B. Goldberg, 1988a, *Getting Disputes Resolved: Designing Systems to Cut the Costs of Conflict.*

Negotiation Strategy

Negotiation expert Dean Pruitt describes five possible negotiation strategies: yielding, contending, problem solving, inaction, and withdrawal. Yielding involves giving up most or all of what you want, because pleasing the other side or avoiding a dispute is more important than winning. This is sometimes true, especially when the issue in dispute is not very important to you but is important to the other side. If maintaining a good relationship with your opponent is more important than winning the argument, yielding is often the preferable approach to take.

Contending means negotiating competitively to win as much as you can. Contending tactics are ones that attempt to use coercion, pressure, or tricks to get the other side to concede. Examples include making demands that far exceed what you really need or want, committing yourself to an immutable position (e.g., "I won't sell for less than $100,000, period!"), making

threats to withdraw or harm the other party if he or she does not concede, or pretending that a decision must be made now when time is not really critical.

Problem solving (also called interest-based bargaining) involves working with the opponent to craft a solution that meets the interests or needs of both parties. This can be done by "expanding the pie" so that both sides can get what they want, or by compensating one side for the costs of giving in. Other problem-solving strategies include logrolling, in which each side gives up something it doesn't care much about to get something that is more important, and bridging, in which a completely new approach is developed that satisfies both parties' major interests in a novel way.

Inaction involves doing as little as possible to negotiate, short of withdrawing. Sometimes this is beneficial if a delay will improve the chances of obtaining an agreement later, but usually such behavior leads to the breakdown of negotiations, as does withdrawal, which terminates the negotiation and forces both parties to rely on their best alternatives to a negotiated agreement (their BATNAs) (Pruitt 1991).

Other authors, such as Joyce Hocker and William Wilmot, add a sixth strategy, compromise, which is an intermediate strategy between problem solving and contending. Compromise involves each side giving up some of what it wants or cutting the pie in half. This is usually different from problem solving, which attempts to give each side close to all that it wants— certainly more than half. Pruitt excludes compromise from his list of strategies because he believes that it is simply "lazy problem solving involving a half-hearted attempt to satisfy both parties' interests" (Pruitt 1991, 31). Lazy or not, compromise is common.

Several factors determine which strategy a negotiator should use, Pruitt maintains. First is a party's concern about its own outcome relative to its concern about the opponent's outcome. If a party is more concerned about itself than it is about the other, contending is generally the strategy of choice. If a party is more concerned about the other than about itself, yielding is preferable. Problem solving should be chosen when a party is equally concerned about both parties' outcomes, and inaction or withdrawal is an acceptable option if the party's concern about a negotiated agreement is low.

Other factors that should influence the choice of strategy are feasibility and cost. If an opponent seems weak or uncommitted, contending is more feasible than it is when the opponent is strong and determined. Problem solving is feasible only when interests are not diametrically opposed. Costs, too, are important—not simply financial costs, but costs in terms of time, resources, and relationships. Contending is usually more expensive in all these dimensions, whereas problem solving is often less so, although it can take a long time.

Another expert on negotiation, Louis Kriesberg, emphasizes different strategic choices. Critical to the success of international negotiation, Kriesberg maintains, are proper selection of issues to be discussed (and the order of discussion), proper selection of the parties to be involved in the negotiating process, and effective use of inducements. Rather than advocating one approach for all situations, strategic choices must be carefully matched to particular circumstances, Kriesberg notes.

Sometimes it is best to consider issues one at a time, starting with the easiest issues first. Once agreement is obtained on the simple disputes, efforts can move on to more difficult issues. At other times, however, it is beneficial to be able to logroll—to trade off one issue for another—in which case multiple issues must be considered at once.

Selecting the parties to be involved is similarly difficult. Sometimes, all the affected parties (or their representatives) should be at the table at once; at other times, so many parties are involved that this becomes chaotic and unwieldy. A better approach might be sequential negotiations with smaller groups, at least in the beginning, deferring a final negotiation with all the parties until the last stages of negotiation, when essentially everything has been worked out already. Also of importance, Kriesberg notes, is the question of whether or not a third-party intermediary—a mediator, for instance—should be used. In highly escalated conflicts, this is helpful, even essential. In less escalated conflicts, it may be unnecessary and may even complicate negotiations.

Finally, Kriesberg examines positive and negative incentives. Although Kriesberg's analysis of the U.S.-USSR conflict and the Israeli-Arab conflict did not show a clear pattern regarding the efficacy of negative sanctions (i.e., threats), it did show that positive sanctions or incentives can encourage effective problem solving, conflict de-escalation, and conflict resolution. To be effective, however, conciliatory gestures must be seen as credible, not as tricks, and they must be seen as a real effort at de-escalation, not simply as yielding to the opponent's superior power (Kriesberg 1988).

See also: Bargaining, Integrative and Distributive; Bargaining, Interest-Based and Positional; International Conflict; Negotiation.

References and Further Reading: Hocker, Joyce L., and William W. Wilmot, 1985, *Interpersonal Conflict;* Kriesberg, Louis, 1988, "Strategies of Negotiating Agreements: Arab-Israeli and American-Soviet Cases"; Pruitt, Dean G., 1991, "Strategic Choice in Negotiation."

The Network: Interaction for Conflict Resolution

The Network: Interaction for Conflict Resolution is a Canadian nonprofit organization that is dedicated to promoting collaborative conflict resolution in Canada. It is a membership organization of people who want to work together, share information and expertise, build public support, and develop more effective approaches to conflict resolution at the community level. The network provides services to mediators, lawyers, teachers, community organizers, researchers, managers, and justice system personnel.

Network activities include workshops and seminars; consultations; conferences; training; publication of a quarterly newsletter, books, and directories; and referrals to conflict resolution professionals within Canada. Its newsletter, *Interaction,* includes articles on new developments in the field, information on new resources, and training programs. It is an excellent source of current information about the conflict resolution field in Canada.

See also: Appendix 1 for contact information.

Neutral Expert Fact-Finding

Neutral expert fact-finding is a process used by a court to clarify scientific or technical questions that are central to a dispute but are beyond the expertise of the typical judge or jury. Examples include cases concerning hazardous waste in which the amount of pollution, its dispersion, and its actual or potential health effects are at issue; cases concerning medical malpractice that involve highly complex medical decisions; or commercial cases in which a manufacturer claims that a supplier's components do not meet industry or contractual standards. Typically, litigants in such technical cases hire their own experts to argue their side. This approach is costly and unpredictable, however. Typically, one expert says one thing, the other says the opposite, and the judge or jury is left to use nonscientific reasoning to conclude who is right.

Neutral expert fact-finding avoids these problems by appointing one neutral expert to examine the facts and testify about them in court. Usually, the expert is appointed by the court, which may act on its own or at the request of one or both of the parties. The judge may consult with the parties to identify an expert acceptable to all or may choose one independently. Either way, the expert studies all the available evidence, comes to a conclusion, and presents it in court; this is used by the judge or jury, along with other evidence, to come to a conclusion. Thus, unlike arbitration, in which the expert arbitrator reaches a binding decision, the neutral expert fact-finder only makes an advisory opinion, which is supplemented with other evidence and used by the judge or jury to render a decision. Neutral experts can also be used by the parties themselves outside the court system. For example, neutral experts can be useful in a mediation process to help clarify technical issues undergoing negotiation. Neutral expert fact-finding can also be useful as a dispute avoidance mechanism if parties turn to a neutral expert to resolve differences before they become severe.

See also: Arbitration; Joint Fact-Finding; Scientific and Technical Disputes.
References and Further Reading: Carpenter, Susan L., and W. J. D. Kennedy, 1988, *Managing Public Disputes;* Dauer, Edward A., 1994, *Manual of Dispute Resolution;* Goldberg, Stephen B., Eric D. Green, and Frank E. A. Sander, 1985, *Dispute Resolution,* chap. 5.

Neutrality and Impartiality

Neutrality, in the context of conflict resolution, refers to conflict interveners who neither have a personal relationship with any of the parties nor stand to benefit personally from a particular outcome. This contrasts with the concept of impartiality, which means that the intervener treats both sides fairly and does not favor one side over the other. Although commonly used in the context of mediation, the terms refer to all dispute resolution professionals—arbitrators, facilitators, and fact-finders as well as mediators.

There are cases, however, in which successful mediators do not claim to be neutral, nor are they perceived as such. If a mediator is perceived to be fair, he or she may be able to mediate effectively even when he or she is not neutral. This situation is common in Latin America, where traditional dispute resolution processes rely on *confianza*, or "insider-partial," mediators who are involved in the conflict and are known to favor one side over the other yet are also perceived to be honest and fair. Oscar Arias Sánchez, the author of the Esquipulas Agreement that ended the civil war in Nicaragua in the 1980s, is a prime example of an insider-partial mediator. Although rarer, partial mediators have also been effective in the United States. Typically, the mediator is not a professional conflict resolver but a well-respected and powerful government leader who uses his or her respect and influence to help the parties forge an agreement.

Some people argue that true impartiality is an impossible goal. They believe that, because of cultural background and personal values, everyone is biased to some degree. For this reason, some observers argue, the success of the mediation should not rest on the unrealistic goal of true neutrality or impartiality. Instead, they believe that intermediaries should make their biases explicit and let the adversaries make an informed and voluntary choice about whether they would like their dispute to be handled by someone with such values. For example, a divorce mediator might reveal that he or she follows certain procedures to empower women who might otherwise be treated unfairly by traditional neutral mediation process.

See also: Mediation, Ethical Issues; Mediator Impartiality and Neutrality.

References and Further Reading: Gibson, Kevin, 1996, "Shortcomings of Neutrality in Mediation: Solutions Based on Rationality"; Moore, Christopher W., 1986, *The Mediation Process;* Wehr, Paul, and Sharon Erickson Nepstad, 1994, "Violence, Nonviolence, and Justice in Sandinista Nicaragua."

NIMBY, LULU, and NOPE

The closely related terms NIMBY, LULU, and NOPE are generally applied to envi-

ronmental conflicts in which land uses proposed by one group (or a governmental entity) are opposed by another group (usually those who live in the immediate vicinity of the proposed activity).

The terms NIMBY (for "not in my backyard") and LULU (for "locally unwanted land uses") are often used synonymously in relation to conflicts that arise when people oppose the siting of an unwanted facility in their immediate neighborhood. Some people, however, make a distinction between the two, saying that NIMBYs are facilities that are unwanted because of the clientele they attract (such as mental health facilities or homeless shelters), and LULUs are facilities that are unwanted because of their nature, not because of the populations they serve (such as highways, landfills, airports, or shopping centers, all of which bring increased traffic and noise to a community). In the case of both NIMBYs and LULUs, the key issue is not whether the facility is needed; rather, the issue is the location, and the goal is to put it in someone else's backyard.

NOPE ("not on planet earth") conflicts generally arise from more extreme environmental positions, in which opponents believe that the facility is unneeded and should not be built anywhere at all. Examples might be nuclear power plants (opposed because they are considered too dangerous) or highways (opposed by some who think that automobiles should be replaced with public transportation).

All three kinds of conflicts are difficult to deal with. They lead to protracted conflicts and result in the failure to site needed facilities for years on end. For example, the federal government's inability to site a high-level nuclear waste repository has resulted in the continued storage of radioactive waste in inadequate temporary storage facilities near several major cities. Similar standoffs over the construction of landfills and highways have led to urban problems as well.

Many approaches have been used to deal with NIMBY problems, with mixed success. Some states have formed governmental siting boards that are charged with investigating the feasibility of several sites and then choosing one. Often, however, the board gets bogged down in the same political problems that prevented successful siting in the first place. Other towns and states have tried market approaches—"paying" communities to accept an unwanted facility. This can be in the form of cash or, more often, in the form of "perks"—new schools or new parks, for instance—in exchange for accepting an unwanted facility. An "insurance policy" to mitigate any negative impacts that do arise diminishes the reluctance of some communities to accept new facilities. Still other states and cities are trying to implement the concept of sharing such necessary but unwanted facilities according to an area's population and need. Cities are told that they must accept their fair share of unwanted facilities; then the conflict is at least transformed into one of what goes where, instead of where to put something that no one is willing to take.

See also: Environmental Conflicts; Public Policy Conflicts.
References and Further Reading: DiMento, Joseph F., and LeRoy Graymer, 1991, *Confronting Regional Challenges: Approaches to LULUs, Growth, and Other Vexing Governance Problems;* Susskind, Lawrence, and Jeffrey Cruikshank, 1987, *Breaking the Impasse.*

Nonnegotiable Issues

Issues are what a conflict is about. They can be simple: for instance, who gets to use the car or where the family will go on vacation. Or they can be complex: for example, how Palestinian autonomy will be structured, or how the Balkan peace plan will be implemented. They can involve interests (what people want to get), values (what they think is good or bad), or needs (what they require to stay physically and psychologically healthy).

Deep-rooted values and fundamental human needs are usually nonnegotiable issues—they are not amenable to compromise. The Palestinians will not compromise their right to exist; nor will the Israelis compromise their right to a Jewish state. (Identity and security are fundamental human needs.) Similarly, pro-life and pro-choice advocates will not negotiate the righteousness or villainy of abortion; nor will homosexuals negotiate about the goodness or sinfulness of homosexuality (a fundamental value).

Conflicts that involve nonnegotiable issues are much more difficult to resolve than ones in which compromise or consensus is feasible. The most effective approach to these situations is often not conflict resolution but rather conflict management, in which the conflict is handled in such a way as to make it more constructive (i.e., beneficial) and less destructive.

Another approach to nonnegotiable issues is analytical problem solving. This conflict strategy provides a means of identifying the nonnegotiable issues in a conflict and considering the costs of ignoring these issues. Since the costs of such inaction are usually high, participants in analytical problem-solving workshops can sometimes be persuaded to consider major social structural changes that are necessary to resolve conflicts based on nonnegotiable issues. Problems often arise, however, when others who were not involved in such workshops have to be convinced to make the major social or economic changes agreed to by the workshop participants. Thus the transfer of workshop agreements to public policy is a major stumbling block to the success of analytical problem-solving efforts.

See also: Compromise; Conflict Resolution, Conflict Management, and Dispute Settlement; Interests and Positions; Needs; Problem Solving, Analytical; Rights.
References and Further Reading: Burgess, Guy, and Heidi Burgess, 1996, "Constructive Confrontation: A Transformative Approach to Intractable Conflicts"; Burton, John, 1987, *Resolving Deep-Rooted Conflict: A Handbook*

Nonviolence

Nonviolence is an approach to conflict that eschews the use of physical force, replacing it with nonviolent protest, noncooperation, and nonviolent intervention. Some advocates of nonviolence call for its use for religious or philosophical reasons. These believers in "principled nonviolence" consider violence to be morally wrong under any and all circumstances—even in response to a violent opponent. (Gandhi, Martin Luther King Jr., and Leo Tolstoy all believed in principled nonviolence.)

Other nonviolent actors prefer nonviolence because they believe that it is strategically or tactically superior to violent ways of confronting and resolving conflict in most, but not necessarily all, circumstances. Their use of nonviolence is based not on religious principle but rather on pragmatic concerns: nonviolence works better than violence, they argue, especially for low-power groups who cannot possibly win a violent confrontation.

Gene Sharp is one of the best-known advocates of pragmatic nonviolence. He argues that nonviolence can overcome even the most oppressive regimes because all government, no matter how tyrannical, is ultimately based on popular consent. If that consent is withdrawn (as it was in the Warsaw bloc countries in 1989, for instance), the power of the government is destroyed, and the government can easily be overthrown.

In his classic three-volume study *The Politics of Nonviolent Action,* Sharp categorizes 198 different forms of nonviolence, which he groups into three fundamental types: nonviolent protest and persuasion (marches, vigils, or picketing, for example), the mildest form of nonviolence; noncooperation, which involves withholding assistance or services (strikes, work slowdowns, or tax resistance, for example); and nonviolent intervention, in which the protester actively intervenes in an ongoing activity or attempts to replace that activity with an alternative one. Sitting on railroad tracks to prevent trainloads of plutonium from reaching nuclear weapons manufacturing sites or chaining oneself to a tree or lying down in front of a bulldozer to prevent logging are examples of nonviolent intervention. This category also includes efforts to set up alternative institutions such as economic enterprises, churches, or communication links or even alternative governmental systems, as was done in much of Eastern Europe in response to the communist regimes.

Although all these examples of nonviolence involve activism and advocacy of a particular point of view, many advocates of nonviolence see it as being consistent with efforts at cooperative conflict resolution and consensus building. The goal of nonviolence is the development of effective nonviolent means for resolving conflict. This includes, therefore, mediation and consensus building; it could even include arbitration or adjudication, although these forms of dispute resolution tend to impose one side's view on the other. Most advocates of nonviolent dispute resolution prefer win-win solutions that encourage the growth of mutual understanding, trust, and consensual solutions.

However it is defined, advocates of nonviolence agree that the benefits are many and almost always outweigh the benefits of violent approaches to conflict prosecution or resolution. First, nonviolence is usually less costly in terms of human life and property damage than is violence. Second, it can be far more effective in bringing about social change, especially when used by otherwise low-power groups. When low-power groups resort to violence, they usually cause a violent reaction, which will likely crush them. Use of violence is seldom successful in forcing negotiations; rather, it tends to create a backlash and further repression. When disputants use nonviolence, the opponent's reaction may still be violent, but it is often less so than it might have been had violence been used initially. The use of nonviolence also tends to elicit sympathy from uninvolved third parties, which can ultimately change the balance of power in favor of the nonviolent group. Martin Luther King Jr.'s use of nonviolence in the 1960s civil rights movement is a good example. Blacks' actions engendered a great deal of violence—houses were bombed; people were imprisoned, beaten, and even killed. But the more such reactions occurred, the more northern whites came to sympathize with the black cause, which eventually prevailed in a series of key civil rights court cases and legislative decisions.

Nonviolence also works by throwing a violent opponent off balance. Sharp and others refer to this effect as moral or political jujitsu. As in the martial art, the aggressor is thrown off balance when the victim fails to counter a physical attack. "Because violent action and nonviolent action possess quite different mechanisms, and induce differing forces of change in the society, the opponent's repression ... can never really come to grips with the kind of power wielded by the nonviolent actionists. Gandhi has compared the situation with that of a man violently striking water with a sword: it was the man's arm which was dislocated" (Sharp 1973, 2:111–13). Thus nonviolence turns a violent opponent's force against itself and leaves the nonviolent actor largely unscathed.

See also: Advocacy; Collaborative Problem Solving; Gandhi, Mahatma; King, Martin Luther, Jr.; Mediation; Montgomery Bus Boycott; Sharp, Gene; Tolstoy, Lev (Leo) Nikolayevich; Violence.

References and Further Reading: Bondurant, Joan V., 1965, *Conquest of Violence: The Gandhian Philosophy of Conflict;* Gregg, Richard B., 1966, *The Power of Nonviolence;* Hocker, Joyce L., and William W. Wilmot, 1985, *Interpersonal Conflict;* Holmes, Robert L., 1990, *Nonviolence in Theory and Practice;* Sharp, Gene, 1973, *The Politics of Nonviolent Action;* Stiehm, Judith, 1972, *Nonviolent Power: Active and Passive Resistance in America;* Wehr, Paul, Heidi Burgess, and Guy Burgess, 1994, *Justice without Violence.*

Ombudsman

An ombudsman (also called an ombudsperson or ombuds practitioner) is an independent person within an organization whose role is to help resolve conflicts between individuals and the organization. Most often the individuals are employees, but they can also be clients, patients, citizens, or customers, depending on the nature of the organization. Thus, corporations have ombuds offices for managing workplace conflicts; hospitals have ombuds offices for managing patient-provider conflicts; and government agencies have ombuds offices for resolving citizen-government disputes. (The IRS, for instance, has an ombuds office to help resolve IRS-taxpayer disputes.)

The U.S. use of the term *ombudsman* differs from the traditional meaning of the word. When ombudsmanship began in Sweden in the 1800s, ombudsmen were completely independent of the organization they served. They were hired by the legislature, for instance, which also paid their salary. This ensured that they could act independently, without fear of being fired if they took an unpopular position. This completely independent role is still used outside the United States, but the concept was altered somewhat in this country, enabling ombudsmen to be hired and paid directly by the organizations they serve.

Ombudsmen began to be used in a few U.S. corporations after World War I, but the concept did not become popular until the 1980s. Since then, the growth in ombudsmanship has been rapid. In an article written in the late 1980s, Massachusetts Institute of Technology ombudsman Mary Rowe reported that there were about 100 ombuds offices in U.S. colleges and universities and 200 such offices in U.S. corporations. Ombudsmanship was even more prevalent in the health care arena. She reported that nearly 4,000 hospitals had patient ombuds offices, and about 1,500 people worked as ombudsmen for nursing homes and other long-term-care facilities (Rowe 1991a, 445).

Services of Ombudsmen

Ombudsmen provide many services; they can act as counselors, facilitators, mediators, fact-finders, consultants, or dispute system designers. They do whatever it takes to solve the client's problem and to keep the organization functioning as smoothly and effectively as possible.

At times, people come to the ombuds office with simple questions that can be handled quickly by providing information about rules, procedures, or resources available within an organization. At other times, the worker simply wants or needs a sympathetic ear—someone who is willing to listen to his or her concerns or fears and can deal with those feelings in an appropriate and helpful manner.

Sometimes ombudsmen receive information rather than give it. Ombuds offices are often the first place whistle-blowers go if they recognize a problem that needs attention but are afraid of reprisals if they go to their own managers to deal with it. Ombudsmen can also see patterns of problems that are invisible to individual managers. For instance, they might start to see a growing number of racial or ethnic problems throughout an organization, which would appear as isolated cases to managers who supervise small numbers of people.

Sometimes these problems cannot be solved without structural or procedural changes in the organization. The ombudsman cannot make these changes, but he or she can strongly recommend them to the appropriate managers. In other cases, the problem can be dealt with successfully by teaching or training. An ombudsman can conduct a workshop on diversity for a whole department without indicating which particular person brought the problem to his or her attention. This approach can help a lot of people without embarrassing any one individual.

As much as possible, ombudsmen try to teach workers how to handle their own problems. They conduct training—both individually and in groups—on effective conflict management skills and common organizational problems. They also help people understand the options available to them in pursuing a conflict. Typically, people are unaware of the range of options available to them. They think that they can ignore the problem, quit, or complain to a superior, but they may be afraid to do the latter for fear of reprisals. The ombudsman can help disputants identify the full range of options open to them, assess the costs and benefits of the different approaches, and, depending on the option chosen, implement the dispute resolution approach.

For instance, ombudsmen can act as mediators, doing either shuttle diplomacy (going back and forth between the disputants without actually getting them together) or traditional mediation (working with the disputants face-to-face) to help

them solve their problems. Alternatively, ombudsmen might act as facilitators of a consensus-building workshop with a large number of people.

Advantages and Disadvantages of Ombudsmanship

Ombudsmen provide a problem-solving resource that is more flexible than similar resources found in organizations. They can operate confidentially, when needed, and can help parties solve their own problems without escalating the conflict, as formal grievance procedures often do. They also can act as an impartial neutral in situations in which none other exists.

Some believe that ombudsmen are unnecessary because the same functions can be performed informally or by other people in the organization (such as employee relations or human resources department staff). However, ombudsmen report that people come to them with problems that they could not bring to those other departments. Just as human resources departments do not serve the function of line managers, ombudsmen do not serve the same function as human resources managers. Each has a different role and collaborates with the other. Another charge is that ombudsmen cannot help because they have no decision-making power. Although it is true that ombudsmen are not decision makers, they do have power to bring about change.

See also: Facilitation; Mediation; Workplace Conflict and Grievance Procedures.

References and Further Reading: Rowe, Mary P., 1991a, "The Corporate Ombudsman: An Overview and Analysis"; Rowe, Mary P., 1991b, "The Ombudsman's Role in a Dispute Resolution System"; Singer, Linda R., 1990, *Settling Disputes: Conflict Resolution in Business, Families, and the Legal System.*

Oslo Accords, Middle East Peace Process

The Oslo Accords represent a breakthrough in Israeli-Palestinian relations. As a result of these negotiations, Israel and the Palestine Liberation Organization (PLO) formally recognized each other, and the PLO formally rejected the use of violence. On 13 September 1993, Israeli Prime Minister Yitzhak Rabin and PLO Chairman Yasir Arafat shook hands on the front lawn of the White House. As Kenneth Stein and Samuel Lewis (1996, 465) observed, "The Oslo Agreement of 1993 between Israel and the Palestine Liberation Organization (PLO) was the first major achievement of Arab-Israel peacemaking achieved without a large component of third-party mediation." For their peacemaking efforts, Rabin and Arafat, along with Israeli Foreign Minister Shimon Peres, shared the 1994 Nobel Peace Prize.

Structure

The Oslo negotiation occurred within the larger context of the Middle East peace process begun in Madrid in October 1991. The Madrid framework established four separate sets of bilateral negotiations. Israel would enter into separate negotiations with Jordan, Syria, and Lebanon, with the goal of achieving peace treaties. Bilateral negotiations would also be pursued between Israel and the Palestinians, with a goal based on a two-stage formula. First, negotiations would seek to establish five-year self-government arrangements for the Palestinians. With a plan in place for interim self-rule, negotiations would then address the issue of the permanent status of Palestine. The Madrid framework also provided for subsidiary, multilateral talks "concentrated on the more practical problems in the region: water sharing, arms control, the economy, the environment and the fate of refugees" (Corbin 1994, 17).

Initial Israeli-Palestinian talks convened in Washington, D.C., but these talks quickly bogged down. At that time (November 1991), Israel refused to recognize the PLO, which it saw as a terrorist organization—violent, untrustworthy, and unreliable. Israel instead attempted to negotiate with a group of socially prominent Palestinians. However, as Jane Corbin observed, over the course of negotiations, "it became apparent that the Palestinians at the peace talks had no independent mandate to negotiate; they were traveling back and forth via Tunis where Arafat authorized every dot and comma" (Corbin 1994, 17). Although U.S. power and influence had been important in bringing the parties to the negotiating table, Arab and Palestinian participants were suspicious of the United States' special relationship with Israel, and Israel resented U.S. pressure.

Norway had a history of good relations with both Israel and the Palestinians dating back to the early 1980s. When Norwegian academic and peace researcher Terje Larsen realized that the formal negotiations in Washington were not progressing, he approached Knesset member Yossi Belin to suggest parallel secret negotiations between Israel and the PLO in Oslo. Belin responded positively. With the election of a Labor government, Yitzhak Rabin became Israel's prime minister, Shimon Peres became foreign minister, and Yossi Belin was appointed deputy foreign minister. On 12 September 1992, Belin met secretly with Norwegian Deputy Foreign Minister Jan Egeland, Terje Larsen, and Norwegian diplomat Mona Juul. Norway offered to provide contact with the PLO and to host secret negotiations. Under Israeli law, it was illegal to make contact with members of the PLO, so Belin refused to send any official representative to Norway. He would, however, support an unofficial representative: Yair Hirschfeld.

In January 1993, Hirschfeld met secretly with Abu Ala, a highly placed PLO official. Following the goals set by the Madrid framework, they began negotiations on a declaration of principles that would lead to transitional self-rule for the Palestinians. The Oslo talks continued through May, with Hirschfeld reporting, still unofficially, to Belin, and Ala communicating with Arafat. The negotiations remained secret, and Norwegian officials took great care to shield the negotiators from the public eye. By May, the Israeli ban against contact with the PLO had been lifted. In May 1993, Prime Minister Rabin, at the request of Foreign Minister Peres, agreed to send Israeli diplomat Uri Savir to participate officially in the Oslo negotiations. Although still a tightly kept secret, the Oslo negotiations were now on an official level.

A final agreement on the declaration of principles was signed in August 1993, and the results were shared with U.S. Secretary of State Warren Christopher. Before the agreement could be publicized, however, Israel and the PLO had to formally recognize each other. The final rounds of the Oslo negotiations centered around crafting a mutual-recognition pact. According to Corbin, negotiators on both sides felt "that the mutual-recognition pact would ultimately prove even more significant than the Declaration of Principles that they had reached in Oslo" (Corbin 1994, 193). These negotiations were successful as well, and they paved the way for the historic moment when Arafat and Rabin shook hands over the declaration of principles on the White House Lawn on 13 September 1993.

timetables. This lack of deadlines gave the parties time to get to know one another, to understand one another's constraints and concerns, and to develop the level of trust necessary to communicate and negotiate effectively. In addition, the negotiations occurred privately and confidentially, allowing the participants to say things that they would not say in public and to explore controversial ideas and options without risk of public censure. Finally, the third party—the Norwegians—had no direct stake in the conflict or the substance of the resolution and had no "real muscle—carrots to dangle or sticks to wave" (Mitchell 1993, 8). An interesting difference between this case and most track two negotiations was that these negotiations took place "parallel to, rather than in preparation for, a formal and official process" (Mitchell 1993, 8). However, the process did evolve into track one (i.e., regular) diplomacy once Israel agreed to meet with the Palestinians on an official basis.

The issues considered included the status of United Nations Resolutions 242 and 338, dealing with Israeli withdrawal from the Occupied Territories, Israeli security needs, the establishment of Palestinian self-government in Gaza and Jericho, and the fate of displaced Palestinians from the 1967 war. Negotiations over the recognition issue focused on the PLO's use of violence and terror.

Deliberative Procedures and Central Issues

The Oslo negotiations were direct, secret negotiations between Israel and the PLO. Unofficial at their opening, the talks became official with the entry of Israeli diplomat Uri Savir, as authorized by Prime Minister Rabin. At the beginning, however, the talks were an almost perfect example of what is called "track two" diplomacy. Like a textbook description of track two negotiations, the process took place over a long period of time, without deadlines or

Outcome

The Oslo Accords were controversial, and the ultimate result of these negotiations remains unclear. Formal recognition between Israel and the PLO has paved the way for further peace negotiations. In September 1995, Rabin and Arafat signed the Oslo II Interim Accord, furthering the process of Israeli troop withdrawal and establishing transitional Palestinian self-rule. Prime Minister Rabin was assassinated in November 1995 by an Israeli extremist. In the subsequent elections, Rabin's Labor government was replaced by the more conservative Likud Party, with Benjamin Netanyahu as the new prime minister.

Analysis

Jan Egeland, one of the Norwegian scholar-diplomats who initiated the Oslo talks, described the advantages that Norway had over other possible third-party facilitators. According to Egeland, Norway's benefits were that (1) it has a compact bureaucracy, which meant that making the decision to undertake the process and carry it out was relatively easy; (2) Norway has a "coherent and consistent foreign policy" (Egeland 1995, 11); (3) Norway had few foreign economic or political commitments that might compromise its impartiality; (4) Norway's small size and simple bureaucratic structure gave it the ability to ensure complete confidentiality; and (5) small nations like Norway and the Netherlands (which has also undertaken back-channel negotiations) "are better at keeping secrets than large ones like the United States" (Egeland 1995, 11).

See also: Amnesty and Forgiveness; Camp David Accords (Israeli and Egyptian); Diplomacy, Citizen, Track Two, and Multitrack; International Conflict; Israeli-Palestinian Women's Workshop; Mediation, International.

References and Further Reading: Corbin, Jane, 1994, *The Norway Channel: The Secret Talks that Led to the Middle East Peace Accord;* Egeland, Jan, 1995, Quoted in "Norway's Back-Channel Success Story"; Mitchell, C. R., 1993, "Track Two Triumphant? Reflections on the Oslo Process and Conflict Resolution in the Middle East"; Stein, Kenneth W., and Samuel W. Lewis, 1996, "Mediation in the Middle East."

Parent-Child Conflict

Conflicts between parents and children happen constantly—from the time a newborn cries and the parent is too tired to respond to conflicts between adult children and their elderly parents. Often these conflicts are struggles for power—to decide who will be in control of which aspects of either the children's or the parents' lives. Although such power struggles are unavoidable, the same rules for effective problem solving that apply to other conflicts can be applied to parent-child conflicts. To the extent that parents and children can identify their interests and needs and then negotiate to satisfy both sides, the dispute will be resolved.

For example, parents can respond to a child's request for a later bedtime with an authoritative or domineering approach—"No way, that is out of the question"—or they can take a compliant approach and say, "Sure, that's fine with me," even when it isn't. Alternatively, they can discuss the child's reasons for wanting a later bedtime—more time to play, more time to read, ability to watch a favorite TV show. Then they can negotiate a way to meet that need while at the same time meeting the parents' need for well-rested children and some time for adult peace and quiet after the children are in bed. As in adult conflicts, parent-child conflicts can often be resolved more effectively and more permanently if parents rely on this kind of interest-based bargaining rather than on power struggles to determine the outcome.

Also important to successful conflict management between parents and children is the acknowledgment of the child's feelings. Parents often deny or dismiss their children's feelings by saying things such as "There's nothing to be afraid of" (which the child hears as "You're dumb because you feel scared") or "Don't get so upset over such a little thing" (which the child hears as "Your problem is unimportant"). If parents listen to and accept their children's feelings and then help them deal with those feelings, they are likely to be more effective at managing conflicts with their children and have better relationships with their children over the long run.

See also: Active Listening; Bargaining, Interest-Based and Positional; Family Conflict; Negotiation.
References and Further Reading: Beekman, Susan, and Geanne Holmes, 1993, *Battles, Hassles, Tantrums and Tears: Strategies for Coping with Conflict and Making Peace at Home;* Faber, Adele, and Elaine Mazlish, 1980, *How to Talk so Kids Will Listen and Listen so Kids Will Talk.*

Parties

The term *parties* refers to the people, groups, organizations, or nations involved in a dispute. Often a distinction is made between first, second, and third parties. First parties are those initiating the dispute—the plaintiff, in legal terms. Second parties are opponents of first parties—the defendant, if the case is being litigated, or simply the opposing side if it is not. Third parties are individuals or groups that are outside of the immediate conflict but are involved in some way. Some third parties act as intermediaries and try to help the disputing parties resolve the conflict—mediators, arbitrators, therapists, or courts, for instance. Other third parties are people or organizations affected by the conflict—the children in a divorce or consumers in a labor-management dispute.

See also: Conflict Assessment; Intermediary or Third Party.
References and Further Reading: Deutsch, Morton, 1973, *The Resolution of Conflict: Constructive and Destructive Processes.*

Partnering

Partnering is a method of preventing or resolving disputes that has been used most frequently in the construction industry in the United States. The idea is to get all the parties together before the construction project starts—before the contract is even finalized—to agree on what is to be done and how it is to be done.

Partnering helps prevent disputes because it encourages the development of trust, cooperation, and teamwork among the project owner, design professionals, general contractors, subcontractors, and suppliers. In a partnering workshop or retreat, a neutral facilitator helps all the involved parties identify their interests, the project goals and objectives, their respective responsibilities, and the time line for the project. Other topics discussed include design specifications, how design changes will be handled, how progress will be monitored and adjustments made, and how potential disputes will be handled. This collaborative problem-solving approach is carried through the entire project. Instead of seeing the others in a competitive "I win–you lose" sort of way, partnering encourages all the parties involved in a project to work together as partners to see the project through to a successful conclusion.

Although used primarily in the construction industry, partnering can be beneficial in any business venture that involves collaboration among multiple organizations. It has also been used by government agencies. The Army Corps of Engineers, for example, has used partnering in over 200 construction projects. As a result, none of these projects resulted in litigated claims. The Arizona Department of Transportation has had similar success, avoiding claims on about 100 projects undertaken since 1991 that used partnering.

See also: Commercial Disputes; Conflict Prevention; Consumer Disputes; Dispute Review Boards.
References and Further Reading: Appel, Mark E., 1993, "Partnering: New Dimensions in Dispute Prevention and Resolution"; Augustine, Mary Jane, 1994, "Dispute Prevention and Resolution in the Construction Industry"; Dauer, Edward A., 1994, *Manual of Dispute Resolution.*

Peace

Peace is an amorphous concept that is defined in many different ways. Some people see peace in a positive way: as order, harmony, and cooperation, for instance. Others see peace in a negative way: as the absence of conflict, tension, or war. Likewise, some view peace as a concept referring to relations between nations, and others extend the notion to relations between individuals or even within one individual (as in "peace of mind").

One's definition of *peace* is important, as it determines whether peace is seen as desirable and, if it is, how it might be obtained. Michael Banks (1987) illustrates this in an essay in which he discusses four conceptions of peace: peace as harmony, peace as order, peace as justice, and peace as conflict management.

Peace as harmony, he observes, is both idealistic and undesirable. It is idealistic in that complete harmony and absence of conflict are impossible; it is undesirable because conflict is necessary for social change and progress. Peace as order, he suggests, is the traditional definition used in international relations. It reflects a stability obtained from an effective political system and balance of power either within a nation or between nations. This conception suggests that force is the primary method used to secure peace and that "peace through strength" is the best approach for maintaining an orderly national and international system.

Peace can also be defined as justice—the absence of poverty, ethnic oppression, and political domination, for example. This concept of peace is similar to that held by Johan Galtung, a leading peace researcher who developed the concept of structural violence (Galtung 1969). Structural violence refers to the situation in which an individual or a group is unable to attain its full potential due to limitations in the social structure imposed because of people's membership in a particular racial, ethnic, or religious group. Peace and justice are often seen in opposition to each other, however, because low-power groups frequently turn to violence to obtain justice. Hence, they see calls for peace as calls to give up their quest for justice.

Last, Banks argues, peace can be seen as conflict management. This view suggests that peace is not an end state but rather a process for obtaining our interests and needs. Further, Banks maintains that peace is a process for obtaining the needs of individuals—not of groups or of states. Peace is obtained not with armies defending national values but with individuals working together for physical well-being, spiritual growth, material fulfillment, and strong interpersonal relationships.

Another leading peace researcher, Kenneth Boulding, made the distinction between stable peace and unstable peace. Stable peace is a positive peace; it is maintained by strong, cooperative relationships when the benefits of peace clearly outweigh the benefits of war. Thus, the peaceful relationship is stable. Unstable peace is a negative peace; it is maintained only through threat or deterrence, not through positive interactions. This kind of peace is tenuous and can easily break down into war. When he wrote the book *Stable Peace* in the late 1970s, Boulding observed that the region of stable peace was growing—by then it encompassed all of North America, Scandinavia, and parts of Europe. By pursuing a carefully designed "policy for peace," Boulding argued, the region of stable peace could be expanded to include ever larger segments of the globe.

See also: Boulding, Kenneth; Galtung, Johan; Justice; Stable Peace; Structural Violence.

References and Further Reading: Banks, Michael, 1987, "Four Conceptions of Peace"; Boulding, Kenneth, 1978b, *Stable Peace;* Galtung, Johan, 1969, "Peace, Violence, and Peace Research."

Peace and Change: A Journal of Peace Research

Peace and Change is sponsored by the Peace History Society and the Consortium of Peace Research, Education, and Development and is published four times a year. The journal publishes scholarly and interpretive articles related to the creation of a peaceful, just, and humane society. It goes beyond national and disciplinary boundaries in an attempt to build bridges between peace research, education, and activism. Common topics covered include peace activists and movements, conflict resolution, nonviolence, internationalism, race and gender issues affecting peacemaking, cross-cultural studies, economic development, imperialism, and post–Cold War upheaval.

See also: Consortium on Peace Research, Education, and Development; Appendix 1 for contact information.

Peace and Conflict: Journal of Peace Psychology

Peace and Conflict is the quarterly journal of the Division of Peace Psychology of the American Psychological Association. Topics addressed by the journal include peace;

nonviolent conflict resolution; reconciliation; and the causes, consequences, and prevention of war and other forms of destructive conflict within nations, communities, and families. Articles represent a mixture of empirical, theoretical, clinical, and historical studies as well as policy analyses, case studies, interpretive essays, interviews, and book reviews.

See also: Appendix 1 for contact information.

Peace Brigades International

Peace Brigades International (PBI) is a nongovernmental, nonpartisan organization that provides unarmed protective accompaniment to people who are threatened by violence—human rights activists, refugees, even whole communities threatened by civil war or state-sponsored repression or terror. A grassroots organization, PBI has volunteers from 15 different countries.

Upon invitation, PBI sends unarmed teams of volunteers into areas of violent repression or conflict. The teams work to reduce the level of violence and support local social justice initiatives. They also foster dialogue and reconciliation between the conflicting parties and provide training in nonviolence and human rights advocacy.

PBI teams have served around the world—in Guatemala, Colombia, Sri Lanka, El Salvador, Haiti, the Balkans, the Middle East, and Southeast Asia. They have also worked in a number of Native American communities in North America.

PBI publishes the monthly newsletter *Project Bulletin* and the quarterly report *PBI/USA Report.*

See also: Dialogue; Peacekeeping; Reconciliation; Appendix 1 for contact Information.

Peace Building

Peace building is the third phase of intergroup or international conflict resolution processes, following the enforced cessation of violence (peacekeeping) and the negotiation of a settlement agreement (peacemaking). Peace building involves the reestablishment or development of normal, peaceful relations between people, organizations, and their societies. It is brought about slowly through socioeconomic reconstruction and development. It focuses more on the people and the context of the conflict than on the issues or the interests being fought over (peacemaking tries to reconcile these).

Almost all approaches to peace building involve increased contact and cooperation between people. Stephen Ryan notes that peacekeeping involves "building barriers between warriors," whereas peace building "tries to build bridges between the ordinary people" (Ryan 1995, 62). For example, he describes Neve Shalom/ Wahat al-Salam (Oasis for Peace), which is a project in Israel that allows Israeli and Palestinian farmers to live and work together. He also describes an Ulster basketball club that was established in Northern Ireland to bring Protestant and Catholic children, teens, and parents together.

Some campaigns, especially those carried out by the peace churches, focus on forgiveness and reconciliation. (The Morovian church in Nicaragua, for instance, worked hard for reconciliation between the Sandinista government and the Indian populations of the eastern coast.) Others involve the pursuit of joint projects that require intergroup cooperation. (For example, the Sarvodaya Society in Sri Lanka created multiethnic teams of volunteers who dig wells and build houses for the needy.) Education for mutual understanding and prejudice reduction is also useful for peace building, as are cross-cultural activities and confidence-building measures. (For example, the Irish have relinquished their claim to Northern Ireland, and justice system reforms have been implemented in Northern Ireland to increase fairness to both sides of that conflict.)

International Alert is one of a number of nongovernmental organizations (NGOs) engaging in peace-building efforts around the globe. An alliance of people working on socioeconomic development, human rights, and international education, International Alert provides "non-governmental bridge-building" to "transform conflict into peace and social justice" in nations torn by ethnic and other internal conflicts. Going further than peacekeeping and peace-building efforts, International Alert "analyzes the cause of internal conflict, enables mediation and dialogue to take place, sets standards of conduct to prevent violence, and helps develop the skills necessary to resolve conflict non-violently" (International Alert 1992, 1).

In many ways, peace building is the most difficult part of conflict resolution, because it involves the most people and the deepest personal and interpersonal feelings, hopes, and fears. It requires widespread attitude and behavior change, usually linked with social and economic changes made at interpersonal, organizational, community, and societal levels. This cannot be done quickly or easily—it takes many years beyond the point when a peace agreement is written, signed, and ratified. Yet only through these processes of peace building can a conflict be considered truly resolved.

See also: International Alert; Peacekeeping; Peacemaking.
References and Further Reading: International Alert, 1992, "Preparing to Promote Peace"; Kumar, Chetan, and Elizabeth Cousens, 1996, "Peacebuilding in Haiti"; Lederach, John Paul, 1994, *Building Peace: Sustainable Reconciliation in Divided Societies;* McFarland, Daniel, 1995, "Consultation on Reconciliation: New Directions in Peacebuilding"; Ryan, Stephen, 1995, *Ethnic Conflict and International Relations.*

Peace of Westphalia

The Peace of Westphalia was a treaty, signed on 24 October 1684, that ended the Thirty Years' War in Europe and in so doing formalized the institution of sovereignty and the nation-state system of international organization. Before that time, political organization in Europe was based primarily on religion and feudal fiefdoms. Europe was ruled by thousands of overlapping lordships that not only challenged one another for religious, political, and economic control but also were challenged by the pope and the Habsburgs, who ruled the Holy Roman Empire. This was also the era of the Protestant Reformation, which created deep-rooted religious schisms between Catholics and Protestants and between different Protestant factions.

The Peace of Westphalia fundamentally changed this political and religious organization. It established Switzerland and the Netherlands as independent states; it greatly weakened the Holy Roman Empire and the Habsburgs by giving each state of the empire full sovereignty and independence from the others; it enabled France to emerge from the wars as a great European power; and it greatly retarded the political unification and economic development of Germany.

The most important and lasting result of the Peace of Westphalia, however, was the recognition it gave to the notion of political sovereignty of nation-states, which remains a guiding principle of international relations.

See also: International Conflict; Sovereignty.
References and Further Reading: Knutsen, Torbjorn, 1992, *A History of International Relations Theory: An Introduction;* Lyons, Gene M., and Michael Mastanduno, 1995, *Beyond Westphalia? State Sovereignty and International Intervention;* Wright, Quincy, 1965, *A Study of War.*

Peace Research

Peace research is an interdisciplinary field of inquiry that investigates the causes and consequences of war and seeks ways that war can be avoided or terminated once it begins. Although scholars have investigated such topics for centuries, modern peace research, as an organized endeavor, began after World War I. This war was exceptionally destructive and apparently even more unnecessary than past wars. It spurred many people to begin thinking about ways that such wars could be avoided in the future. Early scholars, such as Quincy Wright, Pitirim Sorokin, and Lewis Richardson, began to investigate the causes of war in an effort to identify means of prevention.

Interest in this kind of research expanded considerably after World War II, when a group of scientists formed the Research Exchange on the Prevention of War. Most of the initial scholars in this group were not specialists in the field of international relations but were psychologists, economists, and mathematicians—scholars from different disciplines united by their commitment to peace. Among the founders were peace research leaders such as Herbert Kelman, Kenneth Boulding, and Anatol Rapoport. In the early 1950s, this group organized workshops, ran symposia, and published a journal that, in 1957, became the *Journal of Conflict Resolution*—still one of the leading journals in the field.

Publication of the *Journal of Conflict Resolution,* according to Kelman, "represented an important turning point, in that it helped to move the field of peace research into a professional direction" (Kelman 1981, 98). The journal united international relations scholars with the earlier "nonspecialist" scholars who had been involved in the initial Research Exchange. It also led to the creation of the Center for Research on Conflict Resolution at the University of Michigan, a focal point for early U.S. peace research. Other early centers that led the development of the field were the Canadian Peace Research Institute and the Oslo Peace Research Institute, which initiated the *Journal of Peace Research* in 1964.

Although peace researchers are united in their interest in peace, there are distinct divisions within the peace research community. One is a division between those who see the ultimate goal as peace and those who see it as justice. The justice advocates see peace research as a means to achieve social change and human betterment. Others prefer a narrower focus on the avoidance of war and believe that the pursuit of justice is a secondary issue that sometimes actually escalates conflicts rather than mitigates them.

A second division is between those doing basic research and those who engage in applied research. Some peace researchers develop theories and collect data to test those theories—all in a scientifically detached and abstract way. Others pursue applied research with a more immediate goal of affecting current disputes or decisions.

A third division exists between scholars who focus on mathematical analyses to explain human behavior and those who use nonmathematical approaches to address the same problem.

Although the field of dispute resolution has been growing rapidly over the last several decades, peace research has somewhat diminished in popularity. It attracted many scholars just after World War II and again during and after the Vietnam War, which was seen as preventable by many researchers. However, interest in peace research has diminished in recent years, especially since the collapse of the Soviet Union and the end of the Cold War, which seemed to suggest that war was no longer as much of a threat. We are now learning that war is still common—even more so than before—thus necessitating continued peace research.

See also: Boulding, Kenneth; International Conflict; Rapoport, Anatol; Richardson, Lewis.
References and Further Reading: Barash, David P., 1991, *Introduction to Peace Studies;* Galtung, Johan, 1985, "Twenty Five Years of Peace Research"; Kelman, Herbert C., 1981, "Reflections on the History and Status of Peace Research."

Peace Studies Association

The Peace Studies Association (PSA) is an organization of individuals and college and university academic programs that focuses on peace, conflict, justice, and global security. PSA's goal is to address the needs of emerging and existing peace studies programs. It offers faculty workshops, seminars, and consultations and disseminates information about existing programs and courses. It also facilitates communication and collaboration among programs and individuals involved in peace studies and teaching through annual meetings, symposia, and outreach programs. Current membership includes over 100 programs and individuals in the United States, Canada, Europe, and Latin America.

See also: Appendix 1 for contact information.

Peacekeeping

Peacekeeping involves the prevention or termination of violence within or between nation-states through the intervention of third-party neutral military, police, or civilian observers. Unlike peacemaking, which involves the resolution of the issues in conflict, the goal of peacekeeping is simply the cessation of violence. Although often carried out by military personnel, peacekeeping is usually not done in a threatening or coercive manner. Rather, it is usually carried out by simply positioning neutral military units between the warring factions. Peacekeepers are generally taught that they are not to use force unless absolutely necessary, and then to use it only as a deterrent or to maintain a buffer between warring factions. They must not get drawn into the conflict and certainly must not fight on one side against the other. Since the military units are usually small and only lightly armed, they cannot be effective unless the conflicting parties themselves desire a cessation of violence. If they do not (as the Serbs did not in 1994, for instance), peacekeeping is unlikely to be effective.

Also important to effectiveness is a clear mandate that is accepted by all the parties to the conflict. The mandate must be sufficiently precise that the peace-keeper's role is unambiguous and possible to carry out. If the mandate is broad and ambiguous, the peacekeepers themselves can become involved in a conflict over what they can and cannot, or should or should not, do. This seriously jeopardizes their effectiveness.

Although peacekeeping can be done by any national or international force, United Nations (UN) peacekeeping teams are the most well known. The earliest use of UN peacekeeping was in Jerusalem in 1948 to facilitate the end of Israel's war of independence with the Arabs. The concept was considerably expanded in 1956, however, when the first true UN peacekeeping force was deployed to oversee the cessation of hostilities in the Suez war. Overall, the UN was involved in 13 such efforts during its first 40 years of operation.

Beginning in 1989, the number of UN peacekeeping operations increased dramatically. In 1995, over 70,000 UN peacekeepers were involved in 17 locations around the world, including Cyprus, Lebanon, Kuwait, Pakistan, the Golan Heights, the western Sahara, Georgia, Liberia, Haiti, Tajikistan, Angola, Croatia, Bosnia-Herzegovina, and Rwanda. This increased level of activity has strained the UN's ability to organize, train, and deploy peacekeeping teams. Many of the teams do not have adequate access to personnel, funding, or training and cannot carry out their missions as successfully as they would like.

See also: Peace Building; Peacekeeping in Cyprus; Peacemaking; United Nations.
References and Further Reading: Amoo, Sam G., "Frustrations of Regional Peacekeeping: The OAU in Chad, 1977–1982"; Hirsch, John L., and Robert B. Oakley, 1995, *Somalia and Operation Restore Hope: Reflections on Peacekeeping and Peacemaking;* Renner, Michael, "Remaking U.N. Peacekeeping: U.S. Policy and Real Reform"; Ryan, Stephen, 1995, *Ethnic Conflict and International Relations;* Tepper, Alec, "UN Peacekeeping."

Peacekeeping in Cyprus

Cyprus was granted independence from Great Britain in 1960. Populated by both

Greeks and Turks, the island has been the center of almost continuous struggle between those two groups since 1960. The constitution established in 1960 apportioned power between the Greek majority and the Turkish minority according to their relative populations. The differences and distrust between the groups were strong, however, and fighting broke out in 1963 when the Greek president proposed constitutional changes that took away some of the Turks' political rights. As a result, the Turks demanded partition of the island. (The Greek Cypriots still wanted to maintain a single state.) When fighting spread across the entire island, British troops came in to prevent a full-scale war, and the United Nations (UN) appointed a mediator and organized a peacekeeping team to patrol the island. A UN-imposed cease-fire took effect in August 1964 and has been enforced by UN peacekeepers on the island ever since.

Despite the UN presence, fighting broke out again in 1974 following a pro-Greek coup and the subsequent invasion and occupation of the island by Turkish forces. With their help, the Turkish Cypriots gained control of the northern third of the island and in February 1975 proclaimed the establishment of a semi-independent Turkish Cypriot state.

Since the UN troops' mandate was only to keep Greek and Turkish Cypriots apart by patrolling a buffer zone, they could do nothing to stop the invasion by Turkey. They did succeed in reestablishing the buffer zone and the cease-fire, which they police to this day. However, they have not succeeded in socially or politically reuniting the island, despite numerous attempts. There is still almost total division of the island along ethnic lines, and there is no agreement on disarmament or intergroup cooperation.

This is an example in which peacekeeping—the process of keeping the peace by physically separating the warring factions—has been relatively successful. However, Gareth Evans argues that the success of the UN peacekeeping mission may have inadvertently undermined the peacemaking and peace-building efforts needed to bring Cyprus back to a state of stable peace. UN peacekeeping has assured "an indefinite status quo which has to date been more acceptable to both sides than the compromises needed for settlement" (Evans 1993, 93).

See also: Domination Conflicts; Identity Conflicts; Peace Building; Peacekeeping; Peacemaking; United Nations.
References and Further Reading: Evans, Gareth, 1993, *Cooperating for Peace: The Global Agenda for the 1990s and Beyond,* chap. 7.

Peacemaking

Peacemaking refers to a negotiation process that attempts to resolve a conflict between people, groups, or nations. It is contrasted with peacekeeping, which refers solely to activities designed to stop violence, and peace building, which tries to change people's negative attitudes about and social relationships with a former opponent or enemy. Although people may refer to interpersonal negotiation as peacemaking (as in "I am trying to act as a peacemaker in this marriage"), more often the term refers to negotiating a resolution to international conflicts or protracted ethnic conflicts within one nation-state, such as Rwanda, Sri Lanka, or Northern Ireland.

Peacemaking can be done by representatives of the parties negotiating directly, but it is often aided by the intervention of one or more neutral third parties who act as mediators. Sometimes these mediators are high-profile people, such as Jimmy Carter; sometimes they are low-profile people, such as members of the peace churches—the Quakers, the Mennonites, or the Brethren—who engage in peacemaking efforts out of religious beliefs rather than national interests.

No matter what their incentive, however, the goals of peacemakers are the same—to bring about a permanent end to hostilities by reconciling the interests and/or needs of the groups in conflict. Usually this cannot be done until the conflict is "ripe" for resolution, meaning that the parties have determined that they cannot prevail by continuing the violence. Once they have decided that, peacemakers can help craft and implement a settlement agreement that is acceptable to all sides. Any such agreement must then be followed by peace-building efforts, which try to heal the psychological or social wounds created by the conflict and bring the parties back together as partners rather than enemies.

See also: Carter, Jimmy; Mediation, International; Mennonite Conciliation Service; Peace Building; Peacekeeping.
References and Further Reading: Kriesberg, Louis, 1992, "The U.S.-USSR and Middle East Cases"; Ryan, Stephen, 1995, *Ethnic Conflict and International Relations.*

Persian Gulf War

In August 1990, Iraq, under Saddam Hussein's leadership, invaded neighboring Kuwait. Iraq's military action was successful, and Iraq declared Kuwait to be annexed territory. The United Nations (UN) Security Council promptly called for Iraq's complete and unconditional withdrawal from Kuwait. Stiff economic sanctions were imposed. In the face of vigorous encouragement by the United States, the UN Security Council further authorized enforcement action against Iraq, under Article 42 of the UN Charter. An international coalition of military forces, led by the United States, was mobilized to expel Iraq from Kuwait.

Gulf War military action began in January 1991. Within a matter of weeks, Iraq's forces were overwhelmed by the military power of the coalition forces. Under the terms of the resulting cease-fire, Iraq agreed to eliminate its weapons of mass destruction and reduce its conventional weapons capacity. Kuwait's preinvasion government was restored to power. Both Iraq and Kuwait suffered heavy losses during the Gulf War. However, Kuwait's initial wealth left it better able to recover. Damage to the Iraqi infrastructure and the effects of economic sanctions devastated Iraq's already troubled economy.

Central Issues and Deliberative Procedures

Iraq's invasion of Kuwait was a dramatic flare-up of a long-standing but mostly dormant border dispute between the two nations. Iraq had been unable to secure access to the Persian Gulf during its war with Iran. Defeat on that front sparked renewed interest in pursuing long-disputed claims to certain Persian Gulf islands then held by Kuwait. In addition, Iraq charged that Kuwait had been pumping oil from the Iraqi side of the shared Rumaila oil fields. Kuwait had also refused to forgive Iraqi war debts incurred during the war with Iran. Successful annexation of Kuwait would provide a needed boost to Iraq's ailing economy.

The explicit purpose of the subsequent Gulf War was to compel Iraq to withdraw from Kuwait. This action was motivated by an international desire to maintain stability in the region, to oppose military aggression, and to support national sovereignty. Iraq was in violation of international law, and its occupation of Kuwait was particularly brutal. Although many conflict theorists argued that military action was premature and negotiation largely untried, other theorists concluded that swift military action was appropriate

The United States was the primary supporter of military action in the gulf. Although the United States sought authorization, legitimation, and assistance from the UN, it also exercised its substantial influence over neutral members of the Security Council to encourage UN support of the U.S. position. This position was based on a variety of interests, including the desire to eliminate Iraq as a major power in the Middle East region, secure access to low-priced Saudi and Kuwaiti oil, establish a U.S. military presence in the region, and position the United States as guarantor of access to gulf oil, thus securing an advantage over its major economic competitors. Several analysts have argued that, from an ideological perspective, the United States saw the Gulf War as an opportunity to cure its "Vietnam syndrome" and to restore popular confidence in its military abilities. President George Bush also used the Gulf War to introduce his vision of a "new world order," wherein the remaining superpowers, under the auspices of the UN, would assume a much more active role in resolving regional conflicts and enforcing peace.

Some of these interests might have been achieved without military action, but others could not. Although many policy makers within and outside the military advocated a continuation of sanctions before military action, President Bush chose to move to war relatively quickly.

Outcome

Although Iraq's ability to wage war has certainly been curtailed as a result of the Gulf War, the issues underlying Iraq's aggression remain largely unaddressed. In addition, the UN's ability to use force to stop illegal aggression in other areas has not been as successful as many had hoped, although the potential for effective action was clearly demonstrated by the quick success of the Gulf War operation.

References and Further Reading: Evans, Gareth, 1993, *Cooperating for Peace: The Global Agenda for the 1990s and Beyond;* Rubin, Jeffrey, 1992, "Special Issue: Reflections on the War in the Persian Gulf."

Persuasion

Persuasion is the act of convincing another person or group to change its attitude or behavior through the use of argument and reasoning, not coercion or force. Thus, persuasion gets people to change their point of view or their actions because they want to, not because they have to. Martin Luther King Jr. based much of his civil rights campaign on the use of persuasion. He steadfastly refused to use violence or threats to intimidate whites. Instead, he used argument and reasoning in his call for the United States to "live out the true meaning of its creed" (King 1983, 83).

Such positive inducements are usually far more powerful than coercion because they are more stable. People hate being forced to do something against their will. When force is used, the victim usually watches for the first opportunity to lash back at the opponent. If people are persuaded to change their behavior through reason, however, backlash is much less likely to occur.

Although not usually considered a form of power, persuasion is one element of what Kenneth Boulding (1989) calls integrative power—the power to persuade through love or respect, rather than through coercion or trading. Persuasion, he argues, is the most fundamental form of power, because it is based on commonly held notions of legitimacy and fairness.

References and Further Reading: Boulding, Kenneth, 1989, *Three Faces of Power;* King, Martin Luther, Jr., 1983, "'I Have A Dream' Speech Given on August 28, 1963."

Polarization

Polarization is one process that occurs as a conflict escalates. It causes more and more people who had been neutral to take sides (move to the "poles"). It also causes each of the sides to become more clearly defined and opposed to the other (to become polar opposites). Paul Olczak and Dean Pruitt (1995) define four stages of conflict escalation. The first stage is when the conflict is beginning and escalation has not occurred to a significant degree. Perceptions of the opponent and the situation are relatively accurate, the parties' commitment to maintaining the relationship is still strong, and the parties are likely to believe that a win-win solution is possible. The second stage is the polarization stage, in which "trust and respect are threatened, and distorted perceptions and simplified stereotypes emerge" (Olczak and Pruitt 1995, 81). In this stage, parties tend to see the issues in black and white terms: "We are right, they are wrong"; "We are virtuous, they are evil." The ambiguities, the legitimacy of other views, and the benefit of the doubt that might be given to the opponent in the first stage disappear in the polarization stage, as the parties work to more clearly differentiate themselves from their opponents and win the uncommitted over to their side. The third stage is segregation, in which competition and hostility are prevalent and the conflict threatens basic needs (actually a continuation of polarization). The final stage is destruction, in which the primary intent of the parties is to destroy or at least subjugate the other, not just win something for themselves.

In a book on collaborative leadership, Carl Larson and David Chrislip (1994) argue that advocacy processes that were developed in the 1960s (and are still in use today) result in polarization of public policy conflicts, which results in ineffectual leadership and public policy gridlock. "Numerous constituencies from all sectors have formed associations around common grievances, staking out every imaginable position on major issues. Each is convinced of the righteousness of its cause. Paranoid and hostile, they battle each other from mutually exclusive positions, their conflicting aims fragmenting power and political will. Most represent legitimate concerns, but few, unfortunately, speak for the broader interest of society" (Larson and Chrislip 1994, 20–21). This approach, they point out, invites polarization and detracts from our ability to solve complex public policy problems.

Although serious, polarization is easier to reverse than conflicts that have reached the higher stages of escalation, especially if a mediator becomes involved. The mediator should help the parties understand the problems of polarization and escalation and how they distort their perceptions and actions. Once this is understood, the mediator can help the parties reevaluate the situation, reach some common understandings, and then proceed with negotiation. Without third-party intervention, however, conflicts that have reached the second stage of escalation are likely to continue to escalate to the higher stages, making ultimate resolution all the more difficult.

See also: Advocacy; Collaborative Leadership; Escalation; Mediation.

References and Further Reading: Larson, Carl E., and David D. Chrislip, 1994, *Collaborative Leadership;* Olczak, Paul V., and Dean G. Pruitt, 1995, "Beyond Hope: Approaches to Resolving Seemingly Intractable Conflict"; Pruitt, Dean G., and Jeffrey Z. Rubin, 1986, *Social Conflict.*

Police-Citizen Conflicts

Conflicts between citizens and the police are ubiquitous. In one sense, that is what policing is all about: the police watch over us to make sure that we behave properly, and when we don't, they initiate a power-based conflict to make us stop doing whatever illegal thing we have done.

If the police have legitimacy in the community and use their power only when truly necessary, police-citizen conflicts are generally constructive. They help the community maintain order and a sense of security. If the police are distrusted, however—if their presence or actions are seen as illegitimate, or if they are seen as enforcing illegitimate laws—conflicts between citizens and police can quickly escalate and become severe. This happens often both in the United States and abroad when the police are not of the same racial or ethnic group as the people they are policing. Charges of police racism or excessive violence are common in situations in which whites police blacks (in U.S. cities or in South Africa, for example) or in which one ethnic or religious group polices another (the Israelis policing the Palestinians and the British Protestants policing the Irish Catholics in Northern Ireland). In all these examples, racial, ethnic, and religious conflicts exacerbate the normal tension between the police and the local citizenry, leaving the police with almost no legitimacy.

The key to improving destructive police-citizen conflicts is better communication and intergroup understanding. One way to accomplish this is called "community policing," which is now becoming prevalent in the United States. The idea behind community policing is to get the police out of their cars and onto the streets (on foot), into the schools, and into the neighborhoods not just when they are called to investigate a crime but all the time. This gives the police a chance to meet the people of the community in a positive way—to understand who they are, why they are as they are, and what they might want to be. It also gives the community a chance to get to know the police as people rather than as enemies. A linked concept is law-related education that brings the police into the schools to teach students about the law, the justice system, and the role of the police. Again, this is done in a positive way, and the police get to know the kids as students, not just as troublemakers. (Drug Awareness and Resistance Education [DARE] is one example of law-related education.)

When asked what role police officers can play in community conflict management, Denver Police Chief David Michaud said, "It really comes down to the thing that we have been taught over and over again—respect the people that you are dealing with, be open to them, and listen to what they have to say" (Michaud 1993). This is essential, he said, for building trust between the citizens and the police, which is likewise essential if citizen-police conflicts are to be constructive, not destructive.

See also: Communication; Communication, Cross-Cultural; Ethnic and Racial Conflicts; Legitimacy.

References and Further Reading: Kennedy, Leslie W., 1990, *On the Borders of Crime: Conflict Management and Criminology;* Michaud, David, 1993, "The Role of Police in Less-Tractable Conflicts"; Prothrow-Stith, Deborah, and Michaele Weissman, 1991, *Deadly Consequences: How Violence Is Destroying Our Teenage Population and a Plan to Begin to Solve the Problem.*

Policy Dialogues

Policy dialogues are convened to address major public policy disputes. Often used to constructively confront complex environmental conflicts, policy dialogues bring representatives of opposing groups together to open up discussion, improve mutual understanding, and assess the degree of consensus and controversy that exists. Unlike collaborative problem-solving or consensus-building efforts, achieving consensus or reaching resolution is not the objective of policy dialogues. The goal is simply to assess the potential for developing a consensus resolution at some later time.

Despite this limited goal, policy dialogues frequently uncover shared interests and points of consensus that had previously been obscured by the adversarial rhetoric characteristic of escalated policy debates. As in principled negotiation, dialogue facilitators help parties focus on real interests rather than positions and help them sort out different definitions of the problem, areas of misunderstanding, and technical disagreement and uncertainty.

Organizations that conduct numerous policy dialogues include the Keystone Center in Keystone, Colorado, and the Conservation Foundation in Washington, D.C.

See also: Collaborative Problem Solving; Dialogue; Environmental Conflicts; Principled Negotiation and *Getting to Yes;* Public Policy Conflicts.
References and Further Reading: Gray, Barbara, 1989, *Collaborating: Finding Common Ground for Multiparty Problems.*

Power

Like other social concepts, power can be defined in many ways. Stated most simply, power is the ability to get what you want or, as Kenneth Boulding (1978a) put it, to "change the future."

Some social theorists distinguish among "power over," "power to," and "power with." The most common conception of power is "power over," or the ability to dominate another person, group, or nation, thereby forcing it to comply with demands. "Power over" is based on force and threat. If a subordinate fails to comply with a superior's wishes, the superior's ability to hurt the subordinate can force him or her to comply.

"Power to" is the power to accomplish something on one's own, without forcing anyone else to do anything. "Power to" is therefore a function of ability—the power to define problems and solutions, acquire the necessary resources, and solve a problem by oneself or with the willing assistance of others.

"Power with" is similar to "power to" in that it reflects ability, but it involves the power of consensus—the power people develop by working cooperatively to solve problems rather than competitively or coercively, as is done when problems are approached with the power-over framework.

These distinctions are similar to those made by Kenneth Boulding in his theory of power. Boulding argues that power has "three faces"—threat, exchange, and love. Threat power is power over—it is the power of coercion. Exchange power is the power of negotiation and trade: "I'll give you what you want if you give me what I want." Although negotiation is not commonly thought of as power, it is a way of getting what one wants, of changing the future. However, it accomplishes this through cooperation rather than coercion. Exchange power is thus similar to the concept of "power with"; it is the power that one gets by working with, rather than against, another person, organization, or nation. Last is the power of love, or integrative power. When people love others, they help them or do things for them just because they love them, not necessarily because they expect to get something back. In cases in which *love* seems too strong a word, Boulding suggests substituting the word *respect*. Although love and respect have been largely ignored in the academic literature, Boulding argues that love is actually the most significant source of power that a person (or a nation) has. "Without some sort of legitimacy [which is based on respect or love], neither threat power nor economic [exchange] power can be realized in any large degree" (Boulding 1989, 109).

This corresponds to Gene Sharp's conception of power as well. A leading advocate of nonviolent direct action, Sharp contends that nonviolence can be used to overthrow even the most repressive of regimes. According to Sharp, "the exercise of power depends on the consent of the ruled who, by withdrawing that consent, can control and even destroy the power of their opponent" (Sharp 1973, 4). The success of the Norwegian resistance to the Nazis and the Soviet citizens' resistance to the communist rulers in the late 1980s and early 1990s are both examples of how noncooperation with a repressive regime can result in its downfall or (in the case of the Nazis) its inability to control a particular area.

The advantage of using integrative power to accomplish something is that people feel good about what they are doing. When power is based on threats, it tends to generate a backlash, because people do not like being forced to do things against their will. Consequently, they often do what they have to at the moment but then plot how they can "get back at" or otherwise reverse what they were forced to do. When people do something out of love or respect, they do it because they want to do it. Thus the outcome is much more stable and is likely to last over time.

Power is critical to conflict and conflict resolution in many ways. Usually, negotiation is easier to accomplish, and the result is more fair, when the parties negotiating are of relatively equal power. When they are not, the negotiation usually results in the continuation of the existing power relationships. Negotiation is seldom a way to alter power structures. Realizing this, however, mediators sometimes work to equalize power when they recognize that one party is much less powerful than the other. This causes significant ethical problems, because empowering only one party can be seen as a violation of the mediator's impartiality. Transformative mediation solves this problem by working to empower both parties; it works to generate "power with" and "power to" rather than "power over."

See also: Boulding, Kenneth; Collaborative Problem Solving; Empowerment; Mediation, Ethical Issues; Persuasion; Power Balancing; Threats; Transformation.
References and Further Reading: Boulding, Kenneth, 1978a, *Ecodynamics: A New Theory of Societal Evolution;* Boulding, Kenneth, 1989, *Three Faces of Power;* Sharp, Gene, 1973, *The Politics of Nonviolent Action,* Vol. 1, *Power and Struggle.*

Power Balancing

In most conflict situations, one party has more power than the other. This puts the lower-power party at a disadvantage in any negotiation or mediation, unless efforts are made to equalize the power differential. For instance, it is often argued that men typically have more power than women in many divorce mediations. Although women are becoming increasingly sophisticated and financially secure in the 1990s, it is still common for the man to have more business and negotiation experience, more financial knowledge, a more rational and less emotional approach to problem solving (which is often a benefit in mediation), and a prior dominant role in the relationship that is carried into the mediation process. Some people see this power differential as a problem that inhibits a fair outcome from mediation; others do not.

Many mediators believe that mediation itself is a process that empowers the weaker party. It gets people together at a negotiation table, it allows each side to state its concerns and have those concerns heard by the opposing party, and it gives each side an opportunity to design a solution or a settlement that meets its needs. Since most mediation is voluntary, parties are not obligated to accept the result. This gives both parties the power to accept only those agreements that they believe are in their best interests. For these reasons, it can be argued that mediation is an empowering process for all. It gives disputants control over their own conflict and its resolution, which parties do not have if they use adversarial procedures (such as the courts or arbitration).

Others argue that this is not so. Unless the weaker party is actively assisted by the mediator or by another outside party (a lawyer, for instance), the weaker party is simply co-opted or manipulated to the benefit of the more powerful participant. Mediators who hold this view deal with it in a variety of ways. Most at least advise their clients to consult a lawyer about any settlement before it is accepted. Others may urge legal consultation throughout the proceedings. Mediators may also advise one or both parties to seek outside assistance in other areas. For instance, they may advise consultation with a financial adviser, a psychologist, a realtor, or anyone with expertise in an area that is covered in the terms of settlement.

Other mediators try to do the educating themselves. In private meetings (called caucuses) with the weaker party, the mediator asks hard questions about the party's stated beliefs and desires. If the mediator thinks that these beliefs are based on inaccurate information, he or she tries to correct the misperception or urges the party to investigate the situation further. The mediator may even go so far as to suggest a settlement that he or she thinks is preferable to the one being considered (because it is fairer to the low-power party), or he or she may suggest that the settlement being offered be rejected because it is unfair.

Mediators can empower the weaker party in other ways as well. Although mediators do not overtly make decisions, they have a great deal of control over the process. By deciding who talks when, what issues are covered in what order, and which issues are dismissed, mediators can tilt the process in favor of one side or the other. If a mediator perceives one party to be less powerful than the other, he or she may indeed manipulate the process in an effort to equalize the power between the two parties.

Although such active manipulation is common among mediators, it is not accepted as appropriate by all. Some mediators argue that such activities are completely unethical. Mediators are supposed to be neutral; they are process facilitators only. They are not supposed to take sides, give advice on substantive issues, or do anything that could possibly be construed as treating one side differently from the other. Doing so, they claim, calls into question the validity of the process itself.

This debate is by no means resolved. People who are considering using a mediator to help them resolve a conflict should be aware of the potential mediator's views on this question and should feel comfortable with that approach. If they do not, they should seek either a different mediator or a different process.

See also: Divorce Mediation; Empowerment; Mediation, Ethical Issues; Neutrality and Impartiality.
References and Further Reading: Bernard, S., H. Weingarten Folger, and Z. Zumeta, 1984, "The Neutral Mediator: Value Dilemmas in Divorce Mediation"; Bush, Robert A. Baruch, 1992, *The Dilemmas of Mediation Practice: A Study of Ethical Dilemmas and Policy Implications;* Bush, Robert A. Baruch, and Joseph P. Folger, 1994, *Promise of Mediation;* Folger, J. P., and S. Bernard, 1985, "Divorce Mediation: When Mediators Challenge the Divorcing Parties."

Predispute Agreements

Predispute agreements are made before a dispute arises and stipulate how disputes

that do arise will be resolved. For example, many contracts stipulate that disputes relating to the contract will be resolved with mediation or arbitration. They may even go so far as to name the mediator or arbitrator or the organization or process through which such a person would be obtained. This is common in some industries, such as insurance policies, securities sales, and car sales. It is also ubiquitous in labor contracts; labor contracts negotiated through collective bargaining almost always provide for a specific procedure to be followed whenever a dispute occurs relating to that contract or to the relationship between employer and employee. Typically, this involves a series of hearings, culminating with mediation or arbitration of the dispute. By routinizing the handling of labor-management disputes, both sides know what to expect, and conflicts can often be resolved more efficiently and less expensively than might otherwise be the case.

Another form of predispute agreement that is becoming increasingly common is the prenuptial agreement, specifying the terms of a marriage and, in many cases, what will occur should the marriage be dissolved. Advocates of prenuptial agreements argue that they prevent future trouble by specifying in advance what is expected of each party and what will be done if these expectations are violated. Although such agreements may take the romance out of marriage, they can be a practical way to avoid problems in both the marriage and the possible divorce.

See also: Conflict Prevention; Consumer Disputes; Family Conflict.
References and Further Reading: American Arbitration Association, World Wide Web Home Page, http://www.adr.org.

Principled Negotiation and Getting to Yes

Getting to Yes: Negotiating Agreement without Giving In, by Roger Fisher and

William Ury (with Bruce Patton as coauthor on the second edition), can be considered the bible of the dispute resolution movement. First published in 1981, it lays out in straightforward and easy-to-understand language the principles behind integrative or win-win bargaining. Although similar approaches had been advocated before, Fisher and Ury popularized this approach to bargaining, which they call "principled negotiation." This method of negotiation has four principles: separate the people from the problem; focus on interests, not positions; invent options for mutual gain; and insist on objective criteria.

The first rule urges negotiators to separate relationship problems from problems of substance and then deal directly with both. By following the second rule and focusing on interests, not positions, negotiators can determine the underlying reasons that people want what they say they want. Often, interests are compatible, even when opening positions are not. The third rule calls for negotiators to work together to invent solutions to the problem that allow both sides to win. They have to figure out how to "enlarge the pie," or how the pie can be shared in a way that each side gets what he or she needs. Although such win-win solutions may appear illusive at first, parties using principled negotiation can almost always find them, Fisher and Ury maintain. Finally, they urge negotiators to use objective criteria whenever possible. "The more you bring standards of fairness, efficiency, or scientific merit to bear on your particular problem," they say, "the more likely you are to produce a final package that is wise and fair" (Fisher, Ury, and Patton 1991, 83). Agreements based on precedent and standard practice are also less vulnerable to attack.

Getting to Yes has probably influenced the dispute resolution field more than any other book. Most mediators, for example, try to get their clients to use Fisher and Ury's principles to reach a negotiated agreement. However, some critics argue that the book is too simplistic or naive. The most common objection is that it covers only half of the field—that of integrative (or win-win) bargaining. The other half of the field is distributive bargaining, which occurs when there is no win-win solution but a fixed pie that has to be distributed among competing people. Thomas Schelling, Howard Raiffa, and others argue that power is critical to distributive bargaining but is largely neglected by Fisher and Ury, who declare that anything can be negotiated using the integrative approach. Others question Fisher and Ury's rejection of positional bargaining and their reliance on objective criteria, claiming that these rules are unrealistic in a variety of cases. Despite these reservations, a large proportion of people in dispute resolution regard the ideas in *Getting to Yes* as fundamental and these objections as minor issues that can be dealt with through minor adjustments to the approach.

See also: Bargaining, Integrative and Distributive.
References and Further Reading: Fisher, Roger, and William Ury, 1981, *Getting to Yes* (2nd ed. with Bruce Patton, 1991); Raiffa, Howard, 1982, *The Art and Science of Negotiation;* Schelling, Thomas C., 1960, *Strategy of Conflict.*

Private Judging

Private judging (also called court-annexed adjudication, orders of reference, or rent-a-judge) is a private process that is a cross between arbitration and judicial settlement. In private judging, the parties agree to have a private judge (whom they choose and hire themselves) try their case. Like arbitration, the private judge listens to the evidence presented by both sides and then makes a decision. This decision is submitted to the trial court as a judgment and, like arbitration, is binding. Unlike arbitration, however, the decision can be appealed.

Private judging can be either formal or informal, depending on the location of the dispute, the style of the judge, and the wishes of the parties. Some states have specific statutes governing private judging. These statutes may specify the procedures to be used, leaving the parties with little flexibility. Other states let the judge and the parties themselves decide what procedures to use. Although some private judges and parties prefer to follow standard judicial procedures, others greatly simplify the traditional rules of procedure, evidence, and pleading. This tends to speed up the process and lower the cost, although some disputants may feel that such shortcuts interfere with the judge's ability to ascertain the truth.

Private judging has a number of advantages. The ability to use traditional discovery and rules of procedure and evidence maintains some of the avowed advantages of litigation while providing many of the advantages of arbitration. One is the ability to select the judge. In the public process, a judge is assigned to a case; the parties do not get to choose. Most often, the judge selected does not have expertise in the substantive issues; therefore, a lot of time and effort are required to "bring the judge up to speed," and even then, the decision rendered may not be as informed as one that could have been made by a neutral party with expertise in the issue in dispute.

A second advantage is speed. Even with all the alternatives to court-based adjudication that are currently available, the civil court system is still bogged down. Many months or even years can pass before a dispute is brought to trial. With private judging, the case can be heard whenever the parties are ready. In addition, many months may pass between the time of a normal trial and the judge's decision. In private proceedings, however, this delay is minimal. This substantially lowers the cost of the process and enables a decision to be obtained—and applied—quickly.

A third advantage is process flexibility. If the parties want an informal process, in many states they can shortcut many of the court's formal procedures. They can decide which issues they want considered and which they don't. They can even intersperse negotiation or mediation into the process in an effort to obtain a voluntary settlement prior to the judge's decision. (This can happen in pretrial settlement conferences as well, of course.)

A fourth advantage is confidentiality. Once a case is referred to a private judge, the only aspects of the case that need be publicly reported are the judge's findings of fact and conclusions of law. The hearing itself is closed. If a case involves trade secrets or business practices that are best kept hidden, confidential proceedings are appealing.

Private judging does have disadvantages, however. First, it is still an adversarial process. This means that it has the potential of heightening tensions between the parties, just as court adjudication tends to do. It also tends to yield win-lose outcomes rather than win-win outcomes, which might be developed through an integrative process such as mediation.

Some people criticize private judging as "rich-man's justice." It is not fair, they charge, that a speedy, custom-designed process is available to those who can pay and the slow, inflexible process is all that is available to those who can't. Judges can cost up to $1,000 a day, and administrative charges are added to that. This approach is thus inappropriate for minor disputes involving small sums of money. It tends to be used in complex commercial cases and cases in which large amounts of money are at stake. Even with such limited use, some observers believe that private judging and related alternative adjudicatory procedures (such as mini-trials) threaten to destroy our single "integrated system of justice" (Burton and Dukes 1990a). Easy access to private forums may also undermine the reform of the public system, some fear (Gnaizda 1982).

Another criticism is that secret proceedings are inappropriate. All disputes should be settled, some claim, in a public forum. This argument is weak, however, as most filed cases are settled out of court. The court is asked to affirm the settlement, but the settlement negotiations themselves remain private.

See also: Arbitration; Mini-trial; Summary Jury Trial.
References and Further Reading: Burton, John, and Frank Dukes, 1990a, *Conflict: Practices in Management, Settlement and Resolution;* Dauer, Edward A., 1994, *Manual of Dispute Resolution,* 12-1–12-9; Gnaizda, Robert, 1982, "Secret Justice for the Privileged Few"; Goldberg, Stephen B., Eric D. Green, and Frank E. A. Sander, 1985, *Dispute Resolution,* 280–93.

Problem Solving

The term *problem solving* means different things to different people. Many use the term synonymously with consensus building or collaborative problem solving, a process used to resolve multiparty public policy conflicts. In collaborative problem solving, all the parties sit down together with one (or more) neutral facilitators who help the parties jointly define the problem, identify interests, and develop resolution options. The options are evaluated, one is chosen, and it is fine-tuned until an agreement satisfactory to all parties is reached. This agreement is then taken to the parties' constituencies for ratification. Typically, such a process takes several months, or even several years, of weekly, biweekly, or monthly meetings and often small groups working on particular problems between meetings.

The other common use of the term *problem solving* relates to analytical problem solving, or what Herbert Kelman and John Burton refer to as "problem-solving workshops." These are generally weeklong workshops, although successive workshops may be held with the same people over months or years. Most analytical problem-solving workshops have focused on international or internal ethnic conflicts, such as the Palestinian-Israeli conflict, the Northern Ireland conflict, or the South African conflict.

Unlike the process described earlier, the goal of analytical problem solving is to help the parties analyze the conflict thoroughly before trying to develop options for resolution. This analysis involves examining the parties' values and needs as well as their interests. (Collaborative problem solving focuses primarily on interests.) Analytical problem solving also examines each side's frustrations, constraints, perceptions, and fears. Only after these details are understood is an attempt made to develop solutions that address all these aspects of the problem. Unlike collaborative problem solving, which often involves many parties (five or more) meeting together, analytical problem solving is generally limited to only two parties (although multiple people can represent each party). Also different is the goal of collaborative problem solving, which is to come to a decision that is binding once it is ratified. Parties at the table are usually organizational leaders or other representatives who can officially speak for the parties in conflict. Analytical problem solving, in contrast, is unofficial. Parties are usually influential citizens but not government or ethnic group leaders. The discussions are generally considered to be exploratory only; no attempt is made to come to a binding decision.

See also: Collaborative Problem Solving; Problem Solving, Analytical.
References and Further Reading: Burton, John, 1990b, *Conflict: Resolution and Prevention;* Gray, Barbara, 1989, *Collaborating: Finding Common Ground for Multiparty Problems;* Kelman, Herbert C., 1996, "The Interactive Problem-Solving Approach."

Problem Solving, Analytical

Analytical problem solving (also called simply problem solving or interactive problem solving) is "an unofficial, academically based, third-party approach to the analysis and resolution of international and ethnic conflicts, anchored in social-psychological principles" (Kelman 1996, 501). Initially developed by John Burton, Herbert Kelman, and others, this approach is now used by many scholars who seek to apply analytical techniques to the resolution of seemingly intractable international and ethnic conflicts.

Unlike many other forms of conflict resolution, analytical problem solving brings practice, research, and theory building together. The approach is based on theoretical analysis and empirical research on conflict, social, and psychological processes. Thus, the facilitators need to be scholars with a thorough grounding in relevant theory and research. To complete the circle, the experience gained from each intervention then informs the theories and research on which the intervention was based.

The central component of this approach is the problem-solving workshop. These week-long workshops bring together influential members of conflicting parties in a private, confidential setting with a panel of scholar-facilitators. With the help of the facilitation panel, the parties explore each other's perspectives on the problem and examine their own values, interests, needs, prejudices, hopes, and fears as well as the other side's. After doing this, they brainstorm alternative ways of meeting the needs of both parties.

Unlike other forms of conflict resolution, which negotiate interests and use compromise as a means of splitting up incompatible interests, analytical problem solving focuses on meeting groups' fundamental human needs—for security, identity, and self-determination. Most often, such needs are not mutually exclusive but mutually reinforcing. For example, the more positive the Palestinians' sense of identity and security, the more secure the Israelis' identity and security are likely to be, as they will not be as threatened by the Palestinians. In a way, this makes the resolution of needs-based conflicts easier than

the resolution of some interest-based conflicts, because win-win results can be obtained. However, significant political, social, and economic changes are often necessary to achieve such win-win results, which makes the implementation of solutions much harder than their development in principle.

Problem-solving workshops are always unofficial and nonbinding. However, they can be closely linked to and supportive of official negotiations. In the prenegotiation stage, analytical problem solving can help set the stage and encourage the official parties to agree to meet for formal negotiations. During official negotiations, the workshops can be used as a way to develop new options that might not otherwise be considered or to explore more extensively options that had been unofficially discussed. "It is precisely the nonbinding character of the workshops that allows their unique contribution to the larger negotiation process: they provide an opportunity for sharing perspectives, exploring options, and joint thinking—an opportunity not readily available at the official negotiating table [where positional bargaining is the more common approach]" (Kelman 1996, 502).

An example of analytical problem solving is the series of workshops that Kelman and colleagues have conducted with Palestinians and Israelis since 1971. Most of these workshops have been one-time events that took place before official negotiations were convened. The primary goal of the workshops was to create an environment that would encourage formal negotiations and could inform the substance of those negotiations once they started. However, beginning in 1990, Kelman began what turned into a continuing workshop that met periodically for a number of years. Some of the participants in this workshop turned into official representatives of the two sides once official negotiations began in 1991. Although many factors contributed to the success of those negotiations (which led to the signing of the Oslo agreement in September 1993), the personal understandings that had been forged between these individuals and the innovative approaches developed in Kelman's problem-solving workshops were factors in the negotiations' success.

See also: Israeli-Palestinian Women's Workshop; Needs; Oslo Accords, Middle East Peace Process.
References and Further Reading: Burton, John, and Frank Dukes, 1990a, *Conflict: Practices in Management, Settlement and Resolution;* Kelman, Herbert C., 1996, "The Interactive Problem-Solving Approach.

Problem Solving, Collaborative
See **Collaborative Problem Solving.**

Procedural Conflicts

Some conflicts are not about the substance of a decision but about the way a decision is made. For example, if a city council or school board imposes a decision on a resistant constituency without public hearings or any way for the public to have meaningful input, the citizens are likely to be as upset about the lack of input as they are about the decision itself. Although procedural conflicts rarely occur without any substantive conflict, the procedural dispute often becomes bigger than the initial substantive conflict that set it off.

Procedural problems can arise in any of five areas: goals, process design, power relationships, legal issues, and timing. Common goal problems involve acting before the goal of the action is clear, pursuing unrealistic or inappropriate goals, or having the process be the end in itself. (This is what happens when a government agency "solves" a problem by forming an advisory committee, which it then ignores. The process of letting concerned citizens meet and talk is seen to be a "solution," even though the substance of the discussions is not considered important enough to influence subsequent agency decisions.)

Design problems include a decision-making process that is too complicated or lengthy to understand and use or an inflexible process that cannot be altered to meet unanticipated needs.

Power problems are probably the most common source of procedural conflict. Typical power issues include poor or no representation of interest groups in a public decision-making process, the use of power to co-opt an opponent, or the use of power to coerce a weaker party into doing something against its own interests.

Legal issues also give rise to procedural conflicts. The justice system is structured in an adversarial way, which creates conflicts as well as resolves them. The tendency to define problems in terms of rights (one's "right" to a promotion, or one's "right" to a particular kind of education) instead of interests (wanting a better job or a better school) makes conflicts more intense and more difficult to resolve.

Finally, timing can lead to procedural difficulties. Deadlines can force decisions to be made without adequate deliberation, but lack of deadlines can cause action to be delayed forever. Trying to resolve conflicts before the relative power of the parties is determined can be a futile task—mediators speak of waiting until the conflict is "ripe" for resolution.

Although the existence of procedural problems does not mean that conflicts cannot be resolved, superimposing procedural problems over other issues generally makes the conflict resolution process more difficult.

See also: Deadlines; Environmental Conflicts; Negotiation and Mediation, Timing and "Ripeness"; Power; Public Policy Conflicts.
References and Further Reading: Kraybill, Ron, 1993, "Democratic Decision Making: Developing Good Process"; Warfield, Wallace, 1993, "Public-Policy Conflict Resolution: The Nexus between Culture and Process."

Program on Negotiation at Harvard Law School

The Program on Negotiation (PON) at Harvard Law School is an applied research center established for the purpose of improving the theory and practice of negotiation and dispute resolution by people, organizations, and nations. Participants include scholars from four Boston-area colleges and universities: Harvard, MIT, Tufts University, and Simmons College. Activities of PON include eight major research and theory-building projects, postgraduate education and training, and the development and dissemination of teaching materials. The research projects cover a wide range of topics: alternative dispute resolution in general, public disputes, the prevention of war, international compliance, negotiation behavior and strategy, negotiation in the workplace, and the psychological processes of negotiation.

PON publishes *Negotiation Journal,* one of the leading journals in the dispute resolution field. It also publishes *Consensus,* a newsletter focused on environmental dispute resolution and consensus-building processes; the *Harvard Negotiation Law Review;* and the PON newsletter *Negotiation.*

One of the best-known activities of the Program on Negotiation is its clearinghouse, which maintains and disseminates a vast library of negotiation and dispute resolution teaching materials: books, working papers, videotapes, curricula, exercises, and role-plays.

PON offers two semester-length courses that are open to the public: one on negotiation and dispute resolution, and the other on mediators and other facilitative roles in dispute resolution. It also offers short executive education training programs focusing on one particular aspect of negotiation or dispute resolution. Popular topics include negotiation for senior executives, dealing with an angry public, and creating and managing international business relationships. PON also teaches four week-long mediation and negotiation workshops as part of the executive education program.

See also: Alternative Dispute Resolution; *Consensus; Negotiation Journal;* Appendix 1 for contact information.

Propaganda

Propaganda is a technique for advancing one's interests by manipulating the flow of information in self-serving ways. At one extreme, it may involve outright fabrication and the deliberate dissemination of misinformation. At the other extreme, so-called spin doctors may work to place acknowledged facts in the best possible light. Between these two extremes, there is a broad range of strategies designed to encourage people to disregard some facts while focusing on others or to interpret facts in desirable but not necessarily sensible ways.

Usually, the term *propaganda* is used in a negative way, referring to the use of information-manipulation techniques to pursue illegitimate goals. When similar but less extreme techniques are used as part of a competitive relationship, we tend to call it advertising or political campaigning, and we accept it as a legitimate way to pursue one's interests. In its less extreme form, it is also a common component of positional bargaining and advocacy—approaches to negotiation that focus on one side's interests with little regard for the other.

See also: Advocacy; Bargaining, Interest-Based and Positional.
References and Further Reading: Lasswell, Harold D., Daniel Lerner, and Hans Speier, 1979, *Propaganda and Communication in World History.*

Public Conversations Project

The Public Conversations Project (PCP) was founded in 1989 by a group of family therapists who believed that the methods of family therapy could be beneficially applied to highly volatile public policy controversies. In family conflict, people can get caught in intense, destructive power contests. Family therapists help transform the disputants' "dismissive, destructive shouting matches" into "mutually respectful, constructive discussions—the movement from diatribe to dialogue" (Chasin et al. 1996, 324). The founders of the PCP recognized the benefit of doing the same thing in the public policy arena. If debates over volatile issues such as abortion, gay rights, and environmental protection could be transformed from shouting matches to mutually respectful discussions, much more progress toward civility, if not resolution, could be made. PCP founders therefore designed and began to use a method for facilitating dialogues on controversial public topics.

Their first (and most common) dialogue topic was abortion, although they have since branched out into several other areas, including gay rights, population, women's health, the environment, and development.

See also: Dialogue; Family Conflict.
References and Further Reading: Becker, Carol, Laura Chasin, Richard Chasin, Margaret Herzig, and Sallyann Roth, 1994, "From Stuck Debate to New Conversation on Controversial Issues: A Report from the Public Conversations Project"; Chasin, R., Margaret Herzig, Sallyann Roth, Laura Chasin, Carol Becker, and Robert Stains, 1996, "From Diatribe to Dialogue on Divisive Public Issues: Approaches Drawn from Family Therapy."

Public Meetings and Hearings

Public meetings and hearings are the most common way that the public is allowed to participate in government decision-making processes at all levels. Unfortunately, this method is also the least effective form of participation and the one most likely to generate conflict rather than mitigate or resolve it.

Typical public hearings involve people "talking at," but seldom listening to, one another. The government officials explain their proposed actions or decisions to an often hostile audience (as citizens who support a decision are much less likely to take the time to come to the meeting). Citizens then take turns denouncing the proposed action, giving arguments (which may be either rational or highly emotional) for opposing the decision or action. This structure encourages positional statements, not interest-based dialogue. Thus, the process often exacerbates conflicts and makes polarized situations even more so.

Alternative forms of public participation include collaborative problem-solving groups, advisory committees, citizen boards, and similar vehicles for citizen involvement that get citizens, technical experts, and government decision makers working together to examine the nature of a problem and develop a solution that makes sense to everybody involved.

Similar mechanisms can be used by business for handling difficult public-relations problems. In their book *Dealing with an Angry Public,* Lawrence Susskind and Patrick Field urge both government and business to use what they call a "mutual gains" approach to dealings with the public. This approach calls for industry and government to acknowledge, rather than dismiss, the concerns of the public (or other opponent) and to encourage joint fact-finding. Both business and government leaders must act in a trustworthy manner at all times, focusing on building long-term relationships with citizens and other potential opponents. Leaders must be willing to accept responsibility, admit mistakes, and share power. Offering contingent commitments to minimize impacts if they occur and promising to compensate victims for unintended negative effects can go a long way toward developing trust, whereas the adversarial nature of typical public hearings does just the opposite.

See also: Citizen Participation; Collaborative Problem Solving.
References and Further Reading: DeSario, Jack, and Stuart Langton, 1987, *Citizen Participation in Public Decision Making;* Field, Patrick, 1994, "State Legislators Use Consensus-Building to Resolve Issues, Involve Citizens, Develop Legislation"; Susskind, Lawrence, and Patrick Field, 1996, *Dealing with an Angry Public.*

Public Participation
See **Citizen Participation.**

Public Policy Conflicts
Public policy conflicts are conflicts regarding governmental or other decisions that affect members of the public as well as the

primary negotiators. They usually involve one or more levels of government acting either as a party or, more commonly, as the decision maker. Examples include the setting and enforcement of environmental regulations, welfare policies, tax reform, and policies on such diverse topics as affirmative action, abortion, criminal sentencing, and zoning.

Unlike most private disputes, which involve a small number of parties and narrowly defined issues, public policy conflicts often involve many different interest groups with opposing interests and values and myriad interrelated issues. In addition, these conflicts frequently involve a significant element of uncertainty and/or technical complexity. These factors and others make public policy making a challenge. Intense, protracted conflicts are common, and they often lead to stalemates in which no one gets what they want.

Suffering from an increasing number of public policy–making failures in the 1960s and 1970s, many people became interested in the potential of consensus building to solve problems more effectively. Consensus-based processes such as collaborative problem solving, mediation, and regulatory negotiation have been used by many state and federal agencies, often with considerable success. Such techniques are limited, however, by a number of factors. One is convincing the decision maker to try a consensus decision-making process. Although these techniques are becoming increasingly common, there is still a fear among many government officials that participating in a consensus-building process is an abdication of their power and responsibility. In addition, identifying all the appropriate parties can be difficult, as can convincing them to participate. Low-power parties may think that they will be coerced or "railroaded"; high-power parties may think that they can win what they want with traditional power politics, so they choose not to participate in a consensus process in which they might have to compromise or settle for less. Other problems involve binding ad hoc groups to their commitments and providing the necessary resources to allow less-powerful groups to participate on an equal basis.

Although all these limits pose challenges, none is insurmountable, and one can find many examples of successful consensus-based solutions to public policy problems, including the Montreal Protocol on Substances that Deplete the Ozone Layer, transportation planning in Maine, and the Defense Base Closure Commission (all summarized elsewhere in this volume).

See also: Collaborative Problem Solving; Defense Base Closure and Realignment Commission; Environmental Conflicts; Montreal Protocol on Substances that Deplete the Ozone Layer; Negotiated Rulemaking at the Maine Department of Transportation; *Roe v. Wade;* Scientific and Technical Disputes.

References and Further Reading: Carpenter, Susan L., and W. J. D. Kennedy, 1988, *Managing Public Disputes;* Gray, Barbara, 1989, *Collaborating: Finding Common Ground for Multiparty Problems;* Susskind, Lawrence, 1993a, "Resolving Public Disputes."

Pugwash Conferences on Science and World Affairs

The Pugwash Conferences are one of the earliest examples of track two or citizen diplomacy. The first conference was held in Pugwash, Nova Scotia, shortly after the end of World War II. The intent was to provide the opportunity for decision makers and scientists from the West to meet with their counterparts in the Soviet Union (and now their descendants) in an effort to improve relations and reduce the nuclear threat. The ultimate goal of the conferences is to see all nuclear arms destroyed and, beyond that, to develop solutions to international disputes other than war.

Initially, the group was made up of policy makers and physical scientists, as it was thought that they could best understand and deal with questions regarding nuclear weapons and the developing superpower confrontation. Over time, however, participation broadened to include more social and political scientists. Eventually, the group became more like a professional association and was less connected to decision makers in either nation.

In 1995, the Nobel Peace Prize was awarded to Joseph Rotblat, the president of Pugwash and one of its founders, and to the conferences as an organization "for their efforts to diminish the part played by nuclear arms in international politics and in the longer run to eliminate such arms." The Nobel Committee said that it hoped that the prize would "encourage world leaders to intensify their efforts to rid the world of nuclear weapons" (Norwegian Nobel Committee 1996, 113).

In addition to its yearly conferences, the Pugwash organization holds symposia, workshops, and study groups; sponsors many projects; publishes a quarterly newsletter; and has national affiliates and student affiliates (called Student Pugwash) in many nations. Student Pugwash also holds international meetings of youth from around the world who are interested in peace building and nuclear disarmament.

See also: Cold War; Diplomacy, Citizen, Track Two, and Multitrack; Appendix 1 for contact information.

References and Further Reading: Burton, John, and Frank Dukes, 1990a, *Conflict: Practices in Management, Settlement and Resolution;* Council of the Pugwash Conferences on World and Science Affairs, 1992, *Pugwash Newsletter* 29:4 (May); Norwegian Nobel Committee, 1996, "Award of the Nobel Peace Prize for 1995 to Joseph Rotblat and Pugwash Conference on Science and World Affairs."

Railway Labor Act

The Railway Labor Act of 1926 was the first comprehensive piece of labor legislation passed by the federal government. It reduced labor conflicts on the railroads and established a mechanism, later applied in other industries, to regulate and protect the collective bargaining process. The act became necessary because severe labor unrest on the railroads had crippled the country's economy. The 1934 amendments to the act established the National Mediation Board (NMB), which is empowered to conduct certification elections to determine whether employees want a particular union to represent them. The NMB also mediates and arbitrates labor disputes that arise during contract negotiations. The National Railroad Adjustment Board (NRAB) mediates or arbitrates disputes that arise out of the interpretation of an existing contract.

See also: Collective Bargaining; Labor-Management Relations and Conflict.
References and Further Reading: Leap, Terry L., 1995, *Collective Bargaining and Labor Relations.*

Rapoport, Anatol

Mathematician Anatol Rapoport became interested in the problem of international conflict in the 1940s and was one of the early leaders of the conflict resolution field. Born in 1911 in Lozovaya, Russia, Rapoport studied at the University of Chicago, receiving his doctorate in mathematics in 1941. His research emphasized the mathematics of biology and behavioral science. After working at both Stanford and the University of Michigan, Rapoport went to the University of Toronto, where he became professor of peace studies. He received the Lenz International Peace Research Prize in 1976.

Rapoport is best known for his application of game theory to the problems of conflict resolution, specifically, for his distinction among fights, games, and debates. The goal of a fight is to defeat the opponent, by violence if necessary. The goal of a game is to outsmart the opponent within the rules of the game. The goal of a debate is to persuade the opponent. Although conflict resolution should be closest to the model of a debate, he argued, elements of gaming and fighting are often present as well.

See also: Game Theory; Peace Research.
References and Further Reading: Rapoport, Anatol, 1960, *Fights, Games, and Debates;* Rapoport, Anatol, 1974, *Game Theory as a Theory of Conflict Resolution.*

Rationality

Rationality is a decision-making strategy based on the systematic and often scientific identification, evaluation, and selection of options in terms of benefits and costs. In conflict situations, rational approaches can be used by one or more parties to determine which positions will best advance their interests and which dispute handling strategies are most likely to be effective. At the extreme, rational strategies involve a systematic analysis in which the costs and benefits of every possible option are assessed, with the assumption that the most desirable option is the one that produces the greatest possible net benefits. Many contemporary public policy-making processes (such as those involving environmental impact statements) specifically require that the proposed action and its principal alternatives be analyzed in this way. Mediators following the dominant North American problem-solving approach to mediation also use a scientific-rational approach to decision making as much as possible.

The appropriateness of this rational approach is commonly questioned. Political scientist Charles Lindblom, for example, argues that it is almost impossible to conduct the kind of comprehensive analyses that rational approaches require. Such comprehensive analyses are so expensive that society can seldom, if ever, afford them. Furthermore, most problems involve irreducible levels of uncertainty that make it impossible to accurately determine costs and benefits. Added to this are difficult distributional questions over who should receive the benefits and who should bear the costs. There are no generally agreed-upon methods for making such calculations.

Another problem is that people tend not to be completely rational, even when they think they are. It is not rare for a person to like option A better than option B, option B better than option C, but option C better than option A. (True rationality suggests that the person should like A better than C.) Such situations may suggest a misinterpretation of information, or they may suggest that other factors—beyond simple cost-benefit calculations—influence such choices. Indeed, many people argue that rational cost-benefit analysis is only one of several possible approaches to decision making. Although rationality is generally seen as superior in

most Western, democratic, and technologically advanced societies, traditional societies often emphasize relational and emotional factors as being more important than simple cost-benefit determinations. Cost-benefit calculations tend to ignore nonquantifiable issues, such as the importance of a relationship or interpersonal trust, and many traditional societies and people note that rationality is commonly used to disguise largely selfish pursuits with a cloak of scientific impartiality. Consequently, people from traditional cultures tend to distrust any decision-making process, including alternative dispute resolution processes such as problem-solving mediation or consensus building, that are predicated on the rational, cost-benefit approach.

See also: Collaborative Problem Solving; Mediation Models; Negotiation and Mediation, Cross-Cultural.
References and Further Reading: Kondo, Tetsuo, 1990, "Some Notes on Rational Behavior, Normative Behavior, Moral Behavior, and Cooperation"; Lindblom, Charles E., 1968, *The Policy-Making Process;* Simon, Herbert A., 1983, *Reason in Human Affairs.*

Reality Testing

Before agreeing to a settlement in negotiation or mediation, all disputants must determine whether the proposed settlement is better than their best alternative to the negotiated agreement, or BATNA (Fisher, Ury, and Patton 1991). Often, if one party will not agree, it is because that person believes that his or her BATNA is better than the outcome that the settlement provides. If this is true, the agreement will have to be changed before it will be approved. If it is not true, however, the mediator or the opposing party must educate the reluctant party through what is called reality testing. This involves asking hard questions about one's own and one's opponents' power and options. Can you (or they) really get as good a deal as you (or they) think without the negotiation succeeding? Or is one side's BATNA unrealistic?

Ury suggests asking questions such as, "What do you think will happen if we don't agree?" or "If we can't reach an agreement, what would you advise me to do to meet my interests?" or "What will you do to meet your interests if we don't agree?" Often the answers to these questions illustrate that the agreement is better than one or both sides thought and thus should be approved or altered and then approved rather than being rejected outright (Ury 1991).

See also: BATNA; Caucuses; Principled Negotiation and *Getting to Yes;* Ury, William.
References and Further Reading: Fisher, Roger, and William Ury, 1981, *Getting to Yes* (2nd ed. with Bruce Patton, 1991); Ury, William, 1991, *Getting Past No: Negotiating with Difficult People.*

Reconciliation

Reconciliation is the ultimate goal of peace building, when adversaries develop a new relationship of mutual forgiveness, acceptance, and trust. Peace builder John Paul Lederach describes it as "a meeting ground where trust and mercy have met, and where justice and peace have kissed" (McFarland 1995, 10). Thus, reconciliation goes beyond dispute settlement to complete resolution of the underlying conflict and normalization of relations between former adversaries.

Although reconciliation can happen without third-party assistance, in protracted, escalated conflicts, third-party intervention is often essential if reconciliation is to be achieved. Facilitators work with representatives of both sides of a conflict to help them jointly analyze the conflict history, recognize past injustices and suffering, accept moral responsibility, apologize, and forgive. Only then can the parties work together to build a future based on acceptance, cooperation, and trust.

Perhaps the most striking example of reconciliation is that which has occurred since the end of World War II in Europe. Joseph Montville describes a postwar com-

mission of historians who rewrote French and German history books to reflect a joint account of the war's events. The commission's work, reports Montville, "was critical to the post war healing process which laid the psychological foundation for later establishment of the European Community, of which France and Germany are the core" (Montville 1993, 121).

Another approach to reconciliation is citizen diplomacy and analytical problem-solving workshops. With citizen diplomacy, unofficial citizens of disputing countries meet to break down stereotypes, build mutual understanding and trust, and, at times, work on cooperative projects. In analytical problem-solving workshops, influential citizens do the same thing, but facilitators encourage them to move even further to identify the fundamental needs in conflict and to jointly develop new approaches for meeting both sides' needs simultaneously. Although unofficial, such workshops often bring about reconciliation among the members, who then go back to their respective countries to further reconciliation within the larger society.

See also: Amnesty and Forgiveness; Apology; Diplomacy, Citizen, Track Two, and Multitrack; Israeli-Palestinian Women's Workshop; Problem Solving, Analytical; Truth and Reconciliation Commission, South Africa.
References and Further Reading: McFarland, Daniel, 1995, "Consultation on Reconciliation: New Directions in Peacebuilding"; Montville, Joseph, 1993, "The Healing Function in Political Conflict Resolution."

Referendum

A referendum is a process in which a local or state electorate must approve a law (by majority vote) that has already been approved by the local or state governing body. For example, most states require that proposed constitutional amendments be approved by the voters through a referendum. Others require that legislation involving state borrowing be approved by the electorate. In addition to laws that are automatically subjected to a referendum, many states allow the legislature or local government to refer a law for referendum; others allow citizens to file petitions requesting that any law be so approved. The number of petitions required varies from state to state, as does the availability of the referendum process.

See also: Ballot Initiatives; Citizen Participation; Democracy; Legislative Process.
References and Further Reading: Cronin, Thomas, 1989, *Direct Democracy: The Politics of Initiative, Referendum, and Recall.*

Reframing
See **Framing.**

Regulatory Negotiation

Regulatory negotiation (also called negotiated rulemaking or reg-neg) is a process being used by many federal and some state regulatory agencies to involve the parties who will be affected by a proposed regulation in its development. Aided by a neutral convener, the potentially affected parties work with agency staff members to identify the agency's and the affected parties' interests and issues of importance regarding the proposed regulation. The parties then use negotiation to develop the exact wording of the regulation, which is published in the *Federal Register.* Although regulations created in this way are open to challenge as much as any other, challenges are rare, because all the interested parties have been involved in developing the rule from the start. They are much more likely, therefore, to support and comply with the rule.

This approach to rulemaking was first suggested by Philip Harter in 1982, who observed, along with many others, that the traditional approach to rulemaking was ineffective. Before the era of reg-neg, rulemaking was typically done by the federal agency staff working alone. Generally, an agency would propose a rule, interested people would respond, and then, as many cynics observed, the agency would ignore

the responses and issue the rule, and the affected parties would sue to get the rule revoked. Even regulators acknowledged the problem: in 1984, for example, Environmental Protection Agency (EPA) Administrator William Ruckelshaus estimated that 80 percent of EPA rules had been challenged in court, and approximately 30 percent of the rules had been significantly changed as a result (Susskind and McMahon 1985).

Harter argued that these problems could be avoided by involving the affected parties throughout the rulemaking process, not just at the end. This suggestion was adopted by the Administrative Conference of the United States (ACUS), which, in 1986, urged federal agencies to review the areas they regulated to determine regulatory negotiation's potential to increase effectiveness and diminish regulatory costs. A number of agencies experimented with the process with good results, and in 1990, the ACUS convinced Congress to pass the Negotiated Rulemaking Act, which formally authorized and encouraged the use of reg-neg whenever feasible.

Regulatory negotiation is considered by many to be superior to the traditional approach, because it avoids the costly and acrimonious nature of traditional rulemaking and yields rules that are more legitimate and hence more likely to be followed. This saves significant costs for both the federal agencies and the other parties; both avoid the costs of lawsuits to challenge rules, and the agencies avoid the costs of enforcing unpopular rules.

Even if consensus on a rule cannot be reached, regulatory negotiation has benefits. Issues and interests can be clarified, data can be shared and verified, and concerns can be aired. This process helps an agency promulgate a better rule, even if it has to do so on its own.

See also: Adversarial Approach; Federal Use of Alternative Dispute Resolution; Negotiated Rulemaking Act of

1990; Negotiated Rulemaking at the Maine Department of Transportation.

References and Further Reading: Dauer, Edward A., 1994, *Manual of Dispute Resolution;* Goldberg, Stephen B., Frank E. A. Sander, and Nancy H. Rogers, 1992, *Dispute Resolution: Negotiation, Mediation, and Other Processes;* Kolb, Deborah M., and Associates, 1994, *When Talk Works: Profiles of Mediators;* Susskind, Lawrence, and Gerald McMahon, 1985, "The Theory and Practice of Negotiated Rulemaking."

Representation

Representation is often a problem in public policy conflicts, which involve many diffuse interest groups. Typically, a few people negotiate on behalf of large constituencies who may or may not feel that their interests are being adequately represented. For example, a variety of interest-group representatives may negotiate on behalf of citizens in an environmental conflict. If the negotiators agree to a settlement that does not please some of their constituents, those constituents may argue that their interests were not adequately represented, and they may act to block the agreement. In other instances, a person who is chosen to represent an interest group at the negotiating table may not be acceptable to the other negotiators. This can cause the negotiations to break down immediately if an alternative representative who is acceptable to all cannot be found.

See also: Advocacy; Interest Groups.
References and Further Reading: Carpenter, Susan L., and W. J. D. Kennedy, 1988, *Managing Public Disputes;* Gray, Barbara, 1989, *Collaborating: Finding Common Ground for Multiparty Problems;* Susskind, Lawrence, and Jeffrey Cruikshank, 1987, *Breaking the Impasse.*

Richardson, Lewis

Lewis Richardson was a Quaker physicist and meteorologist from Great Britain who became interested in the patterns of human violence and arms races while serving as an ambulance driver in World War I. After the war, he returned to physics and meteorology for a while but retired early to devote his full attention to developing some of the first mathematical models of human violence. After collecting a vast array of statistics on wars and lesser episodes of violence, Richardson tried to develop a model to explain the patterns he saw. Among his findings was the fact that the frequency of conflict is inversely proportional to its magnitude. This means that the higher the magnitude (severity) of the conflict, the less frequently it occurs.

In his study of arms races, he found that three factors tended to influence the speed at which a nation built up its arms: the tendency to react weakly or strongly to threats from other nations, the tendency to be strongly or weakly influenced by the difficulties of producing arms, and the extent of accumulated grievances. Depending on how these factors were assembled, he found four possible outcomes.

First is a situation in which there are considerable grievances, but either cost or other conflict-limiting factors outweigh the countries' reactivity. In this case, the countries move quickly to a stable equilibrium. This might be represented by the current relationship between Japan and the United States. In the second case, goodwill outweighs grievances, and the conflict-limiting factors or cost considerations outweigh the strength of reactivity. This leads quickly to total disarmament, as in the relationship between the United States and Canada. In the third case, there is an accumulation of mutual grievances, and the strength of reactivity outweighs the conflict-limiting factors. This leads to a runaway arms race, as occurred during the Cold War between the United States and the Soviet Union. The last situation is when the nations' reactivity outweighs the conflict-limiting factors, but goodwill outweighs accumulated grievances. This, Richardson said, could lead either to an arms race or to disarmament, depending on the number of arms each side has.

Although Richardson's models are relatively simple, when he compared them with models of human behavior, he (and others who later tested his theories) found a close correspondence between his mathematical predictions and actual human behavior. Thus, his models have received considerable attention, both for their findings and for the impetus his work gave to more sophisticated mathematical modeling.

Although he did his research much earlier, Richardson's two major books—*Arms and Insecurity* and *Statistics of Deadly Quarrels*—were not published until 1960, seven years after his death.

See also: Arms Control and Disarmament.
References and Further Reading: Richardson, Lewis F., 1960, *Arms and Insecurity;* Richardson, Lewis F., 1960, *Statistics of Deadly Quarrels;* Schellenberg, James A., 1996, *Conflict Resolution—Theory, Research, and Practice.*

Rights

In the conflict resolution context, rights are independent standards on which to decide what (or who) is right or wrong. Some rights—such as those guaranteed by the Constitution, by laws, or by contractual agreements—are formalized. Others are simply socially accepted standards of behavior.

According to William Ury, Jeanne Brett, and Stephen Goldberg (1988b), rights are one of three possible ways to resolve disputes; the other two are interests (things people want but aren't guaranteed) and power. They suggest that a healthy dispute resolution system resolves most disputes through the negotiation of interests, using compromise and consensus building. A small segment of disputes need to be adjudicated on the basis of rights (resulting in a win-lose outcome), and an even smaller number need to undergo power contests to determine whose rights will prevail (also a win-lose approach). Distressed dispute resolution systems, in contrast, rely on power- or rights-based decision making, with little or no negotiation of interests and thus few opportunities for compromise or consensus building.

Some rights, such as those embodied in the U.S. Bill of Rights, have a long history of broad public acceptance. These include, for example, the right to due process, freedom of religion, and freedom of speech. In recent years, however, many groups have attempted to expand the initial set of rights guaranteed by the Constitution. Many of these efforts have been controversial: for example, the campaign for women's right to choose (to have an abortion) and the extension of equal rights for minorities and women to include the concepts of affirmative action, race-norming of test scores, and the drawing of congressional districts to favor particular minority groups. Also controversial have been efforts to establish rights for homosexuals, the right to die, and economic rights, such as the right to housing, health care, and food.

This trend, which is well documented in Mary Ann Glendon's book *Rights Talk,* sets up a situation in which cases must be decided in an adjudicatory win-lose structure, with little if any chance for negotiation, compromise, or consensus building. In addition, when problems are defined in terms of rights, the political processes of debate and electoral decision making are bypassed. Instead, issues are resolved through litigation, with the courts making a final determination about whether or not a right exists. This elimination of public participation and deliberation often causes more controversy than it resolves.

For example, *Roe v. Wade,* the landmark Supreme Court decision that established abortion as part of a woman's right to privacy, cannot be overturned by any legislative body, except perhaps through the slow process of changing membership of the Supreme Court. Rather than permanently deciding the abortion debate, *Roe v. Wade* merely increased the intensity of the conflict, forcing abortion opponents to turn to power strategies—even violence—in an effort to be heard. Nevertheless, contending parties often find rights-based approaches to be more attractive than interest-based approaches to conflict, since the rights argument eliminates the need to compromise and offers the possibility of a swift and complete victory.

Quincy Wright's distinction between *rights* and *remedies* is also crucial to the concept of rights. Wright asserts that rights are meaningless unless effective remedies are available to those whose rights have been violated. Rights also entail responsibilities. If there is a right to health care or housing, then someone must be responsible for providing those services. Similarly, someone must be responsible for guaranteeing equal protection, freedom of speech, and other political rights. This means that all rights have costs—often very real, monetary costs—that must be considered when one attempts to define a problem on the basis of rights rather than interests.

See also: Dispute Systems Design; Interests and Positions; Power; *Roe v. Wade.*
References and Further Reading: Glendon, Mary Ann, 1991, *Rights Talk: The Impoverishment of Political Discourse;* Ury, William L., Jeanne M. Brett, and Stephen B. Goldberg, 1988b, *Interests, Rights and Power: Designing Dispute Resolution Systems;* Wright, Quincy, 1965, *A Study of War.*

Ripeness
See **Negotiation and Mediation, Timing and "Ripeness."**

Risk and Uncertainty
In situations characterized by risk and uncertainty, it is impossible for the parties to know ahead of time what will happen if a conflict is resolved in a particular way. Although uncertainties can often be reduced through technical analysis, a significant level of irreducible uncertainty is often unavoidable. For example, it is difficult to predict how a new shopping center will affect a community's traffic patterns; how low-level, heavy-metal soil contamination will affect the public

health; or how a tax cut will affect the overall economy.

In making decisions about whether a particular action is acceptable, people often interpret uncertainties cautiously, using a worst-case approach. For example, citizens living near a proposed chemical plant are likely to base their decisions about whether to oppose the plant on the fear that the worst possible accident might actually occur. At the same time, those who will benefit directly from the proposed facility are likely to take a best-case approach to risk issues and assume that safety measures will effectively eliminate any danger. This sets up a contentious situation in which the principal issue dividing plant supporters and opponents is how they interpret risk estimates.

Efforts to resolve, or at least minimize, such conflicts focus on the establishment of a generally accepted base of technical information. This requires (1) the design and implementation of studies that are worthy of the public's trust, (2) the independent assessment of those studies by trusted outside experts who will then attest to their credibility, (3) communication of those studies to the general public in a way that they can understand, and (4) efforts to help the public sensibly interpret the information.

See also: Citizens' Radiation Monitoring Program; Scientific and Technical Disputes.
References and Further Reading: Fischhoff, Baruch, Sarah Lichtenstein, Paul Slovic, Stephen L. Derby, and Ralph L. Keeney, 1981, *Acceptable Risk;* Rowe, W. D., 1977, *An Anatomy of Risk.*

Roe v. Wade
Roe v. Wade was the landmark 1973 U.S. Supreme Court decision that made abortion legal. It resulted after Norma McCorvey, an unmarried 25-year-old Texas woman, became pregnant in 1969, allegedly as a result of rape. Abortion was illegal in Texas at the time except to save a woman's life. McCorvey agreed to chal-

lenge the Texas ban, on the condition of anonymity. Thus she became "Jane Roe" in *Roe v. Wade,* which was appealed up to the U.S. Supreme Court. Arguments were presented in both 1971 and 1972. In 1973, the U.S. Supreme Court ruled that a woman's choice to end her pregnancy by abortion is constitutionally protected. This ruling invalidated existing abortion laws in 49 states.

Background

During the late 1800s, abortion became increasingly restricted by law. Physicians and the medical establishment were the main force lobbying for abortion restrictions. Generally, the antiabortion statutes of that era made exceptions in the case of "therapeutic" abortions, to preserve the life or health of the woman.

During the first half of the 1900s, abortion was illegal but was widely practiced nevertheless. A number of legal abortions were also performed, under differing interpretations of the "therapeutic" exception. As Laurence Tribe (1990, 35) observes, "In the 1930's poverty became a widely accepted basis for providing a therapeutic abortion. In the 1940s and 1950s some doctors performed abortions for psychiatric reasons." By the 1960s, there was some pressure to reevaluate and ease abortion restrictions, from both the medical establishment and the general population. In 1973, the Supreme Court fundamentally revised the terms of the debate.

Central Issues and Deliberative Procedures

Prior to *Roe,* abortion was regulated by state legislatures on a state-by-state basis. Abortion legislation and the popular debate reflected a broad range of social, moral, and medical concerns. Eugenics, maternal health, religious belief, personal liberty, physician authority and the consolidation of professional power, female sexuality, sexual morality, marriage, the family, quality of life, and even fear of the population explosion all played a role in shaping individual and public opinion.

The U.S. Supreme Court, however, can consider only the issue of constitutionality. In the Court's view, the issue was whether a woman has a constitutionally protected right to decide whether to terminate her pregnancy. In the words of Justice Lewis Powell, the Supreme Court held "that the right of privacy, grounded in the concept of personal liberty guaranteed by the Constitution, encompasses a woman's right to decide." *Roe* largely closed the political debate on abortion by declaring the choice to be the exercise of a fundamental right. The state must have a compelling reason to limit a fundamental right, and the courts have traditionally subjected such proposed reasons to very strict scrutiny.

Structure

In its decision, the Court described the conditions under which the state might limit a woman's choice of abortion. During the first trimester (first three months of pregnancy), the state has no compelling interest that would allow it to restrict the abortion choice. Tribe (1990, 11–12) explains, "In the second trimester government has the power to regulate abortion only in ways designed to preserve and protect the woman's health. The Court wrote that this goal becomes compelling at the end of the first trimester because before that time abortion is less hazardous for the woman than childbirth." After the fetus becomes viable, the protection of fetal life is sufficient reason for the state to restrict abortion.

Outcome

Many believe that the Supreme Court's attempt to resolve the abortion controversy actually inflamed the debate by effectively disenfranchising those opposed to abortion. Since neither Congress nor the state legislatures could overturn the Court, it became impossible to address the core issue through conventional political channels. Instead, legislative action focused on relatively minor side issues, such as parental notification and public funding of abortion. The primary issue, the right to choose an abortion, was framed as an unassailable right—the right to privacy. This has forced abortion opponents to pursue the agonizingly slow process of changing the philosophical makeup of the Supreme Court. Given the likely futility of this effort, they have pursued other options, including efforts to discourage people from performing abortions through protests at abortion clinics, harassment of abortion providers and patients, and occasional acts of violence, including murder. Although some observers believe that abortion would never have become legalized without such a strong Supreme Court ruling, others believe that pursuing it through the political process would have resolved the issue without the uproar that *Roe v. Wade* has generated.

See also: Intractable Conflicts; Public Policy Conflicts; Value Conflicts.
References and Further Reading: Goggin, Malcolm, 1993, "Understanding the New Politics of Abortion"; Tribe, Laurence, 1990, *Abortion: The Clash of Absolutes.*

Rubin, Jeffrey

Jeffrey Rubin was one of the leading figures in the fields of negotiation and alternative dispute resolution (ADR) from the early 1980s until his untimely death in 1995 in a mountaineering accident. At the time of his death, Rubin was a senior fellow at the Program on Negotiation at Harvard Law School, where he directed the Project on the Psychological Processes of Negotiation. He also served as a professor of psychology at Tufts University and a

professor of diplomacy at the Fletcher School of Law and Diplomacy, also at Tufts.

Rubin contributed to the field of ADR in countless ways. He was the founding and acting editor of *Negotiation Journal* from its first issue in 1985 until his death. He was also a consulting editor for the Conflict Resolution book series published by Jossey-Bass of San Francisco.

In addition to writing innumerable journal articles, Rubin wrote or edited 14 books on conflict and negotiation, including *Social Conflict: Escalation, Stalemate and Settlement* (first edition with Dean Pruitt and second edition with Dean Pruitt and Sung Hee Kim); *Dynamics of Third Party Intervention: Kissinger in the Middle East; The Social Psychology of Bargaining and Negotiation* (with Bert Brown), and *When Families Fight: How to Handle Conflict with Those You Love,* which he wrote with his wife, Carol Milligan Rubin.

In addition, Rubin served as executive director of the Harvard Program on Negotiation from 1987 to 1991 and was president of the Society for the Psychological Study of Social Issues and of the International Society for Political Psychology. In 1988, he was faculty chair of the Salzburg, Austria, seminar in American studies. He was the incoming president of the International Association of Conflict Management at the time of his death.

In addition to his scholarly endeavors, Rubin was an avid mountaineer and had climbed mountains throughout the world. Seeking to climb the 100 highest peaks in New England, Rubin had already conquered 99. He was killed in an accident on 3 June 1995 while ascending the final peak—Fort Mountain in Maine—which would have fulfilled his goal.

See also: Negotiation Journal; Program on Negotiation at Harvard Law School.
References and Further Reading: Breslin, J. William, 1995–96, "Negotiation World Saddened by Loss of Jeffrey Rubin."

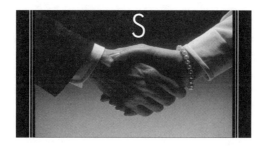

Sadat, Anwar

In the early 1970s, following Henry Kissinger's exercise of shuttle diplomacy between Egypt and Israel, Egyptian President Anwar Sadat shocked the Arab world by offering to meet personally with Israeli Prime Minister Menachem Begin at any place and any time. Begin accepted Sadat's offer, and the two met in Jerusalem. As a result of the initial Sadat-Begin meetings and the subsequent negotiations at Camp David in the United States (as the guests of President Jimmy Carter), peace agreements were negotiated between Egypt and Israel that allowed the return of Egyptian lands in exchange for Egypt's official recognition of Israel. As a result of these efforts, Sadat and Begin were awarded the Nobel Prize for Peace in 1978.

Sadat came to power upon Gamal Nasser's death in 1970 by receiving 90 percent of the vote in the Egyptian presidential election. As president, he reduced the power of the secret police and worked to expel Soviet military experts from Egypt. After meeting with Begin, Sadat's life was threatened by other Arab leaders, most notably Mu'ammar Gadhafi. Sadat was assassinated in October 1981 by Egyptian members of the Muslim Brotherhood, a fundamentalist group opposed to the peace with Israel. Nevertheless, the peace between Israel and Egypt endured.

See also: Camp David Accords (Israeli and Egyptian); Carter, Jimmy; Kissinger, Henry A.

References and Further Reading: Farrell, William, 1981, "Anwar el-Sadat, Daring Pioneer"; Israeli, Raphael, 1985, *Man of Defiance: A Political Biography of Anwar Sadat.*

Saving Face
See **Face Saving.**

School Conflict

Schools are a focal point of most communities, and as such, they tend to become a focal point for community conflicts. In addition to the myriad routine interpersonal disputes that occur between students, schools also tend to generate or reflect the racial, ethnic, class, and value conflicts of the communities they serve. As communities become more diverse, and as schools recruit students from varying backgrounds, more opportunities for conflict are created. This is due, in part, to different behavioral expectations and norms of different groups. It also reflects the tension between the need for some cultural assimilation versus the desire for racial, ethnic, and religious groups to retain their own behavior patterns, beliefs, and customs.

Funding also creates school conflicts. Few schools have as much money as they really need to offer the kind of education they would like or to generate the educational results that are expected of them. Parents clamor for more programs in all areas—sports, art, help for academically challenged and at-risk students, programs for gifted and talented students—while they also lament large class sizes, lack of individual attention, and poor student achievement. Yet in many districts, the electorate tends to vote against tax increases, thereby crippling the schools' ability to provide the services demanded. The result is cutthroat competition between interest groups and beleaguered school boards, administrators, and teachers, who make decisions that are constantly challenged. Ironically, such conflicts detract from the schools' ability to teach effectively, thereby contributing to the problems the disputants are trying to fix. Further, when disputes are settled in an unfair or dictatorial way, they tend to grow in intensity, not go away. This is true when school discipline is perceived to be heavy-handed and unfair. It also occurs when school boards impose decisions and rules that deny the interests or needs of major segments of a school community.

Nevertheless, some school disputes, especially those between students over trivial issues, are easy to resolve. Many schools have instituted peer mediation programs in which students are trained to serve as mediators to help other students resolve playground disputes (at the elementary level) or social disputes (at the secondary level). Evaluations of these programs have generally been positive; most seem to be an effective way for students to resolve their own conflicts without requiring adult intervention. In addition, they teach students skills in conflict resolution and problem solving that will last a lifetime.

Other school conflicts, especially those that reflect larger conflicts in the community, tend to be much more difficult to resolve. Conflicts over school philosophy and teaching approach (for instance, debates over new strategies versus "back-to-basics" approaches) and conflicts over spending choices or value differences (such as whether homosexuality should be taught or whether creationism should be taught

along with evolution) can tear schools and school boards apart. They can be settled temporarily, but the "losers" usually regroup, build support for their own constituency, and come back to challenge the adverse decision later.

Constructive approaches to these problems can be developed, however. The first step is to recognize that the school (or district) has a problem and to identify the nature and source of the conflict. The next step is to formulate a solution that involves all elements of the school community. A team at George Mason University recommends that schools use an inclusive problem-solving approach to do this. "Inclusive" means that all constituencies are involved—students, teachers, administrators, parents, community leaders, taxpayers. The problem-solving approach is one in which problems are identified without placing blame, then collaborative solutions that meet the needs of all affected parties are generated. "These processes . . . are powerful because they are broad, analytical, systematic and creative. You can use them to replace or supplement political processes which are too often blaming, superficial and not open to the full school community. A collaborative assessment and solution-generating process can get various groups' concerns on the table, minimize the danger of rumors and misinformation, build bridges of communication between people, and create new resources and generate options that all can accept" (ICAR 1994, 5).

See also: Collaborative Problem Solving; National Association for Mediation in Education; School Conflict Resolution Programs.

References and Further Reading: Burton, John, and Frank Dukes, 1990a, *Conflict: Practices in Management, Settlement and Resolution*, 165–74; ICAR, 1994, *Understanding Intergroup Conflict in Schools: Strategies and Resources.*

School Conflict Resolution Programs

Conflict resolution programs are becoming increasingly common in schools from the elementary level on up. Although little independent research has evaluated the effects of such programs, widespread anecdotal evidence suggests that these programs have significant benefits. According to the National Association for Mediation in Education (NAME), school mediation programs "decrease violence and fighting; reduce name-calling and put downs; decrease the number of suspensions; increase self-esteem and self-respect among peer mediators; enable teachers to deal more effectively with conflicts; and improve school climate" (NAME brochure).

The institution of conflict resolution programs in kindergarten through grade 12 began in the 1960s and 1970s, when interest in peace issues and conflict resolution processes was growing in many segments of U.S. society. Reflecting this new interest, some teachers began incorporating dispute resolution concepts into their lesson plans. At about the same time, law-related education was becoming an increasingly popular part of social studies curricula, and neighborhood justice centers were becoming more common methods of community dispute resolution. People from all three of these endeavors began to understand the importance of teaching young children better ways of resolving their conflicts.

More and more people—professional educators, conflict resolution specialists, and justice system representatives—now offer a wide variety of programs in elementary, middle, and high schools across the nation. These programs typically follow one of four models: the in-class model, the law-related education model, the schoolwide model, and the peer mediation model.

The in-class model provides conflict resolution training for students within a regular classroom setting. Curricula usually include discussion, experiential activities such as role-plays, and written assignments. The purpose is to teach basic conflict reso-

lution topics (such as separating the people from the problem, active listening, joint problem solving, seeking win-win solutions, and the like). When teachers are provided training, they can then model conflict resolution and problem-solving skills as classroom management techniques. This model can be used in one classroom only, in particular grades, or throughout the school. NAME and many other organizations have curricula available for all grades and even college.

The law-related education (LRE) model can also be implemented in an individual class or schoolwide. Its goal is to educate students about governmental structure and process, the justice system, and alternative methods of dispute resolution that are used in society. These programs are often taught by law-enforcement officers (or by a teacher-officer team), so a side effect is to improve relationships and understanding between youth and the local police. Some LRE programs include mediation training or services; others do not.

The schoolwide model trains selected students, teachers, and administrators as mediators. These trainees then provide mediation for conflicts that develop throughout the school between students, between students and teachers, and among teachers, staff, and administrators; they sometimes even mediate in disputes involving parents. Often this model is combined with the in-class model or the LRE model so that all students gain some familiarity with conflict resolution concepts, with a select group getting in-depth training and experience providing mediation services for the others.

School peer mediation programs are a subset of the broader schoolwide model. Here, selected students are trained to provide mediation for their peers, but the program is implemented in a more limited way than in the schoolwide model. Often schools contract with an outside training organization to train fifth or sixth graders to act as mediators on elementary school playgrounds; likewise, middle school and high school students are trained to provide mediation for their peers. The most successful programs train school employees and parents as well, so that everyone uses a common language and approach to conflict resolution. Even the more limited programs, however, seem to show significant positive effects if the teachers and administrators support them.

Teacher and administrator support and funding are two of the most critical issues facing school conflict resolution programs. Some teachers and administrators are reluctant to give up the time to teach such topics, feeling that they are less important than the ongoing lessons that already take up all the available time. Others feel threatened by such programs, fearing that they will lose control of the classroom or the school overall. Neither fear appears to be justified. Often, conflict resolution curricula can easily be blended into ongoing lessons (especially in social studies and language arts); in addition, effective classroom conflict resolution programs can save so much time by avoiding conflicts and discipline problems that the teachers actually end up with more time to teach the basics, not less. Also, most conflict resolution trainers stress that peer mediation is a supplement to, not a replacement of, the disciplinary authority of teachers. If implemented well, it does not usurp the teachers' or administrators' authority but removes unnecessary problems from their agenda, so that they can concentrate on the more important problems and issues as well as on teaching.

See also: School Conflict.

References and Further Reading: Burton, John, and Frank Dukes, 1990a, *Conflict: Practices in Management, Settlement and Resolution,* 165–74; Umbreit, Mark S., 1995, *Mediating Interpersonal Conflicts: A Pathway to Peace,* 65–86.

Scientific and Technical Disputes

Many environmental and public policy disputes involve scientific and technical issues that cannot be resolved without in-depth scientific analysis. For example, in a dispute about issuing a permit for a local industry to expand, disagreements might center around the health risks associated with a particular industrial process. A dispute over the construction of a new dam might center around the need for the water (which involves both the question of how much water is currently available and what future demands are likely to be) as well as the environmental, social, and economic impacts of converting a free-flowing stream into a reservoir.

These kinds of disputes cannot be resolved without expert analysis. In many cases, however, irreducible scientific uncertainties make it impossible even for scientists to completely resolve such questions. Often, though, scientists can agree to numbers within a certain range of uncertainty. If this range is relatively small, that information can be used to significantly increase the chances that a decision or action will have the desired results. For example, if people do not understand how a chemical threatens human health, it is unlikely that they will be able to mitigate its effects. If they outlaw its use entirely, they may lose a substantial benefit while avoiding only insignificant risk. Or if decision makers do not know how much water they currently have and do not have good forecasts of future needs, they might destroy a valuable free-flowing river ecosystem needlessly. Thus, it is critical that decision makers have accurate technical information on which to base their decisions.

Obtaining such information can be difficult, as science is often used for political purposes. In scientific and technical disputes, contending interest groups often obtain the services of partisan experts who conduct studies that show that the group's interpretation of the technical facts is correct. Sometimes these studies are valid; other times they are not. If the public and decision makers are not scientifically literate, they have no way of knowing which study is good and which is bad. The result is a standoff between contradictory experts. Decision makers—and the public—can get so exasperated with such debates that they ignore the technical evidence completely and rely on other factors (for instance, social, economic, or political interests) to make their decisions. Although these factors are important, in such cases, the potential benefits of fact-finding and technical analysis are completely lost.

This outcome can be avoided by using one of several data mediation or joint fact-finding processes in which the parties jointly design and carry out a research effort to find the answers to technical questions that are in dispute. This can be done in several ways. Each side may agree to accept the findings of an outside technical expert (or expert panel) that is chosen jointly. Or scientists from both sides may meet to critique one another's studies and to collaborate to reduce, as much as possible, any discrepancies among them. These approaches are most commonly used in conjunction with collaborative decision-making processes, although they can be used to support other, more traditional decision-making processes as well.

The key to making either process work is for all parties to have unrestricted access to the advice of technical experts they can trust as well as full access to relevant information. Often, some parties to a scientific dispute have access to data and high-quality expertise. Other parties (often environmental or public-interest groups) do not have such access. In order for collaborative decision making to work, it is important that groups without such access be given technical assistance grants or otherwise be helped to obtain the technical expertise they need to participate intelligently in technical debates.

In all public decision-making processes, it is also important that the public and all the active parties be given accurate summaries of technical findings written in language that is easy for lay (nontechnical) audiences to understand. In addition, parties and decision makers may need assistance in interpreting technically complex findings and in making sensible judgments about scientific uncertainties that still exist.

See also: Citizens' Radiation Monitoring Program; Environmental Conflicts; Fact-Based Disputes; Joint Fact-Finding; Montreal Protocol on Substances that Deplete the Ozone Layer; Neutral Expert Fact-Finding; Public Policy Conflicts.

References and Further Reading: Cormick, Gerald W., and Alana Knaster, 1986, "Mediation and Scientific Issues: Oil and Fishing Industries Negotiate"; O'Brien, David M., 1987, *What Is Due Process? Courts and Science-Policy Disputes;* Susskind, Lawrence, and Jeffrey Cruikshank, 1987, *Breaking the Impasse;* Tillet, Gregory, 1991, *Resolving Conflict: A Practical Approach*, 136–44.

Search for Common Ground

Search for Common Ground (SCG), founded in 1982, is an independent, non-profit, tax-exempt organization based in Washington, D.C. It uses citizen diplomacy to transform conflict into cooperation by helping adversaries work together to design workable solutions to divisive national and international problems.

Search for Common Ground believes that approaching global problems with an adversarial framework is inappropriate, because the problems are too complex and interconnected for the win-lose paradigm to work. For this reason, SCG sees its essential work as the stimulation of a new form of thinking and action that encourages a shift from the win-lose approach to a win-win approach. Recognizing that people and nations will always act to protect their own interests, SCG employs what it terms the "common ground approach," which draws on techniques of conflict resolution, negotiation, collaborative problem solving, and facilitation. The goal is to develop new approaches to problems that satisfy both sides' needs.

SCG focuses primarily on the public policy arena and societal problems. For instance, in the United States, the Common

Ground Network for Life and Choice works to open channels of communication and foster mutual understanding between pro-choice and pro-life advocates. Through facilitated dialogues, cooperative projects, and clearinghouse efforts, the Common Ground Network works to de-escalate the abortion controversy, bringing former foes together to pursue common goals.

Another program in Russia is using workshops, training programs, people exchanges, and TV production to de-escalate labor and ethnic conflicts. Similar projects are under way in the Middle East, Burundi, Macedonia, and South Africa.

Common Ground Productions is the television production division of SCG and has produced several notable PBS series and documentaries, all focusing on the concept of finding common ground and win-win solutions to apparently intractable, win-lose situations.

See also: Adversarial Approach; Common Ground; Win-Win, Win-Lose, and All-Lose Outcomes; Appendix 1 for contact information.

Security

Security means safety—of a person, a group, or a nation. At the individual level, it is a psychological state as well as a physical state. John Burton and other human needs theorists argue that security is one of several fundamental human needs the denial of which leads to deep-rooted and protracted conflict. A child threatened by a bully or a woman threatened by her abusive husband are two examples of situations in which security is absent and a protracted conflict is likely to develop.

Such threats are also common in the international system, where one nation threatens another, or one ethnic or racial group denies another group within the same country security, identity, or other fundamental human needs. This, too, leads to protracted conflicts, as evidenced by the conflicts between Israel and the Palestini-

ans, the Turks and the Greeks in Cyprus, the Catholics and the Protestants in Northern Ireland, and the Tutsis and the Hutus in Rwanda and Burundi.

In the international sphere, security has traditionally been defined in military terms, usually related to maintaining existing state boundaries. This definition became increasingly inadequate, however, as attempts to defend boundaries caused states to build up huge arsenals of weapons, which actually diminished, rather than increased, the security of their populations. (This was caused, in part, by the increasing threat of war by accident, if not by choice, as well as the drain that the arms buildup put on other aspects of the countries' economies, environments, and social structures.) It also neglected the security threats of internal strife between racial and ethnic groups.

Now, security is being more broadly defined to include military, economic, political, and social threats as well as threats to the health of a nation's citizens or its environment. This concept is often referred to as *comprehensive security*, as opposed to *military security*.

Another new term is *common security*. This term, which was coined by the Palme Commission in 1982, refers to the understanding that arms races and their concomitant mutual fear and suspicion do not add to security but detract from it. Common security thus refers to "a commitment to joint survival, to taking into account the legitimate security anxieties of others, and to working cooperatively in a number of ways to maximize the degree of interdependence between nations: in short, to achieve security with others, not against them" (Evans 1993, 15–16). Nevertheless, most discussions of common security maintain the military security, rather than the broader comprehensive security, focus. Attention is paid to the development of nonprovocative defense and military confidence-building measures, rather than broader social, economic, or political ties.

Another military approach to security is *collective security,* which calls on all members of a security community—such as the United Nations or a regional organization—to renounce the use of force against its own members and to guarantee that all members of the community will come to the aid of another if it is attacked either from the outside or from a defecting member of the security group. This idea was fundamental to the League of Nations as well as the United Nations (Boulding 1993; Burton 1990a).

See also: Arms Control and Disarmament; Collective Security; International Conflict; League of Nations; Needs; United Nations.

References and Further Reading: Boulding, Elise, 1993, "States, Boundaries, and Environmental Security"; Burton, John, 1990a, *Conflict: Human Needs Theory;* Evans, Gareth, 1993, *Cooperating for Peace: The Global Agenda for the 1990s and Beyond,* chap. 1.

Settlement
See **Conflict Resolution, Conflict Management, and Dispute Settlement.**

Settlement Conference

A settlement conference is held by a judge or other officer of a court before a trial for the purpose of exploring possible pretrial settlement of the case. Such conferences are authorized by the federal and state rules of civil procedure and are further encouraged by the Civil Justice Reform Act of 1990. This act urged federal judges to implement a variety of time- and cost-saving measures in their courts, including the early involvement of a judicial officer in planning the progress of a case. According to Christine Evans, who carried out an extensive review of the literature on settlement conferences in the United States, Canada, and Australia, the U.S. Civil Justice Reform Act's call for early judicial involvement is "perceived as an unqualified endorsement for an expanded use of settlement conferences and the most substan-

tial reform of federal trial court practice since the rules were first adopted" (Evans 1996).

A settlement conference may involve the participation of only attorneys representing the parties to the dispute, or it may involve the parties as well. Although a conference is not a trial, law and evidence relevant to the dispute are typically reviewed. In addition, possible solutions to the dispute are proposed and discussed. More than one conference may be needed to adequately address the dispute.

Although settlement judges are usually not trial judges or mediators, they are sometimes referred to as "mediators with clout." The clout that they have is their expertise as well as their connection to the court. This enables them to provide meaningful input regarding possible settlements and neutral advice about questions of law. Many judges use private caucuses and shuttle diplomacy as a way of managing communications between parties and moving the parties toward settlement. Although some judges are relatively low-key in this process, others are fairly aggressive. They may actually suggest a particular formula for settlement and then argue for its acceptance.

Although some lawyers object to this practice, Evans reports that most approve of judicial attempts at pretrial settlement. A judge commands respect that another mediator may not, and judges are able to address the strengths and weaknesses of a particular case more effectively than other potential interveners. Also, lawyers may hesitate to suggest discussing settlement for fear of appearing weak. However, they need not worry about such appearances if the settlement discussions are suggested by a judge.

Some lawyers have expressed concerns about judicial involvement in settlement conferences, including the possibility that judges might misuse their power in such circumstances, forcing settlements that are inappropriate. Others have suggested that judicial involvement can exacerbate power differences rather than balance them, and that judges may not be adequately prepared to act as mediators in the case.

Despite these concerns, however, settlement conferences are common. According to Evans, "the settlement conference remains the most common form of dispute resolution in the [U.S.] federal courts, with sixty nine courts explicitly authorizing judicial participation in settlement negotiations" (Evans 1996).

See also: Adjudication; Civil Justice Reform Act of 1990; Settlement Weeks.
References and Further Reading: Bundy, Stephen M., 1992, "The Policy in Favor of Settlement in an Adversary System"; Evans, Christine E., 1996, "The Pre-trial and Settlement Conference in Canada"; Fitzgibbon, Susan A., 1993, "Appellate Settlement Conference Programs: A Case Study"; Galanter, Marc, and Mia Cahill, 1994, "Most Cases Settle: Judicial Promotion and Regulation of Settlements"; Wall, James A., Jr., Lawrence F. Schiller, and Ronald J. Ebert, 1984, "Should Judges Grease the Slow Wheels of Justice? A Survey on the Effectiveness of Judicial Mediary Techniques."

Settlement Weeks

Settlement weeks are specially designated to encourage settlement of cases that have lingered on court dockets for a long time or are particularly suited to pretrial settlement. First used in Orange County, California, where they are part of the regular court calendar, settlement weeks are now held in many judicial districts throughout the country.

Usually the court recruits a large number of judges, officers of the court, and volunteer lawyers to act as mediators or neutral facilitators of settlement conferences scheduled during the settlement week. According to the American Bar Association Standing Committee on Dispute Resolution, 4,218 out of 10,248 cases (41 percent) that tried settlement conferences during settlement weeks held between January 1986 and December 1988 were indeed settled (American Bar Association 1989).

Thus, settlement conferences can limit court congestion and delay.

See also: Adjudication; Civil Justice Reform; Settlement Conference.
References and Further Reading: American Bar Association, Standing Committee on Dispute Resolution, 1989, *Dispute Resolution* 25; Burton, John, and Frank Dukes, 1990a, *Conflict: Practices in Management, Settlement and Resolution*, 97.

Sharp, Gene

Gene Sharp is a world-renowned scholar and advocate of pragmatic nonviolence. Best known for his book *The Politics of Nonviolent Action,* he describes what nonviolent action is, how it works, and how it can be used successfully to overcome social, political, or economic injustice.

Sharp observes that the exercise of power requires human cooperation and assistance. The withholding of this cooperation and assistance by sufficient numbers of people for a long enough time will strip the dominant group of its power. Thus, nonviolent action operates by destabilizing the power of the dominant group and empowering its victims. Sharp stresses that nonviolent action is, indeed, action, not simply pacifism or nonresistance.

Sharp describes three broad classes of nonviolent methods: nonviolent protest and persuasion, noncooperation, and nonviolent intervention. Nonviolent protest and persuasion involve the use of largely symbolic actions with the intention of changing the beliefs of the opponent. Noncooperation is the withdrawal or withholding of social, economic, or political cooperation with the dominant group. Nonviolent intervention may include obstruction or invasion. When successful, nonviolent action produces change through conversion, accommodation, or nonviolent coercion. Conversion occurs when an opponent changes his or her opinions or beliefs. Accommodation occurs when an opponent grants demands without changing his or her views. Nonviolent coercion achieves change against the opponent's will.

Although nonviolent action is not successful in all cases, Sharp argues that violence and war are not always successful either. Nonviolent action has at least as much potential for success as does violence, and it is much less costly. Thus, Sharp advocates its use over violence in almost all situations, although he does so for pragmatic, not philosophical or religious, reasons (such as those held by Tolstoy or Gandhi).

See also: Conversion; Gandhi, Mahatma; Nonviolence; Persuasion; Power; Tolstoy, Lev (Leo) Nikolayevich.
References and Further Reading: Holmes, Robert L., 1990, *Nonviolence in Theory and Practice;* Sharp, Gene, 1973, *The Politics of Nonviolent Action.*

Sibling Conflict

Conflict between siblings is unavoidable. No matter what style of discipline parents use, no matter what age or gender the children, rivalry and conflict between siblings cannot be avoided. It can, however, be controlled and handled in constructive, rather than destructive, ways. When this is done, sibling conflict can even be beneficial: it can teach children how to cooperate and share, how to solve problems in a collaborative way, and how to defend themselves and their interests against attack.

Adele Faber and Elaine Mazlish, authors of *Siblings without Rivalry,* give a number of suggestions on how parents can limit rivalry and conflict between their children: (1) Parents should acknowledge children's feelings about their siblings, even if they are negative, but they should stop hurtful actions. Children need to be allowed to be angry, but they must be taught how to direct and express that anger without hurting the target or escalating the conflict further. (2) Parents must refrain from comparing their children to one another. Each should be praised for his or her own accomplishments and disciplined (or just talked to) about his or her

errors. Children should not be told that they are better or worse than their siblings. (3) Children should not be treated equally, but rather uniquely. This means that each child should be given what he or she wants or needs, not necessarily exactly what the other child got. (4) Children should be encouraged to work through their own problems when possible. If conflicts are minor, let them work it out themselves. If they seem to be having trouble and the situation is heating up, Faber and Mazlish advise the parent to act as mediator, encouraging the children to express their interests and needs and to solve the problem in a collaborative way. Only if the situation is really dangerous should the parent intervene as an authority figure, separating the children and imposing the parent's solution.

Faber and Mazlish recommend using family meetings as a way of resolving frequent conflicts. This approach is also recommended by family therapists Betty Lou Bettner and Amy Lew, who believe that regular family meetings can not only solve sibling conflict but also help "nurture responsible, cooperative, caring, and happy children" who grow into responsible, caring, and capable adults.

None of these techniques eliminates all sibling conflict, however. They just make it more manageable and turn the conflict into a learning experience rather than a destructive and hurtful experience.

See also: Family Conflict.
References and Further Reading: Bettner, Betty Lou, and Amy Lew, 1992, *Raising Kids: Who Can;* Faber, Adele, and Elaine Mazlish, 1987, *Siblings without Rivalry.*

Simmel, Georg

Georg Simmel was a German sociologist who wrote in the late nineteenth and early twentieth centuries. Many of his works were not translated into English and have only recently been used by U.S. theorists and practitioners, but his key work on conflict, *Conflict and the Web of Group Affilia-*

tions, was translated by Kurt Wolff and Reinhard Bendix and published in 1956, the same year that Lewis Coser published *The Functions of Social Conflict,* which draws heavily on Simmel's theory of conflict. Since then, both Simmel and Coser have been considered the founders of modern social conflict theory.

Like Karl Marx, Simmel emphasized a dialectical approach to theory, stressing the importance of harmony and conflict, attraction and repulsion, and love and hate in all social relationships. Human relationships, he said, are always ambivalent. "An entirely harmonious group, Simmel argued, could not exist. . . . It would not partake of any kind of life process; it would be incapable of change and development" (Coser 1971, 184). Conflict is necessary to bind the group together, to allow it to adapt and change. "Conflict," according to Simmel, "can serve as an outlet for negative attitudes and feelings, making further relationships possible; it can also lead to a strengthening of the position of one or more parties to the relationship, thereby increasing the individual's dignity and self-esteem" (Coser 1971, 185). Thus Simmel, along with Marx and later Coser, emphasized the important role of conflict in all social groups. This suggests that conflict should not be feared or repressed but rather encouraged in controlled situations, so that tensions can be released and relationships adjusted as necessary to meet all the parties' interests and needs.

See also: Coser, Lewis; Marx, Karl.
References and Further Reading: Coser, Lewis A., 1956, *The Functions of Social Conflict;* Coser, Lewis A., 1971, *Masters of Sociological Thought: Ideas in Historical and Social Context;* Simmel, Georg, 1956, *Conflict and the Web of Group Affiliations.*

Single-Text Negotiating

Single-text negotiating strategies focus on one draft agreement that is repeatedly revised until all parties find it acceptable. After an initial period of issue identification, fact-finding, option generation, and evaluation, the first draft of an agreement is prepared by the mediator (or other neutral intermediary) or by one of the parties. All the disputants then review the draft agreement, indicating which provisions are acceptable and which are not. If a mediator is conducting the process, he or she listens to the critique and revises the draft accordingly. Sometimes, especially if the parties are negotiating without third-party assistance, the party or parties who object to certain provisions are asked to formulate an alternative draft or section thereof. The revised draft is then reviewed by all the parties, and this back-and-forth process continues until either an agreement is reached or an unbreakable stalemate is encountered.

The principal advantage of this approach is that it forces the parties to think about the problem in the same basic way. Also, as the draft goes through subsequent iterations, there is a tendency for parties to focus only on the issues that are most important to them. This often results in more flexibility on less important issues and increases the likelihood that the ultimate agreement will indeed meet all the parties' interests and needs. The multiple-text approach, in contrast, complicates the situation by approaching the problem from many different perspectives, with people often becoming overly attached to "their" drafts and less willing to accept the ideas of others.

The single-text strategy is especially important in multiparty situations. In environmental and public policy disputes, for instance, there can be 5, 10, or even 50 parties. If each party drafts an agreement and then the group as a whole—or even a mediator—tries to reconcile the different drafts, the task becomes almost impossible. Having an intermediary listen to the interests of all the parties and then fine-tune a draft agreement that he or she writes is often the only way to reach agreement among that many people.

The best-known example of the use of this technique is Jimmy Carter's mediation of the Israeli-Egyptian Accord at Camp David. During the 13-day negotiation, Anwar Sadat and Menachem Begin met only twice—once at the beginning and once at the end. During the rest of the time, Carter shuttled back and forth between Begin and Sadat, writing 23 draft agreements in the process. Eventually—with a lot of arm-twisting, hand-wringing, and implied threat—an agreement was signed and ratified by both parties.

See also: Camp David Accords (Israeli and Egyptian); Carter, Jimmy; Mediation; Negotiation.
References and Further Reading: Fisher, Roger, and William Ury, 1981, *Getting to Yes* (2nd ed. with Bruce Patton, 1991).

Society of Professionals in Dispute Resolution

The Society of Professionals in Dispute Resolution (SPIDR) is an international organization founded in 1972 to represent the interests of third-party neutral dispute resolvers and to enhance the capacity of parties in conflict to achieve rational and equitable solutions without violence or litigation. SPIDR is the only such organization to represent all types of third-party neutrals (mediators, arbitrators, conciliators, fact-finders, hearing officers, and trial examiners, among others) and all sectors of dispute resolution practice. Membership has grown from several hundred in the 1980s to over 3,000 in the late 1990s—a reflection of the growth of the field of dispute resolution itself.

SPIDR's mission is to: "1) enhance public understanding and acceptance of the dispute resolution process; 2) promote the structures through which dispute resolution services are provided; 3) enhance the professional skills of neutrals; 4) promote the development and application of improved dispute resolution methods; and 5) recruit, educate, and nurture a new genera-tion of dispute resolution professionals" (SPIDR 1995).

SPIDR fulfills this mission by providing networking and educational opportunities through annual, regional, and topical conferences. Its members receive the quarterly newsletter *SPIDR News,* published annual conference proceedings, and access to the SPIDR job line. SPIDR also publishes a number of special reports on topics of current interest that can be purchased by both members and nonmembers. One of its reports, "Ensuring Competence and Quality in Dispute Resolution Practice," followed a two-year collaborative effort by SPIDR's Commission on Qualifications. This report is a key statement on the highly controversial issue of accreditation and qualifications of neutral dispute resolvers.

See also: Mediator Qualifications, Certification, and Training.
References and Further Reading: Society of Professionals in Dispute Resolution, 1995, "SPIDR Conference Brochure"; Society of Professionals in Dispute Resolution, 1996, *Ensuring Competence and Quality in Dispute Resolution Practice.*

Sovereignty

Sovereignty is a legal and political concept that defines the nation-state. Sovereign nation-states are capable of entering into treaties and are subject to international law, but they are superior to municipal law. Technically, only sovereign states can wage war (although the concept of sovereignty is being changed as subnational ethnic groups are waging war as well). Nevertheless, sovereignty has been a major strategy for reducing the frequency and destructiveness of international conflict since the Treaty of Westphalia, which ended the Thirty Years' War in Europe in 1648. This treaty granted European kings the right to run their own internal affairs without interference from either other political rulers or the pope. The concept of sovereignty makes it illegitimate—even illegal, in the sense of international law—to intervene in the internal affairs of another country, even if that country is acting in a way that is abhorrent to another.

Respect for the sovereign rights of nations is guaranteed in the charter of the United Nations (UN), which has made it difficult for the UN to deal with the increasing number of conflicts that are now occurring within single nation-states (the UN was designed to deal only with conflicts between two or more sovereign entities). The protection of sovereignty also makes it hard for the UN or individual countries to intervene to stop human rights abuses, even though the UN has passed a variety of declarations and statements upholding the importance of universal human rights.

Increasing numbers of politicians, diplomats, legal scholars, and conflict resolution specialists are now suggesting that the fundamental concept of sovereignty and statehood needs to be changed to reflect the growing fragmentation of nation-states by ethnic groups. Also under consideration are alternative ways to intervene to prevent or limit human rights catastrophes such as those that occurred in the Balkans, Cambodia, and Rwanda.

See also: International Law; Peace of Westphalia.
References and Further Reading: Duke, Simon, 1994, "The State and Human Rights: Sovereignty v. Humanitarian Intervention"; Makinda, Samuel M., 1996, "Sovereignty and International Security: Challenges for the United Nations"; Wright, Quincy, 1965, *A Study of War.*

Special Master Mediation in Prisons

Prison overcrowding in the United States is a nationwide problem. In 1990, the federal system alone was 56 percent over capacity; many local prisons were even worse, and the situation has not improved significantly since that time. The result has been widespread conflict over sentencing, the siting and building of new prisons, prison conditions, and alternative mitigation options. In an effort to solve these problems, a number of courts have ap-

pointed special masters to act as mediators to resolve particular overcrowding problems. Special masters often conduct fact-finding to determine what the current situation really is and what options for remedy are available. They help the judges develop acceptable and effective solutions and help enforce those solutions once they are ordered.

One example of this process was the case of *Ruiz v. Estelle* in Texas. In the early 1980s, the state of Texas was sued because of its overcrowded prisons. It lost the suit, appealed the case, and, after losing that appeal, finally agreed to cap the state prison population at 95 percent of capacity (the other 5 percent is reserved for special uses). In order to accomplish this goal, however, Texas started to "dump" state prisoners in county jails. The problem was particularly acute in the Houston area. According to Kristin Dawkins, "Harris County conceded that conditions in its jails were unconstitutional and begged the federal court to put an end to the way the state was 'solving' its overcrowding problems at the county's expense" (Dawkins 1990, 9).

An appeals court ordered the federal judges in both the state and the county cases to work together. Each judge had already appointed a special master, who then got the parties together to try to resolve the situation. By brainstorming, they realized that they could move felons through the system faster by providing parole hearings in the county jails instead of waiting until the felons got to state prisons. This expedited the parole process, allowing more than 1,500 prisoners to be released, which significantly lessened the overcrowding problem. Since all the prisoners who were released were eligible for parole, there was no public alarm, as there has been in other cases in which dangerous felons have been released.

Special masters have been able to design and implement creative solutions to prison overcrowding in many other localities as well. They have developed a disciplinary system for a women's prison in New York and a plan to improve medical care in an Illinois prison. According to Dawkins, they have also worked to improve the conditions for prisoners in state, county, and local facilities across the nation.

See also: Special Masters and Magistrates.
References and Further Reading: Dawkins, Kristin, 1990, "Prison Overcrowding: Mediation in a Climate of Crisis"; Porter, Bruce, 1988, *Order by the Court: Special Masters in Corrections.*

Special Masters

Special masters are people appointed by a court to help manage complex cases. They may be used to organize evidence, manage pretrial discovery, or for other purposes. Federal court rules recommend that the appointment of masters be limited to exceptional circumstances, as the use of a master may actually increase court delays and costs.

Special masters have been used effectively to help achieve settlement in complex cases involving Superfund litigation, DES (a drug linked to cancer) litigation, and asbestos litigation. In class-action litigation relating to Agent Orange involving 2.4 million injured people and seven defendant companies, three special masters acting as mediators worked with the parties to reach a $180 million last-minute settlement that avoided what would undoubtedly have been a lengthy and costly trial.

See also: Settlement Conference.
References and Further Reading: Dauer, Edward A., 1994, *Manual of Dispute Resolution;* Goldberg, Stephen B., Eric D. Green, and Frank E. A. Sander, 1985, *Dispute Resolution,* 284; Longan, Patrick E., 1994, "Bureaucratic Justice Meets ADR: The Emerging Role for Magistrates as Mediators."

Stable Peace

Economist and peace researcher Kenneth Boulding coined the term *stable peace* to apply to a relationship between nations in which the "probability of war is so small that it does not really enter into the calculations of the people involved" (Boulding 1978b, 13). Stable peace does not require the resolution of all conflict between the contending countries; it simply requires that the parties recognize that the cost of resolving disputes through violent, military confrontations is much greater than any benefits likely to be received.

In his book *Stable Peace,* published in 1978, Boulding described a growing region of stable peace that began with the demilitarization of the U.S.-Canadian border and the end of hostilities between the Scandinavian states in the mid-1800s. It then spread to encompass a great triangle of the developed industrial democracies, reaching from Western Europe through North America to Japan, Australia, and New Zealand. Now we are witnessing efforts to expand this region to include the countries of the former Soviet Union and the Warsaw Pact.

Boulding compares stable peace with three other possible situations: unstable peace, unstable war, and stable war. Unstable peace is that which is brought about by mutual deterrence and threat. The Cold War was a prime example of unstable peace. The United States and the Soviet Union were not truly at war, but the threat of war remained constant, hence peace was unstable. Unstable war occurs when nations go to war but consider it to be an anomaly that will end soon. They do not see it as a way of life. In some difficult situations, war becomes the stable situation, not peace. This has been true in the Middle East since 1948. Until recently, the Palestinians and the Israelis saw themselves as being in a perpetual state of war, even when fighting was not actually occurring. War was seen as the norm; peace, when it occurred, was the anomaly. This is a difficult pattern to break, as social structures, economic structures, and even personal identities become tied up in the war mentality. Nevertheless, the human costs of war are so high that eventually, even in stable war situations, efforts are made to break out of the violent cycle and initiate a "peace spiral" to counter the escalation spiral that usually occurs.

See also: Boulding, Kenneth; International Conflict; Peace.
References and Further Reading: Boulding, Kenneth, 1978b, *Stable Peace.*

Stalemate

A stalemate is a point in a conflict where both sides realize that they cannot prevail, no matter how hard they try. For this reason, they do not try to escalate the conflict further, but they are unable or unwilling to negotiate a settlement either. They are stuck.

Dean Pruitt and Jeffrey Rubin, authors of a book on conflict escalation, stalemate, and settlement, list four reasons that stalemates occur. First is the failure of contentious tactics. "Contentious tactics that were used with some success in the past may begin to fail because they have lost their bite" (Pruitt and Rubin 1986, 127). This happens when too many threats have been made and the opposition no longer believes them, or when adversaries have been fighting for so long that each knows exactly how to counter the other.

A second source of stalemate is the exhaustion of resources: energy, money, or time. "Like two boxers, bloodied and weakened after many rounds of pounding each other against the ropes, the disputants in an escalating conflict simply run out of steam. There is no lack of determination to defeat the adversary. . . . But it just isn't possible" (Pruitt and Rubin 1986, 127).

Loss of social support—which may well result in the loss of people who are willing to fight—is a third reason for stalemate. If one's supporters or constituency aren't behind the fight, it cannot be sustained. The United States, for example, finally withdrew from the Vietnam War because public opposition to the war became too strong to allow U.S. participation to continue.

The last cause of stalemate is unacceptable cost. Often, conflicts have escalated so severely before a stalemate is reached that the parties are no longer willing to sacrifice or risk what has to be risked in order to continue. In the Cuban Missile Crisis, for example, the United States and the Soviet Union reached a stalemate in their nuclear confrontation when neither was willing to push the confrontation further, fearing that nuclear war was imminent.

The result of a stalemate is eventual de-escalation and settlement. Once the parties realize that they cannot win, and they find the current level of conflict too costly, they will work to reduce the level of conflict to a sustainable point, or they will work to settle it entirely.

See also: Cuban Missile Crisis; De-escalation; Escalation.
References and Further Reading: Pruitt, Dean G., and Jeffrey Z. Rubin, 1986, *Social Conflict.*

State Offices of Dispute Resolution

Many state governments now have offices of dispute resolution that design, develop, and implement dispute resolution systems in state government agencies and/or provide training in dispute resolution skills for government employees. Some offer mediation and facilitation services or provide lists of certified providers.

As is true in the federal government, the impetus for such programs is largely cost, efficiency, and quality of government services. So many agencies were wasting time and money in seemingly never-ending lawsuits that alternative dispute resolution (ADR) was seen as a less expensive and more effective way to make decisions that would satisfy all stakeholders.

According to the National Institute for Dispute Resolution, which funded many of these state offices initially, "state governments also see implementation of ADR programs as a way of showing an increasingly skeptical public that they can be innovative and consumer-responsive . . . with ever-shrinking resources" (Khor 1995b, 1). ADR also increases the quality of state agency decision making by increasing citizen participation in government decisions.

See also: Federal Use of Alternative Dispute Resolution; National Institute for Dispute Resolution.
References and Further Reading: Khor, Karen, 1995b, "Cost-Savings Propel Proliferation of States' Conflict-Resolution Programs: Disputants Range from Hindus in New Jersey to High-Plains Ranchers."

Stereotyping

Stereotyping is the process in which one assumes that an individual has a particular set of characteristics because of his or her membership in a group that is assumed (rightly or wrongly) to have those characteristics. Typical stereotypes of Americans, for instance, are that they are generous, friendly, and tolerant but also arrogant, impatient, and domineering. Asians are often seen as shrewd and alert but reserved, close-knit, and less open than others (Breslin 1991, 249).

When stereotypes are inaccurate and negative—as they often are between opposing groups—they can seriously inhibit effective conflict resolution. For instance, if one group assumes that all members of another group are violent, hostile, aggressive, and deceitful, it will be difficult for the two groups to cooperate to resolve their conflict. In order for conflict resolution efforts to be successful, members of both groups must get to know one another well enough that they can dismiss the negative stereotypes and replace them with a more accurate estimation of the other party's interests, concerns, and likely behaviors.

See also: Enemy Image; Misunderstandings.
References and Further Reading: Breslin, J. William, 1991, "Breaking away from Subtle Biases"; Tillet, Gregory, 1991, *Resolving Conflict: A Practical Approach.*

Strategic Arms Limitation Talks

Convened in the midst of the Cold War, the Strategic Arms Limitation Talks (SALT) were a first step in limiting the nuclear arms race between the United States and the Soviet Union. Talks were aimed at limiting both offensive and defensive nuclear arms. SALT I negotiations opened in 1969 and ultimately produced the Interim Agreement on Strategic Offensive Arms and the Anti-Ballistic Missile Treaty, which limited defensive systems.

The SALT negotiations were inspired in part by the Nuclear Non-Proliferation Treaty of 1968, which called on the superpowers to slow the nuclear arms race and negotiate arms limits. Talks were further prompted by the increasing deployment, in both countries, of antiballistic missile (ABM) nuclear defense systems. At the time, both the Soviets and the Americans were pursuing a theory of nuclear deterrence and mutual assured destruction (MAD). Sustaining peace and avoiding a devastating nuclear war depended on maintaining a strategic balance of forces between the two superpowers. It was thought that deployment of a national ABM defense system would give the nation that did so a strategic advantage and upset the delicate balance on which peace depended. Additionally, competition to develop nuclear defense systems further fueled the development and buildup of new offensive weapons. The use of multiple independently targetable reentry vehicles (MIRVs) would dramatically multiply the destructive capacity of existing missiles and promised to be an effective counter to the ABM defense systems.

Structure

The Strategic Arms Limitation Talks opened in Helsinki, Finland, in November 1969 under the Nixon administration. The U.S. and Soviet delegations negotiated directly. Although it was public knowledge that talks were being conducted, their content and progress were kept secret. During the course of the talks, front-channel negotiations were supplemented with high-level back-channel negotiations. The SALT I negotiations culminated with a Moscow summit meeting in May 1972, where Presidents Richard Nixon and Leonid Brezhnev signed the accords. Both treaties were ratified by the U.S. Congress with overwhelming support.

The SALT I Interim Agreement placed limits on land- and submarine-based offensive nuclear weapons and laid out detailed verification procedures. Under the SALT I ABM Treaty, the United States and the Soviet Union agreed not to deploy ABM systems for national defense, except in two sharply defined areas: one centering on the nations' capitals, the other protecting land-based intercontinental ballistic missile sites. However, the treaty limited the ABM systems that could be deployed in these areas. Extensive provisions for verification were included in this treaty.

Central Issues and Deliberative Procedure

Talks on offensive systems quickly deadlocked over differing interpretations of *strategic arms*. The Soviets viewed strategic arms as those capable of reaching the opposing party's territory. With this interpretation, intermediate-range Soviet missiles aimed at Europe would not be limited, but U.S. missiles based in Europe and aimed at the Soviet Union would. The United States defined strategic arms as those with an intercontinental range. Under this interpretation, neither European-based U.S. missiles nor intermediate-range Soviet missiles would be subject to limitation. The Soviets suggested deferring the issue of offensive nuclear arms and focusing instead on defensive systems. However, the Amer-

icans refused to separate offensive and defensive issues.

To resolve this deadlock, Henry Kissinger opened back-channel negotiations with Soviet official Anatoly Dobrynin. These back-channel negotiations succeeded in breaking the deadlock. It was agreed that talks would concentrate on achieving a permanent treaty limiting defensive systems and on reaching an interim agreement regarding offensive systems. Negotiations continued through both front and back channels up to the final summit meeting. Despite escalating violence in Vietnam, the Moscow summit proceeded on schedule, and on 26 May 1972, Nixon and Brezhnev signed both the ABM treaty and the interim agreement.

Outcome

John Newhouse (1989, 233) contends that the "historic essence" of the SALT I ABM treaty was that "each side surrendered any meaningful right to defend its society and territory against the other's nuclear weapons." The verification procedures laid out in the treaty have formed the basis for subsequent arms control. The greatest shortcoming of SALT I was its failure to address MIRVs. MIRV technology allowed for substantial increases in nuclear warhead delivery capability, despite the limits that the interim agreement placed on missiles and launchers.

SALT II commenced in 1972, with the goal of achieving a comprehensive treaty limiting offensive nuclear weapons. Negotiations were completed in 1979 under President Jimmy Carter, and Carter and Brezhnev signed the SALT II treaty at that time. However, in response to the Soviet invasion of Afghanistan, the U.S. Congress suspended the ratification process. In the absence of ratification, the treaty was not legally binding. Nevertheless, both sides stated their intentions to abide by the treaty's provisions.

President Ronald Reagan reopened discussion of strategic defense with his proposed Strategic Defense Initiative (SDI, or "Star Wars"). As a research program, SDI was not in immediate violation of the SALT I ABM treaty. However, its intent was completely opposite to the spirit of the ABM treaty. SDI was halted at the end of the Cold War (brought about by the breakup of the Soviet Union in 1991). The interests and issues at stake in nuclear arms control have now radically changed, with superpower nuclear disarmament and nonproliferation being the topics of greatest concern.

See also: Treaty on the Non-Proliferation of Nuclear Weapons.
References and Further Reading: National Academy of Sciences, 1985, *Nuclear Arms Control;* Newhouse, John, 1989, *War and Peace in the Nuclear Age.*

Structural Violence

The term *structural violence,* introduced by leading peace researcher Johan Galtung, refers to the situation in which an individual or group is unable to attain its full potential due to limitations in the social structure. These limitations might not be noticed; nor are they necessarily physically violent (most often they are not). Rather, the limitations are created by the systematic discrimination against particular groups of people—racial groups, ethnic groups, religious groups, or gender groups. When members of these groups are denied the privileges that the powerful group has, structural violence exists.

Although structural violence is clearly related to the concept of justice, it is also related to the definition of peace. Some argue that peace requires not only the absence of physical violence but also the absence of structural violence.

See also: Galtung, Johan; Justice; Peace; Violence.
References and Further Reading: Galtung, Johan, 1969, "Peace, Violence, and Peace Research."

Summary Jury Trial

A summary jury trial (SJT) is an alternative court process in which a jury issues a nonbinding, advisory verdict after contending parties present it with a synopsis of a case, including opening and closing arguments and a summary of the evidence. The purpose of this much simpler and less expensive court process is to encourage the negotiation of out-of-court settlements by providing the parties with an independent and reasonably accurate forecast of the likely results of a conventional trial. Following a SJT, there is a strong incentive for the parties to negotiate an agreement that closely parallels the advisory verdict, thereby substantially reducing their legal fees and other transaction costs, speeding resolution of the dispute, and limiting the damage to interpersonal and organizational relationships that usually accompanies litigation. If successful, the SJT has the added advantage of relieving some of the congestion in the court system. If the parties cannot reach a mutually agreeable settlement following a SJT, they are free to pursue their case through the regular court process.

Summary jury trials are presided over by a judge or magistrate, using real courtrooms and jurors from the regular jury pool (who may or may not know that their verdict is only advisory). The jury hears only a summary of the evidence, which may, but usually does not, include witness testimony. Since there is not enough time to subject witnesses to full direct examination and cross-examination, the process is often viewed as inappropriate for cases in which the credibility of witnesses is a key issue. After issuing its advisory verdict, the jury may be questioned by contending parties regarding the reasoning behind their decision. Regardless of the outcome of the SJT, proceedings and verdicts are not admissible in any subsequent trial. It is also possible to hold a SJT on only one part of a larger case.

Originally developed by Judge Thomas Lambros of the U.S. District Court in the Northern District of Ohio, SJTs are optional in some jurisdictions, required in others, and completely unavailable in some areas. There are also significant variations in the procedures used in different jurisdictions. The SJT has become highly controversial, as it is sometimes imposed on parties by the court against their will. Although they cannot be forced to settle on the basis of the SJT result, they are forced to reveal their case to the opponent—whom they may have preferred to surprise in a trial setting.

The SJT is only one of many strategies available that provide disputants with an early neutral evaluation of their case that they can use to decide whether to proceed with litigation. Since SJTs involve substantial preparation costs as well as the cost of the proceeding, some of these alternative processes should be considered as a way to get equivalent results at an earlier stage of the dispute and at a lower cost. The principal alternatives to SJTs include mini-trials, ex parte adjudication, advisory arbitration, early neutral evaluation, neutral fact-finding, and arbitration with appeal de novo (the right to appeal the decision to a court).

See also: Alternative Dispute Resolution; Mini-trial.
References and Further Reading: Dauer, Edward A., 1994, *Manual of Dispute Resolution;* Goldberg, Stephen B., Frank E. A. Sander, and Nancy H. Rogers, 1992, *Dispute Resolution: Negotiation, Mediation, and Other Processes;* Nolan-Haley, Jacqueline M., 1992, *Alternative Dispute Resolution in a Nutshell.*

Susskind, Lawrence

Lawrence Susskind is a mediation scholar, trainer, and highly acclaimed mediator who specializes in resolving complex public policy and environmental disputes. A founder of the Program on Negotiation at Harvard Law School, Susskind is also a professor of urban and environmental planning at the Massachusetts Institute of Technology.

Susskind has generated controversy in the field of dispute resolution by rejecting the ideal of mediator neutrality and promoting the idea of activist mediation. He believes that the mediator should become involved in the substance of the discussions as well as the process. When interviewed for *When Talk Works,* Susskind said of himself, "I'm not neutral with regard to the outcome. I'm nonpartisan" (Kolb and Associates 1994, 328). By this, he means that the mediator should not favor the interests of any one party over those of any other. However, the mediator should not remain neutral with regard to the quality of the negotiated outcome. Susskind explains, "I want an outcome that maximizes mutual gain, that does not leave joint gains unclaimed" (Kolb and Associates 1994, 329). Susskind also believes that the mediator should protect the interests of unrepresented parties—the children in divorce mediation or the public in public policy mediation. If the parties at the table come to an agreement that harms unrepresented parties, Susskind believes that the mediator has a responsibility to try to get the parties to remedy the situation.

To encourage quality outcomes, the mediator may need to take an activist role in other aspects of the process as well. In Susskind's view, it can be appropriate for the mediator to take an active role in "recruiting parties, in raising other issues, in asking about the issues, in providing skill building, in cross-examining parties about their alternatives, even in suggesting items to explore that no one has yet brought up" (Kolb and Associates 1994, 328). The mediator must also be sensitive to different levels of power among the parties. In Susskind's view, the mediator has a stake in producing quality outcomes. This stake justifies the mediator's active involvement in the discussions and means that the mediator bears some responsibility for the outcome.

See also: Mediator Impartiality and Neutrality; Program on Negotiation at Harvard Law School.
References and Further Reading: Kolb, Deborah M., and Associates, 1994, *When Talk Works: Profiles of Mediators;* Susskind, Lawrence, and Jeffrey Cruikshank, 1987, *Breaking the Impasse.*

Territorial Conflicts

Territorial conflicts arise out of competing claims to the same piece of land. Although the term generally applies to boundary disputes between nations and between settler societies and indigenous peoples, similar conflicts also arise within nations under the more common name *land-use conflicts*. These conflicts tend to be especially difficult to resolve, because they have a large, irreducible win-lose component. Since the amount of land is fixed, it is impossible for one party to acquire more land without someone else receiving less.

Territorial conflicts often arise because political boundaries differ from natural social boundaries. For example, many national boundaries, such as those established with the dissolution of the European colonies, have failed to honor racial, cultural, and ethnic differences. This has left many minority groups within one country seeking either independence or affiliation with another country that has more similar social characteristics. If the populations of a geographic area are relatively homogeneous, such boundary adjustments may substantially reduce the level of conflict. Dissolution of postcolonial India into mostly Islamic Pakistan and mostly Hindu India is one example. In other cases, contending groups may be so intermixed that the territorial division is extremely difficult, if not impossible. A territorial solution to the problems of Northern Ireland, for example, would require a neighborhood-by-neighborhood division into enclaves to be ruled by Protestant Great Britain or Catholic Ireland. In this case, it makes much more sense for the parties to find a way to live together.

Land-use conflicts within communities are also difficult to handle. They often involve NIMBY ("not in my backyard") or LULU ("locally unwanted land use") disputes. These conflicts are usually framed in a win-lose way: the landfill goes either one place or another—someone has to lose. Creative conflict resolution processes try to change apparently win-lose territorial conflicts into win-win situations by providing offsetting benefits for accepting undesirable land uses and/or insuring the mitigation of impacts.

See also: Environmental Conflicts; Ethnic and Racial Conflicts; NIMBY, LULU, and NOPE; Public Policy Conflicts.
References and Further Reading: Diehl, Paul F., and Gary Goertz, 1988, "Territorial Changes and Militarized Conflict"; DiMento, Joseph F., and LeRoy Graymer, 1991, *Confronting Regional Challenges: Approaches to LULUs, Growth, and Other Vexing Governance Problems;* Rothman, Jay, 1992, *Confrontation to Cooperation: Resolving Ethnic and Regional Conflict.*

Threats

Threats are a dispute resolution strategy in which parties attempt to force their opponents to comply with their demands by intimidating them. Sometimes threats contribute to social welfare by encouraging people to do the right thing. Drivers abide by the traffic laws partly because of the threat of fines and possible imprisonment;

students do their homework to avoid the consequences of revoked privileges; foreign powers do not threaten the United States' interests because of the threat of an overwhelming military response. However, threats can also serve more sinister purposes. Criminals can threaten their victims, militarily aggressive nations can threaten their neighbors, and employers can threaten those contemplating discrimination claims.

Although sometimes yielding a prompt response, threats do not always lead to an opponent's submission. According to Kenneth Boulding, threats can also lead to defiance, in which the threatened party calls the threatener's bluff. This forces the threatening party to either back down and lose credibility, or carry out the threat. Since threats are much cheaper to make than to carry out, defiance dramatically reduces the net benefit that the threatening party can expect to receive.

Another common response to threat is counterthreat, in which threatened parties make threats of their own. Although this approach sometimes produces a relatively peaceful standoff, it often results in a cycle of escalating threats in which contending sides continually try to prove that they are more powerful. This dynamic was the principal force behind the nuclear arms race between the United States and the Soviet Union. The same process also contributes to the escalation of less serious conflicts— for instance, conflicts between siblings or children on the playground. Although mutual threat can lead to "peace" through deterrence, the peace is highly unstable and is likely to break down. When this occurs, the conflict is likely to be severe and costly.

Threats also have the disadvantage of encouraging a backlash. Even if the opposition submits to a threat, people generally do not like being forced to do things against their will. They may comply out of expediency but are likely to try to increase their own power and plot a comeback as

soon as possible. Thus, victories gained through threat are much less stable than victories gained through negotiation or collaboration. They require constant vigilance to make sure that the threatened party continues to comply and makes no attempt to prevail at a later time.

See also: Deterrence; Escalation; Power.
References and Further Reading: Boulding, Kenneth, 1989, *Three Faces of Power;* Fisher, Roger, 1994, "In Theory Deter, Compel, or Negotiate?"

Tolstoy, Lev (Leo) Nikolayevich

Leo Tolstoy, a Russian novelist and social theorist, is considered one of the greatest authors of realistic fiction. His best-known works include *War and Peace* and *Anna Karenina.* In addition to being a great novelist, Tolstoy was one of the nineteenth century's leading advocates of nonviolence.

In the 1890s, Tolstoy experienced a religious epiphany that resulted in the three essays that most clearly express his religious views: "Christianity," "Pacifism," and "The Kingdom of God Is within You." Tolstoy's body of work may be seen as the antithesis of Machiavelli's *The Prince,* as it advocates nonviolence in response to aggression. Machiavelli recommended any tactics, even violent ones, to get and maintain power.

Tolstoy, an anarchist, advocated nonresistance to evil, believing that the fundamental law of the universe is love. He was an antimilitarist, however, not a pacifist, in that he believed that militarism serves only to keep subjects in submission and exploit their labor. The removal of patriotism, Tolstoy professed, would allow the common man to see war for what it is: evil militarism. Tolstoy further asserted that all states are based on the evil of violent force, and the resultant political and social institutions make happiness impossible. War, he believed, is the natural outcome of every political society.

Tolstoy's writings on nonviolence were admired by Mahatma Gandhi, with whom he corresponded.

See also: Gandhi, Mahatma; Machiavelli, Niccolo; Nonviolence.

References and Further Reading: Green, Martin Burgess, 1986, *The Origins of Nonviolence: Tolstoy and Gandhi in Their Historical Settings;* Wasiolek, Edward, 1985, *L. N. Tolstoy: Life, Work, and Criticism.*

Tort

A tort is a personal wrong or injury (other than breach of contract) for which a legal remedy can be sought through the courts. Using tort law, injured persons can seek damages for a variety of wrongs ranging from simple assault to medical malpractice to unreasonable acts that cause injury through defective products or exposure to toxic substances. Although many torts are remedied through formal court-based adjudication, such claims are increasingly being handled through alternative dispute resolution mechanisms such as conciliation, mediation, and arbitration.

See also: Adjudication; Arbitration; Conciliation; Mediation; Tort Reform.

References and Further Reading: Gifis, Steven H., 1991, *Law Dictionary;* Keeton, W. Page, 1984, *Prosser and Keeton on Torts.*

Tort Reform

Tort reform refers to a large number of proposed and actual changes in the way personal-injury cases (torts) are traditionally handled in the U.S. civil justice system. The pressure for reform has come primarily from insurance companies, businesses, and politicians, who charge that the current tort system is inefficient, ineffective, and unfair. Frivolous lawsuits bog down the system, critics contend. Some suits yield huge rewards for some plaintiffs, while other victims with similarly justifiable claims are denied any payment. Product liability and medical malpractice are often cited as particularly problematic. The threat of product liability claims increases insurance costs (and hence consumer costs) and prevents the development of new products, such as new contraceptives and vaccines. Similar complaints are made about malpractice, which has greatly increased the cost of malpractice insurance and therefore medical care overall.

A large number of reforms have been suggested—and many have actually been implemented—in various jurisdictions in an effort to curb these problems. One widely advocated approach is to place a limit on punitive and noneconomic damages. Punitive damages are those charged to a defendant in excess of the amount necessary to compensate the victim. They are intended to punish wrongdoing and to deter future misconduct on the part of the perpetrator and others. Noneconomic damages are damages for "pain and suffering" and "loss of companionship"—items that cannot be quantified and hence sometimes yield wildly high jury awards. By limiting (or forbidding) the payment of such damages, the number of multimillion-dollar awards is substantially reduced.

Other suggestions include the abolition of the rule of "joint and several liability," which means in layman's terms that when two or more parties are each partially at fault for an injury, all are liable for the full amount if, for some reason, the others cannot pay. This means that a party that is only 10 percent responsible for a person's injuries can be forced to cover 100 percent of the costs. Although instituted to make sure that somebody pays injured victims, this rule, many observers charge, has led to grossly unfair results. It has also resulted in "witch-hunts" for parties that may be only peripherally involved in a case but can be forced to bear some or all of the costs.

Another recommended reform is the elimination of the "collateral source rule," which stipulates that juries may not be told if a plaintiff's losses have already been compensated—by an insurance company, for instance. Another suggestion is to limit (or even prohibit) the contingency fees lawyers can charge clients in personal-injury cases. With the U.S. contingency fee system, lawyers work for a percentage—sometimes a substantial percentage—of their clients' awards. If they lose a case, they get nothing. If they win, they can get huge amounts. Some observers believe that contingency fees encourage lawyers to litigate almost anything, hoping that occasionally they will win big. If limits were placed on contingency fees, it is argued, lawyers would not take questionable cases, and juries would not have to award huge amounts to be sure that victims got all that they needed, even after paying the lawyers.

Consumer groups argue that most of these changes are not needed and could actually be harmful to victims, who need the current system for protection. Joint and several liability is important, they argue, to make sure that victims are compensated adequately. The same is true for nonmonetary damages, which, although hard to quantify, are very real. Punitive damages are necessary, they say, to deter future acts of negligence. Because these damages are not paid often, consumer advocates charge that they do not increase costs to society significantly but provide enough of a threat to keep most businesses honest. Finally, the contingency payment approach to personal injury, they argue, is necessary to enable the average person to be able to sue. If people had to pay their lawyers up front for such litigation, most could not afford to do so. In addition, it is argued, lawyers do not take frivolous cases, because they will probably lose and not get paid at all. Thus, contingency fees discourage frivolous cases rather than encourage them.

The issue of tort reform is highly controversial. Some see it as absolutely necessary to "save" the U.S. civil justice system, and others see it as a conspiracy by the insurance companies and unscrupulous businesses to "fleece" the American consumer.

Although such arguments continue unabated, many states have moved forward and have implemented at least some of these changes. According to the American Bar Association, tort reformers have scored significant victories in many states; however, the long-term mission is to get a significant tort-reform bill through Congress, as this is the only way to "bring uniformity to the patchwork structure of 50 different state tort systems" (Raef 1996).

See also: Civil Justice Reform; Discovery; Tort.
References and Further Reading: Abraham, Kenneth S., 1992, "What Is a Tort Claim? An Interpretation of Contemporary Tort Reform"; Daniels, Stephen, and Joanne Martin, 1995, *Civil Juries and the Politics of Reform;* Raef, Susan, 1996, "As Congress Struggles to Rewrite the Nation's Tort Laws, the States Already May Have Done the Job."

Track Two Preventive Diplomacy in the South China Sea

The ownership of the Spratly and Paracel Islands in the South China Sea has been contested for many years. The issues of concern involve both access to resources on these islands and control over sea lanes. Most of the friction has been between China and Vietnam; however, Taiwan, Malaysia, the Philippines, and Brunei have claims on the islands as well. Increasing military activities in the area have led to fears that the issue could escalate into war.

Since January 1990, Indonesia (which does not have any claims on these islands) and the Association of South East Asian Nations (ASEAN) have been sponsoring a series of unofficial workshops on this territorial dispute. Although the workshop participants have been official representatives of the countries involved, they have attended in "their private capacities" (Evans 1993, 7). International relations scholars and other experts have also been in attendance. The goal has been to "promote an informal exchange of views, without putting claimants into any position which could prejudice their respective claims of sovereignty" (Evans 1993, 77).

Although the workshops have not yet resolved the issue, they have established a forum and a framework for an ongoing dialogue, improved relationships between the disputants, and allowed for the exploration of various options that might allow joint resource exploration and economic gains for all sides. This has prevented the escalation of tensions and may lead to official resolution of the conflict in the future.

This case is a good example of what is called track two preventive diplomacy. The term *track two* refers to the fact that this is unofficial—the representatives are participating as individual citizens, not as official representatives of their respective countries. This means that the participants are free to raise new ideas, take risks, and say things that they might be prevented from saying in an official capacity. *Preventive diplomacy* refers to the fact that the negotiations or discussions are taking place before war has broken out, in an effort to prevent war from happening. The case is also a good example of what is called analytical problem solving. By having scholars as well as diplomats involved, the workshop encourages participants to analyze and address the conflict in new ways. By engaging in a cooperative dialogue and examining the underlying sources of the conflict, the participants may be able to create an innovative solution that would never have been found had traditional competitive processes been used to resolve the dispute.

See also: Diplomacy, Citizen, Track Two, and Multitrack; International Conflict; Problem Solving, Analytical.
References and Further Reading: Boutros-Ghali, Boutros, 1995, *An Agenda for Peace;* Burton, John, and Frank Dukes, 1990a, *Conflict: Practices in Management, Settlement and Resolution,* 139–42; Evans, Gareth, 1993, *Cooperating for Peace: The Global Agenda for the 1990s and Beyond;* McDonald, John W., Jr., and Diane B. Bendahmane, 1987, *Conflict Resolution: Track Two Diplomacy.*

Transformation

The term *transformation* is used by conflict theorists and practitioners in at least three ways. Some people refer to transforming conflicts, and others refer to the transformation of individuals or social structures.

Conflict theorists Louis Kriesberg, Terrell Northrup, and Stuart Thorson have written a number of books and articles that discuss the transformation of conflicts from ones that are highly resistant to resolution (i.e., intractable) to ones that can be resolved through traditional or alternative dispute resolution processes. Although many factors contribute to conflict transformation, those that are particularly important include a fundamental change in the relationship between parties (as might occur when conflicting ethnic groups agree to refrain from using violence against each other) and a fundamental change in the parties' mutual identities (for instance, when a dominant group recognizes the legitimate ethnic or national aspirations of a subordinate group) (Kriesberg, Northrup, and Thorson 1989). The concept of "ripeness" is also critical to this type of transformation. Conflicts are ripe for transformation once they reach a stalemate that is hurting all the parties more than it is helping them. Once all sides realize that victory cannot be won at an acceptable cost, the conflict is ripe for resolution (Kriesberg and Thorson 1991). This was one of the major factors that allowed the Dayton, Ohio, negotiations on Bosnia to succeed when earlier negotiations had failed.

A second group of theorists refers to transformation of social structures or societies. C. B. Harrington and S. E. Merry (1988), for instance, refer to transformation as the restructuring of social institutions to redistribute power from high-power groups to low-power groups. Societies, therefore, are transformed when fundamental social and political changes are made to correct inequities and injustice and to provide all groups with their fundamental human needs. According to the human needs theorists, such transformation is a prerequisite to effective and lasting conflict resolution (Burton 1990a).

Transformation is used by a third group of theorists to refer to changes in individual people. R. Baruch Bush and Joseph Folger advocate "transformative mediation," which is designed to bring about a change in the "consciousness and character of individual human beings" (Folger and Bush 1994, 24). When parties to a conflict are transformed, they are empowered to solve their own problems. This personal empowerment also encourages and allows disputants to recognize the legitimate needs, interests, and concerns of the opponent. Often, personal transformation leads to social transformation of the type referred to by Kriesberg and colleagues. The opposite, however, is not necessarily true, which is why changing laws does not necessarily change behavior. The slow transition to racial harmony after the dismantling of apartheid in South Africa is one of many examples of this problem.

See also: Intractable Conflicts; Mediation Models; Needs; Negotiation and Mediation, Timing and "Ripeness"; Stalemate.
References and Further Reading: Burton, John, 1990b, *Conflict: Resolution and Prevention;* Folger, Joseph P., and Robert A. Baruch Bush, 1994, *Promise of Mediation;* Harrington, C. B., and S. E. Merry, 1988, "Ideological Production: The Making of Community Mediation"; Kriesberg, Louis, Terrell A. Northrup, and Stuart J. Thorson, 1989, *Intractable Conflicts and Their Transformation;* Kriesberg, Louis, and Stuart J. Thorson, 1991, "Timing the De-escalation of International Conflicts."

Treaty on the Non-Proliferation of Nuclear Weapons

Nonproliferation treaties attempt to limit the spread of nuclear weapons. Such treaties are based on broad international agreement that the proliferation of nuclear arms would be contrary to all states' national security. Interest in establishing nonproliferation treaties was intensified by the Cuban Missile Crisis of 1962, which threatened to provoke outright war between the nuclear superpowers. In 1963, the United States, United Kingdom, and Soviet Union signed the Limited Test Ban Treaty, which addressed nonproliferation. This treaty was later joined by most of the states that had even the potential capacity to produce nuclear weapons. In 1967, Latin American states formed the Treaty for the Prohibition of Nuclear Weapons in Latin America. The Treaty on the Non-Proliferation of Nuclear Weapons, signed in 1968, was both broader in scope than the Latin American treaty and more explicitly directed toward nonproliferation than the Limited Test Ban Treaty. Although the majority of nations have accepted some form of nuclear control and restraint, some significant holdouts remain.

Structure
The 1968 Nonproliferation Treaty was the result of complex multinational negotiations occurring over several years. Signatories included both nuclear powers and nonnuclear states. Of the then existing nuclear powers, only France refused to join, though it acknowledged its intention to abide by the terms of the treaty. The treaty requires nonnuclear states to agree not to seek or acquire nuclear arms. Nuclear powers agree not to transfer nuclear arms to nonnuclear states or to encourage the development of nuclear weapons capability in those states. The treaty also includes commitments to cooperate in the research and development of peaceful uses of nuclear energy. All parties agree to accept elaborate international safeguards designed to verify that nuclear exports are not used for nuclear explosives programs.

Central Issues and Deliberative Procedure

When the United States was the only nuclear power, its approach to nonproliferation was based on denial. The 1946 MacMahon Act prohibited the U.S. export of nuclear materials, technology, or equipment. By the mid-1950s, four other nations had independently developed nuclear weapons, so the U.S. policy of denial was no longer an effective approach to nonproliferation. The United States then shifted toward a policy of constructive engagement. This meant that the United States would exchange assistance in the development of peaceful applications of nuclear power for commitments to renounce nuclear weapons from the recipient states. The choice between policies of denial and those of constructive engagement remains a central issue in nonproliferation policy.

A second issue is that of capacity versus intention. Should nonproliferation agreements emphasize the parties' intent to forswear nuclear arms, or should treaties seek to limit nations' capacity to produce nuclear weapons? Generally, the materials and capacities needed for a nuclear power program would also support a nuclear weapons program. Thus, an emphasis on limiting nuclear capacity would also limit states' ability to develop and use nuclear power.

Outcome

The 1968 Nonproliferation Treaty adopted a policy of constructive engagement, with an emphasis on states' intentions. In 1974, India, which was not a signatory to the treaty and previously had not been a nuclear state, detonated a nuclear bomb. India insisted that the device was detonated for peaceful purposes. India had used materials and technologies acquired from treaty nations under international safeguards. This incident and others prompted the principal nuclear suppliers to develop the Nuclear Supplier's Guidelines in 1976. The guidelines were an informal agreement that placed stricter restraints on the export of nuclear materials and facilities, particularly to nonparties to the nonproliferation treaty. Since the time of the treaty, there has been some general movement back toward policies of limited denial and toward a stricter scrutiny of nuclear capabilities.

See also: Arms Control and Disarmament.
References and Further Reading: National Academy of Sciences, 1985, *Nuclear Arms Control.*

Trust and Trust Building

When used in reference to dispute resolution, the term *trust* has a variety of meanings. First, it can mean a belief in the veracity of an opponent's statements or promises. Second, it can mean a belief that the opponent is sufficiently concerned about the other party that it will engage in cooperative negotiation or problem solving. Third, it can mean a belief in the fairness of the dispute resolution process itself. All three types of trust are important to successful negotiation, mediation, or cooperative problem solving, although each of these processes can start without such trust, and trust can be built over time as the process goes on.

Often, one or more of the parties involved in a dispute resolution process start out very suspicious of the other party or of the process itself. One of the mediator's (or other third party's) first jobs is to try to allay such fears. This is done by giving a careful explanation of the process and the ground rules for behavior and, as much as possible, allowing the parties to define the process themselves. (The more the parties participate in developing the process, the more they will trust it.) Mediators or facilitators also build trust by helping the parties state their problems clearly and in a nonaccusatory way, and by helping the parties work together as partners to solve a mutual problem instead of working as adversaries trying to defeat the other. Allowing parties time to hear each other's stories—their backgrounds, values, concerns, and fears as well as their interests and positions—also helps develop mutual understanding and trust. This can be done in the context of the formal negotiations, or it can be done in an introductory ice-breaking exercise. Having a meal together before negotiations begin or going through a joint powerful experience, such as an Outward Bound class, can help parties develop trust for the other that was lacking before.

Roger Fisher argues, however, that trust can be a trap. "Behaving in a way that makes oneself worthy of trust is highly useful and likely to be well rewarded. But the more one trusts the other side, the greater the incentive one provides for behavior that will prove such trust to have been misplaced," Fisher cautions. "Other things being equal, the less that an agreement depends on trust, the more likely it is to be implemented" (Fisher 1991, 124). To the extent possible, agreements should be self-enforcing, so that trust in the other side's honesty is not necessary to attain the basic outcomes agreed to in a settlement (e.g., payment of a debt, changes in behavior, distribution of property in a divorce). However, the greater the trust that is developed in the course of mediation or other conflict resolution processes, the better the long-term relationship between the parties is likely to be. This in itself is an important outcome of the process and is likely to diminish the chances that the parties will have similar problems in the future.

See also: Collaborative Problem Solving; Mediation; Principled Negotiation and *Getting to Yes;* Reconciliation.
References and Further Reading: Carpenter, Susan L., and W. J. D. Kennedy, 1988, *Managing Public Disputes;* Fisher, Roger, 1991, *Beyond YES;* Pruitt, Dean G., 1991, "Strategic Choice in Negotiation."

Truth and Reconciliation Commission, South Africa

South Africa made the negotiated transition to full democracy in 1993. Estab-

lished in 1995 by the National Unity and Reconciliation Act, the Truth and Reconciliation Commission fulfills the general promise of amnesty made by the African National Congress (ANC) during the negotiations that brought an end to white rule. The commission is charged with investigating political crimes from the apartheid era. Nobel Peace Prize recipient Desmond Tutu was appointed head of the commission, and his distinctive moral vision has shaped the commission's activities.

The Truth and Reconciliation Commission is made up of three committees: the Amnesty Committee, the Human Rights Violations Committee, and the Reparation and Rehabilitation Committee. The Amnesty Committee offers individuals civil and criminal amnesty for political crimes in exchange for their full and detailed confession. All politically motivated crimes committed between 1960, the year that the ANC was banned, and the signing of the agreements enacting majority rule in December 1993 are eligible for amnesty. Information from these confessions may be used to prosecute those who do not claim amnesty. This provides a powerful incentive for political criminals to come forward and confess.

The Human Rights Violations Committee investigates human rights violations and cases of political violence. As part of these investigations, the committee has held public hearings all over the country. Hearings are held almost daily, are televised, and are covered extensively by the media. Victims whose claims have been substantiated may tell their stories at these hearings.

The Reparation and Rehabilitation Committee assists victims in getting medical or psychological treatment, securing pensions, or educating their children. This committee is also able to recommend "some sort of recognition of hardship, say a scholarship or a health clinic named for the victim" (Rosenberg 1996, 91).

The goals of the Truth Commission are both pragmatic and idealistic. On a practical level, whites still hold substantial military and economic power. As Tutu has observed, "If there were not the possibility of amnesty, then the option of a military upheaval is a very real one." Moreover, much of the evidence needed to prosecute and convict apartheid-era political criminals would not be available in the absence of their confessions. Philosophically, the commission reflects the beliefs of its head, Desmond Tutu. Tutu rejects the notion of retributive justice. Instead, he says that "the justice we hope for is restorative of the dignity of the people" (Rosenberg 1996, 90). Justice is secured when the community is healed. According to Tutu, this restorative sense of justice has roots in both Christianity and the African concept of *ubuntu,* or interconnectedness. Such reconciliation is considered by many to be the ultimate goal of peace building. It allows the normalization of relations based on mutual forgiveness, acceptance, and trust. Leading peace builder John Paul Lederach describes reconciliation as "a meeting ground where trust and mercy have met, and where justice and peace have kissed" (McFarland 1995, 10).

The South African Truth and Reconciliation Commission is an excellent example of how this process can be implemented. The Amnesty Committee encourages the admission of truth and grants mercy; the Reparation and Rehabilitation Committee does what it can to bring justice; and the Human Rights Violations Committee brings victims a sense of peace by allowing them to be recognized and achieve closure of their pain. Altogether, the Truth and Reconciliation Commission has set up a structure that deals successfully with the remaining internal divisions within South Africa, making the long-term success of its new democracy more likely.

The actions of the Truth Commission have generated some controversy. The commission has heard testimony from victims of ANC violence, and Tutu has clashed with ANC members over his demand that the ANC formally acknowledge its own violations of human rights. Some South Africans perceive the Human Rights Violations Committee hearings as simply reopening old wounds and creating new bitterness. Others, especially those who have testified at the hearings, view them as a way of recovering their history, reasserting their dignity, and achieving recognition and closure. Nor does Tutu's conception of justice satisfy all South Africans. Rosenberg (1996, 92) observes that forgoing retribution "seems to be easier for policymakers or for those who have gone through the intense experience of testifying before Tutu's commission than it is for most ordinary black South Africans." There is popular support for the restoration of the death penalty and the prosecution of political criminals.

See also: Amnesty and Forgiveness; Mandela, Nelson; Tutu, Desmond.
References and Further Reading: McFarland, Daniel, 1995, "Consultation on Reconciliation: New Directions in Peacebuilding"; Rosenberg, Tina, 1996, "Recovering from Apartheid."

Tutu, Desmond

Desmond Tutu was a tireless critic of the South African policies of apartheid. Tutu was ordained as an Anglican priest in 1961 and became general secretary of the South African Council of Churches (SACC) in 1978. Under his leadership, the church establishment became more politically active in its opposition to apartheid. Tutu was awarded the Nobel Peace Prize in 1984 for his nonviolent struggle to achieve racial equality and end apartheid. He was elected archbishop of Cape Town and thus head of the Anglican Church in South Africa in 1986.

A charismatic speaker, Tutu emerged as a powerful moral voice opposing racial injustice and advocating nonviolent resistance. Both his opposition to apartheid and his commitment to nonviolence stem from his deep religious faith and his determined recognition that blacks and whites share a common humanity. Domestically, Tutu acted as negotiator and peacemaker during periods of unrest, with mixed success. Internationally, Tutu called for the Western nations to institute economic sanctions against the South African government as a form of nonviolent pressure.

Since the end of apartheid, Tutu has become the head of the Truth and Reconciliation Commission, which is charged with investigating apartheid-era political violence, offering reparation to victims, and dispensing amnesty for apartheid-era crimes in exchange for full confessions. The task of the commission, as Tutu sees it, is to encourage peaceful reconciliation and restore community.

See also: Ethnic and Racial Conflicts; Mandela, Nelson; Nonviolence; Reconciliation; Truth and Reconciliation Commission, South Africa.
References and Further Reading: Du Boulay, Shirley, 1988, *Tutu: Voice of the Voiceless;* Tutu, Desmond, 1984, *Hope and Suffering: Sermons and Speeches.*

Tyranny

Of all the ways of resolving human conflict, the most terrible are those based on tyranny, terror, and violence. There continue to be many societies in which tyran-nical governments maintain power and unjustly resolve conflicts by terrorizing opponents with a virtual monopoly on overwhelming physical violence. Such societies have included Joseph Stalin's Soviet Union, Adolf Hitler's Nazi Germany, South Africa's apartheid, the Chinese Cultural Revolution, and numerous colonial empires. Much of human history can be seen as a struggle against such tyrannies.

The challenge faced by proponents of democratic societies and the peaceful resolution of conflicts is to find effective ways of organizing opposition to such tyranny. Most often, subjugated people rely on force to overwhelm the tyrannical regime, but this method is fraught with danger, as the tyrannical government is almost always more powerful than the opposition. Often, nonviolent resistance is a better approach, though this too is dangerous. The more international pressure that a subjugated group can bring to bear on a tyrant—such as the sanctions against South Africa that eventually brought an end to apartheid—the more effective a campaign of nonviolent resistance is likely to be.

See also: Nonviolence.
References and Further Reading: Wehr, Paul, Heidi Burgess, and Guy Burgess, 1994, *Justice without Violence.*

Uniform Arbitration Act

The Uniform Arbitration Act of 1956 is a model act, intended to guide state arbitration legislation. The act was developed jointly by the American Bar Association and the National Conference of Commissioners on Uniform State Laws and is similar in content to the Federal Arbitration Act. Most states have since adopted state arbitration acts based on this model.

See also: Arbitration; Arbitration, Commercial; Federal Arbitration Act.

References and Further Reading: Dauer, Edward A., 1994, *Manual of Dispute Resolution*, vol. 2.

United Nations

The United Nations (UN) is an international organization of nation-states, formed at the end of World War II for the purposes of "maintaining international peace and security, . . . developing friendly relations among nations," and achieving international cooperation in solving "economic, social, cultural, and humanitarian" problems (UN Charter 1945). The UN is composed of six principal organs: the General Assembly, the Economic and Social Council, the International Court of Justice, the Security Council, the Trusteeship Council, and the Secretariat as well as many associated agencies and programs.

The General Assembly, made up of all UN member-states, is the main deliberative body of the UN. It meets annually and can discuss anything addressed by the UN Charter. However, it has no enforcement authority. Its resolutions are only recommendations, which are carried out by special agencies and programs established by the General Assembly (for example, the United Nations Development Program [UNDP] and the United Nations Children's Fund [UNICEF]) and by the members themselves when they are willing to abide by the General Assembly's recommendations on their own. The General Assembly may also make recommendations to the Security Council for enforcement action, but the Security Council is not obliged to agree. Although the Security Council is more powerful, the General Assembly has played an important role in a variety of peace-building missions. For example, it sent a civilian team to monitor human rights problems in Haiti and has sent election monitoring teams to Haiti and other countries.

The Economic and Social Council, which has 54 member-states, coordinates the economic and social activities of the UN. It oversees a number of specialized agencies, such as the World Health Organization (WHO), the United Nations Educational, Scientific, and Cultural Organization (UNESCO), and the Food and Agriculture Organization (FAO), which contribute to peace building by improving the economic and social status of member nation-states.

The International Court of Justice (ICJ) is the UN's principal judicial body. The ICJ hears cases referred to it by UN members, although the members decide themselves whether they will consider the court's decision binding. In addition to its adjudicatory role, the UN may seek advisory opinions from the ICJ. The ICJ has not been as heavily utilized as had been hoped. By 1990, it had issued only 21 advisory opinions, and just 57 states had accepted its jurisdiction without limitation. Others imposed conditions in agreeing to submit to its jurisdiction (Evans 1993, 27). Nevertheless, the ICJ has issued opinions when both disputants have requested that it do so and has played a significant role in resolving a number of international disputes.

The Trusteeship Council is largely inactive. Originally, it was responsible for supervising the territories placed under international trust at the end of World War II. Once these territories achieved independence or became parts of other states, its function was fulfilled.

The Secretariat is the administrative body of the UN. It is headed by the secretary-general, who is the UN's chief administrative officer and has wide-ranging political responsibilities and powers. He or she is expected to alert the Security Council to matters that "may threaten the maintenance of international peace and security" (UN Charter 1945). Several secretaries have also acted independently to help maintain international peace and justice. For example, U Thant personally intervened between the United States and the Soviet Union during the Cuban Missile Crisis in 1962, and Javier Perez de Cuellar helped negotiate the Iran-Iraq cease-fire in 1988. The secretary-general may also send representatives to provide good offices or mediation in hot spots around the world.

The Security Council is by far the most prominent organ of the UN, and its most influential. Unlike the General Assembly, the Security Council meets continuously. It is composed of five permanent members (the United States, Russia [formerly the Soviet Union], China, France, and Great Britain) and ten nonpermanent members (which each serve for two years).

The Security Council is the body that is primarily responsible for maintaining world peace and security. To do this, it tries to persuade both members and nonmembers to settle disputes through peaceful means and offers assistance in doing so. (Recommendations typically call for negotiation, inquiry, mediation, conciliation, arbitration, judicial settlement, or intervention by regional organizations such as the Organization of African Unity, the Organization of American States, or the Arab League.)

Unlike the General Assembly, which has no enforcement powers, the Security Council may enforce its recommendations with either nonmilitary pressure or military force. Nonmilitary options include economic, social, and/or political sanctions, and military actions may include blockades, the establishment of demilitarized zones or "safe havens," or full-scale military attack.

The Security Council's ability to act effectively has been limited, however, by its operating rules. In order to convince the five permanent members to participate in the UN and uphold the charter, Security Council rules were written to require decisions on nonprocedural matters to be approved by nine members—including all five permanent members. Thus, any of the permanent members can veto any action or recommendation with which it disagrees.

During the Cold War, this veto power prevented the effective utilization of the collective security system in any situation that involved one of the superpowers or their allies. According to Gareth Evans, between 1946 and 1990, 646 Security Council resolutions were passed, and vetoes were cast on 201 occasions. The inability to deal with matters that fell within the superpowers' sphere of influence greatly hampered the UN's credibility and its ability to maintain international peace and security (Evans 1993, 20–21).

The problematic nature of the veto power of the five permanent members has been greatly reduced since the end of the Cold War. Since then, the role of the Security Council, and thus the UN as a whole, has been in continual growth and evolution. The UN has been able to take a more proactive role in world conflicts, moving from limited peacekeeping operations to major efforts in peacekeeping, peacemaking, peace building, and preventive diplomacy. Although initial peacekeeping operations were limited to monitoring cease-fires and protecting borders, UN peacekeeping efforts now do much more. The UN provides security for or even runs elections, monitors police activities, investigates human rights violations, and conducts education programs on human rights issues. UN rehabilitation operations assist in the reconstruction of war-torn states through both long- and short-term social, political, and economic infrastructure projects. The return and resettlement of refugees are the goals of repatriation operations. Finally, administrative operations may control foreign affairs, national defense, public security, finance, and information in an attempt to create, sustain, and monitor a neutral political environment in which elections may take place.

Despite its improved effectiveness after the end of the Cold War, the UN still faces serious obstacles. Funding is a serious problem—the United States and many other nations have failed to pay their dues in full, crippling the UN's ability to provide services where needed. Political struggles between the General Assembly and the Security Council also cause problems, as many third-world members believe that the General Assembly should play a larger role in security matters. Finally, the UN has been criticized by many for having become too large, bureaucratic, and inefficient. Secretary-General Boutros Boutros-Ghali attempted to streamline the bureaucracy but was not sufficiently successful to win a second term due primarily to U.S. opposition. His successor, Kofi Annan, has pledged to continue the streamlining effort while expanding UN work in the areas of peacekeeping, economic development, and social justice.

See also: Cold War; Collective Security; Diplomacy, Preventive; League of Nations; Peace Building; Peacekeeping; Peacemaking.

References and Further Reading: Evans, Gareth, 1993, *Cooperating for Peace: The Global Agenda for the 1990s and Beyond;* United Nations, World Wide Web Home Page, http://www.un.org.

United Nations Institute for Disarmament Research

The United Nations Institute for Disarmament Research (UNIDIR) is an independent institution within the United Nations framework that was established in 1980 to provide the international community with credible, in-depth research on international security, the arms race, and disarmament issues. Current research topics include the evolution of collective security within the context of the United Nations; regional security studies, focusing especially on confidence building and arms control in the Middle East; and nonproliferation. In addition to carrying out research, UNIDIR promotes international participation in disarmament efforts and assists ongoing arms control and disarmament negotiations.

Since it has only a small core staff, most of UNIDIR's research is contracted out to outside experts. On occasion, UNIDIR forms multinational, multidisciplinary teams to undertake its research. It also runs a fellowship program that provides funds for scholars from developing countries to come to its headquarters in Geneva to conduct research. All the research is financed by voluntary contributions from states and from public and private organizations. However, the UN provides funds for the director and core UNIDIR staff (United Nations Institute for Disarmament Research 1996).

See also: Arms Control and Disarmament; Collective Security; United Nations.

References and Further Reading: United Nations Institute for Disarmament Research, 1996, *UNIDIR and Its Activities.*

United Nations Mediation of the Egyptian-Israeli Negotiations at Kilometer 101

In October 1973, Egypt and Israel were at war, as they had been intermittently since Israel's formation in 1948. For the first time, however, instead of being soundly defeated, Egypt believed that it had won the first four or five days of the war and that the war had ended in a stalemate. Although Israel did not agree, it acknowledged that the Arabs were a much more formidable force than they had been.

According to conflict theory, conflicts are most "ripe" for negotiation when the parties have reached a stalemate and the power of the disputants is relatively even. This was true in this case and likely contributed to the success of the negotiations.

Negotiation on disengagement and the separation of forces began right after the war, facilitated by the United Nations (UN). The negotiations were opened at a UN station at kilometer 101 on the Suez-Cairo desert road and continued there and elsewhere until concluding successfully in January 1974.

The talks were significant for several reasons. First, they were the first meaningful encounter between senior Egyptian and Israeli military officials after 25 years of continuing war (Jonah 1990). As such, the talks began to establish a new relationship between the two nations, which paved the way for Anwar Sadat's historic trip to Jerusalem and the Camp David negotiations that followed. Second, the disengagement agreement worked out during these talks provided a pattern for many subsequent disengagement plans and agreements on the separation of forces—in the Golan Heights and the Sinai, for example.

Central Issues and Deliberative Procedures

The talks occurred in five main phases, the first of which occurred at kilometer 101. Although Israel had traditionally insisted on direct negotiations, this time it was persuaded to accept indirect talks held under UN auspices. Initially, the central issue of these negotiations was Egypt's need to resupply its Third Army, which was cut off by Israeli forces. However, talks soon broadened to include other issues: the exchange of prisoners of war, the return to normal civilian life in the Suez Canal Zone, and the disengagement and withdrawal of forces. These topics dominated the subsequent phases of negotiation as well.

The second phase occurred in Washington, D.C., under U.S. Secretary of State Henry Kissinger. In addition to the resupply issue, these talks addressed Egypt's demand that the Israeli forces withdraw to the position they had held when the UN Security Council first issued its call for a cease-fire. It was during this phase that the ideas that would form the core of the final agreement were introduced.

The parties returned to kilometer 101 for the third phase of talks in November. Ideas introduced in the previous phase were formalized into a six-point agreement that was signed on 11 November 1973, and implementation negotiations were concluded. According to James Jonah, the assistant secretary-general of the UN Office of Research and the Collection of Information, "this was the most productive of the five phases and it witnessed a great deal of drama" (Jonah 1990, 58). The agreement signed in the UN tent at kilometer 101 was the first formal agreement between Israel and any Arab state since the armistice agreement in 1949 following the Israeli War of Independence. The parties also began a serious discussion of disengagement issues. By this time, Jonah reports, "the parties began to change the stereotypes they held of each other. Personal friendships began to develop, particularly between the leaders of each delegation" (Jonah 1990, 58). This kind of psychological change often marks a turning point in conflict transformation. Indeed, that theoretical notion appears to be validated in this case.

In December 1973, the United States and the Soviet Union convened and cochaired the Peace Conference on the Middle East. The fourth phase of military talks was subsequently held under conference auspices in Geneva. Both Israel and Egypt sent new delegations, although the UN negotiation team continued as before. At Israel's insistence, negotiations followed the kilometer 101 format and focused on reaching a disengagement agreement. Kissinger also participated in negotiations, focusing on political issues related to the return to normal civilian life in the Suez Canal Zone.

The final phase of the negotiations occurred back at kilometer 101, where the formal disengagement agreement was signed. Subsequent talks focused on implementing that agreement and succeeded in producing a timetable for disengagement.

Outcome

The UN's success as a third party to these talks rested on at least three factors. First, members of the UN's negotiating team were thoroughly familiar with the issues and history involved in the dispute. This helped them be more effective mediators than a less knowledgeable or less involved party might have been. Second, the UN used its ability to call on other member-states to exercise their power and influence on the disputing parties. The United States, for example, was asked to pressure both Egypt and

Israel at several points during the kilometer 101 talks. Third, in a clash over a UN checkpoint on the Suez-Cairo road, the UN peacekeeping forces stood up to Israeli military forces. By refusing to yield, the UN peacekeeping forces demonstrated their commitment to fulfilling the Security Council's instructions. Thus, they proved that they had some clout as mediators, although not the same kind as the superpowers had.

Analysis

Jonah concludes his reflections on this case by noting that recent diplomatic and military efforts of the UN have caused some people to question whether UN intervention as a third party is either appropriate or likely to be successful. This case suggests that it can be both, and this is even more likely now that the Security Council is not split by the standoff between the United States and the Soviet Union. In addition, Jonah suggests, the parties' awareness that the UN supports such efforts encourages parties to accept them, "however grudgingly" (Jonah 1990, 68). Although some negotiations seem to work best when a powerful nation-state, such as the United States, acts as a mediator, others work better when a less powerful nation or the UN does so. "A keen awareness" of the different abilities and disabilities of each kind of international mediation is essential to success, Jonah concludes (1990, 70).

See also: Camp David Accords (Israeli and Egyptian); International Conflict; Kissinger, Henry A.; Mediation, International.
References and Further Reading: Jonah, James O. C., 1990, "The Military Talks at Kilometer 101: The U.N.'s Effectiveness as a Third Party."

United States Bill of Rights

The Bill of Rights is the first ten amendments to the U.S. Constitution, which were adopted in 1791. These amendments protect fundamental human rights, including freedom of religion, speech, press, and assembly; the right to bear arms; the right to due process; and, when accused of a crime, the right to a speedy jury trial. The Bill of Rights also protects citizens against unreasonable searches and seizures and the confiscation of private property without just compensation.

The precedents for these rights came from three different English sources: the Magna Carta, the Petition of Right, and the Declaration of Rights. Although the U.S. Constitution was first drafted without the Bill of Rights, Virginia and Massachusetts had such rights in their own constitutions and insisted (along with Pennsylvania) that such a set of fundamental rights be included in the federal Constitution as well, if they were to ratify it.

Although the protection of individual rights is critical to the U.S. democratic system, the interpretation of what is and is not covered by the Bill of Rights has led to protracted controversy and conflict. According to Mary Ann Glendon, more and more conflicts are being argued on the basis of rights, rather than focusing on interests. At best, this throws the dispute into the adjudicatory system, as opposed to the voluntary dispute resolution system. At worst, it escalates and protracts conflicts, making them more difficult to resolve (Glendon 1991).

Several aspects of the Bill of Rights are particularly pertinent to the conflict resolution field. One is the right of free speech, protected by the First Amendment. Currently, a key dispute is whether "hate speech," speech that ferments conflict and sometimes violence, is a protected right. Another major question is whether alternative dispute resolution procedures such as mediation actually grant disputants due process. Some legal scholars argue that due process is available only through the traditional court system, which has elaborate rules of procedure and evidence—developed over hundreds of years—to protect individual rights and lead to fair decisions.

Many of these rules and procedures are abandoned in alternative dispute resolution processes. Although these processes may be faster and less expensive, some critics argue that they are a violation of the fundamental rights guaranteed by the Bill of Rights and therefore should be forbidden, or at least avoided by most disputants.

See also: Dispute Systems Design; Rights.
References and Further Reading: Fiss, Owen M., 1984, "Against Settlement"; Glendon, Mary Ann, 1991, *Rights Talk: The Impoverishment of Political Discourse.*

United States Institute of Peace

The United States Institute of Peace (USIP) was founded in 1984 as an independent, nonpartisan federal institution funded by Congress to strengthen the nation's capacity to promote the peaceful resolution of international conflict. It assists the executive branch and Congress as well as other organizations, with research analysis and information on issues regarding peace, conflict resolution, violence, and war. It is governed by a 15-member, bipartisan board of directors appointed by the president. Eleven members are drawn from outside the government, and four federal officials serve ex officio.

USIP's objectives are to (1) "mobilize the best national and international talent from research organizations, academia, and government to support policy makers by providing independent and creative assessments of how to deal with international conflict situations by political means"; (2) facilitate resolution of international disputes through citizen, or "track two," diplomacy; (3) "train international affairs professionals in conflict management and resolution techniques, mediation, and negotiating skills"; (4) "strengthen curricula and instruction, from high school through graduate education, about the changing character of international conflict and nonviolent approaches to managing international disputes"; and (5) "raise the level of student and public awareness about international conflicts and peacemaking efforts through grants, scholarships, publications, electronic outreach, and conferences" (USIP Web Site).

To accomplish these objectives, USIP undertakes research, holds conferences, awards fellowships and research grants, does training, and publishes books, monographs, and a newsletter called *Peace Watch*.

See also: Appendix 1 for contact information.

Ury, William

Coauthor with Roger Fisher and Bruce Patton of the best-selling book *Getting to Yes*, William Ury is one of the leading practitioners and scholars in the conflict resolution field. Ury is the associate director of the Program on Negotiation at Harvard Law School. His research focuses on negotiation, mediation, and crisis management.

Ury has served for many years as a mediator and arbitrator in the areas of labor, business, and international conflicts. Together with Jeanne Brett and Stephen Goldberg, he developed the concept of dispute systems design, described in *Getting Disputes Resolved*. Although initially developed for labor-management disputes, this approach to handling large numbers of similar disputes can be applied to many other types of conflicts as well.

Ury also wrote a sequel to *Getting to Yes* entitled *Getting Past No*, which examines how principled negotiation can be used with reluctant or even hostile opponents. In *Getting Past No*, Ury describes a supplemental approach called "breakthrough negotiation" to overcome impediments to principled negotiation.

See also: Dispute Systems Design; Fisher, Roger; Negotiation, Breakthrough; Principled Negotiation and *Getting to Yes*.

References and Further Reading: Fisher, Roger, and William Ury, 1981, *Getting to Yes* (2nd ed. with Bruce Patton, 1991); Ury, William, 1991, *Getting Past No: Negotiating with Difficult People;* Ury, William L., Jeanne M. Brett, and Stephen B. Goldberg, 1988a, *Getting Disputes Resolved: Designing Systems to Cut the Costs of Conflict.*

Value Conflicts

Values are ideas about how things ought to be, about how we differentiate good from bad, better from worse. We have values about family relationships (for instance, that women and men should share family decision-making responsibilities), about work relationships (for example, that deadlines are to be met, no matter what it takes), and about community issues (that open space should be preserved to provide habitat for nonhuman species). We develop our values from our families, friends, schools, religious upbringing, and other life experiences. Since everyone's life experiences are different, their values are likely to be different as well.

Because values are fundamental beliefs that help us make sense of the world, they are very hard to change. "Asking someone to adjust his values," Susan Carpenter and W. J. D. Kennedy explain, "is like asking him to alter his sense of reality" (1988, 198). For this reason, values cannot be negotiated the way interests can. People will negotiate over the price of a car or a house, over the details of a contract, or over the distribution of work in a family or business, but they will not negotiate their values—their concepts of right and wrong.

Although everyone has different values, those value differences do not have to result in conflict. They create conflict only when one person or group tries to impose its value system on another. When that is done, the result is usually a deep-rooted, protracted conflict that is difficult to resolve. Examples of such conflicts include the conflict over abortion in the United States, the conflict between liberals and conservatives regarding the treatment of the poor, and the conflict between fundamentalists and other religious groups over religion in the schools. These conflicts go to the very heart of Americans' value systems and are likely to be hotly disputed issues for years to come.

Value conflicts are additionally difficult to resolve because they are frequently characterized by differing perceptions about how a decision should be made. Not only do disputants "differ about what they want, believe or need, but they also lack shared criteria by which to adjudicate their differences" (Freeman, Littlejohn, and Pearce 1992, 312).

The result is conflicts that tend to persist and escalate. In addition, as Sally Freeman and colleagues point out, the communication in value conflicts (or moral conflicts, as they call them) tends to be impoverished. The moral positions expressed to opponents are usually "shallow, narrow and generally insufficient to reflect the honor that may indeed be felt by the holders of that morality," whereas "the rhetoric used to address one's supporters is usually much fuller, more complex and eloquent.... The parties may eventually say that there is no point in talking to the other side because it is too ignorant or irrational to understand. The result is a form of discourse that is characterized by chants, slogans, signs, song, and slurs rather than eloquent expression of rich moral orders" (Freeman, Littlejohn, and Pearce 1992, 316).

Although many dispute resolution procedures are effective for resolving interest-based conflicts (litigation, mediation, arbitration, or elections, for example), none of these is effective in the case of value conflicts. Such procedures may even exacerbate value conflicts; this occurred when the Supreme Court made a policy statement on abortion in *Roe v. Wade*. Rather than quieting the dispute about abortion, that judicial decision intensified the dispute, because it took the decision-making power away from the states and thus, apparently, away from the people. The response has been widespread civil disobedience and even murder of doctors and other health care providers associated with abortion clinics.

In most cases, value conflicts cannot be resolved—if *resolved* means "made to go away forever." They can, however, be managed in constructive ways. Effective approaches work to break down stereotypes and enhance communication and mutual understanding of differences. Methods that do this include analytical problem-solving workshops (such as those conducted by John Burton and Herbert Kelman), dialogue processes (such as those carried out by the Public Conversations Project), or the encouragement of what Freeman and colleagues call "transcendent eloquence"—a new, more eloquent form of communication that transcends typical rhetoric and diatribe and encourages the expression of one's own values without disparaging others' values. This type of communication is brought about in the National Issues Forums sponsored by the Kettering Foundation. Although they are run differently, each of these processes provides a tightly controlled structure that encourages participants to engage in a "new kind of conversation," as the Public

Conversations Project puts it, one in which people get to understand one another much more deeply than they could in other contexts. Although such understanding seldom changes people's values or even their positions on the key issues, it does allow them to view the debate in a new way, as they come to understand that honest, intelligent, even "good" people can actually have values (and hence positions) different from their own. This tends to increase people's tolerance of difference and to de-escalate conflicts, even if it doesn't lead to complete conflict resolution.

See also: Interests and Positions; Intractable Conflicts; Kettering Foundation and National Issues Forums; Problem Solving, Analytical; Public Conversations Project; *Roe v. Wade;* Stereotyping.

References and Further Reading: Becker, Carol, Laura Chasin, Richard Chasin, Margaret Herzig, and Sallyann Roth, 1992, "Fostering Dialogue on Abortion: A Report from the Public Conversations Project"; Burton, John, 1987, *Resolving Deep-Rooted Conflict: A Handbook;* Carpenter, Susan L., and W. J. D. Kennedy, 1988, *Managing Public Disputes;* Freeman, Sally A., Stephen W. Littlejohn, and W. Barnett Pearce, 1992, "Communication and Moral Conflict."

Venting Anger

When people get angry, they can do several things: they can keep their anger cooped up inside, they can let it out in a verbal or physical way, or they can direct the energy produced by the anger toward problem solving. Most conflict resolution professionals advise the latter course of action, realizing that problem solving is the way to address the situation that created the anger.

Many mediators believe that effective problem solving cannot occur until the anger is released. For this reason, some mediators allow disputants to "vent" their anger before trying to move forward into problem solving. Depending on the mediator's assessment of the likely response of the other party, the mediator has the disputant express his or her anger either in the presence of the other disputant or in a private session with the mediator.

The advantage of venting anger in the presence of the other party is that each party gains a better understanding of how upset and hurt the other is by the situation. The downside is that venting often leads to personal attacks, which may poison the atmosphere for further productive discussions. For this reason, some mediators allow the disputants to vent their anger only in private with the mediator (who can take it). Although this approach is less dangerous, it does not have the benefit of showing opponents the intense feelings of the other.

Further, venting may not diminish the venting party's anger as it is intended to do. Psychologist Gary Hankins argues that venting usually has the opposite effect: letting anger out isn't purging, but practicing. In his view, venting moves people further from reconciliation and understanding and hence further from constructive action (Hankins 1988). This issue is not yet resolved; however, essentially all conflict resolution professionals agree that when venting is used as a prelude to problem solving, it must be carefully limited and controlled by a third-party mediator or facilitator.

See also: Anger and Anger Management; Emotions in Conflict.
References and Further Reading: Hankins, Gary, 1988, *Prescription for Anger;* Moore, Christopher W., 1986, *The Mediation Process.*

number of approvals for the proposed activity. These approvals may include formal permits or the action of various legislative bodies. Generally, this approval process involves a public participation component, which provides a setting in which veto groups can actively oppose an action. Any approvals are also subject to court challenge. As a result, the hurdles required to secure approval for many projects and activities are high and numerous. This makes it relatively easy for veto groups to block projects; it is much harder for developers and innovators to get their projects approved. The result is a political system that tends to favor the status quo, whether it is good or bad.

Disgust with this pathology is leading to an increased interest in collaborative decision making and negotiated rulemaking as alternatives to adversarial interest-group politics. In collaborative decision making, groups work together to identify problems and potential solutions. Decisions are then made by consensus and are thus unaffected by the vetoes that commonly block decisions made through traditional administrative processes.

See also: Adversarial Approach; Collaborative Leadership; Collaborative Problem Solving; Environmental Conflicts; Interest Groups; Public Policy Conflicts.
References and Further Reading: Gray, Barbara, 1989, *Collaborating: Finding Common Ground for Multiparty Problems;* Larson, Carl E., and David D. Chrislip, 1994, *Collaborative Leadership.*

Veto Groups

Because of the structure of the U.S. political and legal system, public-interest groups have considerable power to block the initiatives of others, even though these "veto groups" may lack the power to gain approval for their own counterproposals. Under U.S. law, those proposing a broad range of actions (e.g., shopping center construction, expanded funding for child welfare programs, stricter workplace safety requirements, or establishment of a new national monument) must obtain a large

Victim Offender Mediation Association

The Victim Offender Mediation Association (VOMA; originally called the U.S. Association for Victim Offender Mediation) was created to facilitate networking between practitioners of victim-offender mediation and other interested people from the wider justice and conflict resolution communities.

The purposes of VOMA are to (1) implement a public information and education program about victim-offender mediation and reconciliation programs, (2) provide training materials on the topic, (3) encourage networking by holding international and regional conferences, (4) develop and disseminate guidelines for victim-offender mediation program management, and (5) act as a unified group to promote relevant legislation and influence public policies that enhance opportunities for restorative justice (VOMA brochure).

VOMA publishes a quarterly newsletter, *Victim Offender Mediation*. It also produces an annual directory of members and a job bank, available to members only.

See also: Reconciliation; Victim-Offender Reconciliation Programs; Appendix 1 for contact information.

Victim-Offender Reconciliation Programs

Victim-offender reconciliation was first developed in the 1970s to allow victims of crimes to meet with the offenders to work out some form of restitution for the victims and to achieve reconciliation between the victims and the offenders. Most programs are based on the first victim-offender reconciliation program (VORP), which was established in Elkhart, Indiana, by the Mennonite Central Committee and the Prisoner and Community Together (PACT) organization, both of which are still active in promoting and instituting such programs nationwide.

Typically, VORPs apply only to nonviolent misdemeanors and felonies. However, in some instances, the process has been applied to serious crimes. For example, the Genesee County Community Service and Victim Assistance Program has used VORP for criminally negligent homicide and sexual abuse (Larmer 1986). The rationale is that victims need to express their feelings, understand the event, and work toward closure, which they often cannot do in normal criminal proceedings. The widow of a man killed by a drunk driver affirms

these needs: "It was only at that moment when I was able to confront the man who killed my husband, to express my anger and to see the guilt he was experiencing that I was able to move beyond the bitterness that lay deep in my heart and move toward peace in my life again" (Umbreit 1987, 204).

Origins of VORP

Victim-offender reconciliation grew out of three concerns about the traditional criminal justice system. First was an increased concern for victims. Victims get very little attention within the traditional criminal justice system. They are typically ignored or even mistreated in an effort to bring the criminal to justice. When he or she is prevented from having a significant role in the offender's prosecution, the victim tends to be even more traumatized and feel even more helpless—emotions that were initially caused by the crime itself. Thus, rather than ameliorating these emotions in the victim, the traditional justice system typically makes them worse.

Second is the growing dissatisfaction with the efficacy of punishment as a response to crime. Traditionally, punishment is thought to serve three purposes: to deter others from engaging in criminal behavior, to remove the offender from society so that he or she cannot continue to engage in crime, and to rehabilitate the criminal. Study after study has shown that imprisonment—the most common form of punishment—accomplishes none of these goals. It does not deter crime, it does not rehabilitate criminals, and although it removes them from the streets for a while, it does so at extremely high costs and makes their return to criminal behavior upon release all the more likely. For these reasons, many observers believe that a system that stresses the admittance of guilt and restitution rather than punishment may actually reduce crime and help both criminals and victims more than the standard criminal system.

The third impetus for victim-offender reconciliation comes from the field of alternative dispute resolution. Over the last 20 years, we have come to understand the benefits of collaborative problem solving and mediation in many different conflict contexts. It makes sense that these benefits would apply to criminal problems as well.

Like many other forms of alternative dispute resolution, the use of VORP is growing nationwide. Although only a few programs existed in the late 1970s, as of 1995, there were 125 such programs in the United States, nearly 30 in Canada, and even more in Europe (Umbreit 1987, 136).

How VORP Works

The VORP process is highly variable. In all programs, however, victims and offenders meet face-to-face with a mediator (usually a trained volunteer) to allow the victim to express his or her feelings to the offender and to accept the offender's admission of guilt and (it is hoped) his or her apology. They then work out some way in which the offender can reimburse the victim for his or her loss. This can be done through a financial payment, through service to the victim (perhaps remedying the damage the offender caused), or through service to a third party (the offender might agree to perform a certain amount of community service, for example).

Although most of the VORP literature states that the process is voluntary, this is not always the case. Offenders are sometimes ordered by the court to participate, or they "choose" to participate because participation offers a way out of a prison sentence. Victim participation, however, is always voluntary.

The success of VORP is ambiguous. Many offenders and victims view it as ben-eficial. In one evaluation (Coates 1985), 83 percent of offenders and 59 percent of victims expressed satisfaction with the process; another 30 percent of the victims were "somewhat satisfied." Almost everyone said that they would participate in VORP again if given the choice. However, only one-third of those surveyed reported any positive change in attitude toward the other. (Of course, almost no change in attitude would be expected from a criminal trial.)

Problems tend to revolve around differing expectations. Although the stated goal is reconciliation, the victim's goal is more often obtaining recognition and restitution; the offender's goal is often avoiding a prison term or a harsh sentence. Since neither enter the process with reconciliation in mind, it is not surprising that it does not always occur. That reconciliation occurs as often as it does is a strong endorsement of the program.

See also: Apology; Criminal Justice; Mediation; Reconciliation.
References and Further Reading: Burton, John, and Frank Dukes, 1990a, *Conflict: Practices in Management, Settlement and Resolution;* Coates, Robert, 1985, "Victim Meets Offender: An Evaluation of Victim-Offender Reconciliation Programs"; Larmer, Brook, 1986, "After Crime, Reconciliation"; Umbreit, Mark, 1987, "Victim Offender Mediation and Judicial Leadership"; Umbreit, Mark S., 1995, *Mediating Interpersonal Conflicts: A Pathway to Peace.*

Violence

Violence generally means the intentional infliction of physical harm on another. Some definitions state that the harm must be done to people; others include physical harm to property as well. Still others include psychological harm as well as physical harm—the term *psychological violence* or *psychological abuse* is commonly used to refer to damage that is done to the mind rather than to the body.

Another dimension of violence is what Johan Galtung referred to as structural violence. Structural violence occurs when an individual or group is unable to attain its full potential due to limitations in the social structure—for example, due to widespread racial or ethnic discrimination. According to violence expert Ted Gurr, structural violence can lead to physical violence. This occurs when structural violence causes what he calls "relative deprivation," the sense that one is deprived of benefits given to other individuals or groups. The greater the sense of relative deprivation, Gurr observes, the greater the potential for collective violence, including political violence (Gurr 1970).

Physical violence is also a common result of uncontrolled conflict escalation. This can be prevented by controlling escalation, using many different conflict management or conflict resolution techniques; however, it is best accomplished before violence breaks out. Although conflicts can be resolved after violence has occurred, conflict resolution becomes much more difficult at that point.

See also: Crisis Management; De-escalation; Escalation; Galtung, Johan; Nonviolence; Structural Violence.
References and Further Reading: Gurr, Ted R., 1970, *Why Men Rebel;* Wehr, Paul, Heidi Burgess, and Guy Burgess, 1994, *Justice without Violence.*

Walesa, Lech

Gdansk electrician Lech Walesa was the leader of the Polish trade union Solidarity during labor struggles in the 1980s. As the union's lead negotiator, he pressed for direct dialogue with the Communist Party leadership of Poland. For his efforts toward securing human rights for Polish workers, Walesa received the Nobel Prize for Peace in 1983.

Walesa was notable because he was firm in his beliefs and in his commitment to human rights, yet he relied on negotiation and cooperation rather than violent opposition to the government to obtain his ends. The Nobel Committee honored Walesa as an "exponent of the active longing for peace and freedom which exist, in spite of unequal conditions, unconquered in all the peoples of the world" (Abrams 1988, 239). The Nobel Committee found Walesa to be both "an inspiration and an example."

Realizing that the Communist Party in Poland had to be careful lest it anger the Soviet Union, Walesa advised the members of Solidarity to maintain a moderate approach. Unlike other Solidarity members, Walesa recognized the legitimacy of the Polish Communist Party leadership and sought to work with them, not against them, as much as possible. Through his effective negotiating style, Walesa won the Communist Party's agreement to the right to strike, the right to organize workers without government control, and the right to free expression—all of which were un-precedented freedoms in Soviet-satellite states. He obtained the release of political prisoners as well.

When the government was slow to implement reforms, Solidarity extremists, in opposition to Walesa, called for a national referendum to test the legitimacy of the Communist Party and Poland's association with Moscow. Alarmed, Polish leader General Wojciech Jaruzelski proclaimed martial law, banned strikes, and arrested Walesa and other Solidarity leaders. From 1980 until the legalization of Solidarity in 1989, Walesa was either in prison or the subject of intense surveillance and harassment by the Communist Party.

After the collapse of the Soviet Union in 1989, Walesa forced the Communist Party into a coalition government with the newly legalized Solidarity. Many credit Walesa with a significant role in ending communist rule in Poland. In 1990, he ran for president against Jaruzelski. After a runoff election, Lech Walesa became the president of Poland in the country's first free general election.

See also: Cold War; Nonviolence.
References and Further Reading: Abrams, Irwin, 1988, *The Nobel Peace Prize and the Laureates: An Illustrated Bibliographical History, 1901–1987;* Eringer, Robert, 1982, *Strike for Freedom: The Story of Lech Walesa and Polish Solidarity.*

Wilson, Woodrow

Woodrow Wilson was president of the United States during World War I. He maintained the hundred-year U.S. position of strict neutrality through his first term of office and was reelected to a second term on the slogan "He Kept Us out of War." Unsuccessful in his attempts to end the war or to achieve Germany's recognition of U.S. neutrality, however, he asked for a declaration of war in April 1917 with the famous words, "The world must be made safe for democracy."

In January 1918, Wilson formulated a peace plan based on his Fourteen Points. These points essentially became the surrender terms and formed the basis for the Treaty of Versailles signed in Paris in 1919. The majority of the Fourteen Points pertained to territorial adjustments; most notable of the remainder were the twelfth and fourteenth. The twelfth point recognized the need for national self-determination, and the fourteenth aimed to establish a League of Nations, which was to use the notion of common security to prevent future wars from happening. This provision was adopted by the Allies and included in the Treaty of Versailles. However, despite Wilson's prominent role in forming the league, the U.S. Senate opposed the concept because it required member nations to enter conflicts on the side of any other league nation that was attacked. Thus league membership would have prevented the United States from remaining neutral, as it had tried to do for the past 100 years. For this reason, the Treaty of Versailles was never ratified by the Senate, and the United States never joined the League of Nations. (The United States did conclude a separate peace treaty with Germany in 1921.) President Wilson received the Nobel Peace Prize in 1920 for his efforts to establish the League of Nations.

See also: Collective Security; League of Nations.
References and Further Reading: Ambrosius, Lloyd, 1991, *Wilsonian Statecraft;* Buckingham, Peter H., 1990, *Woodrow Wilson: A Biography of His Times and Presidency.*

Win-Win, Win-Lose, and All-Lose Outcomes

The game theory terms *win-win, win-lose,* and *all-lose* describe possible outcomes of a two-party game or dispute. A win-win resolution leaves both parties feeling better off. Although winnings and losses can theoretically be measured on an absolute monetary scale, it is generally better to measure them against expectations. Wins result when the outcome is better than expected, and losses occur when the outcome is worse than expected. Since expectations and interests differ, calculation of winnings and losses differs from person to person. For example, some people might be more interested in job security than higher wages; others might have the reverse priority. Thus, a win for one person might be a loss for another, even though they received the same outcome. In calculating winnings, it is important to consider transactions costs in addition to the substantive outcome.

People can be expected to voluntarily accept dispute settlements only if they emerge as winners. This is why the goal of dispute resolution is often a win-win settlement. Conversely, the nonexistence of win-win opportunities constitutes one of the principal limits to successful negotiation.

In a win-lose game, it is impossible for the parties to get ahead without making another party worse off. Since win-lose settlements benefit only one party, they are unlikely to be adopted voluntarily. Win-lose disputes, therefore, tend to be resolved through legal, political, military, or other power contests, not through negotiation. (Negotiation may, however, be used to arrange the terms of surrender once the power contests have been decided.) One of the principal approaches to dispute resolution involves showing the parties how to reframe apparent win-lose situations in win-win ways. Instead of fighting over how to divide the "pie," the goal is to work together to enlarge the pie.

Many disputes involve both win-win and win-lose components. In these situations, it is possible to craft one or more agreements that benefit all parties. However, once all these agreements have been concluded, the game reverts to a win-lose mode in which the only way for a party to better his or her position is to take something from another party. This commonly occurs when parties work together to enlarge the pie but then must still divide it up. Although people generally assume that benefits of collaboration will be shared equally, this does not always occur. Sometimes people collaborate to enlarge the pie, but then one powerful party takes more than his or her share in the final distribution of winnings. In this case, a potentially win-win situation is turned into a win-lose situation.

All-lose conflicts arise in situations, such as budget-cutting negotiations, in which all parties emerge with a loss. Here, the key is to demonstrate to everyone that the losses are unavoidable and will be distributed fairly. If expectations are lowered, then negotiators can try to craft agreements that are win-win, at least when compared with expected losses.

See also: Bargaining, Integrative and Distributive; Zero-Sum, Positive-Sum, and Negative-Sum Games.
References and Further Reading: Ury, William, 1991, *Getting Past No: Negotiating with Difficult People;* Weiss, David S., 1996, *Beyond the Walls of Conflict: Mutual Gains Negotiating for Unions and Management.*

Workplace Conflict and Grievance Procedures

Disputes are ubiquitous in the workplace: disputes over performance, disciplinary actions, promotion or demotion, working conditions, hours, benefits, payment, and the like. Most moderate to large-sized organizations have some formal grievance procedures that are designed to be used to resolve such disputes. In unionized companies, the grievance procedures are almost always written into the collective bargaining agreement.

Typically, grievance procedures have a series of steps. The first step is usually for the person with the grievance to take the complaint to his or her immediate supervisor, where it is presented orally. In unionized companies, the complaint is usually presented to both the complainant's immediate supervisor and the shop steward (a representative of the union). At this stage, the three people jointly determine whether the employee has a legitimate grievance. If he or she does, the three can negotiate to resolve the problem at that point, or they can collect evidence to present at the next level of the grievance process.

The second stage of most grievance procedures is to submit the grievance in writing to a higher-level manager. This manager reviews the written evidence and usually hears an oral presentation of the facts. He or she then proposes a solution (which may or may not involve a compromise) or rejects the grievance, holding that management was right and the employee and union were wrong.

If the employee and the union representatives remain unsatisfied, they can continue the process through one or more steps of higher-level committees and hearings until they reach the final stage of almost all labor-management grievance procedures: binding arbitration. Few grievances are taken this far; it has been estimated that only 2 to 20 percent of complaints are actually arbitrated (Feuille and Kolb 1994). However, arbitration is the standard final approach for settling such workplace disputes.

This kind of grievance procedure tends to be highly formal and adversarial. Hence it is relatively slow, expensive, and threatening to both the complainant and the company. As a result, more and more companies are using procedures that rely more heavily on negotiation, mediation, and other integrative approaches to problem solving. Many companies now have ombudsman offices, for example, where employees can go for informal help in resolving workplace problems. Others use mediation in addition to or instead of binding arbitration, believing mediation to be quicker, less costly, and more supportive of interpersonal relationships than arbitration.

These less formal and less adversarial processes have been very successful. Evidence from several studies suggests that mediation is able to resolve 80 to 90 percent of the workplace disputes in which it is used. It costs only one-fifth to one-third as much as arbitration, and it results in far more win-win outcomes than does arbitration, which is structured to produce a win-lose result (Feuille and Kolb 1994). Nevertheless, mediation remains the exception rather than the rule in most workplace grievance procedures. It is not considered as reliable a process as arbitration (which has a much longer history), and parties are reluctant to use mediation when they want to prove that they are right and the other side is wrong.

See also: Arbitration, Labor; Labor-Management Relations and Conflict; Mediation; Ombudsman.

References and Further Reading: Feuille, P., and D. M. Kolb, 1994, "Waiting in the Wings: Mediation's Role in Grievance Resolution"; Leap, Terry L., 1995, *Collective Bargaining and Labor Relations;* Singer, Linda R., 1990, *Settling Disputes: Conflict Resolution in Business, Families, and the Legal System.*

Zero-Sum, Positive-Sum, and Negative-Sum Games

The term *zero-sum* refers to a conflict or dispute in which it is impossible for one party to advance its position without forcing another party to suffer a corresponding loss. Zero-sum conflicts frequently involve distributional issues in which a fixed quantity of resources must be divided among the parties. Since the size of the resource "pie" is limited, the only way for one party to get more is for another party to get less. (This assumes that the resource base is not large enough to satisfy everyone's wants.) Such conflicts are very divisive since, by definition, win-win solutions are impossible. For example, short-term budget-making processes are generally zero-sum, because there is a fixed amount of money that must be divided among competing needs. The more money one party gets, the less there is for another. Another common zero-sum conflict involves competition for social status and position. Since only one person can be elected mayor, serve as office manager, or be voted most valuable player, these situations are zero-sum as well.

The term was developed by game theorists and gets its name from the fact that for every possible outcome, the sum of the winnings and losses of all parties will be zero. By contrast, the term positive-sum refers to games or disputes in which the sum of winnings and losses can be greater than zero. This means that it is

possible to simultaneously advance the interests of all parties. This, in turn, makes win-win solutions a realistic possibility, although it is by no means guaranteed that the parties will be able to achieve it. (If one party greedily tries to take all the benefits of a cooperative activity, then a win-lose situation can persist.) The development of the skills needed to negotiate such win-win agreements is one of the principal objectives of the alternative dispute resolution movement.

In some cases, the existence of a positive-sum situation is relatively obvious. For example, partners in a new business enterprise are likely to recognize the potential advantages of pooling the resources needed to bring a new product to market. In other cases, hidden positive-sum opportunities can emerge from the reframing of an apparent zero-sum conflict in positive-sum ways. For example, parties to a dispute over scarce and fully committed water supplies in the arid western United States might initially view the situation as zero-sum, because newcomers can obtain additional water supplies only by taking water from someone else. This conflict can, however, be reframed in a positive-sum way by recognizing that it is not the physical amount of water that is important but rather the ability to do things that require water. Since much of the West's water supply is used inefficiently, it is possible for newcomers to get relatively low-cost water by purchasing water conservation equipment for existing water users and then buying the water that is saved.

Negative-sum conflicts involve situations in which the resource base is shrinking. This means that the only way a party can maintain (much less advance) its position is by taking something from another party. This produces competitive stresses that are similar to, but more severe than, the stresses associated with zero-sum conflicts. Examples of negative-sum conflicts are allocation of budget cuts within a department and the allocation of gasoline supplies in times of increasing shortage.

In *The Zero-Sum Society,* Lester Thurow argues that U.S. society devotes far too much effort to a competitive, zero-sum struggle to claim existing resources rather than to a cooperative, positive-sum effort to expand the wealth of society as a whole. This echoes the main theme of *Getting to Yes* and its progeny in the dispute resolution field: most conflicts that are considered to be negative-sum or zero-sum can actually be made positive-sum conflicts if the parties will engage in principled negotiation or collaborative problem solving rather than using more traditional competitive negotiating techniques.

See also: Collaborative Problem Solving; Game Theory; Principled Negotiation and *Getting to Yes;* Win-Win, Win-Lose, and All-Lose Outcomes.

References and Further Reading: Fisher, Roger, and William Ury, 1981, *Getting to Yes* (2nd ed. with Bruce Patton, 1991); Thurow, Lester C., 1980, *The Zero-Sum Society: Distribution and the Possibilities for Economic Change.*

Appendix 1

Conflict Resolution Organizations and Publications—Contact Information

Academy of Family Mediators
4 Militia Drive
Lexington, MA 02173
(617) 674-2663

The Alternative Newsletter
James B. Boskey
Seton Hall Law School
1 Newark Center
Newark, NJ 07102-5210
(201) 642-8811

American Arbitration Association
140 West 51st Street
New York, NY 10020-1203
(212) 484-4000

American Bar Association
750 North Lake Shore Drive
Chicago, IL 60611
(312) 988-5000

Association of American Law Schools
1201 Connecticut Avenue
Washington, DC 20036-1206
(202) 296-8851

Association of Family and Conciliation Courts
329 West Wilson Street
Madison, WI 53703-3612
(608) 251-4001

Canadian Law and Society Association
Université du Quebec à Montreal
C. P. 8888, succ. Centre-Ville
Montreal, Quebec H3L P38, Canada
(514) 987-7747

Carnegie Endowment for International Peace
2400 N Street, NW
Washington, DC 20037

(202) 862-7900

Carter Center
One Copenhill Avenue
Atlanta, GA 30307
(404) 420-5151

Children's Creative Response to Conflict
PO Box 271
Nyack, NY 10960
(914) 353-1796

Community Board of San Francisco
Community Board Program
1540 Market Street, Suite 490
San Francisco, CA 94102
(415) 552-1250

Community Relations Service
5550 Friendship Boulevard, Suite 330
Chevy Chase, MD 20815
(301) 492-5929

Conflict Resolution Center International
2205 East Carson Street
Pittsburgh, PA 15203-2107
(412) 481-5559

ConflictNet
Institute for Global Communications (IGC)
P.O. Box 29904
San Francisco, CA 94129-0904
(415) 561-6101

Consensus
See Program on Negotiation at Harvard Law
    School.

Consortium on Peace Research, Education, and
    Development
c/o Institute for Conflict Resolution

George Mason University
4400 University Drive
Fairfax, VA 22030-4444
(703) 993-2406

Council of Better Business Bureaus, Inc.
Alternative Dispute Resolution Division
4200 Wilson Boulevard, Suite 800
Arlington, VA 22203
(703) 247-9318

CPR Institute for Dispute Resolution
366 Madison Avenue
New York, NY 10017-3122
(212) 949-6490

Dispute Resolution Access
See Community Board of San Francisco.

Federal Mediation and Conciliation Service
U.S. Government
Office of Information
Washington, DC 20427
(202) 606-8080

Hewlett Foundation, William and Flora
525 Middlefield Road
Menlo Park, CA 94025-3495
(415) 329-1070

International Alert
1 Gyn Street
London SE11 5HT, UK
44-171-793-7975

International Association of Conflict Management
Tom Fiutak, Executive Officer
Conflict and Change Center
University of Minnesota
252 Humphrey Center
Hubert H. Humphrey Institute of Public Affairs
301 19th Ave. South
Minneapolis, MN 55455
(612) 625-3046

International Negotiation Network
Conflict Resolution Program
Carter Center
One Copenhill Avenue
Atlanta, GA 30307
(404) 420-5151

International Peace Research Association
Karlheinze Koppe
Beethovenallee 4
D53173 Bonn Germany

International Studies Association
324 Social Sciences Building
University of Arizona
Tucson, AZ 85721
(520) 621-7715

Journal of Conflict Resolution
See Sage Publications.

Kettering Foundation
200 Commons Road
Dayton, OH 45459-2799
(513) 434-7300

Law and Society Association
Hampshire House 33615
University of Massachusetts
Amherst, MA 01003-3615
(413) 545-4617

Mediation News
See Academy of Family Mediators.

Mediation Quarterly
See Academy of Family Mediators.

Mennonite Conciliation Service
21 South 12th Street
PO Box 500
Akron, PA 17501-0500
(717) 859-3889

National Association for Community Mediation
1726 M Street, NW, #500
Washington, DC 20036
(202) 467-6226

National Association for Mediation in Education
   (NAME)
1726 M Street, NW, Suite 500
Washington, DC 20036-4502
(202) 446-4764

National Association of Labor Management
   Committees
PO Box 819
Jamestown, NY 14702-0819
(800) 967-2687

National Conference of Peacemaking and Conflict
   Resolution (NCPCR)
Linda Barron, Executive Director
George Mason University
4400 University Drive
Fairfax, VA 22230-4444
(703) 934-5140

National Institute for Dispute Resolution
(NIDR)
1726 M Street, NW, Suite 500
Washington, DC 20036-4502
(202) 466-4764

National Labor Relations Board
1099 14th Street, NW
Washington, DC 20570
(202) 273-1000

National Peace Foundation
1835 K Street NW, Suite 610
Washington, DC 20006
(202) 223-1700

Negotiation Journal
See Program on Negotiation at Harvard Law
School.

The Network: Interaction for Conflict Resolution
Conrad Grebel College
Waterloo, Ontario N2L 3G6, Canada
(519) 885-0880

Peace and Change: A Journal of Peace Research
See Sage Publications.

Peace and Conflict: Journal of Peace Psychology
Lawrence Erlbaum Associates, Inc.
Journal Subscription Department
10 Industrial Ave.
Mahwah, NJ 07430-2262
(201) 236-9500

Peace Brigades International
2642 College Avenue
Berkeley, CA 94704
(510) 540-0749

Peace Studies Association
Drawer 105
Earlham College
Richmond, IN 47374-4095
(317) 983-1305

PeaceNet
3228 Sacramento Street
San Francisco, CA 94115-9907
(415) 923-0900

Program on Negotiation at Harvard Law School
513 Pound Hall
Cambridge, MA 02138
(617) 495-1684

Pugwash
11A Avenue de la Paix
1202 Geneva
Switzerland

Sage Publications
2455 Teller Road
Newbury Park, CA 91320
(805) 499-0721

Search for Common Ground
1601 Connecticut Avenue, NW, Suite 200
Washington, DC 20009
(202) 265-4300

Society of Professionals in Dispute Resolution
(SPIDR)
815 15th Street, NW, Suite 530
Washington, DC 20005
(202) 783-7277

United Nations Headquarters
Attention: Department of Public Information
New York, NY 10017
(212) 963-1234

United Nations Institute for Disarmament
Research (UNIDIR)
Palais des Nations
CH-1211 Geneva 10
Switzerland
(41.22) 917.31.86/917.42.54

United States Institute of Peace
1550 M Street, NW, Suite 700
Washington, DC 20005
(202) 429-3886

Victim Offender Mediation Association (VOMA)
St. Vincent de Paul Center
777 South Main Street, Suite 200
Orange, CA 92668
(714) 836-8100

Appendix 2

Conflict Resolution Conferences

Annual Conference—Academy of Family
  Mediators
Academy of Family Mediators
4 Militia Drive
Lexington, MA 02173
(617) 674-2663; fax (617) 674-2690

Annual Meeting—American Bar Association
American Bar Association
750 North Lake Shore Drive
Chicago, IL 60611
(312) 988-5000

Annual Conference—Association of Family and
  Conciliation Courts (AFCC)
AFCC
329 West Wilson Street
Madison, WI 53703-3612
(608) 251-4001

Annual Meeting—Canadian Law and Society
  Association
Université du Quebec à Montreal
C. P. 8888, succ. Centre-Ville
Montreal, Quebec H3L 3P8, Canada
(514) 987-7747

Annual Consortium on Peace Research Education
  and Development (COPRED) Conference
COPRED Headquarters
Institute for Conflict Analysis and Resolution
George Mason University
Fairfax, VA 22030-4444
(703) 993-2406; E-mail: bwein@gmu.edu

Annual Meeting—International Association of
  Conflict Management
Tom Fiutak, Executive Officer
Conflict and Change Center
University of Minnesota

252 Humphrey Center
Hubert H. Humphrey Institute of Public Affairs
301 19th Ave. South
Minneapolis, MN 55455
(612) 625-3046

General Conference—International Peace
  Research Association
John Synott, Program Director
Locked bag #2, Red Hill Post Office
Brisbane, Qld. 4059, Australia

Annual Meeting—International Studies
  Association
International Studies Association Headquarters
324 Social Sciences Building
University of Arizona
Tucson, AZ 85721
(520) 621-7715; fax (520) 621-5780;
  E-mail: isa@arizona.edu

Annual Meeting—Law and Society Association
Law and Society Association
Hampshire House 33615
University of Massachusetts
Amherst, MA 01003-3615
(413) 545-4617

Annual Meeting—National Association for
  Mediation in Education (NAME)
NAME
1726 M Street, NW, Suite 500
Washington, DC 20036-4502
(202) 446-4764

Biannual National Conference on Peacemaking
  and Conflict Resolution (NCPCR)
NCPCR
George Mason University
4400 University Drive
Fairfax, VA 22230-4444
(703) 934-5140

National Labor-Management Conference
Pam Gowland, Administrator
PO Box 27429
Washington, DC 20038

Annual Conference—The Network for Dispute
    Resolution
The Network
Conrad Grebel College
Waterloo, Ontario N2L 3G6, Canada

Annual Meeting—Society of Professionals in
    Dispute Resolution (SPIDR)

SPIDR National Office
815 15th Street, NW, Suite 530
Washington, DC 20005
(202) 783-7277

Annual International Meeting—Victim Offender
    Mediation Association (VOMA)
VOMA
St. Vincent de Paul Center
777 South Main Street, Suite 200
Orange, CA 92668
(714) 836-8100; E-mail: vorpoc@igc.apc.org

Appendix 3

Directories of Alternative Dispute Resolution Professionals

Academy of Family Mediators (makes referrals to local mediators)
Academy of Family Mediators
4 Militia Drive
Lexington, MA 02173
(617) 674-2663

Conflict Resolution Center International Resource Directory
Conflict Resolution Center International
2205 East Carson Street
Pittsburgh, PA 15203-2107

Consensus (has a good listing of environmental and public policy dispute resolution providers)
Program on Negotiation
Harvard Law School
513 Pound Hall
Cambridge, MA 02138
(617) 495-1684

GAMA's *Directory of Alternative Dispute Organizations and Professionals* (1995)
GAMA at http://www.gama.com/director.htm

Martindale-Hubbell Dispute Resolution Directory (New Providence, NJ: Martindale-Hubbell, 1994–) (includes over 45,000 dispute resolution practitioners)
Martindale-Hubbell
Advertising Sales Department
121 Chanlon Road
New Providence, NJ 07974

Martindale-Hubbell International Arbitration and Dispute Resolution Directory (1996)
Martindale-Hubbell
Advertising Sales Department
121 Chanlon Road
New Providence, NJ 07974

Society of Professionals in Dispute Resolution (SPIDR) *Annual Membership Directory*
SPIDR
815 15th Street, NW, Suite 530
Washington, DC 20005
(202) 783-7277

Appendix 4

Major Conflict Resolution Training Providers and University-Based Teaching Programs

National

ALI/ABA (American Law Institute/American Bar Association Committee on Continuing Professional Education), 4025 Chestnut Street Philadelphia, PA 19104-3099; (800) CLE-NEWS. Offers training in alternative dispute resolution.

American Arbitration Association, 140 West 51st Street, New York, NY 10020-1203; (212) 484-4000; fax (212) 765-4874. Contact: Toni Griffin. The association offers education and training programs worldwide.

James/Endispute, Inc. 73 Tremont Street, Boston, MA 02108; (617) 228-0200; fax (617) 868-8346. Contact: Eric Van Loon. The firm designs and provides training programs for public managers, consumer organizations, and business leaders. Endispute also has offices in New York, Washington, DC, Chicago, and San Francisco.

Mediation Institute of America, 7970 Southwest 86 Terrace, Miami, FL 33143-7025; (800) 659-1976. Contact: Martin I. Lipnack, President. The institute provides civil mediation training from one to five days in duration.

East

Consensus Building Institute (CBI), 131 Mount Auburn Street, Cambridge, MA 02138; (617) 492-1414; fax (617) 492-1919. Contact: Sarah McKearnan or Patrick Field. The institute provides training sessions for both public and private clients.

CPR Institute for Dispute Resolution, 366 Madison Avenue, New York, NY 10017-3122; (212) 949-6490. Contact: Panel Management Group. The institute offers a training service that customizes alternative

dispute resolution training to meet an organization's unique needs.

Interaction Associates, Inc., University Place, 124 Mount Auburn Street, Cambridge, MA 02138; (617) 354-2000. Contact: David Straus. The firm offers training and consulting.

Mennonite Conciliation Service, 21 South 12th Street, PO Box 500, Akron, PA 17501-0500; (717) 859-3889; fax (717) 859-3875. Offers training in conflict management and mediation.

Office of Dispute Settlement, Department of the Secretary of State Advocate, CN 850, 25 Market Street, Trenton, NJ 08625; (609) 292-1773; fax (609) 292-6292. Contact: Eric Max, Director. ODS provides sophisticated training programs to both the public and private sectors.

Program on Negotiation at Harvard Law School, Center for Management Research, 55 William Street, Wellesley, MA 02181; (617) 239-1111. The program offers training in negotiation.

South

Conflict Analysis and Transformation Program (CATP), Eastern Mennonite University, 1200 Park Road, Harrisonburg, VA 22801; (540) 432-4496; fax (540) 432-4449; E-mail zimmermr@emu.edu. Offers training in reconciliation.

West and Rocky Mountains

ADRA, Appropriate Dispute Resolution Applications, Inc., 399 Sherman Avenue, Suite 5, Palo Alto,

CA 94306-1839; (415) 328-2372; fax (415) 328-4049; Internet: ADRA@igc.apc.org. Contact: Nancy Yeend. ADRA trains mediators and provides private coaching.

CDR Associates, 100 Arapahoe Avenue, Suite 12, Boulder, CO 80302; (303) 442-7367 or 1-800-MEDI-ATE. Contacts: Mary Margaret Golten, Christopher Moor, Susan Wildau, or Bernard Mayer. The firm offers three- to five-day training programs in different spheres of mediation.

Confluence Northwest, 342 Union Station, 800 NW 6th Avenue, Portland, OR 97209; (503) 243-2663; fax (503) 243-3683. Contacts: Mary C. Forst and R. Elaine Hallmark.

Mediation Center, 440 East Broadway, Suite 340, Eugene, OR 97401; (541)345-1456 or (800) JDA-GREE; fax (541)345-4024; Internet: agree@conflict-net.org. Contact: James C. Melamed. The center offers mediation and conflict resolution training.

Western Network, 610 Don Gaspar Avenue, Santa Fe, NM 87501; (505) 982-9805; fax (505) 983-8812. Offers training in community leadership and problem solving.

University-Based Degree and Certificate Programs

Conflict Resolution Certificate Program
University of Phoenix
Center for Professional Education
Management Development Center
4615 East Elwood Street, 2nd floor
Phoenix, AZ 85040
(602) 921-0007

Masters Program in Negotiation and Conflict
  Management
California State University
Dominquez Hills Campus
1000 East Victoria Street
Carson, CA 90731
(310) 516-3435
E-mail: dewilliams@dhvx20.csudh.edu

Institute for Dispute Resolution
Pepperdine University Law School (graduate certificate and master's degree)
Malibu, CA 90265
(310) 456-4655

Center on Conflict and Negotiation
Stanford University Crown Quadrangle
Stanford, CA 94305
(415) 723-2696

Institute on Global Conflict and Cooperation
University of California (all campuses)
9500 Gilman Drive
La Jolla, CA 92093
(619) 534-3352

Peace/War and Global Studies
California Institute of Integral Studies
765 Ashbury Street
San Francisco, CA 94117
(415) 753-6100

Center for Peacemaking and Conflict Studies
Fresno Pacific University
1717 South Chestnut Avenue
Fresno, CA 93702
(209) 455-5847; fax (209) 252-4800; Web:
  http://www.fresno.edu/pacs

ADR Certificate Program
University of Denver
2000 South Gaylord Way
Denver, CO 80208-0295
(303) 871-3217

Graduate School of International Studies
University of Denver
School of International Studies
Denver, CO 80208
(303) 871-2989 ext. 2539

Peace and Conflict Resolution Studies
American University
School of International Service
Washington, DC 20016
(202) 855-1622

Mediation Institute
Nova Southeastern University (graduate certificate, master's, and Ph.D.)
School of Social and Systemic Studies
3301 College Avenue
Fort Lauderdale, FL 33314
(800) 541-6682 ext. 5708
E-mail: warters@alpha.acast.nova.edu

Conflict Resolution Program
Carter Center
Emory University
One Copenhill Avenue
Atlanta, GA 30307
(404) 420-5151

Program on Conflict Resolution
University of Hawaii (master's degree in conflict
    resolution, mediation, and peacemaking)
Department of Political Science
242 Maile Way, 717 Porteus
Honolulu, HI 96822
(808) 956-8984

Dispute Resolution Certificate Program
Boise State University, Continuing Education
1910 University Drive, L-104
Boise, ID 83725
(800) 632-6586 ext. 1709 (in Idaho); (800) 824-7017
    ext. 1709 (outside Idaho)

Martin Institute for Peace Studies and Conflict
    Resolution
University of Idaho, I01-X001
Moscow, ID 83843
(208) 885-6527

Peace Studies Program
Associated Mennonite Biblical Seminaries
3003 Benham Avenue
Elkhart, IN 46514
(219) 295-3726

Institute for Peace Studies
University of Notre Dame
PO Box 639
Notre Dame, IN 46556
(219) 239-2970

Loyola College (certificates in conflict resolution
    and prevention of youth violence)
4501 North Charles Street
Baltimore, MD 21210
(410) 617-2000

Peace and World Security Studies (PAWSS)
Hampshire College
West Street
Amherst, MA 01002
(413) 582-5521

Program on Negotiation
513 Pound Hall
Harvard Law School
Cambridge, MA 02138
(617) 495-1684

Defense and Arms Control Studies Program
Massachusetts Institute of Technology
Center for International Studies
#E38-634

Cambridge, MA 02139
(617) 253-7281

Social Economy and Social Justice
Boston College
Department of Sociology
McGwin Hall 426
Chestnut Hill, MA 02167
(617) 552-4130

Peaceable Schools Center
Lesley College
154 Auburn Street
Cambridge, MA 02139
(617) 349-8405

Degree Program in Dispute Resolution
University of Massachusetts, Boston
100 Morrissey Boulevard
Boston, MA 02125-3393
(617) 287-7421
E-mail: krajewski@umbsky.cc.umb.edu

Peace and Conflict Studies
Wayne State University
5229 Cass Avenue, Room 101
Detroit, MI 48202
(313) 577-3453

Dispute Resolution Institute
Hamline University Law School
1536 Hewitt Avenue
St. Paul, MN 55104-1284
(612) 641-2068

Conflict and Change Center
University of Minnesota (minor in conflict
    management)
252 Humphrey Center
Hubert H. Humphrey Institute of Public Affairs
301 19th Ave. South
Minneapolis, MN 55455
(612) 625-3046

Dispute Resolution Program
University of Missouri (St. Louis)
Department of Sociology
8801 Natural Bridge Road
St. Louis, MO 63121
(314) 553-6364

Negotiation and Conflict Resolution Center
Rutgers University
15 Washington Street
Newark, NJ 07102
(201) 648-5048

International Center for Cooperation and Conflict
  Resolution
Columbia University, Teacher's College
Box 171
New York, NY 10027
(212) 678-3274

International Security Policy Specialization
Columbia University
International Affairs Building, Room 3125
School of International and Public Affairs
New York, NY 10027
(212) 854-1754

Peace Studies Program
Cornell University
1800 Uris Hall
Ithaca, NY 14853
(607) 256-6484/6370

Center on Violence and Human Survival
John Jay College of Criminal Justice
City University of New York
New York, NY 10019
(212) 237-8431

New York City Consortium
New York University
East Building, Room 635
239 Greene Street
New York, NY 10003
(212) 998-5494

Analysis and Resolution of Conflicts
Syracuse University (certificate, master's, and Ph.D.)
410 Maxwell Hall
Syracuse, NY 13244
(315) 443-2367

Program in Nonviolent Conflict and Change
Syracuse University
Maxwell School of Citizenship and Public Affairs
305 Sims Hall
Syracuse, NY 13244
(315) 443-3780

Program on the Analysis and Resolution of
  Conflicts
Syracuse University
410 Maxwell Hall
Syracuse, NY 13244
(315) 443-2367

Conflict Resolution Center
University of North Dakota (continuing education)
PO Box 8009

University Station
Grand Forks, ND 58202
(701) 777-3664

Conflict Resolution Program
Antioch University (master of arts in conflict
  resolution)
800 Livermore Street
Yellow Springs, OH 45387
(513) 767-6321
E-mail: mlang@igc.apc.org

Graduate Program in Sociology of Conflict
Bowling Green State University
Department of Sociology
Bowling Green, OH 43403
(419) 372-2294

Applied Peace Studies Certificate Program
Wilmington College
Pyle Center Box 1214
Wilmington, OH 45177
(937) 382-6661

Conflict Analysis and Peace Science
University of Pennsylvania
3718 Locust Walk
Philadelphia, PA 19104
(215) 898-8412

A. A. White Dispute Resolution Institute
University of Houston
College of Business Administration
325 Melcher Hall
Houston, TX 77204-6283
(713) 743-4933; fax (713) 743-4934

Alternative Dispute Resolution Program
University of Utah (graduate certificate program)
Department of Communication
2400 Language and Communication Building
Salt Lake City, UT 84112
(801) 581-7648

School for International Training
Admissions Office
Kipling Road
Brattleboro, VT 05301
(800) 451-4465

Woodbury College (graduate certificate, associate's
  degree)
6600 Elm Street
Montpelier, VT 05602
(800) 639-6039 or (802) 229-0516

Institute for Conflict Analysis and Resolution
George Mason University (master of science and
  Ph.D.)
4400 University Drive
Fairfax, VA 22230-4444
(703) 993-1300
E-mail: mboland@gmu.edu

Institute for Conflict Studies and Peacebuilding
Eastern Mennonite University
Harrisonburg, VA 22801-2462
(703) 432-4450

CORPUS Program
Seattle University
Theological and Religious Studies

Seattle, WA 98122
(800) 426-7123

Justice Institute of British Columbia
4180 West Fourth Avenue
Vancouver, British Columbia V6J 4V1, Canada
(604) 660-1875

Institute for Dispute Resolution
University of Victoria
Begbie Building
PO Box 2400
Victoria, British Columbia
Canada V8W 3H7
(604) 721-8777; fax (604) 721-6607

Appendix 5

Entries Written by Contributing Authors

Most entries in this volume were written by Heidi Burgess and Guy Burgess; however, our research assistants provided initial drafts of many entries. These include the following:

Entries drafted by Tanya R. Glaser: Defense Base Closure and Realignment Commission; Federal Arbitration Act; Galtung, Johan; Israeli-Palestinian Women's Workshop; Kelman, Herbert; King, Martin Luther, Jr.; Laue, James Howard; Machiavelli, Niccolo; Mandela, Nelson; Marshall, George; Myrdal, Alva; Oslo Accords, Middle East Peace Process; Persian Gulf War; Rapoport, Anatol; *Roe v. Wade;* Sharp, Gene; Strategic Arms Limitation Talks; Susskind, Lawrence; Tolstoy, Lev (Leo) Nikolayevich; Truth and Reconciliation Commission, South Africa; Tutu, Desmond; Uniform Arbitration Act; United Nations Mediation of the Egyptian-Israeli Negotiations at Kilometer 101

Entries drafted by T. A. O'Lonergan: Academy of Family Mediators; Community Board of San Francisco; Dispute Systems Design for Families; Dispute Systems Design for Schools; Gorbachev, Mikhail Sergeyevich; International Alert; International Association of Conflict Management; *Journal of Conflict Resolution;* Kissinger, Henry; Law and Society Association; League of Nations; *Mediation Quarterly;* Mother Teresa; National Association for Community Mediation; National Association of Labor-Management Committees; National Coal Policy Project; National Labor Relations Board; National Peace Foundation; Negotiated Rulemaking at the Maine Department of Transportation; *Negotiation Journal; Network: Interaction for Conflict Resolution; Peace and Change;* Peace Brigades International; Sadat, Anwar; Search for Common Ground; Society of Professionals in Dispute Resolution

Entries drafted by Emma Zitter-Smith: Camp David Accords (Israeli and Egyptian); Carter, Jimmy; Carter Center; GATT Negotiations; Walesa, Lech; Wilson, Woodrow

References and Further Reading

Abel, Richard L. 1982. *The Politics of Informal Justice: The American Experience.* New York: Academic Press.

Abraham, Kenneth S. 1992. "What Is a Tort Claim? An Interpretation of Contemporary Tort Reform." *Maryland Law Review* 51:172.

Abrams, Irwin. 1988. *The Nobel Peace Prize and the Laureates: An Illustrated Bibliographical History, 1901–1987.* Boston: G. K. Hall.

Adams, Charles W. 1987. "Final Offer Arbitration: Time for Serious Consideration by the Courts." *Nebraska Law Review* 66:213–48.

Administrative Conference of the United States (ACUS). 1986. *Agencies' Use of Alternative Means of Dispute Resolution.* Washington, DC: Administrative Conference of the United States.

Administrative Conference of the United States (ACUS). 1992. *Recommendations and Reports,* vol. 1. Washington, DC: Administrative Conference of the United States.

Alinsky, Saul. 1969. *Reveille for Radicals.* New York: Vintage Books.

Alinsky, Saul. 1971. *Rules for Radicals: A Practical Primer for Realistic Radicals.* New York: Random House.

Ambrosius, Lloyd. 1991. *Wilsonian Statecraft.* Wilmington, DE: SR Books.

American Arbitration Association. 1989. *A Guide to Mediation for Business People.* New York: American Arbitration Association.

American Arbitration Association. 1991. *A Commercial Arbitration Guide for Business People.* New York: American Arbitration Association.

American Arbitration Association. 1996. World Wide Web Home Page. http://www.adr.org.

American Bar Association. World Wide Web Home Page. http://www.abanet.org/dispute/home.html.

American Bar Association. 1984. "ABA Standards of Practice for Lawyer Mediators in Family Disputes." In *Summary of the Actions of the House of Delegates,* Report of Sections 22–23. Washington, DC: American Bar Association.

American Bar Association, Standing Committee on Dispute Resolution. 1989. *Dispute Resolution* 25.

American Tort Reform Association (ATRA). 1996. "ATRA's Issues." World Wide Web. http:/www.aaabiz.com/ATRA/atri.htm: ATRA.

Amoo, Sam G. "Frustrations of Regional Peacekeeping: The OAU in Chad, 1977–1982." In *Carter Center Conflict Resolution Program* (p. 41). Atlanta: Emory University.

Anglade, Christian. 1988. "President Arias of Costa Rica." *P.S. Political Science and Politics* 21:357–58.

Appel, Mark E. 1993. "Partnering: New Dimensions in Dispute Prevention and Resolution." *Arbitration Journal* (June):47–51.

Arrow, Kenneth, Robert H. Mnookin, Lee Ross, Amos Tversky, and Robert Wilson. 1995. *Barriers to Conflict Resolution.* New York: W. W. Norton and Co.

Association of Family and Conciliation Courts. 1996. "An Invitation [to Join]." Madison, WI: Association of Family and Conciliation Courts.

Augustine, Mary Jane. 1994. "Dispute Prevention and Resolution in the Construction Industry." *New York Law Journal* 105:3.

Austin, Lisa. 1994. "'Public Journalism' Redefines the Media's Role." *Consensus* 24:2.

Avruch, K., P. Black, and J. Scimecca. 1991. *Conflict Resolution: Cross-Cultural Perspectives.* New York: Greenwood Press.

Axelrod, Robert. 1984. *The Evolution of Cooperation.* New York: Basic Books.

Azar, Edward E. 1985. "Protracted International Conflict: Ten Propositions." *International Interactions* 12:59–70.

Azar, Edward E., and John W. Burton. 1986. *International Conflict Resolution: Theory and Practice.* Boulder: Lynne Rienner Publishers.

Babbitt, Eileen F. 1994. "The Power of Moral Suasion in International Mediation." In *When Talk Works,* edited by Deborah M. Kolb and Associates. San Francisco: Jossey-Bass.

Babbitt, Eileen, and Tamra d'Estree. 1996. "An Is-raeli-Palestinian Women's Workshop." In *Managing Global Chaos,* edited by Chester Crocker, Fen Hampson, and Pamela Aall. Washington, DC: United States Institute of Peace Press.

Bailey, R. 1974. *Radicals in Urban Politics: The Alinsky Approach.* Chicago: University of Chicago Press.

Baker, Pauline H. 1996. "Conflict Resolution versus Democratic Governance: Divergent Paths to Peace?" In *Managing Global Chaos.* Washington, DC: United States Institute of Peace.

Banks, Michael. 1987. "Four Conceptions of Peace." In *Conflict Management and Problem Solving: Interpersonal to International Applications,* edited by Dennis Sandole and Ingrid Sandole-Staroste. New York: New York University Press.

Barash, David P. 1991. *Introduction to Peace Studies.* Belmont, CA: Wadsworth Publishing Co.

Barkai, J., and G. Kassebaum. 1989. "Using Court-Annexed Arbitration to Reduce Litigation Costs and to Increase the Pace of Litigation." *Pepperdine Law Review* 16:543–74.

Barnett, Correlli. 1972. "Karl Maria von Clausewitz." In *Makers of Modern Thought.* New York: American Heritage Publishing Co.

Baumann, Melissa, and Hannes Siebert. 1993. "The Media as Mediator." *Forum* (Winter):28–32.

Becker, Carol, Laura Chasin, Richard Chasin, Margaret Herzig, and Sallyann Roth. 1992. "Fostering Dialogue on Abortion: A Report from the Public Conversations Project." *Conscience (A Newsjournal of Prochoice Catholic Opinion)* 13:8.

Becker, Carol, Laura Chasin, Richard Chasin, Margaret Herzig, and Sallyann Roth. 1994. "From Stuck Debate to New Conversation on Controversial Issues: A Report from the Public Conversations Project." *Journal of Feminist Family Therapy* 7:143–63.

Beekman, Susan, and Geanne Holmes. 1993. *Battles, Hassles, Tantrums and Tears: Strategies for Coping with Conflict and Making Peace at Home.* New York: Hearst Books.

Benson, Mary. 1986. *Nelson Mandela.* New York: W. W. Norton and Co.

Bercovitch, Jacob. 1991. "International Mediation and Dispute Settlement: Evaluating the Conditions for Successful Mediation." *Negotiation Journal* 7(1):17–30.

Bernard, S., H. Weingarten Folger, and Z. Zumeta. 1984. "The Neutral Mediator: Value Dilemmas in Divorce Mediation." *Mediation Quarterly* 4:61–74.

Bettner, Betty Lou, and Amy Lew. 1992. *Raising Kids: Who Can.* New York: HarperCollins.

Black, Henry Campbell. 1990. *Black's Law Dictionary.* St. Paul, MN: West Publishing Co.

Bogdonoff, Sandra. 1995. "Consensus Building to Write Environmentally Responsive Rules for Maine's New Transportation Policy." In *Mediating Environmental Conflicts: Theory and Practice* (pp. 151–66), edited by J. Walton Blackburn and Willa Marie Bruce. Westport, CT: Quorum Books.

Bond, Doug. 1993. "Nonviolent Direct Action and the Diffusion of Power." In *Justice without Violence,* edited by Paul Wehr, Heidi Burgess, and Guy Burgess. Boulder: Lynne Rienner Publishers.

Bondurant, Joan V. 1965. *Conquest of Violence: The Gandhian Philosophy of Conflict.* Berkeley: University of California Press.

Bono, Edward de. 1976. *The Greatest Thinkers.* New York: G. P. Putnam's Sons.

Borisoff, Deborah, and David A. Victor. 1989. *Conflict Management: A Communication Skills Approach.* Englewood Cliffs, NJ: Prentice Hall.

Boserup, Anders, and Andrew Mack. 1975. *War without Weapons: Non-Violence in National Defense.* New York: Schocken Books.

Boulding, Elise. 1990. *Building a Global Civic Culture: Education for an Interdependent World.* Syracuse, NY: Syracuse University Press.

Boulding, Elise. 1993. "States, Boundaries, and Environmental Security." In *Conflict Resolution Theory and Practice: Integration and Application* (pp. 194–208), edited by Dennis J. D. Sandole and Hugo van der Merwe. New York: Manchester University Press.

Boulding, Elise, Clovis Brigagao, and Kevin Clements. 1991. *Peace Culture and Society: Transnational Research and Dialogue.* Boulder: Westview Press.

Boulding, Kenneth. 1962. *Conflict and Defense: A General Theory.* New York: Harper Torchbooks.

Boulding, Kenneth. 1973. *The Economy of Love and Fear: A Preface to Grants Economics.* Belmont, CA: Wadsworth Publishing Co.

Boulding, Kenneth. 1978a. *Ecodynamics: A New Theory of Societal Evolution.* Beverly Hills, CA: Sage.

Boulding, Kenneth. 1978b. *Stable Peace.* Austin: University of Texas Press.

Boulding, Kenneth. 1985. *Human Betterment.* Beverly Hills, CA: Sage.

Boulding, Kenneth. 1989. *Three Faces of Power.* Newbury Park, CA: Sage Publications.

Boutros-Ghali, Boutros. 1992. *An Agenda for Peace.* New York. United Nations.

Boutros-Ghali, Boutros. 1995. *An Agenda for Development.* New York: United Nations.

Boutros-Ghali, Boutros. 1995. *An Agenda for Peace,* with the new supplement and related UN documents. New York: United Nations.

Bradshaw, William. 1995. "Mediation and Therapy." In *Mediating Interpersonal Conflicts: A Pathway to Peace* (pp. 237–50), edited by Mark Umbreit. West Concord, MN: CPI Publishing.

Branch, Taylor. 1988. *Parting the Waters.* New York: Simon and Schuster.

Brann, Peter, and Margaret Foddy. 1987. "Trust and Consumption of a Deteriorating Common Resource." *Journal of Conflict Resolution* 31(4): 615–30.

Brecher, Michael, and Patrick James. 1988. "Patterns of Crisis Management." *Journal of Conflict Resolution* 32:426–56.

Breslin, J. William. 1991. "Breaking away from Subtle Biases." In *Negotiation Theory and Practice* (pp. 247–50). Cambridge, MA: Program on Negotiation Books.

Breslin, J. William. 1995–96. "Negotiation World Saddened by Loss of Jeffrey Rubin." *Negotiation Newsletter* (Fall–Winter):1, 12–13.

Breslin, J. William, and Jeffrey Z. Rubin. 1991. *Negotiation Theory and Practice.* Cambridge, MA: Program on Negotiation Books.

Brickman, Lester. 1989. "Contingent Fees without the Contingencies: Hamlet without the Prince of Denmark?" 37 *UCLA Law Review* 29:35–44.

Brown, Brack. 1993. "Public Organizations and Policies in Conflict: Notes on Theory and Practice." In *Conflict Resolution Theory and Practice* (pp. 158–75), edited by Dennis J. D. Sandole and Hugo van der Merwe. New York: Manchester University Press.

Bryson, John M., and Barbara C. Crosby. 1992. *Leadership for the Common Good: Tackling Public Problems in a Shared-Power World.* San Francisco: Jossey-Bass.

Brzezinski, Zbigniew. 1993. "The Cold War and Its Aftermath." In *The Breakup of Communism: The Soviet Union and Eastern Europe* (pp. 10–27), edited by Matthew A. Kraljic. New York: H. W. Wilson.

Buckingham, Peter H. 1990. *Woodrow Wilson: A Biography of His Times and Presidency.* Wilmington, DE: Scholarly Resources.

Bundy, Stephen M. 1992. "The Policy in Favor of Settlement in an Adversary System." *Hastings Law Journal* 44:1–75.

Bunker, Barbara Benedict, Jeffrey Z. Rubin, and Associates. 1995. *Conflict, Cooperation, and Justice: Essays Inspired by the Work of Morton Deutsch.* San Francisco: Jossey-Bass.

Burgess, Guy, and Heidi Burgess. 1996. "Constructive Confrontation: A Transformative Approach to Intractable Conflicts." Working paper no. 96-2. Conflict Research Consortium. (Forthcoming in *Mediation Quarterly.*)

Burgess, Heidi, and Guy Burgess. 1993. "Confronting Intractable Conflicts in Constructive Ways." Conflict Research Consortium.

Burton, John. 1962. *Peace Theory: Preconditions of Disarmament.* New York: Knopf.

Burton, John. 1969. *Conflict and Community: The Use of Controlled Community in Ireland.* New York: Free Press.

Burton, John. 1972. *World Society.* Cambridge: Cambridge University Press.

Burton, John. 1979. *Deviance, Terrorism and War: The Process of Solving Unsolved Social and Political Problems.* New York: St. Martin's Press.

Burton, John. 1987. *Resolving Deep-Rooted Conflict: A Handbook.* Lanham, MD: University Press of America.

Burton, John W. 1989. "On the Need for Conflict Prevention." Center for Conflict Analysis and Resolution, George Mason University, Fairfax, VA.

Burton, John. 1990a. *Conflict: Human Needs Theory.* New York: St. Martin's Press.

Burton, John. 1990b. *Conflict: Resolution and Provention.* New York: St. Martin's Press.

Burton, John. 1993. "Conflict Resolution as a Political Philosophy." In *Conflict Resolution Theory and Practice: Integration and Application* (pp. 55–64), edited by Hugo van der Merwe and Dennis J. D. Sandole. New York: Manchester University Press.

Burton, John, and Frank Dukes. 1990a. *Conflict: Practices in Management, Settlement and Resolution.* In *Community Mediation.* New York: St. Martin's Press.

Burton, John, and Frank Dukes, eds. 1990b. *Conflict: Readings in Management and Resolution.* New York: St. Martin's Press.

Burton, Lloyd, and John McIver. 1991. "A Summary of the Court-Annexed Arbitration Evaluation Project." *Colorado Lawyer* 20(8):1595–98.

Bush, Robert A. Baruch. 1992. *The Dilemmas of Mediation Practice: A Study of Ethical Dilemmas and Policy Implications.* Washington, DC: National Institute for Dispute Resolution.

Bush, Robert A. Baruch, and Joseph P. Folger. 1994. *Promise of Mediation.* San Francisco: Jossey-Bass.

Butfoy, Andrew. 1993. "Collective Security: Theory, Problems and Reformulations." *Australian Journal of International Affairs* 47:1–14.

Carnegie Endowment for International Peace. 1996. "Carnegie Endowment for International Peace: Staff and Projects 1996–97." Washington, DC: Carnegie Endowment for International Peace.

Carpenter, Susan L., and W. J. D. Kennedy. 1988. *Managing Public Disputes.* San Francisco: Jossey-Bass.

Carson, Clayborne. 1991. *The Eyes on the Prize: Civil Rights Reader—Documents, Speeches, and Firsthand Accounts from the Black Freedom Struggle, 1954–1990.* New York: Viking.

Carter, Jimmy. 1982. *Keeping Faith: Memoirs of a President.* New York: Bantam Books.

Carter, L. J. 1977. "Coal: Invoking the 'Rule of Reason' in Energy-Environment Crisis." *Science* (October 21):276–78.

Carter Center. World Wide Web Home Page. http://www.emory.edu/CARTER_CENTER.

Caves, Richard E., Jeffrey A. Frankel, and Ronald W. Jones. 1990. *World Trade and Payments: An Introduction.* New York: HarperCollins College Publishers.

Chasin, R., Margaret Herzig, Sallyann Roth, Laura Chasin, Carol Becker, and Robert Stains. 1996. "From Diatribe to Dialogue on Divisive Public Issues: Approaches Drawn from Family Therapy." *Mediation Quarterly* 13:323–44.

Chawla, Navin. 1992. *Mother Teresa.* London: Sinclair-Stevenson.

Chrislip, David D. 1995. "Transforming Politics." Unpublished paper, p. 29.

Clary, Bruce B., and Regan Hornney. 1995. "Evaluating ADR as an Approach to Citizen Participation in Siting a Low-Level Nuclear Waste Facility." In *Mediating Environmental Conflicts: Theory and Practice* (pp. 121–38), edited by J. Walton Blackburn and Willa Marie Bruce. Westport, CT: Quorum Books.

Clausewitz, Karl von. 1943. *On War.* New York: Modern Library.

Clements, Kevin. 1995. "Elise Boulding, Global Citizen." *ICAR Newsletter* 7:10–11.

Coates, Robert. 1985. "Victim Meets Offender: An Evaluation of Victim-Offender Reconciliation Programs" (report). Valparaiso, IN: PACT (Prisoner and Community Together).

Cohen, Raymond. 1996. "Cultural Aspects of International Mediation." In *Resolving International Conflicts: The Theory and Practice of Mediation* (pp. 107–25), edited by Jacob Bercovitch. Boulder: Lynne Rienner Publishers.

Colaiaco, James A. 1988. *Martin Luther King, Jr.: Apostle of Militant Nonviolence.* New York: St. Martin's Press.

Colas, Bernard. 1994. *Global Economic Co-operation: A Guide to Agreements and Organizations.* Tokyo: United Nations University Press.

Colosi, Thomas R., and Arthur E. Berkeley. 1986. *Collective Bargaining: How It Works and Why.* New York: American Arbitration Association.

Common Ground Network for Life and Choice. 1995. *News from the Common Ground Network for Life and Choice* (spring).

Corbin, Jane. 1994. *The Norway Channel: The Secret Talks that Led to the Middle East Peace Accord.* New York: Atlantic Monthly Press.

Cormick, Gerald W., and Alana Knaster. 1986. "Mediation and Scientific Issues: Oil and Fishing Industries Negotiate." *Environment* 28(10):6–15, 30.

Coser, Lewis A. 1956. *The Functions of Social Conflict.* New York: Free Press.

Coser, Lewis A. 1971. *Masters of Sociological Thought: Ideas in Historical and Social Context.* New York: Harcourt Brace Jovanovich.

Coulson, R. 1985. "Code of Ethics for Arbitrators in Commercial Disputes." In *Dispute Resolution* (pp. 196–201), edited by Stephen B. Goldberg, Eric D. Green, and Frank E. A. Sander. Boston: Little, Brown.

Coulson, Robert. 1993. *ADR in America: Alternatives to Litigation.* New York: American Arbitration Association.

Council of Better Business Bureaus. World Wide Web Home Page. http://cbbb.org/bbb/bbb.html.

Council of the Pugwash Conferences on World and Science Affairs. 1992. *Pugwash Newsletter* 29:4 (May).

Cronin, Thomas. 1989. *Direct Democracy: The Politics of Initiative, Referendum, and Recall.* Cambridge, MA: Harvard University Press.

Cunningham, Helen V., Mark A. Chesler, and Barbara Israel. 1990. "Strategies for Social Justice: A Retrieval Conference: Report on Grassroots Community Organizing and Conflict Intervention." Program on Conflict Management Alternatives, University of Michigan, and the Conflict Clinic, George Mason University.

Curle, Adam. 1995. "Forgiveness?" *Conciliation Quarterly* 14(3):9.

Dahrendorf, Ralf. 1957. *Class and Conflict in Industrial Society.* Stanford, CA: Stanford University Press.

Damas, Kon. 1994. "Mediating Teen Violence in Boulder, Colorado." Working paper no. 94-6. University of Colorado Conflict Research Consortium, Boulder.

Daniels, Stephen, and Joanne Martin. 1995. *Civil Juries and the Politics of Reform.* Chicago: Northwestern University Press.

Dauer, Edward A. 1994. *Manual of Dispute Resolution.* Colorado Springs: Shepard's McGraw-Hill.

Davis, Albie M. 1991. "An Interview with Mary Parker Follett." In *Negotiation Theory and Practice,* edited by J. William Breslin and Jeffrey Z. Rubin. Cambridge, MA: Program on Negotiation at Harvard Law School.

Davis, Albie M., and Janet Rifkin. 1994. "A Conversation between Friends." *Conciliation Quarterly* 13(1–2):2–5.

Davis, Kenneth Culp. 1972. *Administrative Law Text.* St. Paul, MN: West Publishing Company.

Davis, Robert. 1982. "Mediation: The Brooklyn Experiment." In *Neighborhood Justice: Assessment of an Emerging Idea,* edited by Roman Tomasic and Malcolm M. Feeley. New York: Longman.

Dawkins, Kristin. 1990. "Prison Overcrowding: Mediation in a Climate of Crisis." *Consensus* no. 5 (January).

Defense Base Closure and Realignment Commission. 1993. *Report to the President.* Washington, DC: U.S. Government Printing Office.

Defense Base Closure and Realignment Commission. 1995. *Report to the President.* Washington, DC: U.S. Government Printing Office.

Department of Justice, Community Relations Service. 1989. *The Community Relations Service: Assistance in the Resolution of Community Disputes Based on Race, Ethnic or National Origin.* Washington, DC: U.S. Government Printing Office.

Department of Justice, Community Relations Service. 1991. *Avoid Racial Conflict: A Guide for Municipalities.* Washington, DC: U.S. Government Printing Office.

DeSario, Jack, and Stuart Langton. 1987. *Citizen Participation in Public Decision Making.* New York: Greenwood Press.

Deutsch, Morton. 1973. *The Resolution of Conflict: Constructive and Destructive Processes.* New Haven, CT: Yale University Press.

Diamond, Louise. 1994. "On Developing a Common Vocabulary." In *Peace Building* 1(4):3, 11.

Diamond, Louise, and John McDonald. 1991. *Multi-Track Diplomacy: A Systems Guide and Analysis.* Grinnell: Iowa Peace Institute.

Diehl, Paul F., and Gary Goertz. 1988. "Territorial Changes and Militarized Conflict." *Journal of Conflict Resolution* 32(1):103–122.

DiMento, Joseph F., and LeRoy Graymer. 1991. *Confronting Regional Challenges: Approaches to LULUs, Growth, and Other Vexing Governance Problems.* Cambridge, MA: Lincoln Institute of Land Policy.

Dittmer, John, George C. Wright, and W. Marvin Dulaney. 1993. *Essays on the American Civil Rights Movement.* Arlington: Texas A & M University Press.

Donnelly, Jack. 1989. *Universal Human Rights in Theory and Practice.* Ithaca, NY: Cornell University Press.

Downie, Bryan M. 1991. "When Negotiations Fail: Causes of Breakdown and Tactics for Breaking the Stalemate." *Negotiation Journal* 7(2): 175–86.

Downs, George W. 1994a. *Beyond the Debate on Collective Security.* Ann Arbor: University of Michigan Press.

Downs, George W. 1994b. *Collective Security beyond the Cold War.* Ann Arbor: University of Michigan Press.

Doyle, Michael, and David Straus. 1976. *How to Make Meetings Work: The New Interaction Method.* New York: Wyden Books.

Drake, William, and Michael Lewis. 1988. "Community Justice Centers—A Lasting Innovation." In *Dispute Resolution Forum.* Washington, DC: National Institute of Dispute Resolution.

Drivon, Laurence E., and Bob Schimdt. 1990. *The Civil War on Consumer Rights.* Berkeley, CA: Conari Press.

Du Boulay, Shirley. 1988. *Tutu: Voice of the Voiceless.* London: Hodder and Stoughton.

Duffy, K., P. V. Olczak, and J. G. Grosch. 1991. *Community Mediation.* New York: Guilford.

Dugan, Marie A. 1987. "Intervener Roles and Conflict Pathologies." In *Conflict Management and Problem Solving: Interpersonal to International Applications,* edited by Dennis Sandole and Ingrid Sandole-Staroste. New York: New York University Press.

Duke, Simon. 1994. "The State and Human Rights: Sovereignty v. Humanitarian Intervention." *International Relations* 12(2):25–48.

Dunworth, Terence, and James Kakalik. 1994. "Preliminary Observations on Implementation of the Pilot Program of the Civil Justice Reform Act of 1990." *Stanford Law Review* 46(6):1303–38.

Duryea, Michelle Lebaron. 1992. *Conflict and Culture: A Literature Review and Bibliography.* Victoria, BC: University of Victoria Institute for Dispute Resolution.

Dworkin, Joan, Lynn Jacob, and Elizabeth Scott. 1991. "The Boundaries between Mediation and Therapy: Ethical Dilemmas." *Mediation Quarterly* 9:107–20.

Egeland, Jan. 1995. "Norway's Back Channel Success Story." Talk presented March 23, 1995, at Harvard University's Kennedy School of Government, as reported in *Negotiations* (spring–summer):1, 11.

Ellis, Albert. 1996. *Better, Deeper, and More Enduring Brief Therapy: The Rational Emotive Behavior Therapy Approach.* New York: Brunner/Mazel Publishers.

Eringer, Robert. 1982. *Strike for Freedom: The Story of Lech Walesa and Polish Solidarity.* New York: Dodd and Mead.

Evans, Christine E. 1996. "The Pre-trial and Settlement Conference in Canada." World Wide Web. http://www.acjnet.org/docs/127-ch4.html. Department of Justice Canada, Law Reform Division.

Evans, Gareth. 1993. *Cooperating for Peace: The Global Agenda for the 1990s and Beyond.* Sydney, Australia: Allen and Unwin.

Faber, Adele, and Elaine Mazlish. 1980. *How to Talk so Kids Will Listen and Listen so Kids Will Talk.* New York: Avon Books.

Faber, Adele, and Elaine Mazlish. 1987. *Siblings without Rivalry.* New York: Avon Books.

Falk, Richard. 1991. "International Law in a Fragmented World: The Challenge of New Issues and New Actors." In *New Directions in Conflict Theory: Conflict Resolution and Conflict Transformation* (pp. 79–107), edited by Raimo Vayrynen. London: Sage.

Farrell, William. 1981. "Anwar el-Sadat, Daring Pioneer." In *New York Times Biographical Service.* New York: Arno Press, Inc.

Federal Mediation and Conciliation Service. 1995. *Transformation: Forty Eighth Annual Report.* Washington, DC: Federal Mediation and Conciliation Service.

Ferrell, Robert. 1966. *George C. Marshall.* New York: Cooper Square Publishers.

Feuille, P., and D. M. Kolb. 1994. "Waiting in the Wings: Mediation's Role in Grievance Resolution." *Negotiation Journal* 10:249–64.

Field, Patrick. 1994. "State Legislators Use Consensus-Building to Resolve Issues, Involve Citizens, Develop Legislation." *Consensus* 23:4.

Finks, P. David. 1984. *The Radical Vision of Saul Alinsky.* New York: Paulist Press.

Fischer, Frank. 1993. "Citizen Participation and the Democratization of Policy Expertise: From Theoretical Inquiry to Practical Cases." *Policy Science* 26:165–87.

Fischhoff, Baruch, Sarah Lichtenstein, Paul Slovic, Stephen L. Derby, and Ralph L. Keeney. 1981. *Acceptable Risk.* Cambridge: Cambridge University Press.

Fisher, Robert. 1984. *Let the People Decide: Neighborhood Organizing in America.* New York: Twayne Publishers.

Fisher, Roger. 1991. *Beyond YES.* Cambridge, MA: Program on Negotiation at Harvard Law School.

Fisher, Roger. 1994. "In Theory Deter, Compel, or Negotiate?" *Negotiation Journal* 10:17–32.

Fisher, Roger, and Scott Brown. 1988. *Getting Together: Building a Relationship that Gets to Yes.* Boston: Houghton Mifflin.

Fisher, Roger, Elizabeth Kopelman, and Andrea Kupfer Schneider. 1994. *Beyond Machiavelli: Tools for Coping with Conflict.* Cambridge, MA: Harvard University Press.

Fisher, Roger, and William Ury. 1981. *Getting to Yes: Negotiating Agreement Without Giving In.* New York: Penguin Books.

Fisher, Roger, William Ury, and Bruce Patton. 1991. *Getting to Yes: Negotiating Agreement Without Giving In,* 2nd ed. New York: Penguin Books.

Fisher, Timothy S. 1994. "Dispute Review Boards: A Blueprint for Success." *Punchlist* 17.

Fiss, Owen M. 1984. "Against Settlement." *Yale Law Journal* 93:1073–90.

Fitzgibbon, Susan A. 1993. "Appellate Settlement Conference Programs: A Case Study." *Journal of Dispute Resolution* 1:57–111.

Folberg, Jay, and Ann L. Milne. 1988. *Divorce Mediation: Theory and Practice.* New York: Guilford Publications.

Folberg, Jay, and Alison Taylor. 1984. *Mediation: A Comprehensive Guide to Resolving Conflicts without Litigation.* San Francisco: Jossey-Bass.

Folger, J. P., and S. Bernard. 1985. "Divorce Mediation: When Mediators Challenge the Divorcing Parties." *Mediation Quarterly* 10:5–23.

Folger, Joseph P., and Robert A. Baruch Bush. 1994. *Promise of Mediation.* San Francisco: Jossey-Bass.

Folger, Joseph P., and Marshall Scott Poole. 1984. *Working through Conflict: A Communication Perspective.* Glenview, IL: Scott, Foresman.

Folger, Robert, Blair H. Sheppard, and Robert T. Buttran. 1995. "Equity, Equality, and Need: Three Faces of Social Justice." In *Conflict, Cooperation, and Justice,* edited by Barbara Benedict Bunker and Jeffrey Z. Rubin. San Francisco: Jossey-Bass.

Forsythe, David P. 1995. "The UN and Human Rights at Fifty: An Incremental but Incomplete Revolution." In *Global Governance: A Review of Multilateralism and International Organizations* (pp. 297–318). Boulder: Lynne Rienner Publishers.

Fowler, Mary Candace. 1995. "Uncle Sam's In-House 'Efficacy Experts' Report Savings from ADR." *Consensus* 27 (July):1.

Freeman, Sally A., Stephen W. Littlejohn, and W. Barnett Pierce. 1992. "Communication and Moral Conflict." *Western Journal of Communication* 56: 311–29.

Froman, Michael. 1991. *The Development of the Idea of Détente: Coming to Terms.* New York: St. Martin's Press.

Fuller, Lon. 1978. "The Forms and Limits of Adjudication." *Harvard Law Review* 92:353.

Galanter, Marc. 1983. "Reading the Landscape of Disputes: What We Know and Don't Know (and Think We Know) about Our Allegedly Contentious and Litigious Society." *UCLA Law Review* 31:4.

Galanter, Marc, and Mia Cahill. 1994. "Most Cases Settle: Judicial Promotion and Regulation of Settlements." *Stanford Law Review* 46:1339–91.

Galtung, Johan. 1969. "Peace, Violence, and Peace Research." *Journal of Peace Research* 6:167–91.

Galtung, Johan. 1975–80. *Essays in Peace Research.* Copenhagen: Ejlers.

Galtung, Johan. 1985. "Twenty Five Years of Peace Research." *Journal of Peace Research* 25:141–58.

Galtung, Johan. 1995. *Choose Peace.* East Haven, CT: Pluto Press.

Galtung, Johan. 1996. *Peace by Peaceful Means.* Thousand Oaks, CA: Sage Publications.

Gandhi, Mohandas K. 1971. "Non-Violence." In *Civil Disobedience and Violence,* edited by Jeffrie G. Murphy. Belmont, CA: Wadsworth Publishing Co.

Gellhorn, Ernest. 1972. *Administrative Law and Process in a Nutshell.* St. Paul, MN: West Publishing Co.

Gibson, Kevin. 1989. "The Ethical Basis of Mediation: Why Mediators Need Philosophers." *Mediation Quarterly* 7(1):41–50.

Gibson, Kevin. 1992. "Confidentiality in Mediation: A Moral Reassessment." *Journal of Dispute Resolution* 1992:25–66.

Gibson, Kevin. 1996. "Shortcomings of Neutrality in Mediation: Solutions Based on Rationality." *Negotiation Journal* 12:69–80.

Giddens, Anthony. 1971. *Capitalism and Modern Social Theory: Analysis of the Writings of Marx, Durkheim and Max Weber.* Cambridge: Cambridge University Press.

Gifis, Steven H. 1991. *Law Dictionary.* Hauppague, NY: Barron's Educational Series.

Gillie, Michael S. "A State-Level Approach to Community Arbitration and Mediation." *Mediation Quarterly* 5:53–63.

Gircar, B. G., and A. J. Baratta. 1983. "Bridging the Information Gap: Radiation Monitoring by Citizens." *Journal of Applied Behavioral Science* 19:35–41.

Glendon, Mary Ann. 1991. *Rights Talk: The Impoverishment of Political Discourse.* New York: Free Press.

Gnaizda, Robert. 1982. "Secret Justice for the Privileged Few." *Judicature* 66:6–13.

Goggin, Malcolm. 1993. "Understanding the New Politics of Abortion." *American Politics Quarterly* 21(1):4–30.

Goldberg, Stephen B., Eric D. Green, and Frank E. A. Sander. 1985. *Dispute Resolution.* Boston: Little, Brown.

Goldberg, Stephen B., Frank E. A. Sander, and Nancy H. Rogers. 1992. *Dispute Resolution: Negotiation, Mediation, and Other Processes.* Boston: Little, Brown.

Goldschmidt, Arthur. 1988. *Modern Egypt: Formation of a Nation-State.* Boulder: Westview Press.

Goldstein, Susan. 1987. *Cultural Issues in Community Mediation, 1983.* Washington, DC: National Institute for Dispute Resolution.

Gordenker, Leon, and Thomas G. Weiss. 1993. "The Collective Security Idea and Changing World Politics." In *Collective Security in a Changing World: A World Peace Foundation,* edited by Thomas G. Weiss. Boulder: Lynne Rienner Publishers.

Gordon, Thomas. 1970. *Parent Effectiveness Training.* New York: P. H. Wyden.

Gray, Barbara. 1989. *Collaborating: Finding Common Ground for Multiparty Problems.* San Francisco: Jossey-Bass.

Green, Martin Burgess. 1986. *The Origins of Nonviolence: Tolstoy and Gandhi in Their Historical Settings.* University Park: Pennsylvania State University Press.

Gregg, Richard B. 1966. *The Power of Nonviolence.* New York: Schocken Books.

Groom, A. J. 1997. "Approaches to Conflict and Cooperation in International Relations: Lessons from Theory for Practice." Lecture published on the Internet: http://snipe.ukc.ac.uk/international/papers.dir/groom1.html.

Gurr, Ted R. 1970. *Why Men Rebel.* Princeton, NJ: Princeton University Press.

Gurr, Ted Robert, and Barbara Harff. 1994. *Ethnic Conflict in World Politics.* Boulder: Westview Press.

Halpern, Howard Marvin. 1992. *You and Your Grown up Child: Nurturing a Better Relationship.* New York: Simon and Schuster.

Hankins, Gary. 1988. *Prescription for Anger.* Beaverton, OR: Princess Publishing.

Hardin, Garrett. 1968. "The Tragedy of the Commons." *Science* 162:1243.

Hardy, James Earl. 1990. "Silent Minorities: Despite the Huge Impact of Abortion on Minorities, Few Are Active in the Debate. Why?" *Scholastic Update* (April 20):18.

Harrington, C. B., and S. E. Merry. 1988. "Ideological Production: The Making of Community Mediation." *Law and Society Review* 22:708–35.

Heckscher, Charles C. 1993. "Searching for Mutual Gains in Labor Relations." In *Negotiation: Strategies for Mutual Gain: The Basic Seminar of the Harvard Program on Negotiation* (pp. 86–104), edited by Lavinia Hall. Newbury Park, CA: Sage.

Hill, Kenneth L. 1993. *Cold War Chronology: Soviet-American Relations, 1945–1991.* Washington, DC: Congressional Quarterly.

Hirsch, John L., and Robert B. Oakley. 1995. *Somalia and Operation Restore Hope: Reflections on Peacekeeping and Peacemaking.* Washington, DC: United States Institute of Peace Press.

Hitchens, Christopher. 1995. *The Missionary Position: Mother Teresa in Theory and Practice.* New York: Verso.

Hocker, Joyce L., and William W. Wilmot. 1985. *Interpersonal Conflict.* Dubuque, IA: William C. Brown.

Holmes, Robert L. 1990. *Nonviolence in Theory and Practice.* Belmont, CA: Wadsworth Publishing Co.

Honeyman, Christopher. 1993. "A Consensus on Mediators' Qualifications." *Negotiation Journal* 9(4):295–308.

Horwitt, Sanford D. 1989. *Let Them Call Me Rebel: Saul Alinsky, His Life and Legacy.* New York: Knopf.

ICAR (Institute for Conflict Analysis and Resolution). 1994. *Understanding Intergroup Conflict in Schools: Strategies and Resources.* Fairfax, VA: George Mason University.

International Alert. 1992. "Preparing to Promote Peace" (brochure).

Isaacson, Walter. 1992. *Kissinger: A Biography.* New York: Simon and Schuster.

Israeli, Raphael. 1985. *Man of Defiance: A Political Biography of Anwar Sadat.* Totowa, NJ: Barnes and Noble Books.

Johnson, Tim. 1996. "Community Policing: America's Best Chance to End Youth Violence." Community Policing Exchange; Community Policing Consortium. Published on the Internet at http://www.communitypolicing.or/ie-jf96.html.

Jonah, James O. C. 1990. "The Military Talks at Kilometer 101: The U.N.'s Effectiveness as a Third Party." *Negotiation Journal* 6(1):53–70.

Jones, Robert M. 1996. "Navigating through Troubled Waters: The Case for Collaboration in Water Resource Conflicts." In *Solutions in the Process.* Tallahassee: Florida Conflict Resolution Consortium.

Kahn, Si. 1982. *Organizing: A Guide for Grassroots Leaders.* New York: McGraw-Hill.

Kaiser, Robert G. 1991. *Why Gorbachev Happened: His Triumph, His Failure, and His Fall.* New York: Simon and Schuster.

Keeton, W. Page, ed. 1984. *Prosser and Keeton on Torts.* St. Paul, MN: West Publishing Co.

Kelly, Joan B. 1989. "Dispute Systems Design: A Family Case Study." *Negotiation Journal* 5(4):374–80.

Kelman, Herbert, ed. 1965. *International Behavior: A Social Psychological Analysis.* New York: Holt, Rinehart & Winston.

Kelman, Herbert C. 1981. "Reflections on the History and Status of Peace Research." *Conflict Management and Peace Science* 5:95–110.

Kelman, Herbert C. 1982. "Creating the Conditions for Israeli-Palestinian Negotiations." *Journal of Conflict Resolution* 26:39–75.

Kelman, Herbert C. 1996. "The Interactive Problem-Solving Approach." In *Managing Global Chaos,* edited by Chester Crocker, Fen Osler Hampson, and Pamela Aall. Washington, DC: United States Institute of Peace Press.

Kelman, Herbert, and Stephen Cohen. 1976. "The Problem-Solving Workshop: A Social Psychological Contribution to the Resolution of Conflict." *Journal of Peace Research* 8(2):79–90.

Kennan, George F. 1983. *The Nuclear Delusion: Soviet-American Relations in the Atomic Age.* New York: Pantheon Books.

Kennedy, Leslie W. 1990. *On the Borders of Crime: Conflict Management and Criminology.* New York: Longman.

Kennedy, Robert F. 1969. *Thirteen Days: A Memoir of the Cuban Missile Crisis.* New York: W. W. Norton.

Kettering Foundation Web Site. http://www.kettering.org.

Khor, Karen. 1995a. "Conflicting Trends Are Causing Ethical Dilemmas in Health-Care Industry: Hospitals and Nursing Homes Test Mediation for Impartial, Informed Solutions." *Consensus* 26:1.

Khor, Karen. 1995b. "Cost-Savings Propel Proliferation of States' Conflict-Resolution Programs: Disputants Range from Hindus in New Jersey to High-Plains Ranchers." *Consensus* 27:1, 12.

Kidder, Rushworth M. 1994. *Shared Values for a Troubled World: Conversations with Men and Women of Conscience.* San Francisco: Jossey-Bass.

Kilmann, Ralph H., and Kenneth W. Thomas. 1976. "Interpersonal Conflict-Handling Behavior as Reflections of Jungian Personality Dimensions." *Psychological Reports* 37:971–80.

King, Martin Luther, Jr. 1958. *Stride toward Freedom.* New York: Harper and Row.

King, Martin Luther, Jr. 1964. *Why We Can't Wait.* New York: Harper and Row.

King, Martin Luther, Jr. 1966. "Pilgrimage to Nonviolence." In *Nonviolence in America: A Documentary History,* edited by Staughton Lynd. Indianapolis: Bobbs Merrill.

King, Martin Luther, Jr. 1967. *Where Do We Go from Here: Chaos or Community?* New York: Harper and Row.

King, Martin Luther, Jr. 1983. "'I Have a Dream' Speech Given on August 28, 1963." In *The Words of Martin Luther King, Jr.,* edited by Coretta Scott King. New York: Newmarket Press.

Kirshenbaum, Mira, and Charles Foster. 1991. *Parent-Teen Breakthrough: The Relationship Approach.* New York: Plume.

Kissinger, Henry. 1994. *Diplomacy.* New York: Simon and Schuster.

Klein, Lawrence R., Fu-chen Lo, and Warwick J. McKibbin. 1995. *Arms Reduction: Economic Implications in the Post–Cold War Era.* New York: United Nations University Press.

Knutsen, Torbjorn. 1992. *A History of International Relations Theory: An Introduction.* New York: Manchester University Press.

Koch, Koen. 1984. "Civilian Defense: An Alternative to Military Defense?" *Netherlands' Journal of Sociology* 20:1–11.

Kolb, Deborah M. 1994. "Is It Her Voice or Her Place that Makes a Difference? Gender Issues in Negotiation." *Conciliation Quarterly* 13(1–2):7.

Kolb, Deborah M. 1995. "The Love for Three Oranges or: What Did We Miss about Ms. Follett in the Library?" *Negotiation Journal* 11(4): 339–48.

Kolb, Deborah M., and Associates. 1994. *When Talk Works: Profiles of Mediators.* San Francisco: Jossey-Bass.

Kondo, Tetsuo. 1990. "Some Notes on Rational Behavior, Normative Behavior, Moral Behavior, and Cooperation." *Journal of Conflict Resolution* 34(3):495–530.

Koppel, Ted. 1996. "The Perils of Info-Democracy." In *Managing Global Chaos.* Washington, DC: United States Institute of Peace Press.

Kotlikoff, Laurence J. 1992. *Generational Accounting: Knowing Who Pays, and When, for What We Spend.* New York: Free Press.

Kovach, Kenneth. 1987. "New Directions in Labor Relations." In *Conflict Management and Problem Solving: Interpersonal to International Applications,* edited by Dennis Sandole and Ingrid Sandole-Staroste. New York: New York University Press.

Kovach, Kimberlee K. 1994. *Mediation: Principles and Practice.* St. Paul, MN: West Publishing Co.

Kramer, Ralph M., and Harry Specht. 1969. *Readings in Community Organization Practice.* Englewood Cliffs, NJ: Prentice Hall.

Kraybill, Ron. 1993. "Democratic Decision Making: Developing Good Process." *Conciliation Quarterly* 12(4):10.

Kressel, K., and D. Pruitt. 1989. *Mediation Research: The Press and Effectiveness of Third-Party Intervention.* San Francisco: Jossey-Bass.

Kriesberg, Louis. 1988. "Strategies of Negotiating Agreements: Arab-Israeli and American-Soviet Cases." *Negotiation Journal* 4(1):19–29.

Kriesberg, Louis. 1992. "The U.S.-USSR and Middle East Cases." In *International Conflict Resolution: The U.S.-USSR and Middle East Cases.* New Haven, CT: Yale University Press.

Kriesberg, Louis. 1993. "Preventive Conflict Resolution of Inter-Communal Conflicts." Program on the Analysis and Resolution of Conflict (PARC), Syracuse University, Syracuse, NY.

Kriesberg, Louis, Terrell A. Northrup, and Stuart J. Thorson. 1989. *Intractable Conflicts and Their Transformation.* Syracuse, NY: Syracuse University Press.

Kriesberg, Louis, and Stuart J. Thorson. 1991. "Timing the De-escalation of International Conflicts." In *Syracuse Studies on Peace and Conflict Resolution* (p. 303), edited by Harriet Hyman Alonso, Charles Chatfield, and Louis Kriesberg. Syracuse, NY: Syracuse University Press.

Kubey, Craig. 1991. *You Don't Always Need a Lawyer.* Yonkers, NY: Consumers Union of United States.

Kumar, Chetan, and Elizabeth Cousens. 1996. "Peacebuilding in Haiti." In *International Peace Academy: Policy Briefing Series.* New York: International Peace Academy.

Kupchan, Charles A., and Clifford A. Kupchan. 1995. "The Promise of Collective Security." *International Security* 20(1):52–61.

La Feber, Walter. 1994. "Cold War." Microsoft *Encarta.* Microsoft Corporation and Funk and Wagnalls Corporation.

Larmer, Brook. 1986. "After Crime, Reconciliation." *Christian Science Monitor* (June 24).

Larson, Carl E., and David D. Chrislip. 1994. *Collaborative Leadership.* San Francisco: Jossey-Bass.

Lasswell, Harold D., Daniel Lerner, and Hans Speier, eds. 1979. *Propaganda and Communication in World History.* Honolulu: University Press of Hawaii.

Laue, James. 1987. "The Emergence and Institutionalization of Third Party Roles in Conflict." In *Conflict Management and Problem Solving: Interpersonal to International Applications,* edited by Dennis Sandole and Ingrid Sandole-Staroste. New York: New York University Press.

Laue, James H. 1993. "Resolution: Transforming Conflict and Violence." Working paper. George Mason University, Center for Conflict Analysis and Resolution.

Lawler, Peter. 1995. *A Question of Values: Johan Galtung's Peace Research.* Boulder: Lynne Rienner Publishers.

Leap, Terry L. 1995. *Collective Bargaining and Labor Relations,* 2nd ed. Englewood Cliffs, NJ: Prentice Hall.

Lederach, John Paul. 1990. "Training on Culture: Four Approaches." *Conciliation Quarterly* 9(1):6, 11–13.

Lederach, John Paul. 1994. *Building Peace: Sustainable Reconciliation in Divided Societies.* Harrisburg, PA: Eastern Mennonite University.

LeResche, Diane Neumann. 1990. "Procedural Justice of, by, and for American Ethnic Groups: A Comparison of Interpersonal Conflict Resolution

Procedures Used by Korean-Americans and American Community Mediation Centers with Procedural Justice Theories." Ph.D. disssertation, George Mason University, Fairfax, VA.

Lewis, Samuel W. 1990. "Foreword to the Series." In *Conflict: Resolution and Prevention.* New York: St. Martin's Press.

Lindblom, Charles E. 1968. *The Policy-Making Process.* Englewood Cliffs, NJ: Prentice Hall.

Lindskold, S. 1978. "Trust Development, the GRIT Proposal, and the Effects of Conciliatory Acts on Conflict and Cooperation." *Psychological Bulletin* 85:772–73.

Longan, Patrick E. 1994. "Bureaucratic Justice Meets ADR: The Emerging Role for Magistrates as Mediators." 73 *Nebraska Law Review:* 712.

Luttwak, Edward. 1994. "Arms Control, International." Microsoft *Encarta.* Microsoft Corporation and Funk and Wagnalls Corporation.

Lyons, Gene M., and Michael Mastanduno, eds. 1995. *Beyond Westphalia? State Sovereignty and International Intervention.* Baltimore: Johns Hopkins University Press.

Lytle, Clifford M. 1966. "The History of the Civil Rights Bill of 1964." *Journal of Negro History* 51:275–96.

Machiavelli, Niccolo. 1985. *The Prince.* Chicago: University of Chicago Press.

Magleby, David B. 1984. *Direct Legislation: Voting on Ballot Propositions in the United States.* Baltimore: Johns Hopkins University Press.

Makinda, Samuel M. 1996. "Sovereignty and International Security: Challenges for the United Nations." *Global Governance: A Review of Multilateralism and International Organizations* 2(2): 149–68.

Mandela, Nelson. 1965. *No Easy Walk to Freedom.* New York: Basic Books.

Mandela, Nelson. 1986. *The Struggle Is My Life.* New York: Pathfinder Press.

Mandela, Nelson. 1994. *Long Walk to Freedom.* Boston: Little, Brown.

Marx, Karl. 1936. *Capital, A Critique of Political Economy.* New York: Modern Library.

Marx, Karl, and Friedrich Engels. 1955. *The Communist Manifesto.* New York: Appleton-Century-Crofts.

Maslow, Abraham. 1943. "A Theory of Human Motivation." *Psychological Review* 50:370–96.

Mastrofski, Jennifer Adams. 1990. "Mediation in Court-Based Systems: More Variations than Similarities." *Negotiation Journal* 6(3):257–68.

Matthews, Roger. 1988. *Informal Justice?* London: Sage.

Matusow, Allen J. 1984. *The Unraveling of America: A History of Liberalism in the 1960s.* New York: Harper and Row.

McDonald, John W. 1988. "Guidelines for Track Two Diplomats." *Peace in Action* 4:11.

McDonald, John W. 1995. "Why Ethnic Conflict?" *Peace Builder* 3(1):2.

McDonald, John W., Jr., and Diane B. Bendahmane. 1987. *Conflict Resolution: Track Two Diplomacy.* Washington, DC: Center for the Study of Foreign Affairs.

McFarland, Daniel. 1995. "Consultation on Reconciliation: New Directions in Peacebuilding." *Peace Builder* 3(2):1, 10–11.

McGillis, Daniel. 1986. *Community Dispute Resolution—Programs and Public Policy.* Washington, DC: U.S. Department of Justice, National Institute of Justice, Office of Communication and Research Utilization.

McGillis, Daniel. 1987. *Consumer Dispute Resolution: A Survey of Programs.* Washington, DC: NIDR.

McGuire, William, and Leslie Wheeler. 1993. "Alinsky, Saul David." In *American Social Leaders,* edited by Amy Lewis and Paula McGuire. Santa Barbara, CA: ABC-CLIO.

McLauchlan, Gregory. 1996. "Stepping Back: Nuclear Arms Control and the End of the Cold War." *Peace and Change* 21:372–75.

Melman, Seymour. 1970. *The Defense Economy: Conversion of Industries and Occupation Civilian Needs.* New York: Praeger.

Menkel-Meadow, Carrie. 1991. "Pursuing Settlement in an Adversary Culture: A Tale of Innovation Co-Coped or 'The Law of ADR.'" *Florida State University Law Review* 19:1–46.

Merwe, Hugo van der, and Dennis J. D. Sandole. 1993. *Conflict Resolution Theory and Practice: Integration and Application.* New York: Manchester University Press.

Michalak, Stanley J. 1994. "Diplomacy." Microsoft *Encarta.* Microsoft Corporation and Funk and Wagnalls Corporation.

Michaud, David. 1993. "The Role of Police in Less-Tractable Conflicts." Working paper no. 93-34. Conflict Research Consortium.

Mikula, Gerold, Birgit Petri, and Norbert Tanzer. 1990. "What People Regard as Unjust: Types and Structures of Everyday Experiences of Injustice." *European Journal of Social Psychology* 20:133–49.

Milne, A. L. 1983. "Divorce Mediation: The State of the Art." *Mediation Quarterly* 1.

Mitchell, C. R. 1991. "A Willingness to Talk: Conciliatory Gestures and De-Escalation." *Negotiation Journal* 7(4):405–29.

Mitchell, C. R. 1993. "Track Two Triumphant? Reflections on the Oslo Process and Conflict Resolution in the Middle East." *ICAR Newsletter* 5(6):8, 12.

Montville, Joseph. 1987. "The Arrow and the Olive Branch: A Case for Track Two Diplomacy." In *Conflict Resolution: Track Two Diplomacy,* edited by J. McDonald and D. Bendahmane. Washington, DC: Foreign Service Institute, U.S. Department of State.

Montville, Joseph. 1993. "The Healing Function in Political Conflict Resolution." In *Conflict Resolution Theory and Practice: Integration and Application,* edited by Dennis J. D. Sandole and Hugo van der Merwe. New York: Manchester University Press.

Moore, Christopher W. 1986. *The Mediation Process.* San Francisco: Jossey-Bass.

Morgenthau, Hans. 1960. *Politics among Nations.* New York: Knopf.

Morris, Catherine, and Andrew Pirie. 1994. *Qualifications for Dispute Resolution: Perspectives on the Debate.* Victoria, BC: University of Victoria Institute for Dispute Resolution.

Moseley, Leonard. 1982. *Marshall, Hero for Our Times.* New York: Hearst Books.

Murray, John S. 1989. "Designing a Disputing System for Central City and Its Schools." *Negotiation Journal* 5(4):365–72.

Myrdal, Alva. 1980. "Statement by Alva Myrdal upon Receiving the International Award from the Albert Einstein Peace Prize Foundation, 29 May 1980." In *Disarmament: A Periodic Review by the United Nations* (pp. 45–51). Washington, DC: United Nations.

Myrdal, Alva. 1982. *The Game of Disarmament* (revised and updated). New York: Pantheon.

Nader, Laura. 1979. "Disputing without the Force of Law." *Yale Law Journal* 88:1019–21.

Naess, Arne. 1974. "Nonmilitary Defense." In *Preventing World War III: Some Proposals* (pp. 125–35), edited by Quincy Wright, William M. Evan, and Morton Deutsch. New York: Simon and Schuster.

National Academy of Sciences. 1985. *Nuclear Arms Control.* Washington, DC: National Academy Press.

National Association for Community Mediation. 1996. *NAFCM News* (Spring).

"New Democracies Search for Transitional Justice." 1995. In *Peacewatch* 2(1):1.

Newhouse, John. 1989. *War and Peace in the Nuclear Age.* New York: Knopf.

Nolan-Haley, Jacqueline M. 1992. *Alternative Dispute Resolution in a Nutshell.* St. Paul, MN: West Publishing Co.

Northedge, F. S. 1986. *The League of Nations: Its Life and Times 1920–1946.* New York: Holmes and Meier.

Northrup, Terrell A. 1989. "Dynamic of Identity." In *Intractable Conflicts and Their Transformation,* edited by Louis Kriesberg, Terrell A. Northrup, and Stuart J. Thorson. Syracuse, NY: Syracuse University Press.

"Norway's Back-Channel Success Story." 1995. *Negotiation* (Spring–Summer):1, 11.

Norwegian Nobel Committee. 1996. "Award of the Nobel Peace Prize for 1995 to Joseph Rotblat and Pugwash Conference on Science and World Affairs." *Pugwash Newsletter* 33(3):113.

O'Brien, David M. 1987. *What Is Due Process? Courts and Science-Policy Disputes.* New York: Russell Sage Foundation.

Olczak, Paul V., and Dean G. Pruitt. 1995. "Beyond Hope: Approaches to Resolving Seemingly Intractable Conflict." In *Conflict, Cooperation and Justice: Essays Inspired by the Work of Morton Deutsch,* edited by Barbara Benedict Bunker, Jeffrey Z. Rubin, and associates. San Francisco: Jossey-Bass.

Olson, David. 1980. *The Legislative Process: A Comparative Approach.* New York: Harper and Row.

Osgood, Charles E. 1962. *An Alternative to War or Surrender.* Urbana: University of Illinois Press.

Osgood, Charles E. 1966. *Perspective in Foreign Policy.* Palo Alto, CA: Pacific Books.

Ostrom, Elinor. 1990. *Governing the Commons: The Evolution of Institutions for Collective Action.* Cambridge: Cambridge University Press.

Ozone Secretariat. 1996. World Wide Web Home Page. http://www.unep.org/unep/secretar/ozone/abtozsec.htm.

Patfoort, Pat. 1995. *Uprooting Violence: Building Nonviolence: From Nonviolent Upbringing to a Nonviolent Society.* Freeport, ME: Cobblesmith.

Pennock, J. Roland, and John W. Chapman. 1977. *Due Process.* New York: New York University Press.

Perlman, Lawrence, and Steven C. Nelson. 1983. "New Approaches to the Resolution of International Commercial Disputes." *International Law* 17:215.

Plapinger, Elizabeth, Margaret L. Shaw, and Donna Stienstra. 1993. *Judge's Deskbook on Court ADR.* Cambridge: Harvard Law School.

Pogue, Forrest. 1963–73. *George C. Marshall.* New York: Viking Press.

Porter, Bruce. 1988. *Order by the Court: Special Masters in Corrections.* New York: Edna McConnell Clark Foundation.

Prothrow-Stith, Deborah, and Michaele Weissman. 1991. *Deadly Consequences: How Violence Is Destroying Our Teenage Population and a Plan to Begin to Solve the Problem.* New York: HarperCollins.

Pruitt, Dean G. 1991. "Strategic Choice in Negotiation." In *Negotiation Theory and Practice,* edited by J. William Breslin and Jeffrey Z. Rubin. Cambridge, MA: Program on Negotiation at Harvard Law School.

Pruitt, Dean G. 1995. "Process Outcome in Community Mediation." *Negotiation Journal* 11: 365–78.

Pruitt, Dean G., and Peter J. Carnevale, eds. 1993. *Negotiation in Social Conflict: Escalation, Stalemate, and Settlement.* Pacific Grove, CA: Brooks/Cole.

Pruitt, Dean G., and Jeffrey Z. Rubin. 1986. *Social Conflict.* New York: Random House.

Quandt, William B. 1993. *Peace Process: American Diplomacy and the Arab-Israeli Conflict since 1967.* Washington, DC: Brookings Institution.

Raef, Susan. 1996. "As Congress Struggles to Rewrite the Nation's Tort Laws, the States Already May Have Done the Job." World Wide Web: American Bar Association.

Raiffa, Howard. 1982. *The Art and Science of Negotiation.* Cambridge, MA: Belknap Press of Harvard University Press.

RAND Institute for Civil Justice. 1996. "Research Brief: Evaluating the Civil Justice Reform Act of 1990." World Wide Web. http://www.rand.org/publications/RB/RB9022.

Rapoport, Anatol. 1960. *Fights, Games, and Debates.* Ann Arbor: University of Michigan Press.

Rapoport, Anatol, ed. 1974. *Game Theory as a Theory of Conflict Resolution.* Boston: D. Reidel Publishing.

Reich, Kenneth. 1991. "Rallies Losing Intensity." *Los Angeles Times,* 10 February, 1B.

Reinhold, Robert. 1990. "Ballot Becomes a Burden in California. *New York Times,* 24 September, A16.

Renner, Michael. "Remaking U.N. Peacekeeping: U.S. Policy and Real Reform," edited by Worldwatch Institute. World Wide Web. http://www.fas.org./pub/gen/ncecd/reports/ur.html.

Resnick, Judith. 1995. "Many Doors? Closing Doors? Alternative Dispute Resolution and Adjudication." *Ohio State Journal on Conflict Resolution* 10.

Richardson, Lewis F. 1960a. *Arms and Insecurity.* Pittsburgh, PA: Boxwood Press.

Richardson, Lewis F. 1960b. *Statistics of Deadly Quarrels.* Chicago: Quadrangle Books.

Ridolfi, Roberto. 1963. *The Life of Niccolo Machiavelli.* Chicago: University of Chicago Press.

Riskin, Leonard L., and James E. Westbrook. 1987. *Dispute Resolution and Lawyers.* St. Paul, MN: West Publishing Co.

Rivkin, David. 1991. "International Arbitration." In *Commercial Arbitration for the 1990s,* edited by Richard Medalie. Chicago: American Bar Association, Litigation Section.

Roberts, Nancy L. 1991. "Elise Björn-Hansen Boulding." In *American Peace Writers, Editors, and Periodicals: A Dictionary* (pp. 30–32). New York: Greenwood Press.

Rosenberg, Joshua, and Jay H. Folberg. 1994. "Alternative Dispute Resolution: An Empirical Analysis." 46 *Stanford Law Review* 1487.

Rosenberg, Tina. 1996. "Recovering from Apartheid." *New Yorker* (18 November):86–95.

Ross, Marc Howard. 1992. "Ethnic Conflict and Dispute Management: Addressing Interests and Identities, Getting to an Accord." *Studies in Law, Politics and Society* 12:107–46.

Rothman, Jay. 1992. *Confrontation to Cooperation: Resolving Ethnic and Regional Conflict.* Newbury Park, CA: Sage Publications.

Rowe, Mary P. 1991a. "The Corporate Ombudsman: An Overview and Analysis." In *Negotiation Theory and Practice,* edited by J. William Breslin and Jeffrey Z. Rubin. Cambridge, MA: Program on Negotiation at Harvard Law School.

Rowe, Mary P. 1991b. "The Ombudsman's Role in a Dispute Resolution System." *Negotiation Journal* 7:353–62.

Rowe, W. D. 1977. *An Anatomy of Risk.* New York: Wiley.

Rubin, Jeffrey, ed. 1992. "Special Issue: Reflections on the War in the Persian Gulf." *Negotiation Journal* 8(1).

Rubin, Jeffrey Z., and Carol Rubin. 1988. *When Families Fight.* Cambridge, MA: Program on Negotiation at Harvard Law School.

Ryan, Stephen. 1995. *Ethnic Conflict and International Relations.* Brookfield, VT: Dartmouth.

Sadat, Anwar. 1992. "Speech before the Israeli Knesset." Quoted in *From Confrontation to Cooperation* (p. 16), edited by Jay Rothman. Newbury Park, CA: Sage.

Samovar, L. A., and R. E. Porter. 1985. *Intercultural Communication: A Reader.* Belmont, CA: Wadsworth Publishing Co.

Sander, Frank E. A. 1993. "The Courthouse and Alternative Dispute Resolution." In *Negotiation: Strategies for Mutual Gain: The Basic Seminar of the Harvard Program on Negotiation* (pp. 43–60), edited by Lavinia Hall. Newbury Park, CA: Sage.

Sandole, Dennis J. D., and Hugo van der Merwe, eds. 1993. *Conflict Resolution Theory and Practice: Integration and Application.* New York: Manchester University Press.

Sanford, Maine, Police Department. 1996. "Community Policing." World Wide Web Home Page. http://www.biddeford.com/~pdcommun.html.

Saunders, Harold. 1995. "Sustained Dialogue Comes Home." *Connections* 6, 2:5–6.

Schellenberg, James A. 1996. *Conflict Resolution—Theory, Research, and Practice.* Albany: State University of New York Press.

Schelling, Thomas C. 1960. *Strategy of Conflict.* Cambridge, MA: Harvard University Press.

Schmidt, Janet P. 1995. "Mediation and the Healing Journey toward Forgiveness." *Conciliation Quarterly* 14(3):2–4.

Schultz, Beatrice. 1989. "Conflict Resolution Training Programs: Implications for Theory and Research." *Negotiation Journal* 5(3):301–12.

Schwartz, Richard. 1989. "Arab-Jewish Dialogue in the United States: Toward Track II Tractability." In *Intractable Conflicts and Their Transformation* (pp. 180–209), edited by Louis Kriesberg, Terrell Northrup, and Stuart Thorson. Syracuse, NY: Syracuse University Press.

Schwarz, Roger M. 1994. *The Skilled Facilitator: Practical Wisdom for Developing Effective Groups.* San Francisco: Jossey-Bass.

Scimecca, Joseph A. 1993. "Theory and Alternative Dispute Resolution: A Contradiction in Terms?" In *Conflict Resolution Theory and Practice,* edited by Dennis J. D. Sandole and Hugo van der Merwe. New York: Manchester University Press.

Scott, George. 1973. *The Rise and Fall of the League of Nations.* London: Hutchinson.

Segal, Phyllis N. 1993. "'Reinventing Government' Includes ADR." *Consensus* 20:8.

Seifert, Harvey. 1965. *Conquest by Suffering: The Process and Prospects of Nonviolent Resistance.* Philadelphia: Westminster Press.

Sharp, Gene. 1973. *The Politics of Nonviolent Action.* Boston: Porter Sargent.

Sharp, Gene, and Bruce Jenkins. 1990. *Civilian-Based Defense: A Post-Military Weapons System.* Princeton, NJ: Princeton University Press.

Shawcross, William. 1979. *Sideshow: Kissinger, Nixon, and the Destruction of Cambodia.* New York: Simon and Schuster.

Sheehy, Gail. 1991. *Gorbachev: The Making of the Man Who Shook the World.* London: Heinemann.

Sherman, E. 1995. "Court-Mandated Alternative Dispute Resolution: What Form of Participation Should Be Required?" In *1995 Supplement to Dispute Resolution: Negotiation, Mediation, and Other Processes* (pp. 48–57), edited by Stephen B. Goldberg, Frank E. A. Sander, and Nancy H. Rogers. Boston: Little, Brown.

Siccama, Jan G. 1996. "Conflict Prevention and Early Warning in the Political Practice of International Organizations." Netherlands Institute of International Relations.

Silbey, Susan S., and Sally Engle Merry. 1984. "What Do Plaintiffs Want? Re-examining the Concept of Dispute." *Justice System Journal* 9:151–78.

Simmel, Georg. 1956. *Conflict and the Web of Group Affiliations.* New York: Free Press.

Simon, Herbert A. 1983. *Reason in Human Affairs.* Stanford, CA: Stanford University Press.

Simpson, Mary. 1996. "A Story of Victim-Offender Reconciliation." *Interaction* 7(4):13–14.

Singer, Linda R. 1990. *Settling Disputes: Conflict Resolution in Business, Families, and the Legal System.* Boulder: Westview Press.

Singh, Nagendra. 1989. *The Role and Record of the International Court of Justice.* Dordrecht: Martinus Nijhoff.

Slaikeu, Karl A. 1989. "Designing Dispute Resolution Systems in the Health Care Industry." *Negotiation Journal* 5(4).

Slaikeu, Karl A. 1996. *When Push Comes to Shove: A Practical Guide to Mediating Disputes.* San Francisco: Jossey-Bass.

Smith, Anthony. 1986. "Conflict and Collective Identity: Class, *Ethnie,* and Nation." In *International Conflict Resolution: Theory and Practice* (pp. 63–84), edited by Edward E. Azar and John W. Burton. Boulder: Lynne Rienner Publishers.

Smyth, Leo F. 1994. "Intractable Conflicts and the Role of Identity." *Negotiation Journal* 10: 311–21.

Society of Professionals in Dispute Resolution. 1989. *Report of the SPIDR Commission on Qualifications.* Washington, DC: Society of Professionals in Dispute Resolution.

Society of Professionals in Dispute Resolution. 1995. "SPIDR Conference Brochure." Washington, DC: Society of Professionals in Dispute Resolution.

Society of Professionals in Dispute Resolution. 1996. *Ensuring Competence and Quality in Dispute Resolution Practice.* Washington, DC: Society of Professionals in Dispute Resolution.

Stein, Kenneth W., and Samuel W. Lewis. 1996. "Mediation in the Middle East." In *Managing Global Chaos.* Washington, DC: United States Institute of Peace Press.

Stephens, John B. 1992. "Conflict over Sexual Orientation in the Church: The Experience of Two Denominations." Dissertation proposal, George Mason University, Fairfax, VA, p. 9.

Stephens, John B. 1993. "Homosexuality and Faith: The United Methodist Church." Paper presented at Biannual National Conference for Peacemaking and Conflict Resolution, Portland, OR.

Stephens, William O., John B. Stephens, and Frank Dukes. 1995. "The Ethics of Environmental Mediation." In *Mediating Environmental Conflicts: Theory and Practice* (pp. 167–84), edited by J. Walton Blackburn and Willa Marie Bruce. Westport, CT: Quorum Books.

Stiehm, Judith. 1972. *Nonviolent Power: Active and Passive Resistance in America.* Lexington, KY: D. C. Heath.

Strauss, David. 1993. "Facilitated Collaborative Problem Solving." In *Negotiation: Strategies for Mutual Gain: The Basic Seminar of the Harvard Program on Negotiation,* edited by Lavinia Hall. Newbury Park, CA: Sage.

Sur, Serge. 1993. *Nuclear Deterrence: Problems and Perspectives in the 1990s.* New York: United Nations.

Susskind, Lawrence. 1993a. "Resolving Public Disputes." In *Negotiation: Strategies for Mutual Gain: The Basic Seminar of the Harvard Program on Negotiation* (pp. 61–76), edited by Lavinia Hall. Newbury Park, CA: Sage.

Susskind, Lawrence E. 1993b. "When ADR Becomes the Law: A Review of Federal Practice." *Negotiation Journal* 9(1):59–76.

Susskind, Lawrence. 1994. "Activist Mediation and Public Disputes." In *When Talk Works,* edited by Deborah Kolb and Associates. San Francisco: Jossey-Bass.

Susskind, Lawrence, and Jeffrey Cruikshank. 1987. *Breaking the Impasse.* New York: Basic Books.

Susskind, Lawrence, and Patrick Field. 1996. *Dealing with an Angry Public.* New York: Free Press.

Susskind, Lawrence, and Gerald McMahon. 1985. "The Theory and Practice of Negotiated Rulemaking." *Yale Journal of Regulation* 3:133.

Taylor, Anita, and Judi Beinstein Miller. 1994. *Conflict and Gender.* Cresskill, NJ: Hampton Press.

Tepper, Alec. "UN Peacekeeping," edited by United Nations Association in Canada Internet Home Page. World Wide Web. http://www.unac.org/unfaq/peacekee.html.

Thomas, George M., Henry A. Walker, and Morris Zelditch Jr. 1986. "Legitimacy and Collective Action." *Social Forces* 65:23.

Thurow, Lester C. 1980. *The Zero-Sum Society: Distribution and the Possibilities for Economic Change.* New York: Basic Books.

Tillet, Gregory. 1991. *Resolving Conflict: A Practical Approach.* Sydney, Australia: Sydney University Press.

Ting-Toomey, Stella. 1985. "Toward a Theory of Conflict and Culture." In *Communication, Culture and Organizational Processes,* edited by S. Gudykunst and S. Ting-Toomey. Newbury Park, CA: Sage.

Touval, Saadia. 1995. "Ethical Dilemmas in International Mediation." *Negotiation Journal* 11:333–38.

Touval, Saadia, and I. William Zartman. 1985. *International Mediation in Theory and Practice.* Boulder: Westview Press.

Tribe, Laurence. 1990. *Abortion: The Clash of Absolutes.* New York: W. W. Norton and Co.

Trist, E. L. 1983. "Referent Organizations and the Development of Interorganizational Domains." *Human Relations* 36:247–68.

Trolander, Judith Ann. 1986. "Alinsky, Saul David." In *Bibliographical Dictionary of Social Welfare in America* (pp. 20–23), edited by Walter I. Trattner. Westport, CT: Greenwood Press.

Tuchman, Barbara Wertheim. 1962. *The Guns of August.* New York: Macmillan.

Tutu, Desmond. 1984. *Hope and Suffering: Sermons and Speeches.* Grand Rapids, MI: Eerdmans.

Tyler, T. R., and E. A. Lind. 1992. "A Relational Model of Authority in Groups." In *Advances in Experimental Social Psychology,* vol. 25 (pp. 115–92), edited by M. P. Zanna. San Diego: Academic Press.

Umbreit, Mark. 1987. "Victim Offender Mediation and Judicial Leadership." *Judicature* 69(4):202–4.

Umbreit, Mark S. 1995. *Mediating Interpersonal Conflicts: A Pathway to Peace.* West Concord, MN: CPI Publishing.

United Nations. World Wide Web Home Page. http://www.un.org.

United Nations. 1992. *Handbook on the Peaceful Settlement of Disputes between States.* New York: United Nations.

United Nations. 1996. "Boutros Boutros-Ghali United Nations Secretary-General." In *UN Press Release: Biographical Note SG/2015/Rev. 6, 23 April 1996.* New York: United Nations.

United Nations Institute for Disarmament Research. 1996. *UNIDIR and Its Activities.* Geneva, Switzerland: United Nations Institute for Disarmament Research.

United States Institute of Peace. Forthcoming. *Virtual Diplomacy: Conference Proceedings.* Washington, DC: United States Institute of Peace.

Ury, William L. 1985. *Beyond the Hotline: How Crisis Control Can Prevent Nuclear War.* Boston: Houghton Mifflin.

Ury, William. 1991. *Getting Past No: Negotiating with Difficult People.* New York: Bantam Books.

Ury, William L., Jeanne M. Brett, and Stephen B. Goldberg. 1988a. *Getting Disputes Resolved: Designing Systems to Cut the Costs of Conflict.* San Francisco: Jossey-Bass.

Ury, William L., Jeanne M. Brett, and Stephen B. Goldberg. 1988b. *Interests, Rights and Power: Designing Dispute Resolution Systems.* Evanston, IL: Dispute Resolution Research Center.

Ury, William L., Jeanne M. Brett, and Stephen B. Goldberg. 1991. "Designing an Effective Dispute Resolution System." In *Negotiation Theory and Practice,* edited by J. William Breslin and Jeffrey Z. Rubin. Cambridge, MA: Program on Negotiation at Harvard Law School.

USIP Web Site. http://www.usip.org.

Van Bergeijk, Peter A. G. 1994. *Economic Diplomacy, Trade and Commercial Policy.* Cornwall, England: Hartnolls Limited.

Vogele, William B. 1993. "Deterrence by Civilian Defense." *Peace and Change* 18:1:26–49.

Volkan, Vamik. 1985. "The Need to Have Enemies and Allies." *Political Psychology* 6:219–47.

Wall, James A., Jr., Lawrence F. Schiller, and Ronald J. Ebert. 1984. "Should Judges Grease the Slow Wheels of Justice? A Survey on the Effectiveness of Judicial Mediary Techniques." *Journal of Trial Advocacy* 83:94–99.

Wallensteen, Peter. 1985. "Focus on American-Soviet Détente: What Went Wrong?" *Journal of Peace Research* 22:1–8.

Warfield, Wallace. 1993. "Public-Policy Conflict Resolution: The Nexus between Culture and Process." In *Conflict Resolution Theory and Practice: Integration and Application* (pp. 176–93), edited by Dennis J. D. Sandole and Hugo van der Merwe. New York: Manchester University Press.

Wasiolek, Edward. 1985. *L. N. Tolstoy: Life, Work, and Criticism.* Fredericton, Canada: York Press.

Weber, Thomas. 1992. "Conflict Resolution and Gandhian Ethics." *Interdisciplinary Peace Research* (May–June):115–18.

Wehr, Paul. 1979. *Conflict Regulation.* Boulder: Westview Press.

Wehr, Paul, Heidi Burgess, and Guy Burgess. 1994. *Justice without Violence.* Boulder: Lynne Rienner Publishers.

Wehr, Paul, and Sharon Erickson Nepstad. 1994. "Violence, Nonviolence, and Justice in Sandinista Nicaragua." In *Justice without Violence* (pp. 81–98), edited by Paul Wehr, Heidi Burgess, and Guy Burgess. Boulder: Lynne Rienner Publishers.

Weisbrot, Robert. 1990. *Freedom Bound: A History of America's Civil Rights Movement.* New York: W. W. Norton and Co..

Weiss, David S. 1996. *Beyond the Walls of Conflict: Mutual Gains Negotiating for Unions and Management.* Chicago: Irwin Professional Publishing.

Weiss, Thomas G. 1993. *Collective Security in a Changing World: A World Peace Foundation.* Boulder: Lynne Rienner Publishers.

Weissman, Steven. 1996. "'Reg-Neg' Can Work, but Pitfalls Remain." *Consensus* 29:3. 9.

Whalen, Charles, and Barbara Whalen. 1985. *The Longest Debate: A Legislative History of the 1964 Civil Rights Act.* Washington, DC: Seven Locks Press.

White, Ralph K. 1987. "Deterrence and Tension Reduction." In *Conflict Management and Problem Solving: Interpersonal to International Applications,* edited by Dennis Sandole and Ingrid Sandole-Staroste. New York: New York University Press.

Whitman, Alden. 1985. *American Reformers: An H. W. Wilson Bibliographical Dictionary.* New York: H. W. Wilson.

Who's Who of American Women, 1995–1996, 19th ed. 1995. Chicago: Marquis Who's Who

Wilkins, Roger. 1993. "My Friend Jim Laue." *ICAR Newsletter* 5(6):1, 5.

Workskills Program. 1991. "Six Communicating Tricks." In *Better Health and Productivity through Improved Workplace Relationships,* developed by Eileen Derr, Jay Thorwaldson, and Nancy Yeend. Palo Alto, CA: Palo Alto Medical Foundation for Health Care, Research and Education, Department of Community Relations.

Wright, Quincy. 1965. *A Study of War.* Chicago: University of Chicago Press.

Young, Christopher. 1991. *The Role of the Media in International Conflict.* Ottawa: Canadian Institute for Peace and Security.

Zartman, I. William. 1985. *Ripe for Resolution.* New York: Oxford University Press.

Zartman, I. William, and Victor A. Kremenyuk. 1995. *Cooperative Security: Reducing Third World Wars.* Syracuse, NY: Syracuse University Press.

Zillessen, Horst. 1996. "Survey Shows Preparation Must Include Classroom and 'School of Hard Knocks.'" *Consensus* 29:5, 8.

About the Authors

Heidi Burgess and Guy M. Burgess are codirectors of the University of Colorado's Conflict Research Consortium, a multidisciplinary research consortium of graduate students, faculty members, and conflict resolution practitioners who are united by their interest in finding better ways of managing and resolving conflict. The Burgesses both hold Ph.D.s in sociology, obtained from the University of Colorado in 1979. In 1980 they spent a year working on dispute resolution at MIT, after which they returned to Colorado. Guy spent several years working on a series of environmental conflict resolution programs run by the governor of Colorado, while Heidi was a program associate at an environmental conflict management firm. Heidi and Guy then formed their own conflict management consulting firm until 1987, when they collaborated with several faculty members at the University of Colorado to create the Conflict Research Consortium.

Index

Nuclear confrontation, 87
Nuclear disarmament, 279
Nuclear Regulatory Commission, 48
Nuclear Supplier's Guidelines, 287

Ohio State Journal on Dispute Resolution, 14
Olczak, Paul, 90, 238
Ombudsman, 4, 12, 223–224
    advantages and disadvantages of, 224
    definition of, 223
    offices, 127, 308
    services of, 223
Organization of Petroleum Exporting Countries (OPEC), 165
Organizational conflict, 223
Osgood, Charles E., 91, 138
Oslo Accords Middle East peace process, 179, 187, 224–227, 248. *See also* Israel, PLO recognition; Israeli-Palestinian conflict; Middle East
Oslo Peace Research Institute, 234
Ozone Secretariat, 199
Palestine Liberation Organization (PLO), 43, 208, 225, 226
Palestinians, 39, 44, 226
    rights of, 42
    self-rule, 226
    See also Israeli-Palestinian conflict
Panama Canal Treaty, 44
Parent-child conflict, 1, 146, 183, 229. *See also* Family conflict
Parent-teen conflict, 136. *See also* Family conflict
Parks, Rosa, 198
Parties, 75, 229–230
Partnering, 230
Passive resistance, 132. S*ee also* Civilian-based defense
Patton, Bruce, 124, 297
Peace, 27, 131, 230–231, 279
    definition of, 36, 131, 230
    history of, 36
    and justice, 231, 234
    through strength, 231
Peace and Change: A Journal of Peace Research, 79

Peace and Conflict: Journal of Peace Psychology, 231–232
Peace Brigades International (PBI), 232
Peace building, 37, 65, 232–233, 289, 291, 293
Peace Chronicle, 79
Peace churches, 232
Peace History Society, 231
Peace of Westphalia, 233
Peace research, 131, 153, 160, 233–234. *See also* Peace studies
Peace spiral, 276. *See also* De-escalation
Peace studies, 38. *See also* Peace research
Peace Studies Association (PSA), 234–235
Peacekeeping, 37, 65, 101, 119, 232, 235, 236, 293
    in Cyprus, 235–236
Peacemaking, 35, 37, 150, 194, 232, 235–237, 293
PeaceNet, 78
Pearl Harbor, 31
Peer mediation, 179. *See also* School conflict
Perceptions, 154
Peres, Shimon, 225
perestroika, 57
Perez de Cuellar, Javier, 153, 292
Permanent Court of Arbitration, 28, 152
Péron, Juan, 123
Persian Gulf War, 31, 61, 62, 152, 237–238. *See also* Iraq; Kuwait; Middle East
Personal injury disputes, 49, 81, 283
Persuasion, 71, 75, 238
Petitions, 70
Polarization, 7, 238–239, 250
Police-citizen conflicts, 239–240
Police-community relations, 71, 72
Policy dialogues, 240
Political conflict, 92
Political lobbying, 75
Political realism, 200
Politics, international, 200
Positional bargaining. *See* Bargaining, positional
Positions, 6, 33, 46, 75, 129, 147, 210
Power, 31, 240–243

balancing, 3, 7, 50, 178, 242–243
building, 70
contests, 75
definition of, 240
differentials, 89, 182
in families, 124
imbalances, 50
integrative, 241
in negotiations, 34, 211, 33
over, 109, 241
sources of, 34, 54, 75, 270
strategies, 75
threat, 241
to, 109, 241
of unions, 170
with, 109, 241
See also Balance of power
Powerlessness, 112
Precedent, 3, 4, 9
Predispute agreements, 243
Prejudice reduction, 232
Prenegotiation, 91
Preventive deployment, 101
Prisoner's dilemma game, 131
Privacy, 3, 9, 13, 21, 63
    of negotiations, 178, 226, 278
Private judging, 2, 11, 50, 244–246
Problem solving, 246
    analytical, 65, 246–248
    collaborative, 7, 57–59, 61, 70, 79, 83, 126, 248
    mediation, 192
    See also Consensus building
Problem-solving workshops, 18, 38. *See also* Problem solving, analytical
Procedural justice, 161
Product liability disputes, 195, 283
Program on Negotiation (PON) at Harvard Law School, 79, 128, 178, 215, 248–249
Propaganda, 249
Protective accompaniment, 232
Protestant Reformation, 233
Pruitt, Dean, 88, 90, 116, 216, 238, 276
Public Conversations Project, 249–250, 300
Public meetings and hearings, 46–48, 173, 250
Public policy conflicts, 64, 79, 250–251
Public policy making, 7
Public participation. *See* Citizen participation

Pugwash Conferences on
Science and World Affairs,
251–252
Student Pugwash, 252
Punitive damages, 283

Quakers, 150
as mediators, 187
Quebec-Canadian conflict, 65

Rabin, Yitzhak, 40, 225
Racial conflicts, 71, 74, 87,
118–120. *See also* Civil
rights; Ethnic conflicts
Racial injustice, 289
Railway Labor Act of 1926, 169,
253
RAND Institute for Civil Justice,
51
Rapoport, Anatol, 132, 160, 234,
253
Rational emotive therapy, 17
Rationality, 2, 17, 213, 253–254
Reagan, Ronald, 27, 28, 44, 57,
138, 151, 279
Reality testing, 46, 254–255
Realpolitik, 165
Reassurance, 76
Recognition, 38, 181, 191, 208, 303
Reconciliation, 15, 16, 18, 86, 255
in divorce, 108
Referendum, 255–256
Reframing, 37, 46, 113, 212, 256,
306, 309. *See also* Framing
Refugees, 293
repatriation of, 27
Regional conflicts, 44
Regulatory disputes, 126. *See also*
Regulatory negotiation
Regulatory negotiation, 5, 13,
127, 208, 209, 256, 257
Relationship building, 18, 78, 128
in adversarial process, 85
gender differences in, 136
in labor-management conflicts,
26
in mediation, 69, 136, 181, 190
Relationships, 2, 5, 6, 9, 15, 16
Relative deprivation, 304
Relaxation techniques, 17
Religious conflict, 18, 65
Representation, 257
of interest groups, 147
Research Exchange on the
Prevention of War, 160, 234
Reservation price, 107

Resolution, definition of, 77
Respect, 124, 133
Restitution, 86, 303
Retaliation, 16, 134
Revenge, 15
Richardson, Lewis, 234, 257–258
Rights, 5, 258–259
civil and political, 143
human. *See* Human rights
individual, 8
of free speech, 296
social, economic, and cultural,
143
Ripeness, 68, 91, 168, 212–215,
248, 259, 285, 294
of international conflicts, 187
of intractable conflicts, 156
Risk, 122, 141
and uncertainty, 259
Roe v. Wade, 258–261, 300
Rogers Plan of 1969, 40
Roommate disputes, 183
Rothman, Jay, 18, 31, 97, 113
Rowe, Mary, 223
Rowlatt Acts, 133
Rubin, Jeffrey, 88, 116, 261, 276
Ruiz v. Estelle, 274
Rulemaking. *See* Regulatory
negotiation
Rules of engagement, 163
Rules of evidence, 3, 9, 10, 296
Rules of procedure, 3, 9, 188, 296
Rumor-control teams, 197
Rumors, 66, 73, 75
Rush-Bagot agreement, 36
Rwanda, 65, 156
Ryan, Stephen, 232

Sadat, Anwar, 40, 44, 263
trip to Jerusalem, 40
Safety valve institutions, 83
SALT I and SALT II. *See*
Strategic Arms Limitation
Talks (SALT)
Sanctions, 150, 217
Sander, Frank E. A., 28
Satyagraha, 132, 133, 164
Saudi Arabia, 40
Saunders, Harold, 90
Saving face. *See* Face saving
Savir, Uri, 226
Schellenberg, James, 123
School conflict, 12, 63, 72,
263–264
resolution programs, 264–266
See also Peer mediation

Science courts, 122
Scientific and technical disputes,
48, 141, 218, 266–267
Search for Common Ground
(SCG), 267–268
Security, 39, 42, 65, 146, 208, 268
collective, 61, 62, 152, 172, 269,
293
common, 268, 305
comprehensive, 268
international, 56
Security dilemma, 61
Self-awareness, 16
Self-control, 17
Self-determination, 65, 131, 138
Self-enforcing agreements, 288
Self-esteem, 71, 121
Settlement, 269, 276
definition of, 77
of litigation, 211, 213, 216
out of court, 279
potential for, 75
Settlement conference, 49,
269–270
Settlement judges, 269
Settlement weeks, 49, 270
Sexual abuse and harassment,
135
Sharp, Gene, 53, 241, 270–271
Shuttle diplomacy, 41, 43, 122,
165, 224, 269
Sibling rivalry and conflicts, 125,
271
Silbey, Susan, 69
Simmel, Georg, 83, 271–272
Sinai Peninsula, 39, 42
Single-text negotiating, 173,
272–273
Sit-ins, 52
Small-claims court, 80, 171
Social change, 6–8
Social defense, 53
Social justice, 148
Society of Professionals in
Dispute Resolution
(SPIDR), 79, 193, 197, 273
Sorokin, Pitirim, 234
South Africa, 132, 289
Truth and Reconciliation
Commission, 288
Southern Christian Leadership
Conference, 164
Sovereignty, 31, 134, 143, 149, 200,
233, 273–274
Soviet Peace Committee, 89
Soviet Union, 56

Victim-offender reconciliation,
    86
  programs (VORP), 302–303
Violence, 15, 16, 65, 76, 83, 124,
    125, 168, 303–304
  collective, 304
  consequences of, 132
  Palestine Liberation
    Organization use of, 225
  political, 288
  prevention of, 44, 76, 148, 233,
    235
  reduction of, 183
  structural, 131, 231, 279,
    303–304
Wagner Act, 59, 170
Walesa, Lech, 305
War
  crimes, 15
  definition of, 149

  as a method of conflict
    resolution, 55
Warsaw Pact, 61
Washington Naval Conference, 28
Wehr, Paul, 15
West Bank, 39, 42, 44
Wilmot, William, 153, 216
Wilson, Woodrow, 28, 172, 305–306
Win-lose conflicts and situations
    71, 129, 137
Win-lose outcomes, 3, 21, 26, 33,
    157, 208, 306
Win-win approach, 129, 137
Win-win outcomes and solutions,
    155, 306, 307, 309
  in arbitration, 21
  and common ground, 63, 64
  in mediation, 7, 183, 184
  in negotiation or bargaining,
    32, 33, 128

Workplace conflict resolution,
    223, 308
Workplace disputes, 69, 307–308
World Business Organization, 151
World Court, 151
World War I, 28, 87, 152, 172, 233,
    305
World War II, 28, 152, 172, 176,
    234, 291
Wright, Quincy, 149, 234

Yeltsin, Boris, 28
You-messages. *See* I-messages

Zartman, William, 90
Zero-sum, positive-sum, and
    negative-sum games, 167,
    309–310
Zero-sum situations, 6, 32, 309